Support for Asylum-seekers and other Migrants

a guide to legal and welfare rights

Sue Willman is a partner, and head of the public law and human rights department, at Pierce Glynn solicitors, London and specialises in community care, housing, social security law and social welfare provision for migrants, including EU nationals. Sue is regularly consulted as a leading expert in the UK on social welfare law for migrants. She provides training for a number of national organisations and has written widely about issues affecting people from abroad, including the regular law and practice articles on this area of the law in *Legal Action*. In 2007, Sue was awarded immigration 'Legal Aid Lawyer of the Year'.

Stephen Knafler is a barrister at Garden Court Chambers in London specialising in public law. He has appeared in over 100 reported cases, many of which are landmark decisions relevant to community care, housing, asylum support, health and mental health, immigration and human rights. He is general editor of *Community Care Law Reports* and regularly trains and lectures for Legal Action Group, Housing Law Practitioners' Association and others.

With contributions from:
Adrian Berry, Garden Court Chambers (chapter 2)
Adam Hundt, Pierce Glynn solicitors (chapter 10)
Jawaid Luqmani, Luqmani, Thompson & partners (chapter 1)

The purpose of the Legal Action Group is to promote equal access to justice for all members of society who are socially, economically or otherwise disadvantaged. To this end, it seeks to improve law and practice, the administration of justice and legal services.

Support for Asylum-seekers and other Migrants

a guide to legal and welfare rights

THIRD EDITION

Sue Willman and Stephen Knafler

LAG Legal Action Group
2009

This third edition published in Great Britain 2009
by LAG Education and Service Trust Limited
242 Pentonville Road, London N1 9UN
www.lag.org.uk

First edition published 2001
Second edition 2004

British Library Cataloguing in Publication Data
a CIP catalogue record for this book is available from the British Library.

ISBN 978 1 903307 72 4

Typeset and Printed in Great Britain by The Charlesworth Group,
West Yorkshire

Foreword

Alison Harvey, General Secretary, Immigration Law Practitioners Association

Since the second edition of this book in 2004, there have been many changes in the complex field of asylum support law making this new edition most welcome but little change to the combination of poor administration and punitive policies that view destitution as a means of immigration control that have long dogged this area of law. In March 2007 the Joint Committee on Human Rights concluded:[1]

> We have heard countless examples of Home Office inefficiencies in processing support claims, with severe consequences for desperate, vulnerable people who have no other means to support themselves. There is an urgent need to improve the operational performance of the Home Office where decisions are being made about support for asylum seekers. The institutional failure to address operational inefficiencies and to protect asylum seekers from destitution amounts in many cases to a failure to protect them from inhuman and degrading treatment under Article 3 ECHR.[2]

'Muddle and misery' wrote Helen Bamber in her preface to the first edition in 2002 and muddle and misery will do just as well to describe the situation in 2009.

Against this backdrop it is vital that legal representatives assert their clients' rights on the basis of a sound understanding of applicable national and, given its shortcomings, international, law and where necessary defend these rights through litigation. This requires them to negotiate the complex and fast-changing law in not one but several areas: immigration; welfare benefits; community care and housing. It requires them to do so in the face of changes to the legal aid system, implemented and proposed, that militate

1 *The Treatment of Asylum Seekers,* Tenth Report of Session 2006–7, HL Paper 81/I, HC 61/I.

2 *The Treatment of Asylum Seekers,* Tenth Report of Session 2006–7, paragraph 84.

against this cross-over work with a difficult client group, difficult because they may be homeless, hungry, exhausted and ill. It is this book that has given many the courage to do so.

A very welcome extension of the scope of this book so that it covers not only those seeking asylum but also other migrants, recognises the extent to which previous editions have been used by lawyers advising on all areas of support for people under immigration control. The UK has interpreted[3] the powers to limit access to the labour market contained in the treaties governing the admission to the European Union of ten new States in 2004[4] and of Romania and Bulgaria in 2007,[5] as permitting limitations on 'A8' and Romanian and Bulgarian nationals' access to a wide range of social support. This book allows practitioners to negotiate the complex body of law, involving European Court of Justice decisions arising from the support systems of different member states, that has resulted from this.

Meanwhile restrictions on access to support are increasing for migrants from outside the European Economic Area. Now is the time to get to grips with those changes, before the coming into force of the relevant provisions of the Borders, Citizenship and Immigration Act 2009, anticipated for July 2011. These will see migrants pass from limited leave in a particular category to 'Probationary Citizenship' leave, there to remain until they become British citizens or, under a longer timeframe, acquire 'Permanent Residence' leave. Those with Probationary Citizenship leave, other than refugees and those granted humanitarian protection, will face similar restrictions to their access to support as are faced by other migrants with limited leave. The numbers of those with limited or no entitlement is thus set to rise dramatically.

In the field of support for people seeking asylum, there have been significant changes to support for those whose claims for asylum have failed but who cannot be returned to their country of origin, although they are cooperating in attempts so to return them. Support is provided under section 4 of the Immigration and Asylum Act 1999, as amended, following the decision in *Salih and Rahmani v Secretary of State for the Home Department*,[6] by section 10 of the

3 See *Zaleweska v Deparment for Social Development (NI)* [2008] UKHL 67.

4 Treaty of Accession 2003 OJ L 236 of 23 September 2003.

5 Treaty between the member States of the European Union and the Republic of Bulgaria and Romania OJ L 157/11 of 21 June 2005.

6 [2003] EWHC 2273 (Admin).

Asylum and Immigration (Treatment of Claimants, etc) Act 2004.[7] The High Court held the Home Office policy of not informing those whose claims had failed of the policy on 'hard cases' to be unlawful. The amendments to section 4 made provision for regulations to be issued covering section 4 support, and for a right of appeal against refusal of such support to what is now called the Asylum Support Tribunal. By October 2005 more than 7,600 people whose claims for asylum had failed were supported under section 4,[8] compared to 100 people in March 2003.[9] Claims for section 4 support came in particular from those who could not be removed from the UK because there was no safe place to return them. In 2005, of 16,436 applications for section 4 support, 10, 224 were from nationals of Iraq.[10] 'Hard cases' support is support without cash, indeed in 2004 the Government removed any power to pay cash to those supported under section 4.[11]

Those seeking asylum and other migrants have been affected by policies on access to health care for people under immigration control having been under review for the most of the period since the second edition of this book. The decision of the Court of Appeal in *R (YA) v Secretary of State for the Health*[12] is the latest development in the law on when treatment can and cannot be withheld and when the patient will be charged for that treatment. In its written response to the questions posed by the UN Committee on Economic Social and Cultural Rights the UK Government highlighted the entitlements of those seeking asylum to healthcare[13] but remained

7 The Immigration and Asylum (Provision of Accommodation to Failed Asylum Seekers) Regulations 2005 SI No 930.

8 National Asylum Support Service briefing note to members of the National Asylum Stakeholder Forum 12 January 2006, see in particular the analysis in the superb June 2006 report from Richard Dunstan of Citizens Advice, *Shaming Destitution*.

9 *Asylum Applications, Second Report of Session 2003–04, Volume I*, House of Commons Home Affairs Committee, January 2004 (HC 218-I), paragraph 203.

10 National Asylum Support Service briefing note to members of the National Asylum Stakeholder Forum 12 January 2006.

11 Immigration Asylum and Nationality Act 2006 s43 inserting new subsection 4(11)(b) into the Immigration, Asylum and Nationality Act 2009.

12 [2009] EWCA Civ 225.

13 Replies by the Government of the United Kingdom of Great Britain and Northern Ireland to the list of issues (E/C 12/GBR/Q/5) to be taken up in connection with the consideration of the fourth periodic report , E/C12/GBR/Q/5/Add 1 26 March 2009, para 30.

conspicuously silent on the charges levied on those whose claims have failed. The UN Committee was not fooled and recorded its concerns at 'the low level of support and difficult access to health care for rejected asylum-seekers'[14] and recommend that the UK 'review section 4 of the 1999 Immigration and Asylum Act on support and provision regulating essential services to rejected asylum-seekers, and undocumented migrants, including the availability of HIV/AIDS treatment, when necessary'.[15]

Stephen Knafler and Sue Willman have not only recorded the changes to the law in this area in this book, they have worked on many of the cases asserting migrants' and asylum-seekers' entitlements to support. Stephen Knafler's work as editor of Legal Action Group's *Community Care Law Reports* has helped to build recognition of this area of practice. Sue Willman's tireless advocacy for support for people seeking asylum has seen her awarded Immigration Legal Aid Lawyer of the year in 2007 and in 2004 led her, with others, to found the Asylum Support Appeals Project which has gone from strength to strength in providing free legal representation before the Asylum Support Tribunal, where there is no provision for legal aid.[16] There is a desperate need for more lawyers to get involved in this essential work. I commend to them this book.

Alison Harvey
General Secretary
Immigration Law Practitioners' Association
August 2009

14 E/C 12/GBR/CO/5 22 May 2009, Consideration of reports submitted by States Parties under Articles 16 And 17 of the Covenant Concluding Observations of the Committee on Economic, Social and Cultural Rights United Kingdom of Great Britain and Northern Ireland, the Crown Dependencies and the Overseas Dependent Territories, para 27.

15 Ibid, para 28.

16 See *Supporting Justice*, Richard Dunstan, Citizens Advice, June 2009.

Acknowledgements

The authors would also like to thank the following for their ideas, support and direct or indirect contributions to this edition:

Asylum Support Appeals Project, in particular Gerry Hickey and Colin McCloskey; Diane Astin (Public Law Project); Simon Cox (Doughty Street Chambers); First-tier Tribunal (Asylum Support); Garden Court Chambers; staff at Pierce Glynn solicitors for support and editing, in particular Polly Glynn, Stephen Pierce, Joanna Thomson and Sasha Rozansky; the tireless members of the Housing and Immigration Group (HIG); Immigration Law Practitioners' Association (ILPA); Angela Jackman (Fisher Meredith); Ranjiv Khubber (1 Pump Court); Kat Lorenz (Refugee Action); Pip Salvador-Jones; Anne Singh; Solange Valdez (Southwark Law Centre); and the staff at Legal Action Group for their patience.

We are particularly grateful to Jawaid Luqmani (partner, Luqmani, Thompson & partners solicitors) who contributed chapter 1; Adrian Berry (barrister, Garden Court Chambers) who contributed chapter 2; and Adam Hundt (solicitor, Pierce Glynn) who contributed chapter 10.

We have endeavoured to state the law as 12 August 2009.

Sue Willman
Stephen Knafler
August 2009

Contents

Table of cases

R (Blackwood) v Secretary of State for the Home Department [2003] EWHC 97 (Admin)	5.51, 5.68, 7.90
R (Burns) v Southwark LBC [2004] EWHC 1901 (Admin)	8.78
R (C) v Birmingham City Council [2008] EWHC 3036 (Admin), [2009] 1 All ER 1039, June 2009 *Legal Action* 28	8.125, 9.70
R (Conde) v Lambeth LBC (2005) 37 HLR 452, [2005] 2 FLR 198	9.71
R (Conville) v Richmond upon Thames LBC [2006] EWCA Civ 718, July 2006 *Legal Action* 30	8.101
R (Coughlan) v North & East Devon HA [1999] EWCA Civ 1871	10.62
R (Cowl) v Plymouth CC (2002) 5 CCLR 42	9.174, 9.177
R (D & H) v Secretary of State for the Home Department (CO/2096/04 & CO/2106/04; 4 May 2004)	7.31, 8.190
R (DT (Eritrea)) v Secretary of State for the Home Department [2009] EWCA 442	1.105
R (Djamba Kazema) v Asylum Support Tribunal & Secretary of State for the Home Department (interested party) [2002] EWHC 2151	7.94
R (Emeka Omatoyo) v City of Westminster [2006] EWHC 2572 (Admin)	8.95
R (Erdogan) v Secretary of State for the Home Department [2004] EWCA Civ 1087	4.26, 4.35, 7.19
R (Esther Ariemuguvbe) v Islington LBC [2009] EWHC 470 (Admin)	8.140
R (FH) v Secretary of State for the Home Department [2007] EWHC 1571 (Admin)	1.299, 7.10
R (Fetiti) v Islington LBC (CO/2748/00; 19 October 2000)	7.114
R (G) v Southwark LBC [2009] UKHL 26, [2009] 1 WLR 1299	8.61, 9.132
R (G & D) v Leeds CC [2008] EWHC 3275 (Admin)	9.64
R (Gezer) v Secretary of State for the Home Department [2003] EWHC 860	5.47
R (Gjini) v Islington LBC [2003] EWCA Civ 558, EWHC 205 (Admin)	5.84
R (Gnezele) v Leeds CC and Secretary of State for the Home Department (interested party); R (Davina) v Leeds CC & Secretary of State for the Home Department (interested party) [2007] EWHC 3275 (Admin) June 2008 *Legal Action* 19	5.89
R (Gordon Binomugisha) v Southwark LBC [2006] EWHC 2254 (Admin)	9.70, 9.91
R (Grogan) v Bexley NHS Care Trust [2006] EWHC 44 (Admin)	10.62
R (H & D) v Secretary of State for the Home Department CO/2106/04 & CO/2096/04, January 2005 *Legal Action* 13	4.133
R (H) v Kingston upon Thames [2002] EWHC 3158 (Admin)	9.60, 9.98
R (Hetoja) v Secretary of State for the Home Department [2002] EWHC 2146 (Admin)	5.68

Table of statutes

Table of statutory instruments

Table of European legislation

DIRECTIVES AND REGULATIONS

TREATIES AND CONVENTIONS

Table of international legislation

Abbreviations

ACD	Asylum Casework Directorate
AIT	Asylum and Immigration Tribunal
ARC	Application registration card
ASA	Asylum Support Adjudicators
ASAP	Asylum Support Appeals Project
ASP	Asylum Support Partnership
AST	Asylum Support Tribunal (First-tier Tribunal (Asylum Support))
ASU	Asylum screening unit
AVR	Assisted voluntary return
BIA	Border and Immigration Agency
CESC	Council of Europe Social Charter
CFI	Court of First Instance
CIO	Chief immigration officer
CLS	Community Legal Service
CPAG	Child Poverty Action Group
CPS	Crown Prosecution Service
CRD	Casework Resolution Directorate
DES	Department for Education and Skills
DL	Discretionary leave
DLR	Discretionary leave to remain
DWP	Department for Work and Pensions
EA	Emergency accommodation
EC	European Community
ECHR	European Convention on Human Rights
ECJ	European Court of Justice
ECO	Entry clearance officer
ECSMA	European Convention on Social and Medical Assistance
EEA	European Economic Area
EEC	European Economic Community
EHO	Environmental Health Officer
ELR	Exceptional leave to remain
ESC	European Social Charter
EST	Emergency support token
EU	European Union
FACN	Framework for the Assessment of Children in Need; 'the lilac book'

FACS	Fair Access to Care Services
FRE	First Reporting Event
FTAS	First-tier tribunal (asylum support)
HOPO	Home Office Presenting Officer
HP	Humanitarian protection
HMRC	Her Majesty's Revenue and Customs
HRT	Habitual residence test
IAA	Immigration Appellate Authority
IAP	Inter-Agency Partnership
IAT	Immigration Appeal Tribunal
ILR	Indefinite leave to remain
IND	Immigration and Nationality Directorate
INEB	Immigration and Nationality Enquiry Bureau
IOM	International Organisation for Migration
ISDU	Immigration Service Documentation Unit
JCWI	Joint Council for the Welfare of Immigrants
LSC	Legal Services Commission
NAM	New Asylum Model
NASS	National Asylum Support Service
NAT	National Aids Trust
NIAA 2002 Guidance	*Nationality, Immigration and Asylum Act 2002 section 54 and Schedule 3 and the Withholding and Withdrawal of Support (Travel Assistance and Temporary Accommodation) Regulations 2002: Guidance to Local Authorities and Housing Authorities*
NINO	National insurance number
OISC	Office of the Immigration Service Commissioner
PFA	Person from abroad
PSIC	Persons subject to immigration control
RANS	Restricted Access to NASS Support
RAP	Refugee Arrivals Project
RSL	Registered social landlord
RTR	Right to reside
SAL	Standard acknowledgement letter
SEF	Statement of evidence
TEU	Treaty on European Union
TJ	Tribunal Judge
UASC	Unaccompanied asylum-seeker children
UCP	Urgent cases payments
UKBA	UK Border Agency
VARRP	Voluntary Assisted Return and Reintegration Programme
WRS	Worker Registration Scheme

Benefits

Means-tested benefits	
Child Tax Credit	CTC
Council Tax Benefit	CTB
Housing Benefit	HB
Income Support	IS
Minimum Income Guarantee[1]	MIG
Social Fund payments	SFP
State Pension Credit	SPC
Working Tax Credit	WTC
Non-means-tested benefits	
Attendance Allowance	AA
Bereavement Allowance	BA
Carers' Allowance	CA
Child Benefit	CB
Disability Living Allowance	DLA
Incapacity Benefit	IB
Income-related employment and support allowance	IESA
Jobseeker's Allowance	JSA
Maternity Allowance	MA
Retirement Pension	RP
Severe Disablement Allowance[2]	SDA

1 Note that from 6 October 2003, the Minimum Income Guarantee has been replaced by State Pension Credit; SPCs administered by the Pension Service.

2 Note that Severe Disablement Allowance has been abolished for new claimants with effect from 6 April 2001, but remains in payment to existing claimants.

Statutes

AI(TC)A 2004	Asylum and Immigration (Treatment of Claimants, etc) Act 2004
AIA 1996	Asylum and Immigration Act 1996
BCIA 2009	Borders, Citizenship and Immigration Act 2009
CA 1989	Children Act 1989
CC(DD)A 2003	Community Care (Delayed discharges etc) Act 2003
CESC	Council of Europe Social Charter 1961
CJIA 2008	Criminal Justice and Immigration Act 2008
CSDPA 1970	Chronically Sick and Disabled Persons Act 1970
ECSMA	European Convention on Social and Medical Assistance and Protocol 1953
EUAA 2008	European Union (Amendment) Act 2008
HA 1996	Housing Act 1996
HRA 1998	Human Rights Act 1998
HSPHA 1968	Health Services and Public Health Act 1968
IA 1971	Immigration Act 1971
IAA 1999	Immigration and Asylum Act 1999
IANA 2006	Immigration, Asylum and Nationality Act 2006
LGA 2000	Local Government Act 2000
NAA 1948	National Assistance Act 1948
NIAA 2002	Nationality, Immigration and Asylum Act 2002
NHSA 1977	National Health Services Act 1977
NHSA 2006	National Health Service Act 2006
NIAA 2002	Nationality, Immigration and Asylum Act 2002
PFEA 1977	Protection from Eviction Act 1977
SPCA 2002	State Pension Credit Act 2002
SSA 1998	Social Security Act 1998
SSAA 1992	Social Security Administration Act 1992
SSCBA 1992	Social Security Contributions and Benefits Act 1992
UKBA 2007	UK Borders Act 2007

Statutory instruments

A(IWR) Regs	Accession (Immigration and Worker Registration) Regulations 2004
AS Regs	Asylum Support Regulations 2000 SI No 704
CTB Regs	Council Tax Benefit Regulations 1992 SI No 1814
EEA Regs	Immigration (European Economic Area) Regulations 2006 SI No 1003
HB Regs	Housing Benefit (General) Regulations SI No 1971
Homelessness (England) Regs 2006	Allocation of Housing and Homelessness (Eligibility) (England) Regulations 2006 SI No 294
IA(PAFA) Regs	Immigration and Asylum (Provision of Accommodation to Failed Asylum-seekers) Regulations 2005
IAPSF Regs	Immigration and Asylum (Provision of Services or Facilities) Regulations 2007

Interim Regs	Asylum Support (Interim Provisions) Regulations 1999
IS Regs	Income Support (General) Regulations 1987 SI No 1967
JSA Regs	Jobseeker's Allowance Regulations 1996 SI No 207
SPC Regs	State Pension Credit Regulations 2002 SI No 1792
SPC(TMP)A Regs	State Pension Credit (Transitional and Miscellaneous Provisions) Amendment Regulations 2003 SI No 2274
SS(AA) Regs	Social Security (Attendance Allowance) Regulations 1991 SI No 2740
SS(CP) Regs	Social Security (Claims and Payments) Regulations 1987 SI No 1968
SS(DLA) Regs	Social Security (Disability Living Allowance) Regulations 1991 SI No 2890
SS(HR)A Rges	Social Security (Habitual Residence) Amendment Regulations 2004 SI No 1232
SS(IA)CA Regs	Social Security (Immigration and Asylum) Consequential Amendments Regulations 2000 SI No 636
SS(IB) Regs	Social Security (Incapacity Benefit) Regulations 1994 SI No 2946
SS(ICA) Regs	Social Security (Invalid Care Allowance) Regulations 1976 SI No 409
SS(PFA)MA Regs	Social Security (Persons from Abroad) Miscellaneous Amendments Regulations 1996 SI No 30
SSCS(DA) Regs	Social Security and Child Support (Decisions and Appeals) Regulations 1999 SI No 991
TC(I) Regs	Tax Credits (Immigration) Regulations 2003 SI No 653
VOLO 1976	Immigration (Variation of Leave) Order 1976 SI No 1572
WWS(TATA)R 2002	Withholding and Withdrawal of Support (Travel Assistance and Temporary Accommodation) Regulations 2002

CHAPTER 1

Asylum and immigration law

continued

continued

Introduction

1.1 Immigration law is the starting point for most decisions about the entitlements to support for persons from abroad, including asylum-seekers, EEA nationals and those with permission to remain in the UK whether on a limited or unlimited basis. This chapter aims to provide non-immigration specialists with a foundation in immigration law and practice to inform their advice about welfare law issues.

1.2 The chapter begins with an outline of the legal framework and an explanation of commonly used immigration law terms and concepts. The aim is to enable advisers to familiarise themselves not only with these key concepts, but also with the language of immigration decisions.

1.3 Immigration law is subject to regular and rapid changes not only through primary legislation, but frequent changes are made through delegated legislation as well as the immigration rules, which have not been consolidated since Order Paper HC 395 in 1994. Since that time there have been frequent and significant changes.[1] So far as the legislation is concerned, there are also a number of statutory provisions that have yet to be brought into force and it can be confusing to establish whether a particular provision is actually in force at any one time. At the time of writing, proposals were afoot to consolidate a number of the earlier statutory provisions in a simplification bill.

Borders, Citizenship and Immigration Act 2009

1.4 The Borders, Citizenship and Immigration Act (BCIA) 2009 came into force in 2009 with rules affecting migrants and their welfare provision including:

- powers to control all those arriving in the UK from another part of the Common Travel Area (the UK, the Channel Islands, the Isle of Man and the Republic of Ireland);
- restrictions on studying in the UK;
- enabling judicial review applications in immigration cases to be heard by the new Upper Tribunal instead of the Administrative Court, but only those concerning decisions not to treat 'fresh

1 A consolidated version of the rules in force is available on the Home Office website at www.ukba.homeoffice.gov.uk/policyandlaw/immigrationlaw/immigrationrules

claims' or further submissions as an asylum or human rights claim;

- a new duty on the Home Office UK Border Agency (UKBA) to safeguard the welfare of children;
- implementing a new 'path to citizenship' by amending provisions of the British Nationality Act 1981 regarding naturalisation as a British citizen. Government statements suggest 'probationary citizenship' allows full citizenship after five years; otherwise it takes eight years. Those who are recognised as refugees and granted humanitarian protection will be expected to meet the 'active citizenship' test during the probationary period eg by carrying out voluntary work to qualify for citizenship.[2] Those entering the UK on the work route (that is, those highly skilled and skilled workers under tiers 1 and 2 of the points-based system) or the family route, for family members of British citizens and permanent residents, will be expected to support themselves without access to benefits during the probationary period. The detail of how the new scheme will work has been left to regulations.

Reference materials

1.5 Many of the immigration documents referred to in this chapter are reproduced in the appendices. The immigration rules and policy guidance on asylum, immigration, European casework guidance and country guidance are published on the Home Office's UKBA website.[3] They can be found by navigating from 'policy and law' to 'guidance and instructions'.

1.6 Reference materials relied upon by immigration practitioners include Phelan and Gillespie's *Immigration Law Handbook*,[4] which contains the statutory material and seeks to enable the reader to ascertain which provisions are in force although, given the pace of changes, recourse to this book will often only be a starting point. Other useful materials include *Butterworth's Immigration Law Service*, a comprehensive looseleaf volume containing legislative and policy materials, as well as Macdonald's *Immigration Law and Practice*.[5] The

2 *Hansard*, HL col 752, 25 March 2009.

3 www.ukba.homeoffice.gov.uk/

4 6th edition, OUP, 2009.

5 7th edition, OUP, 2009.

Joint Council for the Welfare of Immigrants (JCWI) also publishes accessible handbooks on immigration and asylum law.[6] Additionally, the Legal Action Group publishes handbooks on specific topics and has a regular update on immigration law and practice in *Legal Action*.[7]

The administration of asylum and immigration decisions

1.7 The Home Secretary or Secretary of State for the Home Department is responsible for immigration policy and asylum decision-making through the United Kingdom Border Agency (UKBA).[8] UKBA is based in Croydon but has regional offices where many decisions are made. Often cases are transferred to regional centres such as Liverpool or Leeds even though the individual applicant is based in London or the south east.

1.8 Asylum support was administered by the National Asylum Support Service (NASS) as part of the then Immigration and Nationality Directorate (IND). Although both Home Office staff and representatives continue to refer to NASS, technically it was disbanded in 2006. Asylum support functions are now dealt with by various parts of UKBA. Older 'legacy' cases are dealt with by the relevant Casework Resolution Directorate (CRD) team; newer cases are dealt with by the New Asylum Model (NAM) officer who is responsible for processing the asylum claim. This is explained in more detail in chapter 4.

Leave to enter or remain

Control prior to entry

1.9 For any person from abroad who is not an Irish citizen, it is necessary to obtain leave to enter or remain. EU citizens are in a different category as they are permitted to travel in and out of other EU

6 www.jcwi.org.uk/publications
7 www.lag.org.uk/magazine
8 Previously known as the Border and Immigration Agency and before that the Immigration and Nationality Directorate.

territories without the need formally to seek leave to enter on the basis that their movement between member states is in accordance with EU law and for a regulated purpose such as travel to work, to find work, to study or to provide or receive services.[9]

1.10 For some individuals seeking to travel to the UK it is necessary to seek an entry clearance[10] prior to arriving in the UK, whether because they are citizens of specific listed countries within the immigration rules[11] (known as visa nationals), or because they are seeking entry for a purpose for which an entry clearance is specifically required (for example to set up in business), whether or not they are visa nationals. The decision on whether to grant or refuse entry clearance is taken by an Entry Clearance Officer (ECO), although occasionally the ECO will refer a particular application and seek guidance from UKBA before reaching a decision.

Control on entry

1.11 In practice it is immigration officers that exercise the power to grant leave to enter the UK,[12] although that power is also held by ECOs based outside the UK, who can grant leave to enter at the same time as issuing an entry clearance.

Control after entry

1.12 For decisions relating to persons who seek to extend their leave in the UK, or switch the basis upon which they were originally granted leave, for decisions on deportation, or for asylum, it is generally the Secretary of State through UKBA that exercises these functions.

1.13 In asylum cases, although it is UKBA that reaches a decision as to whether a person has met the criteria for asylum (or humanitarian protection or discretionary leave: see below), for those who have claimed asylum on arrival, or who have evaded immigration control on entry, it will often be an immigration officer who formally issues the leave to enter documents, or the refusal documents where an applicant is unsuccessful.

9 See below for exceptions in the case of citizens of Bulgaria and Romania.

10 Commonly referred to as a visa.

11 See HC 395 appendix 1 as amended.

12 Immigration Act 1971 s4(1).

Immigration service powers

1.14 As well as operating at air and sea ports, immigration officers are also able to exercise functions in designated control areas in France,[13] with reciprocal arrangements for French immigration officials to operate immigration controls for persons seeking to enter that territory.[14]

1.15 Immigration officers have powers to detain, and to question, as well as to give directions for removal to persons deemed to be illegal entrants or persons refused leave to enter.[15]

1.16 Immigration officers also have power to grant temporary admission as an alternative to detention.

The legal framework

Legislation

1.17 The Immigration Act (IA) 1971 continues to form the bedrock of the framework of domestic immigration law. It provides the statutory basis for the grant or refusal of leave to enter or remain, sets out the powers of deportation and provides for the publication of the immigration rules. There have been several significant legislative changes since that Act which have shaped the present legislative landscape.

1.18 A detailed analysis of those changes is beyond the scope of this book but they include:

- the Special Immigration Appeals Commission Act 1997, which provides for a right of appeal in cases involving an issue of national security;
- the Immigration and Asylum Act (IAA) 1999, which amongst other matters created the asylum support scheme and the Office of the Immigration Service Commissioner (OISC);
- the Nationality, Immigration and Asylum Act (NIAA) 2002, which overhauled the immigration and asylum appeals system;
- the Asylum and Immigration (Treatment of Claimants, etc) Act (AI(TC)A) 2004, which created offences for persons subject to

13 Nationality Immigration and Asylum Act 2002 s141.

14 Nationality, Immigration and Asylum Act 2002 (Juxtaposed Controls) Order 2003 SI No 2818.

15 IA 1971 Sch 2 para 16.

control who were liable to be interviewed if they did not produce certain documentation, required persons to seek prior approval from the Home Office if they were subject to immigration control and wished to marry; and removed the entitlement for persons recognised as refugees to seek to backdate their benefit claims to the point of entry to the UK;

- the Immigration, Asylum and Nationality Act (IANA) 2006, which enabled financial penalties to be imposed on employers employing persons from abroad who did not have permission to work;
- the UK Borders Act 2007, which removed appeal rights for those seeking to avoid deportation save for a limited class of persons whose removal would be either a breach of their rights under the Refugee Convention, the ECHR or under EU law; and
- the Criminal Justice and Immigration Act (CJIA) 2008, which enables the Secretary of State to designate an individual who is either a person from abroad who has been convicted in the UK, or the family member of such a person, and who cannot be removed from the UK due to their rights under the Human Rights Act, with special immigration status, the consequence of which can include limited access to support for such a person or their family.[16]

1.19 Some of the detail of these provisions will be examined to enable a better understanding of how immigration legislation presently operates.

Immigration rules

1.20 The immigration rules set out the day-to-day basis upon which applications for leave to enter or remain are to be considered and will change from time to time.

1.21 The shift in recent times has been to move (in certain, primarily economic, categories) towards a points-based system where an individual will need to provide evidence of their ability to meet pre-set criteria in order to seek entry or to continue to remain on the basis of meeting those criteria.

1.22 Another clear shift in recent times has been the removal of the area of discretion from within the rules. Although this might seem to be a positive step by ensuring that an individual knows precisely

16 At the time of writing these provisions within Part 10 of CJIA 2008 had not come into force.

what they need to bring themselves within a particular category, the consequence of the removal of the area of discretion is to ensure that a decision is less likely to be successfully appealed. Refusing to depart from an immigration rule is not to be regarded as the exercise of discretion for the purposes of a tribunal determining an appeal.[17]

1.23 The rules also determine the length of time for which a person is to be granted leave to enter or remain and will determine which categories are going to lead to a person being able to apply for permanent residence.

1.24 Additionally, it is the immigration rules which determine whether an individual meets the criteria for the grant of asylum or humanitarian protection, and the length of residence to accompany a favourable decision.

Statutory instruments

1.25 At the time of writing, the Asylum and Immigration Tribunal (Procedure) Rules 2005 governed the appeals structure for those dissatisfied with immigration or asylum decisions and enable an appeal to be exercised to the Asylum and Immigration Tribunal.[18]

1.26 The Asylum and Immigration Tribunal (Fast Track Procedure) Rules 2005 governed the appeals structure for a limited class of persons whose cases fall within the detained fast track process (see below para 1.114).

1.27 The scope of these appeals relate to the immigration decision as to whether the individual is to be granted leave to enter or remain. A separate appeals structure to a body now known as the First-tier Tribunal (Asylum Support), previously the Asylum Support Tribunal, applies to those persons who believe that they have wrongly been denied support.

1.28 Many of the legislative provisions enable the Secretary of State to issue separate regulations or other delegated legislation. A familiar example to most advisers will be the Asylum Support Regulations 2000[19] and amendment regulations enabling the Secretary of State to determine the level of support to be given to those persons within the scope of IAA 1999 Part VI.

17 NIAA 2002 s86(6).

18 Note that the government has announced an intention to move certain asylum and immigration appeals and judicial reviews to the new tribunal system of first-tier and upper tier tribunals, but see para 1.4.

19 SI No 704.

Policies and guidance

1.29 Many Home Office decisions will seek to conform to a number of polices and guidance issued by the Secretary of State. The majority will operate as instructions to officials within UKBA as to how to carry out certain tasks, including interviews, decision-making, the wording of refusal decisions and factors to consider on an application submitted.

1.30 In the context of asylum, the Secretary of State has produced a number of operational guidance notes or country-specific bulletins in order to inform staff involved in decisions about the human rights conditions in particular countries. Frequently decision letters issued by the Secretary of State will refer to these operational guidance notes and may contain large segments of material taken directly from them.

1.31 Occasionally these policies are the subject of litigation, particularly where it is clear that the conduct of UKBA is not in conformity with their stated position. The failure to have reviews carried out by sufficiently senior staff in conformity with the Home Office's Operational Enforcement Manual led the High Court to award damages to a detainee, albeit refusing to order his release on the basis that by the time of the hearing the detention had been further reviewed.[20]

Immigration law terminology

Subject to immigration control

1.32 The IA 1971 distinguishes between persons who have the 'right of abode' in the UK and those whose right to live, work and settle here is subject to regulation and control under the Act. In broad terms, a person with the right of abode is not subject to any control on their right to move and travel freely in and out of the country, and other persons will be subject to varying degrees of control. Importantly, the fact that a person is permanently resident in the UK does not mean that they are not subject to control. Any person who is subject to control will need leave to enter (issued either on arrival or in some cases prior to arrival or for persons who are permitted to remain having entered irregularly) or leave to remain

20 *R (SK) v Secretary of State for the Home Department* [2008] EWHC 98 (Admin).

(issued after entry by the Secretary of State for the Home Department). Persons exercising EU Treaty rights do not require leave to enter or remain and are not subject to immigration control for the purposes of immigration law.[21]

Public funds

1.33 Most of the immigration rules require an individual to be financially self-sufficient either from their own resources or from resources of their family or sponsor based in the UK. In general terms, there is a restriction on any persons seeking entry to the UK having access to public funds or for a sponsor having recourse to additional public funds as a consequence of an individual being permitted entry to the UK. Consequently the fact that the sponsor is receiving public funds does not automatically bar the individual seeking entry to gain entry, provided that it can be shown that permitting the individual to enter the UK will not increase the financial burden placed on the state.

1.34 Public funds are specifically defined within the immigration rules and para 6 of HC 395 contains a list of those funds that are regarded for the purposes of the rules as being public funds. Paragraph 6A, added in March 2009, contains additional clarification. There is also guidance in chapter 1 of the Immigration Directorate Instructions (IDI).[22]

Leave to enter or remain

1.35 The length of leave to enter or remain may be limited or indefinite (unlimited). Indefinite leave is also referred to as permanent residence or settled status but, as observed above, such a person remains subject to immigration control. Where leave to enter or remain is limited, it may be subject to a variety of conditions, including:

- restriction on employment;
- requirement to maintain and accommodate without reliance on public funds;
- conditions requiring registration with the police;[23]

21 Immigration Act 1988 s7(1).

22 www.ukba.homeoffice.gov.uk/policyandlaw/guidance/IDIs

23 A list of territories of whose nationals are required to register with the police is set out at Appendix 2 to the Immigration Rules.

- conditions requiring the individual to report to the Secretary of State or to an immigration officer;[24]
- conditions on residence.[25]

1.36 A breach of a condition of the leave granted may result in the loss of asylum support as well as the individual being prosecuted, detained and removed from the UK.

Variation of leave

1.37 A person with limited leave (this might include persons with leave to remain as a refugee, with humanitarian leave or discretionary leave) can apply to UKBA for their leave to be extended either in the same capacity for a longer period (for example a student),[26] or for an indefinite period (for example a person who has been lawfully resident in the UK for the requisite number of years in a particular capacity[27]), or to switch to a different capacity (for example a person who had been in the UK as a student who now wishes to remain to work following completion of their degree course).[28]

1.38 A frequent problem faced by many individuals who seek a variation of leave is the length of time taken for a decision to be reached. Often an individual will submit an application for a variation of their leave four weeks before their current leave expires, but not receive a decision until several months have elapsed. They are not required to depart from the UK in the interim and continue to be lawfully present in the UK by virtue of IA 1971 s3C, which provides that as a matter of law their leave is automatically extended until a decision has been made on their application, even if that leave is refused and whilst it remains the subject of any pending appeal.

1.39 Consequently, if the individual were here in a capacity that enabled them to receive state support, that support would similarly continue until the determination of the application and any subsequent appeal. In practice advisers will often encounter practical problems in seeking to persuade either the DWP or a local authority of such an entitlement without further proof from the Home Office.

24 IA 1971 s3(1)(c)(iv).
25 IA 1971 s3(1)(c)(v).
26 HC 395 para 60.
27 HC 395 para 159G.
28 HC 395 para 245Z.

In some cases, where an application has been with the Home Office for a considerable period of time, it may be possible to seek written confirmation from UKBA that a decision remains outstanding.

Ban on return to the UK

1.40 The immigration rules now enable an individual to be barred from return to the UK in circumstances where they had previously overstayed or breached a condition attached to their leave or used or attempted to use deception or been treated as an illegal entrant.

1.41 For persons who overstayed but who left the UK voluntarily and at their own expense, there is no automatic refusal.

1.42 For persons who left the UK voluntarily at their own expense (outside the 28-day period) they are to be refused an application for entry to the UK for a period of 12 months.

1.43 For persons who left the UK voluntarily but at the expense of the Secretary of State, they are to be refused entry for five years.

1.44 For persons who were either removed or deported, or who used deception in an application for entry clearance, the bar on entry is to be for ten years.[29]

1.45 The potentially draconian impact of these provisions will not apply in cases where an individual is seeking entry to join a family member or where the individual who breached the immigration law was under 18 at the date of removal.[30]

1.46 A series of concessions was also announced to the effect that persons who voluntarily left the UK between 17 March 2008 and 1 October 2008, who had overstayed for in excess of 28 days, would not be caught by the provisions, nor would persons claiming to have previously been the victims of trafficking (at the time of removal) and who are recognised as such.[31]

Common Travel Area

1.47 A person resident in or a citizen of the UK, the Channel Islands and the Isle of Man or Republic of Ireland can travel freely within this area, defined as the Common Travel Area. However, a person who is otherwise subject to control who passes through the Common Travel

29 HC 395 para 320 (7B).

30 HC 395 para 320 (7C).

31 Entry Clearance Guidance – General Instructions chapter 26.17.4.

Area en route to the UK would remain subject to control at the UK border.[32]

Deportation/removal directions

1.48 Before issuing removal directions, the Home Office must serve notice of removal which gives rise to a right of appeal. Assuming the appeal is unsuccessful, they may later be followed by removal directions giving a time, route and destination to a third country or the migrant's country of origin. The directions may be challenged by judicial review. Normally, removal would be the process used for a refused asylum-seeker; deportation is used for foreign national criminals, for example.

Deportation is a power exercisable by the Secretary of State to remove persons from the UK after signing a deportation order. The consequence of the signing of a deportation order is that it imposes a ban on the entry of the individual unless and until such time as the deportation order is revoked.

1.49 The power to make a deportation order arises where the Secretary of State deems that the deportation of an individual is conducive to the public good[33] and can also apply to family members of that individual.[34]

1.50 The power to deport also arises in cases in which a court has made a recommendation for deportation following the conviction of a person aged 17 or over who is not a British citizen for any offence for which a prison sentence is imposed.[35]

1.51 The deportation powers can be applied to any person who is not British and consequently can certainly be applied to those persons who have been living lawfully in the UK for many years, including those who have been granted indefinite leave to remain.

1.52 There is an entitlement to appeal against a deportation decision, but at present such an appeal will not be available for individuals sentenced to a term of 12 months or more, or where the sentence was for a lesser period but the offence is one that is designated by the Secretary of State as being sufficiently serious,[36] subject to a finite list of exceptions. The exceptions in these cases mean that an appeal against deportation will still be available for:

32 IA 1971 s9(2).
33 IA 1971 s3(5)(a).
34 IA 1971 s3(5)(b).
35 IA 1971 s3(6).
36 UK Borders Act 2007 s32(1).

- Commonwealth and Irish citizens who have been long resident in the UK;
- where removal would be a breach of the individual's rights under the Refugee Convention or the ECHR;
- where the individual was under 18 at the date of conviction;
- where removal would breach EU law rights;
- where the individual is subject to extradition;
- where a mental health hospital or guardianship order or direction has been made.

1.53 Where a deportation order has been made and an individual seeks to lawfully return to the UK, their first step will be to seek revocation of the deportation order by submitting an application to that effect at the British diplomatic post abroad (an embassy or high commission). In general terms, a deportation order is unlikely to be revoked for at least three years.

1.54 In some cases an individual who is the subject of deportation action will seek to remain in the UK on the basis that their removal will violate their rights under the Refugee Convention or European Convention on Human Rights (ECHR), even though they may not previously have raised a fear of return. Where a deportation order has already been signed, if the application is rejected and gives rise to an appeal, it is the refusal to revoke the deportation decision that gives rise to the appeal.

1.55 In the context of EEA nationals who face removal from the UK, often the term 'expulsion' rather than 'deportation' is used, although the impact of the decision is the same in either case. The Home Office has power to detain EEA nationals prior to expulsion, for example, on reasonable suspicion that they do not have the 'right to reside' (see further paras 1.186 and 2.66).

Overstayers

1.56 As observed above, persons from abroad who are not granted unlimited or settled status will generally have a time limit placed upon their right of residence in the UK, which can in many cases be extended. An individual who remains in the UK after the date on which their leave expires is said to be an *overstayer*,[37] unless prior to the expiry of their leave date an application for further leave was submitted. In most cases such an individual will have no entitlement to appeal against the decision to remove them prior to their removal from the UK, unless the individual is able to show that the removal

37 IAA 1999 s10(1)(a).

would be a breach of their rights under the Refugee Convention or the ECHR, or because they are able to show that removal would breach an EU law right.[38]

Illegal entrants

1.57 An illegal entrant is defined under IA 1971 s33(1) as being a person:

(a) unlawfully entering or seeking to enter in breach of a deportation order or of the immigration laws, or
(b) entering or seeking to enter by means which include deception by another person.

1.58 Caught within the definition of illegal entrant will be individuals who may have been the subject of previous deportation action, now seeking to return many years later. As observed earlier, return at any time while a deportation order is in force renders the individual liable to treatment as an illegal entrant, and as a consequence liable also to detention in accordance with powers exercisable by an immigration officer.[39] The fact that the individual genuinely cannot recall that a deportation order was signed does not make them any less liable to detention or removal as an illegal entrant.

1.59 There is a separate criminal offence of illegal entry and to be convicted it is necessary to show that the person knowingly entered in breach of the deportation order or without leave.[40] A person treated as an illegal entrant for immigration purposes does not have to be prosecuted and the fact that they are not being prosecuted is not a basis for arguing that they should not be treated as an illegal entrant.

1.60 Also within the definition of illegal entrants are those who enter or who attempt to enter on false documents as well as those who evade control altogether, for example by being smuggled on a lorry.

1.61 The definition is wide enough to encompass individuals who state that their intention is to come for one purpose when in reality it is for another, for example an individual seeking entry as a visitor but who subsequently submits an application to remain on the basis of asylum within days of arrival. It is possible that such an individual will be treated as an illegal entrant unless it is possible to demonstrate that at the date of arrival their intention really was to

38 NIAA 2002 s92(4).
39 IA 1971 Sch 2 para 16.
40 IA 1971 s24(1)(a).

stay solely for the temporary purpose for which they sought and obtained leave to enter.

1.62 Entry clearances are not issued for those seeking asylum and consequently it is by no means uncommon for persons seeking entry to the UK for the purposes of making an asylum claim to have utilised some form of deception in their efforts to come to the UK.

1.63 This is also compounded by the fact that not only are there immigration officers exercising powers within the juxtaposed control zones within France, but the imposition of significant penalties through carrier liability provisions upon airlines and freight carriers. Many airlines now employ personnel specifically to carry out the checking of documents to reduce the risk that they would be liable to pay a fine, currently £2,000 per passenger, for carrying passengers who are improperly documented.[41]

1.64 Although in theory there are to be no penalties imposed on persons irregularly seeking entry where their purpose in seeking entry is in order to submit a claim for asylum, in practice there are consequences, not only in terms of potential criminal liability, but also the impact upon the assessment of the asylum claim itself.[42]

1.65 Broadly speaking a person deemed to be an illegal entrant similarly has no entitlement to appeal against their removal other than for the limited exceptions available to overstayers, that is to say for those seeking to argue that removal would be a breach of their rights under the Refugee Convention or the ECHR, or a breach of EU law.

Temporary admission

1.66 Temporary admission (TA) is not the same as being granted leave to enter or remain, but is a practical alternative to detaining every passenger before reaching a decision on whether the individual is to be granted or refused entry. It is a power exercisable by an immigration officer considering the position of any port applicant or any person who has sought entry to the UK without passing through immigration control,[43] that is to say clandestine or illegal entrants. TA can be granted subject to reporting or residence restrictions and is usually also accompanied by a restriction on taking up employment or engaging in any business activity.[44]

41 Carriers Liability Regulations 2002 SI No 2817 reg 3.

42 See para 1.93 below.

43 IA 1971 Sch 2 para 21.

44 IA 1971 Sch 2 para 21(2).

1.67 Although TA does not relate exclusively to cases of individuals seeking asylum, it is certainly commonplace within this field given that there may be weeks if not months before a decision on asylum is taken. The fact of being on TA does not preclude the immigration service from subsequently exercising the power to detain (particularly if there is a change of circumstances), and breach of TA, such as by working without seeking and obtaining prior authority, is likely to lead to the individual being detained.

1.68 While TA is certainly not to be equated with leave to enter or leave to remain, it is still lawful presence in the UK.[45] However, as it is not to be equated with leave, a person on TA who subsequently seeks to remain in some capacity (other than that for which they had originally sought entry) is not given the protection of their leave being extended by virtue of IA 1971 s3C, enabling them to have a right to remaining in the UK whilst the further application is considered or pending any legal challenge against refusal.

Administrative detention

1.69 The powers available to detain individuals subject to immigration control are considerable and are exercisable either by an immigration officer or by the Secretary of State in the following circumstances:

- at the point of arrival to determine whether an individual should be granted leave to enter;[46]
- pending the setting of removal directions for persons refused leave to enter or treated as illegal entrants;[47]
- where persons are in breach of their conditions or are suspected of having obtained leave by deception or whose indefinite leave as a person formerly recognised as a refugee has been revoked.[48]

1.70 Further powers are exercisable by the Secretary of State in the following circumstances:

- persons liable to deportation following a recommendation by a criminal court, even where bail is granted by a criminal court pending appeal against conviction or the recommendation;[49]
- persons served with a decision to deport pending the making of the deportation order;[50]

45 *Szoma v Secretary of State for Work and Pensions* [2005] UKHL 64.
46 IA 1971 Sch 2 para 16.
47 IA 1971 Sch 2 para 16.
48 IAA 1999 s10(7).
49 IA 1971 Sch 3 para 2(1).
50 IA 1971 Sch 3 para 2(2).

- persons in respect of whom a decision to deport is ready to be served but has not yet been served;[51]
- persons in respect of whom a deportation order is signed pending removal.[52]

1.71 In determining whether an individual should be detained, the officer considering release is to have regard to the enforcement instructions and guidance issued by the Secretary of State which provide the criteria for detention.

1.72 A distinction is drawn within the guidance between the 'fast track' cases and the majority of cases. The purpose of the fast track is to detain and process claims for asylum that according to set criteria are likely to be claims that can be resolved very swiftly. Some cases will not give rise to an appeal at all until after removal from the UK.[53] In other cases, whilst it is accepted that an appeal is exercisable, it will be heard on site at the detention centre (as will any bail applications) and the appeals are subject to a different set of procedure rules.[54]

1.73 The guidance for the majority of cases states that:

- there is a presumption in favour of release rather than detention;
- there must be strong grounds for believing that an individual would fail to comply with any conditions attached to the release;
- all reasonable alternatives to detention must have been considered;
- once detention has been authorised it must be kept under regular review;
- each case is to be decided on its own facts.[55]

Bail

1.74 Where an individual is refused temporary admission or is otherwise detained in accordance with one of the powers set out above, there is the possibility of applying for release on bail.

1.75 If seven days have elapsed since the individual was detained with a view to making a decision on whether or not they should be

51 IA 1971 Sch 3 para 2(4).

52 IA 1971 Sch 3 para 3.

53 NIAA 2002 s94.

54 Asylum and Immigration Tribunal (Fast Track) Procedure Rules 2005 SI No 560.

55 Enforcement Instructions and Guidance chapter 55.3.

granted leave to enter and they continue to be detained, power exists for a chief immigration officer to grant bail subject to financial sureties.[56]

1.76 If bail by a chief immigration officer is refused in such a case, and in all other detention scenarios, an individual has the right to apply for bail before an immigration judge at the Asylum and Immigration Tribunal,[57] though in the case of those newly arrived in the UK, they are not entitled to submit an application for bail until after seven days of detention.[58]

1.77 It is for an individual to initiate an application for bail; an individual will not be brought before a detaining authority to have their detention reviewed independently.

1.78 There is however a requirement for persons to have their detention regularly reviewed by immigration personnel, with detention being reviewed by more senior officers the longer the detention.[59]

Immigration offences

1.79 There are a significant number of offences created under the various immigration acts, some of which apply to the individual person from abroad, some of which relate to the individual seeking leave to enter or remain and others which relate to the actions of third parties such as employers or those seeking to provide advice if not regulated to do so.

1.80 Not only has the number of offences increased over time, the Secretary of State has also been empowered to impose civil penalties on third parties such as the carriers responsible for bringing the individual to the UK (even if the carrier were unaware of their presence)[60] and employers.[61]

1.81 The creation of these offences is supported by powers of arrest, detention and search and seizure of documents that are exercisable not just by police officers but also by immigration officers.[62]

56 IA 1971 Sch 2 para 22(1A).
57 IA 1971 Sch 2 paras 22, 29 and 34.
58 IA 1971 Sch 2 para 22(1B).
59 Enforcement Instructions and Guidance chapter 55.8.
60 IAA 1999 s40.
61 IANA 2006 s15.
62 IA 1971 ss28A–28H.

1.82 There are furthermore significant powers available to the Secretary of State to require information from the police and Her Majesty's Revenue and Customs to be shared and for information to be relayed to each of these statutory bodies.[63]

1.83 Additionally, immigration officers have powers to arrest, detain, search and seize in respect of non-immigration offences, including bigamy, theft and handling stolen goods.[64]

1.84 Furthermore the Secretary of State is empowered to designate certain specific immigration officers to exercise even wider powers of detention at a port of entry to the UK, where an individual is liable to arrest or subject to an arrest warrant for any offence, where the individual has arrived at a port or travelled to a port in order to leave the UK.[65] The power to detain is subject to an upper limit of three hours within which time it is expected that the Immigration Service would contact the police.[66]

Asylum-seekers and refugees

1.85 The definition of asylum-seeker for immigration law purposes is different from the asylum support definition (see para 4.22). In the immigration context, an asylum-seeker is an individual who claims that they would be subjected to persecution or serious harm were they to return to their country of origin. They are permitted to remain in the UK until their claims have been determined and, where appropriate, whilst their appeals are considered (apart from those whose claims are deemed to be clearly unfounded).[67]

1.86 A refugee is defined by the 1951 UN Convention on the Status of Refugees and the 1967 Protocol as being a person who has a well-founded fear of persecution for reasons of their race, religion, nationality or for membership of a particular social group or political opinion.[68]

1.87 Some individuals are outside the scope of the protection of the Refugee Convention, for example due to them having committed

63 IANA 2006 s36(2).
64 AI(TC)A 2004 s14.
65 UK Borders Act 2007 s2.
66 UK Borders Act 2007 s2(2).
67 NIAA 2002 s94(1A) and (2).
68 Refugee Convention article 1(A).

war crimes or serious non-political crimes in the country of origin prior to their arrival in the UK.[69]

1.88 Others may have committed offences within the UK and, whilst they may fall within the definition of a refugee, be persons who are unable to benefit from the protection of being removed to the country of origin.[70]

1.89 Such individuals may have the same degree of fear and be likely to face the same degree of serious harm but are outside the protection of the Refugee Convention. They may still present an application for asylum based on ECHR article 3, which provides that no person is to be subjected to torture or inhuman or degrading treatment or punishment. Such a person, if successful, may be granted either humanitarian protection or discretionary leave (see below).

1.90 Asylum-seekers may be those who arrive at a port claiming asylum, or may be persons who have entered the UK illegally or may be persons who now face deportation, or be persons who were granted entry in one capacity, but there has been a change of circumstances in their home country such that they require international protection to prevent them from being subjected to treatment that would otherwise breach their Convention rights if removed.

1.91 Asylum-seeker for support purposes is explained in chapter 4. It includes those who have made a claim under ECHR article 3.

Asylum process

1.92 Regardless of whether the asylum claim was submitted at a port or after entry, the initial step will be that the individual seeking asylum will have their claim screened. The intention of this step is to determine how the application will be processed, for example whether it meets the criteria for the fast track.

1.93 For port entry applicants and for those detected by the Immigration Service seeking to gain entry unlawfully the screening will be carried out at the port. For those seeking to claim asylum after entry the screening will be either at Croydon or Liverpool.

69 Refugee Convention article 1(F).
70 Refugee Convention article 33(2).

1.94 From March 2007, the Home Office introduced what they believed would be an entirely streamlined process known originally as the New Asylum Model (NAM), although it is now simply referred to as the asylum model.

1.95 The intention behind the asylum model was to improve on the significant delays which had blighted the asylum process for many years leading to decisions being routinely delayed for several months if not years, with the intention that within UKBA one single individual would be responsible for the assessment of the claim from initial application through to interview, decision and, if appropriate, even at the appeal.

1.96 The idea is that after screening the case would be allocated to a case owner within UKBA and an initial meeting would be set up between the individual claiming asylum and the case owner, this first meeting being the 'First Reporting Event' (FRE).

1.97 The case owner is then supposed to ensure that the individual claimant understands the process, is aware of their entitlement to seek legal advice and should arrange a date at which the claimant would be interviewed in order that the individual would be able to set out the full basis of their asylum claim.

1.98 Following the interview the individual claiming asylum is given a short period of time within which to make written representations (usually five working days) and a decision is supposed to be made immediately thereafter.

1.99 The process does not appear to be operating entirely as predicted and there remain a very significant proportion of cases that are not determined within the period of 30 days, which is the time frame the UKBA have indicated the introduction of NAM would lead to.[71]

1.100 At the same time as the introduction of NAM, the Secretary of State announced an intention to clear the then backlog, identified as being between 400–450,000 legacy cases, within a five-year period. Part of the backlog was cleared by UKBA issuing legacy questionnaires to individuals, many of whom had been waiting for an initial decision for more than three years.

1.101 Legacy questionnaires are not issued to all claimants who have been waiting for their cases to be resolved, nor does the completion and return of such a questionnaire where it is issued mean that the claimant will be granted permission to remain, although it is certainly likely.

71 www.ukba.homeoffice.gov.uk/asylum/process/processoverview

1.102 Once an application for asylum has been made, UKBA will issue a photocard identification document, the asylum registration card (ARC) which will enable the claimant to access support to which they may be entitled.

1.103 There are a number of positive duties imposed on the Secretary of State under Council Directive 2003/09 of 27 January 2003 laying down minimum standards for the reception of asylum-seekers (the Reception Directive).[72]

1.104 These include, for those not detained, written confirmation of the benefits to which an individual may be entitled while their claim is processed to be given to them within 15 days of the date of the claim being recorded.[73] They also include an entitlement to take up employment (but not self-employment) if the decision on the asylum claim has not been taken within one year of the date on which it was recorded, provided that the delay cannot be attributed to the claimant.[74] Any such permission granted will be limited only until such time as the application has been finally determined.

1.105 The Home Office had interpreted these duties as limited to those who had made a first asylum claim under the Refugee Convention. But the Court of Appeal has decided that they also apply to those who have made a further 'fresh asylum claim' even if it has not been recorded by the Home Office, with the result that such applicants have the right to work if their fresh claim is outstanding after 12 months.[75]

1.106 Often the permission to take up employment will not be limited solely to employment and the permission granted may extend to self-employed activities, which for nationals of Turkey may be very significant.[76]

1.107 In theory with the faster asylum process introduced by NAM, there should be no-one in a position of having to wait for more than 12 months for the initial decision. However the rule applies not only to those who are dealt with under NAM, but also applies to those whose claims fall within the legacy and have yet to be decided, and the average length of time for the processing of asylum applications is presently increasing.

72 Council Directive 2003/09/EC.

73 HC 395 para 358.

74 HC 395 para 360.

75 *R (ZO) (Somalia) and MM (Burma) v Secretary of State for the Home Department* and *R (DT) (Eritrea) v Secretary of State for the Home Department* [2009] EWCA 442.

76 See below para 1.258.

1.108 Financial penalties can be imposed upon an employer employing an adult subject to immigration control who does not have such permission[77] and criminal penalties can be imposed upon employers who knowingly employ a person who has no entitlement to work.[78]

1.109 Consequently although permission to work may be available in theory, in practice finding an employer willing to employ the individual may be far harder. Although a dedicated employers' helpline has apparently been set up by the Home Office, for many employers, the sanctions for getting things wrong and being liable to pay fines will be a significant disincentive.

Unaccompanied minors

1.110 The process for those persons accepted as being unaccompanied asylum-seeking children (under the age of 18) (UASCs) at the date of application for asylum is dealt with differently. In these cases, the child claimant is issued with a statement of evidence form (SEF) which is to be completed and returned to the case owner within 28 days. It is the current invariable practice that the applicant will be interviewed, if aged 12 or above, with the case owners with responsibility for children's cases within the Home Office having undertaken additional training.

1.111 In carrying out the interview, the interviewer is to have regard for the age and sensitivity of the interviewee.[79]

1.112 In many cases the age of the claimant will be an issue of contention and the approach taken by UKBA is that where an individual appears to the case owner to be clearly over 18, the claimant will be treated as an adult in the absence of an age assessment from a local authority which is 'Merton' compliant indicating that the child is a minor, or on some occasions other where evidence is presented such as an original birth certificate or other identity documents or an independent expert report.[80] (For unaccompanied minors and age assessments in the social services context see para 9.131).

1.113 Treatment as a minor can have a significant impact on whether the claimant is likely to be granted some form of leave and is also relevant in assessing the entitlement that they would have access to

77 IANA 2006 s15.
78 IANA 2006 s21.
79 HC 395 para 352.
80 Asylum Process Guidance: Disputed age cases.

in terms of financial assistance, appropriate housing and emotional support.

Fast track

1.114 As observed above, some individuals are subject to a speedier resolution process through the fast track. These cases relate to two sets of fast track cases: the detained fast track and the detained non-suspensive appeals.

1.115 A guidance note has been issued setting out the suitability criteria for cases that might fall within either of these two tracks, the main one being that these are cases that are likely to be resolved swiftly.[81]

1.116 The intention behind the fast track is to resolve cases as efficiently as possible and, given that the assumption is that the individual can have a decision reached speedily, where relevant, to effect their removal from the UK within weeks of arrival.

1.117 Although for the detained fast track cases there is an entitlement to bring an appeal, the time limits are much shorter not only for an appellant within which to bring an appeal,[82] but also for the tribunal to list the appeal and then issue their decision.[83]

1.118 In the case of the non-suspensive appeals, these are cases in which UKBA have concluded that the asylum and/or human rights claim is clearly unfounded and is one which could not succeed before an immigration judge and consequently any appeal is exercisable only after the individual has been removed from the UK.[84]

1.119 Cases that fall within this category include not only those in which it is believed that in general there is no risk of persecution or serious harm (the 'white list' countries), but any case in which the Home Secretary is persuaded that there is no genuine Convention issue to be determined.

1.120 The Home Secretary has not only issued a list of such countries from which it is generally believed that asylum claims will fail,[85]

81 Asylum Process Guidance: Detained fast track and detained non-suspensive appeals intake selection.

82 Asylum and Immigration Tribunal (Fast Track Procedure) Rules 2005 SI No 560 r8(1).

83 Asylum and Immigration Tribunal (Fast Track Procedure) Rules 2005 SI No 560 rr11(1) and 14(2).

84 NIAA 2002 s94(1A) and (2).

85 NIAA 2002 s94(4), the list is also updated from time to time by statutory instrument.

but also has the power to designate part of a territory as being safe,[86] or even by reference to individual characteristics of the claimant, for example their gender, race, language or other such attribute as the Home Secretary considers appropriate.[87]

1.121 The only remedy available to challenge the decision in such cases would be judicial review. Often where such claims were successful, enabling the asylum claimant to bring an in-country appeal right, they were unable to access support. The position has been clarified to the effect that if they become a person who is eligible to exercise an in-country appeal right, then they are entitled to section 95 asylum support under IAA 1999.[88]

Third country claims

1.122 Where an individual has sought asylum either on or after arrival, and has travelled through other countries en route to the UK, the Secretary of State is entitled to consider the extent to which the individual ought to have applied for asylum in that other country prior to seeking protection in the UK and may decline to consider the claim for asylum substantively and refuse the application for leave to enter or leave to remain.[89]

1.123 As between EU territories there is a regulation in force governing the responsibility for the assessment of asylum claims for persons arriving in one EU territory that have passed through other territories[90] commonly referred to as the Dublin II Convention.

1.124 There is no entitlement to bring an appeal against this decision prior to removal from the UK, so the only challenge would be by judicial review.[91] It appears that UKBA accept that such individuals are entitled to receive asylum support under IAA 1999 s95 while they are in the UK.

1.125 The Secretary of State has the power to fingerprint any asylum claimant, or any dependant.[92] Invariably it is the practice of the Secretary of State not only to make comparisons of the fingerprint data with previous applications submitted, but also with other EU

86 NIAA 2002 s94(5).
87 NIAA 2002 s94(5C).
88 UK Borders Act 2007 s17(2).
89 HC 395 para 345.
90 Commission Regulation (EC) No 1560/2003.
91 AI(TC)A 2004 Sch 3.
92 IAA 1999 s141(1).

territories in order to ascertain whether an individual may have travelled through another EU territory prior to submitting a claim for asylum in the UK.

Fresh claims

1.126 In some cases an individual may have made a claim for asylum some considerable time ago that has been refused and may have been the subject of unsuccessful appeals, but as a consequence of a change in their circumstances or a change to the conditions which operate in their former home country they may believe that they should be entitled to bring a fresh claim. Alternatively the individual may have received new evidence prior to enforcement action being taken against them, which they wish to present as a basis for not proceeding with that proposed removal.

1.127 The problem for such individuals may be two-fold. First is the problem of seeking to persuade the Secretary of State that the claim should be reviewed further and second is the issue of whether they have an entitlement to support whilst the claim is being reviewed, bearing in mind that strictly speaking they would no longer fall within the definition of an asylum-seeker for the purposes of s95 support under IAA 1999, unless and until the Secretary of State agreed that the matter should be reviewed in detail and treated as amounting to a fresh claim. In the meantime they qualify for cashless support under IAA 1999 s4, provided the fresh claim does not simply repeat the previous claim (see further para 6.52).

1.128 The immigration rules envisage a situation in which an asylum claimant has more information to provide even after a refusal and even after an appeal may have been determined. Further material or submissions will only amount to a fresh claim if considered significantly different from the material previously considered and, if when taken together with the previous material, they create a realistic prospect of success notwithstanding its rejection.[93]

1.129 The importance to an asylum claimant of the Secretary of State reaching a decision that a claim amounts to a fresh claim, is that an appeal right is triggered, even if the application is rejected, enabling the individual not only to pursue what might be a second appeal to the Asylum and Immigration Tribunal (AIT), but also that the individual falls clearly within the definition of an asylum-seeker for support purposes under IAA 1999 s94.

93 HC 395 para 353.

Irregular documents on arrival

1.130 Many of those persons seeking entry to the UK for the purposes of applying for asylum will be either travelling on no documents, or on false documents, or will have travelled on documents destroyed en route to the UK. Others will have sought to gain entry in other ways, such as by arriving clandestinely.

1.131 Persons arriving in the UK have been subject to criminal prosecution either for the possession and use of false documents or for entering illegally, despite the fact that the Refugee Convention recognises that individuals ought not to be penalised where the individual presents a claim for asylum without delay and can show that there is good cause for their illegal entry or illegal presence.[94]

1.132 The protections afforded by article 31 of the Refugee Convention were watered down following the introduction of IAA 1999 s31, by limiting the availability of a defence in criminal law to a specific number of offences and also by restricting the protection against penalties only to cases in which the individual had come directly to the UK or could not have reasonably been expected to have applied for asylum in a country en route.

1.133 By a majority the House of Lords concluded in *R v Asfaw*[95] that the restriction of protections available under section 31, as opposed to the scope of the protection against penalties under article 31, was unlawful and a conviction obtained against the appellant was unlawful.

1.134 A further offence was created in respect of persons who fail to have a valid identification document to produce at an asylum or leave interview (or within three days of such an interview) for themselves or a dependent child travelling with them.[96]

1.135 The section contains within it a series of potential (and in some cases extremely complex) defences including:

- establishing that the individual is an EEA national or family member of an EEA national;
- proving that the individual travelled all the way to the UK without any such document;
- producing a false document that the individual was able to prove was used for all purposes in connection with the journey to the UK; or

94 Refugee Convention article 33(1).

95 [2008] UKHL 31.

96 AI(TC)A 2004 s2.

- proving that they had a reasonable excuse for not being in possession of such a document.

1.136 In respect of the last of these defences, the legislation specifically precludes a reasonable excuse arising from complying with the instructions of an agent advising what should be done about any such documents, unless it can be shown that it would unreasonable not to comply with those instructions.[97]

1.137 The impact of the legislation, which potentially criminalises any asylum-seeker who is unable to produce an immigration document in connection with their claim, has been lessened by the decision of the Divisional Court in *Thet v Director of Public Prosecutions*[98] in which the court accepted that the 'ill drafted but not ambiguous' statutory provision afforded a defence to the appellant by being able to show that if the individual had only used false documents in order to come to the UK, they could not be culpable of the offence. Only if the individual had used a genuine passport for part of the journey could they be caught within the ambit of section 2.

Credibility

1.138 In the vast majority of asylum claims, success or failure will be determined by the extent to which their account of events as to the past is accepted as being credible. The onus is upon the individual to establish their claim, but given the consequences of removing a person where there is a risk of persecution or serious harm, the burden upon the claimant is to show that the claim demonstrates the existence of such a risk to the lower balance of probabilities. This reduction in the evidential burden is, however, harder to establish than one might think, largely because the asylum claimant will often be unable to provide any evidence or corroboration to substantiate their claim. Such corroboration is not required, but it is worthy of note that in many cases the asylum claimant starts off at a significant disadvantage.

1.139 In determining the credibility of the asylum-seeker, the immigration rules specify that the Secretary of State will apply the provisions in section 8 of the Asylum and Immigration (Treatment of Claimants, etc) Act 2004.[99]

1.140 Section 8 sets out a list of factors that are to be taken into account as damaging an individual's credibility, which include:

97 AI(TC)A 2004 s2(7)(b)(iii).

98 [2006] EWHC 2701 (Admin).

99 HC 395 para 339N.

- failure without explanation to produce a passport on request to an immigration officer;
- production of a false passport;
- destruction, alteration or disposal of a passport or ticket or other document in connection with travel, without reasonable explanation;
- failure to answer a question without reasonable explanation;[100]
- failure to apply for asylum in a safe country en route;[101]
- failure to make a claim for asylum until a negative immigration decision;[102] or
- failure to make a claim for asylum until after arrest, unless there was no reasonable opportunity to do so earlier.[103]

1.141 What makes section 8 so disturbing is that although it is a matter for the Secretary of State to determine which issues are likely to lead UKBA finding against an individual's credibility, the legislation dictates that the AIT is also required to treat these factors as damaging the individual's credibility.[104]

1.142 Perhaps unsurprisingly the Court of Appeal was anxious to avoid judicial independence being undermined by a mandatory provision requiring an assessment of an individual's credibility to be saddled with this statutory proviso. It has attempted to negate the provision largely by qualifying it, using a reminder of the factors that an individual decision-maker should take into account in the general assessment of credibility, and permitting the individual decision-maker to decide on the weight to which any such factors would ultimately have on the general assessment of the individual's credibility.[105]

Favourable decisions in asylum and human rights claims

1.143 The outcomes of asylum applications that can lead to a person being granted leave are:

100 AI(TC)A 2004 s8(3).
101 AI(TC)A 2004 s8(4).
102 AI(TC)A 2004 s8(5).
103 AI(TC)A 2004 s8(6).
104 AI(TC)A 2004 s8(1).
105 *JT (Cameroon) v Secretary of State for the Home Department* [2008] EWCA Civ 878.

- the grant of recognition as a refugee and leave in that capacity;
- the grant of humanitarian protection and leave in that capacity; or
- the grant of discretionary leave.

1.144 Where there is an appeal, if successful this can lead to the grant of status in some capacity, notwithstanding the initial Home Office refusal.

1.145 If the individual has already had leave in the UK and is for example the subject of deportation action, then the grant of status will lead to the individual being granted leave to remain. Where the individual is a port applicant or is a person treated as an illegal entrant, then the individual if successful is granted leave to enter. There are no practical differences between the grant of leave to enter as opposed to the grant of leave to remain: the distinction arises solely in terms of what the individual's immigration status was when the application was submitted.

Grant of refugee status

1.146 If an individual is able to show that they meet the criteria for recognition as a refugee, they must also show they should not be refused protection because the Home Secretary believes that they would constitute a danger to the security of the UK, or have been convicted of an offence in the UK as a consequence of which the individual would be regarded as a danger to the community. They should then be issued with a residence permit for five years.[106]

1.147 The Secretary of State is permitted to review whether the individual remains eligible throughout that five-year period, for example by reference to a significant change in the level of risk that the individual would face if removed to their country of origin, or where they have committed an offence in the UK thereby losing the protection against removal under the Convention.

1.148 Provided that no such changes have occurred during the five-year period, the individual would be entitled to apply for and obtain leave to remain permanently.

1.149 A person granted leave as a refugee is entitled to have a travel document issued to them on payment of a fee and completion of a relevant application form.[107]

106 HC 395 para 339Q(i).
107 HC 395 para 344A(i).

1.150 Such a person is also entitled to be joined in the UK (if not already here) by their spouse or civil partner or unmarried or same-sex partner and any children under the age of 18, provided that they were living together as part of the family unit prior to the person granted recognition as a refugee having left the country of his or her former residence.[108]

1.151 The rules prevent such family members from being admitted to the UK if there is reason to believe that they would be excluded from protection as a consequence of their own actions (having committed a crime against humanity or a serious non-political crime) were they to have applied for asylum in their own right.[109]

Grant of humanitarian protection

1.152 Individuals able to show that they face a real risk of serious harm on return to the country of origin, defined as facing the death penalty or execution, unlawful killing, torture or inhuman or degrading treatment or punishment, or a serious and individual threat by reason of indiscriminate violence in a situation of armed conflict, but who are unable to show that the reason for that harm is for one of the five Refugee Convention reasons (race, religion, nationality, social group or political opinion) may be eligible for humanitarian protection.

1.153 A person will not be eligible for both. First, consideration is given to whether they meet the criteria for recognition as a refugee and for the grant of leave in that capacity. Only if they do not will consideration be given to the grant of humanitarian protection.[110]

1.154 As with persons granted leave as refugees, persons who have been identified as being a danger to the security of the country or, as a consequence of a conviction, a danger to the community, will be excluded from the grant of leave on this basis, but will otherwise be granted leave, also for a five-year period.[111]

1.155 As with those granted leave as refugees, after a period of five years they will be eligible to apply for settlement provided that nothing has occurred that would either suggest that they pose a threat, nor that the risk to them of harm in the other country has diminished.

108 HC 395 paras 352A, 352AA and 352D.

109 HC 395 paras 352A(iii), 352AA(iv) and 352D(v).

110 HC 395 para 339C(ii).

111 HC 395 para 339Q(ii).

1.156 Individuals granted leave on a humanitarian basis can apply for a certificate of travel, but it will only be issued if the individual is unable to obtain a passport or national identity document enabling them to travel. If the individual could obtain a document from their own national authorities, a certificate of travel would only be issued where efforts have been made to obtain such a document and there are serious humanitarian reasons for the person wishing to travel.[112]

1.157 Individuals granted humanitarian protection since 30 August 2005 have an entitlement to be joined by family members, including spouses, same-sex or unmarried partners and children.[113]

Discretionary leave

1.158 For individuals able to show that they face a real risk of harm, but who are excluded from the grant of leave as a refugee or humanitarian protection because they have committed a serious crime prior to arrival or pose a threat in the UK, the individual may be granted discretionary leave. The length of leave granted will usually be not more than six months and will be renewable. If the individual is considered to pose a risk to the UK it is unlikely that they would ever be granted settlement.[114]

1.159 Discretionary leave is also currently issued to unaccompanied minors whose claims do not meet the criteria for the grant of refugee or humanitarian leave and there are inadequate reception arrangements available in their own country.[115] Generally leave would be granted for a maximum period of three years or until the individual is 17.5 years old whichever is shorter. Prior to 31 March 2007, such individuals would be granted leave until 18 but the policy changed at the beginning of April 2007.

1.160 Other persons may also be granted discretionary leave for three years, such as those whose claims do not fall within either the Refugee Convention or the ECHR, and are not otherwise excluded from protection, but where there is some other compelling reason why leave should be granted.

112 HC 395 para 344A(ii) and (iii).

113 HC 395 paras 352FA–352FG.

114 Asylum Policy Instructions – Discretionary leave.

115 At the time of writing, the policy in respect of unaccompanied minors was being reviewed.

1.161 Discretionary leave is also used in cases where an individual, while unable to demonstrate that their removal would be a breach of the Refugee Convention or of the protection elements of the ECHR (arts 2 and 3), would be able to show that removal would breach their rights under art 8 in terms of the unlawful interference with their right to respect for family and private life.

1.162 Other than for persons excluded from protection as a consequence of being perceived as a danger, persons with discretionary leave would normally be eligible to apply for settlement after six years.

1.163 Persons with discretionary leave do not have any entitlement to a travel document, but may qualify for a Home Office certificate of travel.[116] They do not have any entitlement to family reunion. Once granted indefinite leave to remain they may bring their family members if they can satisfy relevant requirements under the immigration rules.

Other human rights applications

Medical cases

1.164 In some cases the individual seeking asylum in the UK does not have a fear from either the state or from particular individuals within their country of former residence, but seeks to remain on the basis that removal would lead to a rapid deterioration in their health, where for example treatment for their illness is not available in their home country.

1.165 Although for a period of time the approach of the Secretary of State had been to grant discretionary leave to such individuals for a finite period, more recently the approach has been to reject these applications outright on the basis that these medical cases do not meet the high threshold set by ECHR article 3.

1.166 The position appears clear following the judgment of the European Court of Human Rights in *N v UK*,[117] that even in cases where the individual is likely to face a slow and painful death due to the lack of availability of medical assistance overseas, other than in exceptional cases, the removal of such a person to their home

116 www.ukba.homeoffice.gov.uk/ukresidency/traveldocuments/types/certificateoftravel/whoqualifies/

117 *N v United Kingdom [GC]* Application no 26565/05.

country would not breach article 3.[118] There may be medical cases where individuals can argue that removal will interfere with their rights under ECHR article 8 or that they fall within the strict 'suicide risk' criteria in the immigration rules.

1.167 There will remain some individuals who, having been granted discretionary leave under the older more generous policy, will be seeking to extend their discretionary leave. Whilst any such applications are under consideration, the individual has their leave extended by operation of law in accordance with IA 1971 s3C until such time as any appeal is finally determined. This ought to mean that such an individual may continue to have access to mainstream support until that stage.

Family life cases

1.168 An individual may have remained in the UK for many years either as an overstayer or as a person who entered illegally or even a person who submitted an application for asylum at the port and who still awaits an initial decision.

1.169 Such individuals may seek to argue that removing them from the UK now would contravene their rights under art 8 ECHR, which is to safeguard respect for family and/or private life.

1.170 Although article 8 is a *qualified* as opposed to an *absolute* right, the Secretary of State and the AIT are required to consider whether the proposed removal would violate the individual's rights having regard to the individual facts of the case.

1.171 In general, the Secretary of State would not seek to remove an individual whilst their application is considered or pending any appeal exercisable from within the UK based on the allegation that the removal would constitute a violation of their human rights, albeit not in the sense of an asylum protection claim. An appeal against a refusal would normally lead to an appeal being exercisable from within the UK.[119]

Seven-year child concession

1.172 The Immigration Minister announced the withdrawal of DP5/96, a concession that has also been referred to as the seven-year

118 *N v United Kingdom* [GC] Application no 26565/05.

119 However, power exists for the appeal to be certified as clearly unfounded: NIAA 2002 s94.

child concession. The concession set out the factors UKBA should take into account when considering the removal of parents of a child who had lived in the UK continuously for seven years. However the minister stressed that the fact that a child has spent a significant period of their life in the UK would continue to be an important relevant factor to be taken into account when considering whether article 8 would be breached by the family's removal.[120]

Victims of human trafficking

1.173 The Council of Europe Convention against Trafficking in Human Beings[121] applies to all forms of trafficking: national/transnational, whether or not related to organised crime, whether the victim is female, male or a child and whatever the form of exploitation: sexual exploitation, forced labour or services. Its aims are to prevent trafficking, protect the human rights of victims and prosecute the traffickers. It requires the UK to have a national referral mechanism for victims or trafficking. Article 10 of the Trafficking Convention provides that a trained 'competent authority' should make the decision about whether or not a person is a trafficking 'victim'. If the person is within the immigration or asylum system (for example, if they have made an ECHR article 3 or 8 claim), a decision should be made by UKBA, if not then by the UK Human Trafficking Centre.[122] A 'victim' may benefit from a 45-day minimum reflection and recovery period and a one-year renewable residence permit.

Appeals to the Asylum and Immigration Tribunal (AIT)

1.174 At the time of writing the government had announced that it planned to transfer the current AIT into the two-tier unified tribunal system by 2010. The first stage of appealing against an asylum or immigration decision would be to appeal to the First-tier Tribunal (Immigration and Asylum Chamber) with an appeal to the Upper Tribunal, replacing the current statutory reconsideration process.

120 HC col 49 WS, 9 December 2008.
121 CETS No 197 in force in the UK on 1 April 2009.
122 www.crimereduction.homeoffice.gov.uk/humantrafficking

But a last minute amendment to the Borders, Citizenship and Immigration Act 2009 limits the transfer of judicial review to fresh claims.[123] Although the right of judicial review would still exist, it is possible that eventually the majority of cases would be heard by the new Upper Tribunal.

1.175 A person served with an immigration decision is entitled to pursue an appeal against that decision subject to certain exceptions and limitations.[124] Immigration decisions are defined as being:

- refusal of leave to enter;
- refusal of entry clearance;
- refusal of a certificate of entitlement to the right of abode;
- refusal of a variation of leave as a consequence of which the individual has no leave;
- variation of their leave as a consequence of which the individual has no leave;
- revocation of their indefinite leave in specified circumstances;
- removal under IAA 1999 s10;
- removal as an illegal entrant;
- decision to make a deportation order;
- refusal to revoke a deportation order;[125]
- grant of leave to remain for in excess of 12 months but refusal of asylum;[126]
- refusal to extend leave or decision to cut short leave previously granted as a refugee.[127]

1.176 In broad terms the exceptions and limitations prevent appeals from being brought for persons who:

- do not satisfy a requirement as to age, nationality or citizenship;
- do not possess an immigration document of a specified type or provide a medical report where required to do so under the rules;
- seek to remain in the UK for a period greater than permitted under the rules or for a purpose outside of the rules;[128]

123 BCIA 2009 s53.
124 NIAA 2002 s82(1).
125 NIAA 2002 s82(2).
126 NIAA 2002 s83.
127 NIAA 2002 s83A.
128 NIAA 2002 s88.

- challenge a refusal of an entry clearance other than as family visitors (except where the individual asserts that the refusal would breach the Human Rights Act or the Race Relations Act);[129]
- challenge a refusal of leave to enter unless the entry clearance was for the purpose of the entry sought (although the appeal is still available if despite that the appeal was on grounds of a breach of the Human Rights Act or the Race Relations Act);[130]
- have had a previous entitlement to bring an appeal against a decision and where the new claim could have been raised previously in the earlier appeal or in a notice inviting the individual to set out their basis for seeking to remain in the UK and where, in the opinion of the Secretary of State, there are no good reasons why it would not have been raised earlier;[131]
- where the Secretary of State has personally directed that a particular individual be refused leave to enter or an entry clearance on conducive to public good grounds;[132] or
- where a deportation decision is made in accordance with the automatic deportation provisions for convicted foreign nationals.[133]

1.177 Where the Secretary of State has personally certified that a decision has been taken in part on national security grounds then it will not proceed to a hearing before the AIT.[134]

1.178 A deportation decision in which an appellant alleged that removal would breach their rights under the Refugee Convention or the ECHR where a certificate as to national security was made by the Secretary of State would still give rise to an appeal, but the appeal would not be to the AIT but instead to the Special Immigration Appeals Commission,[135] the appeals of which are dealt with in an entirely different and far less transparent manner.

1.179 The legislation also limits the grounds upon which an appeal can be brought against an immigration decision. These grounds are that:

129 NIAA 2002 s88A.
130 NIAA 2002 s89(1).
131 NIAA 2002 s96.
132 NIAA 2002 s98.
133 NIAA 2002 s82(3A).
134 NIAA 2002 s97(1).
135 NIAA 2002 s97A(3).

- the decision is not in accordance with the immigration rules;
- the decision is unlawful as being contrary to the Race Relations Act 1976;
- the decision is unlawful under section 6 of the Human Rights Act;
- the decision breaches the EU law rights of an EEA national or the family member of an EEA national;
- the decision is otherwise not in accordance with the law;
- discretion should have been exercised differently where the immigration rules permitted the exercise of discretion; or
- the removal would breach the UK's obligations under the Refugee Convention or the ECHR.[136]

1.180 Where an appeal is available there are time limits for the lodging of the notice of appeal and related documents. In cases where the individual is overseas, the time limit is 28 days. Where the individual is in the UK, it is ten working days, but if the individual is detained the time limit is five working days.[137] In detained fast track asylum cases, the time limit is two working days.[138]

1.181 It is possible for an appeal notice to be lodged out of time and the tribunal will in the first instance consider whether time should be extended by reason of special circumstances and that it would be unjust not to extend time,[139] or in fast track cases whether it had not been practicable to have given notice of appeal within the time limit.[140]

1.182 Appeals will usually be heard in the first instance by a single immigration judge, although in deportation cases (which are not subject to the automatic provisions) the appeals are generally heard before two-judge panels.

1.183 A party who is dissatisfied with the outcome of the initial appeal may seek an order for reconsideration of the decision by application to the tribunal within five working days[141] (the time period is shorter in fast track cases). If that application is refused, there is the

136 NIAA 2002 s84(1).

137 Asylum and Immigration Tribunal (Procedure) Rules 2005 SI No 230 r7.

138 Asylum and Immigration Tribunal (Fast Track Procedure) Rules 2005 SI No 560 r8(1).

139 Asylum and Immigration Tribunal (Procedure) Rules 2005 SI No 230 r 10(5).

140 Asylum and Immigration Tribunal (Fast Track Procedure) Rules 2005 SI No 560 r8(2).

141 NIAA 2002 s103A(3).

opportunity of seeking a statutory review[142] on application to the High Court, from whose decision there is no entitlement to bring a further appeal.[143] This review process is entirely on the basis of written submissions with no entitlement to an oral hearing.

1.184 In unusually complex cases it is possible that the initial appeal will be listed before three or more legally qualified immigration judges, as a consequence of which any challenge will be by way of an appeal direct to the Court of Appeal rather than the reconsideration route.[144]

1.185 If the tribunal orders reconsideration or if the High Court makes such an order, then the matter will proceed to a reconsideration hearing. A further appeal lies to the Court of Appeal from a reconsidered hearing, but only on a point of law.[145] In applications for statutory review, where the tribunal has refused to order reconsideration, the High Court may consider it more appropriate to refer the matter for an appeal to the Court of Appeal instead of ordering reconsideration.[146]

EEA nationals

1.186 The European Economic Area consists of the EU countries and also three other states that, while not members of the European Union, are treated in an identical manner: Norway, Iceland and Liechtenstein. Switzerland, which is neither a member state nor a member of the EEA, is nevertheless treated as if it were, and consequently nationals of that country enjoy the same rights as EEA nationals.[147]

1.187 Many of the citizens of the last two waves of accession have had greater controls imposed upon them, which significantly impact upon their entitlements to receive financial state support. These restrictions, while clearly discriminatory, are lawful as the UK, along with some other EU countries, has chosen to derogate from certain provisions of EU law during the accession period of five years following the accession date. Once the accession period is over,

142 Commonly referred to as an 'opt-in'.

143 NIAA 2002 s103A(6).

144 NIAA 2002 s103E(2).

145 NIAA 2002 s103B(1).

146 NIAA 2002 s103C(1).

147 Immigration (European Economic Area) Regulations (EEA Regs) 2006 SI No 1003 para 2(1) defines EEA nationals as including Swiss nationals.

the treatment of nationals of those countries affected cannot be any different from the treatment of any other EU citizen (but see para 1.217).

1.188 In general terms EEA nationals are able to travel in and out of the UK and have a right to reside pursuant to an enforceable EU law right.[148]

1.189 These rights have been codified by the Free Movement of Persons Directive[149] (Residence Directive), which has been transposed into domestic legislation by the Immigration (European Economic Area) Regulations 2006[150] although, as observed earlier, slightly different regimes apply for the accession states during the accession period.

Recognised treaty rights

1.190 The regulations recognise the entitlement of EEA nationals to reside in the UK as a 'qualified person' either as:

- job seekers (subject to conditions in relation to actively seeking employment);
- workers;
- self-employed persons;
- self-sufficient persons; or
- students.[151]

1.191 Persons admitted as qualified persons are entitled to reside in the UK so long as they remain qualified persons.[152] Workers who have become involuntarily unemployed may be treated as job seekers if they have been employed for more than 12 months, or if they have commenced vocational training, or if they are temporarily unable to work due to accident or illness. Similarly self-employed persons do not cease to be qualified persons as a consequence of a temporary inability through illness or accident.[153]

1.192 EEA nationals are to be given entry to the UK on production of a passport or valid identity document issued by an EEA state,[154] subject to the limited powers available to prevent entry or to expel EEA

148 Immigration Act 1988 s7(1).
149 2004/38/EC.
150 SI No 1003.
151 EEA Regs 2006 SI No 1003 reg 6(1).
152 EEA Regs 2006 reg 14.
153 EEA Regs 2006 reg 6(2) and(3).
154 EEA Regs 2006 reg 11(1).

nationals. They are entitled to reside in the UK for up to three months without being a qualified person, provided that during that time they do not become an unreasonable burden on the social assistance scheme in the UK.[155] There is no time limit imposed on the right to reside of an EEA national who remains a qualifying person.[156]

1.193 EEA nationals may also apply for permanent residence in the UK under a number of circumstances, for instance after having spent a continuous period in the UK for five years in accordance with the regulations.[157]

Family members

1.194 These rights also extend to family members of EEA nationals, with family member being defined as including:

- spouse or civil partner;
- direct descendants under 21 (children, grandchildren) or dependent direct relatives in the ascending line (parents, grandparents) of either the EEA national or the spouse/civil partner;
- dependants of the spouse or civil partner; and
- other members of the household dependent on the EEA national (extended family members).[158]

1.195 In the case of students, unless they are exercising other treaty rights whilst studying (such as working), the family members by whom they can be joined are limited to spouse/civil partner, dependent children of the EEA national or spouse/civil partner or extended family members.[159]

1.196 Extended family members encompass persons living in the household of the EEA national or a family member who requires the personal care of the EEA national or spouse/civil partner, other dependent relatives or a person with whom the EEA national has a 'durable relationship'.[160] There is no EU law definition of durable relationship, nor has there been any attempt to define this term

155 EEA Regs 2006 SI No 1003 reg 13.
156 EEA Regs 2006 reg 14(1).
157 EEA Regs 2006 reg 15(1).
158 EEA Regs 2006 reg 7(1).
159 EEA Regs 2006 reg 7(2) and (4).
160 EEA Regs 2006 reg 8.

within the regulations. It is clear however that it is intended to cover partners where the EEA national and the individual are neither married, nor in a civil partnership.[161]

1.197 The regulations also provide for a continued entitlement to remain in the UK on the breakdown of a relationship with an EEA national where the non-EEA family member retains a right of residence if:

- an EEA qualified person dies; and
- the non-EEA family member had lived with the EEA national for at least 12 months in the UK; and
- is him or herself now either working, self-employed or self-sufficient (or the dependant of such a person);[162]
- they are the child or grandchild of an EEA national qualified person or spouse or civil partner that has died; or
- the EEA national ceased to be a qualifying person when they left the UK; and
- the child or grandchild was attending an educational course (which they are still undertaking) at the date of death or ceasing to reside in the UK;[163]
- a person with actual custody of a child who has retained rights of residence on the basis of their continuing educational course;[164]
- a former spouse or civil partner of a qualified person on termination of a marriage or civil partnership who had previously been residing in the UK in accordance with the regulations and who is themselves now working, self-employed or self-sufficient (or the family member of such a person) where either:
  - the marriage or civil partnership had lasted for at least three years prior to initiating proceedings for termination of the relationship and the parties had lived for at least 12 months in the UK; and
  - the non-EEA national has custody of any children or a right of access to a child under 18 where the access must take place in the UK; or
  - the relationship broke down as a result of 'difficult circumstances', eg domestic violence.[165]

161 EEA Regs 2006 SI No 1003 reg 8(5).
162 EEA Regs 2006 reg 10(2).
163 EEA Regs 2006 reg 10(3).
164 EEA Regs 2006 reg 10(4).
165 EEA Regs 2006 reg 10(5)(iv).

1.198 If the non-EEA family member has already acquired a right of permanent residence (or if they later acquire such right), then they are to be treated as having permanent residence, ie the death, departure or termination of the relationship will not place them in a weaker position so far as their right of residence is concerned.[166]

Residence documents

1.199 The regulations set out the basis upon which an EEA national or family member can seek documentation to demonstrate that they are exercising rights in accordance with the regulations, with registration certificates being issued to EEA nationals who are qualified persons, or to EEA family members who have the retained right of residence or who belong to the family of an EEA national who has been given permanent residence in accordance with the regulations.[167] Such documents must be issued immediately and without a fee being payable, whereas for the majority of applications made to the Home Office (other than an asylum or human rights application, or applications for leave as the victim of domestic violence where the individual is destitute) a fee is mandatory.[168]

1.200 For those close family members who are not EEA nationals, they will be issued with residence cards where they have either acquired a retained right, or the EEA family member is a qualified person or a person with permanent residence. Again no fee is payable and the residence card must be issued within six months. Usually the residence card consists of an endorsement in the passport of the non-EEA family member of either five years or a shorter period if the EEA national is proposing to remain in the UK for a lesser period.[169]

1.201 For extended family members, which includes those in a durable relationship, the Secretary of State is not required to issue a registration certificate and will only do so after conducting an examination of the personal circumstances of the applicant and only if it appears appropriate to the Secretary of State to do so.[170]

166 EEA Regs 2006 SI No 1003 reg 10(8).
167 EEA Regs 2006 reg 16.
168 Immigration and Nationality (Fees) Regulations 2007 SI No 1158.
169 EEA Regs 2006 reg 17.
170 EEA Regs 2006 regs 16(5) and 17(4).

1.202 It is important to appreciate that for EEA nationals and their family members, the registration certificate or residence cards do not themselves give rise to the rights exercisable in accordance with the Treaty; the documents merely confirm the existence of those rights.[171]

Delays in issuing documents

1.203 If the absence of the documentation prevents access to financial entitlements for the EEA or non-EEA national, this can be challenged, by judicial review if necessary.

1.204 A number of successful claims for damages have been brought by those prejudiced by delays in producing documents, eg being unable to travel to work in the EU or to be joined by family members.

Expulsion and refusal of admission

1.205 Given that the rights of residence emanate from the Treaty and not from the issuance of documents from the Home Office, the power of the Secretary of State to refuse to issue those documents, or to refuse entry or to remove an individual who is an EEA national or the family member of an EEA national, is severely restricted.[172]

1.206 Such a decision to refuse entry or to expel either the EEA national or family member may only be taken on grounds of public policy, public security or public health, *or where he or she does not have or no longer has the 'right to reside'*.[173]

1.207 Any such decision is also required to be proportionate and based solely on the conduct of the individual. The individual's conduct must represent a genuine, present and sufficiently serious threat to a fundamental interests of society; general prevention of crime measures do not justify such a decision. Previous convictions in themselves do not justify such a decision.[174]

1.208 There is a sliding scale of protection afforded to the EEA national or family member dependent on the length of residence in the UK.[175]

171 See EU Treaty and European Casework Instructions chapter 2 para 1.1.

172 EEA Regs 2006 SI No 1003 reg 19(1).

173 EEA Regs 2006 reg 19(3) and reg 21(1).

174 EEA Regs 2006 reg 17(5).

175 *MG and VC (EEA Regulations 2006; 'conducive' deportation) Ireland* [2006] UKAIT 00053.

Where the individual has a right of permanent residence under the regulations then removal can only be on serious grounds of public policy or public security.[176] Where the individual has resided in the UK for a continuous period of ten years prior to the decision or is under 18 at the date of the expulsion order, then the decision can only be justified on 'imperative grounds of public policy'.[177]

1.209 Any decision either to refuse admission or to expel would give rise to an appeal to the Asylum and Immigration Tribunal, provided that in the case of an EEA national they produced evidence that they were an EEA national, or in the case of a family member, evidence of the relationship to the EEA national.[178]

1.210 There is an apparent power to detain EU citizens if 'there are reasonable grounds for suspecting that a person is someone who may be removed from the United Kingdom…' So it appears that an EEA national without the right to reside may be detained by an immigration officer on reasonable suspicion that they do not have the right to reside following amendments to the EEA Regulations in 2009.[179] This power appears to be inconsistent with EU law.[180]

Application of EEA Regulations: practical obstacles

1.211 In theory the EEA Regulations 2006 as amended set out a clear framework for decision-making and for the rights of EEA nationals and their family members to be recognised. Problems arise not so much for those seeking entry to the UK to join EEA family members here, but rather for persons already in the UK, whose relationship with the EEA national, commences after either having made a different application, or having overstayed or having never made an application.

1.212 The rights that flow from the EU treaty can trump domestic immigration provisions. For example, the fact that an individual family member of an EEA national has a previous poor immigration history will not in itself necessarily justify either an expulsion or a refusal to grant entry, since the right that the EEA national has to establish themselves in a member state can only be limited on

176 EEA Regs 2006 SI No 1003 reg 17(3).
177 EEA Regs 2006 reg 17(4).
178 EEA Regs 2006 reg 26(1).
179 EEA Regs 2006 SI No 1003 reg 24, as amended by the Immigration (European Economic Area) (Amendment) Regulations 2009, SI No 1117.
180 See *Oulane* (Case C-215/03) 17 February 2005.

grounds of public policy, public security or public health, and cannot be restricted only to family members who had previously had lawful residence there, nor can it be restricted to persons who were already in a relationship with the EEA national when they arrived.[181]

1.213 For the purposes of the regulations, the family member of a UK national who has been exercising treaty rights by working or being self-employed in another member state prior to returning to the UK is entitled to be treated as the family member of an EEA national, provided that in the case of a spouse or civil partner, the marriage or civil partnership has been entered into in another state where they had been living before the UK national returned to the UK.[182] It is likely that the limiting of this provision only to marriages or civil partnerships entered into prior to the return of the UK national to the UK may no longer be lawful.[183]

1.214 At least in part, in recognition of the strength of EU law rights available to non-EEA family members married to EEA nationals, the UK introduced measures to prevent marriages taking place in the UK between persons from abroad where one of the parties to the marriage was neither an EEA national nor settled in the UK (other than for marriages officiated over by the Church of England) without seeking prior approval from the Home Office through the certificate of approval scheme.[184]

1.215 The House of Lords have since ruled that the provision is incompatible with the Human Rights Act in so far as it seeks to prevent persons from entering into marriage that are not marriages of convenience.[185]

1.216 Under the domestic provisions of the immigration rules, the burden remains upon the parties to the marriage to demonstrate that the marriage or civil partnership is subsisting and that they both have the intention to live together permanently with the other.[186] In the EU context, the evidential burden of establishing that a marriage is a sham rests upon the state to assert in the first instance,

181 *Metock and others v Minister for Justice, Equality and Law Reform* (Case C-127/08) (2009) QB 318.

182 EEA Regs 2006 SI No 1003 reg 9.

183 *Metock and others v Minister for Justice, Equality and Law Reform* (Case C-127/08) (2009) QB 318.

184 AI(TC)A 2004 s19.

185 *R (Baiai) and others v Secretary of State for the Home Department* [2008] UKHL 53.

186 HC 395 paras 281(3) and 284(iv).

and then on the individuals to show, that the marriage is not one of convenience.[187]

Accession states: May 2004

1.217 On 1 May 2004, the EU was enlarged by a further ten countries: Hungary, Poland, Czech Republic, Slovakia, Slovenia, Latvia, Lithuania, Estonia, Malta and Cyprus. Special rules were to apply to these States, other than Malta and Cyprus whose nationals got full EU rights, for a period of five years until 30 April 2009. The rules were then extended for a further two years until 30 April 2011.[188]

1.218 These rules impose a requirement on individuals to register their employment with the Home Office within one month unless:

- they were dual UK, Swiss or other EEA nationals (who were not A8 nationals);[189] or
- the family member of a Swiss or EEA national;[190]
- or if they had leave to enter or remain already as at 30 April 2004 without any condition prohibiting them from being employed;[191] or
- if they had been legally working already for a 12-month period prior to 30 April 2004 or any time thereafter;[192] or
- if they were either a member of the diplomatic mission or the family member of a person with the mission who was not exempt from immigration control.[193]

1.219 The obligation to register would be for the 12-month period and if employment with an employer ceased, then the individual would be obliged to apply for a further registration until a complete 12-month period of registered employment, without interruption, had been undertaken. At the end of the period of 12 months' registered employment the individual would cease to be required to register.[194]

187 *IS (Marriages of Convenience) Serbia* [2008] UKAIT 00031.

188 Accession (Immigration and Worker Registration) (Amendment) Regulations 2009 SI No 892.

189 Accession (Immigration and Worker Registration) (A(IWR)) Regulations 2004 SI No 1219 reg 2(5).

190 A(IWR) Regs 2004 reg 2(6).

191 A(IWR) Regs 2004 reg 2(2).

192 A(IWR) Regs 2004 reg 2(3) and (4).

193 A(IWR) Regs 2004 reg 2(5A).

194 A(IWR) Regs 2004 reg 2(4).

1.220 Those exempt from the requirement to register include A8 nationals with leave to enter or remain not subject to restrictions on employment or who had been working lawfully for a 12-month period. This might include persons who prior to accession were granted limited leave on either asylum or human rights grounds, or even those who were on temporary admission who had been given permission to take up employment and had been employed for a full 12-month period prior to accession.

1.221 During the period of time that persons are required to register, an individual is not entitled to come within the definition of a qualified person under the 2006 EEA Regulations if they are in the UK as a jobseeker.[195]

1.222 Similarly they would have no entitlement to be issued with a registration certificate or residence card.[196]

1.223 At the same time as the coming into force of the relevant regulations to coincide with the accession, a series of social security measures were introduced so as to prevent accession state nationals requiring registration to have access to mainstream support. The details of these changes will be covered in detail in the following chapters.

1.224 Importantly, no additional restrictions have been placed upon A8 nationals seeking to exercise other EU law rights such as the right to set up as a self-employed person or the right to enter into vocational training.

1.225 There may well be individuals who as at the date of accession either had pending asylum claims or who had been refused but had not been removed from the UK. The fact of those previous claims or of any refusals would not be a basis upon which such individuals could be removed from the UK since, as at the date of accession, any attempt to expel them from the UK would have to be consistent with EU law, for which the test on expulsion is presently set out within paragraph 21 of the EEA Regulations 2006 (as amended, see appendix B).

Accession states: January 2007

1.226 The second wave of EU enlargement was the accession of Bulgaria and Romania as from 1 January 2007. As with the A8 countries,

195 A(IWR) Regs 2004 SI No 1219 reg 5(2).
196 A(IWR) Regs 2004 reg 5(5).

additional restrictions have been imposed upon nationals of these A2 countries during the accession period of five years ending on 31 December 2011.[197]

1.227 The restrictions imposed on the A2 nationals are however far more stringent than with the A8 nationals. With A8 nationals there was a necessity to register the employment. With A2 nationals the onus is upon seeking prior authorisation for that employment as a means of seeking to control persons arriving in the UK to seek or take up employment.

1.228 Central to the regulations is the concept of 'accession state national subject to worker authorisation' and as with the A8 nationals some persons are outside the scope of the restriction, including:

- A2 nationals with leave under the Immigration Act not subject to a restriction on employment;[198]
- A2 nationals legally working for at least 12 months prior to 31 December 2006;[199]
- A2 nationals who have worked legally for 12 months whether before or after ceasing to be subject to worker authorisation;[200]
- A2 nationals who are dual UK or other EEA nationals (other than A2);[201]
- A2 nationals who have a partner who is either British or has settled status;[202]
- A2 nationals who are members of a diplomatic mission or the family member of such a person;[203]
- A2 nationals who have permanent residence under the 2006 EEA Regulations;[204]
- A2 nationals with an EEA family member who has a right to reside in the UK under the 2006 EEA Regulations;[205]
- A2 nationals who are family members of A2 nationals who are self-employed, self-sufficient or in the UK as students (qualified persons under the 2006 EEA Regulations);[206]

197 A(IWR) Regs 2004 SI No 1219 reg 1(2).
198 A(IWR) Regs 2004 reg 2(2).
199 A(IWR) Regs 2004 reg 2(3).
200 A(IWR) Regs 2004 reg 2(4).
201 A(IWR) Regs 2004 reg 2(5).
202 A(IWR) Regs 2004 reg 2(6).
203 A(IWR) Regs 2004 reg 2(6A).
204 A(IWR) Regs 2004 reg 2(7).
205 A(IWR) Regs 2004 reg 2(8)(a).
206 A(IWR) Regs 2004 reg 2(8)(b).

- A2 nationals holding a registration certificate giving unconditional access to the UK labour market (highly skilled persons);[207]
- A2 nationals who are students and hold a registration certificate confirming an entitlement to work whilst studying, limited to 20 hours a week, other than where the work is part of the course or during vacation;[208]
- A2 nationals who previously had a certificate enabling them to work whilst studying will be exempt from being subject to worker authorisation for a period of four months from the end of their course;[209] or
- A2 nationals posted to work in the UK by their employers.[210]

1.229 These regulations also specify that family members are 'authorised family members' if the A2 national to whose family they belong and who is subject to worker authorisation is exercising a right of residence in the UK under the 2006 EEA Regulations as a worker, but will not include family members of those working as au pairs, under the sectors-based scheme or as seasonal agricultural workers.[211]

1.230 The sectors-based scheme was a category introduced by the Home Office to deal with the shortage of persons wishing to work in particular areas, catering and food processing. Immigration rules were introduced enabling persons to seek entry to the UK to carry out this work. The category is for individuals aged between 18–30 and is restricted to a maximum period of 12 months' employment.[212]

1.231 Seasonal agricultural workers are a category within the immigration rules permitting individuals who are students aged 18 or over to come to the UK for a maximum period of six months to work, but only in accordance with that scheme.[213]

1.232 Highly skilled persons are defined as those who either meet the criteria under the Home Office's highly skilled migrant programme (which is known within the points-based system as tier 1 (general) migrants), other than the language requirement, or who have a

207 A(IWR) Regs 2004 SI No 1219 reg 2(9).
208 A(IWR) Regs 2004 reg 10.
209 A(IWR) Regs 2004 reg 10B.
210 A(IWR) Regs 2004 reg 11.
211 A(IWR) Regs 2004 reg 3(1)(b).
212 HC 395 para 135I.
213 HC 395 para 104.

degree, postgraduate certificate or postgraduate diploma from a UK-based academic institution or a higher national diploma from a Scottish-based institution.[214]

1.233 As with the A8 nationals, A2 nationals who are subject to worker authorisation are not entitled to be treated as qualified persons if seeking to come to the UK as jobseekers.[215]

1.234 Similarly they are not entitled to be issued with registration certificates or residence cards while they remain persons subject to worker authorisation.[216]

1.235 Where a person from Bulgaria or Romania is able to show that they either fall within the definition of highly skilled or that they have been working lawfully for a continuous period of 12 months (in which case they cease to be subject to worker authorisation), they are permitted to apply for a registration certificate in order to take up employment in the UK providing them with unconditional access to the labour market.[217]

1.236 A student is entitled to seek a registration certificate providing confirmation that they may have limited access to the labour market both whilst studying and for the period of up to four months at the conclusion of their course of studies.[218]

1.237 If an accession state national is subject to worker authorisation, then they can only take up employment if they hold an accession worker authorisation document and the work must be in accordance with the conditions set out in the document.[219]

1.238 Such a document can either be:

- a passport endorsed prior to 1 January 2007 (the date of accession) showing leave to remain with a condition of restricted employment;
- a seasonal agricultural work card; or
- an accession worker card.

1.239 As with other seasonal agricultural workers under the immigration rules, the seasonal agricultural work card would cease to be regarded as valid at the end of the six-month period after the A2 national has started their work.[220]

214 A(IWR) Regs 2004 SI No 1219 reg 4.
215 A(IWR) Regs 2004 reg 6(2).
216 A(IWR) Regs 2004 reg 7(1).
217 A(IWR) Regs 2004 reg 7(3).
218 A(IWR) Regs 2004 reg 7(6).
219 A(IWR) Regs 2004 reg 9(1).
220 A(IWR) Regs 2004 reg 9(3)(b).

1.240 An application for an accession worker card by a person subject to worker authorisation is made in writing to the Secretary of State with details of the name and address of the employer and must be within an authorised category of employment.[221]

1.241 The application should be accompanied for the worker subject to authorisation by a letter of approval under work permit arrangements or a letter of offer from the employer.

1.242 Applications can also be made for an accession worker card by authorised family members,[222] with proof that they are an authorised family member.

1.243 Any authorisation issued by the Secretary of State will include a condition restricting the applicant's employment to the employer specified and the authorised category of employment.[223] Slightly less restrictive conditions will be imposed on those meeting the work permit arrangements, but restrictions are still to be imposed preventing employment beyond the type of employment for which approval was granted.

1.244 The regulations create offences for any employer who employs a person subject to worker authorisation where either there is no worker authorisation document or where the authorisation document does not authorise that employment.[224]

1.245 It is also an offence for the worker who is subject to worker authorisation to work either without an authorisation document or in breach of the conditions of the authorisation document.[225]

1.246 A further offence is created of obtaining or seeking to obtain a worker card by deception.[226]

1.247 As with A8 nationals, the restrictions on A2 nationals are largely designed to ensure that they will have limited access to the labour market. The difference here is far starker as the focus is on pre-employment authorisation, whereas for A8 nationals it was on post-commencement registration.

1.248 It is important to observe that not all nationals of Bulgaria and Romania will be subject to worker authorisation (for example they may be married to a person settled in the UK) and similarly to

221 A(IWR) Regs 2004 SI No 1219 reg 10(1)(a).
222 A(IWR) Regs 2004 reg 10(1)(b).
223 A(IWR) Regs 2004 reg 11(5).
224 A(IWR) Regs 2004 reg 12(1).
225 A(IWR) Regs 2004 reg 13(1).
226 A(IWR) Regs 2004 reg 14(1).

observe that the restrictions apply only in respect of those seeking to work and not to the self-employed, the self-sufficient or students.

1.249 Consistent with the government's approach to limiting access to the labour market, many changes were introduced to ensure that access to the benefits system was restricted so as to exclude the EU's newest members.

Turkey: special arrangements

1.250 Although Turkey is not a member of the EU or the EEA it has been in talks about membership since at least the mid 1960s.

1.251 A number of agreements were entered into between the predecessor of the EU, the EEC, and other countries that were in discussions about joining. These agreements were collectively known as the 'association agreements'. One such agreement, the Ankara Agreement, made between the EEC and Turkey, was signed in September 1963 and its aim was the promotion of trade and economic relations including moves towards a freedom of movement for workers.

1.252 Despite the long passage of time since the date on which the agreement was reached and the fact that there is no sign of when Turkey will be admitted to full membership of the European Union, the benefit of the Ankara Agreement can be relied upon for Turkish nationals who are resident in the UK either as self-employed persons, subject to certain conditions, or as employed persons, subject to conditions.

Self-employed persons

1.253 The Additional Protocol to the Agreement came into force on 1 January 1973 and provided that:

> The Contracting parties shall refrain from introducing between themselves any new restrictions on the freedom of establishment and the freedom to provide services.

1.254 This 'standstill' clause sought to prevent any less favourable measures from being introduced, no doubt since at the time it may have been believed that Turkey would soon become a full member of what was then the EEC.

1.255 The Court of Justice has since accepted that the effect of the standstill clause is that an individual is permitted to rely upon the provision of the domestic rules in force in the UK as at that date, which are considerably more favourable than the counterpart provision under the current immigration rules.[227]

1.256 The court was specially invited to consider whether two individuals who had previously applied for asylum at the port of entry, and been refused asylum, should be entitled to take advantage of the standstill clause, or whether the benefit of the standstill clause should be restricted only to persons who had been granted lawful leave to enter the UK. The Court of Justice was clear in accepting that the benefit of the standstill clause would apply to any person either arriving at port of entry or a person already in the UK seeking a variation of leave. It would not, however, be available to a person who had used fraud and consequently could not be used on behalf of those deemed to be illegal entrants.

1.257 The benefit of the standstill clause will consequently apply:

- if a Turkish national is able to show that they are lawfully here (which may include being here on temporary admission);
- whether with or without leave (provided that they have not been deemed to be illegal entrants and provided that if on temporary admission there are no restrictions on engaging in self-employed activities); and
- is able to set up a business, though one which is not large enough to have enabled them to seek entry under the present rules on business visitors (which require a minimum investment of £250,000);

then they cannot be removed from the UK save for grounds of public policy, public security and public health, consistent with the approach to be taken with EEA nationals facing expulsion from the UK.

Turkish workers

1.258 An Association Council was set up by the Association Agreement and on 19 September 1980 adopted Decision 1/80 on the development of the Association. Article 6(1) of Decision 1/80 provides:

> 1. Subject to Article 7 on free access to employment for members of his family, a Turkish worker duly registered as belonging to the labour force of a Member State:
>
> shall be entitled in that Member State, after one year's legal employment, to the renewal of his permit to work for the same employer, if a job is available;

227 *Tum and Dari (External Relations)* [2007] (C-16/05).

shall be entitled in that Member State, after three years of legal employment and subject to the priority to be given to workers of Member States of the Community, to respond to another offer of employment, with an employer of his choice, made under normal conditions and registered with the employment services of that State, for the same occupation;

shall enjoy free access in that Member State to any paid employment of his choice, after four years of legal employment.

1.259 To benefit from the Council Decision it must be shown that the employment is genuine and that there is a true employer/employee relationship and that the work is not so marginal as not to be regarded as real employment.

1.260 Although the employment needs to be remunerative, the amount does not necessarily have to be significant.

1.261 Furthermore, reciprocal arrangements exist between nationals of some countries enabling certain funds to be claimed despite the individuals being subject to immigration control, with Turkey being one of those countries. The fact that a Turkish national may be receiving a financial benefit from the state to 'top up' their earnings does not mean that the individual would be unable to have recourse to Council Decision 1/80.

1.262 In addition, it is necessary that the employee must duly belong to the labour force. A person working without permission to remain would not be able to bring themselves within the decision.

1.263 Finally, it must be legal employment which 'presupposes a stable and secure situation as a member of the labour force of a Member State and, by virtue of this, implies the existence of an undisputed right of residence'.[228] This would tend to rule out persons who are here on temporary admission, even if they had permission to take up employment.

1.264 However, it is not necessary to show that the undisputed right of residence is unconditional, nor that it is permanent; were it required to be permanent, there would be no purpose to the entitlement to renew for the purposes of continued employment.

1.265 A Turkish national working as an au pair or as a student (who would be permitted to work for up to 20 hours without seeking prior authority) can regard themselves as duly registered and belonging to the labour force and consequently can take advantage of the entitlement to renew the permission to take up employment.[229]

228 *Kurzv Land Baden-Wurttemberg* [2002] ECR I-10691.

229 *Payir and Others (External Relations)* [2008] (C-294/06).

1.266 The consequence of this decision is that it provides an entitlement to reside in the UK for persons already here and within the labour force in legal employment. This right is renewable, provided the employment in question remains available and can only be refused on the grounds available for refusal of EEA nationals, namely public policy, public security or public health.

1.267 Furthermore, a person who is able to show that their employment falls within the scope of article 6(1) of Association Council Decision 1/80 and who faces removal from the UK through deportation would be entitled to assert that their right not to be expelled would have to measured by reference to the EU law test and consequently they would not be prevented from bringing an appeal against the automatic deportation provisions following conviction.[230]

Advice and representation

1.268 Providing immigration advice for some people is not only difficult but may lead to prosecution. Part V of the IAA 1999 sought to provide a regulatory framework for those providing advice in this field and created a criminal offence for any person to give advice unless they are either registered with the Office of the Immigration Services Commissioner (OISC) or treated as exempted by the Commissioner, or authorised to provide that advice by a designated professional body such as the Law Society, the Bar Council or the Institute of Legal Executives.[231]

1.269 Employees of either a regulated, exempted or designated body are covered by their employer, but those providing services would potentially be within the ambit of the regulations, for example immigration advisers operating from within a solicitor's firm where they are treated as self-employed contractors.

1.270 Registration with the Commissioner may be at differing levels and for different areas of immigration advice. It is an offence for a person to deliver advice for which they do not have appropriate registration.[232]

230 UK Borders Act 2007 s33(4).
231 IAA 1999 s94(1).
232 IAA 1999 s94(3).

Funding of immigration cases

Legal aid

1.271 It may be difficult to find an adviser willing to assist in a case in which you are providing advice as to an individual's entitlement to support. It may be tempting to provide that advice and assistance instead, but the non-specialist adviser should be wary of taking that step, particularly if they or their organisation are neither registered nor exempted by the OISC and do not fall within the class of organisations regulated by a designated professional body.

1.272 For those who are regulated by a designated body but do not generally provide such advice, it should be observed that while there is no legal impediment on providing assistance in this field, the work undertaken may not necessarily be paid for under the Legal Services Commission (LSC) General Civil Contract.

1.273 In order for immigration advice to be paid for by the Legal Services Commission, the individual undertaking that advice must be an accredited representative. It is not enough that they are employed within an organisation that has a person who is registered. The individual providing the advice may only be remunerated if they have personally been registered.[233] As with the OISC there are different levels at which an individual may be accredited, which limit not so much the work that they can undertake, but the work for which the LSC will make payment.

1.274 Persons who have been accredited by the Legal Services Commission are required to apply for reaccreditation, although to date the process for reaccreditation has been delayed with the consequence that those persons who were due to apply for reaccreditation by the end of 2008 have automatically had their accreditation extended until 31 December 2008.

1.275 Additionally, the General Civil Contract was amended to require that advisers providing assistance on appeals reach a minimum success rate of 40 per cent, with not less than 35 per cent for either asylum/human rights or general immigration appeals.[234]

Fixed fee scheme

1.276 As from October 2007, a new fixed fee scheme operated in respect of most areas of work under the Unified Contract. Asylum and

233 Unified Contract Specification para 11.73.

234 Contract Notice of Amendment Annex A October 2006.

immigration cases were included although there are a limited number of exceptions, including:

- cases involving applications for asylum or human rights where the claim was made prior to 1 October 2007;
- fresh claim cases where the original claim was submitted prior to 1 October 2007;
- cases involving active reviews where the original claim for asylum was made prior to 1 October 2007;
- cases involving minors applying for asylum, regardless of when they make their claim for asylum or human rights (this includes cases where there is an age dispute but it is reasonable to assume the client is a minor);
- cases that were commenced by the adviser prior to 1 October 2007 whether for asylum/human rights or for other immigration advice;
- detained fast track cases where the supplier has an exclusive contract to provide advice under the fast track scheme;
- bail applications before the AIT;
- limited cases where the costs are likely to be lower than the fixed fee limit (advice on the merits of a judicial review or in respect of an application for reconsideration or in respect of advice given to an asylum claimant before they are dispersed); and
- cases which are exceptional and amount to in excess of three times the fixed fee limit.

1.277 The LSC also intends that in future work undertaken for unaccompanied asylum claimants will be subject to exclusive contracting arrangements. A tender process had commenced in respect of the delivery of advice by telephone to detainees at police stations as well as the provision of advice to those detained at prisons.

Retrospective costs

1.278 Whilst advice and representation for an appeal to the AIT is presently within the scope of the Unified Contract, this relates only to appeals at the initial stage, or where the further appeal on reconsideration is by reason of the Secretary of State's application.

1.279 Onward applications for reconsideration to the AIT (or to the High Court on statutory review) are subject to an order for retrospective funding at the conclusion of the proceedings.[235] Fast

235 NIAA 2002 s103D(3).

track detained cases are, however, not subject to this retrospective funding regime.[236]

1.280 The AIT also has power to make an order for funding where the appeal does not conclude at a reconsidered hearing, either because the appellant abandons the appeal or where the appeal is withdrawn by reason of the Secretary of State withdrawing the decision appealed, but only where satisfied that there was a significant prospect that the appeal would be allowed if the matter had proceeded to a reconsidered hearing.[237]

1.281 The AIT is required to make a separate funding determination as to whether costs are payable in respect of the application for reconsideration and in respect of the reconsidered hearing itself.[238]

1.282 The funding order will not be made only in cases where the appellant ultimately succeeds, but essentially in any case in which an order for reconsideration is made as the AIT has concluded that the test for funding which is 'significant prospects of success' is not materially different from the tests for the grant of reconsideration which is 'real possibility'.[239] However, the AIT retains a discretion not to make a funding order where for example there is bad faith such as seeking and obtaining an order for reconsideration without full disclosure of relevant authorities or where the challenge on reconsideration relates to an allegation of improper conduct by the original immigration judge.

1.283 If a funding order is not obtained then no costs may be claimed from the LSC for any of the work undertaken in connection with the reconsideration, except for interpreters' and experts' fees.

1.284 As an incentive for advisers to undertake these cases, the LSC agree that the rate of pay for reconsideration cases is to be at an enhanced rate of 35 per cent above the standard rates applicable on hourly rate appeal cases, although each file is subject to individual assessment by the LSC.

1.285 Given the lack of guarantee of funding, often appellants who are unsuccessful at the first stage have difficulty being able to

236 Community Legal Service (Asylum and Immigration Appeals) Regulations 2005 SI No 966 reg 4(2).

237 Community Legal Service (Asylum and Immigration Appeals) Regulations 2005 SI No 966 reg 6(1A).

238 Asylum and Immigration Tribunal (Procedure) Rules 2005 SI No 230 r33(2).

239 *RS (Funding – meaning of 'significant prospect') Iran* [2005] UKAIT 00138.

persuade their adviser to run the costs risk involved in seeking an order for reconsideration. Similarly an unsuccessful appellant may have difficulty in finding a new representative to assist, particularly as the time limit for the bringing of the application for reconsideration is only five days from the date of the despatch of the original negative AIT decision.

Asylum interviews

1.286 Although the vast majority of those persons seeking asylum will be subjected to an interview, other than in fast track cases, the costs of attendance at the interview will not be met under the Community Legal Service scheme other than where the individual is either a minor (including disputed minors) or person suffering from a mental incapacity.[240]

1.287 There has for some time been a debate about the role to be played by a representative in any interview, with a protocol for interviews having been issued by the Home Office (but never agreed by representatives) in 2002 which largely minimises the opportunity for a representative to interject during the course of an interview and make comment only at the conclusion.[241] In practice it is usually possible to assist with the interview to a greater extent than envisaged by the protocol, particularly as the interviews are likely to be with either minors or vulnerable adults.

1.288 Where an interview is to take place in the absence of a representative, because of the lack of availability of LSC funding, then a request can be made for the interview to be tape recorded by giving at least 24 hours' notice in advance. Interviews on asylum are not routinely tape recorded and a failure to request a taped record will not invalidate the interview. The Home Office have also issued guidance to the effect that the interview will not be recorded if the individual is accompanied by their representative.[242]

1.289 If a representative does attend the interview, they are prohibited from tape recording the interview and if they are suspected of doing so may be excluded from the interview.

240 Unified Contract Specification para 11.103.

241 Asylum Process Guidance: Conducting the interview – Interviewing protocol.

242 Asylum Process Guidance: Conducting the interview.

Remedies

Immigration decisions

1.290 In the majority of cases the remedy against an immigration decision will be by way of an appeal to the AIT.[243]

1.291 The scope of the appeal includes an entitlement to consider whether the decision complained of is a breach of the Race Relations Act 1976, as a breach of the Act is a specific ground of appeal and can be determined by the AIT.[244]

1.292 In some cases the entitlement to appeal will arise only from abroad even for those who were previously in the UK (third country asylum claims or persons whose claims have been certified as being clearly unfounded).

1.293 Where the appeal is only available after removal, or where there is no appeal available at all (fresh claim cases or certain appeals subject to the automatic deportation provisions), then the remedy would be by way of an application for judicial review. The fact that an alternative remedy may be available (an appeal after removal) would not be a bar to the High Court exercising its jurisdiction in a case raising asylum or human rights issues given the potential consequences for the individual. In general, however, the courts would be reluctant to allow judicial review to be utilised for the sake of the convenience of a litigant. Legal aid would be available for either judicial review or habeas corpus applications, subject to the individual being able to satisfy the means and merits tests under the funding code.

1.294 Where there is an appeal exercisable, onward appeals are dealt with under the reconsideration process, which in the case of a further appeal by the claimant is subject to the retrospective funding regime.

1.295 Appeals that proceed to the reconsideration stage are subject to a right of appeal to the Court of Appeal, but only on a point of law[245] and thereafter to the Supreme Court.

1.296 In some cases where an urgent removal is to take place and an individual has exhausted all domestic remedies, it may be possible to seek a remedy from the European Court of Human Rights in Strasbourg, which can include an interim measure requiring the

243 NIAA 2002 s82(1).

244 NIAA 2002 s84(1)(b).

245 NIAA 2002 ss103B and 103E.

individual not to be removed from the UK while the application to the Court is considered.[246]

Delays by the Home Office

1.297 Given that delays are a common occurrence within the Home Office, individuals may seek to challenge the length of time taken either for the making of an initial (or subsequent) application or for the putting into effect of a decision by the AIT.

1.298 In general there is no time limit set either under the immigration rules, the AIT procedure rules (save where they are seeking an order for reconsideration or permission to appeal to the Court of Appeal) or under the legislation within which the Home Office are required to take a particular step.[247]

1.299 The courts are reluctant to grant relief even where the delay has been for several years and have indicated that it is unlikely that such claims would succeed unless it could be shown that delay in a particular case was so excessive as to be manifestly unreasonable or where the individual facts for a particular claimant mean that delay for them caused them to suffer a particular detriment as a consequence of that delay.[248]

1.300 Where the delay relates to the entitlement of an asylum claimant to be issued with documents after the AIT has allowed an appeal, the courts have taken a slightly more robust approach and accepted that a period of more than six months to issue the grant of leave to enter or remain following a successful appeal (which is not being challenged by the Home Office), or if there are exceptional circumstances, would be so excessive as to enable the court to grant relief.[249]

1.301 The justification for granting relief in such circumstances is that otherwise the judicial integrity of the decision allowing the appeal is undermined by the Secretary of State effectively ignoring the consequences of the AIT's decision.

246 European Court of Human Rights Rules of Court r39(1).

247 EEA Regs 2006 SI No 1003 regs 17(3) and 18(2) issuing residence cards for non-EEA nationals within six months is a notable exception.

248 *R (FH) and others v Secretary of State for the Home Department* [2007] EWHC 1571 (Admin).

249 *R (Mersin) v Secretary of State for the Home Department* [2000] EWHC 348 (Admin).

1.302 The AIT is also empowered to make a direction in allowing an appeal in order that the consequences of the decision be given effect, although the Home Office are not required to act upon any such directions whilst the decision is the subject of any further legal challenge.[250]

Unlawful detention

1.303 In some cases an individual may seek to challenge the legality of their detention either through judicial review proceedings or by means of an application for habeas corpus.

1.304 Although an individual is generally unable to rely upon a remedy in judicial review where an alternative remedy would be available (such as an application for bail), this proviso does not apply for claims for habeas corpus and will not rule out claims for judicial review being entertained, particularly where the detention has been significant.

1.305 Where an individual has been detained unlawfully, they may also be able to seek damages either in the High Court or a county court. The AIT does not have jurisdiction to make a financial award to an appellant.

Complaints

1.306 It is possible to bring a complaint, for example about the conduct at an interview by a particular member of UKBA or about delays or inadequate decision-making. There is rarely much prospect of a complaint being upheld although the Border and Immigration Agency Complaints Audit Committee was set up to oversee complaints handling within the department.[251]

1.307 In its latest published annual report, the committee concluded that 89 per cent of the investigations into complaints received were neither balanced nor thorough and 83 per cent of the replies were indefensible.[252]

1.308 The UK Borders Act 2007 created a Chief Inspector of UK Border Agency with responsibility for amongst other matters investigating

250 NIAA 2002 s87(1).

251 See also chapter 7.

252 Border and Immigration Agency Complaints Audit Committee Annual Report 2006–07.

the handling of complaints.[253] Among the Chief Inspector's powers is the ability to serve a 'non-interference' notice on any person who proposes to inspect the work of UKBA on the basis that it would be an unreasonable burden.[254]

1.309 It remains to be seen whether similar robust and independent criticism of UKBA will be made by the new Chief Inspector.

1.310 Complaints are also occasionally pursued through an individual's member of parliament and the Parliamentary Ombudsman has jurisdiction to investigate complaints of maladministration within the Home Office and has power to make financial awards. In the annual report for 2006–07, 76 per cent of complaints against the Immigration and Nationality Directorate were upheld.[255] 85 per cent of complaints against UKBA were fully or partly upheld. The Home Office was in the top five departments complained about and the vast majority of complaints were against UKBA.[256]

253 UK Borders Act 2007 s48.

254 UK Borders Act 2007 s53. Information about the inspector's work can be found at www.ociukba.homeoffice.gov.uk.

255 Now the UK Border Agency.

256 www.ombudsman.org.uk/improving_services/annual_reports/ar08/index.html

CHAPTER 2

EU law and the right to reside

continued

Introduction

2.1 Since the last edition of this book, there has been a significant increase in the numbers of European Union (EU) nationals arriving in the UK, combined with changes to the rules governing their rights to live and work here. There is a growing need for social welfare advisers/lawyers as well as local and central government employees to understand EU law and how it affects domestic law. We have used the term EU law, elsewhere 'EC law' or 'Community law' may be used.

2.2 This chapter gives an introduction to the EU legal system and an overview of the right to reside rules. It should be read with other chapters where they deal with the rights of EU nationals and their dependants to benefits, housing, community care or healthcare. UK legislation in these areas has not quite kept up with the radical recent changes in EU law. EU migrants and their non-EU family members may now be able to use EU law to claim new entitlements.

The key changes

2.3 On 1 May 2004, eight eastern European (A8) countries became part of the EU, followed by the 'A2' countries, Bulgaria and Romania on 1 January 2007. Against a background of tabloid warnings about an invasion by benefit tourists, the government introduced regulations to control A8 nationals' ability to work in the UK, limiting their access to the benefit system. (Cyprus and Malta joined the EU at the same time but were not subjected to these rules.) A stricter habitual residence test was also introduced, affecting any EU national who made a new claim for housing or benefits. So far, the various legal challenges to the restrictions imposed on A8 nationals have failed.

2.4 The second key change was the EU decision to consolidate and strengthen EU rules on the right to reside in the EU, resulting in what is variously known as the 'Residence' or 'Citizenship' Directive, 2004/38/EC.[1] The deadline for implementing the Directive in EU law was 30 April 2006, and on that date the government introduced the Immigration (EEA) Regulations 2006,[2] as well as amending housing and social security regulations. In some respects the EEA

1 Directive 2004/38/EC on the rights of citizens of the Union and their family members to move and reside freely within the territory of the Member States.

2 EEA Regs 2006 SI No 1003.

Regs 2006 are more generous than the Residence Directive; in others it can be argued that they do not fully comply with it.

2.5 In this chapter we will cover:

- introduction to EU law principles and institutions;
- the Residence Directive and EEA Regulations;
- meaning of *right to reside* – worker, self-employed person etc;
- retaining the right to reside – retired workers, family members etc;
- meaning of *dependant* – family member/extended family member;
- initial right to reside – three months;
- permanent right to reside – five years;
- A8 nationals – workers registration scheme;
- A2 nationals – workers authorisation scheme.

2.6 Immigration aspects and the residence documents that an EU national or their family member might apply for are covered in chapter 1. Social security cases involving EEA nationals are in chapter 3.

Introduction to EU law and institutions

Differences between EU and EEA citizens

EEA and EU members

Group 1: the 21 states with 'full rights'

The 21 countries with 'full rights' are: Austria, Belgium, Cyprus, Denmark, Finland, France, Germany, Greece, Republic of Ireland, Italy, Luxembourg, Malta, Netherlands, Portugal, Spain, Sweden, and the United Kingdom. Added to these are Iceland, Norway and Liechtenstein, which are members of the EEA only, and Switzerland, by virtue of its Association Agreement with the EU.

Group 2: the A8 states

Czech Republic, Estonia, Hungary, Latvia, Lithuania, Poland, Slovakia and Slovenia.

Group 3: the A2 states

Bulgaria and Romania.

2.7 All EU nationals are also European Economic Area (EEA) nationals, but some EEA countries have not joined the EU. Austria, Iceland, Finland, Norway, Sweden, Switzerland and Liechtenstein signed the EEA agreement in 1990. They all became EEA members on 1 January 1994, except Switzerland. Austria, Sweden and Finland later joined the EU as full members.

2.8 An agreement between Switzerland and the EU on free movement of persons came into force on 1 June 2002. Since this date, Swiss nationals and their family members have enjoyed similar residence rights to EEA nationals.

2.9 The distinction between EU and EEA nationals is becoming less important in EU law and the recent Immigration (EEA) Regulations 2006 apply the same rights of residence to citizens of all EU/EEA countries and Switzerland while they are in the UK. The difference would be relevant in a case where say a homeless applicant wanted to argue that the EEA Regs 2006 did not fully implement the Residence Directive as only an EU national could rely on the Directive. Nationals of Iceland, Norway and Liechtenstein are not citizens of the EU as defined by EC Treaty art 17, so do not have the general right of free movement provided to EU citizens under article 18.

2.10 An 'EEA national' is defined as a national of a member state other than the UK, Norway, Iceland, Lichtenstein and Switzerland.[3] If a UK national has not travelled to another EU country and exercised freedom of movement rights, eg as a worker, then they and their family members cannot benefit from those rights within the UK. Compare a French national, who travelled to the UK to work and is eligible to claim income support for his Angolan wife as his dependant, with a British man, who would have no equivalent eligibility because he has never exercised his EU Treaty rights by living in another EU country.

The institutions

The main institutions of the EU are the European Commission, the Council of Europe, the European Parliament and the Courts of Justice (European Court of Justice (ECJ) and the Court of First Instance (CFI)). Their powers and duties are contained in a series of EU Treaties.

3 EEA Regs 2006 SI No 1003 reg 2.

2.11 The *European Parliament* is made up of members of the European Parliament (MEPs) who are directly elected by EU citizens. It roughly approximates to the House of Commons. It legislates, authorises the budget and supervises all the EU institutions. The *European Commission* is a politically independent body consisting of Commissioners from member states which proposes legislation and implements decisions (perhaps like the civil service in the UK). The *Council of Europe* consists of one minister from each member state, the Council of Ministers (rather like the Cabinet).

2.12 The European Court of Justice[4] interprets and applies EU law as found in the EU Treaties and legislation. The Court of First Instance (CFI) was created in 1989 to relieve the ECJ's case load and mainly hears cases dealing with competition law, dumping, subsidies and staff grievances. The decisions of the CFI are appealable to the ECJ. The Grand Chamber acts as court of appeal of the ECJ.

2.13 The ECJ has Advocates-General who review the documents submitted in a case and issue an impartial written opinion, advocating a legal position to assist the court before the court issues its own opinion. The ECJ is not bound to follow those opinions. The opinions of the Advocates-General are published separately from the judgments of the ECJ. From 1989, ECJ cases have the prefix 'C' and CFI have the prefix 'T', eg C-386/00, T-201/95.

EC Treaty

2.14 The European Union is based on a series of multilateral treaties between member states, signed and ratified according to their domestic procedures. In 1957, the UK signed the Treaty of Rome establishing the European Economic Community (EEC), now simply the Treaty establishing the European Community.[5] Article 3 of the Treaty established the four main freedoms on which EU law is based:

- free movement of persons;
- free movement of goods;
- free movement of capital;
- free movement of services.

2.15 As a member state, the UK must give effect to the rights enshrined in the treaties, regulations and directives of the European

4 ECJ.
5 The EC Treaty.

Union. EU law takes precedence over UK law.[6] The Act made EU law 'directly effective' and requires courts to take into account EU law when interpreting UK law.

2.16 The rights of free movement contained in the EC Treaty were incorporated into UK law by section 7(1) of the Immigration Act 1988 – a person shall not require leave to enter or remain in the UK 'in any case in which he is entitled to do so by virtue of an enforceable Community right or of any provision made under section 2(2) of the European Communities Act 1972'. This means:

- any EEA (which incorporates EU) national is entitled to be admitted to the UK if they produce, on their arrival, a valid national identity card or a passport issued by the EEA state. Under EU law, an EEA national exercising EU Treaty rights is entitled to the same tax, housing and social advantages available to nationals of the member state, without discrimination. This includes means-tested benefits such as income support;
- the dependant or family member of such an EEA national, as defined, of whatever nationality, does not need leave to enter and remain in the UK. They are not a 'person subject to immigration control' and have the same rights to reside in the UK and access benefits as the EEA national.

2.17 The Treaty of Lisbon amends the EU Treaty and the EC Treaty (which it renames as the Treaty on the Functioning of the European Union) and renumbers articles in both treaties. But member states such as Ireland have been unable to persuade their citizens to accept the constitutional changes, so have not yet ratified the new treaty. In June 2008, the UK passed the European Union (Amendment) Act (EUAA) 2008 assuming ratification, but its provisions are not yet in force.

EU citizenship

2.18 The Maastricht Treaty or Treaty on European Union (TEU) amended the EC Treaty and created the European Union. It also introduced the concept of the EU citizen. The objects of the EC Treaty, as amended over the years, include: the promotion of economic and social cohesion by the establishment of an area without frontiers, the gradual raising of standards of living for EEA nationals, the principle

6 European Communities Act 1972 s2(1).

of 'non-discrimination' on grounds of nationality, and European citizenship (see para 2.32 below).

EU legislation

2.19 A treaty such as the EC Treaty is primary legislation, equivalent to a UK Act of Parliament. Its legality cannot be questioned, but it may be possible to challenge the way in which it is interpreted, whether in EU or UK provisions. Treaties can be found on the EUR-Lex website[7] by selecting the option for treaties.

2.20 The three main forms of secondary legislation are regulations (not to be confused with UK statutory instruments or regulations), directives and decisions. Secondary legislation can be challenged either on the basis that it was made by a defective process, or on the basis that it exceeds the scope of the treaty under which it was made. A recent example was a challenge by the European Commission to an amendment to Regulation 1408/71 on social security, which they argued was based on an error of law. The case concerned the exportability of certain benefits,[8] in the case of the UK of disability living allowance and attendance allowance. The Commission argued successfully that the amendment was unlawful.[9]

Regulations, Directives and Decisions

Regulations

They apply in full to all member states. They have 'direct effect' applying in the UK without the need for any further legislation, eg Regulation 1408/71 covering social security.

Directives

They are addressed to all member states and have an objective to be achieved by a certain date (the date of transposition). It is up to the member state how they are implemented – in the UK it is usually by regulations as with the Immigration (EEA) Regulations

7 http://europa.eu.int/eur-lex/lex/en/index.htm

8 Ie whether an EU national can receive them in another EU country.

9 *Commission for European Communities v European Parliament and Council of the EU, UK, Finland and Sweden intervening* (Case C-299/05).

2006 implementing the Residence Directive. They are binding as to the result to be achieved, so if a UK statutory instrument is inconsistent with the directive it aims to implement, then the directive can override it. If the UK statutory instrument is more generous, then it is lawful, but under UK rather than EU law. Directives are also binding on public authorities. If a directive has not been properly implemented, its provisions can be relied on to help interpret UK law in disputes between private bodies and individuals.

Decisions

These are issued by the European Council or Commission and are specific to particular countries, institutions or individuals on which/whom they have *direct effect* and are binding.

Concepts and principles used in EU law

Supremacy of EU law

2.21 EU law takes priority over any domestic law so the courts must interpret UK law taking into account EU obligations.[10] They must also decide any question about the interpretation of EU law taking account of relevant decisions of the European Court of Justice (ECJ), or where necessary by referring questions of interpretation to the ECJ.[11]

Direct effect

2.22 Many EU provisions in the treaties, regulations and directives give direct rights to EU nationals and their dependants which can be argued in disputes with public authorities and in court proceedings. But only a provision that has 'direct effect' can be used in this way. For a provision to have 'direct effect' it must be:

- clear and precise;
- capable of conferring rights on individuals;
- unconditional – this means it does not need more action/legislation for it to be effective.

10 *Van Gend En Loos* (Case 26/62) (1963) CMLR 105; *Marleasing SA v LA Commercial Internacional de Alimentacion SA* [1990] ECR I-4135.

11 See para 2.48; European Communities Act 1972 s3(1).

2.23 So 'directly effective' provisions create rights and duties between individuals that can be enforced in the national courts.

2.24 Where a Directive is not implemented correctly or in time, a claim for damages, a *Francovich* claim, can be brought against the member state, provided the directive confers rights on an individual, the rights can be identified, and it can be shown that the failure to implement the directive caused the damage. This was established when an Italian worker successfully claimed damages for loss due to the Italian government's failure to implement a directive on the rights of employees on insolvency.[12]

2.25 As well as in the ECJ, a claim for damages can be made against a public authority in a UK court if domestic legislation or guidance does not give effect to directly effective EU rights and the authority has breached an EU national's rights by relying on it. A judicial review letter before claim could include reference to such a damages claim. A declaration for breach of EU rights could be sought in judicial review proceedings, and the claim for damages transferred to or brought separately in the county court. A recent example is a series of claims brought in relation to the Home Office's delay in processing application for EU residence cards and registration certificates.

Certainty

2.26 Another EU law doctrine is 'legal certainty', which means that legal rules (eg internal Home Office instructions) may be unlawful if they are kept secret. An Austrian citizen who was banned from boarding a plane because of an unpublished EU regulation prohibiting tennis rackets, successfully challenged the decision in the ECJ:

> the principle of legal certainty requires that Community rules enable those concerned to know precisely the extent of the obligations which are imposed on them. Individuals must be able to ascertain unequivocally what their rights and obligations are and take steps accordingly. . .[13]

Proportionality and justification

2.27 The principle of proportionality is common to both EU and human rights law. It can be explained as the extent to which an individual's

12 *Francovich v Italy* (Joined Cases C6/90 and 9/90) [1991] ECR I-5357 (1993) 2 CMLR 66, [1995] ICR 722, [1992] IRLR 84.

13 *Gottfried Heinrich* (Case C-345/06) 10 March 2009.

rights may lawfully be interfered with when an EU provision is applied to them. The courts may also consider proportionality when deciding whether a UK law should be allowed to interfere with an EU law right.

2.28 Proportionality has been relied on in challenges to the rules requiring an A8 national to be employed in registered work for 12 months before they can claim any benefit. Where a Polish woman with a child had not worked lawfully for the full 12 months due to domestic violence, the House of Lords found that on balance the requirement that the work of accession nationals must be registered was proportionate. As a result, the Worker Registration Scheme was compatible with EU law.[14]

2.29 To be proportionate, a rule should only be as tough as is needed to achieve its object. The following factors should be taken into account:[15]

- whether the provision is suitable when measured against its objective;
- whether the provision is necessary;
- whether the provision is proportionate given the degree of interference with a person's rights or whether there is a less restrictive alternative.

2.30 A decision that prevents an individual exercising treaty rights also requires *justification*, which is expressed in similar terms to proportionality. It must be suitable for securing the objective it pursues, and it must not go beyond what is necessary in order to attain it.

Purposive approach

2.31 The purposive approach is used by most continental EU countries when interpreting their own legislation, and is the approach that is taken by the ECJ in interpreting EU law. It means considering the intention of Parliament in making the provision, as contrasted with the English courts' traditional approach of relying on precedent and taking a literal approach where the meaning of words is

14 *Zalewska v Department for Social Development (Northern Ireland)* [2008] UKHL 67, December 2008 *Legal Action* 37.

15 *Granaria BV* (Case C-116/76) [1977] ECR 1247; *Brenca and Bakhouche* (Case 8/77) [1977] ECR 1495.

considered. As they have become familiar with interpreting EU law – and human rights law (which also takes a purposive approach) – the UK courts have increasingly adopted a purposive approach to statutory interpretation. In the context of EU law, it means considering wide economic and social aims of the EU, in particular freedom of movement, as well as considering the aims of the particular provision.

Non-discrimination

2.32 The principle of non-discrimination, which is central to EU law, is contained in the EC Treaty as well as various regulations and directives. Discrimination on grounds of EU nationality is prohibited by the EC Treaty article 12. Other forms of discrimination such as on grounds of sex, race or age are also unlawful in various contexts.

2.33 An EU citizen, exercising a treaty right to be in the UK has the right not to be treated less favourably than a UK national in relation to all the areas that come within the material scope of EU law.

ECJ decisions on non-discrimination

- A Spanish national who had worked on and off in Germany for 20 years was refused a benefit because her residence permit had expired. The ECJ found[16] she could rely on article 12 (then article 6):

  > ...a citizen of the European Union, such as the appellant in the main proceedings, lawfully resident in the territory of the host Member State, can rely on Article 6 of the Treaty is all situations which fall within the scope *ratione materiae* of Community law, including the situation where that Member State delays or refuses to grant to that claimant a benefit that is provided to all persons lawfully resident in the territory of that State on the ground that the claimant is not in possession of a document which nationals are not required to have and the issue of which may be delayed or refused by the authorities of that State.

- It was not discriminatory to provide more favourable benefits to illegal migrants such as asylum-seekers than to EU nationals.[17]

16 *Martínez Sala* (Case C-85/96) [1998] ECR I-2691.

17 *Vatsouras and Koupatantze* (Joined Cases C-22/08 and C-23/08).

Ratione materiae and ratione personae

2.34 These Latin terms, which often appear in ECJ case law, literally mean 'material scope' and 'personal scope'. An example of the material scope of EU law would be rights connected to the right to work such as homelessness law because it concerns the right to apply for public housing, as opposed to say disrepair law. An example of the personal scope of EU law would be the rights of an EU national worker, who travelled to the UK, as opposed to the rights of a UK national who has always lived in the UK.

Human rights and other international treaties

2.35 The right of freedom of movement for EU nationals, which is a fundamental objective of EU law, also encompasses the idea of respect for fundamental rights. The concept of fundamental rights or human rights in EU law is broader than under the European Convention on Human Rights (ECHR) and includes equality, dignity and solidarity.

2.36 Respect for human rights is provided for in article 6 of the EC Treaty. EU law may protect human rights, not only those protected under the ECHR, but also those protected by other treaties that have not been incorporated into UK domestic law. If a provision of EU law applies human rights provisions, then it may overcome, and potentially disapply, any incompatible domestic UK law. In that sense EU law may provide greater protection for human rights than the Human Rights Act 1998.

2.37 In its judgments the ECJ has made reference to instruments such as the UN International Covenant on Civil and Political Rights. Other treaties such as UN Convention on the Rights of the Child and the European Social Charter may also be used. So provisions of EU law must be read subject to the requirement to protect human rights.

2.38 The ECHR and the judgments of the European Court of Human Rights define rights that are protected and furthered in EU law. ECHR rights form part of the principles that govern the interpretation and application of EU law. Those rights include a prohibition on torture and inhuman and degrading treatment or punishment (ECHR article 3) and the right to respect for private life, family life, home and correspondence (ECHR article 8). In *Baumbast and R*[18] the ECJ considered whether a Colombian mother who had

18 Case C-413/99.

had divorced her German husband, the EU worker, had the right to continue living in the UK so her child could attend school. Allowing the application, the court specifically referred to the fundamental right of respect for family life contained in ECHR article 8 as forming part of the principles of EU law.

2.39 Sometimes the ECJ develops its own approach to human rights such as the right to a fair hearing and to an effective remedy. In this way the ECJ protects the other rights conferred by EU law.

ECSMA and ESC

2.40 Social security regulations provide access to some benefits for nationals of countries which have ratified the European Convention on Social and Medical Assistance (ECSMA) or the European Social Charter (ESC) (see chapter 3). There were previously similar provisions in the homelessness regulations. Most of the parties are now in the EU (except for Turkey, which has ratified both treaties, and Croatia and Macedonia, which have ratified ESC) so the agreements add little except perhaps in cases of the non-economically active.

2.41 ECSMA was ratified by the UK in 1954. Parties to the convention agree to ensure that the nationals of other parties, who are *lawfully present* in their territory and who are without sufficient resources, are entitled to the same social and medical assistance as their own nationals. Reference to ECSMA is made in article 13, para 4, of the European Social Charter and of the Revised European Social Charter.

2.42 ESC, previously known as the Council of Europe Social Charter, was ratified by the UK in 1962. The UK has not ratified the revised version produced in 7 November 1997. Not to be confused with the Social Chapter, which is not implemented, it governs rights in relation to work, training and social security. Of the rights guaranteed by the charter, the right to work, the right to organise, the right to bargain collectively, the right to social security, the right to social and medical assistance, the right to the social, legal and economic protection of the family, and the right to protection and assistance for migrant workers and their families are regarded as particularly significant. Article 19 covers the right of migrant workers and their families to protection and assistance.

2.43 Neither ECSMA nor ESC has ever been directly implemented in UK law in full in the way that the EC Treaty, has so they are difficult to use. ESC has a collective complaints mechanism but the UK has not signed up to this. It was used by the organisation FIDH[19] when France introduced a new law limiting access to healthcare for undocumented migrants. The Committee on Social Rights of the Council of Europe, which has the task of monitoring the application of the Charter, found the French law contravened art 17 as a:

> legislation or practice that denies entitlement to medical assistance to foreign nationals, within the territory of a State Party, even if they are there illegally, is contrary to the Charter.[20]

2.44 A full list of countries that have ratified both instruments is in the appendix.[21]

2.45 The Reception Directive on treatment of asylum-seekers[22] establishes minimum standards for the reception of asylum-seekers in the EU, which are deemed to be sufficient to ensure 'a dignified standard of living and comparable living conditions in all Member States'. The Directive came into force on 6 February 2003 and required the UK and other member states to comply by 6 February 2005. The immigration rules were amended and new Asylum Support Regulations introduced (see paras 1.104 and 4.13). It has had limited effect until a Court of Appeal decision found that it applied not only to initial asylum claims, but also to second or 'fresh' claims so that refused asylum-seekers with an outstanding fresh claim that had not been considered for 12 months had the right to work, and potentially other rights.[23] At the time of writing this decision is subject to appeal.

Remedies

2.46 There are two ways in which an individual with a complaint that the UK has not complied with EU law may have their case considered; but they may not apply or appeal to the ECJ directly.

19 La Fédération Internationale des Ligues des Droits de l'Homme.

20 The International Federation of Human Rights Leagues *FIDH v France* decision on complaint 14/2033. The Committee of Ministers of the Council of Europe upheld the complaint in 2005: Resolution ResChS (2005)6 of 4 May 2005; *FIDH v France* (2005) 40 EHRR SE25.

21 http://conventions.coe.int/Treaty/Commun/ChercheSig.asp?NT=035&CM=8&DF=4/1/2009&CL=ENG

22 Council Directive 2003/9/EC OJ L31 6.2.03 p18. See further Baldaccini, *Asylum Support: A practitioners' guide to the EU Reception Directive*, Justice, 2005.

23 See para 1.70.

2.47 First they could complain to the Commission or another member state (such as their original member state), which might then bring infringement proceedings under EC Treaty article 226. In 2007 a UK solicitor complained to the European Commission about the UK's interpretation of the permanent right to reside in the Residence Directive. The UK was refusing to take into account lawful periods of residence of A8 nationals which predated EU accession. The Commission agreed to investigate and referred the complaint to the European Parliament which responded on 27 May 2008.

References to the ECJ

2.48 Second, the litigant can argue a point of EU law in any UK court or tribunal. The question may arise as to whether a directive has been properly implemented, for example whether the EEA Regs 2006 fully reflect the Residence Directive. If a question arises about the correct interpretation of EU provisions (eg the definition of 'family member') or the legality of EU secondary legislation, about which the court is uncertain, it should refer the issue to the ECJ to decide.[24]

2.49 A reference may be made by a court or tribunal, for example the county court, the Administrative Court, or First-tier Tribunal. If the court or tribunal is the final court of appeal in the UK, the Supreme Court, it must refer the issue raised. Also a referral should be made if the validity of EU legislation is in question. The national court making the reference can grant interim relief while a reference is made, for example in a homelessness challenge it could order temporary accommodation pending an ECJ decision.

2.50 To decide whether or not to refer a question of interpretation, the UK court should consider whether the issue is 'acte claire', which means sufficiently clear, so that it does not need further consideration, as opposed to obvious. They should exercise their discretion to refer unless the answer would make no difference to the decision, has already been provided, or is free from doubt.

2.51 Once it has decided a question, the ECJ sends its decision to the national court, which must then take it into account in their judgment – as in the habitual residence case *Collins v Secretary of State for Work and Pensions.*[25]

24 EC Treaty article 234.

25 Case C-138/02.

Sources of ECJ decisions

2.52 The Curia website[26] has transcripts of decisions from 1997 onwards. There is a search form enabling a search by date, parties and key words. For cases between 1953 and 1997, searches are only by case number. The numerical lists of cases for the ECJ and CFI are useful as they indicate whether the case is still pending or if it has been removed from the register of cases. The EUR-Lex website[27] has ECJ cases from 1954 onwards. The search is by case number, subject or by date.

Freedom of movement

2.53 The four 'freedoms' enshrined in EU law by the EC Treaty article 3 are:

- free movement of workers;
- free movement of goods;
- free movement of services;
- freedom of establishment and provision of services.

2.54 The basic right of freedom of movement of EU nationals is implemented in UK law by the Immigration Act 1988 s7(1) – a person does not need leave to enter or remain in the UK if they have an enforceable EU right to be here.

2.55 The Residence Directive 2004/38/EC gives practical effect to the aim of article 3. A person who moves under the terms of the Directive, for example as a worker or self-employed person, is within the *personal scope* of EU law. If their activity is within the *material scope* of the Treaty then it will be subject to EU law. The material scope will include their right of access to work, housing and social rights.

2.56 Other EC Treaty provisions such as article 39 and Regulation 1612/68 strengthen the rights of free movement of workers.[28]

Free Movement for Workers Regulation 1612/68

2.57 EEC Regulation 1612/68 on Freedom of Movement for Workers within the Community (the Workers' Regulation) provides for the

26 http://curia.europa.eu/index.htm.

27 http://eur-lex.europa.eu/en/index.htm.

28 See para 2.57.

free movement of EU workers. Articles 1–6 provide for access to employment. Articles 7–9 provide for access to the same social and tax advantages as national workers. Articles 10–12 (now repealed) provided that workers had the right to install their families, defined as spouse and descendants up to age 21 or their dependants, and dependent relatives in the ascending line, ie parents. Subsequent Regulations and Directives dealt with other free movement rights such as of 'self-sufficient' persons, retired people and students.

Social welfare rights[29]

2.58 In EU law, rights to welfare provision are known as 'social advantages' or 'social rights'. Access to housing and welfare provision is seen as essential to enable a worker to exercise their right to move to another EU country to work there. 'Social advantages' include the rights that other UK residents have,[30] for example to apply for child benefit or local authority housing. They also include travel discounts and education benefits if they are 'connected to a person as a worker, his residency in the territory and the appropriateness of the advantages to social mobility.'

2.59 The rights to equal treatment of EU workers and their family members and social advantages are expressed in the Workers' Regulation (above). The Residence Directive is the most recent addition to EU legal provisions protecting social welfare rights.[31]

2.60 However, the Residence Directive should not be treated as an exclusive source of social assistance rights. In a judgment dated 4 June 2009, the ECJ found that a jobseeker can rely on article 39(2) and article 12 of the EC Treaty to qualify for 'a benefit of a financial nature intended to facilitate access to the labour market'.[32] The jobseeker would need to show they had established real links with the labour market, for example by working for a short period and then registering to look for work.

The Residence Directive and the EEA Regulations

2.61 The UK had a deadline of 30 April 2006 by which to implement Directive 2004/38/EC (the Residence Directive) on the rights of EU

29 See also para 2.101, Problems and tactics.

30 *Even and ONPTS* (C-207/78) [1979] ECHR 2019.

31 See further EC Treaty arts 2 and 3, and Title XI.

32 *Vatsouras and Koupatantze* (Joined Cases C-22/08 and C-23/08).

nationals and their family members to move and reside freely in the UK. On that date it introduced the Immigration (European Economic Area) Regulations 2006[33] (EEA Regs 2006), replacing the previous Immigration (European Economic Area) Regulations 2000. In some respects, the EEA Regs 2006 give more rights than the Residence Directive, for example they apply to EEA and Swiss nationals, not simply EU nationals. In other respects, which will be explained below, it can be argued that they do not fully implement the Directive.

2.62 The Residence Directive amended the Workers' Regulation 1612/68 and repealed most of the EU secondary legislation governing freedom of movement. It aimed to incorporate and update previous legislation and case law into one consolidated provision.

2.63 In summary the Directive allows EU citizens and their family members to move and live freely within the member states. It covers the rights of workers and self-employed people (as well as those who have stopped working due to incapacity or retirement), students, self-sufficient people and people receiving services (such as visitors), and the family members of these groups. It covers rights of entry and temporary and permanent residence in the UK and documentation.

2.64 The effects of the Residence Directive and the EEA Regs 2006 include:

- a new right of three months' initial residence in any EEA country for an EEA national and their family member(s) even if they are not exercising an EU Treaty right, for example as a worker. There is no right to social or housing assistance in the UK during this period unless they are exercising other Treaty rights for example working;
- five categories of 'qualified person' with the right to reside in the UK with specified family members – a worker, a self-employed person, a jobseeker, a self-sufficient student, and a self-sufficient person;
- a definition of 'worker' and 'self-employed person' to include those who are temporarily or permanently sick, or those who have lost their job but are looking for work in certain circumstances. Certain family members may retain the right to reside after the death or departure of their relatives;

33 SI No 1003.

- a new definition of 'family member' to include registered civil partner. There is also a new concept in the EEA Regulations – 'extended family member', who has similar rights to a family member if they meet certain conditions;
- new residence documents and a right for them to be issued within a strict time frame;
- a right of permanent residence for the EEA national or their family member, usually after five years exercising the right to reside in the UK.

Summary of the effect of the EEA Regs 2006 and Residence Directive

Right to enter

2.65 An EEA national does not need permission for leave to enter or remain and must be admitted to the UK as long as they can show a valid national passport or ID card.[34] A family member of an EEA national must also be admitted to the UK if they have a valid passport and a family permit, or a registration certificate, or a residence card or a permanent residence card. This includes 'third country' nationals even if they have not previously lived in an EU country.[35]

Right to reside

2.66 Under the EEA Regs 2006, implementing the Residence Directive, there are now three different types of right to reside.

Initial right to reside

- An *initial right to reside* for up to three months for any EEA national and their family member with a valid passport regardless of whether they are exercising EU rights.[36] Those exercising this right are not eligible for homelessness assistance, a housing allocation or most social security benefits unless they are exercising EU Treaty rights, eg as a worker. But there is no bar on them receiving child benefit or disability living allowance.[37]

34 Residence Directive art 5; EEA Regs 2006 SI No 1003 reg 11.

35 See para 1.213; *Metock and others v Minister for Justice, Equality and Law Reform* (C-127/08) (2009) QB 318.

36 Residence Directive art 6; EEA Regs 2006 SI No 1003 reg 13.

37 See para 3.56.

- The Residence Directive provides that during the *initial period* of residence, periods of residence *in excess* of three months should be subject to conditions so that persons exercising a right of residence do not become an *unreasonable burden* on the social assistance system.[38]

Ordinary right to reside

- The most common right to reside is known as an *extended right of residence* for more than three months,[39] which applies to '*a qualified person*' and their family members for as long as they remain qualified persons without the need for leave to remain in the UK under the Immigration Act 1971 (IA 1971). EEA Regs 2006[40] provide that anyone who is admitted to or acquires a right to reside in the UK under those provisions shall not require leave to remain under the IA 1971 during any period when they have a right to reside under these regulations. Family members may retain the right of residence after the qualified person has left.[41]

Permanent right to reside

- *A permanent right of residence* after five years of being a qualified person or family member of a qualified person or, in certain circumstances, a former worker or relative of a former or deceased, qualified person.[42] This is not subject to any conditions about not claiming social assistance.[43]

Who has the right to reside?

Qualified person

2.67 EEA Regs 2006 reg 6(1) provides that an EEA national who satisfies the definition of a *jobseeker, worker, self-employed* or *self-sufficient person*, or a *student*, is to be treated as a *qualified person* for the purpose of the regulations:

38 See para 2.108; 10th Recital.
39 Residence Directive art 7; EEA Regs 2006 SI No 1003 reg 14.
40 EEA Regs 2006 SI No 1003 Sch 2 para 1.
41 See para 2.80.
42 See para 2.117.
43 Residence Directive, 18th Recital.

(a) a jobseeker – defined as someone who entered the UK to look for work and can provide evidence that they are looking for work and have a genuine chance of getting it.[44]

(b) a worker – defined as meaning worker within article 39 of the EC Treaty.[45] This category includes a former worker who has retained worker status in any of the following ways:[46]

  (i) if they are temporarily unable to work due to illness or an accident.[47] This rule also applies to those who were formerly self-employed;[48]

  (ii) if they are involuntarily unemployed and have now registered as a jobseeker (normally by signing on at the local Jobcentre Plus office)[49] and either:
  - worked for a year;
  - worked for less than a year before losing their job but have been unemployed for less than six months; or
  - if they can show they are looking for and have a genuine chance of getting a job in the UK;

  (ii) if they are a former worker who embarks on vocational training;[50]

  (iv) if they stopped working voluntarily, to do vocational training related to the last job.[51]

  The EEA Regs 2006 have a more restrictive definition of a former worker who is looking for work than the Residence Directive. Under the Directive, if an EU national has worked for a year, is recorded as being involuntarily unemployed and has registered as a work-seeker, then they retain worker status.[52] There is no time limit on how long they retain the status and ECJ case-law shows that as long as a host member state treats its own citizens as workers, for example for the purposes of claiming jobseeker's allowance, then the EU national should also be treated as a worker. If the person had been employed for less than a year and is registered as a jobseeker then they retain worker status for six months. ECJ case law suggests that the status can be retained

44 EEA Regs 2006 SI No 1003 reg 6(4).
45 See para 2.81.
46 Residence Directive art 7; EEA Regs 2006 reg 6(2).
47 EEA Regs 2006 reg 6(2)(a).
48 EEA Regs 2006 reg 6(3).
49 EEA Regs 2006 reg 6(2)(b).
50 EEA Regs 2006 reg 6(2)(c).
51 EEA Regs 2006 reg 6(2)(d).
52 Residence Directive art 7(3)(b).

after six months if they have a realistic prospect of getting another job. EEA Regs 2006 reg 6(2)(b) does not make it clear that a year's employment is not a pre-condition to retaining worker status, so it is arguable that article 7 has not been properly implemented in UK law;

(c) a self-employed person, defined under EC Treaty article 43 – see para 2.86 below, including those who are temporarily unable to work as the result of an illness or accident.

(d) a self-sufficient person, defined by regulation 4(1)(c) as a person who has:
  (i) sufficient resources not to become a burden on the social assistance system[53] of the UK during his or her period of residence,
  (ii) and comprehensive sickness insurance[54] cover in the UK;

(e) a student, who must declare that he or she meets the 'no burden' condition, and who has comprehensive sickness insurance. The EEA Regs 2006 reg 4(1) provides that he or she must be enrolled on a course financed by public funds or registered with the Department for Education and Skills' ('DES) register of Education and Training Providers.[55] The Directive provides that the student must be enrolled at a public/private establishment accredited or financed by the member state. The definition of 'family member' for student is more limited than for, say, worker. It has been suggested that this rule might include school students.

Comprehensive sickness insurance

2.68 In some member states sickness insurance is based on residence whereas in others it is based on economic activity. At the time of writing, there was no clear authority on the meaning of 'comprehensive sickness insurance' in the UK context, where we have the NHS, rather than the insurance-based schemes that predominate in other EU countries.

2.69 It has been suggested that since there is no requirement for private insurance, NHS entitlement may satisfy this requirement in the context of an EU national.[56] This is confirmed in HMRC child

53 See para 2.108 below.

54 See para 2.68 below.

55 This is now maintained by the Department for Innovation, Universities and Skills (DIUS) which replaced the DES: www.dcsf.gov.uk/providersregister/ (see EEA Regs 2006 SI No 1003 reg 4(1)(d)).

56 Per Sedley LJ in *W (China) and X (China) v Secretary of State for the Home Department* [2006] EWCA Civ 1494.

benefit guidance interpreting the regulations – 'Comprehensive sickness cover includes the National Health Service (NHS) cover'[57] but this is not essential.

2.70 Alternatively, many EU nationals could comply with this requirement by simply purchasing private health insurance while in the UK.

Family member

2.71 Workers and the self-employed have a complete and unlimited right to have their family members with them when they move around the EU. The definition of *family member* in EU law is far broader than the definitions generally used in UK social welfare law. Family members include the qualified person's:[58]

- spouse/civil partner;
- direct descendants or those of their spouse/civil partner who are under 21 or are *dependants* of the person or their spouse or civil partner (so this could include an older adult disabled child);
- dependent direct relatives in their ascending lines, or that of their spouse/civil partner.

2.72 The exception is for students where family members only include spouse/civil partner and dependent children.[59]

2.73 The family member does not have to be an EEA national. The rights of family members extend to non-EEA nationals who are known in EU law as third country nationals.

2.74 Dependence does not mean total dependence and includes non-financial forms of dependence.[60] Therefore, it is not necessary to show that the family member is fully supported.[61]

2.75 The rights of family members are dependent upon the person exercising the EU law right. Previously, if the person who was working in the UK was an EU national but left the UK, the remaining family members would lose their right to reside unless they had their own EU rights. The Residence Directive means this no longer

57 www.hmrc.gov.uk/manuals/cbtmanual/cbtm10070.htm. An EU national could demonstrate their entitlement to NHS treatment with a European Health Insurance Card (EHIC): see www.ehic.org.uk

58 Residence Directive art 2; EEA Regs 2006 SI No 1003 reg 7.

59 Residence Directive art 7(4); EEA Regs 2006 reg 7.

60 See para 2.91.

61 *Lebon* (Case C-316/85).

applies in all cases,[62] although this is not fully reflected in the EEA Regs 2006.

2.76 The ECJ held that where the child of a German worker had been installed in full-time education in the UK, the child and his primary carer retained a right of residence even after the migrant worker had ceased to work within the EEA.[63] This is partly incorporated into the Directive and EEA Regulations.

2.77 A UK national who has not left the UK and is simply working in the UK will not have exercised any EU law right, and will not fall within any of the above categories. The EEA Regulations specifically exclude UK nationals from the definition of EEA nationals. So if a UK train driver is joined by his mother who is a Dutch Somali national, she will not have the right to reside as the family member of an EEA national because he is not a qualifying person.

Extended family member

2.78 Article 3 of the Residence Directive provides that the member state shall facilitate entry and residence for 'any other family members' who were dependants or members of the household of the EU national before coming to the EU host country, or who need personal care from them on serious health grounds. It also includes a non-married partner who has a durable relationship, duly attested (ie witnessed/evidenced). The UK is entitled to investigate the personal circumstances of the other family member.

2.79 The UK has transposed this into the EEA Regs 2006 by introducing the concept of 'extended family member'. Regulation 8 defines an extended family member as a person who does not fall under the ordinary 'family member' definition, and comes within one of the following categories:

(a) is a relative of the EEA national or their spouse/registered civil partner and was living in an EEA state where the EEA national lives and was dependent upon them or was a member of their household and is now accompanying the EEA national to the UK or wishes to join them there, or has joined the EEA national in the UK and is dependent upon them or is a member of his or her household;[64]

62 See para 2.80.

63 *Baumbast* (Case C-413/99) (see further paras 2.80 and 2.105).

64 EEA Regs 2006 SI No 1003 reg 8(2).

(b) is a relative of an EEA national or their spouse or civil partner and 'on serious health grounds' needs personal care from them.[65] These conditions were found to be met in an immigration appeal where a refused asylum-seeker with a diagnosis of post-traumatic stress disorder and depression needed personal care on a day-to-day basis;[66]

(c) is a relative of an EEA national who would meet the requirements in the immigration rules for indefinite leave to enter or remain as a dependent relative of an EEA national settled in the UK;[67]

(d) is a partner of an EEA national (other than a civil partner) who can prove (to the Home Office) that they are in a durable relationship with the EEA national.

Retaining right to reside as a family member

2.80 A family member keeps the right to reside under EEA Regs 2006 reg 10 in some circumstances after death, divorce or departure of the qualified person. This applies:

- if the family member was living with the EEA national in the UK for a year immediately before their death.[68] To keep this right a person must be a non-EEA national who meets the conditions of a worker, self-employed or self-sufficient person or must be a family member (eg child of such a person);
- if the family member was a child, spouse or civil partner of an EEA national who died or who was a qualified person who left the UK. The child/partner must continue to attend an educational course under article 12 of Regulation 1612/68, that is a general educational, apprenticeship or vocational training course. The parent with custody of the child also qualifies.[69] This attempt to incorporate *Baumbast* into the EEA Regs 2006 does not fully succeed;[70]
- the former family member after divorce/termination of a civil partnership keeps the right to reside in the UK as a family member if: the marriage/partnership had lasted at least three years, of which at least one year was spent in the UK, or the

65 EEA Regs 2006 SI No 1003 reg 8(3).

66 *TR v Secretary of State for the Home Department* [2008] UKAIT 0004.

67 EEA Regs 2006 reg 8(3).

68 EEA Regs 2006 reg 10(2).

69 EEA Regs 2006 reg 10(3)–(4).

70 See para 2.105.

former spouse/civil partner has rights to custody of a child of the qualified person, or a court has ordered access in the UK, or the family member needs to stay in the UK due to difficult circumstances, for example domestic violence during the relationship. But they must now be a non-EEA worker, a self-employed person, a self-sufficient person or a family member of one.[71]

Worker

2.81 The term 'worker' is not defined in the EC Treaty. The meaning of 'worker' is broad and includes persons who are not in work. The following principles have been established in the UK and more particularly in EU case law:

- to be a worker, the EEA national must have been actually employed in the host state;[72]
- a 'worker' includes any EEA national currently employed, unless the work is merely 'marginal and ancillary' as opposed to work which is 'genuine and effective';[73]
- the person must perform services of some economic value. The performance of such services must be for and under the direction of another person; if not they are likely to come within the self-employment definition;[74]
- the term 'worker' includes those who work part-time or whose pay is below subsistence level;[75]
- the source of the remuneration for the work and the limited amount of remuneration are not relevant;[76]
- the work must be a genuine economic activity as opposed to a purely voluntary or leisure pursuit. The provision of services can be an acceptable form of payment, for example food and lodging in return for work;[77]
- work for a short period of time or for only a few hours per week may create 'worker' status;[78]

71 EEA Regs 2006 SI No 1003 reg 10(5).

72 *Collins v Secretary of State for Work and Pensions* (Case C-138/02).

73 *Levin* [1982] ECHR 1035; *Kempf* [1986] ECR 1741.

74 *Lawrie-Blum* (Case C-66/85).

75 *Levin* [1982] ECHR 1035; *Kempf* [1986] ECR 1741.

76 *Vatsouras and Koupatantze* (Joined Cases C-22/08 and C-23/08), para 27; *Bettray* (Case 344/87) [1989] ECR 1621, para 15.

77 *Steymann v Staatssecretaris van Justitie* (Case C-196/87) [1998] ECR 6159.

78 *Ninni-Orasche* (Case C-413/01); *Vatsouras and Koupatantze* (Joined Cases C-22/08 and C-23/08).

- it is for the member state (in this case the UK) to determine whether the work is on such a small scale and/or is on such an irregular or occasional basis that it may be treated as 'marginal and ancillary', but any such decision must be informed by the principles set out in the ECJ's case law;[79]
- the motives of the person employed are irrelevant. A person will be classified as a worker even if their subjective intention was to create a situation where they are classified as a worker for another purpose, for example homelessness assistance.[80]

Decisions on meaning of 'worker' after short periods of work

- A Dutch national who had only worked for two weeks at the Wimbledon tennis tournament in the previous six months was a worker. The length of any particular job was not to be considered decisive in deciding whether work was 'genuine and effective'. Work would be 'genuine and effective' where an employer paid for the services rendered, and where if the person in question had not undertaken them, someone else would have been employed to provide them. The Court of Appeal also found that 'ancillary' referred to a case where the work was a subsidiary part of another relationship between employer and employee, such as where a lodger does a little work as part of his occupancy agreement with a landlord.[81]
- In a recent ECJ decision, two Greek nationals, V and K, had claimed benefits in Germany on the basis they were 'workers' within art 39 of the EC Treaty. V's professional activity brought earnings below the subsistence rate; K was employed from 1 November 2006 until 21 December 2006. The court confirmed previous cases on the meaning of 'worker' emphasising that the concept of 'worker' must not be interpreted narrowly. The fact that income from employment was lower than the minimum required for subsistence did not prevent the person from being a worker, even if they applied for public funds to supplement their income. The fact that the employment was of short duration did not exclude it from the scope of art 39 of the EC Treaty.[82]

79 *Raulin* [1992] ECR I-1027.

80 *Levin* (note 75) and *Ninni Orasche* (note 78).

81 *Barry v Southwark LBC* [2008] EWCA Civ 1440.

82 *Vatsouras and Koupatantze* (Joined Cases C-22/08 and C-23/08).

Pregnancy

2.82 At the time of writing, there is no guidance from the ECJ on whether a pregnant woman counts as a worker. A useful starting point is to consider whether the contract of employment provides for continuous employment during maternity. A woman who has been employed for 12 months has the right to return to work after maternity leave if she gives the required notice.[83] In either case it may be possible to argue that the employee continues to be a worker during the maternity leave.

2.83 A woman who is suffering from pregnancy-related illness may be able to argue that she has retained worker status due to being temporarily incapable of work due to illness under EEA Regs 2006 reg 6(2)(a).[84]

2.84 A French national who left her part-time cleaning job in late pregnancy was refused income support. The Commissioner rejected the ECHR article 14 non-discrimination argument that women unable to work due to pregnancy should be treated in the same way as men and women who are incapable of work as a result of illness or accident.[85]

2.85 It is difficult to see how refusing social assistance to a pregnant former worker complies with the purposive approach required by EU law and the emphasis on non-discrimination and freedom of movement of workers. In the introduction to the Residence Directive, the 31st Recital emphasises that the directive respects fundamental rights and freedoms and observes the principles recognised by the EU Charter of Fundamental Rights and Freedoms. It encourages member states to implement the Directive without discrimination between its beneficiaries on grounds such as sex, race etc.

The self-employed

2.86 The Directive now uses the definition 'self-employed person', whereas self-employment was previously referred to as either the right of establishment or the right to provide services. The self-employment option is particularly important for 'A2' nationals from Romania and Bulgaria whose access to the labour market as employees is limited.

83 Maternity and Parental Leave etc Regulations 1999 SI No 3312.

84 CIS/731/2007 (2 November 2007).

85 CIS/4010/2006 (9 October 2007).

2.87 The Social Security Commissioner has found that a person who has taken preparatory steps to set up a business or provide services qualifies as self-employed.[86]

2.88 The concept of self-employment in EU law is not exactly the same as the meaning in UK employment law, but the domestic approach is relevant in determining whether or not an individual is self-employed. The ECJ has found that a factor to consider when assessing whether an EU national is a worker or a self-employed person is whether or not there is a relationship of subordination:

> Since the essential characteristics of an employment relationship within the meaning of article [39] of the EC Treaty [free movement of workers] is the fact that for a certain period of time a person performs services for and under the direction of another person in return for which he receives remuneration, any activity which a person performs outside a relationship of subordination must be classified as an activity pursued in a self-employed capacity for the purposes of Article [43] of the Treaty.

So arguably anyone who is working for themselves outside of a relationship of subordination (ie who is not being told directly what to do and how to do it) can claim to be self-employed. It is not dependent on the number of contracts or clients the person has.

2.89 Just as in the case of a 'worker', the self-employed activity must not be on such a small scale as to be classified as marginal and/or ancillary. The 'worker' cases (see para 2.81) can be referred to in cases of dispute. There is a broad definition of what constitutes economic activity, including activities carried out as a member of a community religion and, in one case, prostitution.[87]

2.90 It is relatively straightforward to register as a self-employed person by telephoning Her Majesty's Revenue and Customs (HMRC). The website[88] has information about when a tax return should be filed and how to claim exemption from paying Class 2 national insurance contributions for those on a low income. Other evidence of self-employment could include invoices, bank accounts, letters from clients and a record of jobs carried out.

Meaning of 'dependent'

2.91 The concept of dependency in 'dependent relative' is one which has an EU law meaning. A broad approach has been adopted by the

86 CIS/3559/97.

87 *Steymann* (Case C-196/87) and *Jany* (Case C-268/99).

88 www.hmrc.gov.uk/index.htm.

ECJ to dependants, and the relationship of dependency will not be affected by the fact that the worker does not 'wholly or largely' support the dependant. In the leading case[89] the ECJ found that even where a worker was unable to provide financial support to the dependant, that did not undermine the relationship of dependency. The court found that the assessment of whether there is a relationship of dependency was simply a factual one of the emotional and financial situation. It would be discriminatory under EU law if a person were excluded from being considered a dependant of the worker because the dependant was receiving social security benefits.

2.92 The ECJ has considered the meaning of dependency in the immigration context in *Jia v Migrationsverket*.[90] It found that the member state was entitled to look at the material support being provided to the relative in their country of origin, or the member state where the application was being made, in order to determine that the support was being provided and was needed to meet essential needs. There was no set format for providing such evidence, and it could be provided by any means that was appropriate to demonstrating the existence of dependency.

2.93 A Social Security Commissioner has considered the meaning of 'dependent' in the context of the Residence Directive article 2 and EEA Regs 2006 reg 7 and found that:[91]

- a person is only dependent who actually receives support from another;
- there need be no right to that support and it is irrelevant that there are alternative sources of support available;
- support must be material, although not necessarily financial, and must provide for, or contribute towards, the basic necessities of life.

He did not express any opinion on whether support could be emotional.

Students and self-sufficient persons

2.94 Under EEA Regs 2006 reg 4 a self-sufficient person is one who has sufficient resources not to become a burden on the social assistance

89 *Lebon* [1987] ECR 2811.

90 [2007] EUECJ (C-1/05).

91 CIS/2100/2007, www.osscsc.gov.uk/aspx/view.aspx?id=2426

system of the UK during his or her residence and has comprehensive sickness insurance cover.

2.95 By the same regulation a student is a person who:

(a) is enrolled at a public or private establishment included on the Department of Education and Skills' Register of Education and Training Providers or financed from public funds, for the purpose of following a course of study including vocational training;
(b) has comprehensive sickness insurance in the UK; and
(c) assures the Secretary of State by means of a declaration or such equivalent means as the person may choose, that he has sufficient resources not to become a burden on the social assistance system of the UK during the period of residence.

2.96 For a self-sufficient person or a student to be considered self-sufficient they must have, or declare respectively that they have, sufficient resources for themselves, taken together with their family members. Under EEA Regs 2006 reg 4(4):

> The resources of the person concerned and, where applicable, any family members, are to be regarded as sufficient if they exceed the maximum level of resources which a United Kingdom national and his family members may possess if he is to become eligible for social assistance under the United Kingdom benefit system.

2.97 Some of the retained rights of residence under reg 10 also contain a requirement for self-sufficiency.

2.98 By regulation 14 of the EEA Regs 2006, a 'qualified person', defined in reg 6 to include a self-sufficient person and a student, is only entitled to reside thereby for so long as he or she remains a qualified person. Thus, a self-sufficient person or a student may lose the right to reside if he or she cease to be self-sufficient. This also applies to the family members of a qualified person who is a self-sufficient person or a student.

2.99 Article 8 of the Directive concerns administrative formalities for EU citizens. Where a registration certificate may be required, it will only be supplied to a student or other self-sufficient person in circumstances where that person has sufficient resources. Article 8(4) states:

> Member States may not lay down a fixed amount which they regard as 'sufficient resources', but they must take into account the personal situation of the person concerned. In all cases this amount shall not be higher than the threshold below which nationals of the host Member State become eligible for social assistance, or, where this

criterion is not applicable, higher than the minimum social security pension paid by the host Member State.

2.100 In the European Casework Instructions of the UK Border Agency of the Home Office, at chapter 1, para 3.4 it states:

> We cannot apply a set amount of money that is required by an EEA national in order to be considered self-sufficient. Applications should be assessed on a case-by-case basis and should take into account such factors as income vs outgoings.

Right to reside tactics and problem areas

EU citizens who are not economically active[92]

2.101 Does an EU national with no right to reside based on the Residence Directive freedom of movement rights, have rights based on their EU citizenship?[93]

2.102 There has been a series of cases where the ECJ has found that an EU national who is not working or exercising any freedom of movement right has an entitlement to social assistance.[94] The decisions suggest that an EU citizen who is lawfully present or at the very least not unlawfully present in the host member state may be entitled to social assistance in circumstances where no express right to such is conferred by the Directive. There is debate about whether this case law reflects a move towards linking EU rights to EU citizenship, rather than linking them purely to the exercise of Treaty rights.

2.103 These cases pre-date the Residence Directive and the ECJ has not yet considered whether the effect of the Directive is a further move in the direction of the concept of EU citizenship.

2.104 The UK courts have strenuously resisted the EU citizenship approach, particularly in the context of A8 nationals. Two EEA nationals of Somali origin who had entered the UK lawfully but were not economically active were refused benefit on the basis that they had no right to reside because neither was a 'qualified person' within the meaning of the regulations in force at the time of the decision, the EEA Regs 2000.[95] On appeal it was argued that a

92 See also para 2.58.

93 TEC articles 17 and 18.

94 *D'Hoop* (Case C-224/98), *Grzelczyk* (Case C-184/99), *Trojani* (Case C-456/02), and *Bidar* (Case C-209/03).

95 SI No 2326.

refusal of benefit was discrimination on the grounds of nationality within article 12 of the EC Treaty. The Court of Appeal rejected both arguments and refused to make a referral to the European Court of Justice for a preliminary ruling.[96]

Parents with childcare responsibilities

2.105 The Residence Directive provides that the right to reside is only retained by the carer of a child in school if the EU citizen on whom the carer is dependent has died or departed from the UK, and it is subject to them not becoming an unreasonable burden on the member state's social assistance scheme.

2.106 As referred to at para 2.39, in *Baumbast and R v Secretary of State for the Home Department*[97] the ECJ found that where a non-EEA woman had divorced her EEA national husband, the EU worker, she had the right to reside in the UK as the carer of a child so the child could continue attending school. There have been a number of homelessness and benefits applications and appeals relying on *Baumbast* (such as the Social Security Commissioners' joined cases CIS/967/2007, CIS/963/2007 and CIS/2417/2006 currently adjourned).

2.107 In *Harrow LBC v Ibrahim and Secretary of State for the Home Department*[98] a Somali national had come to the UK in February 2003 with her Danish children to join her Danish husband who had been working in the UK for five months. Mrs Ibrahim's homelessness application was rejected on the basis that neither she nor her husband had the right to reside because he had left the UK and returned but was no longer economically active. She argued she had the right to reside as the carer of her older children who were attending school, under the Workers' Regulation 1612/68, article 12 read with *Baumbast*. She also argued that there was a gap in the Residence Directive, which had intended to implement the decisions in *Baumbast* and in *GBC Echternach and A Moritz v Netherlands Minister for Education and Science*,[99] but not fully succeeded. It was

96 *Abdirahman v Secretary of State for Work and Pensions, Abdirahman v (1) Leicester City Council and (2) Secretary of State for Work and Pensions, Ullusow v Secretary of State for Work and Pensions* [2007] EWCA Civ 657.

97 (Case C-413/99) [2002] ECR I-7091.

98 [2008] EWCA Civ 386, June 2008 *Legal Action* 14.

99 (Joined Cases 389 and 390/87) [1989] ECR 723.

pointed out that there was no requirement of self-sufficiency in the context of workers and their dependants either in EU legislation or in the *Baumbast* decision. The Court of Appeal decided to make a reference to the ECJ for guidance.[100]

'Burden on social assistance' and social rights

2.108 The question of a burden on social assistance has been relevant in social welfare cases involving those who are temporarily economically inactive. It is also relevant to the 'right to reside' and 'qualified person' definitions.

2.109 Linked to the Residence Directive's extension of rights to reside to new groups are specified limits on how social assistance rights are attached to the new rights.

- The 10th Recital provides that during the initial period of residence, periods of residence in excess of three months should be subject to conditions so that persons exercising a right of residence do not become an *unreasonable burden on the social assistance system.*
- The Residence Directive (16th Recital) provides some protection against expulsion for those considered to have become an *unreasonable burden on the social assistance system* of the host member state because it implies that a *reasonable* burden may be placed on the host member state. So a mere application for benefits or short-term claim should not lead to automatic expulsion. This may be useful in interpreting the meaning of 'unreasonable burden on the social assistance system' in this and other contexts:

  > The host Member State should examine whether it is a case of temporary difficulties and take into account the duration of residence, the personal circumstances and the amount of aid granted in order to consider whether the beneficiary has become an unreasonable burden on its social assistance system and to proceed to his expulsion.

- The 17th Recital notes that a permanent right of residence for those who have resided in the host member state for five years in compliance with the Directive is a key element in promoting social cohesion. The 18th Recital notes that the permanent right

100 See *Teixeira v Lambeth LBC and Secretary of State for the Home Department* [2008] EWCA Civ 1008. See also para 8.32 below.

of residence should not be subject to any conditions in order to be a vehicle for integration into the host member state. Thus a person with the permanent right of residence may not have that right made subject to a requirement not to be an unreasonable burden on the social assistance system of the host member state.
- The 20th Recital, enforced by article 24, refers to the prohibition against discrimination on grounds of nationality and notes that EU citizens and their family members should enjoy equal treatment with nationals of the host member state in areas within the scope of the EC Treaty subject to the specific provisions of that treaty and secondary legislation.
- The 21st Recital notes that in respect of particular rights to reside, Member States have discretion as to whether or not to confer entitlement to social assistance. This discretion may be exercised in respect of persons with the right to reside (a) during the first three months of residence, or (b) for a longer period in the case of jobseekers, to EU citizens other than those who are workers or self-employed persons or those who retain that status or their family members. There is also discretion as to whether to confer maintenance assistance for studies, including vocational training, before acquisition of the right of permanent residence, on these persons.

2.110 As long as EEA nationals and their family members without a right to reside do not become 'an unreasonable burden on the social assistance system', expulsion shall not be an automatic course of action.[101] The phrase is not defined in the Directive or EEA Regs 2006. In *Grzelczyk*, a student who had been self-sufficient for three years was temporarily without funds. The ECJ placed an emphasis on 'unreasonable' when interpreting the phrase. It was implicit in their judgement that member states must act proportionately and show a degree of financial solidarity with the country of origin so that a residence permit should not be automatically refused because a student needs temporary assistance.

2.111 A person who has acquired a right to reside may be removed from the UK if he or she does not have, or cease to have, a right to reside under them.[102] But such a person must not be removed as the automatic consequence of having recourse to the social assistance

101 Residence Directive article 14.

102 EEA Regs 2006 SI No 1003 reg 19(3).

system of the UK.[103] This would appear to be a reflection of the approach taken by the ECJ in *Grzelczyk*.

2.112 Of course, member states are not obliged to confer social assistance during the first three months of residence or during the period where a person is residing as a jobseeker. In addition, a member state is not obliged, prior to the acquisition of permanent residence, to grant maintenance aid for studies, consisting of student grants or student loans to persons other than workers, self-employed persons, persons who retain status and members of their families. However, all these provisions need to be read in the context of case-law, which has addressed the issues of entitlement to social assistance and assistance for studying in a host member state.[104]

2.113 These cases consider circumstances where there may be, among other things, an entitlement to social assistance, where there is no express right to reside, but where nonetheless an EU citizen may be said to be lawfully present or at the very least not unlawfully present in the host member state. These cases pre-date the implementation of the Directive but they are relevant when considering when a person may be entitled to social assistance in circumstances where no express right is conferred by the Directive or EEA Regs 2006.

The permanent right to reside

2.114 The permanent right of residence arises in a number of ways. In the UK it is regulated by EEA Regs 2006 reg 15. Once obtained it can only be lost only through absence from the UK for a period of more than two consecutive years.[105] The right may also be lost where the Home Secretary has decided that removal is justified on grounds of public policy, public security and public health in accordance with EEA Regs 2006 regs 19 and 21.

Permanent right to reside in the UK – five years

2.115 There is a permanent right of residence where a person has spent five years 'legally residing' in the UK.[106] The five years can

103 EEA Regs 2006 SI No 1003 reg 19(4).

104 See for example *D'Hoop* (Case C-224/98), *Grzelczyk* (Case C-184/99), *Trojani* (Case C-456/02), and *Bidar* (Case C-209/03).

105 EEA Regs 2006 reg 15(2).

106 EEA Regs 2006 reg 15(1)(a), (b) and (f).

include a period which pre-dates the implementation date of the Residence Directive.[107] The Court of Appeal has made a reference to the ECJ on the question of whether article 16 of the Residence Directive entitled an EU citizen to the permanent right to reside where they had been legally resident as a worker under previous provisions of EU law.[108]

2.116 The following may acquire the permanent right to reside via the five-year route:

- an EEA national who has resided in the UK in accordance with the EEA Regs 2006 for a continuous period of five years;[109]
- a family member of an EEA national who is not him- or herself an EEA national but who has resided in the UK with the EEA national in accordance with the EEA Regulations for a continuous period of five years;[110]
- a person who (a) has resided in the UK in accordance with the EEA Regs 2006 for a continuous period of five years; and (b) was, at the end of that period, a family member who has retained the right of residence.[111]

Permanent right to reside in the UK – retired/family members of deceased

2.117 There is a permanent right to reside where a person has spent less than five years in the UK for:

- a worker or self-employed person who has ceased activity (as defined by EEA Regs 2006 reg 5);[112]
- the family member of a worker or self-employed person who has ceased activity;[113] or
- a person who was the family member of a worker or self-employed person where:

107 *Secretary of State for Work and Pensions v Taous Lassal and Child Poverty Action Group (intervener)* [2009] EWCA Civ 157.

108 *Secretary of State for Work and Pensions v Taous Lassal and Child Poverty Action Group (intervener)* [2009] EWCA Civ 157. See also *Secretary of State for Work and Pensions v Marian Dias* [2009] EWCA Civ 807.

109 EEA Regs 2006 SI No 1003 reg 15(a).

110 EEA Regs 2006 reg 15(b).

111 EEA Regs 2006 reg 15(f).

112 EEA Regs 2006 reg 15(1)(c).

113 EEA Regs 2006 reg 15(1)(d).

— the worker or self-employed person has died;
— the family member resided with him or her immediately before his or her death; and
— the worker or self-employed person had resided continuously in the UK for at least the two years immediately before his or her death or the death was the result of an accident at work or an occupational disease.[114]

Meaning of 'worker or self-employed person who has ceased activity'

2.118 To decide who qualifies for the permanent right of residence under regulation 15(1)(c) and (d) it is necessary to consider the definition of 'worker or self-employed person who has ceased activity'. There are three ways in which a person may fall into this category.

- under regulation 5(2), if he or she lived in the UK for three years before stopped working as a worker or self-employed person at the age at which they are entitled to a state pension or in the case of a worker, to take early retirement. He or she must have worked as a worker or self-employed person in the UK for at least 12 months prior to retirement;
- under regulation 5(3), if he or she stopped working as a worker or self-employed person as a result of a permanent incapacity to work; and either had been living in the in the UK continuously for more than two years prior to the termination; or the incapacity was the result of an accident at work or an occupational disease that entitles them to a pension payable in full or in part by an institution in the UK;
- under regulation 5(4), if he or she is active as a worker or self-employed person in another EEA country but keep his or her home in the UK, to which they return as a rule at least once a week; and previously they had been continuously resident and continuously active as a worker or self-employed person in the UK for at least three years.

Accession

2.119 On 1 May 2004, ten new member countries joined the EU's existing 15 members, by virtue of the Treaty of Accession 2003. A distinction

114 EEA Regs 2006 SI No 1003 reg 15(1)(e).

was made between the terms offered to Cyprus and Malta and those offered to the poorer eight accession countries: the Czech Republic, Estonia, Hungary, Latvia, Lithuania, Poland, Slovakia and Slovenia, known as the A8 countries. The existing EU states gave themselves the power to restrict access to their labour markets for up to five years by 'derogations' (or opt-out clauses) in annexes to the Treaty. The same approach was applied to the A2 countries, Romania and Bulgaria when they joined the EU in January 2007.

2.120 The derogations are from art 39 of the EC Treaty and from articles 1–6 of Regulation 1612/68 on freedom of movement for workers, which cover access to the labour market.

Extension of the Worker Registration Scheme – A8 nationals

2.121 The Worker Registration Scheme (WRS) which requires nationals of the A8 countries to register for their first 12 months' work and restricts their access to benefits has been extended for a further two years until 30 April 2011 by the Accession (Immigration and Worker Registration) (Amendment) Regulations 2009.[115] The background to this is that the Treaty of Accession 2003 allowed existing EU member states to impose transitional restrictions on the free movement of labour on the new A8 member states (Poland, Lithuania, Latvia, Hungary, Slovakia, Slovenia, Estonia and the Czech Republic) for a maximum of seven years from 1 May 2004. But the final two years of this period are only lawful if there is a serious disturbance or threat of disturbance to the domestic labour market and the UK government notifies the EU Commission of this (see for example Act of Accession, article 24 and Annex XIII, para 5).

2.122 There is no guidance on the meaning of 'serious disturbance to the domestic labour market'. In response to a government request for advice, the Migration Advisory Committee published a report stating that there was a serious disturbance to the UK labour market due to the economic downturn. Although they concluded that abolition of the WRS or the £90 registration fee would not result in a substantial labour market impact, and should only result in limited additional welfare benefit expenditure, they found that maintaining

115 SI No 892.

the scheme would help address the 'current disturbance' in the UK's labour market.[116]

2.123 Although the right of an A8 or A2 national to work is more strictly controlled than that of other EEA nationals, if they are lawfully working, or have previously worked lawfully and continuously for 12 months, they have the same rights as any other EEA worker. Also, the controls only affect the rights of those working for an employer. Accession nationals exercising other EU rights, such as to be self-employed, are in the same position as any other EEA national (an exception is A2 students).

A8 nationals

2.124 A8 nationals enjoy all the same rights as nationals of other EEA states, except in respect of their status as jobseeker/work seekers and as workers during the first 12 months of employment. Most A8 nationals need to be registered during the first 12 months of working in the UK. Some A8 nationals are exempt from this requirement. Those A8 nationals who are required to register in order to work are subject to the Workers Registration Scheme (WRS) under the Accession (Immigration and Worker Registration) Regulations 2004.

2.125 In order to be lawfully employed, a national of an A8 state who is required to be registered must be:

- working in the UK from a date on or after 1 May 2004; and
- working for an authorised employer.

2.126 For as long as the person is working during the first 12 months under the WRS, that person is treated as a qualified person under the EEA Regs 2006.

2.127 In respect of A8 nationals, there are a number of limitations on the definition of an accession state worker requiring registration.[117]

2.128 An A8 national who legally (with leave to remain) works in the UK without interruption for a period of 12 months falling partly or wholly after 30 April 2004 does not need to register because they

116 'Review of the UK's transitional measures for nationals of member states that acceded to the European Union in 2004, Migration Advisory Committee Report', April 2009, www.ukba.homeoffice.gov.uk/sitecontent/documents/news/wrs-report-final.pdf.

117 Accession (Immigration and Worker Registration) Regulations 2004 SI No 1219.

are no longer an *accession state worker requiring registration*. They will still have to satisfy the ordinary provisions of the EEA Regs 2006 as a 'mainstream' EEA worker.

2.129 A8 nationals who are students or self-sufficient and their family members have access to the labour market without being required to register under the scheme.[118]

2.130 An A8 national who stops working for an authorised employer before they have completed the 12 months stops being a qualified person with the right to reside and will lose social assistance rights such as housing.[119]

2.131 An A8 national must complete a WRS form and pay a fee within a month of commencing employment in the UK.[120]

2.132 After a year's lawful employment under the scheme, an A8 national will have full rights to reside as a worker. This will in practice mean that they will no longer need to register under the scheme and can apply for a registration certificate.

2.133 An employer is an authorised employer in relation to a worker if:

- the worker was *legally* working (with leave to remain) for that employer on or after 30 April 2004 and has not ceased working for that employer after that date; or
- the worker: during the one-month period beginning on the date on which he or she begins working for the employer, applies for a registration certificate authorising him or her to work for that employer; and
  - — has not received a valid registration certificate or notice of refusal in relation to that application or ceased working for that employer since the application was made; or
  - — has received a valid registration certificate authorising him or her to work for that employer and that certificate has not expired.

A2 nationals

2.134 The Accession Treaty for Bulgaria and Romania (signed in Luxembourg on 25 April 2007) provides for existing states to restrict

118 Accession (Worker Authorisation and Worker Registration) (Amendment) Regulations 2007 SI No 3012 reg 3(b) amending Accession (Immigration and Worker Registration) Regulations 2004.

119 See *Putans v Tower Hamlets LBC* [2006] EWHC 1634 (Ch).

120 www.ukba.homeoffice.gov.uk/workingintheuk/eea/wrs/

access to their labour markets[121] until 31 December 2011, provided there are regular reviews. Since Bulgaria and Romania (the A2 countries) joined the EU on 1 January 2007, their nationals have been able to enter the UK without a visa and enjoy free movement rights such as the right to set up a business or to live here as a self-sufficient or retired person or a student. But their access to our labour market has been limited even more than that of the A8 nationals by the Accession (Immigration and Worker Authorisation) Regulations 2006. They may not register under the WRS. They may only work as an employee in the UK if they qualify for the highly skilled migrant programme or under a quota scheme, for example for low skilled workers in food processing and agriculture, or if they are qualifying students. This does not prevent them from working here on a self-employed basis.

2.135 In December 2008, the UK extended these restrictions on access to the labour market. Any member state that intended to continue to apply transitional restrictions on access to their labour markets had to notify the Commission of this intention before that date and justify that decision on the basis that there would otherwise be a serious disturbance to their labour market or a threat of this. In any event all transitional restrictions on workers must end for A2 nationals by 31 December 2013.[122]

Right of entry

2.136 In immigration terms, Bulgarians and Romanians have the right of admission to the UK when they present themselves at British airports or seaports.

Initial and extended right to reside

2.137 On admission, A2 nationals and their family members enjoy an initial right of residence for up to three months. Once admitted it is also possible for them to obtain an extended right of residence based on being either self-employed, self-sufficient or students. The family members of those Bulgarians and Romanians who have an extended right of residence may also have a right to reside as well.

121 By a derogation from article 39, Regulation 1612/68 arts 1–6, and the Residence Directive.

122 COM (2008) 765, 18 November 2008, Commission communication on the impact of free movement.

Permanent right to reside

2.138 Once a Bulgarian or Romanian national, or the family member of such a person, has enjoyed an extended right of residence for a period of time, there are circumstances in which that person may acquire a permanent right of residence. All these rights are available to nationals of Bulgaria and Romania on the same basis as nationals of other EU/EEA states.

Workers and jobseekers

2.139 The Accession (Immigration and Worker Authorisation) Regulations 2006 regulate A2 nationals who seek to work in the UK. Nationals of Bulgaria and Romania cannot directly rely on EU law to be able to work in the UK. They must either satisfy the Home Office and potential employer that they are not an accession state worker subject to worker authorisation or that they are such a person but have an accession worker authorisation document.

Exemptions

2.140 A person may be exempt from worker authorisation in the following cases:

- where he or she had leave to remain without being subject to any restriction on his/her ability to take employment and such leave has expired; and
- where he or she has been legally working for a 12-month period in the UK;
- where he or she is the Bulgarian or Romanian spouse or civil partner of a UK national or a person settled in the UK.

2.141 There are also other categories of persons not subject to the worker authorisation requirements. All such persons are free to take any work and to apply for a Registration Certificate on the same basis as an EU/EEA national. A worker in this situation has an extended right of residence in EU law.

2.142 In addition, where the A2 national fits the criteria for being a highly skilled person, that person is entitled to a registration certificate that enables them to be in the UK as a worker or a jobseeker. They are free to take any relevant employment without being a subject to worker authorisation requirements. Although factually any jobseeker may enter the UK and look for a job, only a highly skilled person will be able to be here with the legal status of a job seeker and take any employment.

2.143 If an A2 national meets the requirements under the highly skilled migrant programme,[123] they will not need authority to work under the worker authorisation scheme and can apply for a registration certificate like any other EEA national. The same will apply if they hold a degree in a subject approved by the Department of Education and Skills, or a master's degree or doctorate in any subject awarded by the UK.[124]

2.144 An A2 student is also not subject to worker authorisation requirements where he obtains a registration certificate entitling him to work 20 hours a week in term time, full time in vacations and for four months after his course ends. This certificate is yellow.

A2 family members

2.145 A family member of a worker not subject to worker authorisation requirements has the same rights to reside as the family member of an EU national from say Spain where that person is a family member of a person exercising a right to reside under EU law.

2.146 However a family member of an accession state national subject to worker authorisation will only be an authorised family member where the worker from Bulgaria or Romania has an accession worker authorisation document. Even if the A2 worker has that document, a family member will still not be an authorised family member able to obtain an accession worker card if the work is as an au pair, a seasonal agricultural worker or under the sectors-based scheme.

2.147 A family member of a self-employed person who has a right to reside here as a self-employed, self-sufficient person or a student is not subject to worker authorisation.[125]

A2 nationals subject to worker authorisation

2.148 An accession state national subject to worker authorisation only has the right to reside in the UK as a worker whilst they have an accession worker authorisation document and are complying with its conditions.

2.149 An accession worker authorisation document may be: (a) a passport or other travel document endorsed with leave to enter or

123 Immigration rules and HC 395 para 135A.

124 Reg 4.

125 Accession (Worker Authorisation and Worker Registration) (Amendment) Regulations 2007 SI No 3012 reg 2.

remain subject to a condition restricting that person to a particular employer or category of employment; (b) a seasonal agricultural worker card; or (c) an accession worker card. One of these documents must be obtained before the work starts.

2.150 A person may apply for an accession worker card where he or she falls within an authorised category of employment or where he or she is an authorised family member. This requirement severely restricts the categories of work for which a person who requires an accession worker card may apply. For an accession worker card to be issued to an accession state national subject to worker authorisation on the basis that that person's work falls within an authorised category of employment, he or she will be required to produce either: (a) a letter of approval where one is required under work permit arrangements; or (b) otherwise a letter from his or her employer confirming that there is a job offer.

2.151 A letter of approval under the work permit arrangements is required for: (a) employment under the Sectors-Based Scheme; (b) employment under the Training and Work Experience Scheme; or (c) employment under the work permit employment scheme.

2.152 Confirmation of an offer of employment is required from the employer for those applying and seeking to work in the following capacities: (a) airport-based operational ground staff of an overseas airline, (b) au pair placement, (c) domestic worker in a private household, (d) minister of religion, missionary or member of a religious order, (e) overseas government employment, (f) postgraduate doctors, dentists and trainee general practitioners, (g) private servant in a diplomatic household, (h) representative of an overseas newspaper, news agency or broadcasting organisation, (i) sole representative, (j) teacher of language assistant, and (k) overseas qualified nurse.

2.153 It is a criminal offence punishable with a fine for an employer to employ a person who requires an accession worker authorisation document and does not have one or who is not working in accordance with its conditions.

2.154 It is a criminal offence punishable by a fine and/or imprisonment to work as a person who requires an accession worker authorisation document and does not have one or as a person who is not working in accordance with its conditions. An immigration officer or constable may offer the A2 national who he has reason to believe is so working the opportunity to avoid liability to conviction by payment of a civil penalty of £1,000.

CHAPTER 3

Benefits

continued

continued

Introduction

3.1 Most PSIC[1] migrants, including most asylum-seekers, are not entitled to state benefits. Asylum-seekers' rights to such benefits have been replaced by an alternative form of state support specifically for those seeking asylum. A very few asylum-seekers remain entitled to state benefits and, if they qualify, they will receive those benefits instead of the specific forms of asylum support explained in chapters 4–6. Asylum-seekers who are granted refugee status, humanitarian protection (HP), or a form of exceptional leave to remain such as discretionary leave (DL) cease to qualify for asylum support and become entitled to state benefits and tax credits. This chapter covers:

- PSIC, including asylum-seekers, who qualify for state benefits;
- persons not subject to immigration control who enjoy a right to reside that enables them to qualify for state benefits;
- the issue of who can claim benefit, and for whom, and the effect of the receipt of state benefits by one household member on the support available to another. In the case of asylum-seekers, some persons may belong to a household where some members qualify for state benefits and some do not;
- the circumstances in which benefit entitlement for asylum-seekers ends; and
- steps to be taken by asylum-seekers who are granted some form of leave to remain.

Categories of persons entitled to benefits

3.2 The main categories of persons who come from abroad and who are entitled to some state benefits are:

- asylum-seekers who had subsisting claims for asylum in February 1996 and fall within transitional protection (1996 transitional protection cases);
- asylum-seekers who had subsisting claims for asylum in April 2000 and fall within transitional protection (2000 transitional protection cases);

1 Persons subject to immigration control.

- EEA nationals who are present in the UK exercising EU Treaty rights[2] and who, where required, are habitually resident in the UK (NB for most benefits other than income-based JSA, EEA jobseeker status does not qualify as a right to reside; for most benefits the EEA initial right of residence for up to three months, does not qualify as a right to reside);
- those (apart from EEA nationals) who are not subject to immigration control and who are habitually resident ie, British citizens, Commonwealth citizens with right of abode, and citizens of the Republic of Ireland;
- persons with indefinite leave to enter or remain who are habitually resident;
- EEA nationals who have leave to enter or remain;
- refugees and those with HP or exceptional leave to enter or remain (including DL);
- persons who have acquired a record of national insurance contributions, for example by past employment;
- persons who have entered the UK under sponsorship arrangements that may no longer be relied upon;
- persons whose funding from abroad is interrupted where they would otherwise be subject to a no recourse to public funds condition;
- asylum-seekers from 'upheaval' countries;
- citizens of ECSMA and ESC countries;
- persons relying on reciprocal agreements with the EU or the UK;
- habitually resident persons with leave to enter or remain (who are not excluded by IAA 1999 s115);
- persons in the UK as a result of deportation, expulsion or other removal from another country to the UK;
- persons in Great Britain who left the territory of Montserrat after 1 November 1995 because of the effect on that territory of a volcanic eruption; and
- persons who arrived in Great Britain on or after 28 February 2009 but before 18 March 2011, who immediately before arriving had been resident in Zimbabwe, and who before leaving Zimbabwe had accepted an offer, made by the British Government, to assist them to move to and settle in the UK.

Each category carries eligibility for specific benefits. We will look at each group in turn, describing the qualifying conditions, and the resulting benefit eligibility.

2 See chapter 2.

Entitlement and disqualification

The legal framework

3.3 The rights of PSICs, asylum-seekers and others with the right to reside to state benefits come from three main sources:

- domestic social security legislation;
- European Union (EU) law;[3] and
- reciprocal agreements[4] entered into by the UK and other countries.

These provisions should be interpreted in the light of the Human Rights Act (HRA) 1998, which incorporates the European Convention on Human Rights (ECHR). In addition, the UK has ratified the European Convention on Social and Medical Assistance (ECSMA) and the 1961 European Social Charter (ESC) (although it has only signed its 1996 successor), which are reflected in some of the provisions of domestic legislation.[5]

3.4 The main relevant social security statutes are the Social Security Contributions and Benefits Act 1992 (for rules of entitlement), the Social Security Administration Act 1992 and the Social Security Act 1998 and the Tribunals, Courts and Enforcement Act 2007 (for the administration of the scheme). The bulk of social security law, however, is contained in secondary legislation and the detailed rules relating to each benefit are contained in regulations. Decisions of the Upper Tribunal (Administrative Appeals), formerly the Social Security Commissioners, are binding on the decision-maker and form part of social security law.

Exclusions from benefit entitlement

3.5 Social security law restricts the availability of state benefits to people who come to the UK from abroad. This is achieved in the following

3 EC Council Regulation 1408/71 co-ordinates social security systems within the European Economic Area (EEA) prohibiting discrimination against EEA nationals who are exercising their rights to freedom of movement to work. This allows certain EEA nationals and their family members to qualify for benefits in the UK on the same basis as British nationals. See para 3.47 onwards. In addition, a person may be eligible to apply for a benefit by virtue of a right to reside arising under EU law.

4 See Department for Work and Pensions (DWP) International at www.dwp.gov.uk/international/ which includes information about contact details. See also, Decision Makers' Guidance (DMG), Chapter 7, Part 1: Agreements with other countries 070310-070341: www.dwp.gov.uk/publications/dwp/dmg/#vol2.

5 See paras 3.10 and 3.23 below.

way. First, claimants are excluded from entitlement if they are a PSIC. On to this structure of exclusions is grafted a series of further rules, which bring back into eligibility sub-groups of persons within the excluded categories. Most asylum-seekers are excluded from eligibility for benefits by being a PSIC. Second, claimants of most benefits (including UK citizens) must satisfy the 'habitual residence test' (HRT), which includes a requirement that a claimant has a 'right to reside' (RTR).[6] Those who do not satisfy the HRT are classified as 'persons from abroad'. On to this structure of exclusions is grafted a series of further rules, which provide for exemptions from the HRT requirement for certain persons. The HRT is dealt with in detail below (para 3.64 onwards).

Meaning of person subject to immigration control

3.6 PSIC is defined[7] as a person *who is not an EEA national* and who:

- requires leave to enter or remain in the UK but does not have it;[8]
- has leave to enter or remain in the UK subject to a condition that they do not have recourse to public funds;[9]
- has leave to enter or remain in the UK given as a result of a maintenance undertaking;[10]
- has leave to enter or remain only as a result of leave being extended while they appeal against a refusal to vary leave.[11]

6 See para 3.64. The Social Security (Habitual Residence) Amendment Regulations (SS(HR)A Regs) 2004 SI No 1232. These regulations introduced the 'right to reside' test into regulations contained in social security legislation in respect of various benefits. Subsequent amendment of those regulations in respect of individual benefits has led to further reordering of their provisions but the right to reside test remains a feature.

7 IAA 1999 s115(9).

8 This includes most asylum-seekers – temporary admission does not amount to leave to enter or remain for the purposes of the Immigration Act 1971 s3.

9 For example, visitors, students, au pairs, tier 2 workers, self-employed people, fiancé(e)s, spouses with limited leave to remain, etc. The provision only applies if the Home Office actually imposes a condition. If leave was granted before 1997 there may be no condition. See paras 1.34–1.35 for a definition of 'recourse to public funds'.

10 By IAA 1999 s115(10) '*maintenance undertaking*', in relation to any person, means a written undertaking given by another person, in pursuance of the immigration rules, to be responsible for that person's maintenance and accommodation.

11 IAA 1999 s115(9) and Sch 4 para 17. This provision refers to a provision that has now been repealed. An extension of leave to remain for those pursuing an appeal against a refusal to vary leave is now catered for by the Immigration Act 1971 s3C where the latter is not subject to IAA 1999 s115(9).

Benefits from which PSICs excluded

3.7 PSICs are also (subject to exceptions) excluded by the Tax Credits Act 2002 s42 and the Tax Credit (Immigration) Regs 2003 reg 3(1) from entitlement to working tax credit (WTC) and child tax credit (CTC). PSICs are (subject to exceptions) excluded from entitlement to state pension credit (SPC) by the State Pension Credit Act 2002 s4(2).

3.8 PSICs are (subject to exceptions) excluded by IAA 1999 s115 from entitlement to:

- attendance allowance (AA);
- carer's allowance (CA);
- child benefit (CB);
- council tax benefit (CTB);
- disability living allowance (DLA);
- health in pregnancy grant;
- housing benefit (HB);
- income support (IS);
- income-based jobseeker's allowance (income-based JSA);
- income-related employment and support allowance (IESA);
- severe disablement allowance (SDA); and
- social fund payments (SFP).

PSICs with some benefits entitlements

3.9 Regulations make provision to take some sub-groups of the PSIC category out of the general exclusion in IAA 1999 s115. The Social Security (Immigration and Asylum) Consequential Amendments Regulations (SS(IA)CA Regs) 2000[12] reg 2 sets out the persons who are not excluded from specified benefits. These are:

- persons specified in the Schedule to the regulations;[13]
- others covered by reciprocal agreements;[14] and
- transitional cases.[15]

3.10 As noted, certain PSICs specified are reincluded so as not to be excluded under section 115 of the IAA 1999 by the Schedule to

12 SI No 636.

13 SS(IA)CA Regs 2000 reg2(1) and (2).

14 SS(IA)CA Regs 2000 reg2(3). DMG, Chapter 7, Part 1: Agreements with other countries para 070831 to 070837. www.dwp.gov.uk/publications/dwp/dmg/#vol2. See also Department for Work and Pensions (DWP) International at www.dwp.gov.uk/international/ which includes information about contact details.

15 SS(IA)CA Regs 2000 reg2(5). See also DMG, Chapter 7, Part 1: Agreements with other countries paras 070838 to 070840 at www.dwp.gov.uk/publications/dwp/dmg/#vol2

SS(IA)CA Regs 2000. For income-based JSA, income support, income-related employment and support allowance, a social fund payment, housing benefit or council tax benefit, the following classes of persons are reincluded:

- A person who has limited leave to enter or remain in the UK under the immigration rules, subject to a condition of no recourse to or no charge on public funds and having, during any one period of limited leave (including any such period as extended), supported himself or herself without recourse to public funds, other than any such recourse by reason of the previous application of this provision, and who is *temporarily without funds during that period of leave because remittances to him or her from abroad have been disrupted, provided there is a reasonable expectation that his or her supply of funds will be resumed.* (NB this does not apply to a person who has been temporarily without funds for any period, or the aggregate of any periods, exceeding 42 days during any one period of limited leave (including any such period as extended). See para 3.13 below).
- A person who has been given leave to enter or remain in, the UK upon *an undertaking* by another person or persons under the immigration rules to be responsible for his or her *maintenance and accommodation* and who has not been resident in the UK for a period *of at least five years* beginning on the date of entry or the date on which the undertaking was given in respect of him/her, whichever date is the later, and the person or persons who gave the undertaking to provide for his or her maintenance and accommodation has, or as the case may be, have *died.*
- A person who has been given leave to enter or remain in the UK upon *an undertaking* by another person or persons pursuant to the immigration rules to be responsible for his or her *maintenance and accommodation* and has been resident in the UK for a period of at least five years beginning on the date of entry or the date on which the undertaking was given in respect of him or her, whichever date is the later.
- A person who is a national of a state that has ratified ECSMA or a state which has ratified ESC and who is lawfully present in the UK.

3.11 'Lawful presence' may include a person admitted on temporary admission.[16]

16 See *Szoma v Secretary of State* [2006] 1 AC 564.

3.12 For attendance allowance, severe disablement allowance, carer's allowance, disability living allowance, a social fund payment, health in pregnancy grant or child benefit, the following classes of persons are reincluded.

- A member of a family of an EEA national.[17]
- A person who is lawfully working in Great Britain and is a national of a state that the EU has a reciprocal agreement with under article 310 of the EC Treaty providing, in the field of social security, for the equal treatment of workers who are nationals of that State and their families.
- A person who is a member of a family of, and living with, a person who is lawfully working in Great Britain and is a national of a state that the EU has a reciprocal agreement with under article 310 of the EC Treaty.
- A person who has been given leave to enter, or remain in, the UK upon an undertaking by another person or persons pursuant to the immigration rules to be responsible for his or her maintenance and accommodation.

3.13 There is an inter-relationship between the Schedule to the SS(IA)CA Regs 2000 and the main eligibility criteria based on habitual residence/right to reside to be found in the social security statutory instruments, see for example regulation 10(4) of the Housing Benefit Regulations 2006 which provides:

> (4) Paragraph 1 of Part 1 of the Schedule to, and regulation 2 as it applies to that paragraph of, the Social Security (Immigration and Asylum) Consequential Amendments Regulations 2000 shall not apply to a person who has been temporarily without funds for any period, or the aggregate of any periods, exceeding 42 days during any one period of limited leave (including any such period as extended).

3.14 An application made on the basis that a person is temporarily without funds must be made while that person is actually without funds and not once funds have been restored.[18]

3.15 Reinclusion of those excluded by section 115 of the Immigration and Asylum Act 1999 does not remove the need to satisfy any further right to reside/habitual test that may also be imposed in other legislation.[19]

17 In respect of para (1) above it has been held that this applies to those who are family members as defined in EU law of those persons who are exercising rights of free movement under EU law, see CDLA/708/2007.

18 See CH/4248/2006.

19 *Yesiloz v Camden LBC* [2009] EWCA Civ 415.

Tax-credits

3.16 The same PSICs are excluded from tax credits. By section 42(2) of the Tax Credits Act 2002 'person subject to immigration control' has the same meaning as in section 115 of the Immigration and Asylum Act 1999. However for tax credit purposes the Tax Credits (Immigration) Regulations 2003 reg 3 provide for the reinclusion of PSICs in the following way:

- A person who has been given leave to enter, or remain in, the UK upon the *undertaking* of another person or persons, pursuant to the immigration rules, to be responsible for his or her *maintenance and accommodation*, and has been resident in the UK for a period of *at least five years* commencing on or after the date of his/her entry into the UK, or the date on which the undertaking was given in respect of him/her, whichever is the later.
- A person who has been given leave to enter, or remain in, the UK upon the *undertaking* of another person or persons, pursuant to the immigration rules, to be responsible for his or her *maintenance and accommodation*, has been resident in the UK for *less than the five years* but the person giving the undertaking has died or, where the undertaking was given by more than one person, they have all *died*.
- A person who has limited leave to enter or remain in the UK; that leave was subject to a condition that he or she does not have recourse to public funds, during that period of limited leave; he or she has, during so much as has elapsed of that period of limited leave (including that period as extended), supported himself/herself without recourse to public funds, other than any such recourse by reason of the previous satisfaction of these conditions; he or she is *temporarily without funds during that period of leave because remittances to him/her from abroad have been disrupted*; there is a reasonable expectation that his/her supply of funds will be resumed; and the period (or aggregate of periods) for which this case applies does not exceed 42 days during any single period of limited leave (including any extension to that period).
- Where the claim is for *working tax credit*, he or she is a national of a state which has ratified ECSMA or of a state which has ratified the ESC (18 October 1961), and is lawfully present in the UK.
- Where the claim is for *child tax credit* he or she is a national of a state which has ratified ECSMA or of a state which has ratified

the ESC, and lawfully present in the UK; where the award of child tax credit would be made on or after 6 April 2004, and immediately before the award is made (and as part of the transition of claimants entitled to elements of income support and income-based jobseeker's allowance, to child tax credit) the person is, or will on the making of a claim be, entitled to any of the amounts in relation to income support or income-based jobseeker's allowance that are described in section 1(3)(d) of the Tax Credits Act 2002.

- Where the claim is for *child tax credit*, he or she is a person who is lawfully working in Great Britain and is a national of a state that the EU has a reciprocal agreement with under article 310 of the EC Treaty providing, in the field of social security, for the equal treatment of workers who are nationals of that state and their families.

3.17 The category of 'person subject to immigration control' *does not* include EEA nationals. It does not include British citizens, Commonwealth citizens with right of abode, or citizens of the Republic of Ireland. It does not include those granted refugee status, HP or DL – unless, exceptionally and, practically speaking not known to happen, HP or DL has been granted subject to a condition of no recourse to public funds. Those who are not PSICs will, nonetheless, be excluded from entitlement to benefit unless they can satisfy the habitual residence test (including the right to reside test), or are exempted from it: persons excluded by the habitual residence test being classified as 'persons from abroad' for benefit purposes.[20]

Persons entering the UK subject to an undertaking by a sponsor

3.18 Advisers should bear in mind that sponsored persons may have leave subject to a requirement that they do not have recourse to public funds, and that claiming benefits may jeopardise their entitlement to remain in the UK. Unless it is clear that a person is not subject to such a requirement, immigration advice should be sought before making a claim for benefit. Paragraphs 6A–6C of the immigration rules should be consulted. It should also be borne in mind that a sponsor who fails to maintain in accordance with their undertaking may be prosecuted.[21]

20 See for example in respect of income support, IS Regs 1987 reg 21AA(1) and (2).

21 IAA 1999 s108.

3.19 A sponsored person who has been here for more than five years or whose sponsor who has given a written undertaking but has died in that five years is entitled to claim the benefits and tax credits mentioned above. An undertaking may continue to run even if a person subsequently leaves and re-enters the UK and is given leave to enter without reference to sponsorship.[22] IS and income-based JSA are paid at the urgent cases rate[23] where the relevant period is less than five years. Sponsored persons who have been here for longer than five years are entitled to ordinary benefits.[24]

3.20 'Sponsorship' here is limited to a written undertaking given by another person under the immigration rules (paras 6 and 35) to be responsible for that person's maintenance and accommodation. The undertaking must be signed and dated by the sponsor and must refer to the immigration rules. The Home Office provides a form for the purpose (currently RON 112 or SET(F)), but use of the form is not essential if the above requirements are met.[25]

Persons funded from abroad whose funding is interrupted

3.21 A person whose leave to enter or remain in the UK is subject to a condition that they have 'no recourse to public funds', but whose funding from abroad has stopped temporarily is entitled to claim benefits and tax credits as set out above.[26] Payments can only be made under this heading for a maximum of 42 days in any one period of leave. IS and income-based JSA are paid at the urgent cases rate[27] (see paras 3.109–3.111). Again, advisers should bear in mind that claiming benefits may jeopardise such persons' entitlement to remain in the UK. Immigration advice should be sought before making a claim for benefit. Paragraphs 6A–6C of the immigration rules should be consulted.

Asylum-seekers from upheaval countries

3.22 A person from an upheaval country who claimed asylum, on or before 3 April 2000, within three months of the Home Secretary's

22 *Shah v Secretary of State for Social Security* [2002] EWCA Civ 285; *Ahmed v Secretary of State for Work and Pensions* [2005] EWCA Civ 535.

23 IS Regs 1987 reg 70(2A); JSA Regs 1996 reg 147(2A).

24 IS Regs 1987 reg 70(2A); JSA Regs 1996 reg 147(2A).

25 CIS/47/2002; CIS/2474/1999; *R (Begum) v Social Security Commissioner* (2003) 6 November, unreported.

26 TC(I) Regs 2003 reg 3.

27 IS Regs 1987 reg 70(2A); JSA Regs 1996 reg 147(2A).

declaration can claim IS, JSA, HB and CTB.[28] Entitlement to benefit continues until the first negative asylum decision. Entitlement does not extend to family members who make their own claim for benefit, for example on death or separation.

Persons who are not EEA nationals but who are citizens of ECSMA and ESC countries

3.23 This category comprises nationals from countries that have ratified ECSMA and the ESC. Albania, Armenia, Moldova and Turkey have ratified the revised Social Charter and Turkey has ratified ECSMA.

3.24 Nationals of these countries are entitled to claim IS at ordinary benefit rates, other benefits (see paras 3.8–3.10) and tax credits (see para 3.16)[29] for themselves and any dependant provided that they are (for nationals of non-EEA countries) 'lawfully present' and (where they are not asylum-seekers) that they meet the 'habitual residence' test (see paras 3.63–3.78).

'Lawfully present'

3.25 For asylum-seeker nationals of Albania, Armenia, Moldova and Turkey the meaning of 'lawfully present' is a key issue. Asylum-seekers are granted temporary admission to the UK. 'Lawful presence' may include a person admitted on temporary admission.[30]

Persons entitled through reciprocal agreements

3.26 'A person who is lawfully working in Great Britain and is a national of a state with which the EU has concluded an agreement under article 310 of the EC Treaty . . .'[31] (or a family member who is living with him/her) is eligible to claim certain benefits and tax credits, as set out above. The EU has agreements with Algeria, Morocco, San Marino, Tunisia and Turkey. Note that for AA, DLA and CA, eligibility depends on being present in the UK for 26 weeks and being ordinarily resident here.[32] However, the agreements also guarantee equal treatment and this extends eligibility to a wider range of social

28 SS(IA)CA Regs 2000 reg 12(4).

29 IS Regs 1987 reg 70(2A).

30 *Szoma v Secretary of State* [2006] 1 AC 564.

31 SS(IA)CA Regs 2000 Sch Part II.

32 SS(AA) Regs 2000 reg 2(1), SS(DLA) Regs 1991 reg 2(1), SS(IA)CA Regs 2000 reg 9(1) and SS(IB) Regs 1994 reg 16.

security benefits,[33] including income-based JSA, employment and support allowance, pension credit, working tax credit, retirement pension, maternity allowance and, possibly, income support.[34] In the context of reciprocal agreements, 'lawfully working' is interpreted by the DWP to mean working or having previously worked in the UK without restrictions on employment and with permission to enter: temporary admission such as is granted to asylum-seekers is not sufficient.[35] However, it has been held in the case of a Turkish national who had worked elsewhere in the EEA that he was eligible even though he had not been employed in the UK.[36] Family member has the same meaning as for EEA nationals (see paras 1.194 and 2.71).

3.27 PSICs are not excluded from benefits that depend for entitlement upon a record of national insurance contributions because IAA 1999 s115 does not apply to them, that is, contribution-based jobseeker's allowance (contributory JSA), incapacity benefit, contribution-based employment and support allowance, retirement pension and maternity allowance. In practice, few asylum-seekers will have worked for long enough to have been paid or credited with sufficient contributions to qualify for these insurance-based benefits.

1996 transitional protection cases

Who falls into the category?

3.28 Asylum-seekers who were entitled to or receiving benefits both on 4 February 1996 (or 6 October 1996 in the case of child benefit) and 3 April 2000 have transitional protection. This means they are entitled to continue receiving benefit until the first negative decision on their asylum claim or until the award of benefit is revised or superseded if that happens first.[37] With the passage of time, very few asylum-seekers still fall into this category. A first negative decision occurs when the Home Secretary records an asylum claim as having been decided and that decision is notified to the applicant or the

33 Those covered by EC Regulation 1408/71; see also CJSA/4705/1999.

34 Following the ECJ case of *Babahenini* (Case C-113/97) [1998] ECR I-00183.

35 CJSA/4705/1999.

36 *Surul* (Case C-262/96); R(FC)1/01.

37 SS(PFA)MA Regs 1996 reg 12; SS(IA)CA Regs 2000 regs 2(4) and 12(10).

claim is abandoned.[38] In cases where an appeal was entered before 5 February 1996, a first negative decision may be the first decision refusing the appeal. If a first negative decision is overturned on appeal, for example if the Asylum and Immigration Tribunal (AIT) (or its predecessor the Immigration Appeal Tribunal) quashes a decision and refers it back to another adjudicator for reconsideration, entitlement to benefit does not revive.[39]

3.29 In the case of non-means-tested benefits (attendance allowance, disability living allowance, carer's allowance, severe disablement allowance and child benefit), entitlement also ends if the benefit award is revised or superseded.[40] This has been interpreted to include the expiry of a time-limited award, even where the award would otherwise be renewed.[41] For these benefits, any break in the claim means that entitlement is lost.[42] In the case of means-tested benefits (income support, housing benefit, council tax benefit), entitlement survives a break in the claim.[43] Therefore, for example, an asylum-seeker may end the benefit claim to work and reclaim at a later date.

3.30 The transitional protection also covers persons who were members of the asylum-seeker's family on 5 February 1996 and 3 April 2000.[44] Thus, for example:

- a child who leaves school can make a claim for income support in their own right;
- in a case of relationship breakdown where one partner was receiving income support on 4 February 1996, the other can claim.

38 SS(IA)CA Regs 2000 reg 12(10); *R (Anufrijeva) v Secretary of State for the Home Department and Secretary of State for Social Security* [2003] UKHL 36 (overruling the Court of Appeal decision in *R v Home Secretary ex p Salem* [1999] 1 AC 450, [1999] QB 805.

39 CIS/3418/1998, Starred Decision No 31/00.

40 SS(IA)CA Regs 2000 reg 12(10).

41 *R (B) v Chief Adjudication Officer* [2001] UKHL 35, [2001] 4 All ER 41; *M (a minor) v Secretary of State for Social Security* (2001) Times 6 July, HL.

42 *R v Chief Adjudication Officer ex p B* [1999] 1 WLR 1695.

43 *Yildiz v Secretary of State for Social Security* [2001] EWCA Civ 309, (2001) Independent, 9 March.

44 SS(PFA)MA Regs 1996 reg 12(1), as amended by SS(IA)CA Regs 2000 reg 12(11).

Which benefits may be claimed?

3.31 This protection applies to asylum-seekers receiving or entitled to IS, HB, CTB, AA, DLA, CA or SDA on 4 February 1996. It does not apply to income-based JSA. IS is paid at the urgent cases rate[45] (see paras 3.109–3.111).

3.32 It is not possible for claimants with this transitional protection to claim benefits additional to those they were receiving on the qualifying day. Thus, for example, an asylum-seeker entitled to IS and HB on 4 February 1996 who subsequently becomes disabled cannot claim DLA. However, an asylum-seeker receiving IS who reaches the age of 60 will qualify for SPC.[46]

2000 transitional protection cases

Who falls into the category?

3.33 Asylum-seekers who were entitled to or receiving means-tested benefits (income-based JSA, IS, HB, CTB) on 2 April 2000 retain entitlement until the first negative decision on their asylum claim.[47] The regulations build on the existing transitional protection provided by the Asylum and Immigration Act 1996.[48] It applies to those who are defined as 'asylum-seekers' within the meaning of the IS, HB and CTB Regulations: that is, an asylum-seeker who made a claim for asylum 'on arrival' in the UK on or before 2 April 2000 and whose claim has been recorded by the Home Secretary.[49]

3.34 Note that the requirement is an asylum claim before 3 April, not a benefit claim. The asylum-seeker may claim benefit for the first time after 2 April 2000. Entitlement survives a break in the claim, so that, for example, an asylum-seeker may end the benefit claim to work and reclaim at a later date. Entitlement does not extend to family members who make their own claim for benefit, for example on death or separation.

3.35 Benefit entitlement ends when the claim for asylum is recorded by the Home Secretary as decided (other than on appeal) and notified

45 IS Regs reg 70(2A).
46 SS(IA)CA Regs 2000 reg 2, as amended by SPC(TMP)A Regs 2003 reg 6.
47 SS(IA)CA Regs 2000 regs 2 and 12.
48 SS(PFA)MA 1996 Regs, which also amended the substantive regulations.
49 SS(IA)CA Regs 2000 reg 12(4).

to the asylum-seeker, or is abandoned.[50] Therefore, it ends if an asylum-seeker withdraws the asylum claim or receives a decision refusing asylum.

3.36 The term 'on arrival' is not defined in the legislation and has been the subject of much litigation. Rival interpretations have found approval before the Social Security Commissioners: it has been taken to mean 'on passing through immigration control at the port of entry', or 'while still within the perimeter of the port of entry'. The notion of an application 'as soon as reasonably practicable' has also been canvassed. The Court of Appeal has added some further guidance.[51]

3.37 Commissioner Howell QC attempted to tackle the problem of a series of inconsistent commissioners' decisions by reviewing all of them in 1999.[52] He adopted the 'factual test' of 'on arrival'. He decided that commissioners who applied a test of whether the claim for asylum had been made within the port of entry, even if this was after passing through immigration control,[53] were mistaken and the appropriate test was an 'immigration control' test:[54]

> It follows in my judgment that the reference in reg 70(3A)(a)[55] to a person submitting a claim for asylum on his arrival (other than on his re-entry) in the UK is concerned with the nature of the application made to be allowed into the UK at the point where a recently-arrived passenger submits, or should submit, himself to examination by an immigration officer at his or her port of first entry into this country.

The commissioner found in both this case and later in 2000[56] that clandestine entrants who had claimed asylum after passing through the port in a lorry had not claimed 'on arrival'.

3.38 However, Commissioner Sanders decided that where a Libyan asylum-seeker was too ill to claim asylum when he reached Heathrow

50 SS(IA)CA Regs 2000 reg 12(5); *R (Anufrijeva) v Secretary of State for the Home Department and Secretary of State for Social Security* [2003] UKHL 36 (overruling the Court of Appeal decision in *R v Home Secretary ex p Salem* [1999] 1 AC 450; [1999] QB 805 and the High Court in *R (Paulo) v Secretary of State for the Home Department and Secretary of State for Social Security* [2001] EWHC 480 (Admin).

51 *Shire v Secretary of State for Work and Pensions* [2003] EWCA Civ 1465.

52 CIS 3867/98, 30 September 1999.

53 CIS 1137/97 and CIS 4341/98.

54 CIS 143/97 and CIS 3231/97.

55 Now contained in SS(IA)CA Regs 2000 reg 12(4).

56 CIS 3646/98, 5 January 2000.

airport due to torture in Libya, this was an exceptional case in which he might fall within the 'on arrival' definition if the facts of his illness could be proven.[57]

3.39 In another case, an applicant for asylum had passed through immigration control at Gatwick airport with an agent without claiming asylum but attempted to claim asylum two hours later with the help of a man from the Third World Refugee Bureau, after waiting in the arrivals hall.[58] Commissioner Williams rejected the 'as soon as reasonably practicable' test but, applying a measure of flexibility to the test of 'on arrival',[59] found that the claimant had claimed 'on arrival'.

3.40 The Court of Appeal has considered the situation of an applicant who does not claim asylum on passing through immigration control because they have placed themselves in the hands of, or are following the directions of, an agent.[60] The court held that such a person voluntarily places him/herself in the control of the agent and adopts their actions, and so fails the test. The court specifically declined to approve or disapprove the 'immigration control', 'port perimeter' or 'as soon as reasonably practicable' approaches. In *Kola and Mirzajani v Secretary of State for Work and Pensions*,[61] the House of Lords held that a claim was made on arrival where a claim could not reasonably have been made earlier. The first practical opportunity had been taken to claim asylum.

Which benefits may be claimed?

3.41 The protection applies to income-based JSA, IS, HB, CTB and a social fund payment. IS and income-based JSA are paid at the urgent cases rate[62] (see paras 3.109–3.111). An asylum-seeker receiving IS or income-based JSA who reaches the age of 60 will qualify for state pension credit (SPC).[63] A claimant may have a choice whether to claim IS or income-based JSA.

57 CIS 3803/98, 7 July 1999.

58 CIS 4341/98.

59 See also CIS 2719/97, CIS 4117/97 and CIS/43/2000.

60 *Shire v Secretary of State for Work and Pensions* [2003] EWCA 1465, (2003) Times, 14 October; the decision concerned the provisions as to claims made 'on arrival' in IS Regs reg 70(3A), since repealed.

61 [2007] UKHL 57.

62 IS Regs 1987 reg 70(2A); JSA Regs 1996 reg 147(2A).

63 SS(IA)CA Regs 2000 regs 2 and 12, as amended by SPC(TMP)A Regs 2003 reg 6.

European Economic Area nationals

3.42 Chapter 2 concerns EU law and the right to reside. It should be consulted to determine whether an EEA national or the family member of an EEA national has a right to reside under EU law. For benefits purposes brief mention is made of the following additional points. An EEA national cannot be a PSIC under IAA 1999 s115, and therefore merely has to meet any habitual residence and/or right to reside test imposed to be eligible to apply for a particular benefit or tax credit. A non-EEA national who asserts a right to reside as the family member of an EEA national, is potentially subject to IAA 1999 s115 but will not be so if they establish a right to reside under EU law. Where a non-EEA national has such a right, it will still be necessary to satisfy any habitual residence and/or right to reside test imposed to be eligible to apply for a particular benefit or tax credit.

3.43 Not all rights to reside enable a person to be eligible to apply for a benefit. Care must be taken to ensure that the EEA initial right of residence for up to three months and/or an EEA right to reside as a jobseeker or the family member of a jobseeker are not expressly excluded in respect of a particular benefit.

3.44 It is possible, although rare, for EEA nationals to have been granted leave to enter or remain. If so, such a person will have a right to reside and will be entitled to equal treatment with a British citizen under article 12 of the EC Treaty (non-discrimination on grounds of nationality).

3.45 The habitual residence/right to reside tests imposed for council tax benefit, housing benefit, income support, income-based JSA, income-related employment and support allowance and pension credit embrace all forms of right to reside arising under UK and EU law.

3.46 An EEA national or the family member of an EEA national who has an EU right to reside may or may not be exempt from the other elements of the habitual residence test (see paras 3.63–3.78) in order to qualify for non-contributory benefits. Those persons exempt from having to satisfy the further elements of the habitual residence test are EEA nationals who are 'workers' or 'self-employed', or have retained such a status, holders of the permanent right of residence other than under the five-year route and additionally family members of such persons.[64]

64 See para 2.61 onwards for information on who has a right to reside.

The co-ordination of social security benefits

3.47 EEA nationals who are insured persons in their state of origin may be able to receive income protection benefits in another EEA state. EEA nationals qualifying under these provisions may be able to avoid having to satisfy the habitual residence test.[65] Further, the right to equal treatment for workers in social security matters under co-operation agreements between the EEA and other states (Algeria, Morocco, San Marino, Tunisia) extends to Turkish nationals by virtue of the EEC–Turkey Association Agreement and EEA Council Decision 3/80.[66]

3.48 European Court of Justice judgments have established a wide definition of 'worker' in the context of the co-operation agreements, which covers most of those who have stopped lawfully working for a valid reason.[67] Nationals of Algeria, Morocco, San Marino, Tunisia or Turkey are to be treated as 'workers' (eligible for benefits) if:

- they have permission to enter Britain and are working here with no restriction on their right to work; or
- they have stopped working in the UK due to sickness, pregnancy, reaching pension age, widowhood, a work-related accident or disease, unemployment or to look after children.

3.49 Regulation 1408/71 co-ordinates the social security systems of EEA states by allowing a person to claim benefits in the EEA country where they last worked, allowing a person to take certain benefits to another EEA state, allowing a person to claim benefits for family

65 These provisions derive from EC Council Regulation 1408/71. This is EU law directly applicable in the UK and designed to support the freedom of movement of EEA nationals. For further information, see *Migration and Social Security Handbook*, 4th edn, CPAG, 2007.

66 In *Surul* (Case C-262/96), the ECJ considered the principle of equal treatment and co-ordination in social security matters, which apply to EEA workers by virtue of EEC Reg 1408/71. It decided that the same 'freedom of movement' principles applied to Turkish workers, their families and survivors by virtue of Council Decision 3/80. The definition of 'worker' and 'family member' was considered, and the court noted that the Decision 3/80 definition of 'worker' corresponds to the concept of worker contained in Reg 1408/71, art 1(a) and that the term 'member of family' has the meaning given to it by Reg 1408/71, art 1(f). See also Social Security Commissioners' decision CFC/2613/1997.

67 See *Kziber* (Case C-18/90) [1991] ECR I-199; *Yousfi v Belgium* (Case C-58/93) [1994] ECR I-1353; *Krid v Caisse Nationale d'Assurance Veillesse des Travailleurs Salariés* (Case C-103/94) [1995] ECR I-719; *Hallouzi-Choho v Bestuur van de Sociale Verzekeringsbank* (Case C-126/95) [1996] ECR I-4807; *Babahenini* (Case C-113/97) [1998] ECR I-183.

members resident in other EEA states, prohibiting discrimination in matters of social security on grounds of nationality and allowing a person to rely on insurance contributions paid and periods of employment and residence in one member state to count towards benefits in another (for example contribution-based JSA) and to override residence conditions. (This is very important for EEA nationals who have been employed or self-employed for a short time in the UK but who have worked prior to coming to the UK.) The regulation applies to a person who is employed or self-employed. This is defined as a person who is insured under a social security scheme in a member state, that is someone who pays, has paid or ought to pay national insurance or the equivalent. It also applies to family members irrespective of nationality. The relevant benefits covered are:

- **Special non-contributory benefits (cannot be exported):** jobseekers' allowance (income-based), DLA (mobility), income support, employment and support allowance (income-based), pension credit.
- **Sickness and maternity:** employment and support allowance (assessment), incapacity benefit, maternity allowance, DLA (care component), attendance allowance, carer's allowance, statutory sick pay, statutory maternity pay, statutory adoption pay, statutory paternity pay.
- **Invalidity:** employment and support allowance (post-assessment and in youth), incapacity benefit, severe disablement allowance.
- **Old age:** retirement pension, additional pension, graduated retirement pension, winter fuel payments and Christmas bonus.
- **Survivors' benefits and death grants:** bereavement benefits, widowed parent's allowance.
- **Accidents at work and occupational diseases:** industrial disablement benefit, constant attendance allowance, exceptionally severe disablement allowance, reduced earnings allowance.
- **Family benefits:** child benefit, guardian's allowance, child dependency increases, child tax credit (these may be paid in respect of family members living in another EEA state but cannot otherwise be exported).
- **Unemployment:** jobseeker's allowance (contribution-based). A person must register at least four weeks before he or she leaves the state he or she was residing in and must register in the second EEA state within seven days. It can only be paid for three months.

The position of EU jobseekers and their family members

3.50 A jobseeker (and the family member of such a person) has a right to reside but a restricted entitlement to non-contributory benefits. Chapter 2 provides information as to who is a job seeker or the family member of a jobseeker under EU law. In respect of council tax benefit, housing benefit, income support, income-related employment and support allowance and pension credit, a right to reside is expressly excluded from being a qualifying right to reside. However, a jobseeker or the family member of a jobseeker may rely upon that right to reside so as to be eligible to apply for income-based JSA. In addition, receipt of income-based JSA renders a person eligible for housing benefit and council tax benefit without having to satisfy the habitual residence test. In *Collins v Secretary of State for the Department of Work and Pensions*,[68] the European Court has criticised the application of the habitual residence test to jobseekers. The court ruled that while it might be appropriate for a member state to have a residence test, such a test would be reasonable and proportionate (and therefore lawful) only if: (a) it was directed at and confined to establishing a link between the person seeking work and the employment market in the member state, (b) it did not discriminate on the basis of the nationality of persons concerned, and (c) it was based on clear criteria, with judicial redress available in case of dispute. The court observed that the other rules of the JSA scheme enabled the UK government to satisfy itself as to (a), with the implication that the (additional) habitual residence test was disproportionate. It also observed that a test was to be considered discriminatory if it were inherently more likely to be satisfied by the member state's own citizens than by other EEA nationals. These rulings of the court are a fundamental challenge to the lawfulness of the habitual residence test in its application to work seekers.

A8 nationals

3.51 From 1 May 2004, ten countries joined the European Union. They are Poland, Hungary, the Czech Republic, Slovenia, Slovakia, Estonia, Latvia, Lithuania, Cyprus and Malta. The UK government introduced regulations[69] to restrict access to benefits for nationals of the eight eastern European countries (but not Cyprus and Malta, whose nationals are treated the same as those of the existing 15 EEA states

68 Case C-138/02, 23 March 2004.

69 SS(HR)A Regs 2004 reg 6.

such as France and Germany). The restriction on A8 nationals of these states works by indirectly limiting the benefit entitlement of employed 'workers' from these countries: they are required to register under a workers' registration scheme, and remain registered until they have been in continuous employment for a period of 12 months.[70] Those registered are able to claim 'in-work' benefits – CB, WTC, CTC, HB and CTB and to have access to social housing. But if they lose their job within the 12-month period, they are barred from claiming IS, income-based JSA, SPC, HB and CTB and cease to be eligible for social housing.[71] There is no bar to DLA, AA and CA beyond the present 26-week residence test. After the period of 12 months' continuous employment, registration is no longer required, and the rights of an A8 national become the same as those of other EEA nationals. The position of the self-employed is that they are not required to register and are eligible for in-work benefits, but if they cease work, they cease to have a right to reside (unless they have applied for and obtained a residence permit), and thereupon lose entitlement. The position of jobseekers is that they are considered to have the right to reside only so long as they can support themselves, and so are debarred from all benefits until they find work. Those who are economically inactive are – like other EEA nationals – also considered to have the right to reside only so long as they are self-sufficient, and so remain debarred from means-tested benefits.

Romanians and Bulgarians – A2 nationals

3.52 When Bulgaria and Romania joined the EU on 1 January 2007, the UK government introduced regulations[72] to restrict their citizens' access to the labour market and benefits system. The restriction works by curtailing the benefit entitlement of employed 'workers'

70 See *Zalewska v Department for Social Development (Northern Ireland)* [2008] UKHL 67.

71 The worker registration scheme is given effect by the Accession (Immigration and Worker Registration) Regulations 2004 SI No 1219. The disqualification from benefits is given effect by the SS(HR)A Regs 2004. Note that there are rules which allow a worker who loses a job during the 12-month period to link employment in a further job to the first in calculating the 12-month period, providing the jobs are not separated by more than 30 days (Accession (Immigration and Worker Registration) Regulations 2004 SI No 1219 reg 2(4), 2(8)). Entitlements to HB, CTB, WTC, CB and social housing are lost as soon as the first job is lost and do not recommence until the next job starts.

72 Social Security (Bulgaria and Romania) Amendment Regulations 2006 SI No 3341.

from these countries: they are required to obtain authorisation under a workers' authorisation scheme, and remain so authorised until they have been in continuous employment for a period of 12 months. Those registered are able to claim 'in-work' benefits, eg CB, WTC, CTC, HB and CTB and to have access to social housing. But if they lose their job within the 12-month period, they are barred from claiming IS, income-based JSA, SPC, HB and CTB, etc and cease to be eligible for social housing.[73]

3.53 Again there is no bar to DLA, AA and CA, beyond the present 26-week residence test. After the period of 12 months' continuous employment, registration is no longer required, and the rights of an A2 national become the same as those of other EEA nationals. The position of the self-employed is that they are not required to register and are eligible for in-work benefits, but if they stop work, they no longer have a right to reside (unless they have applied for and obtained a residence permit), and thereupon lose entitlement. The position of jobseekers is that they are considered to have the right to reside only so long as they can support themselves, and so are debarred from all benefits until they find work. Those who are economically inactive are – like other EEA nationals – also considered to have the right to reside only so long as they are self-sufficient, and so remain debarred from means-tested benefits.

Which benefits may be claimed?

3.54 All EEA citizens are entitled to claim benefits that depend on a record of national insurance contributions (IB, contributory JSA, contributory employment and support allowance, MA and RP). It is also possible to qualify for these benefits on the basis of equivalent or similar contributions made in other EEA states; however, the applicable rules are beyond the scope of this book (see 3.47–3.49).

3.55 All EEA citizens are eligible for benefits and tax credits provided, where material, they satisfy the relevant presence and/or right to reside conditions: see below.

73 The worker registration scheme is given effect by the Accession (Immigration and Worker Authorisation) Regulations 2006 SI No 3317. The disqualification from benefits is given effect by the Social Security (Bulgaria and Romania) Amendment Regulations 2006 SI No 3341. Note that there are rules which allow a worker who loses a job during the 12-month period to link employment in a further job to the first in calculating the 12-month period, providing the intervening periods when not legally working are not more than 30 days in total (Accession (Immigration and Worker Authorisation) Regulations 2006 reg 2(12)). Entitlements to HB, CTB, WTC, CB and social housing are lost as soon as the first job is lost and do not recommence until the next job starts.

3.56 Family members of EEA citizens who are not themselves EEA citizens are *not* excluded from attendance allowance, severe disablement allowance, carer's allowance, disability living allowance, a social fund payment, health in pregnancy grant or child benefit.[74] Note that for AA, DLA and CA eligibility depends on being present in the UK for 26 weeks and being ordinarily resident here.[75] EEA citizens who have worked in other EEA countries can count time spent in those countries towards the 26 weeks' presence (see 3.47–3.49).

Other persons not subject to immigration control

Who falls into the category?

3.57 The remaining broad category of persons who come to the UK who have entitlement to benefits are the following:

- British citizens (as defined by the British Nationality Act 1981);
- Commonwealth citizens with right of abode; and
- citizens of the Republic of Ireland.

Such persons are not subject to immigration control and have a right to reside in the Common Travel Area, but they must satisfy the habitual residence test (see para 3.63–3.78) for most benefits, unless they fall into an exempt category.

Which benefits may be claimed?

3.58 Persons in this category are entitled to claim benefits that depend on a record of national insurance contributions, whether or not they satisfy the habitual residence test (IB, contributory JSA, contributory employment and support allowance, MA and RP).

3.59 Persons in this category who satisfy (or are exempt from) the habitual residence test, and their family members, are eligible for the full range of benefits under the ordinary rules.

Special categories

3.60 There are certain special categories of persons for whom benefit entitlement is allowed or preserved by the regulations. The numbers of persons falling into these groups are generally small.

74 SS(IA)CA Regs 2000 reg 2(2) and Sch Part II.

75 SS(AA) Regs 1991 reg 2(1), SS(DLA) Regs 2000 reg 2(1), SS(IA)CA Regs 2000 reg 9(1), SS(IB) Regs 1994 reg 16.

Persons who have acquired a record of national insurance contributions

3.61 Where a person has been in paid employment in the UK, or has paid national insurance as a self-employed person, they may have built up a sufficient contribution record to qualify for certain contributory benefits (IB, MA, contributory JSA, contributory employment and support allowance and RP). Such benefits are paid irrespective of immigration status. Such persons will have national insurance numbers. If you think a person may have a sufficient contribution record (and otherwise meets the conditions of entitlement) a claim should be made.

Asylum-seekers from designated 'upheaval' countries

3.62 The Home Secretary has power to declare as 'upheaval' countries states where changes in political conditions mean that it becomes unsafe for persons already in the UK to return. Where nationals of such states claim asylum, special rules of entitlement to benefits apply. The only claims for asylum currently affected are those made by Sierra Leone nationals between 16 May 1997 and 16 August 1997, and those made by Democratic Republic of Congo nationals between 1 July 1997 and 1 October 1997. This historical category applies to asylum claims made on or before 3 April 2000.

The habitual residence test and right to reside

3.63 The requirement that a benefit claimant is either habitually resident *or treated as* habitually resident in the Common Travel Area (the UK, Isle of Man, Republic of Ireland or the Channel Islands) applies to a wide range of benefits and tax credits: see below. Different rules apply to contributory benefits, which go beyond the scope of this book.[76] A claimant who satisfies the habitual residence test is not prevented from claiming for a partner or dependents who do not themselves satisfy the test. So where only one of two partners satisfies, or is exempt from, the test, that partner should be the claimant. The DWP applies the habitual residence test to claimants who have not lived in the UK (or the Common Travel Area) throughout the past two years.

76 See *Migration and Social Security Handbook* CPAG, 4th edn, 2007, chapters 22–23.

Meaning of 'habitual residence'

3.64 The test is imprecise, as the term is not defined in domestic law and has a different meaning in EU law.

3.65 The following factors should be taken into account:

- the claimant must have a 'settled intention' to reside in the UK. Events before and after arrival here can be used to demonstrate this. These would include circumstances and arrangements made before arrival in the UK and steps taken after arrival to settle here, for example, children attending school, registering with GPs and other organisations;
- a claimant will need to be resident in the UK for an 'appreciable period' unless they are returning to the UK after a temporary absence abroad, in which case they are 'habitually resident' on the first day back in the UK.

Each claim should be considered on its own merits, taking account of the facts at the date of the claim. A claimant who fails the test may with the passage of time or changes of circumstances come to satisfy it, so that, where a claimant fails the test, consider repeat applications at regular intervals and an appeal against each individual negative decision.

3.66 The meaning of habitual residence has been reviewed by the ECJ in *Swaddling v Adjudication Officer*[77] and by the House of Lords in *Nessa*.[78]

3.67 In *Swaddling*, the ECJ decided that an EEA national who has come to the UK after working in Europe should not need to be in the UK for an appreciable period before being able to establish habitual residence. The DSS (as it then was) then issued guidance, which states that the national of any country who is returning to the UK to 'pick up the pieces of their former life' is habitually resident as soon as they arrive in the UK, that is does not need to be in the UK for an appreciable period. Commissioner Mesher has commented that the guidance incorrectly interprets *Swaddling*.[79] He confirmed that an EEA national who has worked/been insured in the EEA and so falls within EC Reg 1408/71 cannot be excluded from benefit on the basis that the 'appreciable period' requirement is not met. He confirmed that the length of a person's residence in the UK will

77 Case C90/97, [1999] All ER (EC) 217.

78 *Nessa v Chief Adjudication Officer* [1999] 1 WLR 1937.

79 CIS 15484/96, 20 July 1999.

merely be one factor to consider in deciding whether they have a settled intention to remain here, and that in some circumstances other factors could mean that the person concerned was habitually resident on arrival.

3.68 In *Nessa v Chief Adjudication Officer*, the claimant came to the UK after living in Bangladesh all her life and appealed against a DWP decision that she was not habitually resident. The House of Lords attempted to distinguish her circumstances from those in *Swaddling*. The court held that a period of actual residence can be required for those who do not fall within *Swaddling*, that is who have not worked in the EEA, although the appreciable period could be as short as one month. Lord Slynn stated:

> ... as a matter of ordinary language a person is not habitually resident in any country unless he has taken up residence and lived here for a period ... It is a question of fact to be decided on the date when the determination has to be made on the circumstances of each case whether and when the habitual residence had been established. Bringing possessions, doing everything necessary to establish residence before coming, having a right of abode, seeking to bring family, 'durable ties' with the country of residence have to be taken into account. The requisite period is not a fixed period. It may be longer when there are doubts. It may be short.[81]

3.69 Commissioner Jacobs has accepted in the case of two appellants that no appreciable period is necessary to establish habitual residence.[80] An argument that the approach in *Swaddling* – being a decision of the ECJ – should prevail over that of the House of Lords in *Nessa* in a case involving a person who had not spent time in another EEA country before arriving in the UK was unsuccessful before the Court of Appeal.[82]

3.70 The ECJ in the case of *Collins v Secretary of State for the Department of Work and Pensions*[83] criticised the application of the habitual residence test in excluding EEA citizens who are in the UK as work-seekers from entitlement to JSA. The criticisms were based on the right of freedom of movement under the EC Treaty,[84] a right that is

80 CIS/1304/1997 and CJSA/5394/1998.

81 [1999] 1 WLR 1937.

82 *Gingi v Secretary of State for the Department of Work and Pensions* [2001] EWCA Civ 1685.

83 Case C-138/02, 23 March 2004.

84 EC Treaty art 39.

guaranteed to EEA citizens[85] without discrimination.[86] The court found that such a test was potentially unlawful, since it was likely to be discriminatory and disproportionate to its objects. The ruling is likely to give rise to challenges to the lawfulness of the test in other contexts.

3.71 When the A8 countries joined the EU, the government made changes to the habitual residence test that affect all who are subject to it. From 1 May 2004, the habitual residence test is not satisfied by any person who does not also have a 'right to reside' (RTR) in the Common Travel Area (CTA). This marks a significant change, especially for EEA nationals: previously, all EEA nationals could satisfy the habitual residence test by an 'appreciable period' of residence in the CTA and a settled intention to reside; now they are only be able to do so if they have a RTR. Those who fall within the exempt categories described at para 3.46 above are unaffected by this extension of the test.

3.72 A person has a 'right to reside' if they have been issued with an EEA registration certificate or residence card. However, a person also has a right to reside if they have an EEA right to reside (see chapter 2).

3.73 Family members of EEA citizens in the above categories will have the same right to reside.

3.74 It is to be noted that nationals of countries outside the UK and the EEA would also have to establish a right to reside to qualify for benefits, although, as has been seen (paras 3.6–3.17), most are disqualified by IAA 1999 s115 as PSICs.

3.75 Generally speaking, those who are *not* PSIC, as defined by IAA 1999 s115, are excluded from entitlement to benefits under the habitual residence/right to reside tests unless they are:[87]

- EEA nationals who are 'workers' or 'self-employed', or have retained such a status, holders of the permanent right of residence other than under the five-year route, or additionally family members of any such persons (see paras 2.65–2.100);
- persons who have acquired, under the five-year route, the EEA permanent right of residence or their family members where habitually resident;
- EEA nationals or their family members who have other EEA rights to reside and who are habitually resident (see paras

85 EC Treaty art 17.

86 EC Treaty art 12.

87 For PC, by SPCA 2002 s1(2)(a) and SPC Regs 2002 reg 2.

2.65–2.100). (However, for most benefits not those EEA nationals or their family members who rely on the EEA initial right of residence for up to three months or an EEA national's right to reside as a jobseeker, although jobseeker status is sufficient to apply for income-based JSA);

- EEA nationals who have leave to enter or remain and who are habitually resident;
- habitually resident British citizens, Commonwealth citizens with the right of abode, Irish citizens and persons with indefinite leave to enter or remain;
- refugees;
- persons with humanitarian protection or exceptional leave to remain including discretionary leave to remain;
- habitually resident persons with leave to enter or remain (who are not excluded by IAA 1999 s115);
- persons who are in the UK as a result of deportation, expulsion or other removal by compulsion of law from another country to the UK;
- persons in Great Britain who left the territory of Montserrat after 1 November 1995 because of the effect on that territory of a volcanic eruption; and
- persons who arrived in Great Britain on or after 28 February 2009 but before 18 March 2011, who immediately before arriving had been resident in Zimbabwe, and who before leaving Zimbabwe, had accepted an offer, made by the British government, to assist that person to move to and settle in the UK.

The right to reside

The introduction of the right to reside test affecting all new claimants

3.76 Before 1 May 2004, EEA nationals and others who did not have the 'right to reside' could acquire entitlement to benefits by satisfying the habitual residence test. As part of legislative changes introduced as a result of the accession of new countries to the EU on 1 May 2004, the government changed the position so that no person will be treated as habitually resident unless they also have a right to reside in the Common Travel Area.[88] This affected EEA nationals,

88 That is the UK, Channel Islands, Republic of Ireland and the Isle of Man; the changes are made by the SS(HR)A Regs 2004.

British citizens and all other PSICs. In effect, to qualify for benefits applicants have to have the 'right to reside' *and* satisfy the habitual residence test (unless they have a right to reside or qualifying entitlement that exempts them from the further elements of the habitual residence test). There is transitional protection for those EEA nationals already in the UK and entitled to benefit on 30 April 2004 for so long as their claim for benefit lasts (including the period of a repeat claim or a claim to another benefit in succession to the first, provided there is no break).

3.77 The term 'right to reside' as used in benefits and tax credits provisions is without precise statutory definition. It covers a wide group of people who may have right to reside in the UK, Channel Islands, Isle of Man, or the Republic of Ireland. It can embrace any new rights to reside arising out of UK or EU law.

3.78 The following, at least, have a right to reside:

- EEA nationals or their family members with a right to reside under EU law;
- British citizens;
- Commonwealth citizens with the right of abode;
- Irish citizens;
- persons with indefinite leave to enter or remain;
- refugees;
- persons with humanitarian protection;
- persons with exceptional leave to remain including discretionary leave to remain; and
- persons with leave to enter or remain (who are not excluded by IAA 1999 s115).

Presence, ordinary residence and right to reside tests for benefits and tax credits

3.79 Ordinary residence in the context of education and immigration provisions was considered by Lord Scarman to mean:[89]

> . . . in their natural and ordinary meaning the words mean 'that the person must be habitually and normally resident here, apart from temporary or occasional absences of long or short duration'. The significance of the adverb "habitually" is that it recalls two necessary features mentioned by Viscount Sumner in *Lysaght's case*, namely residence adopted voluntarily and for settled purposes . . .

89 *R v Barnet LBC ex p Shah* [1983] 2 AC 309 at 342 and 343.

> ... Unless, therefore, it can be shown that the statutory framework or the legal context in which the words are used requires a different meaning, I unhesitatingly subscribe to the view that 'ordinarily resident' refers to a man's abode in a particular place or country which he has adopted voluntarily and for settled purposes as part of the regular order of his life for the time being, whether of short or of long duration ...

Housing benefit

3.80 Under the Housing Benefit Regulations 2006 reg 10, *a person from abroad* who is liable to make payments in respect of a dwelling shall be treated as if he or she were not so liable. 'Person from abroad' means a person who is not *habitually resident* in the UK, the Channel Islands, the Isle of Man or the Republic of Ireland.

3.81 No person shall be treated as *habitually resident* in the UK, the Channel Islands, the Isle of Man or the Republic of Ireland unless he or she has a *right to reside* in, as the case may be, the UK, the Channel Islands, the Isle of Man or the Republic of Ireland *other than* a right to reside by (a) an initial right of residence for up to three months under EU law (see chapter 2) or a right to reside as a job seeker or family member of a jobseeker under EU law (see chapter 2).

3.82 A person is not further required to satisfy the habitual residence test if he or she has a qualifying right to reside or qualifies is some other way as (NB only (a)–(i) describe rights to reside):

(a) a worker under EU law;
(b) a self-employed person under EU law;
(c) a person who retains the status of worker or self-employed person under EU law;
(d) a person who is a family member of a person referred to at (a), (b) or (c) above;
(e) a person who has an EU right to reside permanently in the UK, where permanent residence has been acquired other than by the five-year route);
(f) a person from an A8 or an A2 state who is treated as a worker for EU law purposes;
(g) a refugee;
(h) a person with exceptional leave to enter or remain, including discretionary leave;
(i) a person with humanitarian protection;

(j) a person not subject to immigration control, in the UK as a result of his deportation, expulsion or other removal by compulsion of law from another country;

(k) a person in Great Britain who left the territory of Montserrat after 1 November 1995 because of the effect on that territory of a volcanic eruption;

(l) a person who arrived in Great Britain on or after 28 February 2009 but before 18 March 2011, immediately before arriving there had been resident in Zimbabwe, and before leaving Zimbabwe, had accepted an offer, made by Her Majesty's government, to assist that person to move to and settle in the UK; and

(m) a person in receipt of income support, an income-based jobseeker's allowance or on an income-related employment and support allowance.

3.83 It is important to remember that for housing benefit purposes, a person who is in receipt of income support, income-based jobseeker's allowance or pension credit is also not considered to be a person from abroad. This is an important point for a jobseeker from another EEA state who is expressly eligible to receive income-based jobseeker's allowance. So an EEA national may qualify for housing benefit.

Council tax benefit, income support, income-based employment and support allowance and pension credit

3.84 Provisions similar to the Housing Benefit Regulations exist in the Council Tax Benefit Regulations 2006,[90] the Council Tax Benefit (Persons who have attained the qualifying age for state pension credit) Regulations 2006,[91] the Housing Benefit (Persons who have attained the qualifying age for state pension credit) Regulations 2006,[92] the Income Support (General) Regulations 1987,[93] the Employment and Support Allowance Regulations 2008[94] and the State Pension Credit Regulations 2002.[95]

90 SI No 215.
91 SI No 216.
92 SI No 214.
93 SI No 1967.
94 SI No 794.
95 SI No 1792.

Income-based jobseeker's allowance

3.85 The Jobseeker's Allowance Regulations 1996[96] also contain similar provisions, except that, in addition, a right to reside as a person seeking work or as a jobseeker can confer eligibility for that benefit where a person is habitually resident. This will only benefit A8 or A2 nationals if they are exempt from registration (for example a Polish national who has been in registered work for 12 months) or authorisation or an A2 national who has a registration certificate as a highly skilled person.

Child benefit

3.86 For child benefit the provisions are different. Under section 146(1) of the Social Security Contributions and Benefits Act 1992 no child benefit shall be payable in respect of a child or qualifying young person for a week unless he or she is *present* in Great Britain in that week. Under regulation 21(1) of the Child Benefit (General) Regulations 2006[97] a child or qualifying young person who is temporarily absent from Great Britain shall be treated as being in Great Britain during, among other things, any period during which that person is absent by reason only of his receiving full-time education by attendance at a recognised educational establishment in an EEA state or Switzerland.[98]

3.87 By section 146(2) no person shall be entitled to child benefit for a week unless he or she is *present* in Great Britain in that week. Thereafter by regulation 23(1) of the Child Benefit (General) Regulations 2006 a person shall be treated as not being in Great Britain if he or she is not *ordinarily resident* in the UK. By regulation 23(4) a person shall be treated as not being in Great Britain for the purposes of section 146(2) where he or she does not have a *right to reside* in the UK. For child benefit purposes, a qualifying right to reside includes the initial right of residence and residence as a jobseeker.

Guardian's allowance

3.88 This is paid to a person entitled to child benefit for a person who is not his or her child where both of the child's parents are dead or, in

96 SI No 207.

97 SI No 223.

98 The question of an EEA national's entitlement to CB where his or her child is outside the UK is considered by the Court of Appeal in *HMRC v Ruas* CI/2009/1288.

more limited circumstances, where only one parent is dead. There is no right to reside test. However, at least one parent must have been born in the UK or at the date of death of the parent whose death gives rise to the claim for guardian's allowance, that parent must have, in any two-year period since the age of 16, spent at least 52 weeks of that period in Great Britain or Northern Ireland, as the case may require.[99]

Tax credits

3.89 Tax credits are governed by the Tax Credits (Residence) Regulations 2003[100] (Tax Credit Regulations). A person needs to be *present* in the UK in order to be eligible. By regulation 3(1) a person shall be treated as not being in the UK if he or she is not *ordinarily resident* in the UK.

3.90 For working tax credit, a person shall be treated as being *ordinarily resident* if he or she is exercising in the UK his/her rights as a worker under Regulation 1612/68/EEC as amended by the Residence Directive or under Regulation 1251/70, or if he or she is a person with a *right to reside* in the UK pursuant to the Residence Directive.[101]

3.91 For child tax credit, by regulation 3(5) a person shall be treated as not being in the UK where he or she (a) makes a claim for child tax credit (other than being treated as making a claim under regulation 11 or 12 of the Tax Credits (Claims and Notifications) Regulations 2002 or otherwise) on or after 1 May 2004; and (b) does not have a *right to reside* in the UK.[102]

3.92 For tax credit purposes, a qualifying right to reside includes the initial right of residence and residence as a work seeker (see para 2.61 regarding the Residence Directive).

Health in pregnancy grant

3.93 A woman must be *ordinarily resident* in the UK and have a *right to reside* in the UK in order to be treated as being in Great Britain so as to qualify.[103] A woman in the UK as a result of her deportation,

99 Guardian's Allowance (General) Regulations 2003 SI No 495 reg 9.
100 SI No 654.
101 Tax Credit Regulations reg 3(4).
102 Tax Credit Regulations reg 3(4).
103 See Health in Pregnancy Grant (Entitlement and Amount) Regulations 2008 SI No 3108 reg 4.

expulsion or other removal by compulsion of law from another country is treated as ordinarily resident.

Contribution-based jobseeker's allowance

3.94 There is no right to reside test for this benefit. But a person must have paid the required number of national insurance contributions or to have had such contributions credited in the two tax years prior to the calendar year in which the claim is made.

Incapacity benefit and now contribution-based employment and support allowance

3.95 There is no right to reside test for these benefits. But a person must have paid the required contributions or to have had such contributions credited. They are work-related benefits. A person must be present in the UK or treated as present.

Retirement pensions

3.96 There is no right to reside requirement, but a person must have made the relevant contributions. For a person present in the UK, category A, B and D pensions are calculated in the normal way, even where not ordinarily resident.[104]

3.97 For category D pensions, there is the additional requirement that a person must be ordinarily resident in Great Britain, and resident in Great Britain for at least ten years in any continuous 20-year period ending on or after the person's 80th birthday.[105]

Bereavement benefits

3.98 For bereavement payment, widowed parent's allowance and bereavement allowance, there is no right to reside test. A person must be present in the UK.[106] Payment depends on whether the contribution conditions are satisfied, although in respect of an accident at work or an occupational disease, a person may qualify where the contribution conditions are not met.

104 Social Security and Benefits Act 1992 s113(1).

105 Social Security (Widow's Benefit and Retirement Pensions) Regulations 1979 SI No 642 reg 10.

106 Social Security and Benefits Act 1992 s113(1).

Maternity allowance

3.99 There is no right to reside condition, nor is the benefit dependent on the record of national insurance contributions. But a person must have been employed or self-employed for a minimum period before the expected birth, earning a minimum threshold amount.

Industrial injuries benefits

3.100 In respect of disablement benefit, reduced earnings allowance, retirement allowance, constant attendance allowance, and exceptionally severe disablement allowance, there is no right to reside test. However, an accident must arise out of and in the course of an employed earner's employment and a disease must be prescribed in relation to an employed earner's employment. A person must also have been in Great Britain when the accident happened or engaged in Great Britain in the employment that caused the disease.

Attendance allowance, disability living allowance, carer's allowance, incapacity benefit for incapacity in youth and employment and support allowance for incapacity in youth

3.101 For attendance allowance, disability living allowance, carer's allowance, incapacity benefit for incapacity in youth and employment and support allowance for incapacity in youth, a person must be *present* in Great Britain, *ordinarily resident* in Great Britain and have been in Great Britain for *26 weeks in the last 12 months.*[107]

3.102 For all these benefits, a PSIC as defined by s115(9) Immigration and Asylum Act 1999 is ineligible for assistance. There is no right to reside test.

3.103 For employment and support allowance for incapacity in youth, the following are expressly included as eligible:[108]

107 Social Security (Attendance Allowance) Regulations 1991 SI No 2740 reg 2(1), Social Security (Disability Living Allowance) Regulations 1991 SI No 2890 reg 2(1), Social Security (Invalid Care Allowance) Regulations 1976 SI No 409 reg 1, Social Security (Incapacity Benefit) Regulations 1994 SI No 2946 reg 16 and Employment and Support Regulations 2008 SI No 794 reg 11.

108 Employment and Support Regulations 2008 SI No 794 reg 11.

(a) a member of a family of an EEA national;
(b) a person who is lawfully working in Great Britain and is a national of a state that the EU has a reciprocal agreement with under article 310 of the EC Treaty providing, in the field of social security, for the equal treatment of workers who are nationals of that state and their families;
(c) a person who is a member of a family of, and living with, a person specified in (b); or
(d) a person who has been given leave to enter, or remain in, the UK by the Secretary of State upon an undertaking by another person or persons pursuant to the immigration rules to be responsible for that person's maintenance and accommodation.

Statutory sick pay and statutory maternity, paternity and adoption pay

3.104 There is no right to reside test. A person must be an employed earner in Great Britain for national insurance purposes, or employed in an EEA state (before or after accession) other than the UK so that if he or she were so employed in Great Britain, he or she would be an employee for the purposes of the benefit in question.

The social fund

3.105 There is no right to reside test.

3.106 Regulated social fund payments are: Sure Start maternity grant, funeral expenses payment, cold weather payment and winter fuel payment.

3.107 Discretionary social fund payments are: community care grant, budgeting loans and crisis loans.

3.108 To qualify for a social fund payment a person must be in receipt of certain qualifying benefits (such as IS). The latter contain residence or presence rules.

The urgent cases rate

3.109 There are a few residual PSICs who are eligible for IS or income-based JSA paid at a reduced rate known as urgent cases payments (UCP).[109] The applicable amount is calculated as 90 per cent of the

109 IS Regs 1987 reg 70(2A); JSA Regs 1996 reg 147(2A).

personal allowance plus full personal allowances for children, any premiums and housing costs.[110]

3.110 The income and capital rules which apply to UCPs are stricter than those which usually apply to IS and income-based JSA.[111] If the claimant has any capital, they will not be eligible – the normal capital limit and rules about disregarded capital do not apply. This means that if a claimant receives arrears of disability benefits or has savings, they will not be entitled to any UCP until the money has been spent or accounted for. Arrears of UCPs or concessionary UCPs are not taken into account as capital.

3.111 Those who will be paid at the UCP rate are:

- asylum-seekers entitled to benefit by virtue of transitional protection (see paras 3.28–3.41);
- PSICs who have limited leave but are temporarily without funds (such as students and visitors) (see para 3.21);
- PSICs whose sponsor has died within five years of their date of entry or the date of the undertaking, whichever is later (such as elderly dependent relatives) (see paras 3.18–3.20).

Those entitled to IS or income-based JSA or ESA because they are nationals of an EEA country or because of a reciprocal agreement are not subject to UCPs and receive benefit at the normal rate.

Mixed households

3.112 Problems arise frequently where there are households in which some family members are entitled to benefits and some are not. In such households, there is often a mix of sources of income including the DWP, the local authority and asylum support. In practice, there is plenty of scope for errors to be made by each of these bodies as to who is responsible for supporting whom. Where there is a dispute about whether persons should be supported by benefits or by asylum support, it should be recalled that persons entitled to social security benefits are excluded from entitlement to asylum support.[112]

110 IS Regs 1987 reg 71; JSA Regs 1996 reg 148.
111 IS Regs 1987 reg 72; JSA Regs 1996 reg 149.
112 IAA 1999 s95(7); Asylum Support Regs 2000 reg 4(4).

Who can be included in the benefit claim?

3.113 The usual position where benefit is claimed is that the claimant claims for him/herself and for any partner and dependent children. However, special rules apply to PSICs. These rules are different for asylum-seekers and other PSICs from those for other persons receiving ordinary benefits.

Where the household includes a PSIC entitled to benefits

3.114 In most cases for asylum-seekers, the entitlement to benefits of such persons derives from transitional protection (see paras 3.28–3.41). The rules differ depending on whether transitional protection derives from entitlement to benefits before 5 February 1996 (or in the case of CB, 6 October 1996), or from a claim for asylum made on arrival before 3 April 2000.[113]

Where the household includes a person entitled to claim ordinary benefits

3.115 Such a claimant who has a partner who is a PSIC cannot receive benefits for that partner or for any children who are themselves PSICs[114] (except in the case of WTC and CTC: see para 3.117). Thus, for example, where one member of a couple is granted refugee status but the other partner and the children of the family still have pending applications for asylum, the refugee partner cannot claim for their partner or the children while they are excluded from benefits by IAA 1999 s115.

3.116 It can be seen from this example that where a partner has been receiving UCPs by virtue of being an asylum-seeker with entitlement under the transitional provisions, the grant of refugee status to that partner can have the effect of ending entitlement to benefits in respect of the other partner and children. Where this happens, an application should be made to the Secretary of State for asylum support for the other partner and children.

3.117 In the case of WTC and CTC, a claimant who is entitled to tax credits can claim for a partner who is a PSIC.[115]

113 See paras 3.28–3.41.

114 IS Regs 1987 reg 21(3) and Sch 7 para 16A; SPC Regs 2002 SI No 1792 reg 5(1), as amended by State Pension Credit (Consequential, Miscellaneous and Transitional Provisions) (No 2) Regs 2002 SI No 3197 Sch para 2.

115 TC(I) Regs 2003 reg 3(2).

3.118 Where both partners in a couple are entitled to claim benefits, they can claim benefit for any dependent children, whether or not the children are PSICs.

3.119 Where the household includes a single parent who is entitled to claim benefits, they are able to claim benefits for dependent children, whether or not the children are PSICs.

3.120 Where the household comprises a single parent or a couple who are PSICs and dependent children who are not PSICs, it is not possible for the parents to claim benefits for the children.

Where the household includes a child born in the UK

3.121 A child born in the UK will not be a British citizen unless one of the parents is a British citizen or has ILR. Such a child is a PSIC who requires leave to enter or remain. Unless sought and granted such a child will not have leave to enter or remain.

Treatment of resources when assessing benefit entitlement

3.122 Where one partner to a couple is entitled to benefits and the other is not because they are a PSIC, the resources of both are taken into account in assessing benefit. The claimant will be able to receive the full amount of any housing costs included in the IS/JSA/ESA assessment.[116]

Treatment of asylum support as income in assessing benefits

3.123 Where a claimant receives means-tested benefits and their partner receives asylum support in kind rather than cash for essential living needs, the asylum support does not count as income for the purposes of income-based JSA, IS or income-based employment and support allowance.[117] Asylum support paid in cash is treated as income.

3.124 Asylum support is treated as income for the purposes of HB and CTB.[118] The full asylum support payment whether in cash or in kind will be treated as income when assessing the amount of benefit. This also includes occasional additional asylum support payments made under particular UKBA asylum support policies.

116 IS Regs 1987 reg 21(3) and Sch 7 para 16A.

117 IS Regs 1987 reg 40(2) and Sch 9 para 21; JSA Regs 1996 reg 103(2) and Sch 7 para 22, ESA Regulations 2008 reg 104(2) and Sch 8 para 22.

118 HB Regs 2006 reg 40(10)(b) and Sch 5 para 23; CTB Regs 2006 reg 30(11) and Sch 4 para 24.

Housing benefit non-dependant deductions[119]

3.125 There is no provision to exempt PSICs, asylum-seekers or those they live with from non-dependant deductions. This means that where a PSIC or an asylum-seeker stays as the guest of someone claiming HB or CTB, the host may be subject to a reduction in their benefit, assuming a contribution from that person. This applies whether an asylum-seeker household is in receipt of asylum support for living expenses or has no income at all. The claimant affected could apply to the local authority to exercise its discretion to award a discretionary housing payment. A discretionary housing payment is an additional payment to recipients of HB/CTB over and above HB/CTB paid under the ordinary rules. A local authority may make such a payment where the claimants 'appear to such an authority to require some further financial assistance (in addition to the benefit or benefits to which they are entitled) in order to meet housing costs'.[120] In this context, 'housing costs' includes council tax. Where a discretionary housing payment is refused, the remedy is an internal review only.

End of entitlement to benefit

3.126 A PSIC who is entitled to state benefits will lose that entitlement in any of the following circumstances:

- the first decision on asylum application for those entitled on the basis of transitional protection. If the decision is favourable it will, nonetheless, amount to a change of circumstances, which should immediately be reported to the DWP and (for HB/CTB) to the local authority (see paras 3.127–3.128 if the decision is unfavourable);
- limited leave to remain (refugee status/HP/DL) expires without an application for extension or variation having been made (see paras 3.128–3.132);
- in the case of non-contributory benefits, where entitlement to benefit is 'reviewed' (see para 3.133).

Unfavourable Home Office decisions

3.127 For asylum-seekers receiving transitional protection, entitlement to benefit ends with the first unfavourable decision on a pending

119 See para 8.209 for council tax liability of persons receiving asylum support.
120 Discretionary Financial Assistance Regulations 2000 reg 2(1)(b).

asylum claim. Such a decision may be a first decision by the Home Office, or – very usually – in cases where there has been a long-outstanding appeal, a decision of the AIT (soon to become the Upper Tribunal). Entitlement ends when the Home Secretary records the asylum claim as having been refused and the asylum applicant is notified of the decision.[121]

3.128 An asylum-seeker whose application for asylum is refused, and who is not granted any other form of leave such as HP or DL, loses any entitlement to benefits unless they fall within a class of PSIC that is not excluded from benefits (see paras 3.3–3.49 above), for example family members of EEA nationals. Asylum-seekers may be eligible for asylum support pending an asylum appeal or, in the case of families, for as long as they have dependent children under 18 living with them in the UK. Childless asylum-seekers who lose IS after an unsuccessful asylum appeal, and other unsuccessful applicants for leave to enter or remain in the UK, may be entitled to help under the community care provisions explained in chapter 9.

Expiry of limited leave to remain

3.129 A grant of asylum as a refugee, HP and DL (as the latter a form of exceptional leave to remain (ELR)) are granted for a specified limited period. Unless HP or DL is granted subject to a condition that there be no recourse to public funds (an extremely unlikely event), all three carry with them entitlement to benefits, but that entitlement ends with the expiry of the period of leave. However, entitlement will not expire if an application is made for it to be extended or varied before the expiry of the existing period of leave.

3.130 A person with leave to enter or remain in the UK who applies for it to be extended or varied before it expires is treated as having leave on the same terms (and carrying the same entitlement to benefits) until the application is decided by the Home Office. This rule previously derived from the Variation of Leave Order,[122] known by its

121 SS(IA)CA Regs 2000 reg 12(5) and (10); *R (Anufrijeva) v Secretary of State for the Home Department and Secretary of State for Social Security* [2003] UKHL 36 (overruling the Court of Appeal decision in *R v Home Secretary ex p Salem* [1999] 1 AC 450; [1999] QB 805 and the High Court in *R (Paulo) v Secretary of State for the Home Department and Secretary of State for Social Security* [2001] EWHC 480 (Admin).

122 See para 1.37.

acronym 'VOLO', although the rule is now contained in IA 1971.[123] Evidence that a relevant application has been made could be provided in the form of a letter from an immigration representative. A letter of acknowledgement from the Home Office or dated receipt from the Home Office should also be acceptable.

3.131 If leave has expired without an application being made to vary or extend and before the grant of asylum, HP or DL and the person was an asylum-seeker with dependent children, the person will continue to be classified as an asylum-seeker and so entitled to asylum support while they have dependent children under 18 living with them in the UK.

3.132 If leave has expired without an application being made to vary or extend and the person is not a former asylum-seeker, they are excluded from entitlement to benefits. Such persons may be entitled to help under the community care provisions explained in chapter 9. If they have children, they may be entitled to assistance under the Nationality, Immigration and Asylum Act 2002 Sch 3 and the Withholding and Withdrawal of Support (Travel Assistance and Temporary Accommodation) Regulations 2002.[124]

Review of entitlement to non-contributory benefits

3.133 Asylum-seekers entitled to 1996 transitional protection (see paras 3.28–3.32) receiving non-contributory benefits (AA, DLA, CA, SDA and CB) will cease to be entitled to those benefits if the award of benefits is reviewed, superseded or if an award made for a specific period expires.[125] Those left destitute by such loss of benefits should apply for asylum support (see chapters 4–6).

123 IA 1971 s3C, as inserted by IAA 1999 s3. Section 3C replaced the Variation of Leave Order (VOLO) 1976 SI No 1572 for all cases where an application to vary leave was made on or after 2 October 2000. See the Immigration (Variation of Leave) (Amendment) Order 2000 SI No 2445. It has been the subject of further, subsequent modification.

124 SI No 3078. See 9.74.

125 SS(IA)CA Regs 2000 reg 12(10); *R (B) v Chief Adjudication Officer* [2001] UKHL 35, [2001] 4 All ER 41; *M (a minor) v Secretary of State for Social Security* [2001] Times, 6 July 2001, HL; *R v Chief Adjudication Officer ex p B* [1999] 1 WLR 1695; *Yildiz v Secretary of State for Social Security* [2001] 28 February 2001, unreported, CA.

Becoming entitled to benefit

Administration, claims and payments

3.134 Asylum-seekers become entitled to benefits following a grant of refugee status, or a grant of HP or DL. Other PSICs may become entitled to benefits if granted HP, DL or ILR or other qualifying leave. EEA nationals and their family members have a right to reside entitling them to benefits. Other PSICs may also be applying.

3.135 Upon the grant of status, it will frequently be necessary to make multiple claims for benefits. Advisers should check through the benefits to which the claimant may be entitled. Consideration should be given to:

- claiming IS or income-based JSA, or employment and support allowance: apply on line, by phone on 0800-055-6688 or at a jobcentreplus, see: www.direct.gov.uk/en/MoneyTaxAndBenefits/BenefitsTaxCreditsAndOtherSupport/index.htm;
- claiming SPC: apply by phone on 0800-99-1234, or by printing out and posting an application form, see: www.thepensionservice.gov.uk/pensioncredit/form.asp;
- claiming HB and CTB: apply at the same time as applying for SPC, ESA, IS or JSA, or claim from a local authority (borough or district council), see: www.direct.gov.uk/en/MoneyTaxAndBenefits/BenefitsTaxCreditsAndOtherSupport/index.htm;
- claiming tax credits – WTC and CTC: apply on the appropriate claim form to Her Majesty's Revenue and Customs (HMRC). An application form can be ordered by phone (0845-300-3900) or downloaded, see: www.direct.gov.uk/en/MoneyTaxAndBenefits/TaxCreditsAndChildBenefit/index.htm;
- claiming interim IS: available where a claim for IS has not been made but a person may be entitled, a claim has been made and the person may be entitled but the claim cannot be determined straightaway or IS has been awarded but cannot be paid on time;
- claiming a crisis loan where there are delays in the administration of other claims: apply to the local jobcentre plus or on an application form, see: www.direct.gov.uk/en/MoneyTaxAndBenefits/BenefitsTaxCreditsAndOtherSupport/index.htm;
- claiming CB where there are children: apply on the appropriate claim form to the Child Benefit Office, see: www.direct.gov.uk/en/MoneyTaxAndBenefits/TaxCreditsAndChildBenefit/index.htm;

- claiming DLA, attendance allowance or CA where there is a disabled claimant (making separate claims for each non-dependant adult in the household): apply online, by phone or by post, see: www.direct.gov.uk/en/MoneyTaxAndBenefits/BenefitsTaxCreditsAndOtherSupport/index.htm;
- claiming a community care grant where there are costs to be met of setting up home: apply by post or at a jobcentre plus, see: www.direct.gov.uk/en/MoneyTaxAndBenefits/BenefitsTaxCreditsAndOtherSupport/index.htm.

The end of asylum support

3.136 Asylum support entitlement ends when an asylum claim is 'determined' for the purposes of IAA 1999 s94(3). A claim is determined at the end of the 'prescribed period'. For prospective benefit claimants, the prescribed period is 28 days (where an asylum claim is granted, a form or leave to enter or remain is granted or an appeal is disposed of by being allowed), which starts either:

- on the date the applicant is notified of the decision, which is two days after posting if the decision is sent by first class post; or
- on the date the appeal is disposed of.

This means asylum-seekers will only receive asylum support for 28 days after notification of a decision on the asylum claim. A favourable decision may arise as a result of an appeal but, in practice, the Home Office will not terminate asylum support until 28 days after it issues its own decision following the appeal. During the 28-day period, the former asylum-seeker will need to sort out any benefits claim and make alternative housing arrangements. The 28-day period is not long enough to process an IS or HB claim in most cases. In many cases the Home Office now issues a national insurance number with the final decision to former asylum-seekers. For other migrants, advisers will need to be familiar with the evidence and national insurance number requirements (see paras 3.141–3.156), rules about interim or other urgent payments (see paras 3.157–3.163) and should consider urgent applications for judicial review. If all else fails, community care help should be sought in cases involving children[126] or adults with needs arising from age, ill-health, etc (see chapter 9).

126 Children Act 1989 s17.

3.137 If a household has been receiving asylum support from the Secretary of State, the asylum-seeker should be issued with a termination of support letter when a final decision is made on the asylum claim. Form NASS 35, which should be issued by NASS when support stops, gives details of the Home Office decision, the names of household members and the period and value of asylum support. It contains a photograph of the main applicant for support. Adult dependants will receive a shorter letter giving details of support received.

3.138 Where an asylum-seeker is granted refugee status HP or DL on appeal, it will not be possible to claim benefits until the Home Office has issued formal letters notifying the grant of status. There are frequently delays in the Home Office issuing such letters. The asylum-seeker's immigration adviser should consider judicial review to compel the Home Office to comply. A common problem is that the Home Office in its asylum support function sends the NASS 35 to the address of the asylum-seeker's asylum support accommodation after they have been evicted from it through the termination of asylum support. Persons who are in asylum support temporary accommodation pending assessment of their asylum support application at the time an asylum decision is made will not be issued with a NASS 35 form at all.

3.139 The duty to offer asylum support ceases if the household is excluded because of eligibility for benefits.[127]

Claims for IS, ESA and income-based JSA

3.140 To make a valid claim for IS and income-based JSA, the claimant must satisfy 'the evidence requirement' and the 'national insurance number requirement'. The information below applies equally to an EEA national coming to the UK for the first time as it does to a former asylum-seeker granted leave to remain.

The evidence requirement

3.141 A claim for income support or jobseeker's allowance may be made by telephone unless in any particular case it is directed that the claim must be made in writing. A telephone claim is defective unless all

127 Note that a destitute asylum-seeker or dependant of an asylum-seeker can claim asylum support if only part of the household is eligible for social security benefit: see para 4.56.

the information necessary to determine the claim is provided during that telephone call. A defective claim may be referred back to the person making it. If the defect is corrected within one month, or such longer period as the DWP considers reasonable, of the date the claim was referred back to the person, the DWP must treat the claim as if it had been duly made in the first instance.

3.142 Where completed in writing, the application form must be completed in full and accompanied by other evidence requested,[128] that is any of the following that the claimant has:

- pay-slips;
- proof of other income (this will be a NASS 35 form provided by the Secretary of State/UK Border Agency in the case of an asylum-seeker who has been receiving asylum support from the Secretary of State, but note that production of a NASS 35 form is not a pre-requisite for benefit to be assessed if other evidence is available);
- proof of any savings or payment from an insurance policy;
- proof of service charges or ground rent.

If the form is not properly completed and the evidence requirement is not met, the DWP should contact the claimant allowing one month from the date of the claim to remedy the problem. If the evidence requirement is not met within that period, the claim may be rejected.[129]

3.143 Where asylum-seekers are unable to meet the evidence requirement within the specified period, or at all, they can ask the DWP for an exemption, for an extension of the one-month period, or to get the information on their behalf.

3.144 If a claimant cannot meet the evidence requirement, a request can be made for exemption on any of the following grounds:[130]

- a physical, mental learning or communication difficulty where it is not reasonably practicable for the claimant to find someone else to assist, for example an isolated asylum-seeker with mental health needs who cannot read or write English;
- the information required does not exist or could not be obtained except with a serious risk of physical or mental harm to the claimant, for example documents are in the country of origin;
- a third party has the information and it is not reasonably practicable to obtain it.

128 SS(CP) Regs 1987 reg 4(1A), (1B).
129 SS(CP) Regs 1987 reg 6(1A) and (4AB).
130 SS(CP) Regs 1987 reg 4(1B).

Where it is decided that the evidence requirement has been met, the regulations[131] state that there is no right of appeal, but the Commissioner has decided otherwise,[132] holding that the exclusion of a right of appeal must be disapplied as being non-compliant with ECHR article 6.

National insurance number requirement

3.145 A claim for benefit should be treated as an application for a national insurance number (NINO); alternatively, an application may be made by phone on 0845 600 0643.[133] An application will lead to an 'evidence of identity' interview, to which documentary evidence should be taken. NINO applications are dealt with by a division of the DWP called the Departmental Central Index (DCI).

3.146 To qualify for benefit, the claimant must provide in respect of every person of 16 and over covered by the claim either:

(a)
- (i) a statement of the person's national insurance number, and information or evidence establishing that that number has been allocated to the person; or
- (ii) information or evidence enabling the national insurance number that has been allocated to that person to be ascertained; or

(b) the person makes an application for a national insurance number to be ascertained that is accompanied by information or evidence enabling such a number to be allocated.[134]

It will be seen that, under (b), a claimant is able to establish entitlement to benefit without a NINO actually being allocated. The evidence required to obtain a NINO is evidence of identity, for example birth and marriage certificates, application registration card (ARC) from the Home Office, passport, national identity card, driving licence, utility bills or tenancy agreement. In practice, originals of documents or notarised copies will be requested, although may not be available to those who have recently arrived in the UK. In addition, the DWP may refuse to accept evidence of

131 SSCS(DA) Regs 1999 Sch 2 para 5.

132 CIS/540/2002.

133 See www.direct.gov.uk/en/MoneyTaxAndBenefits/BenefitsTaxCreditsAndOtherSupport

134 SSAA 1992 s1(1B).

immigration status and identity other than a Home Office letter confirming status, for example not passports with entry stamps. Unreasonable demands should not be made for documents that the claimant is unable to furnish.

3.147 Before a decision on their immigration status, asylum-seekers may have sent the originals of documents proving identity to the Home Office, which is likely to keep them until an asylum decision is made. To obviate this difficulty, claimants can ask the DWP to endorse photocopies of original documents when they first visit the local office with these. If the original documents are later lost or sent to another agency, the photocopies should be relied on.

3.148 The requirement to have a NINO (or be applying for one) as a pre-condition of a claim[135] is one of the main causes of delay for PSICs, asylum-seekers and other migrants claiming benefits for the first time. To avoid this delay, advisers should consider whether an asylum-seeker can obtain a NINO prior to any claim for benefits. Migrants with the right to work who are ineligible for benefits can apply for a NINO if they have a job offer or are registered with an employment agency, although priority is given to processing 'benefits-inspired applications', that is, NINO applications by benefit claimants. (It appears that 'employment-inspired applicants' are dealt with by a separate section of the DWP.)

3.149 Claimants with HP or DL are sometimes refused benefits because DWP or local authority decision-makers misinterpret the immigration documents. HP or DL may initially be granted for a period of one year, but should not be confused with other forms of limited leave. In such cases, advisers can refer to IAA 1999 s115(9), which describes the categories of PSICs and, in particular, section 115(9)(a), which defines a PSIC as a person who 'requires leave to enter or remain in the UK but does not have it'.

3.150 After a decision of HP, DL or full refugee status, a common problem is an error in the spelling of names or the order of names, which the Home Office may take months to correct.

3.151 There have been a number of cases in which claimants have been refused benefits because they do not have a NINO and refused asylum support because they are no longer asylum-seekers. In such cases, interim payments and social fund payments are also often refused. It may be possible to challenge a refusal of benefits by arguing that the claimant is entitled through having applied for a

135 SSAA 1992 s1(1A).

NINO and given all the necessary evidence. Arguably, the DWP should accept the Home Office's confirmation that the Home Secretary is satisfied as to the claimant's identity. In practice, they often do not, but there is scope for judicial review and/or complaints.

3.152 Where a person seeks a NINO in order to work, he or she makes an 'employment-inspired application' and must satisfy the 'right to work' condition.[136] This condition will require satisfaction where a person works, will be working, seeks work or is self-employed.[137] An applicant must demonstrate that they are lawfully able to work in the sense that their immigration status permits them to work.

3.153 There have been frequent problems where a claimant has a spouse who is a person who has no recourse to public funds. Until recently, the DWP have taken the view that any such partner must satisfy the NINO requirement, even if no benefit is going to be paid in respect of that person. However, from 6 April 2009, there is no longer a requirement for a partner who does not have leave to enter or remain to be allocated a NINO.[138]

3.154 Claimants frequently find that their application for a NINO is refused because the DWP states it is not satisfied with the evidence of identity produced, with no reason given. A concurrent claim for benefit may then be refused for failure to meet the NINO requirement. There is no right of appeal against a decision to refuse to issue a NINO, and the only remedy is judicial review. There is a right of appeal against refusal of a benefit claim because of failure to meet the NINO requirement, and the appellant in such an appeal is entitled to raise the issue of whether a refusal to allocate a NINO was correct in fact and law.[139] If the state fails to explain the reasons for refusal to allocate a NINO in its submission to the tribunal, the tribunal should be asked to require the evidence to be produced.[140]

136 Social Security (Crediting and Treatment of Contributions and National Insurance Numbers) Regulations 2001 SI No 769 as amended.

137 Secure National Insurance Number Application Process (SNAP) at www.dwp.gov.uk/foi/2006/oct/

138 Social Security (National Insurance Number Information: Exemption) Regulations 2009 SI No 471; Circular HB/CTB A4/2009.

139 R(IB) 2/04.

140 The DWP and the tribunal should be referred to the findings and observations of the Commissioner in CIS/245/2003.

Claiming other benefits and tax credits

3.155 In the cases of IS, ESA and income-based JSA described above, it has been seen that failure to satisfy the 'evidence requirement' and the 'NINO requirement' prevents there being a valid claim. The commencement of any resulting award of benefit depends upon there being a valid claim. Claims for other benefits, however, should be treated as valid from the date a letter of claim is received by the DWP, HM Revenue and Customs or (for HB and CTB) the local authority, although it will be necessary to complete the relevant application form, to satisfy the NINO requirement[141] and to provide the required evidence before a decision can be made on the claim and benefit can be paid.

3.156 In the case of tax credits, there is a discretion to disapply the NINO requirement where it is considered that the claimant has a reasonable excuse for making a claim without satisfying it.[142] There is no right of appeal against a decision of HM Revenue and Customs that the NINO requirement is not met,[143] and the only remedy is judicial review.

Delays in processing the claim where there is an urgent need

3.157 The process of satisfying the NINO requirement is fraught with delays at every stage, which can leave claimants without resources. As well as repeatedly pressing for decisions to be made, the following interim assistance can be considered.

Crisis loans

3.158 A claimant could consider an application[144] to the DWP for a 'crisis loan' from the discretionary social fund while the claim is being processed. But those who qualify for integration loans (see below) are likely to find it difficult to persuade the DWP to exercise its

141 SSAA 1992 s1, Tax Credits (Claims and Notifications) Regs 2002 reg 5(4), HB Regs 2006 reg 4, CTB Regs 2006 reg 4.

142 Tax Credits (Claims and Notifications) Regs 2002 reg 5(6).

143 Appeal rights are limited to decisions specified in the Tax Credits Act 2002 s14.

144 www.direct.gov.uk/en/MoneyTaxAndBenefits/BenefitsTaxCreditsAndOther Support.

discretion in their favour. Such claims are governed by the Social Fund Directions and the Social Fund Guide. Unlike budgeting loans and community care grants, it is not a pre-condition that the claimant is in receipt of IS, ESA or income-based JSA. Crisis loans are available when required to help meet expenses in an emergency to avoid serious damage or serious risk to the health and safety of the claimant or a member of the household. There is no definition of an emergency and the High Court has ruled that the need and priority of an application should be considered before budgetary considerations.[145] If a crisis loan is refused, a revision within 28 days and written reasons for the decision should be requested.

Interim payments[146]

3.159 There is a discretion to make an interim payment of benefit if the claimant is, or may be, entitled to a DWP benefit, but it is not possible for the claim to be dealt with immediately; including where it is impracticable to satisfy a NINO requirement. There is no right of appeal against refusal of an interim payment: if income is urgently needed a judicial review application should be considered. A formal letter before action under the judicial review protocol to the DWP solicitors will often resolve the matter.

Payments on account of housing benefit

3.160 Private and housing association tenants should ask for a payment on account (or interim payment) if there is a delay in administering the claim.[147] In fact, such payments should be made automatically once all required information and evidence has been provided and if it is not practicable for the authority to process the claim within 14 days. No request is necessary under the regulation but in practice it is usually necessary to ask. Where the required information or evidence has not been provided, a payment on account must still be made if the claimant has 'good cause' for not providing it. It is at least arguable that the lack of a NINO should not prevent a payment on account where there is no fault on the part of the claimant. Failure to make a payment on account may be challenged by judicial review.

145 *R v Social Fund Inspector ex p Taylor* [1998] COD 152, QBD.

146 Social Security (Payments on Account, Overpayments and Recovery) Regulations 1988 SI No 664 reg 2.

147 HB Regs 2006 reg 93.

Community care assistance

3.161 A request to the local authority's social services department for a community care assessment may be appropriate as an emergency measure if the claimant has a health need or has children (see further chapter 9).

Community care grants

3.162 Asylum-seekers who are granted refugee status, HP or DL may be eligible for a community care grant payment from the DWP to enable them to set up home. Social Fund Direction 4(a)(iii) provides for families under exceptional pressure. Social fund guidance suggests that this may be due to the longer term consequences of displacement from a country outside the UK for political or religious reasons so that a grant may be considered where a family whose application for asylum in this country has been successful is moving into the community from temporary accommodation provided by the Home Office.[148] Social Fund Direction 4(a)(v) provides for the payment of a community care grant to help a person 'set up home in the community as part of a planned resettlement programme following a period during which they have been without a settled way of life'. Social fund guidance[149] suggests that those who have been 'staying in temporary accommodation provided by the Home Office pending a decision on their application for asylum in this country' may fall within the definition of an unsettled way of life.

3.163 There may also be asylum-seekers who have been living 'an unsettled way of life' while staying with various friends and relatives who should be considered for a grant. The guidance[150] states that the list given at para 309 is not exhaustive.

Backdated child benefit, guardian's allowance and tax credits and integration loans for refugees

3.164 Asylum-seekers who were notified of a grant of refugee status on or before 14 June 2007 were entitled to claim arrears of IS, HB, CTB and SPC. This provision applied only to those granted refugee status.

148 Social Fund Guidance, para 231.
149 Social Fund Guidance, para 309.
150 Social Fund Guidance, para 310.

For those granted refugee status, HP, or their dependants, on or after 11 June 2007, integration loans are available instead of claims for arrears of those benefits.

3.165 Prior to the abolition of the provision for claiming arrears for IS, HB, CTB and SPC, an asylum-seeker recognised as a refugee was entitled to the relevant benefit or tax credit from the date of the asylum claim. Notwithstanding the abolition provisions for claiming arrears for those benefits, it remains open to an asylum-seeker recognised as a refugee to claim for CB, guardian's allowance, WTC and CTC from the date of the asylum claim.[151]

3.166 In the case of WTC, CTC and CB, the claim for backdating must be made to the HM Revenue and Customs. [152] Tax credits must be applied for within three months of notification of refugee status. There is no provision to extend these periods even if there would usually be 'good cause for a late claim'.

3.167 Evidence of means during the period to which the backdating claim relates will be required for claims for tax credits. For those previously supported by the Secretary of State this should be form NASS 35 issued on the termination of asylum support. For those who have been supported by local authorities, the authority should be approached for a statement of the support provided.

3.168 In assessing backdated awards of CTC and WTC account will be taken of income received in the relevant period under the usual rules. That income includes asylum support[153] and UCP income support paid.

3.169 From 11 June 2007, integration loans were introduced for those granted refugee status, HP or their dependents.[154] The UKBA decides who is eligible for a loan but the loan itself is administered by the DWP. Guidance may be found in the 'Integration Loans Policy Guidance'. A loan can be applied for after 11 June 2007. The application must be made by an adult. The application form and guidance on how to complete it may be found on the UKBA

151 TC(I) Regs 2003 reg 3(4)–(9), Child Benefit and Guardian's Allowance (Administration) Regulations 2003 reg 6.

152 TC(I) Regs 2003 reg 3; Child Benefit and Guardian's Allowance (Administration) Regulations 2003 reg 6.

153 TC(I) Regs 2003 reg 3(9).

154 Asylum and Immigration (Treatment of Claimants, etc) Act 2004 s13, and Integration Loans for Refugees and Others Regulations 2007 SI No 1598.

website.[155] One loan is made per person, although a joint application may be made. Loans may be refused on account of insolvency, that is where a person is, in the Secretary of State's opinion, unable to repay the loan. A variety of factors are taken into account by decision-makers assessing whether to make a loan, including means, ability to repay, the purpose of the loan, the amount of time since leave to remain was granted and the amount left in the budget from which loans are made.

3.170 The loan can be used for needs such as vocational training, a deposit for accommodation, buying essential items for the home, or the purchase of tools of a trade. A loan is to meet integration needs. A loan will not be made where it is intended for certain items prohibited in the guidance.[156] There is a right to have a refusal of a loan reconsidered by a different decision-maker. The Secretary of State must make a written decision on the application. Conditions may be set as to the use of the loan.

3.171 The minimum loan is £100, the maximum £1,000. The terms of repayment are subject to agreement and may be subject to revision by the Secretary of State. Repayment of a loan may be made by the recipient out of his own resources, or where he is in receipt of benefits by way of a deduction from benefits.

155 ww.ukba.homeoffice.gov.uk/aboutus/workingwithus/workingwithasylum/integration/integrationloan/

156 Guidance, para 9.3.

CHAPTER 4

Asylum support: eligibility

continued

Introduction

4.1 Since it was introduced, asylum support under Part VI of the Immigration and Asylum Act 1999, or 'NASS support', has been criticised as an inadequate system which is poorly administered. There are countless reports about asylum-seekers left destitute due to the limitations of the scheme.[1] To some extent the scheme has stabilised: disputes about eligibility, resulting in an asylum support appeal are fairly unusual. The areas in which asylum-seekers continue to experience serious hardship relate to delays and maladministration of support, the more difficult eligibility issues, and the dividing line between Home Office asylum support and local authority community care provision. This chapter gives an overview of the scheme while covering some of these more testing areas.

4.2 Chapters 4–7 describe the scheme of asylum support under the Immigration and Asylum Act (IAA) 1999 in detail. The aim of these chapters is to provide sufficient detail for an asylum-seeker's representative either to find the answer to their question about asylum support, or to have sufficient knowledge of the scheme to know where to find it. For a quick introduction to the scheme see para 4.4 below or the table of entitlements at appendix G.

4.3 This chapter explains who is eligible for asylum support under IAA 1999 Part VI (sections 98 and 95) and covers procedures for applying for support. Chapter 5 covers service provision for those who are eligible, including the type and level of support provided and adequacy (or inadequacy) of accommodation. It also covers asylum-seekers' legal duties while support is provided and the Home Secretary's criminal law powers if those duties are not met. Chapter 6 discusses section 4 support under IAA 1999 for refused asylum-seekers and considers what other options those at the end of the asylum process may have. Chapter 7 explains when UKBA may refuse, suspend or withdraw support and the procedures for appealing to the First-tier Tribunal (Asylum Support) for both section 4 and section 95 support, as well as other potential challenges such as complaints procedures and judicial review.

1 See appendix H.

Rebranding

The National Asylum Support Service (NASS) was established within the Home Office's Immigration and Nationality Directorate (IND), to administer the asylum support scheme. In July 2006, the Home Office announced that NASS no longer existed as a separate department. Asylum support would be administered by two separate routes. Those who made their first asylum claim from 5 March 2007 have their support case processed by the New Asylum Model (NAM) case owner who is processing their asylum claim.[2] Older 'legacy' applicants (who first claimed asylum before 5 March 2007) should have their asylum and support claims dealt with by the Casework Resolution Directorate (CRD). In April 2007, the Home Secretary announced that the Border and Immigration Agency (BIA) had replaced IND. BIA has now been replaced by the UK Border Agency (UKBA). Confusingly, not all of their documentation has been changed and Home Office and voluntary sector staff continue to refer to NASS. In this book, we have mainly referred to UKBA or the 'Home Office' rather than NASS except where NASS applies for historical reasons.

Appeals against refusal of support were initially to the Asylum Support Adjudicators (ASA), renamed the Asylum Support Tribunal (AST) in April 2007. This has become the First-tier Tribunal (Asylum Support), so we will refer to it either as the First-tier Tribunal or by the former acronym AST.[3]

Overview

4.4 The 'asylum support' scheme was introduced on 3 April 2000 by IAA 1999 Part VI, which replaced mainstream welfare provision with a safety net of basic living expenses and/or housing for asylum-seekers and their dependants. A destitute asylum-seeker may receive initial accommodation under IAA 1999 s98, before moving on to section 95 support while an asylum claim or appeal decision is awaited. Support under Part VI has been known as 'NASS support'. Here we refer to it as 'asylum support' or 'section 95 support' to distinguish it from accommodation under IAA 1999 s4 which is for 'failed' asylum-seekers.

2 See para 1.92.

3 See further para 7.2.

Local authorities' role

4.5 From December 1999 until 4 April 2005, local authorities (social services) had a duty to provide households with 'interim support' under the Asylum Support (Interim Provisions) Regulations 1999.[4] Since this scheme has now ended, it is not dealt with here, but local authorities still have a significant role in supporting asylum-seekers with care needs under the National Assistance Act 1948 s21 and unaccompanied asylum-seeking children under the Children Act 1989.[5]

Key points

4.6 The main features of the asylum support scheme are:

- IAA 1999 s115 excludes 'persons subject to immigration control' (PSIC) including asylum-seekers from social security benefits and most other welfare provisions.[6]
- UKBA may provide support under IAA 1999 s95 for an 'asylum-seeker' and any 'dependant' who appears to be destitute or likely to become destitute within 14 days, or 56 days if they are already receiving asylum support.[7]
- 'Asylum-seeker' and 'dependant' are defined by IAA 1999 s94(1). 'Asylum-seeker' includes a person aged 18 or over who has made an asylum claim under the Refugee Convention or a claim under ECHR article 3.
- Migrants outside this definition such as visitors and students are not eligible for asylum support even if they are completely destitute.
- UKBA may not provide support unless their decision-maker is satisfied that the asylum claim was made as soon as reasonably practicable after the person's entry into the UK within NIAA 2002 s55. But this does not apply if support is necessary to avoid a breach of the asylum-seeker's rights under the European Convention on Human Rights (ECHR), eg if the applicant is street homeless. Nor does it apply if the household includes a dependent child under 18 years old.

4 Asylum Support (Interim Provisions) (Amendment) Regulations 2004 SI No 566.

5 See chapter 9.

6 See chapter 3 for asylum-seekers who claimed asylum before 3 April 2000 and whose initial claim is outstanding.

7 IAA 1999 s95(1) and AS Regs 2000 reg 7.

- An unaccompanied asylum-seeker under 18 is not eligible for asylum support but can obtain social services help under the Children Act (CA) 1989 ss17 or 20.[8] Between the age of 18–21 their entitlement will depend on their immigration status. They may need to apply to UKBA or may be entitled to continue receiving assistance as a child leaving care under CA 1989 as amended.[9]
- When the asylum claim or appeal is decided, a childless asylum-seeker's entitlement to IAA 1999 ss95 or 98 support ends after a prescribed period. They are no longer an asylum-seeker for support purposes but may be entitled to IAA 1999 s4 support as a failed asylum-seeker.
- An asylum-seeker with a dependent child under 18 who was born before the final determination of the asylum claim/appeal continues to be treated as an asylum-seeker for support purposes (and so entitled to support) for as long as they and the child are in the UK.[10]
- Under section 54 and Schedule 3 to the NIAA 2002 the UKBA has no power to provide section 95 support to certain groups such as EU nationals. EU refugees or a failed asylum-seeker with a child if they are certified by the Home Secretary as having failed to leave the UK voluntarily.[11]
- A person is destitute if they do not have 'adequate accommodation' or cannot meet other 'essential living needs' for themselves and any dependants during a prescribed period of 14/56 days.[12] A person with care needs will not be destitute if they are 'in need of care and attention' and so entitled to social services accommodation under National Assistance Act 1948 s21. But their able-bodied dependants remain entitled to section 95 support.
- Initial accommodation (that is, temporary support) is arranged on behalf of UKBA by voluntary sector contractors under IAA 1999 s98, while UKBA considers whether an asylum-seeker is eligible for section 95 support.

8 See further para 9.131.
9 See chapter 9.
10 IAA 1999 s94(5).
11 Amendment introduced by section 9 of the Asylum and Immigration (Treatment of Claimants, etc) Act 2004. But see para 4.123.
12 IAA 1999 s95(3) and AS Regs 2000 regs 5, 8 and 9.

- 'Support' under section 95 means accommodation adequate to the household's needs, and/or essential living expenses which are provided in cash.[13]
- An asylum-seeker may appeal to the First-tier Tribunal (Asylum Support) against a decision to end their section 4, 95 or 98 support. The AST currently only considers appeals against the refusal or withdrawal of asylum support. Judicial review must be used to challenge other decisions such as delays.
- Support under IAA 1999 s4 may be provided by UKBA to refused asylum-seekers who have no outstanding claim for asylum or appeal and who meet strict criteria, or to those granted bail.
- If UKBA decides an asylum-seeker is eligible, provision of support is arranged through contracts with the private, public and/or voluntary sectors (see chapter 5).

Legislation and materials

4.7 Part VI of the Immigration and Asylum Act 1999 contains the main provisions, in particular section 95 covering ordinary asylum support and section 98 covering initial emergency support. Every subsequent immigration statute has made some change to support provision. The most significant changes are contained in NIAA 2002. Section 54 read with NIAA 2002 Sch 3 restricts access to various forms of welfare provision, particularly community care assistance, for groups such as certain refused asylum-seekers, those unlawfully in the UK and potentially 'section 9' families who refuse to leave the UK voluntarily. NIAA 2002 s55 restricts access to asylum support for those who do not claim asylum promptly.

4.8 Decisions about eligibility for asylum support are formally made by the Home Secretary who delegates this power to decision-makers in UKBA. They decide whether a destitute asylum-seeker is eligible for 'asylum support' taking into account the above statutes, the AS Regs 2000 and Policy Bulletins (previously known as NASS Policy Bulletins).

4.9 The Asylum Support Regulations (AS Regs) 2000[14] made under powers in IAA 1999 Sch 8, contain the details of the asylum support scheme. Various amending regulations have made minor changes

13 IAA 1999 s96(3) providing that asylum support could only be paid in cash in exceptional circumstances was repealed by the Asylum Support (Repeal) Order 2002 SI No 782.

14 SI No 704.

to the type and amount of support and to the interpretation of IAA 1999. There is usually an annual uprating of the amount of support in line with inflation each April, but unlike income support, for example, there is no statutory requirement for the Home Secretary to increase support levels annually. The most recent regulations are the Asylum Support (Amendment) (No 2) Regulations 2009.[15]

4.10 Policy Bulletins are non-statutory guidance published on the Home Office website. They reflect UKBA's interpretation of the law and are referred to where relevant in the text. UKBA decision-makers also rely on internal, mainly procedural, guidance such as guidance on 'Eligibility and Assessment of Asylum Support' which may be found on the Home Office website or requested under the Freedom of Information Act 2000 s1.

4.11 Decision-makers must take into account the decisions of the First-tier Tribunal (Asylum Support), which are published on the AST website.[16] There is a small number of relevant High Court and Court of Appeal decisions, for example where the Home Office or applicants have challenged the AST's decisions by judicial review.

4.12 For details of organisations which advise and/or represent in relation to asylum support and useful websites, see appendix H.

The EU Reception Directive[17]

4.13 The EU has attempted to implement a common policy for the treatment of asylum-seekers across Europe by introducing the EU Directive laying down minimum standards for the reception of asylum-seekers.[18] It is applied to those who have claimed asylum in the UK on or after 5 February 2005 (but see para 4.15 below) and aims to ensure that asylum-seekers have 'a dignified standard of living' but tends to aid interpretation rather than introduce new duties. The Home Office has implemented the Directive in UK law by amending the immigration rules[19] and by introducing new regulations, which mainly change the circumstances in which support can be refused.[20] Where the Directive might be of assistance, it is referred to in the text.

15 SI No 1388.

16 www.asylum-support-tribunal.gov.uk/

17 For a detailed analysis of the Directive see Baldaccini, *Asylum Support: a practitioners' guide to the EU Reception Directive*, Justice, 2005.

18 2003/09/EC of 27 January 2003.

19 HC 395: see chapter 1.

20 Asylum-seekers (Reception Conditions) Regulations 2005 SI No 7; Asylum Support (Amendment) Regulations 2005 SI No 11.

4.14 The Asylum-seekers (Reception Conditions) Regulations 2005[21] and Asylum Support (Amendment) Regulations 2005[22] were introduced to implement the Reception Directive. It is arguable that the regulations have not fully implemented the directive, so it may be necessary to refer to the Directive on the basis that its provisions have direct effect on the UK government and other public bodies.[23] The Reception Directive has been binding on member states including the UK from 6 February 2005.[24] Key provisions include:

- Reception of groups with special needs should be specifically designed to meet those needs (preamble).
- Asylum-seekers should be informed of their support rights and of legal and other organisations within 15 days of claiming asylum (article 5).
- Family unity should be maintained (article 8).
- A standard of living adequate for asylum-seekers' health should be provided taking account of any special needs and including asylum-seekers in detention (article 13).
- Where there has been an evaluation of a vulnerable asylum-seeker, this should be taken into account (article 17).
- Steps should be taken to trace the relatives of unaccompanied minors.

4.15 The government considers that the Directive only applies to those who claimed asylum (as opposed to an ECHR claim) on or after the UK implementation date, 5 February 2005, but this has been questioned by commentators.[25] The Court of Appeal has decided in the context of the right to work, that it applies to those with unrecorded fresh asylum claims, although their decision is subject to appeal.[26] This could significantly benefit those receiving section 4 support due to a fresh asylum claim, by improving their entitlements.

4.16 The Asylum Seekers (Reception Conditions) Regulations 2005 only apply to those who have made a claim for asylum as a refugee (as opposed to under ECHR article 3) since 5 February 2005, and

21 SI No 7.

22 SI No 11.

23 See para 2.22.

24 It is not binding on Ireland which opted out, or on Denmark.

25 See Baldaccini, *Asylum Support: a practitioners' guide to the EU Reception Directive*, Justice, 2005, para 5.7.

26 *R (ZO (Somalia)) and another v Secretary of State for the Home Department* [2009] EWCA Civ 442, (2009) Times 28 May.

whose claim has not yet been determined. They introduce the family unity principle, the tracing duty, and the duty to take into account special needs. The Asylum Support (Amendment) Regulations 2005 are not so limited, applying to all those supported as an asylum-seeker or their dependants under IAA 1999 s95 including those with article 3 claims. They provide for repayment of support and amend the reasons for refusing support by adding a number of new reasons. They also abolish intentional destitution and absence from accommodation as reasons for refusal of support.

4.17 At the time of writing, the European Commission proposed to repeal the Reception Directive and replace it with a new more specific directive to include new measures such as a right to work after six months and income levels being set at a basic rate similar to income support. The UK had indicated it would not opt in, which may ultimately result in the reception rules no longer applying in the UK.

Eligibility for asylum support

Section 95 support

4.18 Under the Immigration and Asylum Act 1999 s95(1):

> The Secretary of State may provide, or arrange for the provision of support for–
> (a) asylum-seekers, or
> (b) dependants of asylum-seekers,
> who appear to the Secretary of State to be destitute or to be likely to become destitute within such a period as may be prescribed.

4.19 Although this refers to a power to provide support, Stanley Burnton J decided that there is a *duty* to provide support where the criteria for entitlement are met.[27] The power was converted into a duty to provide asylum support under IAA 1999 s98 or s95 by Asylum-seekers (Reception Conditions) Regulations 2005 reg 5 (and see Policy Bulletin 83: Duty to offer support, family unity, vulnerable persons, issued 4 February 2005). Although these regulations only apply to those who have made an asylum claim (not simply an

27 *Husain v Asylum Support Adjudicator and Secretary of State for the Home Department* [2001] EWHC 832 (Admin), (2001) Times 15 November.

article 3 ECHR claim) since 5 February 2005, Policy Bulletin 83 suggests the change makes little practical difference.

4.20 If the asylum claim was made after 7 January 2003, the applicant is subject to NIAA 2002 s55, which is explained below. If an asylum-seeker did not claim asylum at the port and does not have a pregnant woman or dependent child in the household, he or she will only qualify to apply for support by passing the NIAA 2002 s55 threshold (see para 14.105). But support will be provided to avoid a breach of their article 3 rights if he or she is homeless.

4.21 Once the NIAA 2002 s55 requirements have been met, there are three basic steps in assessing whether an applicant is eligible for IAA 1999 s95 asylum support:

(a) Is the applicant an 'asylum-seeker' or the 'dependant of an asylum-seeker'?
(b) Is the applicant excluded from support?
(c) Is the household destitute?

Is the applicant an 'asylum-seeker' or the 'dependant of an asylum-seeker'?

4.22 In the context of asylum support, the terms 'asylum-seeker' and 'dependant of an asylum-seeker' have a different meaning from their ordinary immigration law meaning.[28]

Checklist of who is an asylum-seeker for support purposes:

- 18 years or over; and
- has made a claim for asylum as a refugee or human rights claim under ECHR article 3 which has been recorded; and
- has made the claim at the port of entry or at a designated place eg Asylum Screening Unit;
- is awaiting the result of this claim or appeal (or is within timescale for a further appeal); or
- has a dependent child under 18 born before all asylum claims and appeals were rejected.

4.23 An 'asylum-seeker' for asylum support purposes is a person aged 18 or over who has 'made a claim for asylum that has been recorded by the Secretary of State but which has not been determined'.[29]

28 IAA 1999 s94(1).

29 IAA 1999 s94(1). See also Nationality, Immigration and Asylum Act 2002 (Commencement No 2) Order 2003 SI No 1.

Decisions on the definition of an 'asylum-seeker' dealing with issues such as when an asylum claim has been recorded or determined can be viewed on the AST website[30] by searching the index of decisions.

Amendments to 'asylum-seeker' definition

'Designated place' (claims in person)

4.24 A person making a claim for leave to remain so as to avoid a breach of obligations arising under the Refugee Convention and/or the Human Rights Act 1998 must be made in person at a place designated by the Secretary of State.[31] Section 113 came into force on 10 February 2003.[32] Currently 'designated places' are the Asylum Screening Units (ASU) at Croydon and Liverpool. The Home Office will, in the exercise of its discretion, accept applications by post where for good reasons, such as medical, a person cannot make a claim in person. So for immigration purposes, special permission is needed to claim asylum without travelling to a screening unit. This has presented difficulties for those wishing to apply for asylum who lack the money to travel and who previously would have applied by post.[33] The Home Office agreed to accept a claim after a man who arrived by lorry in Plymouth issued judicial review proceedings arguing the policy was a breach of his ECHR articles 3 and 8 rights because he could not afford to travel to the ASU to claim asylum.[34] The requirement also applies to asylum-seekers who are subject to the requirement to live at an induction centre or elsewhere under NIAA 2002 ss70–71, or to who NIAA 2002 s54 and Schedule 3 applies.[35]

4.25 The background to the rule that a claim must be made in person in asylum support cases is difficult to unravel. Under IAA 1999 s94 a claim for asylum must be recorded but there is no requirement for it to be made at a designated place. However, NIAA 2002 s18 works because the requirement applies to applications covered by NIAA 2002 s55(9), so that 'in-country' asylum applicants must have presented themselves at an ASU to qualify for support NIAA 2002 s18

30 www.asylum-support-tribunal.gov.uk

31 NIAA 2002 s113(1).

32 Nationality, Immigration and Asylum Act 2002 (Commencement No 3) Order 2003 SI No 249.

33 See Inter-Agency Partnership evidence to the Joint Committee on Human Rights: The Treatment of Asylum-seekers, 10th Report of Session 2006–07, Vol II, Ev 384, HL 81-11, HC 60-11.

34 *R (Assoua) v Secretary of State for the Home Department* CO 1712/2003 unreported.

35 NIAA 2002 s18.

states that a person is 'an asylum-seeker' if they have made a claim for asylum at a designated place. A commencement order provided that from 8 January 2003, NIAA 2002 s18 applies to the definition of 'claim for asylum' in NIAA 2002 s55(9). Section 55(9) covers 'late claims' cases which fall within section 55 (see para 14.105 below). So it would seem that an in-country asylum-seeker must generally have made the asylum claim in person at the ASU, or made the claim by post and then presented there, to be eligible for UKBA support. There is no mention of this in the guidance published on the UKBA website for assessing eligibility.

Asylum-seekers appealing against an immigration decision

4.26 UK Borders Act 2007 s17 is intended to resolve a technical problem which arose in the Court of Appeal judgment in *Slough v M*.[36] The Court of Appeal found there was a technical difficulty with the definition of 'asylum-seeker' for support purposes because it was limited to those who are appealing against the refusal of their asylum claim, whereas appeals in asylum cases may arise against a decision which is collateral upon an asylum refusal such as the notified country of intended removal. Section 17 provides that a person becomes or remains an asylum-seeker for support purposes if there is a pending 'in-country' appeal against specified immigration decisions eg where a Somali national is appealing against removal directions giving Kenya as the country of destination, and that the section shall be treated as always having had that effect.

Decisions on meaning of 'an asylum-seeker' for support purposes

- The Court of Appeal has decided that where an asylum-seeker appealed out of time to the (then) Immigration Appeal Tribunal, they are no longer 'an asylum-seeker' for support purposes within the IAA 1999 s94(1) definition. They will only become entitled to section 95 support if the IAT agrees to consider the late appeal. The Home Office has since suggested that people in this category[37] may apply for support under IAA 1999 s4, without giving an undertaking to leave the UK (*R (Erdogan) v Secretary of State for the Home Department*).[38]

36 [2006] EWCA Civ 655.

37 Note that this may in future become an application to the Upper Tribunal for reconsideration.

38 [2004] EWCA Civ 1087.

- A person is entitled to section 95 support if they have made an asylum claim that has been *recorded* but not yet determined (IAA 1999 s94). N had made a second claim for asylum but the Home Office had not yet considered whether it was sufficiently different from his original claim so as to be treated as a fresh claim. Collins J decided that making a fresh claim does not trigger entitlement to support until the Home Office has decided whether or not to treat it as a fresh claim. He also indicated that if an applicant is receiving support, and a fresh asylum claim has been made that is not clearly unmeritorious, some form of NASS support should be provided. NASS responded to this by extending section 4 support to cases where a fresh claim has been made but not recorded (*R (Nigatu) v Secretary of State for the Home Department*).[39]
- In an AST decision, the tribunal judge decided that further representations under ECHR article 3 had been recorded and so the appellant was an asylum-seeker entitled to section 95 support (AST/08/09/18218).

Unaccompanied asylum-seekers under 18

4.27 A child under 18 who claims asylum in their own right is an 'asylum-seeker' for immigration law purposes only. If the child is in the UK without a parent and has an outstanding asylum application as an 'unaccompanied minor' they are entitled to housing and support under CA 1989 s20 and not under IAA 1999 s95 asylum support provisions unless they reach the age of 18 with an asylum or ECHR claim/appeal outstanding.[40]

'Claim for asylum'

4.28 In addition to the above requirement, a claim for asylum for support purposes is defined by IAA 1999 s94(1) as either 'a claim that it would be contrary to the UK's obligations under the Refugee Convention, or under ECHR article 3 for that person to be removed from or required to leave the United Kingdom'. An asylum-seeker whose ordinary claim for refugee status under the Refugee Convention is refused may be able to make a free-standing claim

39 [2004] EWHC 1806 (Admin).
40 See para 9.131.

under ECHR article 3 or may raise article 3 arguments in the appeal and so be an asylum-seeker for support purposes.[41]

Fresh claims

4.29 Where an asylum claim has been refused, and the applicant has made an ECHR article 3 claim or a second asylum claim (further representations which are commonly known as a 'fresh claim') this only triggers entitlement to asylum support under section 95 if the fresh claim is 'recorded', that is if UKBA consider that it is sufficiently different from the original claim to justify consideration.[42] Where an asylum-seeker has made a fresh claim, this entitles him or her to support under IAA 1999 s4 as a failed asylum-seeker, until the fresh claim is 'recorded', unless UKBA decided that the fresh claim is 'entirely without merit'.[43] If they have care needs, they may become entitled to social services accommodation under NAA 1948 s21, if support is needed to avoid a breach of their ECHR rights.[44]

Meaning of 'recorded'

4.30 To trigger an asylum support duty, the ECHR article 3 or fresh asylum claim must be a claim which has been 'recorded' by the Home Secretary (UKBA), but not decided.[45] The Home Secretary may decide not to 'record' a fresh claim if it does not disclose new evidence meeting the test set out in *Onibiyo* and *WM (Democratic Republic of Congo) v Secretary of State for the Home Department.*[46]

4.31 The burden of proof in showing a claim has been made is on the asylum-seeker.[47] They should receive a letter from UKBA stating the fresh claim has been recorded. In practice, it may be months or years before the Home Office considers whether to record a fresh claim. In some cases if the decision is to record further representations as a fresh claim under the immigration rules, para 353, the Home Office will proceed to decide the claim at the same time. If refused, the applicant has an in-country right of appeal. If a fresh claim is

41 See chapter 1.

42 See para 1.126.

43 See further chapter 6.

44 NIAA 2002 s54 and Sch 3.

45 IAA 1999 s94(1).

46 *R v Secretary of State for the Home Department ex p Onibiyo* [1996] QB 768 and *WM (Democratic Republic of Congo)* [2006] EWCA Civ 1495, [2007] Imm AR 337 (see para 1.128). See also *ZT (Kosovo) v Secretary of State for the Home Department* [2009] UKHL 9.

47 ASA 00/11/0111.

recorded, UKBA will also consider the section 55 test before deciding whether the applicant is eligible for section 95 support (see below). A person who has made an unrecorded fresh claim meets one of the conditions for IAA 1999 s4 support (see chapter 6).

4.32 It may be unclear whether or not further representations have been recorded as a fresh asylum claim, for example because the asylum-seeker has changed immigration solicitor, or the immigration solicitor does not respond. A local authority, MP or one-stop provider may contact UKBA to request the information. Unfortunately the UKBA response is not always accurate. A request to UKBA for a copy of the asylum-seeker's Home Office file under the Data Protection Act 1998 s7 may be another way of obtaining the necessary evidence.[48]

Meaning of 'determined' – when entitlement ends

4.33 Entitlement to support ends on the 'date of determination'.[49] This is not simply the date on which the asylum decision is made or received, but variously allows for a statutory appeal to be decided, for a notice period and/or for children to reach 18.

4.34 In a household with no dependent child under 18, an asylum-seeker stops being an 'asylum-seeker' for support purposes 28 days after the Home Secretary notifies them of a favourable asylum decision, or 21 days after notification of a refusal. If there is an appeal, the period ends 28 days after any final appeal is disposed of. An appeal is usually disposed of when any time limit for a further appeal has expired. The time limits for asylum appeals are according to the type of appeal and are explained at para 1.180. There are normally ten working days to appeal against the initial decision to the AIT. If the asylum-seeker is detained, the time limit is five working days, or two working days; in detained fast track asylum cases, the time limit is two working days.[50] 'Appeal' includes an application for statutory review to the High Court or an appeal to the Court of Appeal or Supreme Court, but would not include other judicial reviews eg of a decision not to accept an out-of-time appeal.

48 See para 7.167.

49 IAA 1999 s94(3) and AS Regs 2000 reg 2(2), as amended.

50 At the time of writing the regulations were the Asylum and Immigration Tribunal (Procedure) Rules 2005 SI No 230 para 7; Asylum and Immigration Tribunal (Fast Track Procedure) Rules 2005 SI No 560 para 8(1).

4.35 The then Asylum Support adjudicators allowed an appeal where the Home Office had ended support during the prescribed period.[51] The asylum appeal had been successful but support was withdrawn incorrectly before the expiry of the time limit during which the Home Secretary could appeal. A late appeal will not trigger entitlement to section 95 support while a decision is being awaited on permission to appeal out of time. In *R (Erdogan) v Secretary of State for the Home Department*[52] the Court of Appeal decided that the asylum claim was finally determined even if a decision on an application to appeal out of time was pending. There was no entitlement to support unless the tribunal agreed to consider a late appeal.

4.36 If the decision has been sent to the asylum-seeker or their representative by post, it is assumed it has been received on the second day after the day it was posted.[53] This applies even if it has been posted to the asylum-seeker's representative but not received by the asylum-seeker. However, an adjudicator found that IAA 1999 s94(9) was not satisfied where the asylum decision had been sent to an incorrect address, and so asylum support should continue until the asylum decision had been properly notified.[54]

Refused asylum-seeker with a child

4.37 If an asylum-seeker has a dependent child under 18 in their household, they continue to be treated as 'an asylum-seeker' for as long as the child is under 18 and in the asylum-seeker's household.[55] So a refused asylum-seeker with a dependent child, who is born before their appeal rights are exhausted, is entitled to section 95 asylum support, rather than support under IAA 1999 s4 or CA 1989 s17[56] for as long as the family is in the UK. If the child is born after the asylum claim/appeal is finally determined (see para 4.33), then the former asylum-seeker does not qualify for support under IAA 1999 s95, but may qualify under IAA 1999 s4 or CA 1989 s17.

Parent in custody

4.38 The child must be 'in the household' of the asylum-seeker for the family to qualify for section 95 support. Where a family had been

51 ASA 03/01/5489.
52 [2004] EWCA Civ 1087.
53 IAA 1999 s94(9).
54 ASA 02/03/2349.
55 IAA 1999 s94(5).
56 Unless the Children Act duties are triggered by the risk of harm or neglect or the child's special needs.

receiving section 95 support and the asylum-seeker (father) was imprisoned, the Home Office withdrew support on the basis that the child was no longer part of the asylum-seeker's household. In such circumstances the mother as a dependant of a former asylum-seeker would qualify for support under IAA 1999 s4, if she met the conditions, for example by having an outstanding fresh claim or being unable to travel due to pregnancy.[57] Depending on the individual facts, it may be possible to argue that the Home Office's interpretation is incorrect, and that a child remains part of the father's household despite a temporary separation. Alternatively it may be possible to argue that the rules should be read in conjunction with the article 8 right to respect for family and home life, or are incompatible with article 8, again depending on the facts.

Other exceptions

4.39 If an asylum-seeker has been refused asylum and has either failed to appeal in time or appealed unsuccessfully, they will no longer be an asylum-seeker for support purposes if the child leaves the UK or reaches 18. They will no longer be an asylum-seeker for support purposes if asylum or leave to enter or remain in the UK is granted, in which case the 28-day prescribed period applies (see para 4.34). An asylum-seeker may also lose entitlement if the Home Office certifies them as having failed to leave the UK without reasonable excuse under s9 Asylum and Immigration (Treatment of Claimants) Act 2004, which amends NIAA 2002 Sch 3 (see further para 7.27).

Meaning of 'dependant'[58]

4.40 'Dependant' in relation to an asylum-seeker or supported person is as the dependant of 'an asylum-seeker, the supported person or an applicant for asylum support' by virtue of IAA 1999 s94 and AS Regs 2000 reg 2(4). The categories are listed below. The dependant's own immigration status is not relevant, for example an asylum-seeker may claim asylum support for his wife, even if her asylum claim has been rejected. So coming within the 'dependant' definition may be a way of accessing support for a PSIC who would otherwise be excluded.

57 See chapter 6.
58 AS Regs 2000 reg 2.

4.41 Whether the family member is 'a dependant' should be judged at 'the relevant time', which is the date of the application for asylum support. Where another family member arrives in the UK or joins the supported household after arrival, the relevant time is the date of joining a person who is already a supported person. So if the dependant applies for support a few days before their 18th birthday, that is the relevant date for assessing whether or not they are a dependant, not the date when the application is considered.[59]

4.42 The Home Office has introduced the 'overarching principle of family unity' to the provision of asylum support accommodation so that families should be housed together.[60] The aim is to implement the Reception Directive,[61] so it is limited to those covered by the Directive, that is those who since 4 February 2005 have made an asylum claim rather than a claim under ECHR article 3. In the light of the *ZO Somalia* decision (see para 4.15 above) this may include section 4 applicants who have made a fresh claim.

4.43 'Family members' are limited to[62] a spouse or partner in a stable relationship and any unmarried dependent minor children of either the asylum-seeker him or herself or of the couple, although this is a narrower definition than the usual asylum support definition of dependant.[63]

Tribunal decisions on meaning of dependant

- Support was refused because a birth certificate had not yet been obtained. The tribunal decided that there was no requirement formally to register the child's birth to obtain support if the birth had been notified to the Home Office.[64]
- M was an asylum-seeker receiving subsistence-only support while living with her sister and young nephew who were both British citizens. She contributed to the household's living expenses. She appealed against the withdrawal of support by

59 AS Regs 2000 reg 2(6).

60 See the Asylum Seekers (Reception Conditions) Regulations 2005 SI No 7 and Policy Bulletin 83.

61 Council Directive 2003/09/EC laying down minimum standards for the reception of asylum seekers.

62 Asylum Seekers (Reception Conditions) Regulations 2005 SI No 7 reg 3.

63 AS Regs 2000 reg 2, or the definition of family member in EU law. See para 2.71.

64 ASA/05/04/9203.

NASS after she lost her asylum appeal. The ASA found firstly that her nephew was a child who was a member of her close family and so a dependant under AS Regs 2000 reg 2(c) and secondly that the child formed part of her household, following the approach of Lord Hailsham in *Simmons v Pizzey*.[65]

- An unborn child of a pregnant asylum-seeker is not a dependant.[66]

Categories of dependants

Husband or wife or civil partner

4.44 The regulations initially referred only to 'spouse' by reference to a 'married couple', defined as 'a man and woman who are married to each other and are members of the same household'.[67] The rules have been updated to include a 'civil partnership couple' defined as 'two people of the same sex who are civil partners of each other and living as part of the same household' by amending the AS Regs 2000.[68] Policy Bulletin 87 confirms that the Home Office will treat registered civil partners in the same way as a married couple. Other same-sex partners who are cohabiting are treated in the same way as an unmarried couple.

4.45 A husband or wife, unlike a partner in an unmarried couple, would be treated as a dependant even if the couple had not been living together before they applied for support together. In cases where a husband or wife arrives in the UK after a spouse who is receiving asylum support, a new application for support could be made. Both husband and wife may have made an asylum claim in their own right, in which case UKBA may require some evidence of the marriage. If the spouse is treated as a dependant for the purposes of the husband's or the wife's asylum claim, then the evidence accepted for the purposes of the asylum claim should be accepted for support purposes. The marriage must be valid in the country of residence at the time of the marriage so an Islamic marriage ceremony in Somalia should be treated as a lawful marriage, but not

65 [1979] AC 37, ASA 04/05/8109.
66 ASA 03/02/5731.
67 AS Regs 2000 reg 2(1).
68 Civil Partnership Act 2004 (Amendments to Subordinate Legislation) Order 2005 SI No 2114.

if it took place in the UK where a civil ceremony would be needed.[69]

Dependent child under 18

4.46 The child must be under 18 on the 'relevant date', which means the date of the application for asylum support or on the date when they joined a supported household. For example, if an only son joins his mother's household at age 17, support should continue when he reaches 18 unless he wants to form a separate household or his mother's asylum claim and appeal has been refused. A child will qualify as a dependant if:

- they are a child of the applicant, or of the applicant's spouse, and dependent on the applicant; or
- they are a member of the close family of the applicant, or the applicant's spouse, provided the child has been living as part of the applicant's household since birth or for six of the 12 months before this application for support.

4.47 A child who has been adopted, whether formally or informally, should come within the definition of 'close family'.

Disabled family member over 18

4.48 The family member will qualify as a dependant if they are 'in need of care and attention from the applicant or a member of his household by reason of a disability' and:

- they are a child of the applicant or of the applicant's spouse and dependent on the applicant; or
- they are a member of the close family of the applicant or the applicant's spouse provided they have been living as part of the applicant's household since birth or for six of the 12 months before this application for support.

4.49 So an adult with a disability or mental health condition may be treated as part of the household, despite the fact that they are over 18.[70] The term 'in need of care and attention' reflects NAA 1948 s21(1)(a) and is explained at para 9.59. Where a household includes a disabled adult, a community care assessment should be carried out and NAA 1948 s21 accommodation provided for that family

69 Marriage Act 1949 s26.
70 AS Regs 2000 reg 2(1).

member and possibly for their carer following a carer's assessment, living with other household members receiving IAA 1999 s95 support.[71] The local authority makes the provision and should receive a subsidy from UKBA.

Unmarried or same-sex couple

4.50 An unmarried couple means a heterosexual or same-sex couple who can show they have been living together for two of the three years before the application for support or before the joint application if they arrived in the UK separately. 'Unmarried couple' is defined as 'a man and woman who though not married to each other, are living together as if married'. The Civil Partnership Act 2004 gives same-sex couples the right to enter a legally binding civil partnership and various amendments have been made to the AS Regs 2000 to bring them into line with that Act. Policy Bulletin 87: 'The Civil Partnership Act 2004' explains the changes and reproduces the amendments. The bulletin suggests that asylum-seeking same sex couples are likely to come within the 'unmarried couple' category. 'Same sex couple' is defined as 'two people of the same-sex who, though not civil partners of each other, are living together as if they are'.[72]

4.51 An unmarried partner who does not meet the two years rule may come within the 'dependant' definition if they are a dependent on the asylum claim (see below). ECHR arguments may be available where an unmarried partner in a long-term relationship has a good reason for not satisfying the rule, for example where they have been separated in civil war or while fleeing from their country of origin. It could be argued that it would be disproportionate not to read the AS Regs 2000 so as to be compatible with ECHR article 8 (right to respect for home and family life) and article 14 (discrimination on the basis of unmarried status), and see para 4.42 in relation to the effect of the Reception Directive.

4.52 In an ASA appeal,[73] a gay man had refused to travel to a dispersal area because his partner, with whom he had come to the UK, was subject to NIAA 2002 s55 and so was not to be accommodated with him. The adjudicator remitted the decision back to the decision-maker to 'reconsider the appellant's case in conjunction with that of

71 See para 9.102.

72 AS Regs 2000 reg 2(1) and 2(4)(ff) as amended by the Civil Partnership Act 2004 (Amendments to Subordinate Legislation) Order 2005 SI No 2114.

73 ASA 03/06/6654.

his partner', apparently on the basis that there was a reasonable excuse for the failure to travel.

4.53 The Equality Act (Sexual Orientation) Regulations 2007 which prohibit discrimination in relation to housing, apply where it can be shown that a heterosexual applicant would be treated differently. It seems they are unlikely to assist a same-sex asylum-seeking couple as they are treated in the same way as a mixed gender couple, having to live together for two of the past three years to qualify as a dependant. The UKBA's Race, Disability and Gender Equality Scheme[74] states that whenever a new policy, procedure or a significant change to an existing policy or procedure is proposed that identifies the need for consideration of sexual orientation an equality impact assessment will be conducted that takes this into account (see paras 45–46 of the scheme).

Dependent on the asylum claim

4.54 Anyone who has made a claim for leave to enter or remain in the UK, or for variation of any such leave, which is being considered on the basis that they are dependent on the asylum-seeker, will automatically be treated as a dependant of the asylum-seeker for asylum support purposes.[75] This will normally be demonstrated by the applicant's immigration documents. If the asylum-seeker has an application registration card (ARC), the number of their dependant(s) will appear on the back of the card, but a dependant over the age of five will have their own card that records the ARC reference of the main asylum applicant. There may be difficulties if the dependant has only recently arrived and has not yet been added to the ARC. In such cases evidence will be needed from their immigration solicitor or the Home Office that they are a dependant. This category extends to dependants for the purposes of the immigration claim such as a brother or sister who would otherwise be excluded from qualifying as dependants for support purposes. Note that where a family member is applying for 'leave in line' with an asylum-seeker who has been granted refugee status, they are not a dependant of an asylum-seeker.[76]

74 www.ukba.homeoffice.gov.uk/sitecontent/documents/aboutus/workingforus/Three-strand_Equality_Scheme.pdf.

75 AS Regs 2000 reg 2(4)(i).

76 AST 03/08/6919.

Challenging a decision regarding a dependant

4.55 It has been suggested that the definition of dependant contained in the AS Regs 2000 does not fully reflect the definition of dependant in EU law which includes dependent children up to 21 and parents/grandparents for example (see para 2.71). If UKBA refuses to accept a family member as a dependant, they should be asked to take into consideration article 8 of the Reception Directive,[77] which requires the UK government to ensure that the principle of family unity is maintained. They are also required to take into account the ECHR article 8 right to respect for family life.

The destitution test

4.56 An asylum-seeker may be 'destitute' either due to a lack of 'adequate accommodation' or if they cannot meet the household's 'essential living needs' during a prescribed period of 14 days (if they are applying for support) or 56 days (if they have been receiving support).[78] So a new applicant for support may be treated as destitute if they are living with friends and simply need help with food, or if they have some money but not enough to cover their housing needs for the next 14 days. The destitution test in applications for s4 support is explained further in chapter 6.

4.57 The UKBA approach to the destitution test is as follows:

(a) What income and assets are available to the applicant during the prescribed period?
(b) Can the applicant meet the essential living needs of the asylum-seeker and any dependant(s)?
(c) Does the applicant have adequate accommodation for themselves and any dependant(s)?
(d) Can the applicant meet essential living needs and secure adequate accommodation until after the end of the prescribed period?

What income and assets are available to the applicant?[79]

4.58 Any asylum support provided by UKBA, including initial accommodation provided under IAA 1999 s98, must be ignored in assessing resources. But support provided by a local authority such

77 See para 4.13.

78 IAA 1999 s95(3); AS Regs 2000 regs 5–9.

79 AS Regs 2000 reg 6(4).

as social services accommodation under NAA 1948 s21 must be taken into account.[80] Assets outside the UK are taken into account if they are available or might reasonably be expected to become available.[81]

Tribunal decisions on destitution

- An appellant had a home in Sri Lanka that he was reluctant to sell. A community organisation was paying his £750 per month rent in the UK, but not his living expenses. The Chief Asylum Support Adjudicator decided that the family should receive asylum support for three months to allow him time to take steps to sell the house.[82]
- At the date she lodged her appeal, the appellant was living with her husband who had £2,000 and a six-month tenancy agreement at a monthly rent of £606.66. They had spent £23,000 on a combination of medical treatment, hotel bills and their essential living needs. These included extensive transport costs to hospital, prescription charges and dietary needs due to the husband's condition (he had had half his tongue removed). By the date of the tribunal hearing, they had £729 left. The adjudicator decided that the appellant had sufficient means to meet their essential living needs for at least 14 days.[83] Of course, this does not prevent an applicant from reapplying when their circumstances have changed.
- Where a mother had a sick child, the adjudicator took into account the need to spend extra money on sanitary towels, clothes and travel.[84]

4.59 It is difficult to quantify notional help from friends and family in practice and there is no specific provision for this in the regulations. The explanatory notes to the IAA 1999 (para 282) suggest that this includes resources to which an asylum-seeker might be expected to have access, for example from friends and family in the UK. The

80 *R ((1) AW (2) A (3) Y) v (1) Croydon LBC, (2) Hackney LBC* [2007] EWCA Civ 266, (2007) 10 CCLR 189, (2007) Policy Bulletin 82.

81 AS Regs 2000 reg 6(4).

82 ASA 02/08/4018.

83 ASA 00/05/0006.

84 ASA/01/03/0234.

intention seemed to be to take account of support that family and friends are willing and can reasonably afford to provide. This should be distinguished from the emergency support that family or friends cannot really afford, but may offer on a humanitarian basis to prevent physical or mental injury. The schedule to the regulations asks applicants to provide information about any support that friends or relatives are giving at the time of the application, as well as any financial support that friends or relatives can give.

Resources that must be taken into account

4.60 Only those assets listed in AS Regs 2000 reg 6(5) may be taken into account:

- cash;
- savings;
- investments;
- land;
- cars or other vehicles; and
- goods held for the purposes of a trade or other business.

4.61 The NASS 1 application form requires the person claiming support to list all the household's assets and then explain why they are not 'available' to them, for example assets that are abroad. An asylum-seeker is eligible for support while they take steps to recover property not currently available. Where assets are realised the Home Secretary may recover sums paid in support, for example if the Sri Lankan house referred to at para 4.58 above were sold.[85]

Resources which are not taken into account

4.62 UKBA will not take into account jewellery (including watches), personal clothing, medical items and bedding.[86] The asylum-seeker must inform UKBA if the value of jewellery owned by the household is more than £1,000 in total. If jewellery or other belongings are sold for cash, they become an asset and the supported person has a duty to report this to UKBA as a change of circumstances.[87] The guidance notes to the asylum support application form explain this.

85 AS Regs 2000 reg 17.
86 AS Regs 2000 Sch notes.
87 AS Regs 2000 reg 15(2)(b).

Can the applicant meet essential living needs?

4.63 Policy Bulletin 4 contains a table (see the Home Office website) showing the thresholds that are applied when working out an asylum-seeker's essential living needs. UKBA's approach is to calculate the total amount the household would receive if receiving subsistence-only support and adding this to the household's reasonable accommodation and utility costs. UKBA will only decide that the household is destitute if its resources or income fall below the threshold. Despite the decisions referred to below it appears that UKBA continues to apply the thresholds fairly rigidly.

4.64 The rates in Policy Bulletin 4 are currently based on the local reference rate for board and lodgings. There is no authority in the IAA 1999 or the AS Regs 2000 for applying fixed thresholds, although this is the approach routinely taken in AST appeals. But each case should be looked at on its individual circumstances; for example, a newly arrived asylum-seeker in London would normally need more than the ordinary threshold amounts to secure accommodation and subsistence for 14 days since they would need to pay higher housing costs. Bed and breakfast at that rate might not be available or suitable for some asylum-seeking families, in which case the local cost of rent and deposits/rent in advance should be taken into account. Evidence of the cost of housing (by reference to the local housing allowance) and essential living needs should be provided at AST appeals to support these arguments.

Decisions on whether asylum-seeker's living costs are met

- Where an asylum-seeker came to the UK to join a partner with leave to remain, Gibbs J found there was no mathematical formula for calculating entitlement. The household's existing obligations (such as fuel debts and work expenses) as well as their income should be taken into account. 'NASS should exercise a sensible discretion within the scheme to take account of relevant factors so as to ensure that essential needs are met'. In each case the income, living expenses and housing costs must be examined individually.[88]

88 *R (Secretary of State for the Home Department) v Asylum Support Adjudicator and (1) Berkadle (2) Perera* [2001] EWHC 811 (Admin); and see below.

- Where an asylum-seeker was working on a low income so could not afford to pay for subsistence and accommodation, the adjudicator found that the thresholds had been applied too rigidly, failing to take into account accommodation costs and allowed his appeal.[89]

4.65 There are no items specified to be taken into account to decide whether living needs are met, but a number of items may not be taken into account, such as travel and communication expenses.[90]

4.66 If UKBA decides that an applicant who has some resources is destitute, either because they cannot meet his or her essential living needs or has inadequate accommodation, the question of income and assets will be considered to decide what level and kind of support should be provided.[91]

Mixed households

4.67 An asylum-seeker may have a dependant with a different immigration status, or different needs, or vice versa resulting in eligibility for different types of support. A common scenario is where an asylum-seeker joins the household of a partner or parent with leave to remain. Policy Bulletin 11 outlines the approach to mixed households, and Policy Bulletin 4 the approach to the partner's income. As the cases below demonstrate, if an asylum-seeker comes to the UK to join his or her partner, their income, accommodation and expenses will be taken into account when calculating whether the asylum-seeker is destitute for the purposes of entitlement to asylum support.

Decisions on mixed households

- Where an asylum-seeker came to the UK to join his wife, the court decided that the income of the existing UK resident should be taken into account in assessing eligibility for section 95 support, but should not simply be compared with the ordinary support thresholds so that a couple would be reduced to 'NASS' rates of subsistence (70 per cent of income support).[92]

89 ASA 02/04/2341.

90 IAA 1999 s95(7) and AS Regs 2000 reg 9.

91 AS Regs 2000 reg 12.

92 See para 4.63; *R (Secretary of State for the Home Department) v Asylum Support Adjudicator and (1) Berkadle (2) Perera* [2001] EWHC 811 (Admin).

- Where a woman on maternity leave was supporting her child and asylum-seeker husband, the adjudicator remitted the appeal for reconsideration because there was no evidence that Gibbs J's guidance (above) had been taken into account.[93]

4.68 The same approach should apply when UKBA is considering whether a mixed household has adequate accommodation. Policy Bulletin 11 proposes that a mixed household in overcrowded accommodation should attempt to seek private rented accommodation and claim housing benefit. But para 22 goes on to say:

> If it is determined that the accommodation is not adequate, and the household have not been able to obtain alternative accommodation and they have taken reasonable steps to find alternative accommodation then the UK Border Agency may provide the accommodation.

Does the applicant have 'adequate accommodation' for the household?

4.69 For the purposes of this section, a person is destitute if:[94]

> (a) he does not have adequate accommodation or any means of obtaining it (whether or not his other essential living needs are met).

4.70 So an applicant is destitute if they are homeless, that is with no adequate accommodation or no means of obtaining any adequate accommodation.[95] The accommodation must be adequate for both the applicant and any dependant(s).[96]

4.71 The test of whether the asylum-seeker has 'adequate accommodation' when UKBA is deciding whether or the household is eligible for support (IAA 1999 s95(6)) is slightly different from the question of whether the accommodation that UKBA has provided for a supported household is adequate (IAA 1999 s97). The meaning of 'adequate accommodation' in the context of housing provided by UKBA is discussed in chapter 5.

93 ASA 02/04/2522.
94 IAA 1999 s95(3)(a).
95 IAA 1999 s95(3).
96 IAA 1999 s95(4).

Tip

Where an asylum-seeker has been staying with a friend or relative in unsuitable accommodation, it may be simpler for them to apply for support with evidence that they have now been asked to leave (where this applies) rather than to prove that it is not adequate.

The meaning of 'adequate accommodation'

4.72 The approach to assessing whether asylum-seekers have adequate accommodation is similar to the test of homelessness in the Housing Act (HA) 1996 ss175–177.[97] The Court of Appeal has indicated there is little difference between the meaning of 'suitable accommodation' in homelessness law and 'adequate accommodation' in the IAA 1999.[98] The main difference is that an asylum-seeker is not treated as destitute simply because they have 'no enforceable right to occupy' the accommodation.[99] So a homeless applicant who has an eviction order to take effect within 28 days is 'threatened with homelessness' and entitled to assistance. An applicant for section 95 support may have to wait until 14 days before the eviction order before they are awarded support because that is the prescribed period under AS Regs 2000 reg 7(a).

4.73 Although IAA 1999 provides that asylum-seekers should have 'no-choice' about the accommodation they are given, the regulations are worded to reflect the test of 'accommodation which is reasonable to continue to occupy' (as developed in homelessness law). Both the IAA 1999 and the AS Regs 2000 appear to use terms from the homelessness provisions in HA 1996 Part VII.

4.74 To decide whether accommodation is adequate, UKBA must have regard to prescribed matters and may not have regard to matters listed at IAA 1999 s95(6) or to other prescribed matters. The AS Regs 2000 include factors that must be taken into account. So far the Home Secretary has not made regulations with prescribed factors that may not be taken into account.

97 See chapter 8.

98 See *R (A) v National Asylum Support Service and Waltham Forest LBC* [2003] EWCA Civ 1473, (2003) 6 CCLR 538.

99 IAA 1999 s95(6)(a).

Factors which may not be considered

4.75 There are four specified factors that should not be taken into consideration by UKBA in deciding whether an asylum-seeker's accommodation is adequate under IAA 1999 s95(6):

(a) there is no enforceable right to occupy the accommodation;
(b) all or part of the accommodation is shared;
(c) the accommodation is temporary;
(d) the location of the accommodation.

4.76 These factors will need to be interpreted broadly to make sense of the provisions, for example if an applicant has no enforceable right to occupy accommodation under IAA 1999 s95(6)(a), they may not be able to secure entry to it, which is a relevant matter under AS Regs 2000 reg 8(d). The government gave various assurances that asylum-seekers would not be expected to remain in accommodation that was severely overcrowded or subject to racial harassment when the IAA 1999 was debated.[100]

4.77 In the context of homelessness eligibility under HA 1996 s186, the Court of Appeal considered whether an asylum-seeker had 'any accommodation in the United Kingdom, however temporary available for his occupation'. They decided that an asylum-seeker who was living in accommodation in an appalling state of repair was homeless.[101] Many of the asylum support appeals where support has been withdrawn because asylum-seekers have adequate accommodation are due to them having income from employment.[102] Their success or failure depends on whether the asylum-seeker can show their income is insufficient to cover reasonable accommodation and subsistence costs.

Factors which must be considered[103]

4.78 The following matters must be taken into account in deciding whether the asylum-seeker with any dependant is destitute because they do not have adequate accommodation:

(a) whether it would be reasonable for the person to continue to occupy the accommodation;

100 Lord Williams of Mostyn, *Hansard*, HL Debates cols 1159–1160, 20 October 1999.
101 *Lismane v Hammersmith and Fulham LBC* (1999) 31 HLR 427.
102 See ASA 02/04/2752 and ASA 02/09/4414.
103 AS Regs 2000 reg 8(3).

(b) whether the accommodation is affordable;
(c) whether it is initial accommodation provided as IAA 1999 s98 temporary support while a claim of support is being considered;
(d) whether the person can secure entry to the accommodation;
(e) where the accommodation is a vehicle or caravan, whether the applicant has a place where it can be parked and lived in;
(f) whether the accommodation is available for occupation by the person's dependants together with him or her;
(g) whether it is probable that the person's continued occupation of the accommodation will lead to domestic violence against him/her or any of his or her dependants.

4.79 Where the family is a split household living separately, but wants to live as one household, it can be argued that the applicant is destitute because they do not have adequate accommodation for all those who come within the definition of dependant (see para 4.40).

4.80 When UKBA considers whether the current accommodation is 'reasonable to continue to occupy', '... regard may be had to the general circumstances prevailing in relation to housing in the district of the local housing authority where the accommodation is'.[104] These concepts are taken from homelessness legislation[105] so homelessness case-law may be relevant. Consideration of local housing conditions may be an advantage in some cases; for example, UKBA should not decide that it is reasonable for an asylum-seeker family to continue to occupy a bed and breakfast hotel in an area where there was a plentiful supply of empty council housing.

4.81 To decide whether the accommodation is affordable, UKBA must have regard to income or assets which are available or might be expected to be available, the cost of the accommodation and the applicant's other reasonable living expenses.[106]

4.82 Other factors that UKBA may take into account when it considers whether accommodation is reasonable to continue to occupy are listed in the notes to the NASS 1 application form. These are racial harassment or attacks, physical violence, sexual abuse or sexual harassment or harassment because of the asylum-seeker's religion.[107]

104 AS Regs 2000 reg 7(4).
105 HA 1996 s175(3).
106 AS Regs 2000 reg 8(5).
107 See www.ukba.homeoffice.gov.uk/asylum/support/apply/

4.83 Domestic violence means violence or threats of violence that are likely to be carried out by a close family member or someone who was formerly a close family member.

4.84 If an asylum-seeker claims subsistence-only support, they will be expected to show that the household has adequate accommodation. The Home Office's policy requires that it must not be section 95 accommodation occupied by another asylum-seeker. An asylum-seeker would not normally be permitted to live in 'expensive accommodation' and claim subsistence-only support while paying for the unaffordable accommodation from other resources.[108]

Can the applicant meet essential living needs and secure adequate accommodation for the prescribed period?

4.85 Support may be provided for asylum-seekers or their dependants who 'appear to the Secretary of State to be destitute or to be likely to become destitute' within a specified period.[109] Two different periods are prescribed by the regulations, depending on whether the applicant is making a new claim or is already in receipt of support:[110]

- if the asylum-seeker is not already receiving support, 14 days beginning with the day on which the UKBA makes a decision about support;
- if the asylum-seeker is already receiving asylum support but support is being reviewed, for example due to a change of circumstances, the relevant period is 56 days beginning with the day on which the support decision is made.

4.86 The assessment of destitution is an ongoing assessment while support is provided to the 'supported person(s)'. The supported person has a duty to report changes of circumstances such as income or assets becoming available. AS Regs 2000 reg 15 lists the relevant changes of circumstances.

4.87 Support should only be withdrawn if an asylum-seeker has sufficient resources to support him or herself and any dependant for more than 56 days from the date on which destitution is reconsidered. The capital and income thresholds for supported households

108 See AST 02/08/4018.
109 IAA 1999 s95(1).
110 AS Regs 2000 reg 7.

and arrangements for contributing to section 95 support are outlined in Policy Bulletin 4. A supported asylum-seeker could obtain very short-term employment or receive a small lottery win without loss of accommodation and support. AS Regs 2000 reg 10 allows an asylum-seeker who has an income or is working to make contributions to their support.

Procedures

Applying for support

A note of caution

The system of support and compliance with conditions of support is closely linked to immigration control; for example an asylum application may be processed more quickly if the applicant is receiving asylum support. Any information given to UKBA may be passed on to a wide range of agencies from the police, government departments and local authorities, to private landlords and the Post Office. There is a risk of prosecution in cases of failure to provide accurate information or notify relevant changes of circumstances. UKBA has wide powers to require information and make further enquiries of the applicant about any matter connected with the application. There are various offences connected to the provision of support (see para 15.133). The Home Office's powers are supplemented by UK Borders Act 2007 s18, which provides that an immigration officer may arrest without warrant a person whom the immigration officer reasonably suspects has committed an offence under IAA 1999 ss105 or 106.

4.88 UKBA's procedures for considering support applications are mainly in internal guidance, some of which is published as Policy Bulletins or 'Process guidance'. These can be accessed from the Home Office website.[111]

111 www.UKBA.homeoffice.gov.uk/policyandlaw/guidance/asylumsuppbull/?version=1

Voluntary sector agents

4.89 The Home Office funds voluntary organisations such as Refugee Action, the Refugee Council and Migrant Helpline[112] to carry out some of the following functions as its agents under IAA 1999 Part VI:

(a) 'reception assistance' which includes arranging and managing IAA 1999 s98 initial accommodation and assisting clients to apply for s95 support by completing the NASS 1 application form.

(b) 'One Stop Service' front-line advice and assistance to asylum-seekers who are receiving IAA 1999 s95 support (normally those who have been dispersed).

4.90 Where special needs are identified, the applicant should be referred to a local authority (social services department) for an assessment of community care needs. Where the applicant claims to be under 18, but this is disputed by the Home Office, they should be referred to a social services department for an age assessment (see further chapter 9). The reception assistant is expected to refer the asylum-seeker to the Medical Foundation for the Care of Victims of Torture where appropriate.

Accessing initial section 98 accommodation

4.91 The Home Office requires each asylum applicant and any dependant(s) to participate in a screening process at which they are photographed, fingerprinted and issued with an identity card or ARC (see further 1.92). The procedures for screening and authorising access to initial accommodation are covered in Policy Bulletins 73 and 75.

Eligibility for section 98 initial accommodation

4.92 An asylum-seeker may be in urgent need of accommodation after making an asylum or ECHR article 3 application whether on arrival at the port of entry, or 'in-country' having recently arrived in the UK, or at a later stage. Initial accommodation under IAA 1999 s98, which UKBA refers to as 'initial accommodation' is provided pending a

112 See appendix E for full list.

decision on full section 95 asylum support. Initial accommodation may be provided for:

(a) asylum-seekers; or
(b) dependants of asylum-seekers,
who it appears to the Secretary of State may be destitute.[113]

4.93 An asylum-seeker is only eligible for initial accommodation if the household appears to have an *immediate* need for housing and support. An asylum-seeker who appears likely to become destitute within 14 days, but not immediately, is entitled to asylum support under IAA 1999 s95 but not to initial accommodation under section 98. This would apply where an asylum-seeker who has just arrived in the UK is able to stay briefly with friends or community members. IAA 1999 s98 support is provided as a stop-gap until there is time to carry out a full assessment, and in every other respect the test of eligibility is the same as for the full section 95 duty set out above.[114]

Port applicants

4.94 An asylum-seeker who claims asylum at the port of entry on arrival in the UK should be issued with form IS96 endorsed with 'applied on arrival' as evidence of this. If there is not time to carry out a screening interview and issue an application registration card (ARC) on arrival, the IS96 should be presented to the relevant voluntary organisation to allow access to initial accommodation for one night. Such applicants do not need a NIAA 2002 s55 decision (see below) since the asylum-seeker is treated as having applied for asylum 'as soon as reasonably practicable'.

'In-country' applicants

4.95 'In-country' applicants need to attend the asylum screening unit (ASU) to obtain a Home Office letter and ARC card to access initial accommodation. This complies with the requirement for them to claim asylum at a designated place (see para 4.24) currently the ASU in Croydon or Liverpool. There are difficulties because the ASUs have limited opening times. If the ASU is closed, the voluntary organisation may accommodate 'vulnerable applicants' until the

113 IAA 1999 s98(1).
114 IAA 1999 s98(3) and s95(2)–(11).

next working day when the applicant is expected to attend to claim asylum and/or participate in the screening process. These are defined in Policy Bulletin 73 as applicants who are pregnant, have a child under 18, are disabled (but with insufficient clear and urgent care needs to obtain immediate social services assistance), or 'individuals whose needs require special consideration'. Other applicants may be admitted if the ASU has closed at a time when it is normally open, but they will need an ASU2 letter provided by the skeleton ASU staff (see UKBA internal 'Eligibility and Assessment of Support' guidance).[115]

Section 55 procedures

4.96 UKBA will then consider the information on the Home Office file including from the original screening process to assess whether the applicant applied for asylum as soon as reasonably practicable under NIAA 2002 s55(1). If they decide the applicant did not, or if they are in doubt, they must proceed to consider whether section 55(5) applies, ie is the applicant exempt from section 55 due to having a dependent child in the household, or are they in need of accommodation to avoid a breach of rights under article 3 ECHR? If the caseworker cannot decide whether or not section 55(5) applies, the asylum-seeker will be invited to a section 55 interview. The interview will involve questions about their reasons for delaying in applying for asylum (section 55(1)) and explore whether a refusal of support would result in a breach of his or her ECHR rights (section 55(5)).

4.97 An interview is likely if a childless applicant has applied for asylum more than three working days after arrival and is claiming 'subsistence-only support'. Policy Bulletin 75, Version 7 suggests that if an asylum-seeker has accommodation, it may be assumed they also have access to sanitary facilities and food, or can obtain food from a charity. An asylum-seeker who is subject to a section 55 interview should produce any evidence they have about their reasons for delay and about their lack of access to food/sanitary facilities (see para 14.119 below) either at the interview or as soon as possible afterwards. If an asylum-seeker fails to attend such an interview without good reason, support may be refused either under NIAA 2002 s55 or s57 (see para 14.121).

115 www.ukba.homeoffice.gov.uk/sitecontent/documents/asylumprocess guidance/asylumsupport/

Applying for section 95 support

4.98 The first step in applying for section 95 support is to complete the NASS 1 application form which is available on the Home Office website or at the offices of voluntary sector agents. But it is not necessary to complete this form to access initial accommodation. Where an asylum-seeker is admitted to initial accommodation, the voluntary sector agent is contracted with UKBA to assist the asylum-seeker to apply for section 95 support within two days of arriving in the initial accommodation. In other cases, an asylum-seeker may have made their own application, perhaps with voluntary sector assistance while staying with a friend or relative.

Application for section 95 asylum support

4.99 The procedure for applying for support is to complete the NASS 1 application form. Copies of the form and guidance notes are available by telephoning or writing to UKBA, or can be downloaded from the UKBA website. There are several pages of notes explaining to the applicant how the form should be completed. The form should be faxed to UKBA followed by a hard copy, supporting documents and four photographs in the post. If the form is completed with help, for example from a community or advice worker, one photograph should be signed by any adviser who helps with the completion of the form.

4.100 UKBA has arranged for voluntary organisations known as the 'One Stop Service' to assist asylum-seekers with completing the NASS 1 form and provide an interpreter if necessary.[116] Legal help funded by the Community Legal Service (CLS) is not normally available for form-filling, but it may be reasonable to assist a client with the NASS 1 form if an issue of law arises, for example about whether they should apply for asylum support or social services assistance, or if they are particularly vulnerable. Legal help is available for advice about legal rights in relation to asylum support, for example whether the client is eligible under the contract for housing, welfare benefits or 'tolerance', depending on the type of problem. The immigration contract allows for half an hour to be spent on an asylum support problem before it should be treated as a separate matter.

116 See appendix E for list.

Who should make the application for support?

4.101 The household can choose whether the person applying for support should be the asylum-seeker or their dependant. One factor to take into account is that the supported person will need to attend a post office regularly to obtain support. The explanatory notes to IAA 1999 (at para 270) give the example of a dependant claiming support if the asylum-seeker is in detention. There are a number of other circumstances where a dependant may need to claim or continue to receive support while temporarily or even permanently separated from the asylum-seeker. A dependent wife can claim support for herself and her dependent children after a relationship breakdown, although she should be advised of the implications for her immigration status.

4.102 UKBA initially stated that it aimed to make a section 95 decision within two working days of receiving the NASS 1 form but this target has not been met. Despite improvements and a reduction in the backlog, there are delays in processing the forms. Some applicants, such as those needing special accommodation or women who cannot be dispersed due to pregnancy, may stay in IAA 1999 s98 initial accommodation for several weeks while awaiting an offer of IAA 1999 s95 support. Where the accommodation is inadequate, it may be possible to apply for a judicial review of the delay to obtain a decision about section 95 support, or of the quality of the section 98 accommodation, to obtain alternative section 98 accommodation. See chapter 7 for tactics on dealing with delays.

UKBA decision to grant IAA 1999 s95 support

4.103 When UKBA has processed the NASS 1 application form, it writes to the applicant with a decision to provide or refuse support, or a request for more information. If UKBA decides to provide support to an asylum-seeker under IAA 1999 s95, a support package is sent to the applicant enclosing a letter with details of the travel arrangements and the location of the accommodation.

4.104 The support pack should contain a support details letter, outlining the regular support and any emergency support ordered, an HC2 form granting exemption from prescription charges, and a support agreement. The emergency payment is £90 per household member, to last three weeks[117] normally paid at any general post office via the

117 The same amount as when the second edition of this book was published in 2004.

ARC. The support letter explains the amounts of weekly support entitlement and explains amounts and periods of emergency support. Once arrangements have been made with the local post office, an asylum-seeker must attend with their ARC identity card to obtain cash there each week. UKBA monitors the collection of support so that an investigation is triggered into whether the asylum-seeker has left their accommodation or is working if receipts are not cashed regularly. The arrangement also enables UKBA to end support promptly when an asylum-seeker receives a decision on the asylum claim.

Exclusions from support

Section 55

Overview

4.105 IAA 1999 was amended by the Nationality, Immigration and Asylum Act (NIAA) 2002 Part 3 which made radical changes to eligibility for asylum support. Section 55 of that Act excludes childless asylum-seekers from the right to claim asylum support unless they can show they claimed asylum 'as soon as reasonably practicable' or that the refusal of support is breaching their human rights. Thousands of asylum-seekers were left destitute as the interpretation of section 55 was fought over in the courts, culminating in the House of Lords decision in *Limbuela*. Since then, asylum-seekers without accommodation have generally been provided with support to avoid a breach of their ECHR article 3 rights, but UKBA continues to use section 55 to refuse support to the smaller number of applicants who apply for 'cash only' support whilst staying with friends or relatives. Note that the European Commission is proposing to remove article 16(3), the provision contained in the Reception Directive 2003/09/EC (see para 4.13) which allowed support to be withdrawn from those who failed to claim asylum as soon as reasonably possible, but the government has stated it will opt out of the revised directive.

4.106 NIAA 2002 s55(1) provides that the Home Secretary (UKBA) may not provide or arrange for the provision of support under IAA 1999 ss4, 95 or 98 unless they are satisfied that the asylum claim was made 'as soon as reasonably practicable after the person's arrival in the UK'. NIAA 2002 s55(5) provides that this does not prevent support being provided to an asylum-seeker with a dependent child. Section 55(5) also requires UKBA to provide support or exercise other powers 'to the extent necessary for the purpose of avoiding a breach of the person's [ECHR] rights'. So if an asylum-seeker is left with no food or accommodation after being refused support under NIAA 2002 s55(1), they will be entitled to support under section 55(5) if they can show support is necessary to avoid 'inhuman and degrading treatment' in breach of ECHR article 3.

4.107 Policy Bulletin 75, Version 7, 16 July 2007 sets out UKBA's current policy and procedures following the House of Lords decision in *Limbuela*. Their approach is that homeless asylum-seekers who apply for accommodation are granted support to avoid a breach of their ECHR article 3 rights under section 55(5), but those who apply for 'subsistence-only support' are assumed not to reach the threshold and are generally refused.

Tactics

If an asylum-seeker is staying with a friend or relative and is refused subsistence-only support, options include:

- they may be able to challenge the section 55(1) decision by judicial review if there are good reasons for the delay in claiming asylum, such as being held in captivity by a trafficker;
- they may be able to show that although they have accommodation, they need subsistence to avoid a breach of their ECHR rights, for example a medical condition or lack of washing facilities, or where there is evidence that the person they are staying with cannot feed them;
- if the person housing them asks them to leave, then the asylum-seeker can notify UKBA that there has been a change of circumstances and apply for accommodation and subsistence. Support will then be needed to avoid a breach of article 3 under section 55(5), but the accommodation offered will be in a dispersal area unless there are exceptional reasons to stay in a particular area (see para 15.40).

Section 55(1): the case law

4.108 In *R (Q and others) v Secretary of State for the Home Department*[118] the Court of Appeal considered what is 'as soon as reasonably

118 [2003] EWCA Civ 364, (2003) 6 CCLR 136.

practicable' and gave guidance as to what is a fair procedure for the Home Office to apply. In making decisions under NIAA 2002 s55(1), the Home Office must take into account the asylum-seeker's personal circumstances, including their state of mind on arrival. The Court of Appeal decided that the procedures operated by the Home Office in implementing section 55 were unfair and did not comply with ECHR article 6 but could be improved so as to be compatible with the Human Rights Act 1998. The judgment contains a useful summary of the correct approach both to NIAA 2002 s55(1) and (5) and to decision-making by public authorities. The court set out the section 55(1) approach as follows:

> The test whether an asylum-seeker claimed asylum 'as soon as reasonably practicable' under section 55(1) may be framed in this way: on the premise that the purpose of coming to this country was to claim asylum and having regard both to the practical opportunity for claiming asylum and to the asylum-seeker's personal circumstances, could the asylum-seeker reasonably have been expected to claim asylum earlier than he or she did?

4.109 In *R (S, D and T) v Secretary of State for the Home Department*[119] D, an Ethiopian man who had arrived by air and claimed asylum the next day was found to have met the 'as soon as reasonably practicable' requirement. Maurice Kay J noted a number of propositions about immigration procedures at airports and the general circumstances of asylum-seekers. The decision was not appealed on NIAA 2002 s55(1) and is useful for an asylum-seeker with a possible challenge to a section 55(1) decision. He recorded the following points:

- many refugees know little or nothing of asylum procedures, of airport procedures, airlines, etc;
- many asylum-seekers are illiterate and rely on oral information;
- most asylum-seekers using an agent depend completely on him;
- it is common for asylum-seekers not to know the details in their travel documents;
- it is common for immigration officers at airports not to ask questions or to ask the agent;
- it is common for a person to pass through immigration control with a forged EU passport;
- many asylum-seekers do not understand the concept of claiming asylum as soon as reasonably practicable;
- it is common and quite likely for asylum-seekers not to see posters in airports.

119 [2003] EWHC 1941, (2004) 7 CCLR 32.

4.110 The issues were later reviewed at a permission hearing which looked at the procedure for challenging NIAA 2002 s55 decisions. In *R (Q, D and others) v Secretary of State for the Home Department (Shelter intervener)*[120] Maurice Kay J made it clear that he did not consider that it was necessary for UKBA to require asylum-seekers to provide evidence in every case to support the generic issues that were covered in *S, D and T*.

Policy Bulletin *75* and the *72*-hour rule

4.111 The Home Office's current interpretation of the 'as soon as reasonably practicable' test, which allows an asylum-seeker a notional 72 hours after arrival to claim asylum, is explained in Policy Bulletin 75, Version 7. This states that 72 hours normally means three working days but the rule should be applied flexibly; for example, if an asylum-seeker arrives on the Friday night before a bank holiday and claims asylum on the following Tuesday this will normally be reasonable. If they claim on Wednesday or Thursday, the decision will depend on the reasons for that delay. The three-day time limit is a guideline that should not be strictly applied as a deadline. So the individual circumstances of an asylum-seeker when they arrived should be considered. Were they exhausted, traumatised, in need of medical treatment? It will be more difficult to challenge a decision under section 55(1) if the delay arises solely because the client has waited for an appointment with an immigration solicitor.

4.112 UKBA may apply section 55(1) to applicants who initially claimed promptly but whose asylum claim was refused and who later made a fresh asylum or ECHR article 3 claim based on new evidence such as a medical report or information from their country of origin. To challenge a refusal of support in these cases, the applicant will need to show that they acted promptly as soon as the evidence came to light, or had a good reason for not making the new claim earlier, for example serious health problems, but in practice since it is necessary to be destitute to qualify for section 4 support, such applicants will qualify due to section 55(5).

Section 55(5) and ECHR article 3: the case law

4.113 NIAA 2002 s55(5) enables the Home Secretary to provide support, despite a late claim, 'to the extent necessary to prevent a breach of the person's ECHR rights and to provide support where the applicant has a dependent child under 18. The type of 'treatment' that falls

120 [2003] EWHC 2507 (Admin).

within the scope of ECHR article 3 would include 'ill-treatment' that attains a minimum level of severity and involves actual bodily injury or intense physical or mental suffering. Where treatment humiliates or debases an individual showing lack of respect for, or diminishing, his or her human dignity or arouses feelings of fear, anguish or inferiority capable of breaking an individual's moral and physical resistance, it may be characterised as degrading and also fall within the prohibition of article 3. The suffering which flows from naturally occurring illness, physical or mental, may be covered by article 3, where it is, or risks being, exacerbated by treatment whether flowing from conditions of detention, expulsion or other measures for which the authorities can be held responsible.[121]

4.114 In *R (Q and others) v Secretary of State for the Home Department*[122] the Court of Appeal agreed that the refusal of support under NIAA 2002 s55 could amount to 'treatment' under ECHR article 3, but it was not enough that there was 'a real risk' that an asylum-seeker would be reduced to a state of degradation. To breach article 3, the asylum-seeker's condition must be 'verging on' that described above in the *Pretty* case.

4.115 In *R (S, D and T) v Secretary of State for the Home Department*[123] Maurice Kay J gave a detailed and considered judgment as to what circumstances would constitute a breach of ECHR article 3 in relation to NIAA 2002 s55(5). He found that there was little or no charitable support available so it is inevitable that most asylum-seekers refused section 55 support will be reduced to a state of destitution and 'within a short period of time the demands of article 3 require the relief of damage to human dignity which is caused by a life so destitute that . . . no civilised nation can tolerate it . . .'.[124] The Home Secretary did not produce evidence of the existence of charitable support to disprove this. Maurice Kay J's decision was eventually appealed only in relation to T, and not in relation to the claimants S and D.

4.116 In *R (T) v Secretary of State for the Home Department*[125] the Court of Appeal decided that T's rights under ECHR article 3 had not been breached and he did not meet the NIAA 2002 s55(5) threshold because he had shelter and cash for food and access to sanitary

121 *Pretty v United Kingdom* (2002) 35 EHRR 1.
122 [2003] EWCA Civ 364.
123 [2003] EWHC 1941 (Admin), (2004) 7 CCLR 32.
124 [2003] EWHC 1941 (Admin) at [33].
125 [2003] EWCA Civ 1285, (2004) 7 CCLR 53.

facilities, whilst living in Heathrow airport, and he was not so unwell as to need immediate treatment. The court found that the art 3 threshold fell somewhere between T and S. S, a Somali asylum-seeker who was found by Kay J to qualify for support under NIAA 2002 s55(5), had been sleeping rough and begging, had lost weight almost to the point of malnutrition, had a swelling on his neck and had a GP's report about psychological disturbance. The Court of Appeal stressed that a case did not have to reach the same level of severity as S's to reach the threshold.

Limbuela

4.117 in *R (Limbuela) v Secretary of State for the Home Department (Shelter intervener)*,[126] the House of Lords accepted evidence that there was not enough charitable support for the numbers of asylum-seekers refused support under section 55, so to refuse them support would interfere with their rights under article 3. They found that there would be a breach of article 3:

> when ... an individual faces an imminent prospect of serious suffering caused or materially aggravated by denial of shelter, food or the most basic necessities of life.

The court went on to say that if there were persuasive evidence that an asylum-seeker was being forced to sleep rough or was seriously hungry, or unable to satisfy the most basic requirements of hygiene, that would reach the article 3 threshold. The Home Office has interpreted the judgment as meaning that it must provide support unless the asylum-seeker has accommodation. But the judgment also requires the decision-maker to be satisfied that the asylum-seeker has some means of meeting their need for food and washing facilities.

Challenging NIAA 2002 s55 decisions: procedure

4.118 Policy Bulletin 75: Section 55 (Late Claims) 2002 Act Guidance gives an outline of UKBA's policy and practice. There was previously a team within UKBA dealing with section 55 screening procedures, which has been disbanded. Currently the NAM case-owner will carry out the section 55 screening, or regional UKBA staff for CRD applications (see para 4.3). UKBA currently only carries out a screening interview where a single adult is subject to NIAA 2002 s55(1), that is has not claimed asylum as soon as reasonably

126 [2005] UKHL 66, (2006) 9 CCLR 30.

practicable after arrival. Asylum-seekers should be provided with a copy of the screening notes after interview. UKBA will now issue a section 55 decision letter and/or a letter allowing access to initial accommodation based on information gathered at the initial (screening) interview.

4.119 If UKBA decides not to provide section 95 support because section 55 applies, a decision letter should be provided. To challenge the decision, a letter should be sent in response requesting a reconsideration of the section 55(1) and/or section 55(5) decision. Representations should address any errors in the section 55(1) decision if that is to be challenged. They should then explain how the client meets the ECHR article 3 threshold, for example problems getting access to food with details of the resources of the person accommodating them such as proof they are on benefits, a low income, in debt, medical evidence about ill-effects on the asylum-seeker such as weight loss, evidence of problems accessing toilet/washing facilities, etc. Policy Bulletin 75 indicates they should be provided with section 98 accommodation pending the section 55 interview or any reconsideration decision.

4.120 In *Limbuela* the limited availability of charitable support was accepted, but a section 55(5) case would be strengthened by evidence that local charities are not able to provide adequate nutritious food seven days a week, for example by witness statements or research.

Failure to provide information or co-operate with enquiries: NIAA 2002 s57

4.121 UKBA has the power to refuse to consider an application for section 95 or section 98 support if they are not satisfied that the information is complete or accurate or that the applicant is co-operating with enquiries. When NIAA 2002 s57 came into force, the Home Office amended the NASS 1 application form so that it includes questions about the applicant's route to the UK and method of entry.[127] Where UKBA makes enquiries about any matter connected with the application for support, the applicant has five days to reply. If they fail to do so without reasonable excuse, support may be ended.[128]

4.122 So if UKBA decides that an asylum-seeker is not giving a full account of their route here, they may refuse asylum support. Policy

127 AS Regs 2000 reg 3(4)–(5) as amended by Asylum Support (Amendment) (No 3) Regulations 2002 SI No 3110.

128 NIAA 2002 s57 and AS Regs 2000 reg 3(5) as amended by Asylum Support (Amendment) Regs 2005 SI No 11.

Bulletin 79 'Application for support: false or incomplete information 2002 Act guidance' gives more examples. NIAA 2002 s57 is normally applied at the stage where an asylum-seeker has submitted his or her NASS1 application form and UKBA believes the information is inaccurate or incomplete. As explained in Policy Bulletin 79, UKBA should then write to the applicant to give them a chance to explain or offer more information. If they fail to do this, support may be refused. Like section 55, there is no right of appeal against a refusal of support so the remedy would be judicial review. Unlike section 55, there is no exemption where refusing support would breach an asylum-seeker's human rights. This may mean that section 57 is incompatible with the Human Rights Act 1998 and the ECHR.

Section 9: families failing to leave the UK voluntarily

Overview

4.123 Section 9 of the Asylum and Immigration (Treatment of Claimants, etc) (AI(TC)A) Act 2004 is a highly controversial provision that remains on the statute book at the time of writing. In January 2005, the Home Office piloted the rules that withdraw support from a refused asylum-seeker with a dependent child. The scheme led to a public outcry from organisations such as the British Association of Social Workers and in a series of reports,[129] and it also failed to meet its objective of encouraging such families to leave the UK.

4.124 In June 2007, the Immigration Minister, Liam Byrne MP, announced[130] that it would be retained for use on a case-by-case basis by NAM case-owners:

> I have therefore decided that the section 9 provision should be available to case owners dealing with cases under our new end-to-end asylum process. While it will not be suitable on a blanket-basis, it is important that we retain an ability to withdraw support from families who are wilfully not co-operating in the process. Going forward it should be for case owners to take a view, based on an established relationship with the family and an intimate knowledge of the asylum claim which has not been successful, of which approach to

129 See 'The State of Children's Rights in England: Annual Review of UK Government action on 2002 Concluding Observations of the UN Committee on the Rights of the Child', Children's Rights Alliance for England, November 2005 (www.crae.org.uk); Cunningham and Tomlinson, *'Starve them out': does every child really matter? A commentary on section 9 of the Asylum and Immigration (Treatment of Claimants, etc) Act 2004*, Critical Social Policy Ltd, 2005.

130 *Hansard* HC, Written Answers col 10, 25 June 2007.

> encouraging departure is most likely to be effective. Case-specific close working with appropriate officials from the local authority will normally be required if the use of the section 9 provision is being considered.

4.125 Section 9 amended NIAA 2002 s54 Sch 3, para 7(A) to provide there is no power to provide asylum support (or social services assistance under CA 1989 s17) if the applicant is a refused asylum-seeker with a dependent child who is refusing to leave the UK and has been certified under specified procedures. However, the Home Office must still provide support if it is necessary to avoid a breach of ECHR rights or to enable the applicant to exercise their EU Treaty rights (see paras 7.25 and 7.114). Although social services authorities have duties under CA 1989 this is only if assistance is needed to avoid a breach of the family's rights under the ECHR, eg under article 3.

4.126 After the introduction of section 9 on a pilot basis, a number of families had their asylum support withdrawn. The first tribunal decision[131] on the interpretation of section 9 involved a failed Iranian asylum-seeker. Both he and his wife suffered from lower back pain and depression. They had children aged six and seven months; the baby was born with a congenital abnormality of the intestines which might require further treatment. Dismissing the appeal, the Chief Asylum Support Adjudicator rejected the argument that withdrawal of support would interfere with ECHR articles 3 and 8 because she considered that if the appellant took reasonable steps to leave the UK the support would be reinstated. She also made the assumption that:

> one of the likely consequences of a decision [to withdraw support] is that the two children may be accommodated by the Local Authority under section 20 of the Children Act or taken into care under section 31. A family in this position is not eligible for Local Authority support under section 17 of the Children Act . . .

Since the asylum process had been exhausted, she considered that the withdrawal of support was both proportionate and legitimate.

4.127 This approach was followed in subsequent appeals.[132] An application for judicial review challenging that decision and the s9 policy in general was refused permission.[133]

131 ASA 05/03/9119.

132 ASA 05/08/9824 and ASA 06/09/05. January 2006 *Legal Action* 14.

133 *R (K) v Asylum Support Adjudicators and Secretary of State for the Home Department* CO/7074/05, 13 June 2006.

Asylum decisions and end of support entitlement

4.128 An asylum-seeker is only entitled to support for as long as they come within the definition of asylum-seeker in IAA 1999 s94(1) explained at the start of this chapter. Entitlement to support ends if the asylum-seeker withdraws the asylum claim or if the claim is refused and there is no outstanding appeal. Entitlement also ends if leave to remain is granted, at the end of a prescribed period of 28 days.

4.129 Where an asylum-seeker is refused asylum, they remain 'an asylum-seeker' eligible for IAA 1999 s95 asylum support as long as the household includes a dependent child under 18 (see para 4.37 above). If there is no dependent child, community care provision or IAA 1999 s4 support may be available as a last resort (see para 4.137).

Effect of withdrawal of support

4.130 There is no prescribed notice period for withdrawal of UKBA support except that entitlement continues for the 21/28-day grace period explained above at para 4.34. Any notice to quit may be limited to seven days.[134]

New applications after withdrawal of support

4.131 Where an award of asylum support has been suspended or discontinued under AS Regs 2000 reg 21, UKBA may refuse to accept another application unless:

- there has been a material change of circumstances of the kind that the asylum-seeker would have to report if they were receiving support, for example arrival of a new household member or a reduction in income/capital to below the eligibility thresholds (see para 15.123); or
- UKBA considers there are exceptional circumstances.

Notices to quit and security of tenure

4.132 Where a supported person is living in accommodation provided by UKBA, there are special rules about notices to quit and eviction. These are described in more detail in para 8.184.

134 AS Regs 2000 reg 22.

Options where applicant is ineligible for section 95 asylum support

A reasonable notice period/fair decision

4.133 On 30 April 2004, NASS wrote to refused eastern European asylum-seekers with children ending their section 95 support in anticipation of their becoming EU nationals on 1 May and so excluded from entitlement.[135] Two of the asylum-seekers, who were settled in the UK with school-age children, argued that the lack of notice was procedurally unfair because they had less than four weeks' notice. They also argued that the potential breach of their ECHR article 8 right to respect for family life was discriminatory under article 14. After the High Court granted permission to apply for judicial review[136] NASS agreed to carry out assessments of all those affected by the decision. Similar arguments about procedural fairness may be useful in other cases where support is withdrawn without proper notice.

Unaccompanied and former unaccompanied children[137]

4.134 An asylum-seeker child under 18 who came to the UK without a parent is not eligible for asylum support because they are not classed as 'an asylum-seeker' for support purposes.[138] They should apply for social services help under CA 1989 s20. If the Home Office disputes the child's given age, an age assessment should be carried out by the local authority.[139]

4.135 When the child reaches 18, whether or not they are still an asylum-seeker, they may be entitled to continue receiving Children Act 1989 support until the age of 21. If he or she has an outstanding asylum claim or appeal, he or she could apply for section 95 support, but may be subject to NIAA 2002 s55 (see para 4.105). Policy Bulletin 29 'Transition at Age 18', the Children Leaving Care Act 2000 Regulations and Guidance paras 7–11 explain how UKBA deals with applications. It should not disperse an asylum-seeker who has been supported under CA 1989 s20 but take over financial responsibility for support. They would be excluded from CA 1989 help if there are pending removal directions, or if they are unlawfully in the UK and

135 NIAA 2002 s54 and Sch 3.

136 *R (H and D) v Secretary of State for the Home Department*, CO/2106/04 and CO/2096/04 (unreported) and January 2005 *Legal Action* 13.

137 See further chapter 9.

138 IAA 1999 s94(1).

139 CA 1989 s17 and Sch 2 Part 1 para 4.

have not made a fresh asylum or human rights claim (see NIAA 2002 Sch 3 and para 9.91, below). An 18-year-old former asylum-seeker is entitled to claim mainstream benefits and housing if leave to remain in the UK has been granted.

Households with children

4.136 An asylum-seeker with a dependent child is excluded from the right to accommodation or subsistence under CA 1989 s17 help if the household is entitled to section 95 asylum support.[140] This is explained below at para 9.7 onwards. Where a person is 'subject to immigration control' and the household contains a child under 18 years old, the family may be eligible for CA 1989 s17 help, provided it is needed to avoid a breach of their ECHR rights (see para 9.70).

Able-bodied adults

4.137 A refused childless asylum-seeker with no outstanding asylum claim or appeal may be entitled to support under the IAA 1999 s4 scheme (see chapter 6). Section 4 will also apply if they have a child born after the asylum claim or appeal was finally determined.[141]

Adults with mental health needs

4.138 Anyone who has been detained in hospital as a mental patient to receive treatment under sections 3, 47 or 48 of the Mental Health Act 1983 is eligible for 'aftercare' when they leave, regardless of their immigration status. This can include housing and support, whatever his or her immigration status and for an unlimited period (Mental Health Act 1983 s117).[142]

Adults with community care needs[143]

4.139 Where a destitute asylum-seeker would be eligible for UKBA support but has a care need, they may ask a local authority to provide a community care assessment[144] and an assessment of their entitlement to accommodation under NAA 1948 s21. An asylum-seeker who is in need of care and attention, not otherwise available to

140 IAA 1999 s122.

141 See para 14.33 for meaning of 'finally determined'.

142 See further para 9.123.

143 See para 9.13.

144 NHS and Community Care Act 1990 s47.

them, due to old age, mental illness, ill health, disability or other special reason may be entitled to NAA 1948 s21 accommodation.[145] The local authority may not refuse to help on the basis that section 95 asylum support would be available. If the adult has other dependants, UKBA should finance their proportion of the accommodation and support.[146]

Comparison of IAA 1999 s95 Home Office Support v NAA 1948 s21 social services support

Support under IAA 1999 s95	**Accommodation under NAA 1948 s21**
Accommodation is normally in a dispersal area.	Accommodation is normally in or near the area of the local authority applied to, enabling the applicant to maintain ties with the community/ relatives there.
Support may be subsistence only or subsistence and accommodation, enabling applicant to live with friends or relatives and claim cash support.	Section 21 support may only be provided as accommodation with subsistence. Subsistence-only support is not normally available.
Subsistence is provided in the form of cash, normally collected from a local post office with a card, allowing greater autonomy.	Subsistence may be in the form of vouchers or full board provision and is normally collected from the local authority's offices.
The support package is limited to subsistence and adequate accommodation. Extra help, if needed would have to be sought from other sources.	The support package can include a carer to provide personal care or domestic care if needed.
For a childless adult, support ends 21/28 days after the asylum claim is finally determined depending on whether the decision is negative or positive. For an applicant with a child under 18, support normally continues after a final negative decision as long as they are in the UK.	If the applicant made their asylum claim 'on arrival' at the port of entry, they remain entitled to section 21 accommodation for as long as it is needed, unless removal directions are issued. If they claimed in country, it will end after the refusal of asylum or final appeal, unless the applicant needs support to avoid a breach of their ECHR rights, for example they have made a fresh claim or cannot travel home due to pregnancy.

145 *Westminster CC v NASS* [2002] UKHL 38; (2002) 5 CCLR 511.

146 See chapter 5.

CHAPTER 5

Asylum support: service provision

continued

Introduction

5.1 This chapter outlines the entitlements of asylum-seekers who are eligible for asylum support under the Immigration and Asylum Act (IAA) 1999 Part VI, s95 and s98, including accommodation and cash payments. Remedies for inadequate service provision are discussed towards the end of the chapter, but specific challenges relating to each topic are referred to throughout the text. Finally, the responsibilities of the asylum-seeker or dependant while they are supported, and the powers of the Home Office if those responsibilities are not met, are outlined.

5.2 The government has consistently stressed that the asylum support scheme offers basic provision, aimed at meeting asylum-seekers' essential needs only. It is slightly more generous than the cashless support provided to 'failed' asylum-seekers under IAA 1999 s4, described in chapter 6. At the time of writing, UKBA was considering whether the differences between the two schemes should be reduced. Substantial evidence about inadequate service provision in both schemes, such as poor quality accommodation, was received by the Parliamentary Joint Committee on Human Rights Inquiry into the Treatment of Asylum-seekers.[1]

5.3 This chapter should be read in conjunction with chapter 4 which explains who is eligible for section 95 and section 98 support. Chapter 7 deals with appeals against refusal or withdrawal of support, but it includes more information about other remedies, such as judicial review and complaints procedures, which are relevant to service provision.

> We refer here to the UK Border Agency (UKBA) as the body currently administering asylum support provision on behalf of the Home Office, but the National Asylum Support Service (NASS) is referred to where it applies for historic reasons (see para 4.3 'rebranding'). For the Asylum Support Tribunal, now the First-tier Tribunal (Asylum Support), the acronym we use is AST.

5.4 Since the last edition of this book, the (relatively few) changes to service provision include:

1 The treatment of asylum-seekers, tenth report of session 2006–07, HL81-I/HC60-I, March 2007.

- accommodation centre proposals have not gone ahead;[2]
- the six-monthly payment of £50 to asylum-seekers has been withdrawn;
- additional criminal offences have been introduced.

Legal framework

5.5 The framework for the kind of support that may be provided to destitute asylum-seekers who meet the eligibility rules is contained in IAA 1999 Part VI. The Asylum Support Regulations (AS Regs) 2000[3] contain more detailed rules about support. Guidance and instructions are published on the Home Office/UKBA website,[4] currently in the 'Policy and Law' section that has policy bulletins and other internal guidance about how the UKBA interprets and implements the law. Some policies such as guidance on compensation are unpublished but can be obtained by a Freedom of Information Act 2000 s1 request to UKBA.[5]

Key features

5.6 The key features of asylum support provision are:

- The three main forms of support under IAA 1999 are s98 temporary support (initial accommodation), s95 or 'NASS' support and s4 support.
- An adult asylum-seeker with care needs may be receiving social services support under s21 National Assistance Act (NAA) 1948, but housing and support for any dependant(s) is financed by the Home Office under s95 IAA 1999.
- Unaccompanied asylum-seekers under 18 are supported under s20 Children Act 1989 (CA 1989) by a social services authority (see chapter 9).

2 NIAA 2002 Part 2 introduced a scheme of accommodation centres. In June 2005 the Immigration Minister announced there were no plans to build any centres in the next five years (*Hansard* HC col 653 W 9 June 2005). Although Part 2 has not been brought into law with a commencement order, it has not been repealed, so in theory the proposals could be revived. We have not included details of the scheme here as this seems unlikely.

3 SI No 704.

4 www.ukba.homeoffice.gov.uk

5 See para 7.168.

- When an asylum-seeker applies for support, and has no alternative accommodation, they may be accommodated in initial hostel-style accommodation under IAA 1999 s98 while the application for section 95 support is considered.
- Section 95 support may be 'essential living needs and/or adequate accommodation' under IAA 1999 s96(1). So an asylum-seeker may apply to UKBA for 'cash-only' support if they have accommodation with friends or relatives.
- Section 95 support is the only support provided in the form of cash, at rates fixed by the AS Regs 2000 as amended. It is paid by a local post office on production of the asylum-seeker's application registration card (ARC).
- The section 95 power to provide support must be met by having regard to 'the desirability, in general, of providing accommodation in areas in which there is a ready supply of accommodation'. So most asylum-seekers are dispersed to areas outside London and the south-east.
- Although the Home Secretary, acting by the UKBA, makes decisions on entitlement, which is responsible for ensuring that provision is then made, it does not own or directly manage accommodation. UKBA makes arrangements for accommodation and/or living expenses through contracts with public, private and/or voluntary sector suppliers. Local authorities may provide section 4, 98 or 95 accommodation.[6] There is no security of tenure (see paras 5.20 and 5.184).
- The whole household's income and assets are taken into account in assessing the level of support. An asylum-seeker with other resources, for example working part-time, may receive a lower rate of support or may be asked to contribute to their support.
- The remedy for poor service provision is usually an application for judicial review, not an appeal to the First-tier Tribunal (Asylum Support) (AST). The AST may only hear appeals at present where section 4, 95 or 98 support has been refused or withdrawn (see chapter 7).

Forms of support

5.7 The first step in dealing with any problem about support provision is to identify which form of support is being provided because the quality of provision will depend on this. It is also advisable to check

6 Immigration and Nationality Act 2006 s43.

the client's immigration status to ensure they are receiving the correct form of support and to ensure that action about service provision will not lead to a termination of support (see para 4.22). The level of subsistence or type of housing to which an asylum-seeker is entitled depends on whether they are receiving IAA 1999 ss4, 98 or 95 support, or whether they are being accommodated by social services under NAA 1948 s21.

Section 98 initial support

5.8 The Home Secretary may arrange to provide support under IAA 1999 s98, which is referred to as 'initial accommodation', to destitute asylum-seekers and their dependants under IAA 1999 only until a decision is reached on eligibility for support section 95. It may also be provided where a supported asylum-seeker has left their accommodation in an emergency, such as due to racial harassment, pending an investigation[7] or as interim accommodation for section 4 support – as per UKBA's July 2009 pilot.

5.9 There is little case-law interpreting section 98. The remedy for a refusal to provide section 98 support is judicial review. The schedule to the AS Regs 2000 provides that initial accommodation may be provided for up to three months in a case where an applicant has assets such as property abroad, but needs time to realise them.

5.10 Section 98 initial accommodation is usually in a hotel or hostel, arranged by a voluntary sector agent (see para 5.13). This may be referred to by the Home Office as an induction centre even if it is more than one building. An asylum-seeker may be required to live at or near an induction centre for up to 14 days after they claim asylum.[8]

5.11 The induction process should include briefing asylum-seekers on the immigration and support processes, health screening and referral of asylum-seekers with special needs to a local authority for a community care assessment. The immigration rules have been amended to comply with the Reception Directive article 6.[9] So an asylum-seeker has the right to receive information within 15 days of making an asylum claim about the 'benefits and services' that they may be eligible to receive and about the rules and procedure with

7 See Policy Bulletin 73.

8 NIAA 2002 s70.

9 See below and see para 4.14.

which they must comply. An asylum-seeker is also entitled to a document confirming his or her asylum application, within three days of them making the application.[10]

Access to initial accommodation

5.12 Policy Bulletin 73 describes the procedures for admittance and readmittance to initial (section 98) accommodation. Any asylum-seeker wishing to access initial accommodation is subject to 'section 55' NIAA 2002 procedures.[11] This means that an asylum-seeker who has made an 'in-country' asylum or European Convention on Human Rights (ECHR) article 3 claim must go to at a Asylum Screening Unit (ASU) or 'designated place'[12] to obtain the necessary documentation in order to access initial accommodation. An asylum-seeker with a dependent child under 18 or pregnant woman in the household will need to provide evidence either that they applied for asylum at the port or a letter from UKBA to confirm that they are exempt from section 55. A childless adult asylum-seeker must provide evidence that they claimed at the port of arrival or a 'decision letter' to show that UKBA has agreed to allow access to emergency accommodation, or they will need an injunction ordering the Home Secretary to provide support until a judicial review application is considered. Overnight accommodation may be provided to vulnerable applicants before the section 55 screening interview.

5.13 The Home Office funds voluntary organisations, known collectively as the Asylum Support Partnership (ASP), to carry out some of its functions as agent for UKBA. The Asylum Support Partnership provides 'reception assistance', which involves wrap-around advice services for those in initial accommodation including assisting clients to apply for section 95 support by completing the NASS 1 application form. A list of the organisations is provided in appendix E.

Problems and delays in accessing initial accommodation

5.14 A childless destitute asylum-seeker who has claimed asylum in-country must satisfy the 'section 55' test to access emergency accommodation under IAA 1999 s98 unless they applied for asylum at the port. The exceptions are if there is a visibly pregnant woman

10 Statement of Changes in Immigration Rules HC 194, 11 January 2005, HC 395, Part 11B paras 357–361.

11 See para 4.105.

12 NIAA 2002 s18 and see para 4.24.

in the household or someone with a special need.[13] Where there is a delay in accessing initial accommodation, the section 55 case-law may help.

5.15 In *R (Q, D and others) v Secretary of State for the Home Department*,[14] Maurice Kay J decided UKBA had the power to provide initial accommodation under section 55(5)(a) and issued this guidance as to the procedure to follow in section 55 cases.

- The Home Secretary must establish an adequate and efficient decision-making procedure, applying the law as set down in *Q* and *T*, doing so within a timescale which meets urgent needs.
- The aim should be for the Home Office to provide resources to produce decisions on further representations within the timescale previously set by the Home Secretary (on the same day if representations are received before 2pm, otherwise by the next day).

5.16 Section 98 accommodation is basic, hostel-style, and unsuitable as medium-term accommodation, particularly for families. Delays in processing section 95 support applications may mean a household remains in section 98 accommodation for weeks or even months. These delays can be challenged by a letter warning of judicial review and, if necessary, an application for judicial review and an injunction.

Problems with initial accommodation

5.17 There is no definition of the form or quality of section 98 accommodation in IAA 1999; the explanatory notes to the Act suggest it 'may take any form'. Unlike section 95 accommodation which must be 'adequate',[15] there is no mention of adequacy in relation to section 98. If initial accommodation is of very poor quality, unsuitable or if insufficient food or subsistence is provided, the following could be considered:[16]

(a) a complaint to the accommodation provider or organisation managing the accommodation, followed by a complaint to UKBA;[17]

(b) a request for an inspection by the local council's environmental health officer. As with accommodation provided under the

13 Policy Bulletin 73.

14 [2003] EWHC 2507 (Admin).

15 IAA 1999 s96.

16 These suggestions apply equally to accommodation under IAA 1999 s4.

17 See further para 7.170.

section 95 duty, there are no specific requirements for adequate standards in initial accommodation, but ordinary environmental health law provisions apply, in particular a property in multiple occupation should be registered.[18] A complaint to the local authority's environmental health officer if the accommodation is 'prejudicial to health' or 'hazardous' may compel repairs by the landlord, particularly if backed by the threat of enforcement action;[19]

(c) if the accommodation is extremely unsuitable for the household and/or the above approaches fail, a judicial review of the Home Office's decision to accommodate in that accommodation, or of its delay in processing a section 95 claim to transfer the household to more adequate accommodation could be considered. In some circumstances, it may be possible to bring a judicial review of the decision to provide inadequate temporary support based on ECHR articles 3 or 8, or sex/disability discrimination arguments;[20]

(d) any complaint or judicial review should consider whether there is an adverse impact on the asylum-seeker's child eg of sharing accommodation with adult males – the Home Office must take into account its own code of practice in relation to children.[21]

(e) the Reception Directive 2003/09/EC lays down minimum standards for the reception across Europe and is binding on the UK. It should be taken into account in decision-making.[22] Key provisions relevant to accommodation include:
- the reception of groups with special needs should be specifically designed to meet those needs (preamble);
- family unity should be maintained (article 8);
- a standard of living adequate for asylum-seekers' health should be provided taking account of any special needs and including asylum-seekers in detention (article 13);
- where there has been an evaluation of a vulnerable asylum-seeker, this should be taken into account (article 17 and see para 5.43 below).

5.18 The Directive only applies to those who claimed asylum or made a fresh asylum claim on or after 6 February 2005 but the government

18 See para 8.197 onwards.

19 See para 8.205 onwards.

20 See para 7.111.

21 See para 7.109 below.

22 See further para 7.105.

has implemented parts of the Directive[23] so that the new provisions apply to all section 98/95 supported persons including those with an ECHR article 3 claim, in particular the family unity principle, and the duty to take into account special needs.

Delays in initial accommodation

5.19 When the IAA 1999 was passed, the Home Secretary indicated that initial accommodation would be for a couple of days while the NASS section 95 application was processed. At the time of writing, delays in processing section 95 applications were reported as long as several weeks. During this period, the asylum-seeker has no cash for basic needs such as travel and communications and a delayed ability to register with a doctor, or for children to attend school. It may be possible to speed up a decision by writing to the UKBA threatening judicial review. Delays may particularly prejudice pregnant women who need consistent ante-natal care during their pregnancy (see para 7.84).

Eviction from initial accommodation

5.20 There is no formal notice period for an asylum-seeker who has been asked to leave section 98 accommodation. UKBA guidance suggests it should be terminated as soon as is reasonable, normally after one day, or seven days at most.[24] If the reason for the termination is a positive or negative final asylum decision, the period is 28 days or 21 days respectively. If the reason for termination is that an asylum-seeker has failed to travel to a dispersal area, the period is two days, or five days if there is a child under 18 in the household.

5.21 If section 95 support has been refused, and an applicant has appealed to the AST there is no legal right to support pending the appeal (although UKBA may permit the appellant to remain in section 98 accommodation in practice). It may be possible to obtain 'interim relief' by judicial review, for example in a dispersal case where there is both a High Court challenge about the adequacy of the accommodation and an appeal about the decision to withdraw support. Social services provision could be considered if the appellant has community care needs or a dependent child.[25] In exceptional circumstances, asylum-seekers will be allowed access

23 Asylum Seekers (Reception Conditions) Regulations 2005.

24 Policy Bulletin 73: Provision of Initial Accommodation para 4.

25 See chapter 9.

to initial accommodation after their section 95 support has been withdrawn, for example where they have left accommodation due to domestic violence, racial or other forms of harassment and their complaints are being investigated.[26]

5.22 If an asylum-seeker is present in the accommodation at the time of eviction, refusing to leave, it is an offence under the Criminal Law Act 1977 s6 to use or threaten violence to secure entry to the initial accommodation if the occupier is present and is opposed to the entry. Therefore, an offence could be committed, for example if the accommodation-provider had to break into premises to physically remove an asylum-seeker against their will, without a court order.[27]

5.23 In a recent line of housing cases it has been argued that for a public body to compel a person to leave their home without a court hearing about the issues may interfere with their rights under ECHR article 8. This argument could be considered in asylum support cases.[28]

Section 95 support

5.24 UKBA should arrange for the applicant to be offered section 95 support once it has decided they are eligible. IAA 1999 s96 limits the 'ways in which support may be provided' to:

- accommodation adequate for the household's needs;
- essential living needs;
- expenses connected to the asylum claim;
- expenses of attending bail hearings;
- other forms of support if there are exceptional circumstances.

5.25 Before deciding what form of support to provide or to continue to provide, UKBA must take certain matters into account and ignore others.[29] The applicant's resources must be taken into account in deciding the kind and level of support.[30] The supported person's compliance with any conditions subject to which support is provided may be taken into account.[31] Because this is discretionary, ECHR issues would be relevant.[32]

26 See Policy Bulletins 70, 73 and 81.
27 See further para 8.193.
28 See further para 8.183.
29 IAA 1999 s97(1), (2) and (4).
30 AS Regs 2000 reg 12.
31 AS Regs 2000 reg 19(1)(b).
32 See para 7.111.

'Adequate' accommodation under section 95

5.26 Accommodation will be offered on a no-choice basis just as it may be in respect of UK residents who present themselves as homeless, usually where accommodation is more readily available outside London and the south-east. That does not mean that asylum-seekers will be placed in isolated or derelict accommodation.[33]

Overview

5.27 Where UKBA decides that an asylum-seeker is destitute, it may provide accommodation that appears 'to be adequate for the needs of the supported person and his dependants (if any)'.[34] Section 97 then sets out the factors that must and may not be taken into account in providing housing. The supported person's 'preference' as to the type and location of their accommodation must not be taken into account, but their 'individual circumstances' must be taken into account:[35]

> The legislation does not allow us to take asylum-seekers' preferences as to location of accommodation into consideration. But if there is a particular reason ... why an individual, or one of his dependants needs to be placed in a certain area, for example for ease of access to a specialised hospital to meet specific health needs, that will be taken into consideration by the directorate before reaching a decision.
>
> ... We shall have regard to any special needs, not least the safety, welfare and protection of children ....

5.28 The above approach is reflected in Policy Bulletin 31: Dispersal Guidelines. It has further been strengthened by the Reception Directive, as interpreted by Policy Bulletin 83: Duty to offer support, family unity, vulnerable persons, withdrawing support.

5.29 Accommodation may be provided on a self-contained, bed and breakfast, full or half-board basis, in a hostel, flat or house without regard to the asylum-seeker's 'preference'. In practice, since individual circumstances, such as the asylum-seeker's health needs, are relevant, the question of 'preference' has limited relevance. Policy Bulletin 31 suggests that UKBA must take into account

33 Ministerial statement, second reading IAA 1999, HC Debates col 45, 22 February 1999.

34 IAA 1999 s96(1)(a).

35 Lord Williams of Mostyn, *Hansard*, HL Debates col 1163, 20 October 1999.

circumstances such as the location of other family members, education, medical and other social welfare needs when reaching a decision about where to accommodate a supported household. Detailed questions about the household's needs are asked in the NASS 1 application form.

5.30 As with section 4 and section 98 accommodation, the local authority has a duty to ensure that environmental housing standards are met so if the property is in a state of disrepair or prejudicial to health, a request for an inspection by a local environmental health officer should be made.[36]

The standard of section 95 accommodation – adequate or suitable?

> We consider that in some cases the quality and terms of accommodation provision under section 95 of the 1999 Act interferes with the rights of asylum seekers and their children to respect for family and home life under Article 8 ECHR, and the right to adequate housing under Article 11 ICESCR (The International Convention on Economic, Social and Cultural Rights).[37]

5.31 There is limited guidance on the standard of accommodation that should be provided to supported persons. Both the IAA 1999 and the AS Regs 2000 use the word 'adequate' rather than 'suitable', reflecting the 'no-choice' policy. However, ministers have repeatedly suggested that the 'no-choice' approach to the housing of asylum-seekers is the same as the 'one offer' approach to the housing of homeless families. The Home Office gave this ministerial reply to a parliamentary question:

> The accommodation provider will have a contract with the National Asylum Support Service. They will ensure that the accommodation is 'suitable' in that it will be of an adequate standard; the relevant standard. The relevant standards are the same applied by local authorities when rehousing any homeless residents.[38]

5.32 This suggests that offers of inadequate accommodation to asylum-seekers may be challenged by judicial review using grounds similar to those used to challenge offers of unsuitable accommodation to homeless persons, but there is limited guidance or case-law to support this approach.

36 See para 8.205.

37 Tenth Report Session 2006–7, The Treatment of Asylum Seekers (HL Paper 81, HC 60) JCHR para 103.

38 HC Written Answers vol 348, col 593, 20 April 2000.

5.33 The Court of Appeal has found there is no material difference between the meaning of 'adequate' accommodation for asylum-seekers under IAA 1999 and 'suitable' accommodation in the context of the National Assistance Act (NAA) 1948 s21 or in the homelessness provisions.[39] The court found there was no justification for providing a different standard of provision for disabled children as compared with disabled adults under NAA 1948 s21. To do so could be discriminatory under ECHR article 14, read with article 8. It explained that any difference in the test of adequacy lies in the context, and the context of asylum support is that the accommodation is intended to be temporary accommodation to prevent destitution. The court found that article 8 was engaged due to the effect of the housing conditions on the physical and psychological integrity of the family, but the breach was justified by the financial cost and effect on other families (on the council waiting list) if Mrs A's family was suitably housed.

Section 95 accommodation – irrelevant factors

5.34 In exercising its power to provide accommodation, UKBA may not have regard to 'any preference that the supported person or his dependants (if any) may have as to the locality in which the accommodation is to be provided'.[40]

5.35 Section 97 provides for regulations to prescribe factors which must or may not be taken into account. The AS Regs 2000 reg 13(2) excludes from consideration any preference as to the 'nature of accommodation' to be provided and as to 'the nature and standard of fixtures and fittings', but the regulation continues:

> ... this shall not be taken to prevent the person's individual circumstances as they relate to accommodation needs being taken into account.

5.36 The government has drawn a distinction between preference and individual circumstances stating:[41]

> ... it is not required to have regard to preferences but we can have regard to circumstances. So we can look at the background circumstances of a group of asylum-seekers to disperse all those with a common ethnic, linguistic or territorial origin to a place common to all of them. That is looking at the circumstances and not preferences.

39 *R (A) v (1) NASS and (2) Waltham Forest LBC* [2003] EWCA Civ 1473.

40 IAA 1999 s97(2).

41 HL Debates cols 1200–01, 20 October 1999.

5.37 This approach is reflected in Policy Bulletin 31: Dispersal Guidelines and clearly requires UKBA to take into account the location of other family members, education, medical and other social welfare needs when deciding on accommodation provision. However, provided UKBA can show the considerations have been taken into account, its decisions will be difficult to challenge (see dispersal decisions below).

Section 95 accommodation – relevant factors

When exercising his power under section 95 to provide accommodation, the Secretary of State must have regard under section 97(1) to:

- the fact that the accommodation is to be temporary pending determination of the asylum-seeker's claim;
- the desirability, in general, of providing accommodation in areas where there is a ready supply of accommodation; and
- such other matters as may be prescribed.

5.38 To date, no matters have been prescribed. Although the Home Office has dramatically speeded up asylum decision-making and cleared much of its backlog, many asylum-seekers are in UKBA accommodation for years rather than months and the notion that section 95 accommodation is 'temporary' remains a policy aspiration. During the passage of the IAA 1999, the Home Secretary gave a 'two plus four' assurance, indicating that asylum decisions would be made within two months of the claim, and appeals processed within four months. There has since been a reduction in the numbers of new asylum applications, more of which are processed in two months. There remains a backlog in relation to appeals. The latest statistics are published at www.homeoffice.gov.uk/rds/immigration-asylum-stats.html.

5.39 When challenging the adequacy of support under section 97(1)(a) evidence of any specific needs in their own case and general evidence to demonstrate that the provision is not temporary (assuming the delays are not resolved) may be relevant factors for UKBA to take into consideration.

Dispersal challenges/refusing an offer of accommodation

5.40 Challenges to dispersal are explained in detail in chapter 7. In cases where an asylum-seeker has refused an initial offer of accommodation, considering it inadequate, support can be refused[42] or withdrawn[43] on the ground of breach of conditions. The asylum-seeker has the right to appeal, submitting evidence that the accommodation is inadequate, or of other reasons for refusal but will need to show these amount to a 'reasonable excuse' for refusal in order to succeed and be offered further accommodation. Any new offer may also be in a dispersal area. If the asylum-seeker has a child, an offer of accommodation will be left open in the dispersal area. UKBA may refuse to entertain a new application for support unless there is a change of circumstances.[44] Some asylum-seekers have successfully argued that their new decision to accept accommodation in a dispersal area is a change of circumstances, but this would be easier to argue if there has been a gap where the household stayed with friends for example.

5.41 The target section 95 accommodation contract published on the UKBA website provides that if a 'service user' refuses accommodation, the accommodation provider should arrange temporary dispersal accommodation for one day until UKBA can adjudicate as to the suitability of the accommodation.

A note of caution

The threshold for 'adequate' accommodation is a low one. UKBA's general practice is to disperse unless a member of the household is a torture survivor receiving regular treatment from a specialist agency, or there are serious medical needs which can only be met in a particular place. It is very difficult for an asylum-seeker successfully to challenge their one offer of section 95 accommodation. If they refuse to be dispersed, their initial accommodation will be withdrawn and they may be left homeless/without any support.

5.42 The approach to deciding where and how to accommodate is contained in Policy Bulletin 31: Dispersal Guidelines.[45] There are other policy bulletins dealing with particular needs which are also

42 AS Regs 2000 reg 19.
43 AS Regs 2000 reg 20.
44 See para 7.157 and Policy Bulletin 84.
45 See para 7.74 onwards for the factors listed in Policy Bulletin 31 and their interpretation.

relevant, in particular Bulletin 85: Dispersing asylum-seekers with health care needs, and Bulletin 83 relating to family unity and vulnerable asylum-seekers. In order for UKBA to have lawfully reached a decision that accommodation in a dispersal area is adequate, it should have properly considered this guidance. We set out here some of the more persuasive reasons for arguing that accommodation is not adequate.

'Special needs'/pregnancy

5.43 The Asylum-seekers (Reception Conditions) Regulations 2005[46] transposing the Reception Directive[47] provide that a *vulnerable person* supported under section 98 or section 95 IAA 1999 should have their special needs taken into account but only if there is an *individual evaluation* of their needs. There is no statutory definition of individual evaluation but Policy Bulletin 83 suggests it could include a social services assessment, or a Medical Foundation report. Vulnerable person is widely defined as including a child, a disabled person, an elderly person, a pregnant woman, a lone parent, or 'a person who has been subjected to torture, rape or other serious forms of psychological, physical or sexual violence', which covers a large number of asylum-seekers.

5.44 It is UKBA policy not to disperse a woman in the late stages of pregnancy or if the journey is over four hours or she is at risk of miscarriage.[48] There may be scope for arguing that a woman in an earlier stage of pregnancy should not be dispersed based on her particular needs (eg if there is evidence of complications), or based on the generic evidence referred to at para 7.85.

Racial or other harassment/domestic violence

5.45 The UKBA's approach to harassment is contained in Policy Bulletin 81, on Racist Incidents, confirming the definition of a racist incident as 'any incident which is perceived to be racist by the victim or any other person'.[49]

46 SI No 7.

47 See para 4.13.

48 See Bulletin 31.

49 See further Home Office Code of Practice on reporting and recording racist incidents at www.homeoffice.gov.uk/police/about/race-relations or www.homeoffice.gov.uk/documents/coderi.pdf

5.46 Policy Bulletin 70 covers domestic violence and Policy Bulletin 73 covers readmittance to initial accommodation for households fleeing violence and harassment. Tactics for dealing with cases where asylum-seekers have experienced racial harassment are explored at para 7.47 onwards.

5.47 In *R (Gezer) v Secretary of State for the Home Department*,[50] NASS had housed a Turkish Kurdish asylum-seeker who was a torture survivor in an area in Glasgow where another Kurdish asylum-seeker had been murdered a month earlier. He was placed in initial accommodation by the police after experiencing serious racial harassment, including his 13-year-old son being threatened with a knife. NASS cut off his support because he had left his accommodation. After he applied for judicial review, NASS agreed to reinstate support, pay backdated support and provide alternative accommodation. The court was left to consider a claim for damages for breach of ECHR article 3. Moses J rejected the damages claim and this issue was the subject of an appeal to the Court of Appeal.[51] They accepted NASS's evidence that it was not aware of the level of racial violence on the estate and would not have dispersed the family there if it had been. But the court also found that there was no 'positive obligation' arising from article 3 to ensure there was no risk.

5.48 *R (Thiab) v NASS*[52] concerned an asylum-seeker who left the Sighthill estate with his family after the Glasgow murder referred to above and brought a judicial review of NASS's decision not to admit them to initial accommodation, in particular of its failure to follow the guidance in Policy Bulletin 18 (now Bulletin 81). There was evidence of 100 racially motivated incidents reported by asylum-seekers prior to the murder. While the judicial review was still pending, the claimant was offered different accommodation in Glasgow and had to return there, later finding a part-time job. Some steps had been taken by the police and community to improve the situation at Sighthill and the family did not report any further harassment after their return. The court found there was undisputed evidence that community relations had significantly improved in the area. There was also limited evidence that the family had complained about the original harassment. The Administrative Court decided that the application was academic by the time it reached a full hearing, some seven months later and dismissed the application.

50 [2003] EWHC 860.

51 [2004] EWCA Civ 1730, June 2005 *Legal Action* 13.

52 [2002] EWHC 205.

Health

5.49 Accommodation that does not meet the supported household's physical or mental health needs, or is in disrepair, so represents a significant risk to health, may not meet the definition of 'adequate'. If an asylum-seeker considers that accommodation is inadequate, eg because it is in a dispersal area, they should send a letter explaining why together with any supporting evidence such as a doctor's report, social services' assessment, counsellor's letter, evidence of medical appointments to UKBA who should then forward it to their medical officer for advice. If the evidence simply shows a medical condition, this will not be sufficient as the response is likely to be that NHS treatment for that medical condition is available throughout the UK. It needs to show either that medical treatment is only available in the area of origin, eg for a rare tropical disease, or that the applicant is part way through an important course of treatment that should be completed, eg for skin grafting or a serious mental illness where there is a relationship with the therapist.

5.50 Shared accommodation may be inadequate if sharing would adversely affect health or interfere with the asylum-seeker or their family's right to respect for family life under ECHR article 8. Accommodation may be inadequate if the supported person has an essential need to be near friends, family or members of the same refugee community for practical or emotional support, for example if social services residential accommodation would otherwise be needed.

5.51 In *R (Blackwood) v Secretary of State for the Home Department*[53] a 22-year-old Jamaican woman had lived in London since the age of ten without regularising her immigration status and then made an application to the Home Office that to remove her from the UK would interfere with her ECHR article 3 rights. She had applied for section 95 support for her and her baby, including rent on her council tenancy. When NASS decided to disperse her outside London, away from family, friends and her support network, she brought a successful judicial review of the decision. Collins J found that article 8 was engaged because the adverse effect on her health, increasing her dependence on social and mental healthcare services, would directly affect her and her child's psychological well-being. Respect for private and family life under article 8 included physical and psychological integrity.

53 [2003] EWHC 97 (Admin).

Specialist medical needs/Medical Foundation treatment

5.52 The availability of specialist support from organisations such as the Medical Foundation for the Care of Victims of Torture or the Helen Bamber Foundation should be taken into account when decisions are taken about where asylum-seekers should be accommodated. This is documented in Policy Bulletin 19 (now withdrawn from the UKBA website) as well as in correspondence between the Medical Foundation and the Home Office and in the parliamentary debates on the IAA 1999:[54]

> I pay tribute to the very fine work of the Medical Foundation for the Care of Victims of Torture. Where it is clear that someone needs specialised services which cannot be delivered other than through a body of that sort, and the location of that body does not fit in with our normal cluster arrangements, we shall consider the possibility of finding accommodation adjacent to those services . . .

5.53 The asylum-seeker will need to show that they are actually receiving treatment from the Medical Foundation, not merely awaiting an assessment, or with a one-off appointment.[55]

5.54 In *R (Wanjugu) v Secretary of State for the Home Department*[56] W, a woman with mental health needs, who was referred to local counselling because there was a nine-month waiting list for the Medical Foundation, brought a judicial review of her dispersal, arguing that the policy should be applied to her because she was receiving treatment analogous to that provided by the Foundation. Elias J rejected this argument, finding that the services offered by the Foundation were linked to the particular nature of the institution and the treatment it provided. He was reluctant to extend the policy simply because W suffered from a serious illness of the same kind as some of those treated by the Foundation. However, the court found that NASS needed to reconsider its decision to disperse W because of new medical evidence she had produced. It remains possible to argue that accommodation in a dispersal area is not adequate accommodation if an asylum-seeker is receiving highly specialised treatment elsewhere, which is analogous to that provided by the Foundation, or under the 'health' consideration which is contained in Policy Bulletin 31.

54 Lord Williams of Mostyn, HC Debates col 1112, 21 July 1999.

55 See Policy Bulletin 85.

56 [2003] EWHC 3116 (Admin).

HIV status

5.55 Where the claimant is in need of care and attention due to their medical condition, a request to social services for a community care assessment and provision of accommodation under NAA 1948 s21 should be considered.[57] This has been a solution for many asylum-seekers and refused asylum-seekers living with HIV who needed to stay in a particular area for medical treatment and support networks. Following *R (M) v Slough LBC*,[58] it has become more difficult to show that an applicant with HIV is 'in need of care and attention', rather than simply medical attention if they have no or few symptoms. So the approach to dispersal of those with HIV may need to be revisited.

5.56 By 2006, a number of reports highlighting the effects of dispersal on people with HIV had been published.[59] Research based on a questionnaire sent to leading clinicians in genito-urinary clinics in England[60] attributed two deaths and three cases of mother to child transmission to dispersal. The clinicians were critical of the short notice of dispersal and failure to make adequate arrangements for transfer to medical treatment in the dispersal area.

5.57 In response, the Home Office changed their policy to dispersal in such cases, so that dispersal should only take place after consultation with the treating clinician and provided arrangements are made for a smooth transfer of treatment.[61]

5.58 The National Aids Trust (NAT) reviewed the implementation of the new policy in 2007 and found it wanting in over 50 per cent of cases. With the British HIV and AIDS Association, they have produced 'The Dispersal Process for Asylum seekers living with HIV: Advice for Healthcare and Voluntary sector professionals, NAT and BHIVA, 2006'.

5.59 It has been the practice to disperse to areas of the country where HIV and AIDS treatment is available, making such decisions difficult to challenge unless there are additional factors such as a high level of mental health needs. In *R (Muwangusi) v Secretary of State for the Home Department*[62] a woman with 'full-blown AIDS'

57 See chapter 9.

58 See para 9.62.

59 See for example 'Migration and HIV: improving lives in Britain, an inquiry into the impact of the UK nationality and immigration system on people living with HIV', the All-party Parliamentary Group on AIDS, July 2003.

60 S Creighton, G Sethi, S G Edwards and R Miller, 'Disperal of HIV positive asylum-seekers: national survey of UK healthcare providers', *British Medical Journal*, August 2004.

61 See Policy Bulletin 85.

62 [2003] EWHC 3116 (Admin).

who had been in London for a short period but was obtaining appropriate medical and psychological support was unsuccessful in her judicial review of a dispersal to Leeds. Goldring J found that medical treatment was available in Leeds, and that NASS's decision was rational. He decided that although her article 8 rights could be engaged, it was proportionate for NASS to disperse in the circumstances of the case.

5.60 There has been some success in challenging decisions that dispersal accommodation is adequate where it can be shown that the effect of disruption to medical or other service provision is so severe that it cannot be justified.[63]

5.61 To challenge dispersal, asylum-seekers with AIDS or HIV would need clear medical evidence that appropriate treatment was not available in the dispersal area or that dispersal would be detrimental to their health for other reasons. UKBA should be asked to produce evidence of HIV services in the area to which the household is being dispersed.

Education/children/family life

5.62 Family members receiving section 95 or section 98 support should be housed together by virtue of regulation 3 of the Asylum-seekers (Reception Conditions) Regulations 2005[64] implementing article 8 of the Reception Directive.[65] The directive may also apply in section 4 cases based on a fresh asylum claim[66] but does not apply where the asylum-seeker's asylum or ECHR claim has been rejected and there is no further appeal.

Children

5.63 The policy of not dispersing some families with a child who has been in school for 12 months no longer applies. Dispersal will be temporarily deferred where a child has started the final year of school or college year leading up to GCSE, AS or A level exams or their equivalents, provided they have been enrolled for at least a term of the previous academic year.[67] The policy does not apply to other exams or if the family has been 'unco-operative'. Dispersal may be delayed to allow a transfer of a child with special educational needs to an appropriate school.

63 See *R (M) v Secretary of State for the Home Department* at para 5.65 below.

64 SI No 7.

65 See para 7.86.

66 See para 7.106.

67 See Policy Bulletin 31.

5.64 The 'UK Border Agency Code of Practice for keeping children safe from harm',[68] issued under the UK Borders Act 2007 s21, came into force on 6 January 2009. It requires UKBA to take appropriate steps to ensure that children are safe from harm while in the UK. The Agency is required to have regard to the Code in exercising its own functions[69] and to take appropriate steps to ensure that those providing services on its behalf, such as contractors, also have regard to the Code.[70] In addition the Borders, Immigration and Citizenship Act 2009 includes a provision that the Home Office's immigration and nationality functions shall be carried out having regard to the need to safeguard and promote the welfare of children in the UK. The Home Office considers this is equivalent to the safeguarding duty in CA 1989 s11.[71]

5.65 To date, the judicial reviews of dispersal which have had the greatest degree of success are those where it has been shown that dispersal would interfere with the welfare of the child. A torture survivor with AIDS, whose medical needs were being met in London, successfully challenged his dispersal to Middlesbrough.[72] While the court rejected the father's argument about inadequate HIV services in the dispersal area, it accepted that NASS had failed to take into account the evidence of the needs of his son, S, which included letters from his school and social services. S had settled in school in London despite his trauma after having observed some of his father's torture and was then racially harassed in Middlesbrough. Richards J stated:

> The question was whether the disruption to the services being provided would be liable to have such deleterious consequences for the asylum-seeker that dispersal was inappropriate ... There was no evidence ... that the available services in Middlesbrough could be provided in such a way as to compensate for the problems arising out of the disruption to the services provided in London ...

Adequate accommodation for children with special needs

5.66 In *R (A) v (1) NASS and (2) Waltham Forest LBC*[73] Mrs A lived with her husband and two disabled teenage children in a flat that did not

68 UKBA, December 2008.

69 UK Borders Act 2007 s21(2)(a).

70 UK Borders Act 2007 s21(2)(b).

71 See Code of Practice para 1.4.

72 *R (M) v Secretary of State for the Home Department* [2002] EWHC 1924 (Admin); November 2002 *Legal Action* 25.

73 [2003] EWCA Civ 1473.

meet their special needs, including the need for wheelchair access. The bedrooms were upstairs and the toilets were downstairs. The Court of Appeal decided that the family's needs for suitable accommodation had to be balanced against the context of the Home Secretary's duty to provide adequate accommodation for destitute asylum-seekers in an area where there was a scarcity of accommodation. The court described these duties in finding adequate accommodation as including:

- to make arrangements with a local authority under IAA 1999 s99;
- to request one or more local authorities to assist under IAA 1999 s100 and to ensure they complied with the request;
- to make its own enquiries of registered social landlords (RSLs) or estate agents.

5.67 Although local authorities did not have the primary responsibility for accommodating the disabled children of asylum-seekers, their responsibilities included:

- to co-operate in giving the Home Office such assistance as is reasonable in the circumstances;
- generally to look outside its own stock, but there are circumstances where it should use its own stock, for example where the accommodation is extremely inadequate.

Family life under article 8

5.68 In *R (Hetoja) v Secretary of State for the Home Department*[74] a Kosovan grandmother was living in Leicester with her son and providing considerable childcare for her grandson with whom she lived as an extended family. She challenged her dispersal to Barnsley, arguing this would interfere with her ECHR article 8 rights by separating her from her son and grandson. NASS compromised, agreeing to house her in Leicester in a hostel. The court then rejected her claim that the hostel accommodation breached her article 8 rights because visitors were not allowed and so she could not care for her grandson adequately. It decided that while the Home Office must consider the claimant's personal circumstances, article 8 did not require the provision of particular accommodation.[75]

74 [2002] EWHC 2146 (Admin); (2002) 24 October, unreported.

75 See also *R (Blackwood) v Secretary of State for the Home Department* (at para 5.51 above).

Former unaccompanied minors

5.69 It is UKBA's policy not to disperse a young person of 18 who has been supported by a local authority as a 'looked after' child under CA 1989 s20.[76]

Challenges and complaints about inadequate service provision

5.70 There are suggestions about tactics and different types of complaints at para 7.167, but in a complaint about accommodation, the asylum-seeker should first contact the accommodation provider. The local 'one stop service' (see appendix E) should offer help with this, and with contacting UKBA if the accommodation provider fails to take action. If either UKBA fails to provide adequate accommodation or support, the remedy is judicial review. The limited statutory provisions governing the quality of service provision make it more difficult successfully to challenge low standard provision. It may be possible to refer to the standards within the target accommodation contract for section 95 and section 4 accommodation and argue that the terms agreed between UKBA and the accommodation provider have not been met, relying on the Contracts (Rights of Third Parties) Act 1999.

Human Rights Act considerations

5.71 As public bodies, UKBA or a local authority, including where they are using an agent to provide support on their behalf, must take into account the Human Rights Act (HRA) 1998 and ECHR when making decisions about asylum support. The provisions must also be taken into account by the courts and the AST when interpreting the AS Regs 2000. Complaints about inadequate service provision and requests to make alternative provision should include reference to relevant ECHR articles, with a request to the provider to take those articles into consideration when making a decision.

5.72 Throughout this chapter we have referred to articles 3 (freedom from inhuman and degrading treatment) and 8 (right to respect for private and family life, home and correspondence, which is qualified to allow interference where this is necessary in a democratic society, for example on economic grounds). The Court of Appeal has

76 See Policy Bulletin 29.

accepted that article 8 could be engaged if a property were in an extremely poor state of repair.[77]

5.73 Other relevant ECHR articles include article 9, the right to freedom of thought, conscience and religion. The First Protocol contains article 1, which provides for the protection of property and the right to the peaceful enjoyment of possessions, and article 2 provides the right to education. All the ECHR rights must be interpreted in accordance with article 14, which prohibits discrimination, including discrimination on the ground of 'other status', which could include asylum-seeker status. HRA 1998 s8 also provides for a free-standing damages claim where there have been serious breaches of human rights.[78] The Administrative Court has considered a case where a local authority was accommodating a disabled claimant and her carer in wholly inappropriate accommodation which was not adapted to meet her needs, and decided there was a breach of article 8, but not of article 3, and awarded damages.[79]

Essential living needs

5.74 The phrase 'essential living needs' in IAA 1999 s95(1) was considered by the Administrative Court in *R (Ouji) v Secretary of State for the Home Department*[80] a case that considered whether the Home Office or social services were responsible for providing extra support to a disabled child. Collins J held:

> What was being considered within the phrase 'essential living need' were those needs which had to be met for a person to live in a reasonable fashion. Those needs included sufficient food, nourishment, clothing and warmth so as to prevent that person falling into illness. They were the kinds of needs that people in general had so as to prevent that person falling into illness.

Level of support

5.75 The proposed provision is set at 70 per cent of the equivalent income support because the asylum support system is intended to be on a

77 *Lee v Leeds CC* [2002] 34 HLR 367.

78 See *R (Kanidagli) v Secretary of State for the Home Department* [2004] EWHC 1585 (Admin) and para 9.180.

79 *R (Bernard) v Enfield LBC* [2002] EWHC 2282 (Admin).

80 [2002] EWHC 1839 (Admin).

short-term basis, a safety net arrangement, and it should be possible to live on these amounts for short periods only.[81]

5.76 Where the household has no other income, the levels for maximum asylum support were set by the AS Regs 2000 at approximately 70 per cent of income support levels (excluding premiums) and 100 per cent of the income support level for a child at the time the IAA 1999 came into force. Because premiums for age and disability and parenthood are not included, section 95 support levels are often considerably lower than 70 per cent of the income support level for an equivalent household.

5.77 The rates are contained in a table in the schedule to the AS Regs 2000 as amended (and see UKBA website). Unlike the annual uprating of income support and other social security benefits, there is no statutory provision for a periodical review, although there was a government commitment 'to make regular annual reviews of the level at which support is provided to asylum-seekers'.[82]

Annual increase?

5.78 The rates have been increased in response to lobbying and court decisions, most recently by the Asylum Support (Amendment) Regulations 2008.[83] In 2009, the Home Secretary repealed the amendment regulations, pending a review, citing the economic downturn.[84] The reason given in an explanatory memorandum was the need 'to consult further with other government departments'. The memo continued:[85]

> Previous practice has been to increase all asylum support rates in line with inflation. In view of the current economic situation in the country as a whole and the present downward inflation trend, this year consideration is being given to the structure of asylum support payments to ensure that the essential living needs of asylum seekers are met within current budgetary constraints. We are also considering whether existing support categories may be simplified.

5.79 Subsequently the Home Office announced that some of the rates would be increased, in line with the Consumer Prices Index, by 5.2 per cent, but there was no increase for lone parents or single persons of 25 or over who were receiving £42.16 a week. Also the support rate

81 Home Secretary Jack Straw MP, *Hansard*, Vol 333 col 475, 15 June 1999.

82 Lord Williams of Mostyn, *Hansard*, HL Debates col 1164, 20 October 1999.

83 SI No 760.

84 Asylum Support (Amendment) (Revocation) Regulations 2009 SI No 641.

85 www.opsi.gov.uk/si/si2009/em/uksiem_20090641_en.pdf

for new applicants over 25 would be reduced to £25.13, the rate for those aged 18 or over (excluding lone parents). The changes took effect on 6 July 2009.[86]

5.80 Apart from the planned temporary nature of support, the initial explanation given for setting asylum support at a lower level than income support was that asylum-seekers would not have overheads such as the need to replace household items or utility bills.[87]

5.81 If a supported household is not being provided with the above, it may be possible to challenge the level of support provided (see below). Where accommodation is provided under the section 95 duty (or by a local authority under NAA 1948 s21), it is the landlord and not the asylum-seeker who is liable for council tax.[88]

5.82 When specifying the levels of support, AS Regs 2000 reg 10 states that section 95 support may be expected to be provided at these levels as a general rule. This allows UKBA scope for greater or lesser amounts to be provided where appropriate, but in practice it does not appear that the discretion is considered, eg in cases where an asylum-seeker has extra expenses because of a medical need to follow a special diet. The government suggested that regulations would be made under the IAA 1999 to specify the circumstances in which the Home Secretary could make payments to meet special needs, for example where a medical condition gives rise to special needs.[89] Similarly, IAA 1999 Sch 8 allows for regulations to provide for particular items falling outside the definition of 'essential living needs'. Ten years on, no such regulations had been issued: the AS Regs 2000 do not expressly make any such provision. The IAA 1999 s96(1)(b) provision for essential living needs would allow UKBA to make payment at an appropriate level, for example a higher payment may be appropriate if an asylum-seeker can produce evidence of a need for additional clothing or extra expense on washing due to incontinence.

5.83 The Reception Directive[90] requires the UK to 'ensure a standard of living adequate for the health of the applicants and capable of ensuring their subsistence'.[91] It is proposed that the replacement directive will define the level of support more specifically, for example by providing that it should be equivalent to national income support levels. At the time of writing the UK was not proposing to

86 Asylum Support (Amendment) (No 2) Regulations 2009 SI No 1388.
87 Lord Williams of Mostyn, *Hansard*, HL Debates col 251, 29 June 1999.
88 See para 8.209.
89 IAA 1999 Sch 8 paras 3 and 4, and explanatory notes para 281.
90 See para 7.105.
91 Article 13.

opt in to the new directive, but if the 2003 Reception Directive is not repealed, this may be a means of demonstrating the purpose of the former article.

Challenges to the levels of support

5.84 There have been various attempts to challenge the level of support which was previously provided by local authorities under the former interim asylum support scheme, as well as that provided by the Home Office under IAA 1999 s95, which indicate the approach that the courts take.

Judicial review decisions on support level

- A lone parent with one child challenged the reduction of her weekly income to £42. In addition to this, her utility bills and some travel expenses were paid and her son received free school meals, and a school clothing grant of £35 every six months. The council argued that the total was equivalent to 72 per cent of income support. The Administrative Court found that a policy of paying interim support at the rate of 72 per cent was irrational and unlawful, although a fixed daily rate of £5 for single adults and £3 per person for families was lawful. The Court of Appeal then dismissed the appeal and decided the 72 per cent policy was lawful.[92]
- A lone parent brought a judicial review claiming that her low level of support was irrational and in breach of ECHR article 8. She was getting £78.64 for an adult and two children and had to pay utility bills, whereas a similar household supported by NASS received £89 per week with utility bills paid. The High Court refused her application. The decision was upheld by the Court of Appeal, which rejected the argument that the Interim Regulations were ultra vires and dismissed her appeal. The court found that, to succeed she would need to have shown that taking all the relevant matters, including the cost of providing support, the rate paid was not a rate that could have appeared to the local authority to meet the claimant's essential living needs.[93]
- The Child Poverty Action Group (CPAG) supported a (successful) challenge to the levels of support paid by NASS to nursing mothers as well as an (unsuccessful) challenge of the

92 *R (Gjini) v Islington LBC* [2003] EWCA Civ 558.

93 *R (Satu) v Hackney LBC* [2002] EWCA Civ 1843, [2002] All ER (D) 86.

Department of Health's refusal to provide asylum-seekers with milk tokens. T, who was HIV positive, did not want to risk breast-feeding her new baby because there was a risk of HIV transmission and she could not afford powdered milk from her section 95 support. It was also argued that additional support could be paid under section 96 in these exceptional circumstances. The case led to an increase in weekly support rates for pregnant mothers and children under five years old.[94]

Extra support

Extra payments in exceptional circumstances

5.85 If an asylum-seeker needs an occasional or regular additional payment, for example to cover a special diet, UKBA may provide support in other ways if it considers that the circumstances of a particular case are exceptional.[95]

5.86 Although section 96(2) provides for a discretion rather than a duty, it could be read in conjunction with the requirement to take into account special needs and article 13 of the Reception Directive.[96] This should allow more extensive provision in the form of cash or by other means, for example where a supported person has a physical disability or HIV positive status if this gives rise to additional costs.

Provision for pregnant and nursing mothers

5.87 A pregnant woman or woman with a child aged one to three years is entitled to an extra £3 or £5 during the first year after birth.[97] It is not paid automatically. To receive this payment, the asylum-seeker must write to UKBA with evidence of the pregnancy/birth of the child, which is a change of circumstances, to ensure the provision of increased weekly support.

94 *R (T and another) v Secretary of State for Health and Secretary of State for the Home Department* [2002] EWHC 1887 (Admin). See also November 2002 *Legal Action* 12 and 35.

95 IAA 1999 s96(2).

96 See para 5.83 above.

97 See para 5.84 above and Bulletin 78. Asylum Support (Amendment) Regulations 2003 SI No 241.

5.88 A supported person may claim a one-off maternity payment of £300 for themselves or their dependant if they are receiving section 95 support. The claim should be made four weeks before the birth or two weeks after, with medical evidence of the expected week of confinement or an official copy of the birth certificate from the local register of births. A difficulty arises because where women are too pregnant to travel long distances they may remain in initial accommodation on section 98 support until the child is born. If a woman in initial section 98 accommodation only receives an emergency payment of £50, this may be challengeable if they are not able to transfer to section 95 support shortly afterwards and claim the full grant.

5.89 Dispersal of pregnant women is covered at para 5.44 and see para 7.85. Local authorities have discretion to accommodate pregnant and nursing mothers under NAA 1948 s21(1)(aa). The High Court considered the position where refused asylum-seekers who were in receipt of support under IAA 1999 s4 applied for social services' assistance. Mitting J decided that in normal circumstances a pregnant or nursing mother is not 'in need of care and attention' other than by virtue of their destitution and so will not qualify for accommodation under NAA 1948 due to section 21(1A).[98]

5.90 A pregnant woman, or a woman with a child under one year old is entitled to an HC2 exemption certificate entitling her to free prescriptions and exemption from dental charges by applying to the Prescription Pricing Authority, regardless of immigration status.[99]

Travel expenses for reporting

5.91 Most asylum-seekers or refused asylum-seekers now have a duty to report or 'sign' regularly at the local office of the Immigration Service or police. Section 95 support may be withdrawn if the asylum-seeker does not report 'without reasonable excuse'. The Home Office has power to finance their travel expenses under NIAA 2002 s69. Their published policy provides that such expenses may be paid to those with a journey of three miles or more or with exceptional needs.[100] It

98 *R (Gnezele) v Leeds CC and Secretary of State for the Home Department (interested part 1); R (Dayina) v Leeds CC and Secretary of State for the Home Department (interested party)* [2007] EWHC 3275 (Admin), June 2008 *Legal Action* 19. Permission to appeal was granted by the Court of Appeal but not pursued.

99 www.ppa.org.uk.

100 Travelling expenses policy. Contact management policy, process and implementation, June 2006, Version 5: see www.ind.homeoffice.gov.uk/6353/6356/policydocv51.pdf

is interpreted as excluding asylum-seekers or refused asylum-seekers who are not receiving support under IAA 1999 ss4, 98 or 95 but there is no clear exclusion within the policy and there is provision for a review if an applicant does not meet the main criteria. An alternative solution for those with difficulty attending, eg due to being in late pregnancy or having mobility needs, is to ask the Immigration Service (IS) to suspend reporting temporarily or agree to make it less frequent. In some cases the IS will allow reporting by (landline) telephone.

Expenses connected with the asylum claim or bail hearings

5.92 The supported person may be provided with expenses other than legal expenses, which are incurred in connection with the asylum claim.[101] The provision covers the cost of travel to interviews at the Home Office or port of entry, and to appeal hearings. It also covers travel to appointments at the Medical Foundation for a medical assessment connected to the claim and arguably should cover other similar medical appointments.[102]

5.93 The LSC will usually finance the cost of travel to an immigration solicitor as a legal help disbursement, although the asylum-seeker may be required to prove they cannot find a local representative.[103] The asylum-seeker and their dependants should receive travel costs to enable them to attend bail hearings of either an asylum-seeker or dependant who is detained under any provision of the Immigration Acts.[104]

Travel expenses to hospital appointments

5.94 A supported asylum-seeker can claim a refund for attending hospital appointments from the NHS Trust, provided they have the HC2 certificate.[105] This applies to any migrant on a low income.[106] The cost of travel to medical appointments can also be claimed from UKBA

101 IAA 1999 s96(1)(c)–(e).

102 Policy Bulletin 28.

103 LSC Manual Vol 2.

104 Section 96(1)(d) and(e) which enables the whole supported household to travel back to the dispersal area after a court hearing.

105 See Policy Bulletin 43.

106 For details see para 10.22.

provided there is evidence of them. Policy Bulletin 28 applies in section 95 cases; there is a separate application form in section 4 cases.

Funeral costs

5.95 UKBA's policy is not to pay for the funeral costs of an asylum-seeker who dies while receiving support on the ground that there is no power to provide for them, because they are no longer an asylum-seeker within the meaning of IAA 1999 s94(1).[107] If a close relative of the deceased is in receipt of income support, jobseeker's allowance, housing benefit, council tax benefit or tax credits, they may be eligible for a social fund payment towards funeral costs.[108] Otherwise, the local council's environmental health department or NHS may be responsible for cremation costs.

Subsistence-only support

5.96 An asylum-seeker who is able to live in accommodation provided by friends or relatives may claim cash-only support while living at an authorised address, provided that address is not itself section 95 accommodation. The provision has been used by asylum-seekers whose support is cut off and who have lost asylum support appeals, often in dispersal cases. They may reapply for 'subsistence-only' support, notifying UKBA there has been a change of circumstances. Periodic inspections are carried out to check that asylum-seekers are actually living at their given address and residence at a specified address may be a condition of support entitlement.[109] UKBA has refused to provide section 98 temporary support to those who are claiming cash only. Where an asylum-seeker has faced a long delay while their claim for cash-only support is processed, they could bring a judicial review of the delay.[110]

Section 55 and subsistence-only support[111]

5.97 An asylum-seeker without a dependent child who claims subsistence-only section 95 support is likely to be refused if they did not apply for

107 Policy Bulletin 59: Help with funeral costs.

108 Social Fund Maternity and Funeral Expenses (General) Regulations 1987 SI No 481 as amended.

109 See paras 5.118 and 7.60.

110 See para 7.8.

111 See further para 4.105.

asylum 'as soon as reasonably practicable' under NIAA 2002 s55(1).[112] This is because UKBA's approach is to assume that applicants who apply for housing are homeless and meet the ECHR article 3 threshold, so qualify for support due to section 55(5), whereas people staying with friends or relatives usually have access to food and washing facilities. So such applicants will need to provide evidence that support is needed to avoid a breach of their ECHR rights because their hosts cannot cover their needs. Such evidence might include:

- letters from the DWP or wage slips to show that their hosts are in receipt of benefits or on a low income;
- letters or court orders from creditors to show that their hosts are in debt;
- a breakdown of the host's income and expenditure to show they cannot finance the asylum-seeker household;
- evidence of the asylum-seeker's extra needs due to ill-health, for example a medical report about a special diet, or travel expenses to regular medical appointments;
- a letter from the host to say they cannot afford to finance personal items such as sanitary towels and/or laundry facilities.

5.98 Tactics for dealing with a section 55 refusal are covered in para 4.107. It may also be necessary to apply for a judicial review of any delay in providing a section 55(1) interview or reaching a decision on section 95 support. If an asylum-seeker is staying with a friend or relative and cannot meet the section 55(5) requirements, the host may decide to provide a letter ending accommodation, but in most circumstances this will lead to an offer of accommodation in a dispersal area.

5.99 This right to claim subsistence-only support may be ended in part or in full by NIAA 2002 s43, if the Home Secretary introduces an order, but he has not done so to date. This requires an affirmative resolution by parliament and so would have to be debated.[113]

Payment problems and procedures[114]

Claiming additional support for special needs

5.100 If an asylum-seeker or dependant wants to claim a one-off or regular additional payment on the ground of exceptional circumstances

112 See para 4.105.

113 *Hansard* HC WA 259, 9 June 2003.

114 See further para 7.167.

under section 96(1), a letter outlining the need should be sent to UKBA with a supporting letter, for example from their doctor and/or social services.

Payment of support

5.101 When the asylum support scheme was introduced, support was provided in vouchers that could be exchanged at specified shops. After a national campaign against the stigmatising effect of the scheme, IAA 1999 s96(3), which provided that support could only be paid in cash in exceptional circumstances, was repealed, so that section 95 support is now provided in cash, but at the time of writing support under IAA 1999 s4 was still paid in vouchers. UKBA has indicated plans to move to a debit card system for section 4 only but the card could only be used in exchange for goods at specified supermarkets and shops, not for cash. The standard amounts of section 95 support as at the date of publication are listed on the UKBA website.[115]

5.102 The procedure for claiming section 95 subsistence is to attend a specified local post office and produce the identity card issued to asylum-seekers by the Home Office, known as the application registration card (ARC). The post office then pays the weekly cash amount unless it has instructions from UKBA to terminate payment.

Action if payment is not received

5.103 If the post office informs the asylum-seeker that there is no payment for them, they should issue a receipt with a code that indicates the reason for the refusal, for example if there is a problem with the ARC. The asylum-seeker should ask them to try for a second time and to provide the two receipts. These receipts should be faxed to UKBA with a request to resolve the problem. Where an expected payment has not arrived, whether an emergency payment by post, a dispersal travel package, or the regular cash payment at the post office, the procedure is to phone the UKBA hotline 'Support Discontinuation and Voucher Enquiries'. The telephonist should 'log' the call and notify the relevant section of UKBA. A written

115 www.ukba.homeoffice.gov.uk/asylum/support/cashsupport/currentsupport amounts/

acknowledgement of this call should be received by post. In cases where there is no apparent justification for cessation or non-payment of support, UKBA should send emergency vouchers to the household until the problem is resolved.

Lost or stolen ARC or payments

5.104 The asylum-seeker should report the loss or theft of an ARC to the police and Home Office as soon as possible and then phone the Sodexho helpline. UKBA should then arrange emergency support tokens until the Immigration Service has notified them that the ARC has been replaced. The Immigration Service usually takes about four weeks to replace the ARC. They will invite the asylum-seeker to attend the nearest reporting centre or local enforcement office for a fingerprint check and replacement ARC. The ARC holder should keep receipts for any related journeys of three miles or more to claim a refund from UKBA.

5.105 Where emergency vouchers or 'support notifications' have been stolen, the asylum-seeker should notify the police, and then UKBA, by fax.

The amount of support where household has an income

5.106 The Home Secretary may decide that an asylum-seeker is destitute due to inadequate resources or accommodation even though the household has some income or assets. In deciding what kind and level of support to offer, AS Regs 2000 reg 12 repeats the list of relevant factors at reg 6(4). Any income, assets or support for the applicant or their dependant(s) may be taken into account in deciding what kind of support should be offered and at what level. Support provided under IAA 1999 is excluded but other resources are relevant, whether in or outside the UK, if they might reasonably be expected to be available to the household.

Contributions to support

5.107 Where an asylum-seeker has resources, the Home Secretary may:

- set the asylum support at a level to reflect the resources; or
- set the asylum support at the standard level but require the supported person to make payments to UKBA in the form of 'contributions'.

5.108 AS Regs 2000 reg 12 should be read in conjunction with reg 16. Prompt payment of contributions may be made a condition of continued asylum support.[116] Asylum Process Guidance on the UKBA website explains the arrangements for an asylum-seeker with income or capital to make weekly payments to UKBA as a contribution to their support.

Overpayments[117]

5.109 Where section 98 or section 95 asylum support has been overpaid due to an error by the Home Secretary, the Home Secretary may recover the overpayment as a deduction from asylum support, or as a debt by bringing an action against the asylum-seeker in the county court.[118]

5.110 Overpayments due to a misrepresentation or fraud are recoverable under IAA 1999 s112. The Home Secretary may request a person in receipt of asylum support to refund support if it transpires that he or she was not destitute.[119] If it is not repaid it can be recovered as a debt in the county court.

5.111 Where overpayment is due to a criminal misrepresentation by the applicant or a third party, recovery may be ordered by the court, even if there is no finding of fraud.[120]

Backpayments and delays in processing claims for section 95 support

5.112 A payment should be made under IAA 1999 s96(2) as an exceptional payment where a delay in payment is caused by the UKBA. Where support has not been paid due to an official error, the asylum-seeker can claim a backpayment.[121] If the agency fails to respond to complaints, a complaint and request for compensation could be made to the Parliamentary Ombudsman.[122] There is no specific power to 'backdate' support, but the AST may order payment from

116 IAA 1999 s95(9) and AS Regs 2000 reg 16(4).

117 See also Policy Bulletin 67: Overpayments.

118 IAA 1999 s114; AS Regs 2000 reg 18.

119 AS Regs 2000 reg 17A inserted by para 4 of the Asylum Support (Amendment) Regulations 2005 SI No 11.

120 IAA 1999 s112.

121 See Policy Bulletin 80: Backpayment of asylum support.

122 See chapter 7.

the date of the original UKBA decision in exceptional circumstances if refusal of payment leads to a tribunal appeal.[123]

5.113 An asylum-seeker who had waited several weeks with no income after claiming section 95 support, obtained permission to apply for judicial review of the delay in processing his claim and an injunction ordering NASS to provide subsistence and accommodation under section 98.[124] Evidence was presented of NASS delays and maladministration in other cases but since NASS then processed the section 95 application, the case was settled.[125]

5.114 There is a practical difficulty that commonly arises where an asylum-seeker is provided with emergency support tokens (ESTs) after a delay in receiving support. UKBA may advise that the tokens will be delivered in the next one to five working days. The asylum-seeker must be at home to receive the ESTs in person. The courier company may then say they have delivered the vouchers, whereas the asylum-seeker may not have received them, for example if they have been delivered to the wrong address. If the courier does not leave a card, the asylum-seeker has no evidence that the vouchers have not been delivered, but UKBA's approach is to insist that the client must provide evidence to qualify for backdated/replacement ESTs.

Asylum-seekers' responsibilities and UKBA's powers

5.115 The provision of asylum support under IAA 1999 is linked to the Home Office's immigration control functions by powers contained in Part VI of the Act. Support is provided subject to conditions and asylum-seekers may be prosecuted if they fail to report a relevant change of circumstances, as well as having their support withdrawn. IA 1971 Sch 2 para 21(2C) allows for regulations to require residence in particular accommodation and to prohibit a person's absence from the accommodation. UKBA has wide powers to obtain and exchange information, and to enter premises. The effect of these provisions is that a supported asylum-seeker and members of their household have a duty to disclose fully to UKBA any information

123 ASA 08/05/17697.

124 *R (Koch) v NASS* CO 735/01 (Admin); January 2002 *Legal Action* 26.

125 See also para 7.8 on tackling delays.

affecting their entitlement to support throughout the period of the claim. A number of criminal offences aim to deter fraud and misrepresentation by asylum-seekers or those who seek to profit from them. To date, there have been few prosecutions. For example in 2005–06 there were only 15 out of approximately 100,000 supported households, below the rate for DWP prosecutions. In 2007, the Home Secretary suggested this may change.[126] But UKBA has withdrawn support where they suspect that a criminal offence has been committed under IAA 1999 Part VI, for example if the asylum-seeker is claiming support while failing to declare that they are working, leading to a number of appeals.[127]

Asylum-seekers' responsibilities

Reporting

5.116 IA 1971 Sch 2 para 21(2C) allows for regulations to require residence in particular accommodation and prohibiting a person's absence from the accommodation. See para 5.91 for travel expenses for reporting.

Offences

5.117 It is a criminal offence for the asylum-seeker or their dependant to fail to provide accurate information or notify a relevant change of circumstances.[128]

Conditions of support[129]

5.118 Support is provided subject to written conditions.[130] The extent to which the household has complied with any conditions is specified as a factor that may be taken into account in deciding the level or kind of support to be provided.[131] A breach of conditions also allows support to be withdrawn.[132] An example of this is that the asylum

126 The treatment of asylum-seekers, tenth report of session 2006–07, HL81-I/HC60-I, March 2007.

127 See para 7.66.

128 IAA 1999 s105(1).

129 AS Regs 2000 reg 15.

130 IAA 1999 s95(9).

131 AS Regs 2000 reg 19(1).

132 AS Regs 2000 reg 19(1).

support agreement provides that travel to accommodation in the dispersal areas is a condition of support. If an asylum-seeker fails to travel, UKBA may terminate support on the basis that conditions have been breached, although its current policy is to leave the accommodation available where the household includes a child under 18. The qualification that conditions have been breached 'without reasonable excuse' applies explicitly in cases of suspension or termination of support due to breach of conditions. The question of when it is possible to challenge the withdrawal of section 95 support due to a breach of conditions is discussed in detail in chapter 7.

5.119 The leading case on how to approach the withdrawal of support after an asylum-seeker has breached conditions is *R v Kensington and Chelsea RBC ex p Kujtim.*[133] Although this related to support provided under NAA 1948 s21, the guidance has been widely applied and approved in later court and tribunal decisions. It was held that section 21 accommodation for destitute asylum-seekers should only be withdrawn after a thorough investigation. The Court of Appeal also indicated that a discharge of duty could only occur after a persistent refusal to comply with requirements and a warning letter. It is arguable that UKBA should take these considerations into account when exercising its discretion to reduce the level of support or change the form of support.

Complying with conditions of support

5.120 A written copy of the asylum support conditions should be provided to the supported person by UKBA or their agent and a copy could be requested if it is alleged that conditions have been breached.[134] It is arguable that these conditions should be translated into the asylum-seeker's first language or interpreted where possible, particularly for newly-arrived households. Some asylum support appeal decisions have supported this approach, depending on the circumstances. But the principal tribunal judge has found that it is an asylum-seeker's duty to ensure they get assistance in getting such documents translated and this approach has not been challenged by judicial review.[135]

5.121 In relation to accommodation, conditions are likely to be in the form of a licence agreement. In relation to living expenses, the

133 [1999] 4 All ER 161, (1999) 2 CCLR 340, CA.
134 IAA 1999 s95(9)–(11).
135 ASA/01/06/0435.

conditions will be based on the duty to notify a change of circumstances, for example if the asylum-seeker gets income from a job or moves house.

Notifying UKBA of a change of circumstances

5.122 The supported person or a dependant must notify NASS by letter or fax, without delay, of any relevant change of circumstances.[136] There are 22 relevant changes listed in AS Regs 2000 reg 15(2), which range from pregnancy to death via moving house. If a person (not simply the applicant) does not notify relevant changes, they face suspension or termination of support and/or prosecution.

5.123 In summary, the relevant changes of circumstances in relation to the supported person or a dependant are:

- a new dependant joins him or her in the UK;
- new assets/income;
- gaining/losing employment;
- marriage/divorce/cohabitation/separation/civil partnership;
- name change;
- pregnancy/childbirth;
- leaving school;
- sharing accommodation with someone new;
- moving house/leaving accommodation;
- hospital/prison admission;
- leaving the UK;
- death.

5.124 There is a power to make further inquiries and request further information from the supported person or their dependant(s) if UKBA considers that it affects the future provision of asylum support.[137]

UKBA's powers

Exchange of information about asylum-seekers

5.125 Information held by the police, the National Criminal Intelligence Service, the National Crime Squad, or HMRC may be supplied to the Home Office for use in the provision of support to

136 AS Regs 2000 reg 15(1).
137 AS Regs 2000 reg 15(3).

asylum-seekers.[138] Similarly, the Home Office can pass on information to those agencies.[139]

Arrest, search and seizure

5.126 There are wide powers of arrest, search and seizure of documents where there is a suspected asylum support offence.[140] An immigration officer may arrest *without a warrant* a person who they reasonably suspect has committed the offence of false or dishonest representation to obtain support under IAA 1999 ss105–106.

Warrants under IAA 1999 s125

5.127 The Home Secretary has the power to obtain a warrant to enter section 95 or section 98 accommodation that has been provided to a supported household. The warrant can be executed 'at any reasonable time . . . using reasonable force'. A justice of the peace may grant a warrant to a person authorised in writing by the Home Secretary if satisfied that there is reason to believe that:

(a) the supported person or any dependants of his for whom the accommodation is provided is not resident in it;
(b) the accommodation is being used for any purpose other than the accommodation of the asylum-seeker or any dependants of his; or
(c) any person other than the supported person and his dependants (if any) is residing in the accommodation.

Information from property owners

5.128 The power to obtain a warrant forcibly to enter asylum-seekers' homes is supplemented by a power to obtain information about where supported persons live. IAA 1999 s126 enables the Home Secretary to obtain information from friends, relatives or others providing accommodation to asylum-seekers who are receiving section 95 cash-only support. Information may be required from any person appearing to the Home Secretary to have any interest or be involved in any way in the management or control of the accommodation.

138 IAA 1999 s20.
139 IAA 1999 s21.
140 IAA 1999 s109 as amended by UK Borders Act 2007 s18.

5.129 The Home Secretary can demand 'such information with respect to the premises and the persons occupying them as he may specify'. The only limitation is that information obtained may only be used in the exercise of his functions under IAA 1999 Part VI (the support provisions), as opposed to in the asylum and immigration decision-making process.

Information from postal services

5.130 The Home Secretary may track down persons who have moved while receiving support under IAA 1999 Part VI by requiring the postal services to give details of any forwarding address. The terms of the power are that the information is:

> (a) for use in the prevention, detection, investigation or prosecution of criminal offences under this Part;
> (b) for use in checking the accuracy of information relating to support provided under this Part;
> (c) for any other purpose relating to the provision of support to asylum-seekers.

5.131 Unlike section 126, there is no limit on the use of the information obtained, provided it is obtained for one of the above purposes. So such information could be passed on to those responsible for deciding the asylum claim.

Information from financial institutions

5.132 The Home Secretary may require a financial institution such as a bank or building society to supply information (such as bank statements) about a person if UKBA reasonably suspects that the person has committed an offence under IAA 1999 s105(1)(a)(b)(c) or s106(1)(a)(b)(c) by making false or dishonest representations to obtain asylum support.[141]

Criminal offences

5.133 A series of criminal offences that relate to the provision of asylum support was established by IAA 1999 ss105–108. Prosecution is in the magistrates' court. The most serious offence has a maximum sentence of seven years' imprisonment.

141 NIAA 2002 s135.

5.134 It is not merely the asylum-seeker or applicant for support who is liable to prosecution. Any person or body corporate, such as a private or public sector landlord, may be found guilty of the offence. This renders an asylum-seeker's representative, friend, relative or housing-provider potentially liable if they fail to pass on information. In the case of a body corporate, it will be liable if an offence has been committed with the consent or connivance of an officer (director, manager, secretary or similar) or due to their neglect. Both the relevant officer and the organisation may be prosecuted and sentenced.[142]

False or dishonest representations[143]

5.135 The first two offences in IAA 1999 Part VI cover misrepresentations or failure to notify a change of circumstances. The wording reflects the misrepresentation provisions governing homeless and housing register applicants.[144] There is no express requirement in the IAA 1999 to explain to every applicant their duties and potential liability in ordinary language, as required by the Housing Act 1996. The ASA considered the effect of section 105(1) in an appeal where section 95 support had been withdrawn after a young asylum-seeker gave incorrect information about her age and identity. The adjudicator decided that no offence had been committed under section 105(1)(a), because there had been no warning.[145]

5.136 A distinction is drawn between false and dishonest representations:

- 'False representations under section 105 are where the aim is 'obtaining support for himself or any other person'. The offence is triable in the magistrates' court, with a sentence of up to three months and/or a fine of up to scale 5 (currently £5,000). Perhaps the most notable of the new offences is section 105(c), which makes it an offence not to notify a relevant change of circumstance 'when required to do so'. AS Regs 2000 reg 15 imposes an onerous requirement to notify specified changes of circumstances 'without delay'.[146] Asylum-seekers should be informed of these when they claim support. If there are any prosecutions under this clause, one possible defence may be that the relevant

142 IAA 1999 s109.
143 IAA 1999 ss105 and 106.
144 Housing Act 1996 ss171 and 125.
145 ASA 00/09/0061.
146 See para 5.122.

circumstances and the duty to notify were not explained to the supported person in their first language.

- 'Dishonest representations' under section 106 are where the aim is 'obtaining any benefit or other payment or advantage for himself or any other person' and the conduct must be dishonest. The sentence if tried in the magistrates' court is up to six months' imprisonment and/or the statutory maximum fine. In the case of more serious offences it can be tried in the Crown Court with imprisonment of up to seven years and/or a fine.

5.137 According to the explanatory notes to IAA 1999, the section 106 'dishonest representations' offence is aimed at serious and calculated fraud 'such as where someone makes a plan to extract as much from the Home Office as possible by deception'.

5.138 In the case of either IAA 1999 s105 or s106, the person may be guilty of an offence under any one of four heads:

- making a statement or representation knowing it is false;
- producing or arranging for the production of false documents or information;
- failing to notify a change of relevant circumstances when required to do so in accordance with any provision made by or under Part VI (this is qualified by 'without reasonable excuse' in the case of false representations only);
- knowingly causing another person's failure to notify a change of relevant circumstances (without reasonable excuse in the case of section 105).

Delay or obstruction

5.139 Section 107 introduces a vague and broad offence of 'delay or obstruction without reasonable excuse', which is punishable in the magistrates' court by a fine of up to scale 3 (£1,000). Any person may be guilty of this if that person:

- intentionally delays or obstructs a person exercising functions conferred by or under this Part; or
- refuses or neglects to answer a question, give any information or produce any document when required to do so in accordance with any provision made by or under this Part.

5.140 There is considerable scope for prosecuting asylum-seekers and their associates under this provision. The broad framing of the provision may indicate an aim of deterrence rather than conviction.

Failure of sponsor to maintain

5.141 Section 108 introduces the offence of a refusal or neglect of a sponsor to maintain his/her spouse or dependent relative. The failure must result in asylum support being provided and there is a defence of 'reasonable excuse' or being on strike. Sponsorship and public funds is discussed at para 1.33. The provision is aimed at cases where someone obtains leave to enter the UK on the basis of sponsorship and subsequently claims asylum. The sentence is up to three months' imprisonment and/or a fine up to level 4 (£2,500).

Challenges and complaints[147]

5.142 The Home Office's powers outlined above may breach various articles of the ECHR, both in relation to the supported person and those who accommodate him/her including friends, relatives or voluntary sector organisations. However, as yet, there have been no challenges to these parts of the Act, on the basis that they are incompatible with ECHR article 8, or article 1 of Protocol 1. The provisions for arrest without a warrant and to enter property respectively are extremely wide. Depending on the manner of use they could be subject to a claim for damages under the Human Rights Act 1998 and the ECHR article 5 right to liberty or article 8 right to respect for private life and correspondence. Where an asylum-seeker believes any such power has been used unfairly, the Home Office's complaints procedure could be used followed by a complaint to an MP, and/or the Parliamentary Ombudsman.

147 See further 7.XX.

CHAPTER 6

Section 4 support

continued

Introduction

6.1 The Home Office may accommodate a destitute refused asylum-seeker and their dependant(s), or a former detainee under section 4 of the Immigration and Asylum Act 1999 (IAA 1999). This very basic form of support, which was originally known as 'hard cases' support, is now known colloquially as 'section 4' support.[1] In the first edition of this book, the arrangements only merited a couple of paragraphs, but as asylum claims are now processed more quickly, there are thousands of refused asylum-seekers who are unable to leave the UK through no fault of their own, and so are reliant on section 4.

6.2 There are two routes to section 4 support. Any migrant who is granted temporary admission or released from immigration detention may qualify for support under IAA 1999 s4(1) without meeting other conditions. A refused or 'failed' asylum-seeker may qualify under section 4(2) if they are destitute and meet one of five criteria, usually having made a fresh asylum claim that has not yet been considered.

6.3 A refused asylum-seeker with a child in their household remains entitled to support under IAA 1999 s95 until their child reaches 18. So those supported under section 4 are either childless or have a child who was born after their asylum claim and appeal were finally decided.

6.4 Section 4 support is cashless, consisting of accommodation and 'facilities for accommodation. This may mean board and lodging, or a private rented room with supermarket vouchers, to be replaced by a 'section 4 payment card' or a store card. The rate is £35 per person per week. Extra vouchers may be provided on application for children under five, pregnant women or applicants with special needs.

6.5 Where a refused asylum-seeker has 'non-destitution' needs due to a physical or mental health need, they may be entitled to social services support and accommodation under National Assistance Act (NAA) 1948 s21, which takes precedence over IAA 1999 s4 support. They will need to show that they claimed asylum on arrival in the UK or that support is needed to avoid a breach of their ECHR rights, for example if they have made a fresh claim.[2]

6.6 As explained in chapter 4, the National Asylum Support Service (NASS) no longer exists so here we refer to it only for historical

1 Note that IAA 1999 refers to 'accommodation' rather than support.

2 See further *R (AW) v Croydon LBC; R (1)(A) (2)(D) (3)(Y) v Hackney LBC and Secretary of State for the Home Department (interested party)* [2005] EWHC 2950 (Admin), June 2006 *Legal Action* 29 and para 9.

reasons and otherwise to the Home Office or UK Border Agency (UKBA).[3]

6.7 This chapter covers:

- eligibility for section 4 support;
- application procedures and challenging delays;
- appeals to the First-tier Tribunal (Asylum Support) (AST);
- support provision;
- how to get extra support.

Resources

6.8 In comparison with other areas of asylum support, the legislation is relatively straightforward, consisting of IAA 1999 s4 and currently two statutory instruments covering eligibility for support and extra provision respectively.[4]

6.9 Home Office or NASS guidance for making decisions about section 4 support was previously published in Policy Bulletin 71. This bulletin has been withdrawn. At the time of writing, there is only internal guidance for decision-makers, published on the Home Office website as 'asylum process guidance'.[5] There are two sections, one entitled 'section 4 support instructions' and the other 'section 4 support review'. Here we refer to it simply as 'Home Office guidance' since it may be renamed and is internal guidance only, which is not legally binding.

6.10 The website of the independent voluntary organisation, Asylum Support Appeals Project (ASAP), publishes detailed guidance on section 4 support and section 4 appeals.[6]

Eligibility for section 4 support

The legal framework

6.11 The power to provide section 4 support is contained in IAA 1999 s4. Section 4(1) provides for accommodation for those with temporary

3 See para 4.3: 'rebranding'.

4 The Immigration and Asylum (Provision of Accommodation to Failed Asylum-seekers) Regulations 2005 SI No 930 and Immigration and Asylum (Provision of Services and Facilities) Regulations 2007 SI No 3627.

5 www.UKBA.homeoffice.gov.uk/sitecontent/documents/policyandlaw/asylumprocessguidance/asylumsupport/

6 www.asaproject.org.uk.

admission under IA 1971, Sch 2 para 21, or released from immigration detention or released on bail. There is no requirement that such a person must have claimed asylum in the past or that they must be destitute. Until April 2008, Home Office guidance suggested that where a person in this category is also a failed asylum-seeker, then the IAA 1999 s4(2) criteria applied – so they must be destitute and meet one of the five conditions. There is no authority for this in the legislation and the Home Office agreed in March 2008 to change the guidance on its website to state that in applying for section 4(1) support a failed asylum-seeker in detention does not have to show they are destitute or that they qualify under one of the five criteria.

6.12 As originally enacted, the provision went no further than the existing section 4(1). But the Act was amended in 2002, by adding section 4(2), which states that support may be provided to a person who is no longer an asylum-seeker and whose claim has been rejected. His or her dependant(s) may be accommodated under section 4(3). Asylum-seeker is as defined by IAA 1999 s94(1), so section 4(2) is referring to those who are 18 or over and have made an unsuccessful claim either for asylum or under ECHR article 3.[7] An asylum-seeker with a dependent child under 18 in his or her household is still an 'asylum-seeker' under section 94(5) so cannot qualify for section 4 accommodation.

6.13 A former unaccompanied minor whose claim for asylum was rejected before their 18th birthday who is now 18 years or older does not normally fall within section 4(2). They are outside the IAA 1999 s94 'asylum-seeker' definition because they were never an asylum-seeker of 18 years or more. Usually the Home Office will have granted limited leave until the age of 17.5 years and will then have made an application to extend their leave, which is not treated as an asylum application.[8] They may be entitled to Children Act (CA) 1989 assistance as a child leaving care.[9] Otherwise it may be arguable that they fall within IAA 1999 s4(1) if they have temporary admission.

6.14 NASS Policy Bulletin 71 was first issued after Stanley Burnton J found that the Home Secretary's policy of not informing asylum-seekers of his policy on section 4 support was unlawful.[10] At that time there was no statutory instrument or other website information. But it may be arguable that without any policy bulletin or equivalent,

7 See para 4.18.

8 See chapter 1.

9 See para 9.139.

10 *R (Salih and Rahmani) v Secretary of State for the Home Department* [2003] EWHC 2273 (Admin).

the internal guidance published on the website does not meet the Home Office's legal obligations to explain its policy to potential applicants (although the notes to the amended section 4 application form may serve this purpose in part).

6.15 Section 55 of the Nationality Immigration and Asylum Act 2002 (NIAA 2002) applies to section 4 accommodation.[11] This means that support may be refused under NIAA 2002 s55(1) if the original asylum claim was not made 'as soon as reasonably practicable' after arrival in the UK, unless it is needed to avoid a breach of ECHR rights (under section 55(5)). This has little practical effect since an applicant must be destitute to qualify for section 4 accommodation, and so support would be needed to avoid a breach of ECHR article 3.

6.16 Section 4(5)[12] permits the Home Secretary to make regulations specifying the criteria to be used in deciding whether an applicant qualifies for section 4 support.

6.17 The Immigration and Asylum (Provision of Accommodation to Failed Asylum-seekers) (IA(PAFA)) Regulations 2005[13] list the eligibility criteria for 'a failed asylum-seeker'. These criteria only apply to applicants under section 4(2)–(3) so do not affect those released from detention. The regulations provide for support to be provided subject to conditions such as living at the section 4 address and reporting.

6.18 The Home Office intended to make section 4 support subject to 'participation in community activities', effectively compulsory unpaid work. This is provided for in section 4(6)[14] and in IA(PAFA) Regs 2005 regs 4–5. It has not been implemented because no voluntary organisation has so far agreed to operate such a scheme and so we do not discuss the arrangements here, but it only applies to section 4(2)–(3) support so does not affect those who receive support following detention.

6.19 The Home Office has been consistently lobbied about the problems with voucher-only support. The alternative of cash payments has been strongly argued for, as well as provision for travel and other essential needs. In response, the Immigration and Asylum (Provision of Services and Facilities) Regulations 2007[15] were introduced to

11 See chapter 5.
12 Inserted by Asylum and Immigration (Treatment of Claimants, etc) Act 2004.
13 SI No 930.
14 Introduced by AI(TC)A 2004 s10(7)–(8).
15 SI No 3627.

provide extra support in kind (ie still not cash) for maternity and baby items, travel to medical appointments, and other additional expenses – but a specific application has to be made for each item of extra support. In 2009 UKBA began to pilot a 'section 4 payment card' that avoids the need for vouchers and can be used at more than one outlet. One of the reasons given for this development was the stigmatisation caused by vouchers; another was to prevent people from exchanging their vouchers for cash.

Dependants

Note that a person who qualifies for support under section 4(1), for example as a former detainee may not be provided with section 4 support for a dependant, unless the dependant also meets the section 4(2) criteria as a destitute former asylum-seeker. A person who qualifies for support under section 4(2) as a former asylum-seeker can apply for support for him- or herself and any dependant. But the dependant is not eligible to apply for support in his or her own right, because it can only be provided as part of the former asylum-seeker's household (section 4(3)). If the dependant is an former asylum-seeker qualifying for section 4(2) support, he or she could make a separate application for support. In either case, a dependant who cannot qualify for section 4 support and has a child under 18, may be entitled to CA 1989 s17 assistance. 'Dependant' is defined in the same way as 'dependant' for section 95 support (see para 4.40).

Outline of eligibility criteria for those who have been detained or granted temporary admission (IAA 1999 s4(1))

6.20 Under section 4(1) the Home Secretary may provide facilities for accommodation of persons:

(a) temporarily admitted to the UK under IA 1971 Sch 2 para 21;
(b) released from detention under that paragraph;
(c) released on bail from detention under any provision of the Immigration Acts.

6.21 So the Home Secretary has wide powers to grant section 4(1) support to anyone who has arrived in the UK and been granted temporary admission or who has been detained, whether or not they are also a former asylum-seeker.

6.22 The APAFA Regs 2005 reg 3 only applies to those supported under IAA 1999 s4(2) or (3) so a detainee applying for bail is entitled to a grant of section 4(1) accommodation even if they do not meet one of the five criteria.

Outline of eligibility criteria for failed asylum-seekers (IAA 1999 s4(2))

6.23 For applications under IAA 1999 s4(2), there is a two-stage test under the IA(PAFA) Regs 2005. First the failed asylum-seeker must appear to the Home Secretary to be destitute.[16] Second, they must satisfy *one* of the following five conditions:

(a) *Reasonable steps*: he is taking all reasonable steps to leave the UK or place himself in a position in which he is able to leave the UK, which may include complying with attempts to obtain a travel document to facilitate his departure.
(b) *Obstacle to travel*: he is unable to leave the UK by reason of a physical impediment to travel or for some other medical reason.
(c) *No safe route of return*: he is unable to leave the UK because in the opinion of the Home Secretary there is currently no viable route of return available.
(d) *Judicial review of asylum decision*: he has made an application for judicial review of a decision in relation to his asylum claim and (except in Scotland where there is no permission stage) has been granted permission to proceed by the court.
(e) *Support needed to avoid human rights breach (eg due to fresh claim)*: the provision of support is necessary for the purpose of avoiding a breach of the person's Convention rights within the meaning of the Human Rights Act 1998.

Destitution test

6.24 To qualify for support, an applicant must appear to the Home Secretary to be destitute.[17] The test of destitution for section 4(2) accommodation is the same as for an applicant for section 95 support: '"destitute" is to be construed in accordance with section 95(3) of the 1999 Act . . .'.[18]

16 IA(PAFA) Regs 2005 reg 3(1).
17 IA(PAFA) Regs 2005 reg 3(1)(a).
18 IA(PAFA) Regs 2005 reg 2.

6.25 Under section 95(3):

> . . . a person is destitute if–
> a) he does not have adequate accommodation or any means of obtaining it (whether or not his essential living needs are met); or
> b) he has adequate accommodation or the means of obtaining it, but cannot meet his other essential living needs.

6.26 The factors to be taken into account in deciding whether a person's accommodation is adequate and whether their 'essential living needs' are met are contained in other subsections of section 95, which then refer to the Asylum Support Regulations 2000 (AS Regs 2000).[19] The AS Regs 2000 contain a 'prescribed period' of 14 days for new applicants[20] so UKBA must consider whether the applicant has adequate accommodation and living expenses for this period in section 95 asylum support cases. In section 4 cases the position is unclear since the AS Regs 2000 appear only to relate to support under IAA 1999 s95. However UKBA internal guidance on section 4 refers to AS Regs 2000 regs 5–9 in the context of assessing destitution.

6.27 Any dependant should be taken into account when assessing whether accommodation and living needs are met[21] so, for example a nursing mother may be destitute if she is living in shared accommodation that presents a health risk to her baby.

Evidence of destitution

6.28 For section 4(2) applicants, showing that they are destitute has proved unexpectedly difficult. The Home Office frequently decides that applicants are not destitute and so are ineligible for section 4 accommodation.[22] The issue has arisen in numerous asylum support appeals and tribunal judges tend to apply a fairly restrictive approach, requiring appellants to produce evidence to 'prove' destitution.

6.29 Typically a refused asylum-seeker will have lived at a series of temporary insecure addresses for months or even years after the refusal of their asylum claim, with frequent moves. They may have lived with other migrants on the floors of hostels, sharing food and attempting to keep their presence secret because they have no

19 SI No 704.

20 AS Regs 2000 reg 7.

21 IAA 1999 s95(4).

22 See *Not Destitute Enough*, Asylum Support Appeals Project (ASAP) Report, January 2009.

lawful right to live there. They may have obtained food from soup kitchens, mosques, casual acquaintances, churches and/or voluntary organisations. In some cases, in desperation, an asylum-seeker may have unlawfully worked some time in the past. For the current support application, this should be irrelevant if now they have no money left. The test is whether the applicant is currently destitute. It is strongly arguable that where an applicant gives a consistent account of their *recent* accommodation history and where there is no evidence that they can meet their essential living and accommodation needs, the decision-maker should be satisfied that they are destitute.

6.30 If the decision-maker is not satisfied that the applicant is destitute then any decision should include individualised reasons, rather than the standardised ones which are commonly issued.[23]

6.31 The best evidence of destitution might be a letter from a reputable voluntary organisation that the applicant visits regularly who can confirm, for example, if his or her physical condition is deteriorating. The following list indicates the type of evidence that may be available to an applicant to demonstrate they are destitute. It is not suggested that applicants should be required to provide all or any of this information:

- letters from friends or family members saying what support/accommodation has been provided and how long it was/can be provided for. If the applicant is still residing with them, it is usually necessary to state the date on which they are required to leave. If no date is given the Home Office often will presume that accommodation remains available and refuse the application;
- letters from voluntary, charitable or faith organisations stating what food, shelter or other assistance has been provided and whether it can continue. Where appropriate the writer should give their opinion on the appearance of the refused asylum-seeker, eg if they have lost weight or appear homeless;
- if there is a bank account, the last bank statement and preferably statements covering the previous three months;
- letter from doctor, counsellor or practice nurse commenting on applicant's physical or mental condition;
- letter from voluntary organisation, adviser or solicitor giving details of the availability or otherwise of charitable food and shelter in the locality;

23 See *Failing the Failed*, Asylum Support Appeals Project Report, 2007.

- letter from any other person who knows the applicant or has regular contact with them who is able to confirm their account ie that they do not have access to essential living needs and shelter;
- a detailed letter or statement from the applicant explaining their recent circumstances.

The five conditions

6.32 An applicant for section 4(2) support only needs to meet one of the following five criteria. (There is a common misconception that all applicants for section 4 support must agree to leave the UK and apply for voluntary return to be eligible.)

Taking all reasonable steps to leave the UK (reg 3(2)(a))

6.33 The applicant must satisfy the Home Secretary that they are taking all reasonable steps to leave or are placing themselves in a position in which they are able to leave the UK. The regulation[24] adds: 'This may include complying with attempts to obtain a travel document', but the Home Office guidance sets out lengthy additional criteria for the decision-maker to consider, including whether the applicant has applied for assisted voluntary return (AVR), whether they have supplied evidence to support an application to the Immigration Service Documentation Unit (ISDU) for an emergency travel document and, if so, whether they could leave the UK more quickly if they applied for AVR instead.

6.34 The International Organisation for Migration (IOM) is an independent body that receives state funding to operate the Voluntary Assisted Return and Reintegration Programme (VARRP). Their role is to assist in obtaining travel documents, make travel arrangements and provide limited financial assistance to help with education, training or employment on return. Asylum Support Policy Bulletin 71, which previously contained the Home Office guidance on section 4 eligibility, required confirmation of a travel document application or an application to IOM.[25]

6.35 The AST case law suggests they have interpreted the legislation based on the Home Office guidance, finding that 'reasonable steps' would normally include registering with IOM for voluntary return. So in ASA 05/10/10339 the Chief Asylum Support Adjudicator

24 IA(PAFA) Regs 2005 reg 3(2)(a).
25 Policy Bulletin 71, Version 2.0, para 5.3 (i).

found that an appellant who had not registered with IOM had failed to take all reasonable steps to leave the UK.

6.36 Where a deportation order or removal directions have been issued, a refused asylum-seeker is not eligible to apply for voluntary return. This was recognised by the adjudicator in AST 07/04/15054. In such cases, they must rely on other 'reasonable steps' such as co-operating with the Home Office's attempts to obtain travel documents.

6.37 In AST 07/11/16508, a Somali applicant had made two applications to IOM, which advised him it was their policy not to accept a third unless they found there were exceptional circumstances. Section 4 support was refused and he appealed. He explained to the tribunal he had no evidence of his identity because he was an orphan and had been brought up in a refugee camp in Kenya. He said the Somali embassy in London was closed and he had approached the Kenyan embassy that would not provide travel documents in these circumstances. The adjudicator found that the applicant was taking all reasonable steps to return. He observed that section 4 entitlement might be reviewed in future, at which time the appellant would again need to show he was taking reasonable steps.

6.38 Attempts have been made by Iraqi refused asylum-seekers to show they are taking all reasonable steps to return, in the context of the lack of safety of the return route. In *R (Rasul) v Asylum Support Adjudicator and others*[26] the court found that the safety of return under reg 3(2)(c) was a matter for the Home Office, but they left open the possibility of the argument being used in the context of reasonable steps under reg 3(2)(a). Soon after *Rasul* the Chief Asylum Support Adjudicator found herself unable to follow Wilkie J's suggested approach because she considered that the tribunal was limited to considering the reasonableness of any steps which the appellant had actually taken, not whether it was reasonable to take a proposed step due to an unsafe route.[27]

6.39 Subsequently a refused Iraqi asylum-seeker from outside the Kurdish controlled KRG area applied for support under reg 3(2)(a) with evidence of the dangers of travel along the proposed return route. The Asylum Support Tribunal dismissed the appeal on the basis that they had no jurisdiction to consider the safety of travel within Iraq, even within the context of reasonable steps. He applied for judicial review arguing that the correct approach to reg 3(2)(a) was to consider not simply whether he could reach Iraq, but whether

26 [2006] EWHC 435 (Admin).

27 ASA 06/03/12859.

he could reach his home in central Iraq. Silber J dismissed the application finding there was a lack of evidence and the wording of the regulation limited it to matters arising in the UK. But significantly it was accepted on behalf of the Home Office that refused asylum-seekers unable to travel home might be able to show a potential ECHR article 3 breach and so come within reg 3(2)(e). This could apply if there was a real risk that the applicant would suffer ill-treatment reaching the article 3 threshold either on the journey back to their home country, or on the journey to the safe area within their home country. In such cases the breach would arise because the article 3 threshold would be reached if the claimant was without food and/or shelter whilst unable to travel home. The claimant was granted permission to appeal to the Court of Appeal, but the appeal was not pursued because he was granted leave to remain in the UK.[28]

6.40 Nationals of certain countries such as Eritrea may find their embassy is not willing to issue them with a travel document because they cannot prove they are Eritrean. Examples of 'reasonable steps' in this and other situations could include:

- attending the embassy (with a witness if necessary);
- contacting the Red Cross to ask them to search for family members in the country of origin, who might be able to provide identity documents;
- completing the IOM application, furnishing IOM with information and attending an appointment with them;
- writing to relatives or agencies in the country of origin or authorising IOM to do so if appropriate.

Obstacle to travel

6.41 The applicant must show they are '*unable*' to leave the UK due to a '*physical impediment to travel*' or for some other medical reason. It is not sufficient for an applicant to have a medical need. Arguably, 'physical impediment' could include a situation where there is no available means of travelling to the home country, for example in the case of Gaza at a time when all borders were sealed and there were no flights allowed. But there do not appear to have been any appeals in which this has been argued.

6.42 In the maternity context, a relevant factor is whether an airline would carry a woman on a long-haul flight at a late stage of her

28 *R (Ahmed) v Asylum Support Adjudicator and Secretary of State for the Home Department* [2008] EWHC 2282 (Admin), December 2008 *Legal Action* 38.

pregnancy, which is often interpreted as from seven months of confinement onwards. Home Office guidance suggests that this criterion covers cases where a woman is in the late stages of pregnancy or has a baby under six weeks old. The guidance indicates that late stages of pregnancy is usually limited to cases where the expected date of confinement is within six weeks, and could only be at an earlier stage if there were complications with the pregnancy.

Decisions on 'impediment to travel'

- Applying their guidance, UKBA refused to provide section 4 support to a pregnant woman whose baby was due nine weeks later. Their approach was challenged on the basis that the six-week limit is arbitrary and there may be a margin of error of between 37-42 weeks according to NHS guidance.[29] The tribunal judge allowed her appeal noting she had a history of miscarriages and that the section 4 guidance did not establish a legal test.[30]
- The High Court reviewed the test in the context of ill-health in a case where the applicant was not represented at the tribunal or in the judicial review. The court decided that a two-stage test should be applied, asking first whether the applicant was 'unable to leave the UK'. Second, the Home Office should consider whether the inability was 'by reason of a physical impediment or other medical reason'. The judge refused to define the word 'unable' but appeared to approve (at para 16 of the judgment) the reference in the NASS Policy Bulletin 71 to being 'unfit to travel . . . .'.[31]

6.43 So the emphasis is on showing a link between the health need and inability to travel, whether for a physical or psychological reason. The refusal of airlines to carry a passenger with a contagious disease such as certain forms of TB would be relevant. The lack of medical treatment in the country of origin (even if fatal) will not generally meet the condition. The current practice of the AST is to issue directions seeking detailed information from the appellant's medical advisers.

29 NHS Choices – Pregnancy Overview.

30 AST 09/02/1904 (see para 7.84).

31 *R (Secretary of State for the Home Department) v Asylum Support Adjudicator and Mohammed Osman and others (interested parties)* [2006] EWHC 1248 (Admin).

6.44 The adviser should specifically point out the test to the appellant's medical adviser, explaining that the expression of sympathy or general support by the medical adviser for the appellant is not of assistance unless their medical opinion, confirmed in writing, is that the appellant is 'unable' to travel.[32]

6.45 This may present practical problems where a doctor requires payment for any such report. Arguably it should be sufficient to produce specific evidence that the appellant has a particular medical condition together with general evidence about its effects but the AST has not adopted this approach.

6.46 The revised section 4 application form allows the applicant to provide a 'medical declaration'. The declaration form is published on the UKBA website. The new tribunal procedural rules[33] which allow the tribunal judge to order a person such as a doctor to provide information also.

No safe route of return: reg 3(2)(c)

6.47 Currently there are no countries to which the Home Secretary considers there is no viable route of return, but between January and July 2005 this criterion applied to Iraq.

6.48 It has been argued unsuccessfully in the case of an Iraqi former asylum-seeker that the AST has jurisdiction to consider the safety of the return route.[34]

Permission granted to apply for judicial review: reg 3(2)(d)

6.49 This applies only to a judicial review of the asylum decision and is not generally controversial. The Administrative Court will issue a court order when they grant permission that should accompany the section 4 application. (The Treasury solicitor is also notified but often communication between them and the Home Office section 4 team can be poor.) On occasions, the Home Office has confused this criterion with an application for judicial review of the section 4 decision.

6.50 In Scotland there is no permission stage in judicial review. So in Scotland it is sufficient simply to apply for judicial review to qualify for section 4 under this ground.

32 ASAP has a model letter on its website setting out the test for a medical adviser.

33 See para 7.115.

34 *R (Rasul) v Asylum Support Adjudicator and others* [2006] EWHC 435 (Admin); and see para 6.35 above.

6.51 If the judicial review application is successful, and this leads the Home Office to 'record' representations as a fresh asylum claim, then the applicant becomes an asylum-seeker again and so should apply for (and will be entitled to) support under IAA 1999 s95.

Support needed to avoid a breach of human rights

6.52 This criteria needs to be considered in the context of whether or not the applicant can avoid a human rights breach by leaving the UK. So in *R (Limbuela) v Secretary of State for Home Department*[35] the court found support was needed to avoid a breach of ECHR article 3 rights where asylum-seekers were faced with street homelessness.[36] Since they had an outstanding first asylum claim, they could not leave the UK to avoid destitution.

6.53 In their guidance the Home Office gives two examples of where this criterion would apply:

- the applicant has made further representations that have not yet been considered, and those representations do not simply repeat previously considered material or contain no detail;
- the applicant has submitted an out of time appeal against a refusal of asylum and the AIT is considering whether to allow the appeal to proceed out of time.

6.54 The main group of applicants in this category are those who have made a fresh asylum or ECHR article 3 claim or representations, which have not yet been recorded. Other examples are:

- the applicant has applied for leave to remain under another ECHR ground, such as the article 8 right to respect for family life, for example arguing they cannot leave the UK because they have a British spouse or child living here;
- the applicant needs to remain in the UK temporarily because of court proceedings (article 6) or care proceedings (article 8);[37]
- the applicant has applied for judicial review in England or Wales and has an arguable case, but permission has not yet been considered (see AS 09/06/19865);
- the applicant is stateless (AST 06/03/13043).

35 [2005] UKHL 66, (2006) 9 CCLR 30.

36 See para 4.105.

37 See *R (PB) v Haringey LBC* [2006] EWHC 2255 (Admin), January 2007 *Legal Action* 17.

6.55 Before the five conditions for accessing section 4 accommodation were placed on a statutory footing, the High Court considered, in *R (Nigatu) v Secretary of State for the Home Department*,[38] whether a refused asylum-seeker who had made a fresh claim was entitled to support. Collins J found that the claimant would not become entitled to support under IAA 1999 s95 until the fresh claim was recorded by the Home Office. He suggested that in the meantime section 4 accommodation should be provided.

6.56 There is considerable case law about when the Home Office should record a fresh claim.[39] Similarly there has been debate in the support context about the extent to which the section 4 decision-maker should scrutinise the fresh claim to assess whether it has merit.

6.57 The Administrative Court considered this in the community care context.[40] Lloyd J observed:

> In many cases – possibly the great majority – it may well be inappropriate for a public body to embark on any consideration of the purported fresh grounds. However, there may be cases where the purported fresh grounds are manifestly nothing of the sort and where it would be appropriate for the public body to take account of that fact in arriving at its decision in relation to asylum support.

6.58 The law was reviewed by the tribunal in a landmark decision,[41] which decided that each case should be determined on a case-by-case basis and that NASS caseworkers may refuse applications for section 4 support if further representations '*simply rehearse previously considered material or contain no detail whatsoever*'.[42]

6.59 The question was then revisited in another community care judicial review, *R (B) v Southwark LBC*.[43] Deputy Judge Andrew Nicol QC considered that a local authority's role was simply to consider whether an outstanding human rights application was 'manifestly unfounded', not to assess the general merits of the application, which must be left to the immigration authority. See also the approach in *R (Yogathas) v Secretary of State for the Home Department*.[44]

38 [2004] EWHC 1806 (Admin).

39 See chapter 1.

40 *R (AW) v Croydon LBC; R (1)(A)(2)(D)(3)(Y) v Hackney LBC and Secretary of State for the Home Department (Interested party)* [2005] EWHC 2950 (Admin).

41 ASA 05/01/11695.

42 See also ASA 05/07/9572 and ASA 05/12/11497.

43 [2006] EWHC 2254 (Admin), January 2007 *Legal Action* 17.

44 [2003] 1 AC 920 at [34].

6.60 After NAM was introduced in March 2007, case owners are expected to decide on both asylum and support issues. It is therefore foreseeable that in future the Home Office will argue that the caseworker can make a valid preliminary decision on the asylum claim which will affect the outcome of the support application. This approach could be challenged on the basis that the asylum process does not allow for such preliminary decisions.

Procedures

Applications

6.61 The procedure for refused asylum-seekers to apply for section 4 support is to complete a lengthy form which is available on the Home Office website. There are two different forms/procedures depending on whether the applicant is a New Asylum Model (NAM) or a legacy (CRD) case.[45]

6.62 Where the applicant applied for asylum before 6 March 2007 and does not have a case owner, their case is classed as a 'legacy' case, being processed by the Casework Resolution Directorate (CRD). They must complete a 'casework resolution' application form for section 4 support, which was processed by the UKBA's section 4 team, but should now be processed by CRD. The one stop agencies can provide the forms and assist in completing and submitting the application.

6.63 Applicants who applied for asylum after 5 March 2007 (when NAM was in place) or who have a case owner must complete an 'asylum team' application form, which is processed by the relevant case owner/asylum team.[46] This will normally be the same official who refused their original asylum application and so will be familiar with their circumstances.

6.64 In either case, the form should be sent/faxed to the address that appears on the form with as much supporting documentation as is available. It should have enough information to show the applicant is destitute and meets one of the five criteria.

6.65 When completing the form, an important consideration is that an applicant for section 4 support may have no safe postal address or be

45 See para 1.74.

46 Pre 6 March 2007 applicants can attempt to find out the identity of their case-owner by phoning the Home Office or completing a query on the UKBA website.

facing eviction. If possible, an address should be put on the form where post can be promptly received, for example c/o a local refugee organisation. UKBA may write requesting further information within a short timescale or may refuse support, in which case there are only three working days to appeal (see below).

Applicants in detention

6.66 Applicants who are in detention/claiming support under section 4(1) are not required to complete an application form, but it may save time.

6.67 A new procedure for processing applications from detainees was introduced in June 2009. The process enables accommodation to be provided quickly if bail is granted and for the detainee to be moved into initial accommodation. From there they will be dispersed to alternative accommodation, depending on their needs.

6.68 There has been some debate about whether a detainee who is also a failed asylum-seeker must apply for support under section 4(2) rather than under section 4(1) and so must meet one of the five criteria. In the past UKBA's approach has been variable, only occasionally granting section 4 support to a detainee without any of the criteria being met and thus providing an address on which a bail application can be based. Until a court has considered the issue, it is reasonable to argue that section 4(1) provides that a failed asylum-seeker who is a detainee is eligible for support without meeting the criteria in IA(PAFA) Regs 2005 reg 3(2). In fact UKBA in April 2008 published amended section 4 guidance on its website confirming it accepts this argument.[47]

Procedure after grant of section 4 accommodation

6.69 At the time of writing, the procedure was as set out here, but it is subject to change. UKBA will usually send or fax the applicant a 'grant letter' setting out the conditions of support, for example to live at the section 4 address and that support will be withdrawn is these conditions are not met. The applicant is required to telephone to confirm the offer of support. UKBA will then fax a 'booking form' to an accommodation provider, requesting that an offer of accommodation is made within 48 hours. The applicant will then receive a letter from UKBA with an address. If necessary the accommodation

47 See also AST 09/02/19288.

provider will collect the applicant from their current location and transport them to their section 4 address. This will normally be shared private rented accommodation outside London. There are very limited circumstances in which it is possible to challenge the location or quality of the accommodation.[48]

6.70 UKBA procedure involves regular reviews of section 4 support. There is policy guidance governing their approach to such reviews. A review would include the decision-maker checking whether one of the five criteria still applies, for example has the fresh claim been rejected or have further reasonable steps been taken to leave the UK by co-operating with IOM. If it appears to them that the criteria no longer apply, the procedure is that UKBA should write to the applicant requesting a response within the next 14 days, explaining why they still consider themselves eligible.

6.71 At the time of writing, UKBA has indicated that they plan to review section 4 support every three months, and in the context of those within reg 3(2)(a) will require applicants to reapply. Representations were made that this appeared to be unlawful in view of the wording of the regulations.

Delays

6.72 Delays of days or weeks may be experienced at any of these points in the process:

- in making a decision about the initial application for section 4 accommodation;
- after a grant of section 4 accommodation, before a property is offered;
- after a successful appeal to the AST, before section 4 accommodation is provided.

6.73 As any section 4(2) applicant must be destitute, even a short delay may have severe consequences. Home Office policy is that an application for accommodation should be decided within 48 hours if it is a priority case. There is substantial evidence that this target has consistently not been met.[49] Although UKBA has improved procedures for processing claims, the current administrative arrangements do not provide adequate protection for destitute households.

48 See para 6.92.

49 See for example 'The Treatment of Asylum-Seekers', Tenth report of session 2006–7, HL Paper 81-I, HC 60-I, 30 March 2007.

A particular problem is the absence of any equivalent to IAA 1999 s98 emergency accommodation if enquiries need to be made before an initial decision.

6.74 The remedy for delay is to apply for judicial review and an emergency injunction. In *R (Matembera) v Secretary of State for the Home Department*,[50] M applied for judicial review because he was destitute and had not received a section 4 decision in the 48-hour period. An injunction was granted ordering section 4 accommodation to be provided immediately. But because M's fresh claim was then recorded, he became entitled to support under IAA 1999 s95 so his claim was academic and permission was refused. M applied to renew the application with evidence that as many as 83 per cent of cases were not decided in two days, arguing there was a duty under ECHR article 3 to provide interim accommodation pending a section 4 decision. Hodge J refused permission but made observations urging the Home Secretary to sort out the system.[51]

6.75 This means individual applicants are left to challenge delays on a case-by-case basis unless evidence is gathered to support a further 'academic' challenge. An alternative remedy would be to make a formal complaint to UKBA and ask the Parliamentary Ombudsman to investigate current systems, but this will not provide the urgent relief needed by an individual who is without food and shelter.

ID cards

6.76 In preparation for the introduction of compulsory identification cards for foreign (and eventually British) nationals, the Home Office introduced the definition of an immigration registration card. This can include a card issued to an asylum applicant (an application registration card or ARC) or a document issued in connection with those seeking or eligible to receive section 4 support.[52] It is an offence to interfere with such a card or use it for the purposes of deception.[53] By letter dated 28 March 2008, the Asylum Policy Unit of the Home Office wrote to stakeholders announcing its intention to make section 4 support conditional on the applicant attending an appointment to be issued with a registration card and producing

50 CO/6401/2006, December 2007 Legal Action 19.

51 See also *R (Salih and Rahmani) v Secretary of State for the Home Department* [2003] EWHC 2273 (Admin) para 65.

52 IA 1971 s26A(1) as substituted by Immigration (Registration Card) Order 2008 SI No 1693.

53 IA 1971 s26A(2).

the card when support was provided. The letter stated that the Immigration and Asylum (Provision of Accommodation to Failed Asylum-seekers) Regulations 2005[54] would be repealed and replaced with new regulations that would also amend the conditions for section 4 support. At the time of writing, the legislation had not been changed but applicants were being required to produce the card.

Appeals to the First-tier Tribunal (Asylum Support)

6.77 If section 4 support is refused there is a right of appeal[55] to the First-tier Tribunal (Asylum Support), formerly known as the Asylum Support Tribunal (AST), and before that the asylum support adjudicators (ASA).[56]

6.78 An applicant may appeal against a decision not to provide, or not to continue to provide, accommodation under section 4. There is no right of appeal in relation to location or quality of accommodation, which can only be challenged by judicial review.

6.79 The appeals procedure for section 4 appeals is the same as for other appeals as described in chapter 7. The following points apply in particular to section 4 appeals:

- To succeed in an appeal, the section 4(2) applicant will need to show they are destitute and that they meet one of the five criteria. So any representations or extra evidence in support of this should be included with the appeal form.
- The tribunal judge is likely to issue directions addressing the reasons for refusal. These will normally be sent or faxed to the applicant (often with a day or two in which to respond), unless they have a named representative.
- The appeal form asks if the appellant has a representative. If a voluntary/advice organisation or solicitor gives their details as 'representative' they are acknowledging responsibility. They are likely to receive formal directions from the tribunal judge requesting extra information within a short timescale. So before agreeing to be the recorded representative, they should consider whether/how they can remain in contact with the appellant and respond promptly to any such directions. One approach would be

54 SI No 930.

55 IAA 1999 s103(2A) as inserted by AI(TC)A 2004 s10.

56 See para 7.115 onwards regarding the changes to the tribunal procedure and constitution.

for the organisation to indicate on the form that they are assisting but not 'representing ' the appellant and simply offer themselves as a contact address.

- The appeal stage is an opportunity to provide extra evidence in support of the claim, for example evidence that the applicant has contacted IOM, or has made further representations, or has a medical condition preventing them from travelling. If the appeal fails and judicial review is considered, it will be useful if all the available relevant evidence was before the adjudicator.

Provision of section 4 support[57]

6.80 The problems for section 4 applicants in supporting themselves with vouchers and sharing poor quality accommodation are well-documented.[58]

6.81 If an applicant qualifies for support under section 4, they will receive a package of accommodation and support. The support is usually vouchers for living expenses with a room in a communal private rented house arranged by an accommodation provider. Sometimes the package is 'full board' in hostel accommodation. The applicant may be expected to share with another adult of the same sex, unless they can produce evidence such as a doctor's report explaining why they need their own room, or unless they have a child. The accommodation provider will issue weekly supermarket vouchers, which may be delivered or the applicant may need to collect them from an office.

6.82 The power to provide support under IAA 1999 s4 is expressed as 'facilities for accommodation' so it may only be provided in the form of accommodation with living expenses attached. Unlike support under IAA s95, it is not possible for an applicant to stay with a friend and claim subsistence only.

Living expenses

6.83 In *AW (Kenya) v Secretary of State for the Home Department*,[59] a Somali nursing mother applied for judicial review of the decision to limit section 4 support to £35 per week food vouchers, arguing

57 See also chapter 10 regarding healthcare for refused asylum-seekers.

58 '*Shaming Destitution*', Citizens Advice, June 2006.

59 [2006] EWHC 3147 (Admin).

that she should be provided with clothing and baby items. She had been receiving section 4 support for over two years. NASS argued they had no power to provide her with clothing. The court agreed, finding that the section 4 terminology 'facilities for accommodation' could only be read so as to include facilities linked to accommodation, which could include food but did not extend to clothing. The Home Office then introduced IAA 1999 s4(10) and (11) which prohibit the provision of cash under section 4 (IANA 2006 s43(7).

6.84 The Home Office's consistent position has been that they are not willing to provide section 4 support in the form of cash. In evidence to the JCHR, the Home Office suggested that this is justified by the temporary nature of section 4 support, despite conflicting evidence that many applicants are supported under section 4 for months or even years.

6.85 On 31 January 2008, the Immigration and Asylum (Provision of Services or Facilities) Regulations (IA(PSF) Regs) 2007[60] came into force, to allow for extra support to be provided in kind to those supported under section 4, including for travel, clothing, baby items and extra payments for children.

Travel and communications

6.86 'Facilities for travel' may be provided to the applicant and their dependent child for a journey of not less than three miles to receive medical treatment or register a birth.[61] A full birth certificate may also be financed.[62]

6.87 Facilities may be provided for phone calls, stationery and postage to specified agencies such as doctors, a Citizens Advice Bureau, the voluntary organisations funded by the Home Office to provide reception advice and immigration solicitors/advisers.[63] It is envisaged that the applicant will receive a voucher for £2.50 (when applying for stationery expenses) or a £5 telephone card and can apply again for a telephone card six months later if necessary.[64]

Mothers and children

6.88 A pregnant woman is eligible for a £250 payment but must claim in the period of eight weeks before her expected week of

60 SI No 3627.
61 IA(PSF) Regs 2007 reg 3.
62 IA(PSF) Regs 2007 reg 4.
63 IA(PSF) Regs 2007 reg 5.
64 UKBA s4 guidance.

confinement[65] or within the six weeks after the birth.[66] Time limits are strict. She is entitled to an extra £3 voucher a week during her pregnancy.[67] She may claim an extra £5 voucher per week for her baby until he or she reach the age of one year. £3 per week is then payable until the child's third birthday.[68] Extra vouchers may be claimed for a child's clothing up to the value of £5 per week.[69]

Other needs

6.89 There is a 'catch all' provision where the supported person can satisfy the Home Office that they have an exceptional need for travel, phone calls, stationery/postage, or 'essential living needs'.

6.90 It is important to note that no payments are made without a specific application on the correct form. At the time of writing, these provisions were relatively new and the mechanism for processing applications had not been ironed out. The procedure (under the IA(PSF) Regs 2007) is to complete an application form available on the Home Office website and send it to the Home Office with supporting evidence. It is difficult to see how this can work in practice if the applicant has no money for postage or is illiterate and cannot finance travel to attend a refugee organisation for help with the form. Given delays in processing section 4 applications, it is also difficult to see how this arrangement will enable a sick pregnant mother attend an urgent medical appointment for example, especially as she will need evidence to demonstrate that the journey is 'necessary'.

6.91 There is no right of appeal against the refusal of extra support, so the remedy would normally be to use the UKBA complaints procedures, or Ombudsman (see para 7.170).

Accommodation

6.92 Unlike accommodation under IAA 1999 s95, there is no requirement for section 4 accommodation to be 'adequate'. This means that the main methods for challenging an offer of accommodation are by

65 IA(PSF) Regs 2007 reg 6(1) and see specific Home Office asylum support guidance.
66 IA(PSF) Regs 2007 reg 6(2).
67 IA(PSF) Regs 2007 reg 7(1).
68 IA(PSF) Regs 2007 reg 7.
69 IA(PSF) Regs 2007 reg 8.

relying on UKBA policy, public law or ECHR arguments. For those receiving section 4 support after making further representations/a fresh asylum claim, it may be arguable that the Reception Directive applies.[70] The Reception Directive article 14(4) adds support to arguing that asylum-seekers (including those with fresh claims) should not be moved unnecessarily and so should not be moved from existing section 95 accommodation or from one dispersal location to another. But generally, if accommodation is refused, no further offer will be made unless there is new evidence.

6.93 The conditions in the accommodation would need to be extremely poor to meet the article 3 threshold of inhuman and degrading treatment. A more effective remedy may be to ask the local council's environmental health officer to inspect and to consider whether there are any breaches of health and safety or fire regulations.[71]

6.94 It is UKBA's policy not to disperse section 4 applicants if they are receiving Medical Foundation treatment, as for IAA 1999 s95 cases.[72] If there are other strong reasons to challenge the offer of accommodation, for example an essential medical need which can only be met by housing in a particular area, then representations should be made to UKBA who will probably refer the case to their medical adviser. Judicial review will only be available in cases where UKBA has failed to take into account all the relevant factors, or follow a fair procedure or where the move would interfere with ECHR rights. For example, if accommodation were offered in Glasgow and the applicant has a young child in Bristol with whom he has regular contact, he might be able to argue the accommodation would interfere with his art 8 right to respect for family life as he would be unable to visit his child.

6.95 If the supported person has physical or mental health needs, then it may be appropriate for him or her to ask the local authority in the area where they are living for a community care assessment and accommodation under National Assistance Act 1948 s21 on the basis that they have 'non-destitution' needs.[73]

70 See para 7.105.

71 See para 8.197.

72 See Policy Bulletins 31 and 85.

73 See chapter 9.

CHAPTER 7

Appeals and remedies

continued

continued

Introduction

7.1 This chapter considers the remedies available to challenge an asylum support decision, from complaints procedures to asylum support appeals and judicial review. The focus is on Home Office decisions about asylum support under section 4, 98 or 95 of the Immigration and Asylum Act (IAA) 1999, as covered in the previous three chapters. Remedies relating to immigration, benefits, housing, community care and healthcare decisions are dealt with in the relevant chapters. But those parts of this chapter covering general issues, access to information and complaints, and judicial review may also be useful in tackling adverse decisions by any public authority.

7.2 At the start of the NASS asylum support scheme on 3 April 2000 appeals were mainly about entitlement to support under IAA 1999 s95. As the scheme has bedded down and asylum decision-making speeded up, there has been a reduction in such appeals, and an increase in the number of appeals relating to entitlement under IAA 1999 s4. The other main development is new procedural rules from 2009, when the tribunal became the First-tier Tribunal (Asylum Support) of the Social Entitlement Chamber. We include a full overview of potential reasons for refusing section 95 support and earlier decisions because the approach taken remains relevant to the new First-tier Tribunal. We also highlight changes introduced by the EU Reception Directive.

Rebranding

Appeals against refusal of support were initially to the Asylum Support Adjudicators (ASA), renamed the Asylum Support Tribunal (AST) on 2 April 2007. This became the First-tier Tribunal (Asylum Support) of the new Social Entitlement Chamber on 3 November 2008 (still referred to here as the AST). Earlier appeal decisions are referred to as *ASA* 04/04/7885 or *AST* 08/02/4215. The 'adjudicator' is now referred to as the 'tribunal judge' (TJ). The Chief Asylum Support Adjudicator and Deputy Chief Asylum Support Adjudicator are now principal judge asylum support (PJ) and deputy principal judge asylum support (DPJ) respectively.

Refusal or withdrawal of support

Procedures for ending support

7.3 Formally decisions are made by the Home Secretary, but here we refer to decision-makers in the UK Border Agency (UKBA) who act as agents for the Home Office. Where asylum support under IAA 1999 s4 or s95 is refused or withdrawn, the procedure which the UKBA decision-maker should follow is to send the applicant a refusal letter with reasons, together with a notice of appeal form and explanatory letter.[1]

7.4 In practice, an asylum-seeker may discover their support has ended in a variety of ways, such as when the post office refuses to cash their receipt book or when an accommodation-provider asks them to leave. If the reason for withdrawing support is unclear, the first step may be to phone the 'termination of support' telephone number at UKBA[2] to establish the reason why support has stopped. In the case of the post office refusing to provide section 95 support, they should ask for two receipts from the post office which have a code on them to indicate the reason for refusal. If UKBA is investigating the case or believes it has made an error, emergency support tokens may be sent to the asylum-seeker until the problem is resolved.

7.5 If UKBA is refusing even to consider an application for section 95 support because of non-co-operation with enquiries, they must write to the applicant, giving him or her five working days to reply before refusing support.[3]

7.6 Any decision to end support must be taken 'individually, objectively and impartially and reasons shall be given'.[4] It should be based on the particular situation of the person concerned and particular regard should be had as to whether the person is a 'vulnerable person' as defined by regulation 4 of the Asylum Seekers (Reception Conditions) Regulations 2005.[5] If the person concerned is vulnerable within the meaning of the Reception Directive, for example a lone parent, that should also be taken into account.[6]

7.7 If support is not reinstated, or if there is a delayed response, an appeal to the tribunal is likely to result in UKBA re-examining the case and possibly withdrawing their decision. But the problem may be a delay in getting any decision at all.

1 See Policy Bulletin 23.

2 See appendix H for contact details.

3 Asylum Support Regs 2000 reg 3(5A).

4 See paras 7.23–7.25.

5 SI No 7.

6 See para 7.105 onwards; Asylum Support Regulations 2000 SI No 704 as amended by Asylum Support (Amendment) Regulations 2005 SI No 11 and NASS Policy Bulletin 83.

Delays in decision-making[7]

> We have heard countless examples of Home Office inefficiencies in processing support claims, with severe consequences for desperate, vulnerable people who have no other means to support themselves .... The institutional failure to address operational inefficiencies and to protect asylum seekers from destitution amounts in many cases to a failure to protect them from inhuman and degrading treatment under Article 3 ECHR.[8]

Section 95 delays[9]

7.8 At the time of writing, delays as long as three months were reported in processing applications for section 95 asylum support. A threat of, or application for, judicial review of the delay is likely to result in a decision being made and accommodation offered, but this does not resolve the wider problem. Attempts to challenge Home Office/UKBA operational failures and policies that cause delay, in the context of section 4 delays, have generally failed.[10] An alternative approach is to use the Home Office complaints scheme or the Ombudsman (see below). This is unlikely to get a quick response but could lead to some compensation, and even policy changes if a significant number of complaints are received.

Delays in issuing Home Office decisions/status documents

7.9 Many *initial* asylum decisions are now made within six months of the application,[11] but there are lengthy Home Office delays in recording or making a decision on a fresh asylum or human rights claim, which may have an impact on an asylum-seeker's access to support. The courts have taken a restrictive approach to attempts to judicially review these delays, but may grant relief in exceptional cases.

7 See also para 5.14 regarding section 98 delays and para 6.72 regarding section 4 delays.

8 Joint Committee on Human Rights, The treatment of asylum-seekers, tenth report of session 2006–07, HL81-I/HC60-I, March 2007.

9 See also paras 1.203 and 6.72 regarding section 4 delay.

10 See para 6.72.

11 Control of Immigration, Quarterly statistical summary UK, first quarter 2009, RDS www.homeoffice.gov.uk/rds/pdfs09/immiq109.pdf

7.10 In *R (FH and others) v Secretary of State for the Home Department*[12] the claimants were refused asylum-seekers who had submitted fresh asylum or ECHR claims based on new evidence. Their claims had not been decided for two or three years (apart from in one case) and in the case of H, for five years. They applied for judicial review arguing that the system of dealing with the backlog was unfair and also unlawful. Collins J found that the delays were 'excessive, unsatisfactory and undesirable', but with the exception of H's case he did not consider they reached the exceptional threshold so as to be declared unlawful. In deciding that the Home Office's new system for processing backlog cases was not irrational, he took into account that the claimants' initial claims had been decided, that there were past problems with removals, and that the Home Office had to process large number of unmeritorious fresh claims. He concluded:

> Claims such as these based on delay are unlikely, save in very exceptional circumstances to succeed ... It is only if the delay is so excessive as to be regarded as manifestly unreasonable and to fall outside any proper application of the policy or if the claimant is suffering some particular detriment which the Home Office has failed to alleviate that a claim might be entertained by the court.

7.11 Where there has been a delay in issuing Home Office documents after a successful asylum appeal, it is possible to apply for judicial review of the delay.[13] As a rule of thumb, the asylum-seeker should wait six months before applying for judicial review but the period may be shorter if there are urgent or exceptional reasons.[14] If the family is about to be evicted and needs status documents to apply for rehousing, then a judicial review could be considered within two months of the appeal decision.

7.12 Where the Home Office's maladministration in failing to issue accurate immigration status documents meant that A waited a year subject to an incorrect 'no recourse to public funds' condition and K waited nine months after his asylum appeal for a status letter, Keith J found the Home Office owed each of them a duty of care and awarded damages in negligence to compensate them for their lost income support.[15]

12 [2007] EWHC 1571 (Admin).

13 See para 1.203 onwards.

14 *R (Mersin) v Secretary of State for the Home Department* [2000] EWHC 348 (Admin).

15 *R ((1) A and (2) Kanidagli) v Secretary of State for the Home Department* [2004] EWHC 1585 (Admin).

Challenging asylum support decisions

7.13 A suggested approach where section 4, 98 or 95 support has been refused or withdrawn is as follows:

- establish UKBA's reason;
- check client's current immigration status (chapter 1);
- check whether they are entitled to section 95 or section 4 support (chapter 4 or 6);
- check whether UKBA has followed its own procedures and guidance;
- review whether any general considerations apply, eg if it would be a breach of human rights to withdraw support (see para 7.104 below);
- if there is entitlement to support, consider whether the remedy is an asylum support appeal, judicial review or both (see para 7.160 below).

Reasons for refusing or withdrawing support

7.14 Support may be refused under Nationality, Immigration and Asylum Act (NIAA) 2002 s55 where a late claim has been made or under NIAA 2002 s57 for failure to provide information, and challenged by judicial review.[16]

7.15 Support may be refused or withdrawn if the applicant does not meet the criteria explained in chapter 4. This may be because the applicant is not an 'asylum-seeker'[17] or the 'dependant' of an asylum-seeker[18] or is not 'destitute'[19] or is in receipt of benefits.[20] Support may also be withdrawn if the applicant is excluded by NIAA 2002 s54 Sch 3 cases, for example as a person who is unlawfully in the UK or an EEA national or occasionally in section 9 cases.[21]

Not an 'asylum-seeker'[22]

7.16 In brief, an asylum-seeker for support purposes is a person of 18 or over who has made a claim for asylum or under ECHR article 3 in person which has been recorded but not yet been finally decided.[23]

16 See para 4.105.
17 See para 4.18.
18 See para 4.56.
19 See para 7.23.
20 AS Regs 2000 reg 4(4).
21 See para 4.123.
22 IAA 1999 s94(1).
23 See full definition at para 4.18.

7.17 If asylum support is refused or withdrawn for this reason and there is an appeal to the First-tier Tribunal (Asylum Support) (AST), the judge must first consider whether the appellant is an asylum-seeker (or dependant). The Home Secretary argued that the AST has no jurisdiction in the case of a refused asylum-seeker because the appellant had no right of appeal under IAA 1999 s103(1). The Chief Asylum Support Adjudicator rejected his argument, deciding that she had jurisdiction to hear an appeal in order to consider whether or not the appellant was an 'asylum-seeker'. The Home Secretary applied for judicial review.[24]

7.18 The High Court dismissed the application. They decided that the AST may hear an appeal which relates to the existence or otherwise of the factual circumstances that lead to support being granted under section 95, such as whether or not the appellant is an asylum-seeker.[25]

Asylum-seekers whose asylum appeal is late

7.19 If an asylum-seeker appeals against a refusal of asylum after the time limit has expired, there is no legal right to support until they have been granted permission to appeal out of time. In *R (Erdogan) v Secretary of State for the Home Department*[26] the Court of Appeal decided that the asylum claim was 'finally determined' even if a decision on an application to appeal out of time was pending. The Home Office has since agreed that asylum-seekers in this category can apply for section 4 support.

Appeal decisions in 'not an asylum-seeker' cases

- Where an Iranian national sent his application for a review of his AIT asylum decision to the tribunal rather than to the High Court, so it did not reach the court within the 14-day deadline, the ASA found he was not an 'asylum-seeker' within the IAA 1999 s94(4) definition so there was no jurisdiction to consider his appeal.[27]
- Similarly, the tribunal found it had no jurisdiction where a wife had applied for 'leave in line' with her husband who had indefinite leave to remain, but there was no evidence of a separate asylum claim.[28]

24 *R (Secretary of State for the Home Department) v Chief Asylum Support Adjudicator and Flutura Malaj (Interested Party)* [2006] EWHC 3059 (Admin).

25 The approach in such cases is also referred to in ASA 03/01/5461 and ASA 02/08/4215, ASA 05/09/10048.

26 [2004] EWCA Civ 1087.

27 ASA 05/03/9124.

28 ASA 02/03/2052.

- Where a claim had been made which referred to a fear of persecution but did not specifically refer to ECHR article 3, the adjudicator found that the statement disclosed an article 3 claim, so the appellant was an 'asylum-seeker' for support purposes.[29]

Not destitute

7.20 The destitution test requires the application of IAA 1999 s95(3) and AS Regs 2000 regs 5–9. The tribunal's usual approach is to apply the guidance in Policy Bulletin 4 in calculating whether an appellant's capital and income mean they are destitute within the next 14 days (or 56 days if the appellant was receiving section 95 support). There are cases in which it may be arguable that the Policy Bulletin 4 thresholds are inapplicable since it is non-statutory guidance and so merely a relevant factor.[30] The tribunal needs to apply section 95(3) and the regulations.

7.21 The judge has to consider the position as at the date of the decision to refuse support, not the date of the tribunal. So an appellant may have their appeal dismissed but be able to show they are destitute as at the tribunal date (if their assets have since reduced) and make a new support application (but see para 7.157).

7.22 According to Policy Bulletin 4, the same destitution test applies to section 4 support as applies to section 95 support. Commentators have criticised the Home Office's strict approach to the test, effectively requiring applicants to prove their destitution, particularly in section 4 cases, where they may have been living a hand-to-mouth existence for months or years with no fixed address.[31] Suggestions about the type of evidence that may satisfy UKBA, or at least the tribunal in such cases are at para 6.128.

Exclusions from support

Receiving social security benefits

7.23 An asylum-seeker must be refused IAA 1999 s98 or s95 support under AS Regs 2000 if the whole household is eligible to claim

29 ASA 02/03/2053.

30 See para 4.131.

31 See for example 'Not destitute enough: A report documenting UKBA's failure to apply the correct legal definitions of destitution in asylum support decisions', Asylum Support Appeals Project, December 2008.

means-tested social security benefits.[32] This might apply if the asylum-seeker is the dependant of an EEA national with the right to reside.[33] The relevant social security benefits are income support, income-based jobseeker's allowance, housing benefit and council tax benefit. Tax credits are not referred to, but would be taken into account as income for the purposes of assessing destitution.

Mixed households where there is a benefit claim

7.24 If a non-asylum-seeker is in receipt of benefits, for example a husband with discretionary leave to remain in the UK, he cannot include his wife and children in his income support claim if she arrives in the UK and claims asylum for herself and her children. She could apply for section 95 (or even section 4) asylum support, and his benefits would be taken into account when assessing destitution (see para 6.26). An application for section 95 support should not necessarily be excluded on the ground that some, but not all, of the household are eligible for means-tested benefits. This enables an asylum-seeker to claim asylum support, including housing for the whole family, including family members who are already in the UK receiving benefits.

Schedule 3 exclusions

7.25 There is no power to provide section 95 support if the applicant comes within certain categories set out in NIAA 2002 s54 and Sch 3.[34] The excluded categories include anyone who is unlawfully in the UK or subject to removal directions, an asylum-seeker who is an EEA national or refugee or his or her dependant, and a 'section 9' refused asylum-seeker with a dependent child who has been certified. However the Home Office must provide support if it is necessary to avoid a breach of ECHR rights or to enable the applicant to exercise their EU Treaty rights.[35]

7.26 If the Home Office or tribunal finds that an asylum-seeker is ineligible for support, the question of whether it is necessary to provide support to avoid a breach of ECHR article 3 needs to be considered before support is withdrawn or the appeal rejected.[36] If

32 AS Regs 2000 reg 4(4).

33 See chapter 2.

34 See chapter 9 for full explanation.

35 See para 7.114.

36 See para 7.111 below.

one of the supported persons is under 18, a local authority may have duties to the family under the Children Act (CA) 1989. If the applicant is 'in need of care or attention' for a reason that does not arise solely out of the physical effects of destitution, for example where there are also other factors such as age, disability, illness, mental illness or pregnancy, they may be entitled to help under the National Assistance Act (NAA) 1948 s21.

Section 9[37]

7.27 Where a failed asylum-seeker with a dependent child refuses to leave the UK voluntarily, they may be certified and excluded from asylum support or CA 1989 s17 provision by Sch 3, para 7A of NIAA 2002, inserted by Asylum and Immigration (Treatment of Claimants, etc) Act 2004 s9. A family falls into this category of ineligible persons 14 days after the Home Secretary has certified that the former asylum-seeker has failed 'without reasonable excuse' to take reasonable steps to leave the UK. Like the other ineligible categories under Schedule 3, support must still be provided if it is needed to avoid a breach of ECHR or EU Treaty rights (para 2(3)). Policy Bulletin 73 provides for admission to emergency accommodation in urgent cases. There is a right of appeal to the AST which may annul the certificate or require the Home Secretary to reconsider it.

7.28 In the first appeal against the withdrawal of support under section 9, the Chief Asylum Support Adjudicator dismissed the appeal setting out the approach which should be followed. The same approach was applied in the appeal of a Congolese asylum-seeker mother, whose eldest child had recently joined her and was making an ECHR claim based on sexual abuse.[38] Her application for permission for judicial review in which she challenged the ASA approach and the section 9 policy in general was rejected at an oral hearing.[39] Although she then applied to the Court of Appeal, she withdrew the application because the Home Office then agreed to consider a fresh claim.

7.29 During the period when 'section 9' was piloted, the majority of appeals were dismissed. This was partly because of the careful assessment procedure prior to withdrawal of support, and partly because it can be argued that a refused asylum-seeker can avoid an ECHR breach by returning to their country of origin.

37 See further para 4.123.

38 ASA 06/09/05.

39 *R (K) v Asylum Support Adjudicators and Secretary of State for the Home Department* CO/7074/05, 13 January 2006.

7.30 However, because research showed that the section 9 pilot had failed to encourage families to leave the UK, the Home Office indicated that it will only be used on a limited case-by-case basis by NAM case owners.[40] The government has the power to repeal NIAA 2002 Sch 3 para 7A by statutory instrument.[41]

EEA nationals[42]

7.31 In April 2004, NASS withdrew support from former asylum-seekers who were nationals from the new 'A8' accession countries when their countries of origin joined the European Union (EU). It was argued that as EU nationals they were excluded from support by NIAA 2002 s54 and Sch 3. In a series of asylum support appeals and in the judicial review *R (D and H) v Secretary of State for the Home Department*[43] the claimants argued that the withdrawal of support interfered with their rights under articles 3, 8 and 14 of the ECHR and so the Home Office had a duty to continue providing support (see also ASA 04/04/7885 and ASA 04/04/7894). Collins J granted permission to apply for judicial review of the Home Secretary's decision to withdraw section 95 support from A8 nationals both on procedural grounds and on the basis of possible discrimination under articles 8 and 14. The Home Office then agreed to carry out individual assessments before deciding whether or not support should be withdrawn.

7.32 The ASA has considered whether there was a potential breach of the article 3 and 8 rights when support was withdrawn from A8 EU nationals and found that in some cases there was and the cases should be remitted to NASS for reconsideration.[44] The benefit and housing rights of EEA nationals are described in chapters 2, 3 and 8.

Appeal decisions in EEA national cases

- A Polish mother with an outstanding asylum appeal who had four children, one with cerebral palsy who was awaiting an operation, succeeded in showing that the withdrawal of support

40 Family Asylum Policy: the section 9 implementation project, BIA. See www.ukba.homeoffice.gov.uk

41 Immigration, Asylum and Nationality Act 2006 s44.

42 This section is also relevant to withdrawals of housing or community care provision from EEA nationals due to NIAA 2002 Sch 3.

43 CO/2096/04 and CO/2106/04, 4 May 2004, unreported.

44 See for example ASA 04/04/7885, 7894.

would interfere with her rights under ECHR article 8. The Chief Asylum Support Adjudicator allowed the appeal, taking into account the fact that she could not work lawfully under the Workers Registration Scheme without withdrawing her asylum application.[45]

- Appeals were dismissed in other cases where the adjudicator concluded on the evidence that the appellants had other options, whether getting a job or through friends or social services.[46] It should be noted that these decisions all pre-date the House of Lords' decision in *Limbuela*.
- NASS withdrew support from a 66-year-old Polish widow with an outstanding asylum claim who had mental and physical health problems and was living with her adult son. He was in receipt of income support and was unfit for work. It was argued that a withdrawal of support would constitute an unjustified interference with her physical integrity under ECHR article 8 that was not justified as support was only needed for a short period until her claim for attendance allowance had been processed. Evidence was produced that all her family members were in the UK and they could not afford to support her. The ASA remitted the appeal to NASS to consider what support was available to her from third parties and the effect of termination of support on her article 8 rights.[47]

Suspension or withdrawal of support

7.33 Apart from the reasons set out above, the AS Regs 2000 provide that section 95 support may only be *refused* if there has been a breach of conditions in relation to the provision of support.[48] The circumstances in which IAA 1999 s95 support may be *suspended* or *discontinued* are listed in reg 20. A number of changes were made by the AS (Amendment) Regs 2005[49] aimed at implementing the

45 ASA 04/10/8719.
46 ASA 04/07/8315; ASA 04/09/8659.
47 ASA 04/08/8497.
48 AS Regs 2000 reg 19.
49 2005 SI No 11.

Reception Directive article 16.[50] AS Regs 2000 reg 20 now reflects the Reception Directive and should be interpreted in the light of EU law. A commentary on each rule now follows.

Breach of the rules in collective accommodation and seriously violent behaviour[51]

7.34 Both these reasons apply where the Secretary of State has reasonable grounds to believe a serious breach of the rules or seriously violent behaviour has occurred, placing the burden of proof on the Home Office. 'Collective accommodation' is defined by AS Regs 2000 reg 20(6)(b). It refers to accommodation where the supported household shares facilities with another supported person, for example in a hostel, a hotel, an induction centre, or shared house. This is an attempt to interpret the Reception Directive references to 'accommodation centres' in a way that makes sense in the UK where there are no accommodation centres.

7.35 H's support was terminated on the grounds of nuisance, which was a breach of his occupancy agreement after he allegedly caused a disturbance including making threats to kill in the residential home where he was accommodated. He was unsuccessful at his AST appeal, at which he was unrepresented but then brought a successful judicial review of the decision. In *R (Husain) v Asylum Support Adjudicator*,[52] Stanley Burnton J found that a single incident of assault in the common parts could not constitute 'use of the demised premises' since the 'demised premises' did not include the whole building. The change in the rules means this argument would no longer succeed.

7.36 An asylum-seeker who was evicted due to nuisance in his accommodation claimed subsistence-only support and appealed against the withdrawal of accommodation. The adjudicator found that the eviction was brought upon him by his own conduct and the withdrawal of support did not interfere with his rights under art 3 because he still had subsistence.[53] But this decision pre-dated *Limbuela*.[54]

50 See para 7.105 below.

51 AS Regs 2000 reg 20(1)(a) and (b).

52 See para 7.111.

53 ASA 02/12/5284.

54 See para 4.117.

Reasonable excuse

7.37 Unlike some other reasons for ending support, there is no explicit defence of 'reasonable excuse' in relation to AS Regs 2000 reg 20(1)(a) and (b), but it can be argued that one should be implied. In appeals involving the withdrawal of support for unauthorised absences from accommodation, the tribunal has implied a 'reasonable excuse' defence by analogy with the explicit defence in other cases of breach of conditions, since the decision about whether or not to end support is discretionary.[55] In support of this approach it should be noted that before this new reason for withdrawing support was introduced, similar cases were dealt with simply as a breach of conditions. So appeals relating to breach of conditions arising from problems in shared accommodation are relevant.

7.38 An asylum-seeker's support was terminated after he had been arrested while trying to set fire to himself after allegedly setting fire to his NASS hostel.[56] The adjudicator found that these actions gave rise to questions about the appellant's mental health and remitted the case back to NASS for further consideration with a direction that a psychiatric report should be provided. Relying on *R v Kensington and Chelsea RLBC ex p Kujtim*[57] she found that conduct will need to be shown to be persistent and unreasonable in all the circumstances. The *Kujtim* case, which involved a 'disruptive' asylum-seeker whose social services support was withdrawn, is also authority for giving at least one warning before withdrawing support and conducting a thorough investigation. Other factors to be taken into consideration are whether the asylum-seeker received a written copy of the rules and understood them.

Offences connected to provision of asylum support[58]

7.39 Support may be withdrawn where the supported person or any dependant has committed an offence under IAA 1999 Part VI. These offences are discussed in more detail at para 5.33. The relevant offences are:

55 ASA 00/11/0100.
56 ASA 01/01/0107.
57 [1999] 4 All ER 161, (1999) 2 CCLR 340.
58 AS Regs 2000 reg 20(1)(c).

- where false or dishonest representations were made to obtain support;[59] or
- where an applicant has caused intentional delay or obstruction of asylum support functions;[60]
- where an applicant refuses or neglects to answer a question, to give any information or produce any document when required to do so in accordance with provisions under IAA 1999 Part VI;[61]
- where an applicant fails to provide accurate information or notify a relevant change of circumstances.[62]

7.40 'Representations' include an omission, such as a failure to notify a change of circumstances. The relevant changes of circumstances are listed in AS Regs 2000 reg 15.[63] Previously it was only necessary for the Home Office to show a suspected offence. The requirement to show that an offence has been committed suggests the need for a successful prosecution, of which there have been very few. At the very least, the Home Office would need to show that all the elements of the offence have been met 'beyond reasonable doubt'. It is difficult to see how this can be done in the context of a support tribunal, where there is usually no representation of the appellant and none of the protection of the criminal evidence rules, without an interference with ECHR article 6, since it would appear to pre-empt any criminal trial. Advisers should consider whether the withdrawal of a family's support could lead to a breach of the ECHR. For these reasons, case-law under the old 'reasonable suspicion' ground appears inapplicable.

Abandonment of authorised accommodation[64]

7.41 Support could previously be withdrawn either if one or more of the supported household was not living at the authorised address or was away from the address for a certain period. This is now modified so support may only be withdrawn where the Home Office has reasonable grounds to believe that the supported person or any supported dependant has *abandoned* the authorised address without

59 IAA 1999 s106.
60 IAA 1999 s107(a).
61 IAA 1999 s107(b).
62 IAA 1999 s105.
63 See para 5.122.
64 AS Regs 2000 reg 20(1)(d).

informing UKBA, or, if requested, without permission. So intention and a deliberate act is implied. No time period is mentioned. If the supported person or dependant are traced by or report to the police, Home Office or an immigration officer, a new decision must be made about their support, taking into account the reasons for the disappearance.[65] This also applies to cases where a supported person has failed to comply with their regular reporting requirement. Because the amendment arises from article 16 of the Reception Directive, any decision under this ground must be proportionate.[66]

7.42 This requirement underlines the monitoring role of UKBA as part of immigration control. An asylum-seeker who moves house is also required to inform the Home Office or immigration officer at the port of entry for immigration purposes and records will be amended to show the new address. It is a condition of section 95 support that an asylum-seeker lives at 'the authorised address'. IAA 1999 s125 gives a power to obtain a warrant to enter the supported household's home using reasonable force. A warrant may be granted where there is a reasonable belief that one or more of the supported household is not living in accommodation provided by UKBA.[67] Where an asylum-seeker abandons accommodation, UKBA may rely on 'suspected breach of conditions' in AS Regs 2000 reg 20(1)(k) as well as reg 20(1)(d) as a reason for withdrawing support, so the case-law on this, in particular AST decisions on failure to travel, may be relevant.[68]

Authorised address

7.43 'Authorised address' includes cases where the asylum-seeker has found their own accommodation with friends or relatives and is claiming subsistence only support, as well as cases where they are accommodated by UKBA under section 98 or section 95. The supported person is required to notify UKBA if the household moves to a new address even if it is provided by friends or family. UKBA may visit the authorised address to check that the supported household is living there and may terminate support, both under this ground and on grounds of breach of conditions, if it believes they have left.

65 AS Regs 2000 reg 20(5).
66 See para 2.29.
67 See further para 5.127.
68 See para 7.60 onwards.

7.44 Since asylum-seekers are dispersed around the UK, it is not unlikely that they will need to be absent from accommodation at some point, for example to visit friends or legal representatives in other parts of the country. An asylum-seeker may write to UKBA to inform them of the reasons for leaving the accommodation and/or to request permission to be absent to avoid a breach of AS Regs 2000 reg 20(1)(d). The regulation does not specify that permission must be obtained in advance, although supported persons should be advised to do so. Where necessary, there is an argument that permission should be granted retrospectively, for example if the asylum-seeker needed to travel urgently to visit a sick relative.

7.45 Although there is no reference to 'reasonable excuse' for leaving accommodation under the old AS Regs 2000 reg 20(1)(d) and (e), the ASA has implied one, finding that since the Home Office has a discretion when deciding whether or not to terminate support in those paragraphs, the approach should be analogous to the 'reasonable excuse' approach to AS Regs 2000 reg 20(1)(a).[69] 'It is equally open to an appellant under para (d) or (e) as under para (a) to seek to discharge the burden of proof upon him by showing that his actions were reasonable in the circumstances.'

Appeal decisions about leaving accommodation

- Where an asylum-seeker was absent from an authorised address due to isolation aggravating mental and physical effects of torture, the case was remitted to obtain medical evidence about the availability of treatment and impact on health of a further move.[70]
- An appeal was allowed where an asylum-seeker who had been beaten up and hospitalised for 13 days temporarily moved in with a friend to convalesce.[71]

Domestic violence

7.46 Domestic violence is another reason why a supported person or asylum-seeker might abandon their accommodation or breach their conditions of support 'with reasonable excuse'. Policy Bulletin 70 explains UKBA's procedures for investigating domestic violence and allowing access to initial section 98 accommodation where

69 ASA 00/11/0100.
70 ASA 02/12/5224.
71 ASA 02/06/3555.

someone has left domestic violence. It covers domestic violence from 'associated persons' so is not limited to domestic violence from a partner within the home. As with racial harassment, it is advisable that evidence is collected about any incidents by reporting them to the police, GP, or local 'one stop service' and keeping a diary. An asylum-seeker or dependant who is considering leaving domestic violence should obtain independent legal advice about whether it will have any effect on her immigration status. Domestic violence cases have not generated many appeals, which is consistent with UKBA's comment in Policy Bulletin 70 that only a small number of cases of domestic violence are reported. But the ECHR case *Opuz v Turkey*,[72] may be useful in case of dispute.

Racial harassment

7.47 A common reason for 'abandonment' is racial harassment. Racial harassment may also be a factor where asylum-seekers have breached conditions of support by leaving authorised accommodation in a dispersal area and refusing to return. UKBA's approach to complaints of racial harassment and its investigation procedures are outlined in Policy Bulletin 81 on racial incidents. Policy Bulletin 73 confirms that where an asylum-seeker has left accommodation due to a racial incident, or other harassment or serious property defect, they may be admitted to initial section 98 accommodation in exceptional circumstances.

7.48 Asylum-seekers have faced a relatively high standard of proof to show they have 'a reasonable excuse' for leaving their accommodation due to harassment. It is not uncommon for asylum-seekers to leave accommodation with little or no evidence of recorded incidents because of a lack of interpreting facilities in organisations such as the police in dispersal areas. The following steps are recommended where asylum-seekers are experiencing racial or other harassment in their accommodation or have left accommodation:

- Every incident should be reported to the police. If the police appear not to have recorded the incident as racially motivated or at all, a report should be made even if the incident occurred some time in the past. If necessary an informal police complaint should be made to ensure there is a record if the police refuse to record an incident properly.
- The asylum-seeker should report and seek advice about incidents at any relevant official agency, for example local race equality

72 Application no 33401/02, 9 June 2009.

council, Citizen's Advice Bureau or advice centre, local authority, community organisations. They could also contact the local councillor or MP.
- The asylum-seeker should keep a diary of incidents and report them to the accommodation provider, to UKBA and to the local one stop service.
- The asylum-seeker should visit their GP with any household member whose health is adversely affected and ask the doctor to make a record.
- Evidence should be collected of whether there is a history of incidents in the area, for example through local newspaper reports, by word of mouth in refugee and minority communities, by searching the Home Office website of recorded crime, or by contacting the local race equality council, Refugee Forum or similar bodies.

Tribunal decisions on racial harassment

7.49 The tribunal has approached the question by emphasising the relevance of the effect of the harassment on the individual or household. In ASA 00/08/0036, a case where an asylum-seeker had suffered serious racial harassment, the factual background included:

- verbal abuse of the appellant who also had an egg and banana skin thrown at him;
- a British National Party demonstration outside the accommodation followed by the assault of two asylum-seekers nearby after which the appellant had acted as interpreter for one of the victims;
- the robbery and assault of an asylum-seeker occupying the same accommodation;
- local and national media coverage;
- offers of support by the police and service provider.

7.50 The adjudicator decided 'in looking at questions of reasonableness I should be concerned not with the general efforts made to combat racial harassment but with how the situation affects this appellant in particular'. She followed *R v Brent LBC ex p McManus*,[73] a judicial review by a family who were found to be intentionally homeless after fleeing the psychological effects of sectarian violence in Northern Ireland. In *McManus* the High Court decided the correct approach

73 (1993) 25 HLR 644.

was to investigate the individual circumstances, including medical evidence and that the council was wrong simply to take account of the prevailing situation of violence in Belfast.

7.51 Looking at the asylum-seeker's circumstances, the adjudicator decided 'in this case the appellant did have reasonable excuse ... very real fear of risk of attack'. She went on to set out an approach to racial harassment which has been followed in later appeals, stating:

> No matter how ethnically and culturally mixed the local population may be, there is unlikely to be any area of the UK in which freedom from racial harassment can be guaranteed. In reaching a decision I have therefore had regard to the nature, degree, frequency, persistence and organisation of the harassment involved and its immediacy to the appellant.

7.52 Where a torture survivor left accommodation after racist abuse, which he did not understand at the time, and incidents of racial harassment affecting other occupiers, the adjudicator stated:[74]

> There exists sufficient protection against racial harassment in this country in the form of a system of criminal law which makes violent attacks by persecutors punishable and a reasonable willingness to enforce that law on the part of law enforcement agencies ... I am satisfied that the police have provided protection to the appellant when called upon to do so.

7.53 An appeal was allowed where a Roma family from Romania returned to London from accommodation in Cleveland where they were experiencing racial harassment and slept in a park. The adjudicator found that UKBA had not complied with the Policy Bulletin 18 (now 81) procedures for investigating racist incidents and that the withdrawal of support interfered with their ECHR article 8 and article 3 rights.[75]

7.54 The conclusion from the tribunal decisions is that there must be convincing evidence of the asylum-seeker's circumstances and/or of the local situation for an appeal to succeed. This is consistent with the approach in *R (Thiab) v UKBA*[76] where an asylum-seeker left Sighthill estate in Glasgow with his family after a racist murder and presented at initial accommodation in London. Four months later, when his judicial review was heard, the family had been

74 ASA 00/09/0044.

75 ASA 03/06/6684.

76 [2002] EWHC 905 (Admin).

dispersed back to Glasgow where steps had been taken to tackle the harassment. He failed in challenging the decision since the family had not experienced further racially-motivated incidents, he was in part-time work and community relations had improved.

Failure to provide information/attend an interview regarding eligibility, or provide information about asylum claim[77]

7.55 The supported person has only five working days from the date on which the request is received to respond to a request for information about their asylum support eligibility, eg provide information about any resources. There are ten days to produce asylum claim information. This may present difficulties if the supported person is not able to get a reply from his or her immigration solicitor and may be disproportionate since UKBA can access information about the asylum claim from the Home Office database. The five working days' notice of an interview[78] may present difficulties if the asylum-seeker has other pressing appointments such as urgent medical appointments, young children or difficulty travelling. All these grounds are subject to proportionality and ECHR considerations, and arguably a 'reasonable excuse' defence.[79]

7.56 While these provisions allow for a right of appeal, UKBA has power to consider the support application with no right of appeal if they consider the information provided is inaccurate and/or that the asylum-seeker is failing to co-operate with enquiries, for example failing to attend a section 55 interview, in which case the remedy would be judicial review.[80]

Reason to believe financial resources have been concealed[81]

7.57 To withdraw support for this reason, UKBA needs to show the supported person or their dependant has 'unduly benefited' from the receipt of asylum support as a result. This ground could be used

77 AS Regs 2000 reg 20(1)(e), (f), (g).
78 AS Regs 2000 reg 20(2).
79 See para 7.37.
80 NIAA 2002 s57 and AS Regs 2000 reg 3(4).
81 AS Regs 2000 reg 20(1)(h).

where support was previously withdrawn due to a suspected offence or breach of conditions, eg where an asylum-seeker is found to be working and claiming support at the same time.[82] AS Regs 2000 reg 17A provides for UKBA to claim a refund of support.[83] If the asylum-seeker is successfully prosecuted, a refund may be sought under IAA 1999 s112.

Failure to comply with a reporting requirement[84]

7.58 Most asylum-seekers and their dependants now have a weekly or monthly duty to report at a local immigration office or police station as explained in chapter 1. It is possible to apply for travelling expenses to attend if the asylum-seeker lives three miles or more away from the centre, or in other exceptional circumstances, eg mobility needs.[85] It is also possible to apply to suspend or reduce the regularity of reporting, or to report by phone in limited circumstances eg during the final stages of pregnancy or due to ill-health. The most serious consequence of a failure to report is the risk of detention, but it may also lead to a withdrawal of support. If the supported person or dependant is traced by or reports to the police, Home Office or an immigration officer, a new decision must be made about their support, taking into account the reasons for the disappearance.[86] Support should be reinstated if an asylum-seeker can give a 'reasonable excuse' for non-attendance, eg produce a doctor's letter to say they were unwell, or if they can show they would otherwise suffer 'genuine and considerable hardship'.[87]

Reason to believe applicant has made a previous asylum claim in a different name[88]

7.59 This condition only applies where the first claim has not yet been decided.

82 See para 7.66 below.
83 See para 5.109 below.
84 AS Regs 2000 reg 20(1)(i).
85 See para 5.91.
86 AS Regs 2000 reg 20(5).
87 See Policy Bulletin 80, Backpayment of asylum support; Policy Bulletin 84, Entertaining a further application for support.
88 AS Regs 2000 reg 20(1)(j).

Breach of conditions without reasonable excuse[89]

7.60 This encompasses a range of actions, from failing to travel to the dispersal area, to working while claiming support. IAA 1999 provides for support to be provided subject to conditions, which should be set out in writing and given to the supported person.[90] Previously support could withdrawn where there were reasonable grounds to *suspect* that the supported person or any dependant had failed to comply with any condition subject to which support is provided. Support can now only be withdrawn under IAA 1999 s20(1)(k) if the supported person or a dependant has failed to comply with a relevant condition 'without reasonable excuse', placing a heavier burden of proof on the Home Office.

7.61 The 'reasonable excuse' criterion has enabled the tribunal some discretion to allow or remit appeals where an asylum-seeker has a valid reason for their behaviour. An asylum-seeker may be able to challenge a decision by UKBA to withdraw support for breach of conditions if they were not provided with a written copy of the conditions or they were not translated or interpreted. If this is in dispute, the representative could ask UKBA to produce a copy of any conditions signed by the applicant. The tribunal has recognised the importance of conditions being properly notified to the supported person before UKBA can withdraw support for a breach of conditions.[91]

7.62 The contract between UKBA and its section 95 and section 4 accommodation providers requires them to provide the asylum-seeker with certain information. If this has not been provided, it may be possible to argue 'reasonable excuse' eg for failure to travel to dispersal accommodation.

7.63 There have been a number of (largely unsuccessful) appeals where support has been stopped due to an asylum-seeker's failure to notify UKBA that they are working, on the grounds of breaching conditions and potentially committing an offence.

Not understanding the conditions

7.64 The conditions of support include the duty to notify a change of circumstances as specified by AS Regs 2000 reg 15. Failure to do

89 AS Regs 2000 reg 20(1)(k). Decisions where a breach of conditions causes a nuisance are at para 7.35 above.

90 IAA 1999 s95(9)–(11).

91 See para 7.73.

so is also a criminal offence under IAA 1999 ss105(d) and 106(c). When UKBA decides to provide IAA 1999 s95 support, it should provide the asylum-seeker with a pack containing the UKBA agreement with conditions of support. The agreement is often provided at the same time as a lot of other information in English, such as leaflets about local services and access to healthcare. It is not necessarily interpreted to the supported household. Also the Reception Directive requires the Home Office to provide certain information within 15 days of the asylum claim, which may support a 'reasonable excuse' argument if it is not provided.[92]

7.65 The tribunal has at times taken a strict approach to an asylum-seeker's responsibility to ensure the agreement is interpreted to them and that they understand it, particularly in cases where applicants have worked and claimed UKBA support. In some cases it may be possible to challenge this approach, arguing that a traumatised asylum-seeker who has recently arrived in the UK has a reasonable excuse for not being able to understand the UKBA agreement or identify which parts are important. Obviously this will depend on other factors such as their level of education, the availability of translation and interpreting facilities in the dispersal area and the seriousness of the alleged breach of conditions.

Appeal results in 'breach of conditions' cases

- An appeal was dismissed because it was the asylum-seeker's duty to ensure he obtained assistance in getting documents translated and the fact that he had failed to do so and misunderstood did not amount to a reasonable excuse for breaching the conditions of support.[93]
- An appeal was allowed where the asylum-seeker had informed the Home Office, but not NASS of a change of address – this was enough to show no breach of conditions in relation to absence from an authorised address.[94]

Working cases

7.66 Home Office investigation teams discovered a number of cases of asylum-seekers working while claiming support by carrying out

92 HC 395 immigration rules.

93 ASA 01/06/0434.

94 ASA 02/08/3979.

investigations at particular workplaces and employment agencies in dispersal areas. In some cases asylum-seekers had stopped working or did not have Home Office permission to work. The tribunal has generally dismissed appeals in working cases and as yet there have been no judicial reviews to test their approach.

Appeal decisions in 'working' cases

- An appeal was allowed where an asylum-seeker had reported his employment to the accommodation provider and was unaware of the requirement to report it to UKBA.[95]
- An appeal was remitted to UKBA where the appellant was on a low income, often below the UKBA threshold, and his pregnant wife gave evidence she might miscarry if support were terminated.[96]
- An appeal was allowed where the appellant with a dependent wife and son had stopped work due to an injury and it was argued that withdrawal of support would breach ECHR articles 3 and 8, following *Husain*.[97]

Dispersal

7.67 This section covers the law and practice where section 95 support has been terminated after an asylum-seeker fails to travel to a dispersal area, both tribunal decisions and judicial review dispersal decisions.

Appeal or judicial review?

7.68 Since the test of adequacy is different from the test of 'reasonable excuse for failure to travel', there is a higher rate of success in indirect challenges to dispersal through the AST appeal mechanism.

7.69 Where an asylum-seeker with a dependent child refuses to travel to a dispersal area, the remedy is judicial review since there is no

95 ASA 01/10/0928.

96 ASA 02/052939.

97 *R (Husain) v Asylum Support Adjudicator and Secretary of State for the Home Department (Interested Party)* [2001] EWHC 582 (Admin); (2001) Times 15 November.

right of appeal, following *R (Secretary of State for the Home Department) v Chief Asylum Support Adjudicator and Ahmet Dogan (interested party)*.[98] UKBA approaches such cases by ending the IAA 1999 s98 initial accommodation, arguing there is no right of appeal to the tribunal because section 95 support is available in the dispersal area and so has not been terminated.

7.70 There may be an advantage to an asylum-seeker appealing to the AST against dispersal since if the judge finds there is no reasonable excuse not to travel, it has become the tribunal practice to suspend support pending compliance with the UKBA instructions to travel, instead of dismissing the appeal. In *R (Lik Cani) v Asylum Support Tribunal and Secretary of State for the Home Department (interested party)*[99] the appellant applied for judicial review because the adjudicator had dismissed the appeal outright. The judicial review was settled by setting aside the AST decision by consent and remitting the case back to the AST for rehearing.

Dispersal procedure

7.71 UKBA Policy Bulletin 17, Failure to travel, explains the procedure in dispersal cases. Normally the asylum-seeker is in IAA 1999 s98 initial accommodation when they receive the UKBA decision letter, support package and notice of dispersal. If the asylum-seeker fails to leave, they are allowed 24 hours to explain the reasons to UKBA, after which UKBA sends a 'withdrawal of support' decision letter. Initial accommodation normally ends on the fifth working day after that letter was served for asylum-seekers with a child under 18, and the third working day for childless adults. If the letter is posted, the date of service is two working days after the date of postage. A childless adult may appeal to the tribunal.

7.72 There is no right of appeal for an asylum-seeker with a dependent child because the offer of accommodation is simply left open.[100] Families and childless adults are given a second chance to travel if they had a reasonable excuse not to travel, for example they were sick on the day of the journey, misunderstood or otherwise missed the opportunity to travel and are willing to be dispersed as soon as it can be rearranged. If the Policy Bulletin 17 procedure has not been

98 [2003] EWCA Civ 1674.
99 CO/4768/2002 unreported.
100 See para 5.40.

followed in any significant respect, there is a reasonable chance of success at an appeal, but this will normally just provide a short respite before a further dispersal.

Challenging dispersal on procedural grounds

7.73 Dispersal appeals have succeeded where UKBA has not followed its own procedures or complied with public law standards of fairness, but where the challenge is based on procedure alone, it is likely that a further decision to disperse will be promptly issued.

Appeal results in cases of procedural mistakes

- There was a reasonable excuse not to travel where arrangements and a warning of the consequence of failure to travel were not properly communicated.[101]
- An Albanian single mother who was illiterate and had two children under five years old, one of whom was sick, had not understood the dispersal requirement or had an opportunity to have it translated.[102]

UKBA dispersal criteria

7.74 Dispersal may be challenged if UKBA has failed to take into account its own criteria for providing accommodation in dispersal areas. Policy Bulletin 31 outlines UKBA's approach to dispersal, reinforcing the IAA 1999 s97 presumption that UKBA accommodation is 'temporary' and that it is desirable to provide it in areas where there is low demand, that is outside London and the south-east. The Policy Bulletin provides a checklist of factors that UKBA should take into account. UKBA decisions usually list the factors that it is meant to consider, so they appear to have complied with the public law requirement of taking individual and relevant circumstances into account in each case. If UKBA has carried out a 'group dispersal' or the decision letter withdrawing support is clearly standardised, this is a potential ground for judicial review, but is unlikely to be enough on its own.

101 AST 01/04/0269.
102 AST 00/09/0046.

Medical treatment

7.75 Policy Bulletin 85, Dispersing asylum-seekers with healthcare needs, December 2005 outlines UKBA's approach and reflects some of the earlier tribunal decisions in this area. Para 6 of the Bulletin lists the circumstances in which dispersal may be delayed, eg infectious diseases, HIV, TB, mental health needs. The Bulletin makes reference to UKBA staff seeking advice from their medical adviser. The medical adviser's involvement in decision-making has been controversial, partly because it appears that his recommendations are treated as decisions, rather than a relevant factor to guide the UKBA case owner. Also there is a tendency simply to consider the availability of medical treatment in the dispersal area. The tribunal has taken a broader approach, deciding that the disruption to the medical treatment that a supported person is receiving could constitute a reasonable excuse for failing to travel.

7.76 The Reception Directive[103] requires that accommodation provided to asylum-seekers must be 'adequate to health'.

Appeal decisions in medical cases where appeals allowed/remitted

- An asylum-seeker had serious physical injuries that were being treated in London.[104]
- An elderly Polish Roma couple with multiple physical health needs depended on their extensive family network for support. Relying on *Secretary of State for the Home Department v Abdi*[105] the Chief Asylum Support Adjudicator found dispersal would be an ECHR article 8 breach. Although dispersal was a legitimate aim, it was not necessary or proportionate in the circumstances of the case.[106]
- Where there was evidence of continuity of care from a GP and Croatian speaking therapist over a lengthy period, the adjudicator saw this as an exceptional case and distinguished it from similar cases. She was influenced by evidence of 'severe signs of psychological distress' with 'overwhelming' anxiety and fear.

103 See para 7.105 below.
104 ASA 01/01/0166.
105 [2009] Imm AR 148 CA.
106 ASA 00/11/0095.

> Ms [X] described the appellant as [being] 'on the edge of total collapse' and refers twice in her letter to the appellant's 'suicidal ideation'.[107]

Mental health

7.77 The general approach to asylum-seekers with mental health needs is that the dispersal process should not adversely affect the mental health of an individual and the care they receive since mental health treatment is available anywhere in the UK, but Policy Bulletin 85 also highlights some of the specific difficulties that asylum-seekers may face and when there is a need to arrange for a transfer of treatment. It also allows for deferral of dispersal where there is an existing course of treatment:

> The disruption of therapy with a trusted clinician may be detrimental to an individual's mental health and compromise their capacity for recovery in the long term. Where an asylum seeker is engaged in physiological and psychiatric services, consideration should be given to deferring dispersal in order to allow treatment to continue and be completed, based on the opinion of the therapist or clinician providing the intervention.

So medical treatment may result simply in a decision to defer dispersal until an assessment, investigation or course of treatment is completed, as in ASA 02/07/4305, where the adjudicator decided it was reasonable to defer dispersal pending an ultrasound investigation.[108]

Counselling for torture survivors[109]

7.78 UKBA's stated policy in former Policy Bulletin 19, The Medical Foundation for Care of Victims of Torture, was not to disperse those who 'have been accepted for treatment' by the Medical Foundation. The Bulletin is referred to in current Policy Bulletins 31, Dispersal, and 85, Dispersing asylum-seekers with healthcare needs, but is no longer published at the time of writing. However it is understood that the policy continues to apply to both section 4 and section 95 dispersal cases, where the patient is receiving ongoing treatment that is unavailable elsewhere (the Medical Foundation now has centres in Manchester, Newcastle and Glasgow).

107 ASA 02/09/4292.

108 See also ASA 01/06/0365.

109 See also paras 5.52 and 7.107.

7.79 UKBA will not defer dispersal because the asylum-seeker is on the Foundation's (lengthy) waiting list for treatment, awaiting assessment, or has a report from them. Policy Bulletin 28 gives details of UKBA's arrangements for paying travel expenses of a supported asylum-seeker to attend a Medical Foundation assessment. In some cases UKBA may go ahead with the dispersal, but offer travel expenses to the appointment.

7.80 If a torture-survivor is receiving treatment analogous to Medical Foundation treatment, such as intensive counselling after sexual assault, it could be argued that this is a 'reasonable excuse' for failure to travel. The UKBA appears to accept that treatment by the Helen Bamber Foundation is analogous to that of the Medical Foundation, or it may be that such cases come within this criteria, also referred to at para 5.52 above.

Appeal and judicial review results in torture survivor cases

- The adjudicator found a reasonable excuse not to travel where an asylum-seeker was receiving counselling due to psychological problems following torture, rape and beatings. There was also a GP's letter stating dispersal should be postponed due to abdominal pain.[110]
- An asylum-seeker (W) who was receiving counselling for post-traumatic stress disorder unsuccessfully argued that her case should be treated in the same way as those covered by the Medical Foundation (MF) exception. Elias J refused to extend the exception to cases where asylum-seekers had illnesses similar to those suffered by some MF patients. He decided that the policy was linked to the particular nature of the institution and the kind of treatment that it provided. But he found that W's medical evidence justified reconsideration of the dispersal decision.[111]
- An appeal was remitted to allow another decision to disperse after NASS provided an undertaking to pay the appellants' travel expenses to the Medical Foundation and hospital appointments.[112]

110 AST 01/06/0365.

111 *R (Wanjugi) v Secretary of State for the Home Department* [2003] EWHC 3116 (Admin).

112 ASA 02/02/1907.

HIV treatment

7.81 Policy Bulletin 85 sets out in detail UKBA's approach to asylum-seekers living with HIV. The emphasis is on planned dispersal, following expert clinical advice from the treating clinician. The policy of dispersing asylum-seekers with HIV to parts of the UK where it states that HIV treatment is available has been found to be lawful. The tribunal's approach is to consider the availability of HIV services in the dispersal area and the effect of disruption.

Appeal decisions on HIV

- Where a woman was receiving anti-retroviral therapy and treatment for depression, the tribunal found she had a reasonable excuse not to travel because UKBA had not made the necessary arrangements for the transfer of her treatment.[113] They decided her dispersal should be deferred until this had been done.
- The adjudicator has found that it was not enough to say that suitable medical and support services existed in the dispersal area where UKBA's medical adviser had entirely failed to consider any harm the appellant might suffer as a result of dispersal: 'there must be evidence that these services can be provided in such a way as to compensate for the problems arising out of the disruption to services provided in London'.[114]
- An appeal against dispersal was also allowed in a case where medical evidence was lodged to show dispersal would be detrimental to the appellant's health.[115] The High Court's decision in *Muwangusi*[116] was considered but the adjudicator did not find UKBA's decision to disperse was proportionate. The ongoing medical care could not be replicated outside London without detriment to the appellant's health.
- Where an HIV positive couple was receiving treatment in Liverpool the appeal was strengthened by the fact that the appellant was already in a dispersal area.[117]

113 ASA 03/04/6334.
114 ASA 03/07/6850.
115 ASA 03/09/7004.
116 *R (Muwangusi) v Secretary of State for the Home Department* [2003] EWHC 813 (Admin).
117 ASA 03/07/6831.

Special needs

7.82 Where an adult asylum-seeker has a 'need of care and attention' due to age, disability, mental illness etc they may be the responsibility of a local social services authority rather than UKBA.[118] Disabled children are UKBA's responsibility, though they may ask the local social services authority for assistance. Where an asylum-seeker with two disabled children had failed to travel to dispersal accommodation, the court decided that it would be reasonable for UKBA to place the family in lower standard accommodation in London while it looked for other accommodation.[119]

Victims of trafficking

7.83 The Reception Directive provides that where there has been an evaluation of a vulnerable asylum-seeker, this should be taken into account. A victim of trafficking would come within the 'vulnerable' definition. She may also be able to argue that she needs to remain in a certain area to access services there and attend solicitors/police interviews/court hearings. Safety may also be a factor, though this may make dispersal more desirable. Accommodation under NAA 1948 s21 may be an option if there is a need for care and attention, eg due to mental health needs.[120] See also para 1.73.

Pregnancy

7.84 Policy Bulletin 85 on dispersal of asylum-seekers with care needs states that it covers 'some pregnancies or certain stages of pregnancy and related obstetric conditions', and it cross-refers to Policy Bulletin 61 on pregnancy. At the time of writing, Policy Bulletin 61, which contains guidance on the dispersal of pregnant women, was no longer available on UKBA website. It stated that during the final weeks of pregnancy, UKBA should attempt to limit the dispersal journey time to four hours. Where a woman in a late stage of pregnancy refused dispersal to Stockton-on-Tees, a journey of 10 hours 40 minutes, the appeal was successful.[121]

7.85 It has been successfully argued that support under IAA 1999 s4 should be provided at a stage earlier than six weeks before the

118 See chapter 9.

119 *R (A) v (1) UKBA and (2) Waltham Forest LBC* [2003] EWCA Civ 1473; (2003) 6 CCLR 538.

120 See para 9.92.

121 ASA 02/02/1840.

expected week of confinement because NHS guidance suggests that the average date for giving birth varies between 39–42 weeks of pregnancy (see chapter 6).[122] This argument could be expanded on in dispersal cases. Deferral of dispersal would be relevant both to avoid a long journey and to avoid a move, where a woman is receiving ante-natal care/has a support network that may improve her and her baby's chances of a healthy birth. Research shows the risk of preterm delivery in UK Africans and Afro-Caribbeans is higher than among women of other ethnic groups.[123]

7.86 There is also considerable evidence that migrant women, including asylum-seekers, are affected by poor maternity outcomes such as stillbirth and maternal morbidity and mortality (eg black African women are six times more likely to die than white women, and other ethnic groups are also at increased risk). Infant mortality rates are highest for babies whose mothers were born in Pakistan, followed by those with mothers born in the 'Rest of Africa', in other words former colonies in West Africa and in the Caribbean.[124] Also women from some minority ethnic groups, particularly migrant women are at above average risk of dying themselves in and around childbirth.[125]

7.87 The evidence referred to above may also be relevant to a speedy dispersal from unsuitable section 98 initial accommodation, early in pregnancy. Where an appellant argued it was unreasonable to expect her to share a room with her mother and her one-month-old baby the adjudicator remitted the appeal.[126]

Family ties

7.88 The Reception Directive art 8 introduced a requirement of family unity, implemented by the Home Office in Asylum Seekers (Reception Conditions) Regulations 2005 reg 3[127] and Policy Bulletin 83.

122 AST 09/02/1904.

123 Aveyard and others, 'The risk of preterm delivery in women from different ethnic groups' *International Journal of Obstetrics and Gynaecology*, August 2002.

124 Office for National Statistics, *Mortality statistics, childhood infant and perinatal. Series DH3*. published annually.

125 *Why mothers die 2000–02: the sixth report of confidential enquiries into maternal deaths in the United Kingdom*, RCOG Press, 2004.

126 ASA 02/07/3729.

127 SI No 7.

Family members should be accommodated together when in section 95 or section 98 accommodation, provided they want to be. The requirement arguably also applies to those receiving section 4 support who have made a fresh asylum claim,[128] but not to applicants whose only claim is under ECHR article 3. The meaning of dependant is explained at para 4.40.

7.89 Policy Bulletin 31 (Dispersal) para 5 considers the effect of ECHR article 8:

> An asylum seeker may request accommodation in London or the South East because he or she has a relative there. The person's individual circumstances and the nature of the relationship with that relative should always be carefully taken into account. But in the absence of exceptional circumstances, dispersal will generally be appropriate.

The adjudicator has found that NASS had not considered this discretion properly, allowing the appeal of a frail elderly man and his wife who were dependent on a daughter in London for help with shopping and housework.[129]

7.90 UKBA must consider whether dispersal will interfere with the household's right to respect for private, home and family life under ECHR article 8. In *R (Blackwood) v Secretary of State for the Home Department*[130] an asylum-seeker who had lived in London for 12 years relied on ECHR article 8 to show that dispersal accommodation was not adequate. In ASA 01/06/0368 an asylum-seeker was divorced from her husband (who had leave to remain in the UK) but her children had daily contact with him. She argued that dispersal would interfere with the children's article 8 rights. The tribunal decided the relevant question was whether the father could afford contact:

> . . . provided that the father is able to visit the children at weekends, during school holidays, and bank holidays, there is no interference with the family life of the children. If however, his earnings are so limited that he would effectively be prevented from visiting his children then there may be an interference under article 8 . . .

7.91 There have been some cases where a combination of medical needs and a need for family support have provided a reasonable excuse not to travel.[131]

128 See paras 6.92 and 7.95 above.
129 ASA 01/08/0714.
130 [2003] EWHC 97 (Admin).
131 See ASA 01/08/0714 and ASA 01/11/130.

Education

7.92 The policy that if a child of the household has attended the same school for 12 months, the family should not normally be dispersed has been abolished. But dispersal may be deferred if the child has started the final school or college year leading up to their GCSE, AS or A level exams and the family has not previously been 'unco-operative' by delaying dispersal.[132] Dispersal can also be deferred for a child with a statement of special needs who is attending an appropriate school until a school has been found in the dispersal area.

Appeal decisions on education

- Where an asylum-seeker wanted to complete an HND course in IT and business, the adjudicator dismissed the appeal, noting that ECHR of the First Protocol article 2 applies mainly to primary and secondary education, but recommending that dispersal be postponed for six weeks until the course had been completed.[133]

Unaccompanied minors

7.93 The UKBA's policy is not to seek to disperse those young people who reach the age of 18 without a final decision being reached on their asylum claim if they have been accommodated by the local authority under CA 1989 s20 and qualify as 'former relevant children' under section 23C of the Children (Leaving Care) Act 2000.[134]

Religion

7.94 There have been a number of tribunal cases considering whether difficulties in practising religion in a dispersal area amount to a reasonable excuse not to travel and/or a breach of ECHR article 9, that protects the right to hold or adhere to religious beliefs and manifest them in worship. In ASA 02/04/2665, a Congolese

132 Policy Bulletin 31.

133 ASA 02/05/2924. See also ASA 02/02/2002.

134 See Policy Bulletin 31 and Policy Bulletin 29, Transition at age 18. See further chapter 9.

asylum-seeker gave as one of the reasons for failing to travel that he needed to attend a catholic church that was French-speaking. The tribunal found that the most important feature of participating in mass was physical attendance at the service. The decision was upheld by the Administrative Court in *R (Djamba Kazema) v Asylum Support Tribunal and Secretary of State for the Home Department (interested party)*, which noted that the words of the mass recurred each week.[135] The tribunal's approach is to reject the argument that the first language of the asylum-seeker should be spoken, provided there is a place of worship within a reasonable travelling distance of the dispersal accommodation.[136]

Lawful employment

7.95 An asylum-seeker or a member of their household might be working in the south-east and claiming a top-up of UKBA support. This could justify failure to travel. Where an asylum-seeker has been waiting 12 months for a decision on their asylum claim or fresh asylum claim, they may apply for the right to work (see para 1.105).[137]

Dispersal from dispersal area

7.96 Where an asylum-seeker is already living in a dispersal area and wishes to remain there, it is UKBA's policy not to disperse.[138] In ASA 02/08/4239, a young asylum-seeker had appealed against dispersal from Birmingham. The adjudicator noted that IAA 1999 s97(1)(b) requires UKBA to take into account the desirability of providing accommodation in areas where there is a ready supply of accommodation.[139] The Reception Directive article 14(4) adds support to arguing that asylum-seekers (including refused asylum-seekers on section 4 support with outstanding fresh claims) should not be moved unnecessarily.

135 CO/2674/02.

136 ASA 03/09/4414.

137 Reception Directive art 11 and *R ((1) ZO (Somalia) (2) MM (Burma)) v Secretary of State for the Home Department; R (DT (Eritrea)) v Secretary of State for the Home Department* [2009] EWCA Civ 442.

138 See para 2.3 of Policy Bulletin 31 as referred to in ASA 02/08/4233 where the decision to disperse from Glasgow was overturned.

139 See also ASA04/06/8224; ASA 03/04/6367.

Judicial reviews of dispersal decisions where accommodation is inadequate

7.97 If an asylum-seeker refuses to travel to accommodation in a dispersal area, UKBA may withdraw support. The remedy will then be an appeal to the AST. Another method of challenging dispersal directly is to apply for judicial review on the basis that the accommodation is not 'adequate'. Asylum-seekers should be clearly warned of the possible consequences of failure to travel. In some cases, it may be advisable for them to move briefly to the dispersal area until the court has considered whether to grant permission to apply for judicial review.

7.98 IAA 1999 s97(1) sets out the presumption in favour of dispersing asylum-seekers around the UK. An asylum-seeker can challenge dispersal if accommodation has been offered without taking into account individual circumstances and/or if the accommodation offered is not adequate for the household within the meaning of section 96(1)(a). Although UKBA cannot take into account 'preferences' as to locality, it should take personal circumstances into account. So to bring a judicial review of dispersal, an asylum-seeker can argue provision in a dispersal area is not 'adequate accommodation' claiming that the decision does not adequately take account of their personal circumstances or of the ECHR.

7.99 The first dispersal judicial review was brought by a Turkish Kurdish family who argued that they should be accommodated in London where they received medical treatment and support from the Kurdish community.[140] The case is often referred to as evidence that dispersal cannot easily be challenged, but note should be taken of its particular facts. Mr Altun was a depressed, refused asylum-seeker who had exhausted all his appeal rights. He had lived in London for about eight years but the judicial review and section 95 application were made in the name of his wife who had only recently arrived in the UK with their children and claimed asylum. So it was difficult to demonstrate that they were settled in London or that there was no justification for dispersal under ECHR article 8 in those circumstances.

Tactics in dispersal cases

7.100 Any decision to end support under regulation 20(1) 'shall be taken individually, objectively and impartially and reasons shall be

140 *R (Altun) v Secretary of State for the Home Department* [2001] EWHC 296 (Admin), August 2001 *Legal Action* 24.

given . . .'.[141] As a matter of public law, 'reasons' implies adequate reasons.[142] So if support is ended without any reasons, or with insufficient or incomprehensible reasons, that may be grounds for appeal. Such cases should at the very least be remitted back to UKBA to provide reasons.

7.101 AS Regs 2000 reg 20(3) also provides that 'decisions will be based on the particular situation of the person concerned and particular regard shall be had to whether he is a vulnerable person as described by article 17 of the [Reception Directive]'. Article 17(1) lists who is a vulnerable person and then provides that their specific situation should be taken into account in healthcare and welfare provision. The list includes children, unaccompanied minors, disabled people, elderly people, pregnant women, lone parents and people who have experienced torture, rape or other forms of psychological, sexual or physical violence. The list is not exhaustive so it could be argued that other similar groups should be included. Article 17(2) provides that article 17(1) only applies if there is an individual evaluation showing that such a person has special needs. An individual evaluation is not defined in UK or EU law. It has been suggested that it could include a medical report, a community care or Children Act assessment, or a report by the Medical Foundation for the Care of Victims of Torture.[143]

7.102 The difficulty here is that the Home Office has expressly provided that it does not have any obligation to carry out an assessment.[144] In practice many local authorities are reluctant to carry out social services assessments unless there is a clear obligation to provide services so vulnerable asylum-seekers may not be able to get an individual evaluation unless they can find a community care solicitor willing to threaten judicial review. So where an asylum-seeker is vulnerable, eg visibly pregnant or disabled but does not have an 'evaluation', it seems arguable that regulation 20(3) still applies because of proportionality.[145] An example might be where support is withdrawn because they are failing to comply with a reporting requirement due to mobility needs or being heavily pregnant. In addition there is no express requirement for an evaluation in

141 AS Regs 2000 reg 20(3) and Policy Bulletin 83.
142 *South Bucks DC v Porter (No 2)* [2004] UKHL 33.
143 See Policy Bulletins 19 and 82.
144 Asylum Seekers (Reception Conditions) Regulations 2005 SI No 7 reg 4(4).
145 See para 2.27.

regulation 20(3), as contrasted with regulation 4(3) of the Asylum Seekers (Reception Conditions) Regulations 2005.[146]

7.103 A couple that had refused dispersal accommodation applied instead for accommodation under NAA 1948 s21. The Court of Appeal found Mrs Pajaziti was 'in need of care and attention' due to a 'major depressive episode'.[147]

General considerations where support is refused

7.104 There are a number of general arguments and considerations that may apply where support has been withdrawn or refused (see also para 7.38). These are potentially relevant when making representations to UKBA about sections 4, 98 and 95 support, in AST appeals, and in judicial reviews:

- decision to end support not taken individually, objectively and impartially/no reasons given (applies to section 95);[148]
- UKBA has not taken into account the Reception Directive considerations, eg that the person concerned is a lone parent, torture survivor (ie vulnerable within the meaning of the Reception Directive (applies to section 98, section 95 and possibly to section 4 cases where there is a fresh asylum claim);
- UKBA has not taken into account its Code of Practice and duties in relation to a child's welfare (applies to section 95, section 98 and section 4);
- withdrawal of support will result in breach of ECHR, eg articles 3 and 8 (this can only be used in section 4 appeals if the appellant is unable to leave the UK eg due to pregnancy/illness/a fresh claim).

The Reception Directive

7.105 Council Directive 2003/09/EC laying down minimum standards for the reception of asylum-seekers (the Reception Directive) aims to harmonise housing and support provision across Europe and has been binding on all member states since 6 February 2006. The impact of a directive on UK law is explained in chapter 3. Key provisions include:

146 SI No 7.

147 *R (Pajaziti) v Lewisham LBC and Secretary of State for the Home Department (Interested Party)* [2007] EWCA Civ 1351. But see further para 9.62.

148 See para 7.100.

- reception of groups with special needs should be specifically designed to meet those needs (preamble);
- asylum-seekers should be informed of their support rights and of legal and other organisations within 15 days of claiming asylum (article 5);
- family unity should be maintained (article 8);
- a standard of living adequate for asylum-seekers' health should be provided taking account of any special needs and including asylum-seekers in detention (article 13);
- where there has been an evaluation of a vulnerable asylum-seeker, this should be taken into account (article 17).

7.106 The Reception Directive only applies to those who have made a claim for asylum, as opposed to under ECHR, on or after 5 February 2005, but the Court of Appeal has decided that it covers fresh asylum claims as well as initial asylum claims.[149] The European Communion is planning to repeal and replace the Reception Directive and the UK government has indicated that it will opt out of the proposed new directive.

7.107 The Asylum Seekers (Reception Conditions) Regulations 2005[150] are aimed at implementing the Directive and provide limited new rights, if any. They only apply to a person whose claim for asylum is under the Refugee Convention (so not ECHR article 3 claims), has been recorded on or after 5 February 2005 and has not yet been decided or whose appeal is outstanding. The changes are explained in Policy Bulletin 83, Duty to offer support, family unity, vulnerable persons, withdrawing of support. The regulations provide:

- Family members should be accommodated together when NASS is providing asylum support under IAA 1999 s95 or s98, provided they want to be.
- A vulnerable person supported by NASS under IAA 1999 s95 or s98 should have their special needs taken into account, but only if there is 'an individual evaluation' to confirm that they have special needs. 'Vulnerable person' is widely defined to include a child, a disabled person, an elderly person, a pregnant woman, a lone parent, or a person who has been subjected to torture, rape or other serious forms of psychological, physical or sexual violence. These categories could include most

149 *R ((1) ZO (Somalia) (2) MM (Burma)) v Secretary of State for the Home Department: R (DT (Eritrea)) v Secretary of State for the Home Department* [2009] EWCA Civ 442.

150 SI No 7.

asylum-seekers, but there is no statutory duty or provision for carrying out an evaluation. Policy Bulletin 83 suggests an evaluation could include a community care assessment or a report by the Medical Foundation.

- The Home Office now has a duty to provide asylum support under IAA 1999 s95 or s98 to eligible asylum-seekers, not just a power.

7.108 The Home Office has implemented some parts of the Reception Directive so that the provisions apply to both asylum-seekers claiming under the Refugee Convention and those with an ECHR article 3 claim. The Asylum Support (Amendment) Regulations 2005[151] go further than the Reception Directive, changing and expanding the reasons for refusing asylum support under IAA 1999 s95 and s98, by amending the Asylum Support Regulations 2000.[152] Policy Bulletin 83 describes some of the changes. The main changes are:

- If UKBA is refusing to entertain an application for support because of non-co-operation with enquiries, it must write to the applicant person, giving them five working days to reply before withdrawing support.
- Any decision to end support must be taken 'individually, objectively and impartially and reasons shall be given'. If the person concerned is vulnerable within the meaning of the Reception Directive (see above) that should also be taken into account.

Children

7.109 UKBA 2007 s21 provides that the Home Secretary shall issue a code of practice designed to ensure that, when exercising functions in the UK, the UKBA takes appropriate steps to ensure that children are safe from harm while in the UK. The Borders, Citizenship and Immigration Act 2009 s55 introduces a duty to safeguard and promote the welfare of children who are in the UK. The duty extends to contractors performing certain functions.

7.110 Complaints involving children's rights such as the failure to implement this duty could be made to the Children's Commissioner.[153]

151 SI No 11.
152 SI No 704.
153 www.11million.org.uk.

Human rights

7.111 The Human Rights Act 1998 s3(1) means that courts and tribunals must interpret regulations and guidance so that they are 'human rights compliant'. So even if a judge decides that UKBA has withdrawn or terminated support correctly within the strict terms of the AS Regs 2000, they must interpret the regulations so they are compatible with the Human Rights Act 1998 and the ECHR.

7.112 The first full judicial review of an ASA decision, *R (Husain) v Asylum Support Adjudicator and Secretary of State for the Home Department (interested party)*[154] established various useful principles. It was argued that the ASA was not an independent tribunal as required by the ECHR article 6 right to a fair hearing because adjudicators were then appointed and funded by the Home Office. Stanley Burnton J decided that asylum support was a 'civil right' within the meaning of ECHR article 6. He found that appellants' rights to a fair hearing were satisfied by the current arrangements, applying the test of what an informed observer would think about the process. But he went on to find that the withdrawal of support may interfere with an asylum-seeker's right to freedom from inhuman and degrading treatment under ECHR article 3.

7.113 This approach to ECHR article 3 and asylum support has been extended in the cases which deal with asylum-seekers affected by NIAA 2002 s55.[155] In *R (Q and others) v Secretary of State for the Home Department*[156] the Court of Appeal found there was no real difference between a refusal of support and a withdrawal of support. Either could constitute 'treatment' that might interfere with an asylum-seeker's ECHR article 3 rights.

7.114 If UKBA decides to withdraw support where ECHR or the EU Reception Directive applies, it must consider whether to do so is proportionate.[157] For example, where support is suspended or withdrawn because an asylum-seeker has failed to attend an interview, it would be disproportionate to the aim of ensuring asylum-seekers provide the necessary information about their support claim if the asylum-seeker has good reasons for failing to attend such as a lack of finance to travel, ill-health, a sick child etc.

154 [2001] EWHC 582 (Admin); (2001) Times 15 November.
155 See para 4.105 below.
156 [2003] EWCA Civ 364 (2003) 6 CCLR 136.
157 See also para 2.27.

Appeal decisions on whether refusal/withdrawal of support is human rights breach

- An asylum-seeker father had breached the conditions of support by repeatedly failing to travel to dispersal addresses. The adjudicator allowed the appeal because he decided that ending support would interfere with the six-month-old baby's rights under ECHR article 8.[158]
- The adjudicator remitted a case back to NASS to consider whether the withdrawal of support would interfere with the articles 3 and 8 rights of a widow with health problems and a 12-year-old son.[159]
- Where support had been refused on the former 'intentional destitution' ground, the Court of Appeal granted permission to apply for judicial review of a decision to withdraw support under the Interim Regs 1999, in a case where the appellant had left his accommodation before the IAA 1999 came into force *R (Fetiti) v Islington LBC*.[160] It was argued that being left without support might cause indefinite destitution and so violate Mr Fetiti's ECHR rights (articles 3, 6, 8 and 14).

Procedure in appeals to the First-tier Tribunal (Asylum Support) (AST)

> . . . this is an inquisitorial jurisdiction in which strict rules of evidence do not apply.[161]

Background

7.115 Initially the tribunal was known as the asylum support adjudicators (ASA); it was part of the Home Office which funded it. A review by Sir Andrew Leggatt published in 2001 recommended that a new agency be created known as the Tribunals Service to administer what became the Asylum Support Tribunal (AST), and other tribunals, under the authority of the Lord Chancellor. On 2 April 2007, the function was transferred to the Lord Chancellor (now the Minister of

158 ASA 01/03/0229.
159 ASA 04/04/7902.
160 CO/2748/00 19 October 2000 (unreported).
161 ASA 04/06/8224.

Justice) with the power to make rules for asylum support adjudicators under IAA 1999 s104 and the power to appoint adjudicators and staff (Sch 10).[162]

7.116 The second part of the reforms established a new generic tribunal structure consisting of a First-tier Tribunal and an Upper Tribunal.[163] The functions of existing tribunals were transferred to this structure and assigned to chambers within the new tribunals. The First-tier Tribunal's main function is to hear appeals against decisions of the government where the tribunal has been given jurisdiction. It is intended that the First-tier Tribunal will eventually exercise the jurisdictions exercised by most of the tribunal jurisdictions administered by central government. It has been suggested that ultimately the jurisdiction of the Administrative Court to hear a judicial review of an AST decision will be transferred to the Upper Tribunal (Administrative Appeals).

7.117 On 3 November 2008, the AST's functions were transferred to the new Social Entitlement Chamber, which also deals with social security and various medical appeals.[164] The previous Asylum Support Appeal Procedure Rules were abolished.[165] There are new generic rules governing the practice and procedure to be followed in all proceedings that have been allocated to the Social Entitlement Chamber, but they do not appear to make far-reaching changes.[166] Apart from the name change, the main changes are:

- there is an overriding objective to enable the tribunal to deal with cases fairly and justly (r2) (see para below);
- there is a power to issue a witness summons (r16);
- there is a power to strike out or set aside proceedings (r8; r37);
- there is a specific power to adjourn proceedings (r5);
- the First-tier Tribunal judge has power to grant the right of appeal to the Upper Tribunal (this would become relevant if the judicial review jurisdiction is transferred[167] (rr38–39).

162 Ministers of the Crown and the Transfer of Functions (Asylum Support Adjudicators) Order 2007 SI No 275.

163 Part 1 of the Tribunals, Courts and Enforcement Act (TCEA) 2007.

164 First-tier Tribunal and Upper Tribunal (Chambers) Order 2008 SI No 2684.

165 TCEA 2007 Sch 2.

166 Tribunal Procedure (First-tier Tribunal) (Social Entitlement Chamber) Rules (Tribunal Procedure Rules) 2008 SI No 2685.

167 See para 7.116.

Resources

7.118 UKBA has issued an updated Policy Bulletin 23, Asylum support appeals process, with their interpretation of the amended procedures.

7.119 Apart from the legislation, previous tribunal decisions and policy bulletins are the most useful resources to rely on at an appeal. Some tribunal decisions can be found at www.asylum-support-tribunal.gov.uk/ under the reference number. They can also be searched under specific categories, under keywords and under the name of the adjudicator. Appeals that appear likely to be legally complex cases are often decided by the principal or deputy principal judge. Another way of finding decisions in a specific subject area on the internet is to use a search engine, to search within results, for example by typing in the AST website address and then adding the words that you would like to search, eg 'dispersal and HIV' to find all decisions involving the dispersal and HIV. This is also a means of finding decisions in which specific cases have been referred to, for example, by adding 'Husain'.

7.120 The AST website contains a range of information including notice of appeal forms, decisions and an explanation of how the tribunal works. There is currently a daily duty scheme at the tribunal, operated by a voluntary organisation, the Asylum Support Appeals Project (ASAP), which also has a useful website.[168]

Jurisdiction

7.121 The First-tier Tribunal (Asylum Support) may only hear appeals against a decision by UKBA to refuse or withdraw support under IAA 1999 s4 or s95, not against the type, level or adequacy of support.[169] This leaves many decisions outside its remit. In such cases judicial review will be the appropriate remedy. There is no right of appeal where support is refused under NIAA 2002 s55 or s57, so judicial review is the remedy.

7.122 An applicant has a right of appeal to the tribunal under IAA 1999 s103 either:

> (a) if, on an application for support under s95 [UKBA] decides that an applicant does not qualify for support under that section . . . or
> (b) if [UKBA] decides to stop providing support for a person under section 95 before that support would otherwise have come to an end . . .

168 www.asaproject.org.uk

169 IAA 1999 s103.

7.123 There is also a right of appeal introduced by the Asylum and Immigration (Treatment of Claimants, etc) Act 2004 s9 for failed asylum-seeker families refused support on grounds they have failed voluntarily to leave the UK. The right of appeal against refusal of section 4 support was introduced by section 10 of that Act.

Possible outcomes of an AST appeal

7.124 When considering an appeal the tribunal may:

- remit the appeal to the Home Office to reconsider (IAA 1999 s103(3)(a));
- substitute its decision for the Home Office's decision (s103(3)(b));
- dismiss the appeal (s103(3)(c));
- strike out the case (see above).

The appeal process

7.125 The table below gives a guide to the possible timescale in which an appeal may be considered. The appeals procedure is designed as a fast-track procedure, with a tribunal decision or 'reasons statement' provided within 12 working days of the AST receiving the appeal if an oral hearing is requested, and nine in cases considered on the papers. The speed is necessary because the tribunal has no power to order temporary support until an appeal is decided so an appellant may be without subsistence or housing until the appeal decision. In some cases it may be possible to obtain interim relief from the High Court by issuing judicial review proceedings, for example in dispersal cases where it is argued that accommodation is not adequate.

Day 1	**Date of UKBA decision.** UKBA posts decision letter refusing or withdrawing support with details of how to appeal. Letter is treated as served (received) two days after posting unless hand-delivered.
Days 3–5	**Appeal deadline.** Appellant should fax a valid, signed appeal notice to be received by the AST within three working days of the date decision was served by UKBA, ie within five days of the UKBA decision letter. If the appeal is late, explain reasons and ask for an extension of the time-limit.
Days 3–7	**AST fax appeal to UKBA.** The AST must fax the appeal to UKBA on the day it is received or within two working days.

Days 4–9	**UKBA faxes appeal bundle to AST and appellant.** UKBA must either withdraw decision or fax an appeal bundle to the AST within two days. UKBA should also fax or post the appeal bundle to the appellant or their representative (this doesn't always take place).
Days 4–10	**Consideration Day.** The day after receiving the appeal bundle, the AST must consider whether to order an oral hearing. If the appeal is to be decided on the papers, the tribunal judge must make a decision within five days. If the appellant has requested an oral hearing, it should take place within five days.
Days 9–15	**Appeal hearing.** The appellant may attend in person or may be represented by whoever they choose. The AST should arrange an interpreter. The tribunal judge may allow or dismiss the appeal or substitute their decision for UKBA's decision. The decision must be announced at the hearing.
Days 5–17	**Reasons statement.** The AST must send a full statement of the reasons for their decision to the appellant and to UKBA no later than three days after their determination.

The overriding objective

7.126 It could be said that the approach of the overriding objective has already been followed in appeals implicitly, but it may be useful to refer to it in support of procedural arguments. It includes a duty on the parties to co-operate generally with the tribunal and help further the overriding objective. Its aim is to enable the tribunal to deal with cases fairly and justly by:

- dealing with cases in ways that are proportionate to the importance of the case, the complexity of the issues, the anticipated costs and the resources of the parties;
- avoiding unnecessary formality and seeking flexibility in the proceedings;
- ensuring, so far as practicable, that the parties are able to participate fully in the proceedings;
- using any special expertise of the tribunal effectively;
- avoiding delay, so far as compatible with proper consideration of the issues.

7.127 The 'overriding objective' is a principle first introduced to civil litigation and is contained in the Civil Procedure Rules (CPR) r1.1. Case-law on the use of the principle there may be relevant, but a 'plain English' application of the rules to the facts of the case is likely to be most useful.

Completing the appeal notice

7.128 The notice of appeal form is published on the AST website. It is fairly simple to complete but, if not completed correctly, it may be rejected as invalid. The form must be completed in full and in English. The Home Office reference number must be included and the grounds of appeal. It must be signed by the applicant or his or her representative. It should be sent or faxed to the AST to arrive within the three-day time limit.[170] If it is late, then reasons should be given for the delay. The appellant should provide an address where they can be sure of receiving correspondence about the appeal – so not the UKBA address if eviction is imminent.

7.129 The appellant needs to state on the appeal notice whether they want an oral hearing. An oral hearing will mean the appeal takes longer than if it is decided on the papers but allows the appellant to attend the hearing and give evidence. An appellant may decide to submit written evidence such as medical reports and submissions from their legal adviser instead of attending the hearing. After the notice is filed, the judge may issue directions that have to be complied with in a short timescale, for example requesting further evidence. If the notice of appeal is completed to state that a legal representative is representing the appellant, the representative will then be responsible for the progress of the appeal, including compliance with these directions. Note also that if the form has the name of a representative, then the duty representative of the ASAP will not be able to represent without further written authorisation, changing the name of the representative.

Common errors with appeal forms

- omitting the UKBA reference number;
- forgetting to indicate whether an oral hearing is requested;
- forgetting to enclose the decision letter;
- failing to reply to the two questions:
  - What are the grounds of your appeal?
  - What matters in the UKBA decision letter do you disagree with?

170 See para 7.130.

Time limits

7.130 The notice of appeal must be received by the adjudicator within three working days after the date on which the appellant received written notice of the decision being challenged.[171]

7.131 The judge may extend the time limit[172] if this complies with the overriding objective, for example the requirement to ensure that the parties are able to participate fully in the proceedings. But the appellant must provide a request for an extension of time on the appeal form,[173] for example illness, difficulties obtaining interpretation/legal advice or non-receipt of the letter.

7.132 The previous test for an extension was whether or not the judge considered it in the interests of justice and if the appellant or his or her representative was prevented from appealing in time 'by circumstances beyond his control'. Reasons for a late appeal should be included. If the decision-making procedure explained at para 7.3 above is not followed, an applicant may have a valid ground for requesting an extension of the three-day time limit for submitting an appeal to the AST.

7.133 The adjudicator extended the time limit in a case where the asylum-seeker was not informed of the right of appeal.[174]

Tribunal's powers

7.134 During the appeal process, the tribunal judge's powers include:

- *extending the time limit* for entering the appeal;
- *case management powers* such as making directions/summonsing witnesses;[175]
- *striking out the appeal*[176] – this applies if a direction has not been complied with, there has been serious non-co-operation or if the appeal has no reasonable prospect of success. If the judge is considering using this power they must write to the party and give them up to a month to respond, so it is difficult to see how this could work within the 'fast track' timetable that asylum support appeals require. Presumably the tribunal will not use these powers except where there is flagrant breach of the Procedure Rules;

171 Tribunal Procedure Rules 2008 r22.
172 Tribunal Procedure Rules 2008 r5(3)(a).
173 Tribunal Procedure Rules 2008 r22(6).
174 ASA 00/07/0030.
175 See para 7.135 below.
176 Tribunal Procedure Rules 2008 r8.

- *setting aside the appeal* – this is a power which either the appellant or the respondent (UKBA) could try to use, but again it seems unlikely to be ordered apart from in exceptional circumstances, for example if an appellant had an accident on the way to the tribunal so could not attend, or there was clear evidence of fraud at the tribunal;
- *adjournments*[177] – the difficulty with this new power is that there is no power to order support pending an appeal so it is usually not in an asylum-seeker's interest to adjourn. Previously in *R (Secretary of State for the Home Department) v Chief Asylum Support Adjudicator*,[178] Toulson J found that the ASA has an inherent power to adjourn an appeal in the interests of justice. He also found that they could refuse to accept a request by the decision-maker to substitute the decision appealed against with a fresh decision that raised new issues if this would cause prejudice to the appellant. NASS's remedy was to withdraw the decision and make a fresh decision allowing the asylum-seeker a fresh right of appeal;
- *summonsing witnesses and/or ordering them to produce information*[179] – this could be useful, for example where a medical report is needed and the doctor refuses to assist without payment.

Case management

7.135 The adjudicator must fax the notice of appeal to UKBA on the date of receipt of the appeal or the following day. UKBA may decide to withdraw its decision after receiving the appeal.

7.136 UKBA will review their decision[180] but must send the appeal bundle by fax or by hand to the tribunal no later than two days after the tribunal received notice of the appeal. It must be sent back to the tribunal by fax or by hand and to the appellant or their representative by first class post or fax on the same day.

7.137 The day after UKBA sends the appeal bundle to the judge, the judge must decide whether there should be an oral hearing. If the appeal is to be decided without a hearing it should be decided that day or as soon as possible thereafter and not later than five days later.

7.138 There must be an oral hearing if the appellant has requested one in the notice of appeal or if the judge considers it necessary to

177 Tribunal Procedure Rules 2008 r5(3)(h).
178 [2003] EWHC 269 (Admin).
179 Tribunal Procedure Rules 2008 r16.
180 See Policy Bulletin 23.

dispose of the appeal justly. The adjudicator must give notice of an oral hearing to the appellant and to UKBA. If the appellant wants to provide additional evidence after entering the notice of appeal they must send it to both the tribunal and UKBA.

7.139 If neither UKBA nor the appellant attends the oral hearing, the appeal can be considered in their absence provided a notice of the date, time and place of hearing has been served.

Directions

7.140 The tribunal has always had the power to make relevant directions, but these powers are extended and clarified in the new Procedure Rules. Rule 5 provides that the tribunal may give a direction in relation to the conduct or disposal of proceedings at any time, including a direction amending, suspending or setting aside an earlier direction. For asylum support purposes the most relevant of these are that the tribunal may:

- extend or shorten the time for complying with any rule, practice direction or direction;
- consolidate or hear together two or more sets of proceedings or parts of proceedings raising common issues, or treat a case as a lead case (whether in accordance with rule 18 (lead cases) or otherwise);
- permit or require a party to amend a document;
- permit or require a party or another person to provide documents, information, evidence or submissions to the tribunal or a party;
- adjourn or postpone a hearing;
- require a party to produce a bundle for a hearing;
- stay proceedings.

7.141 So the appellant and their representative should be prepared for the judge to issues detailed directions containing a request for documents and information to both parties.

The hearing

7.142 The appellant and any representative should be given at least one day's and at most five days' notice of the hearing.[181] Hearings are held in public unless the judge directs that all or part of a hearing should be held in private.[182] They are relatively informal and a

181 Tribunal Procedure Rules 2008 r29.

182 Tribunal Procedure Rules 2008 r30.

decision must be provided at the end of the hearing, with reasons statements to follow within three days.[183]

7.143 In 2009, the hearing centre was to be moved from Croydon to east London. ASAP representatives are usually present at the tribunal running a duty scheme and will aim to represent or advise where possible.[184] It is desirable for appellants to arrive early so they can give instructions if they wish to be represented.

7.144 Interpreters are provided by the tribunal. Hearings are generally inquisitorial, partly due to the frequent lack of representation. The judge may take into account matters that they consider relevant even if they arose after the date of the UKBA decision. Evidence may be given by witnesses on oath. The appellant and Home Secretary are entitled to receive and consider copies of any documents if they have not received them in advance.

7.145 The judge must inform the appellant or their representative of the decision at the end of the hearing. If neither party is present the judge should send their decision to the appellant on the same day, with a 'reasons statement' not later than three days after the appeal.

7.146 The possible decisions open to a tribunal judge are listed above. If an appeal is dismissed a further application for support will only be considered if there is a material change of circumstances.[185]

7.147 If an appeal is dismissed, the appellant may be able to bring judicial review proceedings of the decision arguing ordinary administrative law principles, for example if the tribunal judge has not applied the law correctly, or if UKBA's procedures have not been followed.

Backdating of support

7.148 Where an appeal has been successful, support is normally payable from the date of the hearing, but the tribunal judge has power to award backdated support in exceptional circumstances. In *R (Secretary of State for the Home Department) v Asylum Support Tribunal and (1) Berkadle (2) Perera*[186] Gibbs J decided that section 95 support could only be backdated by relying on the Home Office's power to provide support in other ways 'in exceptional circumstances' in IAA 1999 s96(2). A tribunal judge is entitled to rely on that section and use their power to substitute a decision and so decide to backdate

183 Tribunal Procedure Rules 2008 rr33–34.

184 See appendix H.

186 See para 7.157 below.

186 [2001] EWHC 881 (Admin).

support, eg to the date of the UKBA decision or of the date the application for support was received. This approach was followed in an appeal where NASS had taken 18 months to process the application for support.[187]

7.149 UKBA's policy on backpayments is in Policy Bulletin 80, Backpayment of asylum support. A backpayment of section 95 support will normally be paid where the delay is due to fault on the part of UKBA. An alternative would be to consider making a complaint and claim compensation from UKBA, followed by an Ombudsman complaint if necessary.[188]

Practical aspects of appeals

> It should never be forgotten that Tribunals exist for users, and not the other way round. No matter how good tribunals may be, they do not fulfil their function unless they are accessible by the people who want to use them, and unless the users receive the help they need to prepare and present their cases.[189]

Representation and public funding

7.150 Some appellants have had difficulty in attending or failed to attend hearings because of UKBA delays in paying travel costs in advance. The majority of appellants continue to be unrepresented because of the lack of public funding, the short time limits and the complexity of asylum support law. UKBA is normally represented by a Home Office Presenting Officer (HOPO), or occasionally by a solicitor and/or counsel. AST appeals are outside the scope of a Community Legal Service (CLS) public funding for representation certificate. The Asylum Support Appeals Project (ASAP) is a small voluntary organisation providing a duty scheme but this does not allow for advance preparation or meet the full extent of the need.

7.151 *Supporting justice: The case for publicly-funded representation before the Asylum Support Tribunal*[190] makes a compelling case for legal aid funding with evidence of the improved prospects of success and the vulnerability of appellants. *Failing the Failed? How NASS Decision-making is letting down destitute rejected asylum-seekers*[191] demonstrates

187 ASA 02/04/2462.

188 See 7.170.

189 The Leggatt Review of Tribunals, August 2001.

190 June 2009, Citizens Advice.

191 Asylum Support Appeals Project, February 2007, www.asaproject.org.uk.

the effect of the lack of public funding for representation before the tribunal, with 99 per cent of appellants unrepresented in 2004–05. 60 per cent of those represented by ASAP during this period had their appeals allowed or remitted, compared to only 20 per cent of unrepresented appellants.

7.152 Legal help under a CLS contract for housing,[192] welfare benefits, public law or 'tolerance' can be used to advise and assist appellants. This could cover drafting a written appeal and corresponding with the tribunal and obtaining further evidence. The adviser could attend the hearing as a 'Mackenzie friend' under the legal help scheme and claim travel, waiting and assisting at the hearing. LSC guidance allows for this in cases where the need can be demonstrated due to the difficulty of the case, its importance to the client or the inability of the client to act on their own without legal assistance, for example learning or other relevant disability, language difficulties.

7.153 In this case, the adviser should not be on the record as the appellant's representative and it would be desirable for the adjudicator to be asked at the hearing to record that the adviser is there in the capacity of Mackenzie friend. As described above, a serious obstacle to asylum-seekers wishing to exercise their appeal rights or attend an oral hearing is that there is no statutory provision for emergency or other support while the appeal is being decided. It may be possible to apply separately for interim relief by judicial review.[193]

7.154 It is arguable that the absence of public funding for representation or controlled legal representation is a breach of an appellant's rights under ECHR art 6, particularly in a complex case that requires representation. Referring to support appeals, the Reception Directive[194] provides: 'Procedures for access to legal assistance in such cases shall be laid down in national law.'

7.155 To date there has been no attempt to judicially review the exclusion from scope of AST appeals. In theory it might be possible to obtain 'exceptional public funding' under the Access to Justice Act 1999 s6(8)(b) on the ground of 'overwhelming importance to the client', and possibly 'significant wider public interest' but the application process makes it almost impossible for funding to be obtained in time.[195] There have been various challenges to the

192 Housing will apply if the case concerns the client's right to occupation of their home, eg if their support is being ended due to breach of conditions or failure to travel.

193 See para 7.160.

194 Article 21(2): see appendix B.

195 See www.legalservices.gov.uk for more information about exceptional funding.

absence of public funding for representation in the context of council tax and inquests which provide guidance.[196] Limited funding is now available for some inquests.

Travel expenses

7.156 UKBA is responsible for sending a travel warrant to the address the appellant gives on the appeal form to enable travel to the AST appeal. A failure to facilitate travel has been accepted as a good reason to order an adjournment of an appeal.[197] In the same case, the Chief Asylum Support Adjudicator ordered a rehearing of the appeal before a different adjudicator where inadequate travel arrangements had been made by UKBA. The hearing had gone ahead without the appellant and had been dismissed. Although there was no express provision to order a rehearing, the adjudicator considered that she had a duty to interpret the procedure rules then applying so that they were compatible with the ECHR article 6 right to a fair hearing. The overriding objective in the new procedural rules that includes 'ensuring, so far as practicable, that the parties are able to participate fully in the proceedings', would appear to have a similar effect. The appellant later won his appeal.

Unsuccessful appeals – other options

Fresh applications for support

7.157 UKBA has discretion to refuse to consider a new application for support if it has previously suspended or withdrawn under the AS Regs 2000 reg 20 and there is no material change of circumstances. There is no right of appeal against this decision so the remedy would be judicial review. In exercising this discretion, as a public authority interpreting the AS Regs 2000, UKBA must take Human Rights Act 1998 and ECHR considerations into account.

7.158 Policy Bulletin 84, Entertaining a further application for support, explains the Home Office approach if section 95 or section 4 support is refused or withdrawn, and if any appeal to the AST is unsuccessful. They may refuse to accept a new application unless there has been a change of circumstances, or there are exceptional circumstances,

196 See *R (Tobias Main) v Minister for Legal Aid* [2007] EWCA Civ 1147 and *Julie Beet and Others v UK; Raymond Lloyd and Others v UK* (2005) App No 00047676/99 ECHR, 2 March 2005.

197 ASA 00/11/0116.

or unless support is needed to avoid a breach of the ECHR. Policy Bulletin 84 introduces two exceptions to this where section 95 support has been withdrawn because UKBA accommodation has been 'abandoned without permission' or where the asylum-seeker has failed to comply with a reporting requirement. In those cases, if the asylum-seeker is traced or reports to the police, UKBA may accept a new application or reinstate support depending on the reasons for the disappearance.

7.159 An asylum-seeker whose support stops after they fail to travel to a dispersal area may be able to arrange to stay with a friend and apply for subsistence-only support, notifying UKBA of a change of circumstances. It has also been argued that a change of circumstances includes the situation where an asylum-seeker's address has changed after the termination of support because they have left UKBA accommodation. If UKBA has ended support and there has been no appeal or an unsuccessful appeal, UKBA need not consider a further application 'unless the Secretary of State considers there are exceptional circumstances which justify it being entertained'.

Judicial review or tribunal appeal?

7.160 Much of the tribunal's current workload consists of s4 appeals. Previously, cases where UKBA had withdrawn section 95 support on the ground that the asylum-seeker had breached conditions without reasonable excuse were common. The breach of the condition that support is provided subject to the requirement to live at, or travel to, a specified address was also a common reason for the withdrawal of support.

7.161 A childless asylum-seeker may exercise the right to appeal against withdrawal of support for 'failure to travel' and also bring a judicial review of the decision that the accommodation is adequate. There is a different legal test for each remedy so it would be possible to succeed in an appeal but not in a judicial review and vice versa. The disadvantage of using an appeal as an indirect challenge to the adequacy of accommodation, rather than judicial review, is that if the appeal (and any subsequent judicial review of the adequacy of accommodation or the AST decision) is unsuccessful, UKBA has discretion not to consider a further application for support unless there has been a material change of circumstances.[198]

198 See Policy Bulletin 84.

7.162 An asylum-seeker could move to the dispersal area and challenge the adequacy of accommodation while bringing a judicial review. Alternatively, if a judicial review and interim relief are applied for urgently when the decision is made to disperse, but before support is withdrawn, an asylum-seeker may be able to postpone the decision about whether to move until after the outcome of the judicial review. If the review were unsuccessful, they could accept the accommodation. See also the paragraph below on the AST practice of suspending support pending dispersal.

Judicial review

7.163 To challenge a UKBA decision about the type or level of support, the appropriate remedy at the time of writing is judicial review. It is possible that in future the remedy may be an appeal to the Upper Tribunal (Administrative Appeals). The defendant will be the First-tier Tribunal (Asylum Support) in a judicial review of an AST decision. The Secretary of State for the Home Department will generally be an interested party unless they are the defendant. The Secretary of State for the Home Department is the defendant in a challenge to a UKBA decision about service provision. In either case, a letter before action should be sent to UKBA and court documents served on the Treasury Solicitor after proceedings are issued (in Scotland, the Home Secretary is represented by the Scottish Office). UKBA's procedure for dealing with judicial review applications is set out in Policy Bulletin 47. CLS public funding for representation is available, subject to the merits of the case. Cases are likely to involve ECHR arguments, be of exceptional importance to the client, and/or be of public interest, making it easier to obtain public funding if the prospects of success are low.

7.164 The AST does not have jurisdiction to hear appeals about the adequacy of accommodation or the kind and level of support provided. If a supported household is provided with accommodation that is not adequate, an application for judicial review should be made of the decision by the Home Secretary (that is, by UKBA decision-makers) to provide the accommodation, on the basis that they have failed to take into account relevant circumstances or have acted unlawfully. UKBA will be represented in any such action by the Treasury Solicitor, who should be notified of any hearing.

7.165 UKBA eligibility decisions that can be challenged by judicial review (instead of a tribunal appeal) include:

- NIAA 2002 ss55 or 57 decisions refusing access to support under IAA 1999 ss4, 98 or 95;
- a decision that an applicant is not 'an asylum-seeker', and/or that the Home Office has not recorded an asylum or ECHR article 3 claim (this may also arise in an AST appeal where there is a question about whether or not the AST has jurisdiction).

7.166 Judicial review may be brought on the usual administrative law grounds:

- procedural irregularity, for example if UKBA's own procedures have not been followed;
- illegality, for example if UKBA has not correctly interpreted the IAA 1999 and AS Regs 2000 or case-law;
- irrationality, for example if UKBA has failed properly to take into account all the relevant facts and reached a perverse decision;
- breach of the Human Rights Act 1998 and ECHR, for example where UKBA's decision interferes with ECHR article 3 right to freedom from inhuman and degrading treatment (as in NIAA 2002 s55 cases), or where there is a serious breach of an asylum-seeker's ECHR article 8 rights to respect for family, home and private life and correspondence that cannot be justified.

Other remedies

Access to information from UKBA

7.167 Anyone is entitled to copies of information held on them within 40 days, for example on their Home Office (or social services file) under Data Protection Act 1998 s7. The procedure is to send £10 (payable to the Accounting Officer, Home Office or relevant local authority) and specific authorisation signed by the client with their Home Office reference number. Some councils do not charge. The law requires that the information should be provided within 40 days. The UKBA address is Data Protection Unit, Lunar House, 40 Wellesley Road, Croydon, CR9 2BY.

7.168 Another tactic for dealing with problems is to request general information under section 1 of the Freedom of Information Act 2000, to which a public body must reply within 20 working days. For example, a question could be put about how many complaints they have received about a particular landlord or housing provider, for internal policies/procedures, or for target timescales for processing applications. UKBA's Central Freedom of Information Team is at 5th Floor, Whitgift Centre Block C, 15 Wellesley Road, Croydon, CR9 3LY.

7.169 If there is no response to requests for a file or general information in the above periods, the next step is a complaint to the Information Commissioner's Office whose website[199] has information about rights of access to information. Alternatively a formal complaint may be made through the UKBA's complaints procedures.

Complaints about UKBA

7.170 UKBA's service has improved in many respects, but there are still serious difficulties with administration and decision-making. Suggestions for resolving these whether at an individual or policy level include:

- writing to the Director of UKBA, relevant section head or assistant director;
- using the Home Office complaints procedure.[200] There is no specific complaints scheme for asylum support or NASS complaints. It appears that a complaint should initially be made to the relevant case owner in NAM if the asylum application was made from March 2007. (Their address should appear on correspondence about the asylum or support claim.) Otherwise it should be sent to the Case Resolution Directorate Customer Service Unit (CSU). UKBA has internal 'compensation guidance' on their approach to compensation claims, covering financial and non-financial loss. This can be obtained on request to the CSU, or if necessary via a Freedom of Information Act request:[201]
- if the complaint does not succeed, the next step is to complain to the Ombudsman. The complaint referred to below against Hackney council also involved a complaint to NASS because they had given Hackney incorrect information. NASS agreed to reimburse subsistence costs of £1,507.59 for two children from the date of the original section 95 support application until the date that H was granted leave to remain;
- if the complaint is about the UKBA/Home Office it should be sent to the client's local MP to forward to the Parliamentary Ombudsman. Their website[202] has forms and advice. There are

199 www.informationcommissioner.gov.uk

200 See www.ukba.homeoffice.gov.uk/contact/makingacomplaint which has a complaint form and explains the procedure.

201 See para 7.168 below.

202 www.ombudsman.org.uk

usually long delays in processing Ombudsman complaints, so it is worth sending a copy of the complaint to UKBA, which may result in a positive response;

- if the complaint is about a local authority, their internal procedures must be exhausted before complaining to the local government Ombudsman. On 17 January 2006, a complaint was made by an asylum-seeker, H, against Hackney council for a delay of one year and two months in ensuring her two children received subsistence payments from 'NASS' under IAA 1999 s95. This resulted in an offer through the Ombudsman on 25 May 2007 from Hackney of £1,751.28 backdated subsistence and £2,000 compensation (£1,500 for delay, £250 for time and trouble and £250 for interest);
- note that there are special statutory complaints schemes for health and social services complaints;[203]
- ask the local MP to write to the Home Secretary.

Complaints about Home Office policy

7.171 At a policy level, complaints about the Home Office may be made through the National Asylum Stakeholder Forum at which national bodies such as Citizen's Advice, the Refugee Council and ILPA are represented,[204] or at another relevant stakeholder forum.

7.172 The independent Chief Inspector of the UK Border Agency was established by the UK Borders Act 2007 s48 to inspect and report to Parliament on the performance of UKBA.[205] One of the main areas of responsibility is customer service (including complaints handling), which is a key area during 2009–2010.

7.173 An MP or member of the House of Lords could be contacted to ask a parliamentary question.

7.174 Complaints about the implementation of EU law may be made to an MEP or directly to the European Commission.

Complaints about accommodation

7.175 Problems with the standard of accommodation and harassment or similar complaints are discussed in chapter 8 at para 8.182 onwards.

203 See chapters 9 and 10.

204 See appendix H.

205 www.ociukba.homeoffice.gov.uk

Policy Bulletin 81 gives details of the steps which should be taken where an asylum-seeker wants to complain about racial or other forms of harassment. Where accommodation is damaging to the health of the household or there is a safety hazard, a complaint should first be made to the local authority's environmental health officer.[206] If they refuse to act, an asylum-seeker could threaten judicial review to compel them to take action or bring proceedings in their own name in the magistrates' court under the Environmental Protection Act 1990 s82.

206 See para 8.197.

CHAPTER 8

Housing

continued

Introduction

8.1 This chapter covers migrants' mainstream housing options, in particular their rights to homelessness assistance and social housing under the Housing Act 1996. In summary, only those granted leave to remain or European citizens with a right to reside can access mainstream housing (or housing benefit).[1] But other migrants, even a person unlawfully in the UK, may be able to access housing as the dependant of one of these categories in some circumstances.

8.2 The special Home Office schemes of accommodation for asylum-seekers and refused asylum-seekers under the Immigration and Asylum Act (IAA) 1999 are outlined in chapters 4–6. Those living in such accommodation have limited rights to repairs and can be evicted more easily. Asylum-seekers and refused asylum-seekers must generally access housing from the Home Office. Adults with care needs or unaccompanied asylum-seeking children should apply to a social services authority (see chapter 9).

8.3 A local authority must not offer homelessness assistance to an *ineligible* person,[2] or rehouse them under their allocation scheme.[3] If an eligible homeless applicant depends on a dependent partner or child to be in priority need, he or she will not be entitled to homelessness assistance unless his or her dependant is eligible. This resulted in the Court of Appeal declaring that the law was incompatible with the Human Rights Act 1998.[4]

8.4 In response, the government introduced a new category of eligible homeless households, known as 'restricted cases' in 2009.[5] A restricted case is where the applicant is an eligible British, European or Commonwealth citizen with the right of abode, but the dependant, on whom they rely for priority need, is ineligible. Other categories of eligible migrant, such as a person with leave to remain, continue to have no right to homelessness accommodation unless they are in priority need. In a restricted homelessness case, the applicant has limited rights. The local authority is expected to try to identify a private sector tenancy, rather than offer a public sector tenancy. At the time of writing, it was too early to know how the changes would work in practice, or whether there would be an ECHR challenge of the new rules.

1 See para 3.86.
2 Housing Act (HA) 1996 Part 7.
3 HA 1996 Part 6.
4 See para 8.50.
5 See more detailed explanation at para 8.51.

8.5 In a number of other areas including in self-financed private rented accommodation or in getting help from local authority environmental health services where the accommodation is hazardous or damaging to health, the rights of migrants, including those in Home Office accommodation, are unaffected by their immigration status.

8.6 This chapter considers:

- who is eligible and who qualifies for housing as a homeless person;
- who is eligible to apply for an allocation of social housing;
- an eligible applicant with an ineligible dependant (restricted cases);
- in outline the application process and procedures;
- housing duties, including to 'restricted' persons;
- discrimination and the equality duties;
- the essential reference materials;
- other housing options for migrants;
- tenancy rights and exclusions;
- harassment and eviction;
- problems with bad housing conditions and disrepair;
- council tax.

Earned citizenship[6]

The 'Path to Citizenship' Green Paper[7] proposed that migrants should earn the right to British citizenship by speaking English, 'working hard and paying taxes', obeying the law and being 'active citizens'. This has translated in the Borders, Citizenship and Immigration Act 2009 as 'probationary citizenship' which results in full citizenship after five years, and eight years for others.[8] In response to concerns that this would mean migrants such as refugees would be excluded either from housing and benefits, or from citizenship, the government stated that as regards access to services or benefits, there was to be no change.[9] Parliament was told that those who are recognised as refugees and granted humanitarian protection will still get access to benefits and

6 See also para 1.4.
7 Home Office, February 2008.
8 See chapter 1.
9 *Hansard*, HL 2 March 2009 col 509.

services as now, and there was no requirement that a refugee must be employed in order to naturalise. However, they would be expected to meet the 'active citizenship test', for example by doing voluntary work.[10] Those entering the UK on the work or family routes (that is, those highly skilled and skilled workers under tiers 1 and 2 of the points-based system, and the family route, for family members of British citizens and permanent residents) should be expected to support themselves without access to benefits.[11]

As with much of immigration law, the detail will be provided by future secondary legislation. It may become necessary when advising migrants of the effect of obtaining homelessness assistance or public sector housing to refer them to an immigration solicitor for advice about the impact on a future citizenship application.

Homelessness and allocations

Legal framework[12]

8.7 The statutory rules about entitlement to homelessness assistance and local authorities' duties to homeless households are in the Housing Act (HA) 1996 Part 7. The rules about allocation to social housing, that is rehousing in council or housing association tenancies are in HA 1996 Part 6. The Act is supplemented by regulations. The Allocation of Housing and Homelessness (Eligibility) (England) Regulations 2006[13] and various amending regulations govern eligibility.

8.8 There are slightly different rules for homelessness applications made in Wales. From 9 October 2006, the Homelessness (Wales) Regulations 2006[14] apply. These regulations retain categories that have been repealed in the English provisions (see below).

8.9 When making homelessness decisions, local authorities should take into account the Homelessness Code of Guidance for Local

10 *Hansard*, HL 25 March 2009 col 752.

11 www.publications.parliament.uk

12 For detailed guidance, see Luba and Davies, *Housing Allocations and Homelessness*, Jordans, 2006 and Arden, *Homelessness and Allocations*, 7th edition, 2006, Legal Action Group (new edition in 2010).

13 Homelessness (England) Regulations 2006 SI No 294.

14 SI No 2646.

Authorities (Homelessness Code of Guidance).[15] The section on eligibility is at paras 91–95. The most recent guidance in Wales is the Code of Guidance for Local Authorities in Wales, April 2003. In this chapter references to the Code of Guidance are to the English code.

Effect of a housing application on immigration status

8.10 Housing as homeless under HA 1996 Part 7 or an allocation of social housing under HA 1996 Part 6 counts as 'recourse to public funds'. Where a client has immigration documents with 'no recourse to public funds' this alone does not entitle a housing authority to refuse assistance, but such clients should be advised to obtain immigration advice about the effect on their immigration claim of pursuing a housing application.[16]

8.11 The Homelessness Code of Guidance contains the following sections on European applicants: Annex 11: European groupings (EU, A8, EEA, Switzerland); Annex 12: Rights to reside in the UK derived from EU law; Annex 13: Worker Registration Scheme.

8.12 When making allocation decisions, authorities must take into account the Allocation of Accommodation Code of Guidance for Local Housing Authorities which was issued on 11 November 2002.[17] Annex 4 deals with eligibility for allocation but has not been updated to take into account changes such as the EU rules explained below. Allocation of Accommodation: Choice Based Lettings – Code of Guidance for Local Housing Authorities[18] is also a relevant consideration. Where the homelessness and allocation eligibility rules are the same, the relevant parts of the Homelessness Code of Guidance could be used as an alternative.

8.13 Finally, every local housing authority must have a homelessness strategy and take it into account when making decisions and exercising housing functions.[19] This may assist in cases of ineligible households and prevention of homelessness. It can usually be

15 July 2006, in force 4 September 2006: www.communities.gov.uk/publications/housing/homelessnesscode

16 See para 1.33.

17 www.communities.gov.uk/publications/housing/allocationaccommodationcode.

18 CLG, August 2008.

19 Homelessness Act 2002 s1.

found on the local council's website. However at the time of writing, the government had indicated that 'beacon councils' would no longer need to produce a strategy, suggesting that this duty may go in future.

When is the eligibility test relevant?

8.14 There are three stages at which the question of eligibility applies. First the authority must consider whether the applicant is eligible to apply as homeless or for a housing allocation. Second, when the authority considers for homelessness purposes whether the household has accommodation to occupy, ie 'homeless', it can only take into account eligible household members. Third, when considering whether the applicant is in priority need, the authority can only take into account eligible family members. The exception is where the applicant is a British, Irish, a Commonwealth citizen with the right of abode or EEA nationals with the right to reside. Their ineligible dependant(s) may now be taken into account,[20] but once the authority has decided it has a duty to provide the applicant with homelessness assistance or an allocation, it must take into account ineligible family members when deciding on how to exercise the duty. This is explained in more detail below.

Homelessness

8.15 To qualify for long-term housing, an applicant must be:

- eligible;
- homeless;
- in priority need;
- not intentionally homeless.

8.16 Each of these areas is considered from the perspective of a migrant applicant, looking at the housing rights that apply and procedural issues, with tips for tackling common problems.

Is the applicant eligible?

8.17 The main groups eligible for homelessness assistance (HA 1996 Part 7) and rehousing under an allocation scheme (HA 1996 Part 6) are:

20 See para 8.50.

- *British and Irish citizens, and Commonwealth citizens with a 'right of abode'*[21] who are habitually resident in the UK. Many Commonwealth citizens do not have a right of abode and so are not eligible. This should be evidenced by a certificate of entitlement or endorsement in passport/ID card;
- *EEA nationals with specified types of right to reside* such as workers, self-employed people, certain people with the right of permanent residence and their dependants.[22] They are not subject to the habitual residence requirement;
- *people with leave to enter or remain in the UK*, such as former asylum-seekers with discretionary leave or humanitarian protection. They are not generally subject to the habitual residence requirement;
- *other EEA nationals with the right to reside for other reasons*, for example who have retained the right to reside or are an extended family member. They must be habitually resident to qualify.

8.18 The eligibility rules are drafted in a complex way. They work by excluding a wide class of applicants from eligibility, and then 'reincluding' people in certain classes. To help find a way through this maze, there is a quick reference table at para 8.214 to show who is eligible for homelessness assistance/a housing allocation and what documents they may need. The table refers to relevant statutory provisions. But for those needing to consider the rules in detail, we set out below the concepts and the three main groups of applicants, in line with the legislation.

Overview of eligibility

'Person from abroad' or 'person subject to immigration control'

8.19 An applicant is ineligible if they are 'a person from abroad'.[23]

8.20 The terms 'person from abroad' (PFA) and 'person subject to immigration control' (PSIC) have a housing-specific meaning which is different from their meaning in social security law.

8.21 There are two categories of person from abroad. First 'persons subject to immigration control' within the meaning of the Asylum and Immigration Act (AIA) 1996 and second, persons who are not

21 See para 1.32.

22 See para 2.101.

23 HA 1996 s185(1).

PSICs but are 'other persons from abroad', for example a British or Commonwealth citizen who has failed the habitual residence test.

8.22 Applicants in either category may still be eligible as they can be 'reincluded'.

8.23 Where an applicant is required to be 'habitually resident' this means in the area known as the Common Travel Area that consists of the UK, Channel Islands, Isle of Man and the Republic of Ireland. The meaning of 'habitually resident' is explained in more detail at para 3.63.[24]

Category 1: applicants who are not PSICs

8.24 A 'person subject to immigration control' is defined as a person who under the Immigration Act (IA) 1971 requires leave to enter or remain in the UK (whether or not such leave has been given).[25] Broadly speaking, PSIC means people from non-EEA countries and EEA nationals who do not have the right to reside. The following do not need leave to enter or remain and so are not treated as PSICs:

- British citizens;
- Commonwealth citizens with the right of abode;
- citizens of the Republic of Ireland;
- diplomats and serving members of certain armed forces;
- specified EEA nationals who are exercising their right to reside such as 'workers', self-employed people and their family members.

8.25 To be eligible, all of the above groups except the specified EEA nationals must be habitually resident[26] or they will be treated as an ineligible 'person from abroad'[27] for example a Commonwealth citizen who has just arrived in the UK for the first time. British citizens, Commonwealth citizens with right of abode, and citizens of the Republic of Ireland must pass the habitual residence test to be eligible.

8.26 A person who is in the UK after deportation, expulsion or removal from another country is exempt from the requirement. There are also occasional exemptions relating to those fleeing civil conflicts. This applied to those arriving from Lebanon between 25 July 2006

24 See also Homelessness Code of Guidance, Annex 10: The Habitual Residence Test.

25 AIA 1996 s13(2).

26 See para 3.63.

27 Homelessness (England) Regulations 2006 reg 6(1)(a).

and 31 July 2007,[28] and from Zimbabwe between 28 February 2009 and 18 March 2011, who had been offered settlement.[29]

8.27 An EEA national with a right to reside in one of the categories below is not subject to the habitual residence test and so is not treated as a person from abroad and is eligible.[30] Note that the terms 'worker' and 'family member' have particular meanings in EU law:[31]

- a worker or their family member;
- a self-employed person or their family member;
- an accession state (A8) national who is subject to the worker registration scheme, who qualifies as a worker under the Immigration (European Economic Area) Regulations 2006[32] and the Accession (Immigration and Worker Registration) Regulations 2004.[33] So they must be working in registered employment or have previously worked lawfully for 12 months in registered employment;[34]
- a person with a permanent right to reside in the UK[35] as a worker or self-employed person who has 'ceased activity'[36] or their family member. This relates to cases where a worker has retired after 12 months working and three years living lawfully in the UK, or has been permanently incapacitated whilst working here after two years living lawfully in the UK;
- a person with a permanent right to reside in the UK as the family member of a worker or self-employed person who has died due to an accident/occupational disease, or after living in the UK for two years before they died.[37] The family member must have been living with the EEA national immediately before they died.

8.28 An EEA national whose only right to reside is as a 'jobseeker' or under the initial three months' right to reside, or as their dependant is an ineligible PFA.[38] Note that 'jobseeker' generally refers to an

28 Homelessness (England) Regulations 2006 SI No 2007.
29 Allocation of Housing and Homelessness (Eligibility) (England) (Amendment) Regulations 2009 SI No 358.
30 Homelessness (England) Regulations 2006 regs 4(2) and 6(2).
31 See further chapter 3.
32 EEA Regs 2006 SI No 1003.
33 A(IWR) Regs 2004 SI No 1219 reg 5.
34 See A(IWR) Regs 2004 reg 3.
35 EEA Regs 2006 reg 15(c) or (d).
36 EEA Regs 2006 reg 5.
37 EEA Regs 2006 reg 15(e).
38 Homelessness (England) Regulations 2006 reg 4(1)(c).

EEA national who has never worked in the UK. A person who has previously worked but is now unemployed and looking for work may come within the definition of 'worker'.[39] A jobseeker with links to the labour market may be eligible for housing assistance to help him or her access work following a recent ECJ case.[40]

Category 2: persons subject to immigration control who are eligible

8.29 The following PSICs are eligible for homelessness assistance or a housing allocation and are not subject to the habitual residence test:[41]

- *Class A: a refugee*, recorded as such by the Home Office, and with leave to enter or remain in the UK;
- *Class B: a person with exceptional leave to remain (ELR)* granted outside the Immigration Rules whose leave is not subject to a 'no recourse to public funds' condition. From 1 April 2003 the grant of exceptional leave to remain was replaced by humanitarian protection (HP) (which was granted outside the rules until 8 October 2006), and discretionary leave (DL). This category also covers other leave outside the rules (LOTR);
- *Class C: a person with indefinite leave to enter or remain (ILR)*, described as leave to enter or remain which is not subject to any limitation or condition, and who is habitually resident in the Common Travel Area, other than sponsored migrants who have been here for less than five years and whose sponsor is still alive;
- *Class D: a person who has humanitarian protection (HP)* granted under the Immigration Rules;[42]
- *Class E (applies only to homelessness assistance under HA 1996, Part VII)*: an asylum-seeker aged 18 or over whose claim for asylum was made before 3 April 2000, either on arrival, or within three months of a 'country of upheaval' direction and has not been decided, or who claimed before 4 February 1996 and was entitled to housing benefit on that date. There are now few if any homeless households in this category.

39 See para 2.81.

40 See para 2.60.

41 Homelessness (England) Regulations 2006 reg 5.

42 For applications made before 9 October 2006, the previous Class D applies – a person who left Montserrat after 1 November 1995 because of the volcanic eruption. They were not subject to the habitual residence test.

Category 3: EEA nationals with other rights to reside[43]

8.30 There are a number of other EEA nationals with the right to reside under the Residence Directive and EEA Regs 2006 who are not excluded from eligibility by the Homelessness (England) Regulations. They are eligible but subject to the habitual residence test. They include:

- an EEA national who is a student and their family members. An EEA student must be on a recognised course, have comprehensive sickness insurance in the UK and have made a declaration that they have sufficient resources not to become a burden on the UK social assistance system whilst living here. This is different from the definition in relation to a self-sufficient person below who has to actually show they have sufficient resources not to become a burden. An example of where an EEA student would be eligible to apply as homeless would be if funding from home suddenly stopped temporarily. A student's family members do not include parents (dependants in the ascending line). The definition of 'extended family member' is more limited in the case of a student;
- an EEA national who is self-sufficient and their family members. 'Self-sufficient' means a person who has sufficient resources not to become a burden on the UK social assistance system whilst living here and have comprehensive sickness insurance in the UK. An example of where such a person might apply as homeless would be where they were temporarily in need of assistance if payments from abroad were delayed;
- extended family members. To have the right to reside as a family member they must have been issued with an EEA family permit, registration certificate or residence card by the Home Office.[44] There are four possible types of extended family member:[45]
  - a relative of the EEA national, their spouse or civil partner who was dependent on them in another EEA state and has accompanied them to the UK;
  - a relative of the EEA national, their spouse or civil partner who needs personal care from them 'on serious health grounds';

43 For more explanation of the meaning of each EEA category see chapter 3.

44 EEA Regs 2006 reg 7(2).

45 EEA Regs 2006 reg 8.

- a relative of an EEA national who would meet the requirements of the immigration rules for the grant of indefinite leave to remain as a dependent relative;
- the partner of an EEA national who can show they are in a 'durable relationship';

- an EEA national who has lived in the UK with the right to reside for five years and so has the permanent right to reside under reg 15(1)(a) or their non-EEA family member under reg 15(1)(b);
- a family member who has retained the right of residence under reg 15(1)(f) having living in the UK lawfully for a continuous period of five years.

Right to reside outside the Directive: carer of EU school-child

8.31 An EEA national may have the right to reside based on EU law, even though they are not referred to in the Residence Directive. This is because the Residence Directive was introduced to codify existing directives, regulations and case law on rights of residence. Inevitably it did not succeed in incorporating all the case law. Also it dates from 2004 but did not come into force until 2006 so does not include case law since 2004. The main type of homeless applicant who has argued that they have the right to reside is the EU parent/carer of a child who is attending school in the UK. These applications are inspired by a case brought by the self-supporting, divorced, Colombian wife of a German national. He had worked and lived with her for some time in the UK. The ECJ accepted that she had the right to continue residing in the UK with their child who was attending school.[46] The Residence Directive has not fully implemented *Baumbast* because the right to reside is only retained by the carer of a child in school if the EU citizen on whom the carer is dependent has died or departed from the UK, and is subject to them not becoming an unreasonable burden on the member state's social assistance scheme.

8.32 Although it could be some time before the ECJ issues guidance in this area, it may be possible to argue that until then, homeless assistance should be provided to similar applicants who are the carers of an EU school-age child, relying on the following cases.

46 *Baumbast and R* (C-413/99) [2002] ECR I-7091.

Decisions on whether a parent of school-age child has the right to reside

- A Somali national joined her Danish husband who had been working in the UK for five months. He stopped work due to incapacity in June 2003, and left the UK in 2004, separating from his wife. He returned in December 2006 but did not exercise any EU Treaty right to reside in the UK. In 2007, she made a homelessness application that was rejected. The county court allowed her appeal on the basis that she had the right to reside as the carer of her two older children who were attending school.[47] It was pointed out that there was no requirement of self-sufficiency in the context of workers and their dependants either in EU legislation or in the *Baumbast* decision. The Court of Appeal decided to make a reference to the ECJ for guidance.[48]
- In a similar case the questions were whether an EU national mother who was not self-sufficient has the right to reside even if her child started school when she was not a worker. A reference has been made to the ECJ on whether she has a right to reside in the UK within art 12 and whether any such right to reside ceases when the child reaches 18.[49]
- A Polish national who had not had the 12 months of registered work needed for a right to reside, appealed against the council's refusal of her homelessness application, based on her child's right to education under art 12 of Regulation (EEC) 1612/68 as interpreted in *Baumbast*. HHJ Knight QC ordered a stay of the appeal to await the outcome of the reference in *Ibrahim* (see above). He found that he could not dismiss the appeal before the conclusion of the appeal in the *Ibrahim* case.[50]

47 Under art 12 of the Workers' Regulation (EEC) No 1612/68 together with *Baumbast* and *GBC Echternach and A Moritz v Netherlands Minister for Education and Science* (Joined Cases 389 and 390/87) [1989] ECR 723.

48 *Harrow LBC v Ibrahim and Secretary of State for the Home Department* [2008] EWCA Civ 386, 21 April 2008, June *Legal Action* 2008. Case C-310/08 listed for 2 September 2009, Grand Chamber.

49 See para 2.105; *Teixeira v (1) Lambeth LBC and (2) Secretary of State for the Home Department* [2008] EWCA Civ 1088. Case C-480/08 listed for 2 September 2009, Grand Chamber.

50 *Parker v Brent LBC*, Central London Civil Justice Centre, 1 August 2008.

Homelessness eligibility in Wales[51]

8.33 The eligibility rules in Wales are slightly more generous than those applying in England. Eligible PSICs are listed below. Note that they are not eligible if they are excluded from entitlement to housing benefit by IAA 1999 s115:[52]

- class A, B and C: are the same as England;
- class D: a person who left Montserrat after 1 November 1995 because of the volcanic eruption and who was not subject to the habitual residence test;
- class E: a person who is habitually resident in the Common Travel Area and who is either:
  - lawfully present and a national of a state which has ratified the European Convention on Social and Medical Assistance (ECSMA) or the European Social Charter (ESC); or
  - who continues to be owed a duty that arose prior to 3 April 2000, under HA 1985 Part 3 (old homelessness scheme) or HA 1996 Part VII (new homelessness scheme) and who are nationals of a state which is a signatory to ECSMA or ESC;[53]
- class F and G: an asylum-seeker whose first claim was recorded before 3 April 2000, as per the English class E;
- class H: an asylum-seeker whose asylum claim was made before 5 February 1996. There are other conditions which are not set out here as in practice this category is not likely to have any practical effect;
- class I: a person who is in receipt of income support or income-based JSA, and those covered by the Temporary Protection Directive;[54]
- class J: a person with humanitarian protection (as in class D of the Homelessness (England) Regulations).

Tip

It has been suggested that since the eligibility rules are more generous in Wales than in England,[55] some migrants might prefer

51 See also para 8.17 above.

52 HA 1996 ss160A(4) and 185(2A).

53 Further detail is not provided as this historic category appears unlikely to apply.

54 See chapter 1.

55 See para 8.24.

to make their homeless applications there. In practice a Turkish homeless family in north London is likely to have difficulty in travelling to, say, Wrexham with their belongings to apply as homeless. There is also a risk that if the application is made in an area of plentiful housing, the applicant might be rehoused in Wales, rather than referred back to an area with which they have a 'local connection'.

Applications made in England before 20 April 2006

8.34 The eligibility rules for England[56] were more generous for applications made before 20 April 2006 because they included the classes E and I, which are in the Welsh rules below. The regulations were amended to delete those classes,[57] partly in response to *Abdi v Barnet LBC, Ismail v Barnet LBC*.[58] In that case, the Court of Appeal decided that an EEA national without the right to reside was a 'person subject to immigration control' for the purposes of the housing provisions. This meant that an EEA national who was not economically active could qualify for homelessness assistance. The rules were changed within a week of the decision, but an EEA national who applied for homelessness assistance before April 2006 and was eligible then, as a jobseeker for example, remains eligible for assistance based on the rules at that time. We have not explained the old provisions in detail here because they are now of mainly historical significance.

8.35 See para 8.214 for eligibity tables.

Is the applicant 'homeless'?

8.36 After considering eligibility, the local authority should consider whether an applicant is homeless or 'threatened with homelessness'. To be considered homeless[59] a person must have no accommodation available for their occupation in the UK or elsewhere that they are entitled to occupy. If the applicant is an unlawful occupier or 'squatter' they are considered homeless. If a relative has agreed they can temporarily stay in a spare bedroom, they have a licence and will

56 Allocation of Housing (England) Regulations 2002 SI No 3264 and the Homelessness (England) Regulations 2000 SI No 701.

57 Allocation of Homelessness (Amendment)(England) Regulations 2006 SI No 1093.

58 [2006] HLR 23, CA.

59 HA 1996 s175.

not usually be considered homeless unless the relative ends the licence by giving them notice to leave in the next 28 days or less.

8.37 A person may be homeless if they have accommodation but it would not be 'reasonable for them to continue to occupy'. It is not reasonable for a person to continue to occupy accommodation if it is probable that this will lead to violence against him, or her, or a member of the household.[60]

8.38 The House of Lords has recently considered whether a woman who is living in a refuge or a household who is 'homeless at home' in overcrowded conditions should be treated as homeless. They decided that in most cases a woman who has left her home because of domestic, or other, violence within it remains homeless even if she has found temporary haven in a women's refuge. A family may be homeless because it is not reasonable to remain in their present accommodation indefinitely, but accommodation which might be unreasonable for a person to occupy for a long period could be reasonable for that person to occupy for a short period.[61]

8.39 When deciding whether or not accommodation is reasonable to continue to occupy, the council can take into account local housing conditions such as a severe shortage of housing, but not in cases involving domestic violence as referred to above. Where a family with health needs was statutorily overcrowded, the Court of Appeal upheld the council's decision that they were not homeless because it was reasonable for them to continue to occupy their house in view of the prevailing housing conditions.[62]

8.40 A person is 'threatened with homelessness' if it is likely that he or she will become homeless within 28 days. Most local authorities approach this condition by insisting on a court order before they will process a homelessness application, relying on the case of *R v Newham LBC ex p Sacupima*.[63] The code of guidance, which post-dates that case, confirms authorities should not have a general policy either of accepting or of refusing to accept an applicant as homeless until a court order has been made. But if the applicant has received a valid two months' notice[64] on their assured shorthold tenancy, the tenant has no defence and if it is clear the landlord intends to evict, the authority should take these factors into account.[65]

60 HA 1996 s177.

61 *Birmingham City Council v Ali and others; Moran v Manchester City Council* [2009] UKHL 36.

62 *Houda Harouki v Kensington and Chelsea RLBC* [2007] EWCA Civ 1000.

63 (2001) 33 HLR 1, CA.

64 Under HA 1998 s21.

65 Homelessness Code of Guidance para 832.

8.41 A person is defined as 'homeless' if they have no accommodation in the UK 'or elsewhere': in practice, a refugee or person granted leave to remain based on the situation in their country of origin will not be considered to have accommodation available in the country they have fled from. But this may be an issue for an EEA national if they or their dependants still have accommodation in their country of origin. If a person cannot afford to travel to the accommodation that would otherwise be reasonable for them to continue to occupy, then that factor would make it unreasonable to occupy the accommodation.[66]

8.42 In a more recent case, involving a Ugandan with indefinite leave to remain based on marriage, the council found that his accommodation in Uganda was 'available for his occupation' despite there being a repossession order. The Court of Appeal disagreed with this approach, deciding that the council had to consider whether it was reasonable for the family to continue to occupy the accommodation, taking into account the specific facts, including its location in Uganda.[67]

8.43 Accommodation will only be considered to be available for occupation if it is available for the applicant and any other person who usually resides with them as a family members or any other person who might reasonably be expected to reside with them. When a 17-year-old applied as homeless, the council accepted a duty to accommodate him but refused to accommodate his aunt who previously lived with him. The High Court quashed that decision. The aunt was a member of the claimant's family with whom he normally lived so the council had to accommodate them together.[68]

8.44 If the eligible applicant is not a person subject to immigration control, ie is a British or Commonwealth citizen with a right of abode or an EEA national with a right to reside, then any PSIC dependant can be taken into account when considering homelessness.[69] That dependant is referred to as a 'restricted person' and the household has more limited rights to long-term housing.[70]

66 *Begum v Tower Hamlets LBC* (2000) 32 HLR 445.

67 *Maloba v Waltham Forest LBC* [2007] EWCA Civ 1281.

68 *R (Ogbeni) v Tower Hamlets LBC* [2008] EWHC 2444 (Admin), [2008] All ER (D) 67 (Aug).

69 Housing and Regeneration Act 2008 s314 and Sch 15 amending HA 1996 s185(4).

70 See para 8.50.

8.45 Eligible applicants who are PSICs, for example applicants with leave to remain, cannot include an ineligible family member in their household when the council decides if they are homeless or threatened with homelessness.[71] To qualify as homeless, those applicants must be without accommodation for themselves and eligible members. So if a Somali refugee living in a hostel wants to live with his partner, an asylum-seeker with a two-year-old son, he will not be treated as homeless even though they cannot live in the hostel together because she is ineligible.[72] But if he is joined from Somalia by his wife and son with leave to remain under family reunion rules, he may be treated as homeless because they are eligible and he does not have accommodation available for them. Similar rules apply to priority need. If the Somali refugee were disabled so the hostel was unsuitable for him, he will be homeless and in priority need in his own right. If he then applies as homeless with the ineligible asylum-seeker and her son, the dependants must be taken into account by the authority when it decides on what type of accommodation to offer.[73]

> *Tip*
>
> Where an applicant is eligible, homeless and in priority need, the local authority must house the eligible applicant and anyone who can reasonably be expected to live with them, including household members who are themselves ineligible.

8.46 Where an applicant is not 'homeless' under these rules, but being joined in the accommodation by an ineligible spouse, partner or dependants results in the accommodation becoming inadequate (for example, overcrowded), then the whole household may be eligible for Home Office accommodation under the asylum support provisions. Assistance is provided depending on whether the existing accommodation is 'adequate', applying IAA 1999 ss95–96 and Asylum Support Regulations 2000 reg 8.[74]

8.47 If an asylum-seeker is recognised as a refugee or granted another form of leave to remain, the UKBA will normally notify them that

71 HA 1996 s185(4).

72 But see para 8.46 below.

73 See Tip and para 8.86 below.

74 SI No 704 (AS Regs 2000).

their asylum support will end in 28 days. But that notification does not necessarily mean they are homeless. Accommodation providers in dispersal areas – whether hard-to-let public sector properties in areas of low housing demand or private rented properties – may want occupiers to remain. Households which leave such accommodation and, for example, apply as homeless to London authorities, are likely to be found 'not homeless' (or, if the accommodation then ceases to be available, 'intentionally homeless'[75]). They may also be referred back to the dispersal area under the local connection provisions. In some cases it may be possible to argue that the dispersal accommodation was not reasonable for the family to continue to occupy, eg if they experienced racial harassment damaging to health.

Is the applicant in 'priority need'?

8.48 Only those applicants with a priority need for accommodation have the right for the council to secure housing for them. The following have a priority need for accommodation:[76]

- a pregnant woman or a person with whom she resides or might reasonably be expected to reside;
- a person with whom dependent children reside or might reasonably be expected to reside;
- a person who is vulnerable as a result of old age, mental illness, handicap or physical disability or other special reason, or with whom such a person resides or might reasonably be expected to reside;
- a person who is homeless or threatened with homelessness as a result of an emergency such as flood, fire or other disaster;
- in England only:
  - a person who is 16 or 17 years old, and who is not a 'relevant child' for the purposes of local authority duties under Children Act (CA) 1989 s23A (certain 16 to 17-year-olds formerly looked after by a local authority), or owed duties under CA 1989 s20 (16 to 17-year-olds currently looked after by a local authority);
  - a person who is 18 to 20 years old and has been in care between ages of 16 and 18 (as defined by CA 1989 s24(2), as amended),

75 See para 8.64 below.

76 HA 1996 s189; Homeless (Priority Need) (Wales) Order 2001 SI No 607 (W30); Homelessness (Priority Need for Accommodation) (England) Order 2002 SI No 2051.

or 21 years and over who is vulnerable as a result of being in care;
  - a person who is vulnerable as a result of ceasing to occupy accommodation by reason of violence from another person, or threats of violence from another person which are likely to be carried out;
  - a person who is vulnerable as a result of having been a member of the armed forces;
  - a person who is vulnerable as a result of having been in custody (by way of either sentence, or committal, or remand);
- in Wales only:
  - a person who is 16 or 17 years old;
  - a person who is 18 to 20 years old and who either is at particular risk of sexual or financial exploitation, or has been in care at any time;
  - a person who has been subject to domestic violence, or is at risk of domestic violence, either now or if they return home;
  - a person who formerly served in the armed forces and has been homeless since leaving those forces;
  - a person who is a former prisoner who has been homeless since leaving custody and has a local connection with the local authority.

8.49 When deciding whether a former asylum-seeker is in priority need, there are particular factors that need to be taken into account. The Homelessness Code of Guidance para 1035 makes specific reference to the possibility that former asylum-seekers may be vulnerable as a result of persecution in their country of origin and severe hardship in their efforts to reach the UK:

> In assessing applications from this client group, housing authorities should give careful consideration to the possibility that they may be vulnerable as a result of another special reason.

The Morris *case and 'restricted cases'*

8.50 Previously a homelessness applicant was not entitled to rely on persons who are ineligible for housing assistance to establish a priority need.[77] This was considered in the case of Ms Morris, a British citizen from Mauritius who came to the UK with her child who was not British and so was ineligible. Her homelessness

77 HA 1996 s185(4).

application under HA 1996 was refused on the basis that she was not in priority need because her daughter was ineligible under HA 1996 s185. The Court of Appeal made a declaration of incompatibility under the Human Rights Act 1998 finding section 185(4) was incompatible with ECHR articles 8 and 14.[78]

8.51 This declaration led eventually to the Housing and Regeneration Act 2008 s314 and Sch 15, providing for regulations to introduce a new class of eligible person known as a 'restricted person' for the purposes of eligibility for homelessness assistance and housing allocations.[79] The amendment came into force on 2 March 2009.[80] Communities and Local Government (CLG) wrote to chief housing officers of all local housing authorities in England reminding them that the change only benefits those who are not persons subject to immigration control (PSIC), such as British citizens and EEA nationals with a right to reside in the UK.[81]

8.52 The amendment works by providing that in the case of a household containing a restricted person, the local authority may discharge its duty by providing a suitable private sector assured shorthold tenancy of 12 months. By letter dated 16 February 2009, the CLG wrote to chief housing officers of all local housing authorities in England confirming that the change only benefits person, not subject to immigration control such British citizens and EEA nationals with a right to reside in the UK. This means applicants with leave to remain will still be excluded from assistance if the dependant who would confer priority need is a person subject to immigration control. Such an applicant could ask the court to consider whether this means the law is still incompatible with ECHR articles 8 and 14 Similarly a household offered an assured shorthold tenancy might apply for a judicial review arguing the amendment still discriminates under article 14. The key question seems to be whether the discrimination is proportionate or justifiable under ECHR article 8.

8.53 Because the reforms do not apply to applicants with leave to remain, it may still be useful to refer to a case which was heard with *Morris*[82] by the same Court of Appeal Panel, sitting as the

78 *R (1) Westminster CC (2) First Secretary of State v Morris; R (Badu) v (1) Lambeth LBC and (2) First Secretary of State* [2005] EWCA Civ 1184, January 2006 *Legal Action* 18.

79 HA 1996 Part 7 and Part 6 respectively.

80 Housing and Regeneration Act 2008 (Commencement No 1 and Savings Provisions) Order 2009 SI No 415.

81 By letter dated 16 February 2009.

82 See para 8.50.

Administrative Court. B was a Ghanaian homelessness applicant with indefinite leave to remain who was caring for his son who was a person subject to immigration control. The court remitted his case back to the local authority to consider the exercise of alternative powers – to secure accommodation for the unintentionally homeless whether under HA 1996 s192(3), assisting under CA 1989 s17; or promoting welfare under Local Government Act 2000 s2.

8.54 Subsequently, a Nigerian applicant with indefinite leave to remain applied as homeless arguing she was in priority need because her nephew, who was born in the UK, formed part of her household. The Court of Appeal decided that a child born in the UK who was not a British citizen required leave to remain under IA 1971 s1(2) and so was an ineligible person subject to immigration control. Under HA 1996 s185(4), members of this household could not therefore rely on him as a dependent child to show that they had a priority need for accommodation.[83]

8.55 Where an applicant is not in priority need under these rules, but wants to live with an ineligible asylum-seeker spouse, partner or dependant, the asylum-seeker could apply to UKBA for asylum support accommodation for the whole household. If the presence of the asylum-seeker results in the accommodation becoming inadequate (for example, overcrowded), then the household will be eligible for accommodation under IAA 1999 s95. To qualify for accommodation under section 95 the asylum-seeker will need to show the existing accommodation is not 'adequate', applying AS Regs 2000 reg 8, but the accommodation offered will be ordinary s95 accommodation in a dispersal area, unless there are particular reasons to stay in another area.[84]

Tip

The reforms mean applicants with leave to remain are still excluded from assistance if the dependant who would confer priority need is a PSIC. Such an applicant could ask the court to consider whether the law remains incompatible with the Human Rights Act and ECHR articles 8 and 14. A household offered an assured shorthold tenancy might apply for a judicial review arguing the amendment still discriminates under art 14 and is disproportionate. It seems that a PSIC family who has not applied as homeless, but has applied for an allocation under HA 1996 Part 7 only, does not fall within the 'restricted case' definition.

83 *Ehiabor v Kensington & Chelsea RLBC* [2008] EWCA Civ 1074, 9 May 2008.

84 See para 5.24.

Vulnerable

8.56 A former asylum-seeker who has no eligible dependent child may qualify as being in priority need in their own right. Many asylum-seekers will satisfy the test of being vulnerable as a result of old age, mental illness, handicap or physical disability or other special reason. Case law has defined vulnerability: a person is 'vulnerable' when he or she is 'homeless, less able to fend for himself than an ordinary homeless person so that injury or detriment to him will result when a less vulnerable man would be able to cope without harmful effects'.[85] It should be considered in a housing context, and so means less able to fend for oneself in finding and keeping accommodation. This is now explicit in the Homelessness Code of Guidance para 1013 so the question is whether the applicant *would* be less able to fend for himself so that they *would* suffer injury or detriment.

8.57 Lack of English[86] or lack of money will not by itself amount to vulnerability, but a combination of factors is capable of amounting to 'other special reason'.[87] The need for a composite assessment was reiterated by the Court of Appeal in *Kamel Belouti v Wandsworth LBC*[88] although they refused to interfere with the council's decision that a 43-year-old refugee who had lived in private rented accommodation for a number of years and had diabetes, depression and backache was not 'vulnerable'.

8.58 Councils have a wide discretion in vulnerability cases so it may be easier to challenge them where there is a procedural mistake. Where a council found that a drug user with depression and hepatitis C was not vulnerable, the Court of Appeal decided that the decision letter had not properly considered and weighed up all the factors to consider whether he might be vulnerable for special reasons.[89] In the context of competing medical evidence, a local authority had concluded that two Kosovan refugees were not in priority need despite their medical evidence of severe post-traumatic stress disorder and depression. The court quashed the decision and expressed concerns about the local authority's preference for their own medical advisor who had no psychiatric experience and had

85 *R v Camden LBC ex p Periera* (1999) 31 HLR 317, CA; and see *Griffin v Westminster CC* [2004] HLR 32.

86 *R v Bath CC ex p Sangermano* (1984) 17 HLR 94.

87 *R v Kensington and Chelsea LBC ex p Kihara* (1996) 29 HLR 147, CA.

88 [2005] EWCA Civ 602.

89 *Crossley v Westminster CC* [2006] EWCA Civ 140.

never spoken to the patient.[90] *Shala* was followed by a county court appeal where a review officer found that a Liberian former asylum-seeker with post-traumatic stress disorder and depression was not vulnerable because he considered that anyone who experienced the same trauma would have these symptoms.[91] The court found this was not the correct test and the review officer had failed to take into account guidance from *Shala* about the difference in quality of a medical report from the treating doctor and one from a doctor regularly commissioned by local authorities.

8.59 Asylum-seekers who fall short of 'mental illness or handicap or physical disability' may exhibit a combination of factors that, added together, amount to 'other special reason', such as post-traumatic stress disorder, the effects of torture and detention, and the loss of family members.[92]

8.60 A dependent child cannot make an application as homeless in their own right,[93] but their birth or presence in the household may give rise to priority need if they and one of the adults in the household are eligible.

8.61 Asylum-seekers who are 16 or 17 years old and (in England) are either 'relevant children' or are currently in care will have their accommodation needs met by the local authority under the CA 1989[94] or under the Children (Leaving Care) Act 2000.[95] Care leavers who are 18 to 20 years old will have priority need in Wales and – if vulnerable as a result – in England.[96] This will include those asylum-seekers who arrived as unaccompanied minors, are granted leave to remain and have until now been looked after by the local authority.[97] Where there is a dispute about whether the child was looked after under CA 1989 s17 or s20 see *R(G) v Southwark LBC*.[98]

8.62 Where the eligible homeless applicant is in priority need and not intentionally homeless, the duty upon the local authority is to secure accommodation for the eligible applicant and anyone

90 *Shala and Another v Birmingham CC* [2007] EWCA Civ 624.

91 *Sesay v Islington LBC*, Clerkenwell and Shoreditch County Court, 2 July 2008, September 2008 *Legal Action* 25.

92 Homelessness Code of Guidance, para 1013.

93 *R v Oldham MBC ex p Garlick* [1993] AC 509, 25 HLR 319, HL.

94 See para 9.131.

95 See para 9.139.

96 See para 9.139.

97 See para 9.165.

98 [2009] UKHL 26, [2009] 1 WLR 1299.

who can reasonably be expected to live with him or her, including household members who are themselves ineligible.[99]

8.63 If an applicant is homeless or threatened with homelessness, but is not in priority need, only limited duties are owed to them.[100]

Is the applicant intentionally homeless?

8.64 A person becomes intentionally homeless if they have deliberately done or failed to do anything in consequence of which they ceased to occupy accommodation that is available for their occupation and that it would have been reasonable for them to continue to occupy.[101] The act or omission will not be considered 'deliberate' if the person was unaware of any relevant fact and any act or failure to act was done in good faith. So where a tenant left when the landlord told her to because she did not realise he would need to apply for a court order, the Court of Appeal found she was acting in good faith so was not intentionally homeless.[102]

8.65 An applicant may be intentionally homeless by leaving accommodation abroad.[103] Although local authorities are unlikely to conclude that a former asylum-seeker is intentionally homeless for leaving accommodation in the country they fled from, the question may arise for other migrants, particularly EEA nationals.

8.66 The Court of Appeal refused to interfere with the decision that a Spanish citizen with a wife and two children was intentionally homeless.[104] After losing his job in Spain, the applicant had found work in the UK and then surrendered his Spanish tenancy and brought his family to the UK without having found suitable accommodation for them.

8.67 In *Aw-Aden v Birmingham CC*,[105] a Belgian national had come to Birmingham to look for work. He relied on HA 1996 s191(2) arguing that he was unaware of his true job prospects there. The Court of Appeal upheld a review decision that section 191(2)

99 See para 8.86.

100 See para 8.84 below.

101 HA 1996 s191(1). See also guidance at www.communities.gov.uk/documents/housing/pdf/1304826

102 HA 1996 s191(2); *Ugiagbe v Southwark LBC* [2009] EWCA Civ 31.

103 HA 1996 s175(1).

104 *Osei v Southwark LBC* [2007] EWCA Civ 787.

105 [2005] EWCA Civ 1834 July 2006 *Legal Action* 29.

did not apply, finding his job prospects were based on 'a wing and a prayer'. They applied the analysis in *R v Westminster CC ex p Obeid*[106] which distinguishes between a case where an applicant has investigated housing or employment prospects, but is unaware of a relevant fact, and a case of mere aspiration that they will be able to afford accommodation.

8.68 As mentioned above, there is a risk of an 'intentional homeless' decision if an asylum-seeker leaves accommodation that they have a legal right to occupy after they have been granted leave to remain, but where they no longer have a tenancy or licence nor any kind of statutory protection (occupation in section 4 and section 95 accommodation being 'excluded' within the meaning of the Protection from Eviction Act 1977) it can be argued there is no intentional homelessness.

8.69 Applicants who are in priority need but intentionally homeless are owed only limited duties, which are explained below. Applicants found intentionally homeless but not in priority need are entitled only to 'appropriate' advice and assistance.

Does the applicant have a local connection?

8.70 The local connection provisions are considered below in connection with local authority duties to the homeless.[107]

Procedures

Making an application

8.71 A homeless person may apply to any local housing authority (borough councils in cities, and district councils elsewhere). A person does not have to apply to the authority where they are or were last living; however, upon a decision being made on the application, an authority may refer the applicant to another authority for housing.[108]

8.72 Although an application is normally made by going in person to the local council's homelessness office, it may also be made in

106 [1996] 29 HLR 389.

107 See para 8.114.

108 See para 8.114.

writing, by a third party such as an adviser or social worker, and to more than one housing authority.[109] Many homeless applicants find it difficult to persuade their cash-strapped local council to consider their application. Migrants in particular may find that if they do not have relevant documents such as Home Office documents and an eviction order, they are quickly turned away by the receptionist. This is unlawful.

8.73 The homelessness duties under Part 7 are triggered when a person applies to a housing authority and the authority 'has reason to believe' that they 'may be' homeless or threatened with homelessness.[110] The Code of Guidance confirms that this is a lower test than 'being satisfied'.[111]

8.74 A homeless applicant is entitled to have their case investigated and receive a written decision letter and so this approach should be challenged by a formal complaint to the local authority and/or judicial review.

Ombudsman decisions

- Where a council failed to investigate a homelessness application or provide interim accommodation, leaving a family homeless and staying separately with friends and relatives for 11 weeks including the Christmas period, the Local Government Housing Ombudsman awarded £3,000 compensation.[112]
- A council that refused to accept a homelessness application from a pregnant woman who had fled domestic violence in Nigeria was required to pay £2,250 compensation.[113]

8.75 The housing authority is required to 'make such inquiries as are necessary to satisfy themselves' whether or not the person is eligible, homeless, in priority need, and intentionally homeless; the authority *may* also inquire about whether they have any local connection. Whether any duty is owed by the authority to the person depends on the outcome of each of these inquiries.

109 Code of Guidance paras 66, 67.

110 HA 1996 s183.

111 Para 65.

112 *Re Eastleigh Borough Council (06/B/7896)*, 10 September 2007.

113 *Re Thurrock Council (05/A/09461)*, 24 October 2006.

Evidence of immigration status/contacting the Home Office

8.76 If a migrant makes a homelessness application, the local authority may contact the Home Office UK Border Agency (UKBA) to request information about an applicant's immigration status and UKBA must respond in writing if the request was in writing.[114] If UKBA provides such information, it has a duty to notify the local authority in writing of any changes affecting the applicant's status. The procedure is contained in the Homelessness Code of Guidance.[115] In practice, UKBA may not update on immigration status changes. If it provides incorrect information, or there is delay, a homeless applicant who is prejudiced as a result could make a formal complaint through the Home Office complaints procedure and from there seek compensation from the Parliamentary Ombudsman.[116]

Documents

8.77 It is common for mistakes to be made by both advisers and housing officers in understanding the effect of the Home Office documents that a migrant may or may not have. The table at para 8.214 below shows which documents are needed by applicants according to their immigration status. Common Home Office documents are referred to in chapter 1 and we have included examples in the appendix. The Homelessness Code of Guidance[117] has examples of a worker's registration card and certificate for 'A8 nationals'.

Tip

Tactics for obtaining a Home Office document include:

- requesting a copy of the file from a former immigration representative;
- requesting a copy of the Home Office file under Data Protection Act 1998 s7;
- making a formal complaint to the Home Office;
- involving the local MP;
- threatening/applying for judicial review of the Home Office, for example if there has been a successful asylum appeal but the status documents have not been issued.

114 HA 1996, s187.
115 Annex 8.
116 See para 7.167.
117 Annex 13.

8.78 The local authority must make its own decision about eligibility, but it is entitled to rely on information from the Home Office about an applicant's immigration status. A Nigerian homeless applicant who had separated from her EEA national husband believed she was entitled to a residence permit which the Home Office had refused. She applied for judicial review of the council's refusal to exercise its discretion to provide temporary accommodation pending further inquiries into whether or not she was eligible. The court found that the authority was entitled to rely on the Home Office's decision in these circumstances and their decision had not been irrational.[118] This case presents difficulties because the Home Office may give out of date information. The solution is for the applicant to seek their own evidence from their immigration representative or directly from the Home Office, if necessary making a formal complaint.[119]

8.79 In the majority of EEA cases, the Home Office is not likely to have a file on the applicant so the local authority will need to make its eligibility decision without assistance.

Tip

If the council refuses to offer temporary accommodation until immigration documents are provided/delays in making a decision, send a letter threatening judicial review or a formal complaint referring to:

- the failure to conduct adequate enquiries into the claimant's application as homeless under HA 1996 s184(1);
- the failure to provide suitable interim accommodation pending enquiries under HA 1996 s188(1);[120]
- the failure to provide a written decision under HA 1996 s184(3); and/or
- the delay: the Homelessness Code of Guidance para 616 provides that authorities should deal with applications as 'quickly as possible', and should aim to complete their enquiries and notify the applicant of their decision within 33 working days of the application.

118 *R (Burns) v Southwark LBC* [2004] EWHC 1901 (Admin).

119 See para 7.170.

120 See para 8.83.

Homelessness decisions

8.80 Authorities must make inquiries and, on their completion, notify the applicant in writing of their decision, with reasons for any adverse finding, sometimes known as a section 184 decision.[121] The decision letter must advise the applicant of their right to request a review and of the time limit for doing so.[122] These requirements apply to decisions about homelessness, eligibility, priority need, intentional homelessness and local connection. They also apply to a decision that a final offer of homelessness accommodation under HA 1996 Part 7 is suitable, but they do not apply to any other decision that an offer of accommodation is suitable, for example in relation to interim accommodation pending a decision, review, appeal or local connection referral. For remedies available in the case of an adverse homelessness decision, see para 8.146 below.

Changes in status/eligibility

8.81 The relevant date for deciding eligibility is the date of the homelessness (or allocation) decision or review. For example, if an A8 worker who has applied as homeless only on the basis that they are working and registered to work becomes unemployed after only six months in work, they will be ineligible until they find another job and re-register. If the local authority decides to provide homelessness assistance but has not yet offered a housing allocation, their duty ends if the household stops being eligible. So if an applicant stops being eligible before a homelessness decision is made, they have a duty to notify the authority of a change of circumstances. The same rule applies if a homelessness duty has been agreed but there has not yet been an allocation of permanent accommodation. An applicant for an allocation or homelessness assistance commits a criminal offence if they knowingly withhold information which the authority has required them to give.[123] The complexity of the eligibility rules means that an applicant may simply have misunderstood the effect of a change in their circumstances. In relation to homelessness there is a defence of 'reasonable excuse' for non-compliance.

121 HA 1996 s184.
122 HA 1996 s184(5).
123 HA 1996 ss171 and 214.

Homelessness: what are the duties owed?

Restricted cases

8.82 If a household is homeless, not intentionally homeless but the priority need is because of a restricted person, for example a child who is an ineligible restricted person, it is now known as a 'restricted case'.[124] The housing authority must inform the applicant that they are considered to be a restricted case and why. They should try to bring the homelessness duty to an end by arranging for the family to be offered an assured shorthold tenancy of 12 months or more by a private landlord, so far as reasonably practicable.[125] If this is not possible, the authority may still offer interim accommodation in the usual way as described below but should continue looking for a private sector tenancy. This applies to applications made from 2 March 2009 onwards.[126]

Temporary accommodation pending decision

8.83 An asylum-seeker granted leave who has been asked to leave their accommodation by UKBA, the local authority or relatives will be classed as 'threatened with homelessness' as soon as they are within 28 days of the date when they have to leave the accommodation, and 'homeless' on the day they do have to leave. Such an applicant will be eligible for assistance. If they are in priority need, the local authority will have a duty to secure interim accommodation for them and anyone who can reasonably be expected to live with them, until the conclusion of inquiries.[127] If the local authority decides the applicant is homeless, eligible for assistance, in priority need, and not intentionally homeless, they will have a duty to secure accommodation.[128] If the applicant has no local connection with the authority they apply to there may be a local connection referral to another area.[129]

8.84 If the applicant is not 'in priority need', there is no duty to arrange temporary accommodation. The authority is still under a duty to

124 HA 1996 s193(3B); see para 8.50.

125 HA 1996 s193 (7A)–(7D) as amended by Housing and Regeneration Act 2008 s314 and Sch 15.

126 Housing and Regeneration Act 2008 (Commencement No 1 and Savings Provisions) Order 2009 SI No 415.

127 See para 8.92.

128 See para 8.96.

129 See para 8.114.

make inquiries into the applicant's circumstances and to provide a written decision.[130] If it is decided that the applicant does not have a priority need, the authority must assess the person's housing needs and provide appropriate advice and assistance in the applicant's attempts to secure their own accommodation. In practice, this usually means advice and information about private sector housing and may include a scheme for providing deposits and rent in advance. These duties are explained at para 8.121 above. Such a person, even though not *entitled to* accommodation as a homeless person, should nonetheless make a housing allocation application. An asylum-seeker granted refugee status, discretionary leave or humanitarian protection will also be eligible to apply to the DWP for an integration loan for a deposit or rent in advance to secure private rented accommodation[131] and to claim housing benefit.

8.85 A person who applies as homeless to a local authority is entitled to temporary or 'interim' accommodation while the authority investigates their case. The duty applies until a homelessness decision is issued to an applicant under HA 1996 s184. It is triggered:[132]

> If the local housing authority have reason to believe that an applicant may be homeless, eligible for assistance and have a priority need, they shall secure that accommodation is available for his occupation pending a decision as to the duty (if any) owed . . .

8.86 The accommodation must be suitable[133] for the applicant and anyone else who can reasonably be expected to live with the applicant (including 'ineligible persons' – see para 8.104 below). The suitability requirement is the same for interim accommodation as it is for the full housing duty explained below, but what is deemed suitable might be of a lower standard as the occupation is meant to be for a shorter period of time.[134]

8.87 The Code of Guidance discourages authorities from using bed and breakfast accommodation except for very short-term stays. Where hostel accommodation is used to accommodate families with children or vulnerable young people, it would be inappropriate to accommodate these groups alongside adults.[135] The extent to which particular temporary accommodation must suit an applicant's needs

130 HA 1996 s184.
131 See chapter 3.
132 HA 1996 s188(1).
133 HA 1996 ss205(1) and 206(1); *R v Ealing LBC ex p Surdonja* (1999) HLR 686.
134 Homelessness Code of Guidance para 172.
135 Homelessness Code of Guidance para 1625.

will vary according to how long it is occupied.[136] Shared bed and breakfast accommodation should only be used for up to six weeks for an applicant with a child or who is pregnant.[137] A hotel or hostel is not classified as bed and breakfast accommodation if it is owned or managed by a local housing authority, registered social landlord or voluntary organisation as defined by HA 1996 s180(3).

8.88 Bed and breakfast accommodation is still used for childless adults, but the particular circumstances of a former asylum-seeker may make such accommodation unsuitable even in the short term. Evidence would be required to challenge a decision that such accommodation is suitable, for example that an applicant has post-traumatic stress disorder following detention and needs self-contained accommodation.[138]

8.89 The authority may not refer the applicant to another authority for accommodation under this section, but may find temporary accommodation for the applicant outside its own area. If an applicant's household needs an essential service such as social services support or a specialist counselling service, they should be given priority for accommodation within the authority's own area.[139]

8.90 If the local authority refuses to provide interim accommodation or to provide suitable interim accommodation the remedy is judicial review.

8.91 The duty continues until ended by one of a series of specified events[140] where the temporary accommodation secured is refused, or intentionally lost, or the applicant leaves, or the applicant accepts or refuses to accept Part VI accommodation, or in certain circumstances if the applicant accepts an offer of an assured shorthold tenancy. The duty also ends if the applicant stops being eligible.

Interim accommodation pending review or appeal

8.92 When an authority issues its HA 1996 s184 decision about whether or not an applicant is eligible, homeless, in priority need, intentionally homeless etc, there is a right to request a review within 21 days

136 *R v Exeter CC ex p Gliddon* (1984) 14 HLR 103.

137 Homelessness (Suitability of Accommodation) (England) Order 2003 SI No 3326.

138 *R v Newham LBC ex p Sacupima* [2001] 33 HLR 1 and 18.

139 Homelessness Code of Guidance para 169.

140 HA 1996 s193(3) and (5)–(8).

of notification of the decision. Similarly there is a right to appeal to the county court within 21 days of the review decision. If asked, the authority must consider whether to exercise its discretion to provide accommodation pending the review[141] or appeal.[142] There is a list of factors they must take into account when considering this power, such as the applicant's personal circumstances, the strength of their case and the consequences if accommodation is not provided.[143] The Administrative Court reviewed the *Mohamed* test in the context of an applicant who had been found not habitually resident, criticising the local authority for the lack of explanation or proper reasons in their decision letter, in *R (Paul-Coker) v Southwark LBC*.[144]

8.93 The High Court found that a council had acted unlawfully by refusing to provide a mentally ill young man with accommodation pending review of the decision that he was not in priority need.[145] They had not taken into account their own homelessness strategy or the strong merits of the review.

8.94 There is a further obstacle to migrants who are seeking accommodation pending review or appeal in the form of the Nationality Immigration and Asylum Act (NIAA) 2002 s54 and Sch 3 paras 1–2. The main group affected are EEA nationals and their dependants. They are ineligible for such help unless it is needed to avoid a breach of their rights under the ECHR or the EU treaties. So where an EEA national is arguing that they have a right to reside and so are eligible, they face being refused interim accommodation on the same basis as they have been found ineligible in the original decision.

8.95 In *R (Maryam Mohamed) v Harrow LBC*[146] a Dutch national had worked part-time for two short periods before her children joined her. She applied as homeless when she was later evicted from her temporary accommodation. The court refused to overturn the council's decision that she was not entitled to accommodation pending the review of the homelessness decision that she was ineligible. They considered the EU arguments and concluded that she had not retained worker status because she had been unemployed for 15 months after working for only a short time. See also *Putans v Tower Hamlets LBC*[147] where an accession national who became

141 HA 1996 s188(3).
142 HA 1996 s204(4).
143 *R v Camden LBC ex p Mohamed* (1998) 30 HLR 315.
144 [2006] EWHC 497 (Admin), May 2006 *Legal Action* 34.
145 *R (Emeka Omatoyo) v City of Westminster* [2006] EWHC 2572 (Admin).
146 [2005] EWHC 3194 (Admin).
147 [2006] EWHC 1634 (Ch), 20 June 2006, August 2006 *Legal Action* 38.

incapacitated after working for less than 12 months was refused interim accommodation pending his homelessness appeal.

The 'full housing duty'

8.96 If the authority is satisfied that an applicant is homeless, eligible, in priority need and not intentionally homeless then a duty arises to ensure that accommodation is available to the applicant.[148]

8.97 The duty is to secure that accommodation is available for the applicant and anyone else who usually resides with the applicant as a family member, or anyone else who can reasonably be expected to live with the applicant.[149] 'Anyone else' here includes persons subject to immigration control who would fail the eligibility requirement in HA 1996 s185: once an applicant is owed the housing duty, that duty extends to securing accommodation for the whole of their household whether or not they are eligible. The accommodation will be temporary accommodation, since such accommodation cannot be let on a secure or assured tenancy. However, in many local authority areas, an offer of permanent accommodation under HA 1996 Part VI will follow eventually, depending on supply and the local allocation policy.[150]

8.98 The accommodation secured must be 'suitable'.[151]

Other housing duties

8.99 If an applicant is homeless and in priority need, but found intentionally homeless, the authority has a duty under HA 1996 s190(2) to:

> (a) secure that accommodation is available for his occupation for such period as they consider will give him a reasonable opportunity of securing accommodation for his occupation; and
> (b) provide him with such advice and assistance as they consider appropriate in the circumstances in any attempts he may make to secure that accommodation becomes available for his occupation.

8.100 The provision of advice and assistance must follow an assessment of housing need.[152] This should identify any factors that make it

148 HA 1996 ss193 and 206.
149 HA 1996 s176.
150 See para 8.136 below.
151 See para 8.104 below.
152 HA 1996 s192(4).

difficult for the applicant to secure accommodation, such as illiteracy, English as a second language or long-term health needs.

8.101 It has been common for local authorities to allow a 28-day period in all cases, taking into account their limited resources, but this approach was found to be unlawful where a single woman with a 13-year-old son had no money for a deposit or rent in advance to secure private rented accommodation.[153] The Court of Appeal decided that the council was not entitled to have regard to its own resources or the other demands on it when deciding what constituted a reasonable opportunity for an applicant to secure their own accommodation but should have regard to the applicant's circumstances and the possibilities open to them.

8.102 Applying this approach, a migrant family with children in London would arguably require a longer period to give them the 'reasonable opportunity', particularly if they have language needs, are unemployed or do not have friends or family who can assist. Accommodation secured under section 190(2)(a) must be 'suitable'.[154]

Tip

If a homeless applicant is found intentionally homeless and asked to leave their temporary accommodation in 28 days, send a letter threatening judicial review or a formal complaint and:

- request a copy of the assessment under HA 1996 s192(4);
- make a Freedom of Information Act 2000 s1 request for a copy of the council's policy for the exercise of the HA 1996 s190(2) duty;
- refer to any general equality duties or specific duties contained in the council's equality scheme;
- refer to the council's homelessness strategy;
- describe any particular needs of the household affecting their ability to find alternative accommodation;
- provide evidence of the local private rented housing supply for this type of applicant, eg who is on benefits, no references or has a child under two.

8.103 If an applicant is homeless (whether or not intentionally), but not in priority need, the authority owes the 'advice and assistance'

153 *R (Conville) v Richmond upon Thames RLBC* [2006] EWCA Civ 718, July 2006 *Legal Action* 30.

154 See para 8.104 below.

duty described in section 190(2)(b). Local authorities have a power (not a duty) to secure accommodation for such applicants who are not intentionally homeless and their homelessness strategy may make reference to it.[155] There is no duty on local authorities to give written decisions or reasons for decisions not to exercise the power, and no right of review of such a decision.

Is the accommodation suitable?

8.104 Accommodation secured by the local authority must be suitable[156] for the applicant and anyone else who usually resides with the applicant as a family member, or anyone else who can reasonably be expected to live with the applicant.[157] 'Anyone else' here can include persons who would fail the eligibility requirement in HA 1996 s185.

8.105 In deciding what is suitable, the authority must take into account slum clearance, overcrowding and houses in multiple occupation.[158] The Code of Guidance[159] recommends that local authorities should, as a minimum, ensure that all accommodation is free of category 1 hazards (under the housing health and housing safety rating system).[160] This covers a wide range of problems and the occupant's personal circumstances are taken into account in assessing each potential hazard, so for example a higher standard would be applied to a faulty plug socket where a family had young children.

8.106 The circumstances of migrants may give rise to special consideration in relation to suitability. For example, the courts have quashed suitability decisions where an asylum-seeker refused a basement flat on an estate that reminded her of a prison where she had been tortured;[161] and where an asylum-seeker refused an offer where she would be in contact with Turkish and Kurdish communities in circumstances where she had a genuine terror of such contact and where her daughter's mental health would be damaged by acceptance.[162]

155 HA 1996 s192(3).
156 HA 1996 ss193 and 206.
157 HA 1996 s176.
158 HA 1996 Parts IX, X and XI; HA 1996 s210.
159 Paragraph 1715.
160 www.communities.gov.uk/housing/rentingandletting/housinghealth/.
161 *R v Brent LBC ex p Omar* (1991) 23 HLR 446.
162 *R v Haringey LBC ex p Karaman* (1997) 29 HLR 446.

Location

8.107 In *R v Newham LBC ex p Sacupima,*[163] the Court of Appeal decided that the location of accommodation was relevant to its suitability. The use of privately-owned or managed bed and breakfast accommodation will not be considered suitable for families including dependent children or pregnant women for more than a six-week period, or if any other accommodation is available.[164] In this context, 'bed and breakfast accommodation' means accommodation where more than one household shares toilet, washing or cooking facilities.[165]

8.108 So far as is reasonably practicable, authorities must accommodate the homeless person within their own district.[166] Authorities should have regard to the importance of housing homeless people as close as possible to where they previously lived so that they can keep the same schools, doctors, social workers and other support. Any journey to work should also be taken into account,[167] but a local authority may take into account cost when deciding whether to make an 'out of area' placement.[168]

8.109 A Turkish asylum-seeker with ILR made a homelessness application after living with relatives in overcrowded accommodation in the Enfield area for over five years. When he made a homelessness application, Enfield council told him that he met the criteria for their 'out-of-borough' policy and offered him accommodation in Luton, Bedfordshire, which he refused on two occasions. His appeal succeeded because despite the duty imposed by HA 1996 s208 to secure accommodation in its own area 'so far as reasonably practicable', the evidence showed that the council had been determined throughout to deal with him under the 'out-of-borough' policy. There was no evidence that the availability of housing in-borough had been established before reoffering the Luton property. The council had also failed to give the claimant notice in writing, when making the offer, that he had a right to a review of the decision on suitability.

163 (2001) 33 HLR 18.

164 Homelessness (Suitability of Accommodation) (England) Order 2003 SI No 3326.

165 SI No 3326 r2.

166 HA 1996 s208.

167 Code of Guidance para 1741.

168 *R (Tekin Calgin) v Enfield LBC* [2005] EWHC 1716 (Admin).

Affordable accommodation

8.110 Housing authorities should consider accommodation as unaffordable if the rent is so high the applicant would be left with an income lower than the income support level, or would need to claim housing benefit, if they are in low paid employment and the high cost of the accommodation makes it difficult for them to work or acts as a disincentive to find work/continue working.[169]

Wales

8.111 The rules are more favourable in Wales where regulations set out the factors that should be taken into account when deciding suitability and provide for a gradual end to the use of bed and breakfast accommodation.[170]

Challenging unsuitable accommodation

8.112 The Code of Guidance suggests that applicants should be given the chance to view accommodation before being asked to accept it and sign a tenancy. If an applicant refuses a property, the local authority must advise the applicant of the consequences of refusal and that it considers the duty discharged.[171]

8.113 If accommodation is unsuitable the remedy is then to request a review under HA 1996 s202, within 21 days, whether or not the applicant accepts the accommodation. Usually applicants should be advised to accept a property even if they consider it unsuitable and then to request a review, to protect their position.

Local connection referrals

8.114 Where a person is owed the full housing duty, the authority may transfer the duty to house to another housing authority where the applicant has a local connection by 'referring the case'.[172] Under HA 1996 s198(2), a local authority may only refer an applicant to another authority if these conditions are met:

(a) neither the applicant nor any person who might reasonably be expected to reside with him has a local connection with the district of the authority to whom his application was made;

169 Code of Guidance para 1740.
170 Homelessness (Suitability of Accommodation) (Wales) Order 2006 SI No 650.
171 HA 1996 s193(5).
172 HA 1996 s198(1).

(b) the applicant or a person who might reasonably be expected to reside with him has a local connection with the district of that other authority; and

(c) neither the applicant nor any person who might reasonably be expected to reside with him will run the risk of domestic violence in that other district.

(2A) But the conditions of referral mentioned at subsection (2) are not met if:

(a) the applicant or any person who might reasonably be expected to reside with him has suffered violence (other than domestic violence) in the district of the other authority; and

(b) it is probable that the return to that district of the victim will lead to further violence of a similar kind against him.

8.115 The term 'local connection' is defined in HA 1996 s199 and the duties on referring are set out more fully in HA 1996 s200. A person has a local connection with an authority area if they meet one of four criteria:

- they are or were in the past usually resident in it, and their residence is or was of their own choice;
- they are employed in it;
- they have family associations;
- there are special circumstances.

8.116 There is an additional criterion which applies only to former asylum-seekers who have been housed under asylum support provisions. HA 1996 s199[173] now provides that a person will have a local connection with the district of a housing authority if they were (at any time) provided with accommodation in that district under IAA 1999 s95. The relevant authority is the last one in which they received section 95 accommodation. These provisions reverse the effect of the House of Lords decision in *Al-Ameri v Kensington and Chelsea RLBC; Osmani v Harrow LBC*[174] that decided that asylum-seekers dispersed to Glasgow had no local connection there, because it was not accommodation 'of choice'.

8.117 The provision does not apply to cases where accommodation was provided under National Assistance Act 1948 s21. Where a former asylum-seeker has been accommodated by the Home Office under IAA 1999 s4, they cannot be referred back to that area under this provision. But if they were previously supported under IAA 1999

173 As amended by the Asylum and Immigration (Treatment of Claimants, etc) Act 2004 s11.

174 [2004] UKHL 57.

s95, they could be referred back to the area where the section 95 accommodation was situated.

8.118 Different rules apply to asylum-seekers who were dispersed to Scotland and apply to an authority in England and Wales. The authority has a discretion to provide accommodation for a temporary period giving the applicant a reasonable opportunity of finding accommodation, plus advice and assistance in doing so. It would thus be open to such applicants to reapply in Scotland.

8.119 The local connection criteria are developed in the Code of Guidance chapter 18, and the Local Authority Association Joint Local Connection Agreement contains guidelines for resolving disputes between local authorities as to where homeless persons have local connections. The criteria and the guidance should not be applied rigidly however, so that the ordinary meaning of the term 'local connection' is lost.[175] The relevant time for considering whether the local connection conditions are satisfied is the date of decision, or the date of review (even if the applicant has acquired or lost a local connection in the meantime).[176] Guidance to local authorities suggests that 'normal residence' will be established by residence for six of the last 12 months, and that 'family associations' will exist where there are parents, adult children, brothers or sisters residing for at least five years in the area in question. The criterion of 'other special circumstance' leaves open a wide range of considerations which may give rise to a local connection.

8.120 The effect of these provisions can be seen in two Court of Appeal decisions where former asylum-seekers have left the dispersal areas where they were accommodated under section 95.

Local connection High Court decisions

- A former asylum-seeker moved his family from Portsmouth to join relatives in Ipswich when he was granted leave to remain, arguing unsuccessfully that he had a local connection there due to family associations. The Court of Appeal accepted that it was possible to have a local connection where relatives had lived in an area for less than five years, even if they were not close relatives, but in O's case his brothers had lived in Ipswich 'for nothing like the five year period'.[177]

175 *R v Eastleigh BC ex p Betts* [1983] 2 AC 613; (1983) 10 HLR 97, HL.
176 *Mohamed v Hammersmith and Fulham LBC* [2001] UKHL 57.
177 *Ozbek v Ipswich BC* [2006] EWCA Civ 534, January 2007 *Legal Action* 17.

- An asylum-seeker had left Swansea after he had been mugged and racially abused. The council rejected his argument that he should not be referred back there because of the theat of violence and the court upheld their decision. The test was not whether he subjectively feared violence but whether there was a probability of him suffering actual violence if he were referred back.[178]
- When a refugee who had been dispersed to Sunderland by NASS applied as homeless to Kensington and Chelsea RLBC (K&C), they housed her in temporary accommodation in Tower Hamlets LBC for 18 months. When K&C referred her back to Sunderland under the local connection rules, she applied to Tower Hamlets LBC for accommodation and they also referred her to Sunderland. She appealed arguing the council's decision had failed to address whether or not her period of normal residence in temporary accommodation had given her a connection with that area. The appeal was allowed. The court found there was no rule that residence in interim accommodation could never be 'residence of choice'.[179] Each case was fact-sensitive. Also, the claimant had chosen to remain in Tower Hamlets area after K&C's duties to her had ended.[180]

Tip

An asylum-seeker may be able to avoid a local connection referral to the area where they received IAA 1999 s95 accommodation if any of the following apply to them or a member of their household:

- they have paid employment in the local authority area they wish to live in;
- they have relatives who have lived there for a few years;
- they lived in the local authority's area for six months or more to acquire a local connection there based on residence before making a homelessness application;

178 *Kensington and Chelsea RLBC v Danesh* [2003] EWCA Civ 1404.
179 HA 1996 s199(1)(a).
180 *Melka v Tower Hamlets LBC* Bow County Court, 7 July 2008.

- they have a local connection there based on other special circumstances, eg the need to receive treatment for HIV/AIDS at a hospital in that area which is not available elsewhere, or a statemented child whose welfare may suffer if they have to change schools;
- they cannot return to the previous area due to a proven risk of racial violence.

Housing options for ineligible applicants[181]

8.121 If an applicant is ineligible then the main homelessness duties do not apply. But they still have a right to receive advice and information about homelessness and the prevention of homelessness.[182]

8.122 There is a guide explaining the entitlements of asylum-seekers and former asylum-seekers at appendix G.

8.123 Asylum-seekers and other migrants with care needs or who are pregnant or nursing mothers[183] may be eligible for assistance from the local authority social services department under community care legislation, in particular NAA 1948 s21.[184] A former unaccompanied asylum-seeker may have rights as a child leaving care under CA 1989,[185] but in either case, social services must consider NIAA 2002 s54 and Sch 3, which applies if the applicant is unlawfully in the UK or an EEA national.[186] Schedule 3 provides that social services may only act if assistance is needed to avoid a breach of the applicant household's rights under the ECHR or their EU treaty rights. Examples would be where the applicant is a destitute disabled Palestinian refused asylum-seeker who cannot travel home,[187] or where a young Polish mother has a job offer to start in a month's time and needs temporary accommodation.[188]

8.124 If the ineligible applicant has a child, the housing authority has a duty to ask the applicant to consent to them making a referral to

181 See also para 2.101.
182 HA 1996 ss183(3) and 179(1).
183 But the maternity provision is discretionary.
184 See chapter 9.
185 See para 9.139.
186 See para 9.53.
187 ECHR article 3.
188 See further para 9.70.

the social services department in the area where they are living.[189] The social services authority should then carry out an assessment of whether the child is in need under CA 1989 s17.[190] Again this is subject to NAA 1948 Sch 3, above.

8.125 Where a Jamaican overstayer applied for CA 1989 assistance on the basis that she had an outstanding application for leave to remain based on her children living in the UK for seven years, the council offered her a ticket home. Charles J allowed her application for judicial review because the council had failed to have regard to Home Office policy that no enforcement action would be taken against those with irregular immigration status who had been in the UK for more than seven years. The council should reconsider its decision having regard to the claimant's rights under ECHR article 8 (right to respect for private and family life).[191]

8.126 The social services department may ask the housing authority for reasonable advice and assistance to enable them to discharge their CA 1989 duties.[192] The duties of housing and social services authorities to co-operate in relation to children are discussed in the Homelessness Code of Guidance at chapter 13.

8.127 Housing authorities have a duty to publish a homelessness strategy,[193] which should be taken into account by the social services authority when carrying out their functions. It is worth checking the strategy to see if there is any local provision for homeless households to whom no duty is owed, such as a rent deposit scheme.

8.128 In a Scottish case, the council had housed an ineligible Iraqi family under general housing powers, but the family then fell foul of the 'no recourse to public funds' requirement in their immigration appeal.[194] On 7 August 2008, the government introduced regulations[195] that apply to England, Scotland and Northern Ireland, but not to Wales. In England their main effect is to prevent housing authorities from granting a tenancy or licence under HA 1985 Part 2 to a person subject to immigration control simply because they are a national of

189 HA 1996 s213A.

190 See chapter 9.

191 *R (C) v Birmingham City Council* [2008] EWHC 3036 (Admin), June 2009 *Legal Action* 28.

192 HA 1996 s213A(5).

193 Homelessness Act 2002 s1.

194 *KA and others (Public funds (housing) Iraq)* [2007] UKAIT 00081, 14 August 2007.

195 Persons subject to Immigration Control (Housing Authority Accommodation and Homelessness) Amendment Order 2008 SI No 1768.

a country that has ratified the European Convention on Social and Medical Assistance 1953 (ECSMA) or the European Social Charter (ESC), who is also lawfully present and habitually resident in the UK. This potentially affects EEA nationals without the right to reside and nationals of Turkey, Macedonia and Croatia.[196] EEA nationals with the right to reside are unaffected.

8.129 An asylum-seeker or refused asylum-seeker who is homeless but ineligible under the above provisions should seek assistance with accommodation from UKBA.[197]

8.130 A person who is ineligible to apply may nonetheless be accommodated if there is another member of the household (or another person with whom they may reasonably be expected to live) who is eligible to apply. To qualify for assistance the eligible person will have to be homeless in their own right without taking into account the housing needs of ineligible household members[198] and in priority need without reliance upon ineligible household members.[199] Where the eligible person qualifies, the duty upon the local authority is to secure accommodation for the eligible applicant and anyone who can reasonably be expected to live with them, including household members who are themselves ineligible.[200]

8.131 There is no 'immigration test' applying to a mentally ill person who has been detained under the Mental Health Act 1983.[201] They are entitled to 'aftercare' that can include accommodation.

8.132 HA 1996 Part 6 covers the 'allocation' of housing accommodation by local housing authorities. A housing authority 'allocates' accommodation when it selects a person to be a secure or introductory tenant of council accommodation, nominates a person to be a secure or introductory tenant of other accommodation (for example, owned by a body that can grant a secure or introductory tenancy, such as a housing action trust); or nominates a person to be an assured tenant of a registered social landlord.[202] Note, however, that the grant of a tenancy by a local authority (but not the nomination of a person to be an assured tenant of a registered social landlord), which is made in order to provide accommodation under the

196 See chapter 2.
197 See chapters 4–6 and table in appendix E.
198 See para 8.45 below.
199 See para 8.50 below.
200 See para 8.104 below.
201 Mental Health Act 1983 ss 3, 47 or 48.
202 HA 1996 s159.

asylum support provisions of IAA 1999 is not an allocation under HA 1996 Part 6.[203] Allocation includes a transfer made at the request of an existing tenant. For the granting of tenancies or other rights of occupation in local authority housing stock falling outside the scope of allocation under HA 1996 Part 6, see para 8.161 below.

8.133 The allocation of accommodation must take place in accordance with rules as to priorities and procedure devised by the housing authority and set out in its 'allocation scheme'.[204] The schemes are usually 'points based' or in bands. There are statutory groups who are entitled to 'reasonable preference' in an allocation scheme, such as people to whom a homelessness duty is owed, and people who need to move on medical or welfare grounds.

8.134 A homeless applicant who had been in temporary accommodation for years argued that the ten points she had been given under the waiting scheme was not a 'reasonable preference' because it meant she might never be rehoused.[205] The Court of Appeal decided that 'reasonable preference' simply meant a 'head start' and it was quite possible for a lawful allocation scheme to give a reasonable preference and for that person never to be allocated housing. The House of Lords has further limited the prospects of challenging allocation schemes, finding that the courts should be slow to interfere with decisions about reasonable preference and did not have to do a detailed exercise to work out priority between different households with a reasonable preference.[206] This makes it difficult to challenge a decision about priority unless, for example, the procedure is unfair, the council has not applied its own policy, or relevant evidence has not been taken into account.

8.135 A scheme may be challengeable by a migrant if it appears to discriminate on grounds of race.[207] Local authorities are subject to equality duties that include having due regard to the need to promote good race relations.[208] However one of the permitted reasons for giving reasonable preference is a local connection with the authority's district.[209] This allows an authority to give extra priority to applicants

203 HA 1985 Sch 1 para 4A, as amended by IAA 1999 Sch 14 para 81.

204 HA 1996 s167.

205 *Lin v Barnet LBC* [2007] EWCA Civ 132.

206 *R (Ahmad) v Newham LBC* [2009] UKHL 14.

207 See Allocations Code of Guidance para 310.

208 See para 8.154.

209 HA 1996 s167(2A).

who have lived in the area for a long time, even though this may indirectly discriminate against migrant applicants.

Allocations

Eligibility and allocations

8.136 A housing authority may only allocate accommodation to 'eligible persons'. The rules about eligibility for the purposes of allocation are almost identical to the homelessness rules and so are explained at para 8.19 above. The table at para 8.214 also shows when an applicant is eligible for an allocation. The difference is that the allocation rules have not included asylum-seekers, even those who claimed prior to 3 April 2000 and so all asylum-seekers are excluded from eligibility for the allocation of public housing, unless they fall within another category, for example dependant of an EEA national with the right to reside.

8.137 The route to working out whether an applicant is eligible for an allocation is initially the provisions of HA 1996 s160A, then regulations made under section 160A, in particular the Homelessness (England) Regulations 2006 as amended and finally by the exercise of powers given to local authorities under that section to treat persons as ineligible. These powers enable local authorities to decide that an applicant is ineligible on the ground that they are guilty of unacceptable behaviour making them unsuitable to be a tenant.[210] As with the homelessness rules, there is a general exclusion of all persons subject to immigration control, modified by the 'reinclusion' of people falling within classes specified in the regulations. The general exclusion does not apply to transfer applicants.[211]

8.138 Where a local authority decides that an applicant is ineligible, it must give notice of its decision in writing and with reasons[212] and there is a right of a review of a decision that an applicant is not eligible[213] but there is no statutory procedure for the review and no appeal so the remedy if the local authority fails to review the decision within a reasonable period would be judicial review.

210 HA 1996 s160A(7).
211 HA 1996 s160A(6).
212 HA 1996 s160(A)(9).
213 HA 1996 s167(4A)(d).

Mixed households

8.139 A child born in the UK who has a parent who is ineligible, but who has a spouse or partner who has indefinite leave to remain or who is a British citizen, can claim British nationality and so would not be an ineligible 'person subject to immigration control'.[214] There is nothing in HA 1996 Part VI to exclude children from applying for housing, although local authority allocation schemes may exclude them.

8.140 Where a joint application for housing is made by two or more persons, and one of those persons is ineligible, then all applicants will be treated as ineligible,[215] but there is nothing to prevent eligible applicants applying on their own, and including ineligible persons in their household for rehousing purposes.[216] The council can consider whether the ineligible persons form part of the household, provided they take their allocation policy into account. The High Court found it was lawful for a council to refuse to allow a Nigerian applicant to include five adult children aged between 22 and 31 in her application.[217] The council had a wide discretion and were entitled to refuse to treated the children as part of the household given their age and insecure immigration status. At the time of writing, the decision was being appealed. Where problems arise, the council's equality duties should be considered.[218]

Restricted cases[219]

8.141 In a 'restricted case' where there is a homelessness duty[220] if the local authority has not been able to arrange for the family to be offered an assured shorthold tenancy by a private landlord, they can bring their 'full' homelessness duty under HA 1996 s193(2) to an end by offering an allocation under HA 1996 Part 6. But any restricted person cannot be taken into account when assessing reasonable preference (priority).[221]

8.142 The cases at para 8.140 now needs to be read in conjunction with the rules on restricted cases.[222] It seems the rules would not

214 See para 8.21.

215 HA 1996 s160A(1)(c).

216 *R v Tower Hamlets LBC ex p Kimvono* (2000) 5 December, QBD; February 2001 *Legal Action* 27.

217 *R (Esther Ariemuguvbe) v Islington LBC* [2009] EWHC 470 (Admin).

218 See para 8.154.

219 See para 8.50 above.

220 HA 1996 s193(3B); see para 8.82.

221 HA 1996 s167(2ZA) as amended by the Housing and Regeneration Act 2008 s314 and Sch 15.

222 See also para 8.50.

affect property size, as opposed to priority. Nor should they apply to a family who has not applied as homeless but has applied for an allocation only.

8.143 If ineligible family members are included, liability for rent and 'non-dependant deductions' of housing and council tax benefit may present a difficulty, for example if there is a large family and only the applicant is eligible for housing benefit.[223]

Choice-based lettings schemes

8.144 The procedure for allocation is usually via a choice-based lettings scheme. Provision for this is made in HA 1996 s167(1A).[224] In theory this allows an applicant to choose a property by bidding for properties that are advertised, normally via the internet or phone. In practice the high demand for social rented housing means choice it limited, but as soon as an applicant has been accepted as eligible for an allocation, they should be provided with details of the local scheme.

8.145 If an applicant needs help bidding due to language needs or disabilities, the local authority should provide this to comply with its race and disability equality duties.[225]

Remedies in homelessness and allocation cases

Challenging homelessness decisions

8.146 Detailed provisions about the review of homelessness decisions and appeal to the county court are set out in HA 1996 ss202–204, and the Allocation of Housing and Homelessness (Review Procedures) Regulations 1999.[226] A brief summary is given here. A review can be requested by the applicant or by an advisor or solicitor on their behalf.

8.147 The applicant has a right to request a review of decisions made by local authorities concerning eligibility,[227] whether duties to secure accommodation, advice and assistance are owed, and what those

223 See para 3.112.

224 See also Allocation of Accommodation: Choice Based Lettings – Code of Guidance for Local Housing Authorities, CLG, August 2008 and the Allocation of Accommodation Code of Guidance chapter 5.

225 See para 8.154.

226 SI No 71.

227 HA 1996 s202.

duties are; whether the applicant is to be referred to another authority; and whether or not the final accommodation offered under HA 1996 s193 is suitable.

8.148 The review must be requested within 21 days of the decision. The review must be carried out by a more senior officer and be completed within 56 days of the request. If it is not completed in that period, the applicant can appeal within 21 days or agree an extension in writing. The applicant must be informed in writing of the review decision. If the review officer decides to uphold the original decision, the applicant has a right of appeal on a point of law to the county court.[228] The applicant has 21 days from the review decision (or from the expiry of the 56 days if no decision is made within that time) to lodge the appeal.[229] If the local authority refuses to continue the provision of temporary accommodation pending hearing of the appeal, the applicant can appeal to the county court against that decision also.[230]

8.149 Not all decisions made on homelessness applications have a right of review and appeal. The most important exceptions are the failure to accept a homelessness application and/or make a decision and decisions about the provision of temporary accommodation pending assessment or review. Such decisions may be challenged by judicial review.

8.150 Where there is a right to a statutory review of a suitability decision, an applicant may both accept an offer of accommodation and seek a review of its suitability.[231] Where an applicant wishes to challenge an offer, it will therefore usually be advisable to accept it and ask for a review, rather than refuse it, since if an offer is refused and the review is unsuccessful, there is a risk of being left with no accommodation at all.

Challenging allocation decisions

8.151 There is a statutory right to review of a decision of a housing authority as to whether or not a person is eligible.[232] Authorities must include in their allocation schemes a right to request a review, and a right of the applicant to be informed of the review decision and the

228 HA 1996 s204(1).
229 HA 1996 s204.
230 HA 1996 s204A.
231 HA 1996 s202(1A).
232 HA 1996 s202(1)(a).

grounds for it.[233] The local authority must publish the allocation scheme itself,[234] and applicants are entitled to be given information about assessments, likelihood of being rehoused and the length of time they are likely to have to wait.[235]

8.152 There is a similar right to request a review of a decision that accommodation allocated under HA 1996 Part 6 is suitable,[236] so as to discharge a local authority's obligations under Part 7 towards a homeless applicant.

8.153 There is no right of appeal to the county court against a review of an allocation decision: it may only be challenged by an application for judicial review. Other decisions of local authorities in relation to allocation, including the lawfulness or otherwise of allocation schemes, may only be challenged by judicial review.

Discrimination/equality duties

8.154 The issue of discrimination may arise at any point in the homelessness process from the application stage onwards. Procedures for assessing eligibility and entitlement to homelessness assistance and allocations should be compliant with the local authority's equality duties and policies. The Homelessness Code of Guidance[237] provides that authorities should adopt a formal equality and diversity policy relating to all aspects of their homelessness service, to ensure equality of access and treatment for all applicants.

8.155 There is a *general* legal duty on public authorities, such as local councils to have 'due regard' to the need to eliminate unlawful discrimination and promote equality of opportunity in relation to race,[238] sex[239] and disability.[240] There is a *specific* duty on certain public authorities, including local councils, to take certain steps, which include publishing an equality scheme.[241]

8.156 Although there are no equality duties relating to religion or sexual orientation, there is a prohibition on discrimination by

233 HA 1996 s167(4A)(d).
234 HA 1996 s168.
235 HA 1996 s167(4A)(a).
236 HA 1996 s202(1)(f) as amended by the Homelessness Act 2002 s8(2)(a).
237 Para 7.
238 Race Relations Act 1976 ss19B, 71 and Sch 1A.
239 Sex Discrimination Act ss1, 76A–E; Equality Act (EA) 2006, Part 4.
240 Disability Discrimination Act 1995 ss1, 21B and 49A–F.
241 See 'The Equality Duties and Public Authorities', July 2008 *Legal Action* 24 and September 2008 *Legal Action* 43.

public authorities on grounds of religion or belief[242] and sexual orientation.[243]

8.157 In the housing context, the equality duties could be used to support a challenge to service provision in a variety of ways. Suggestions include:

- suitable facilities from the application stage onwards such as British sign language/other interpreting facilities, or home visits for housebound applicants;
- suitably adapted temporary accommodation for disabled people;
- access to a fridge in hotel/hostel accommodation to enable storage of halal or kosher food;
- help with bidding for properties for migrants who have special needs or English as a second language.

8.158 The Homelessness Code of Guidance reminds authorities that the disability equality duty means taking steps to take account of the disabled person's disabilities even where that involves treating disabled people more favourably than others.[244]

8.159 In order to avoid race discrimination, a local housing authority should ask all applicants for homelessness assistance or an allocation the same questions in relation to eligibility. The Homelessness Code of Guidance[245] makes reference to staff training on this.

8.160 Any significant change of policy, for example a decision to change priorities under an allocation scheme so that there is a long residence requirement, should be subject to an impact assessment. Local authorities have a duty to publish their equality schemes, which should include details of when impact assessments are carried out and may be useful background if it appears that discriminatory policies are being applied. The remedy for discriminatory treatment may be a damages claim in the county court or an application for judicial review in the Administrative Court to quash a particular policy or for a declaration that it is unlawful.

The use of social housing as accommodation for asylum-seekers

8.161 Although an asylum-seeker or person from abroad cannot usually access social housing under HA 1996 Parts 6 and 7, a local authority

242 EA 2006 s52.
243 Equality Act (Sexual Orientation) Regulations 2007 SI No 1263 reg 8.
244 DDA 1995 s49(A); Homelessness Code of Guidance, para 11.
245 Chapter 9.

may use its own housing stock to accommodate such persons in certain circumstances.

8.162 The requirement that all lettings be through HA 1996 Part 6 only affects allocation by local authorities of secure or introductory tenancies, nomination by local authorities to registered social landlords for letting on assured tenancies, and transfers requested by tenants. It does not cover:

(a) the grant of or nomination to a tenancy or licence by a local authority which is exempt from security;[246]
(b) the nomination of a person to a tenancy or licence which is exempt from assured status.[247]

8.163 A local authority can let properties under (a) that are exempt from security including a tenancy or licence granted to provide accommodation under IAA 1999 Part 6,[248] that is accommodation for asylum-seekers through the asylum support provisions. Initially this only applied to IAA 1999 s98 and s95 accommodation, but it has now been extended to cover section 4.[249] There is parallel provision exempting tenancies or licences granted by registered social landlords from assured status.[250] The reference to private landlord in para 12A includes registered social landlords. So local authorities may nominate asylum-seekers to registered social landlords, or lease accommodation from a registered social landlord to provide temporary accommodation.[251]

8.164 UKBA may require registered social landlords to provide 'reasonable assistance' in providing accommodation under IAA 1999 Part 6.[252] So if UKBA states it cannot find suitable accommodation for an asylum-seeker who needs to be in a particular area, it can ask the local authority to assist. Neither the exemption from security of accommodation for asylum-seekers, nor the powers to require assistance, extend to accommodation provided for other persons subject to immigration control. Leasing from housing associations or private landlords may, however, be used to accommodate such persons.

246 See HA 1985 Sch 1 for the classes of occupation exempt from security.
247 HA 1988 Sch 1.
248 HA 1985 Sch 1 para 4A as amended by IAA 1999 Sch 14 para 81.
249 IAA 1999 s99 as amended by IANA 2006 s43.
250 HA 1988 Sch 1 para 12A, as inserted by IAA 1999 Sch 14 para 88.
251 HA 1985 Sch 1 para 6.
252 IAA 1999 s100; see also *R (A) v Waltham Forest LBC* [2003] EWCA Civ 1473, (2003) 6 CCLR 538.

8.165 These provisions are complemented by IAA 1999 s118, which requires that housing authorities avoid 'so far as practicable' granting tenancies or licences to persons subject to immigration control as defined by IA 1971 ss2 and 3,[253] unless they do so to provide accommodation for asylum-seekers under IAA 1999 s95 or for persons falling within classes specified by the Home Secretary. The classes specified[254] are the same as those applied to allocation under HA 1996 Part 7[255] plus:

- those owed a duty under NAA 1948 s21;[256]
- those owed a duty under CA 1989 s17;[257]
- those owed housing duties under homelessness legislation;[258]
- students in accommodation provided under arrangements between colleges and local authorities.

8.166 Interpreting IAA 1999 ss100 and 118, the court has said that 'reasonable assistance' will require the local authority to look first outside its own housing stock, but to use its own stock where an applicant's present accommodation is so inadequate as to make it unreasonable not to use their own stock.[259]

8.167 Local authorities also have the power to provide IAA 1999 s4 accommodation to refused asylum-seekers on behalf of the Home Office.[260]

Succession and assignment

8.168 Successions to a tenancy after a death and assignments of tenancies are unaffected by immigration status. The rules that exclude asylum-seekers from housing allocation do not apply to successions and assignments. In local authority housing stock, successions and assignments are excluded from the scope of allocation under Part 6[261] and, in that they do not involve the 'grant' of rights of occupation by a local authority, are not covered by the restrictions in IAA 1999 s118, above.

253 See para 8.121 above.

254 IAA 1999 s188(1)(a) and Persons Subject to Immigration Control (Housing Authority Accommodation and Homelessness) Order 2000 SI No 706.

255 See para 8.136 above.

256 See para 9.105.

257 See para 9.128.

258 See para 8.96.

259 *R (A) v Waltham Forest LBC* [2003] EWCA Civ 1473, (2003) 6 CCLR 538.

260 IAA 1999 s99 as amended by IANA 2006 s43.

261 HA 1996 s160.

Effects of changes in immigration status

8.169 This section considers housing issues which arise when an asylum-seeker or other migrant is granted leave to enter or remain, and briefly deals with the situation where an unaccompanied asylum-seeking child reaches the age of 18.

Grant of refugee status or HP or DL

8.170 A successful asylum application will conclude with a decision by the Home Secretary to grant the applicant refugee status or HP or DL.[262] If an asylum applicant wins their appeal, they will then need to wait for the UKBA to issue a decision to grant them refugee status or leave to enter/remain. This should follow but there are often delays and sometimes policy reasons for the Home Secretary not to make such a decision, as in the 'Afghan hijackers' case. See chapter 1 for how to deal with such delays.

8.171 People who have refugee status or HP or DL are eligible to apply for assistance under HA 1996 Parts 6 and 7. But to qualify for homelessness assistance, they will need to meet the conditions explained above – be in priority need, not intentionally homeless etc. This means that an able-bodied childless asylum-seeker who has been recognised as a refugee may be faced with street homelessness within 28 days, after months or years in UKBA accommodation.

8.172 Where the person is in section 95 accommodation provided by UKBA under IAA 1999, at the point when such a decision is made, the entitlement ends 28 days from the date of notification of the Home Secretary's decision or, where an appeal has been made, from the appeal decision. If the applicant has a child under 18, entitlement continues. Where an applicant is in receipt of section 4 accommodation, there is no statutory notice period but guidance on the UKBA website suggests a 21-day notice period if leave to remain is granted.

8.173 Where the household of the person whose asylum claim has been decided includes a person with an outstanding asylum claim, for example their adult disabled sister, that person may be able to argue that the section 95 accommodation should continue. They would need to be able to show they are not entitled to accommodation for the whole household under the homelessness provisions so they are without adequate accommodation for asylum support purposes.[263]

262 See para 1.43.
263 See para 4.69 above.

8.174 Where the asylum-seeker whose claim is determined is accommodated by the local authority under community care law (usually NAA 1948 s21 or CA 1989 s17), then, unless the asylum-seeker needs residential care, the social services department is likely to take steps to terminate that support and transfer responsibility to the housing department. However, there is no requirement to end support within 28 days as is the case with asylum support. The local authority should not terminate support until satisfied that, as the case may be, the applicant's needs are otherwise being met[264] or that the child is no longer a child in need.[265] The local authority should review the community care or section 17 assessment and care plan before ending accommodation or changing service provision. If services are suddenly withdrawn, the remedy is judicial review.

8.175 Where an asylum-seeker who has been staying with relatives wishes to apply for homelessness assistance after they are granted leave, they will have the right to continue to occupy that accommodation until their licence to do so is terminated by the tenant or owner. The housing authority is likely to ask for evidence of this, for example a letter from the owner/relative asking them to leave the accommodation by a certain date.

8.176 For the reasons explained above, most asylum-seekers granted leave will not have a tenancy, but merely a licence of some kind. Examples of where they might have a tenancy agreement are where they had an income from relatives to finance a private rented flat, or they claimed asylum some years ago and so were eligible for housing benefit, or they were supported under social services provisions and entered a direct agreement with a landlord, financed by the local authority. Assuming the accommodation is suitable for them to continue to occupy, they should claim housing benefit to avoid the risk of being found intentionally homeless. To qualify for housing benefit, the claimant will need to show they are liable for the rent. Where the tenancy or occupation agreement is between the local authority or UKBA and the landlord and the former asylum-seeker wishes to remain there, they could contact the landlord directly to ask if they are willing to issue a new agreement.

8.177 The former asylum-seeker should also apply promptly to the local authority allocation scheme to register for public sector housing. If they are informed that their accommodation provided by UKBA or the local authority is to be terminated, they should apply to the local housing authority for assistance under HA 1996 Part 7 as a homeless person.

264 NAA 1948 s21.
265 CA 1989 s17.

8.178 An asylum-seeker granted leave should not leave accommodation provided by UKBA or the local authority or by relatives until it is terminated. If they do, they risk a decision that they are not homeless (if the accommodation remains available to them) or are intentionally homeless. This is particularly likely to occur where asylum-seekers who have been dispersed are granted status and then return to London and apply to local authorities as homeless persons.

8.179 A common practical problem arises when the Home Secretary has decided to grant an asylum-seeker leave to remain, but the applicant does not receive the decision, perhaps where it has been delivered to the incorrect address. The asylum support accommodation may then be ended but when the applicant applies to the local authority as a homeless person, they are told that they will not be assisted until they can produce the standard documents. The remedy is a judicial review of the failure of the Home Office to provide a decision, or of the local authority for breach of its duty under HA 1996 ss184 and 188. The threshold for challenging the local authority is a low one – it is only necessary to give the local authority 'reason to believe' that the applicant 'may' be eligible for assistance.

8.180 Similar problems arise in claiming benefits,[266] and housing authorities frequently refuse to assist applicants unless they can show proof of benefit entitlement or of the allocation of a national insurance (NI) number. Given the time taken to process benefit claims and NI number applications, such requirements arguably place the threshold under HA 1996 s188 too high. It should be recalled that people with refugee status or HP, DL or ELR are not subject to the habitual residence test.

Where a person whose asylum application is refused has a tenancy

8.181 Where the person has an assured tenancy (shorthold or otherwise) or a secure tenancy, ordinary housing law applies. A change in immigration status, whether grant or refusal of leave, does not affect security of tenure.[267] The person will be entitled to remain until a possession order is obtained and lawfully executed. The fact that a refused asylum-seeker ceases to be entitled to housing benefit and so may be unable to pay the rent does not alter this position.[268]

266 See para 3.134.

267 *Akinbolu v Hackney LBC* (1997) 29 HLR 259.

268 See para 1.183 below.

Asylum-seekers reaching 18 years of age

8.182 Unaccompanied asylum-seekers aged under 18 are the responsibility of the social services department; current UKBA policy is to grant him or her discretionary leave until reaching the age of 17.5.[269] If they apply in time for an extension of this leave and are still waiting for a decision when they reach 18, they should be eligible in their own right for assistance as homeless persons. If they have not received an asylum decision at the age of 18, they should be entitled to continuing accommodation under the children leaving care provisions until they reach 21 or until a negative Home Office decision is received.[270]

Recovery of possession, protection from eviction and harassment

Security of tenure

8.183 The ordinary law relating to the recovery of possession of land applies to tenants who are EEA nationals, asylum-seekers or persons subject to immigration control, just as it applies to other tenants.[271] Changes in a person's immigration status do not affect the rights of such tenants in relation to security of tenure and protection from eviction. This applies to those tenants who acquired their tenancy through arrangements made before 6 December 1999 or who have acquired their tenancy since that date otherwise than through arrangements made by UKBA or the local authority.

8.184 However, where accommodation is provided to accommodate asylum-seekers under the asylum support provisions, tenancy rights are restricted. A tenancy or licence granted by a local authority to provide accommodation under IAA 1999 Part 6 (that is, to provide UKBA asylum support) is not a secure tenancy or licence under HA 1985.[272] Similarly, a tenancy or licence granted by a private landlord or housing association to provide accommodation under IAA 1999 Part 6 is not an assured tenancy under HA 1988.[273] Any

269 See chapter 1.

270 See further para 9.139.

271 *Akinbolu v Hackney LBC* (1997) 29 HLR 259.

272 HA 1985 Sch 1 para 4 as amended by IAA 1999 s169(1) and Sch 14 para 81.

273 HA 1988 Sch 1 para 12A as amended by IAA 1999 s169(1) and Sch 14 para 88.

tenancy or licence granted in order to provide accommodation under IAA 1999 Part 6 is an excluded tenancy or licence under the Protection from Eviction Act 1977.[274] This means, that a landlord is not required by law to obtain a court order to recover possession or to provide a minimum of four weeks' notice to quit. It has been suggested that these provisions may be in breach of HRA 1998 and ECHR articles 8 and 14 on the ground that they discriminate between different classes of occupier on the basis of asylum-seeker status, but this has not been tested.[275]

8.185 These restrictions do not apply in the following circumstances:

- where the tenancy or licence was granted before the tenant or licensee made their claim for asylum;
- where the tenancy or licence was initially self-funded by the asylum-seeker (with or without housing benefit) and subsequently the rent was subsidised by UKBA or the local authority;
- where the tenant or licensee is not an asylum-seeker or dependant of an asylum-seeker;
- where the tenancy or licence has been granted as part of provision made under CA 1989 s17 or NAA 1948 s21.

8.186 In this last case, it may not be easy to establish under what statutory provisions a local authority is providing accommodation. Where a request for assessment has been made under the National Health Service and Community Care Act (NHSCCA) 1990 s47 to establish whether a person has a need for services, for example under CA 1989 s17 or NAA 1948 s21, the local authority has power to make emergency provision under NHSCCA 1990 s47(5), but may instead provide accommodation by arrangement with and on behalf of UKBA.

Recovery of possession of accommodation provided under the asylum support scheme

8.187 There is a special procedure for ending UKBA accommodation. It applies where a person 'has' a tenancy or licence 'as a result of asylum support'.[276] This does not appear to cover cases regarding accommodation is provided under IAA 1999 s4. There is also

274 Protection from Eviction Act 1977 s3A(7A), as inserted by IAA 1999 s169(1) and Sch 14 para 73.

275 *Larkos v Cyprus* (1997) 7 BHRC 244.

276 IAA 1999 s95 and Sch 8 para 9; AS Regs 2000 reg 221.

guidance on withdrawing support from vulnerable persons in Policy Bulletin 83.

8.188 The procedure provides for a notice to quit to be served where one or more of the following conditions apply:

- asylum support is withdrawn under AS Regs 2000 reg 20;[277]
- the asylum claim or appeal has been determined;
- the supported person is no longer destitute;
- the supported person is to be moved to other accommodation.

8.189 The notice to quit must be in writing and the notice period must not be less than seven days, except in the case of determination of an asylum claim or appeal, where it must be not less than 21 days. Where the decision is posted, the 21 days run from the second day after UKBA posted the decision on the asylum claim.[278] Despite these provisions, a period of less than seven days is allowed if 'the circumstances of the case are such that the notice period is justified'.[279]

8.190 In cases where at least seven days or at least 21 days is allowed, how long should the notice period be? It was found to be arguable in *R v Newham LBC ex p Ojuri*[280] that a housing authority was under a public duty to act reasonably in terminating temporary accommodation provided to a homeless person with dependent children under HA 1996 s188. In the circumstances of that case, the High Court decided that a 28-day period was reasonable. In *R v Secretary of State for the Environment ex p Shelter and Refugee Council*,[281] it was decided that local authorities were under a public law duty to act reasonably in evicting asylum-seekers from accommodation in cases where the statutory duty to provide accommodation had been withdrawn. Subject to consideration of individual cases, the court suggested that at least 28 days was generally appropriate. Similar arguments were made (together with ECHR arguments) in an application for judicial review when former asylum-seekers who were due to become EU nationals on 1 May 2004 faced losing their accommodation at very short notice.[282] They were granted permission to apply for judicial review but the case was then settled before a final hearing, with their notice period extended.

277 See para 7.33.

278 AS Regs 2000 reg 22(3).

279 AS Regs 2000 reg 22(4).

280 (1999) 31 HLR 631.

281 [1997] COD 49.

282 *R (D and H) v Secretary of State for the Home Department* CO/2096/04; CO/2106/04, 4 May 2004, June 2004 *Legal Action* 14.

8.191 If it is found that UKBA or a local authority is allowing a notice period of less than seven days, for example in relation to accommodation under IAA 1999 s4 or NAA 1948 s21, representatives may also wish to consider ECHR arguments in relation to respect for private and family life, peaceful enjoyment of possessions, discrimination etc (articles 8 and 14, and article 1 of the First Protocol). There is also an old domestic authority for the proposition that having to cope in a foreign country should be taken into account. In *Ministry of Health v Belotti*,[283] Lord Green said:

> They find themselves removed to this country and provision made for them by the government under a licence of this kind, and it must surely be the implied intention of the parties that, if they were turned out by the ministry, they should be given such an opportunity as strangers in the land might require, to enable them to find other accommodation. That consideration ought to be taken into account in deciding what time is to be allowed to such licensees as those in this case to comply with the notice determining their licences.

8.192 In summary, a short notice period is probably only lawful in limited circumstances, for example where the basis of the decision is that the supported household has adequate accommodation otherwise available.

Harassment and domestic violence[284]

8.193 Much of the statutory protection from harassment afforded to tenants and licensees has been taken away from asylum-seekers if they are in UKBA accommodation. Such tenancies and licences are excluded from the protection under the Protection from Eviction Act (PEA) 1977 s3, which requires landlords to apply for a court order to permit them to recover possession.[285] However, while such tenancies or licences continue, the tenants/licensees are 'residential occupiers' and so have the protection of PEA 1977 s1. Under section 1, it is an offence for any person unlawfully to deprive the occupier of occupation, or to commit acts of harassment with intent to gain possession or to obstruct the occupier's exercise of their rights and remedies. The protection under section 1 for tenancies and licences excluded under section 3A ends when the right to occupy ends, for

283 [1944] 1 KB 298.

284 See Policy Bulletin 70 on domestic violence and Policy Bulletin 81 on racist incidents.

285 PEA 1977 s3A, as amended by IAA 1999 s169(1) and Sch 14 para 73.

example by the expiry of a notice to quit, a fixed term or a notice of termination of licence. This means the accommodation provider of section 4 accommodation cannot lawfully end the occupation without first serving a notice. Breaches of section 1 should be referred to the tenancy relations service of the local authority if there is one: there is no direct remedy available to the individual, though if a tenancy relations service unlawfully fails to act, it may be subject to judicial review.

8.194 Asylum-seekers suffering harassment may also complain to the accommodation provider under its complaints procedure, or directly to UKBA, or to the police. There is a 'statement of requirements' in relation to both section 95 and 4 housing provision, which was published on the Home Office website at the time of writing.[286] The accommodation provider is required to comply with Policy Bulletins 70 on Domestic Violence and 81 on Racist Incidents.[287] The contract between UKBA and the accommodation provider requires the latter to have a complaints procedure to deal with allegations of harassment, in the same way as complaints about sub-standard accommodation.[288] The supported person can contact UKBA directly if they have been harassed by the housing provider.

8.195 UKBA's policy guidance[289] states that its role in investigating racist incidents is to establish whether it is appropriate to provide alternative accommodation because there is a significant risk of violence occurring if the person were to remain. It goes on to say that 'the responsibility for tackling harassment lies with the police and the relevant local authority'. The guidance lists the various legal remedies, which asylum-seekers who are suffering racial harassment can pursue. UKBA's approach has been to consider whether there is an immediate and significant risk to the household.

8.196 If a supported person needs to leave UKBA accommodation due to domestic violence or racial or other harassment, they should make an immediate complaint to the housing provider. Internal instructions specifically provide for consideration of a move in such circumstances. If UKBA does not provide alternative accommodation, judicial review (of the decision not to provide adequate accommodation) would be the appropriate remedy. There have

286 'National Asylum Support Service Accommodation 2005 Project–Target Contracts' Schedule 3 Statement of Requirements, www.homeoffice.gov.uk.

287 Ibid Mandatory requirements para 2113.

288 See para 8.198 below.

289 Policy Bulletin 81.

been a number of appeals to the First-tier Tribunal (Asylum Support) where UKBA has terminated support in cases of racial harassment on the ground that the asylum-seeker has breached a condition of support by failing to travel back to the accommodation from which they fled. These are discussed at para 7.46 onwards.

Housing conditions[290]

8.197 Many asylum-seekers are housed in sub-standard accommodation, particularly where the accommodation is provided under IAA 1999 s4.[291] On 21 February 2007, the Immigration Minister, Liam Byrne, announced to the committee that the Home Office planned to bring the standards and contracts for s4 accommodation in line with those for accommodation under IAA 1999 s95 by the end of 2007.[292]

8.198 There is a document addressed to accommodation providers entitled 'Section 4 Accommodation Standards' published on the UKBA website which sets out their responsibilities. It outlines what should be provided at the address, from bedding and number of people per bathroom to security arrangements. It stipulates what should happen when accommodation is offered and that repairs should be carried out within a reasonable timescale.

8.199 The contractual basis of accommodation provision by UKBA is an 'occupancy agreement', which the supported person should have been asked to sign when they moved into the accommodation provided on behalf of UKBA by a contractor. It should contain details of the landlord's obligations to maintain and manage the property. It may contain an express contractual duty to maintain the accommodation or carry out repairs.

8.200 The housing provider will also have entered a contract with UKBA containing terms about the condition of the property. The 'statement of requirements'[293] sets out timescales for responding to complaints. Contractors who are providing accommodation on behalf of UKBA are expected, as a term of their contract, to have an internal complaints procedure to enable the supported person(s) to

290 See further Luba and Knafler, *Repairs: tenants rights*, 3rd edn, LAG, 1999 (new edition December 2009).

291 See 'The treatment of asylum-seekers', tenth report of session 2006–07, HL 81-1/HC 60-1, March 2007, Joint Committee on Human Rights.

292 Ibid. Ev 87 Q483.

293 See para 8.194 above.

make a complaint about harassment or about the service provided, for example where utilities are not provided, furniture is missing, or the property is in disrepair. The housing provider should respond to the complaint within seven days and record the outcome in a logbook. If the supported person is not satisfied, it is the function of the landlord to make a referral to the nearest 'one stop service' for advice and advocacy, and from there to UKBA. The terms of such agreements between UKBA and the housing provider may be enforceable by the asylum-seeker who is accommodated despite their not being a party to the agreement. A term will be so enforceable under the Contracts (Rights of Third Parties) Act 1999 s1 if it purports to confer a benefit on the asylum-seeker.

8.201 IAA 1999 s96 provides for accommodation 'appearing to the Secretary of State to be adequate' for the needs of the supported person and any dependants. The adequacy requirement applies only to accommodation provided under section 95, not to section 4 or to section 98 (initial emergency) accommodation. 'Adequate' suggests that the accommodation should be in basic repair and (in a non-technical sense) fit for human habitation with basic facilities such as adequate space, and with water, heating, sanitation and cooking facilities in proper working order. It is part of UKBA's role to inspect accommodation to ensure contracts are being fulfilled. Commentators have pointed out the difficulty of the Home Office carrying out a function more suited to the local authority housing and environmental health departments with local knowledge of landlords. UKBA has a contract with the property advisors to the civil estate to inspect properties to ensure that the physical standard of accommodation provided complies with the terms of the contract. This programme of inspections is supplemented by UKBA's performance monitoring inspections team. Its role is 'to ensure that accommodation providers are complying with the contract requirements for effective housing management and access to support services'.

8.202 The courts seem likely to treat an occupation agreement entered into under IAA 1999 as a licence to occupy accommodation rather than a tenancy. The Landlord and Tenant Act 1985 s11 implies an obligation upon the landlord to repair into a tenancy but not into a licence.

8.203 This does not mean that property owners have no legal duties to asylum-seeker occupiers. Licensors of dwellings may have retained sufficient control of the dwelling to be liable to the occupiers in negligence for personal injury or property damage, or to justify an implied term as to repair or fitness for purpose, depending on the circumstances of the case. In *Greene v Chelsea LBC*[294] the council exercised statutory powers to requisition housing accommodation. Those powers made it impossible to grant occupiers a tenancy, only a licence. When one occupier was injured after a ceiling collapsed, the council was held liable in negligence. It had been informed about the bulging ceiling but had failed to repair it. The case is significant because landlords do not usually owe a duty of care in negligence to licensees.

8.204 Even if a county court action is available, there are difficulties for an asylum-seeker in bringing it because they will not generally have any security of tenure. An award of compensation could temporarily remove eligibility for support because the household would have some money. Unless an emergency injunction is available, another problem is that occupation of the accommodation is intended to be short term. An asylum-seeker may prefer to use the speedier Environmental Protection Act 1990 procedures explained below.

Accommodation that is damaging to health

8.205 If an asylum-seeker is placed in accommodation that is 'prejudicial to health' (for example with loose electric wiring which could injure a child, or with black mould) in a poor state of repair, lacking adequate amenities or means of escape from fire, a request could be made to the local authority's environmental health officer (EHO) to inspect with a view to taking action under the Environmental Protection Act 1990 s80 if the accommodation appears to be prejudicial to health or a nuisance. If the landlord refuses to do repairs after the local authority has served a notice, the authority can take enforcement action, doing the works itself and recouping the cost from the landlord. If the EHO will not act promptly or at all, an asylum-seeker could consider a judicial review of the EHO's decision. The EHO will not take action where the landlord is the same local authority.

8.206 The EHO should also act if the accommodation is a hazardous dwelling under HA 2004. In brief, a hazard is a risk of harm which arises due to a failure to maintain or repair a building, or because of its construction. Under a rating system, the local authority must take action if it finds a category 1 hazard.

294 [1954] 2 QB 127.

8.207 In cases where the EHO will not act, the asylum-seeker can take individual action under the Environmental Protection Act 1990 s82, by serving a 21-day standard notice at the landlord's registered office, supported by evidence of the prejudice to health. If the landlord does not do the necessary repair works to 'abate the nuisance' within 21 days, the asylum-seeker can start a fast track procedure to prosecute the landlord in the magistrates' court. Community Legal Service legal help funding will be needed for an independent EHO's report to support the action. This may be justified by demonstrating that the local authority EHO will not intervene, but it may be difficult to get help from a solicitor due to the lack of public funding to cover representation in the magistrates' court.

8.208 Where a migrant is being housed by a private sector landlord, and considering action to enforce repairs, advice should be given about the risk of the landlord responding with possession proceedings to which there may be no defence if there is only a licence agreement or an assured shorthold tenancy.

Council tax

8.209 Asylum-seekers occupying accommodation provided by UKBA under IAA 1999 s95 are not liable for council tax. The reason for this is that liability for council tax falls upon owners rather than occupiers in certain prescribed categories of dwelling.[295]

8.210 Migrants provided with accommodation under NAA 1948 s21 should not be liable for council tax. Liability should fall onto the owner rather than the occupier. Most councils have an arrangement whereby they pay a slightly increased amount of rent that covers all bills (utilities, council tax etc), but some councils leave individuals to sort out the council tax themselves. If the client is sent a council tax bill for any period when they were provided with s21 accommodation, a suggested approach is to write to ask the council tax department to reconsider the client's liability:

> We consider that our client's accommodation comes within Class A of the Council Tax (Liability for Owners) Regulations 1992 (as amended by the Council Tax (Liability for Owners) Regulations 2003) because it is part of a building in which residential accommodation

295 Council Tax (Liability for Owners) Regulations 1992 SI No 551 reg 2, as amended by the Council Tax (Liability for Owners) (Amendment) Regulations 2000 SI No 537 reg 2.

is provided under section 21 of the National Assistance Act 1948. Therefore liability for Council Tax due on this property falls on the owner rather than the occupier of the dwelling under section 8 of the Local Government Finance Act 1992.

If you consider our client remains liable for Council Tax, please treat this letter as notice of appeal to the Valuation Tribunal established under section 16 of the Local Government Finance Act 1992.

8.211 If the council decides that the client is still liable then the next step is to appeal to the valuation tribunal. The deadline to lodge the appeal is two months from the date of the council's new decision. The client must inform the council on notice that they intend to do this. If the council simply does not respond the client has four months from the date of their request for a revision to lodge an appeal with the valuation tribunal. The council should be asked to delay any enforcement proceedings pending the tribunal's decision.

8.212 Asylum-seekers and other migrants such as EEA nationals who have arranged their own accommodation will be liable for council tax unless they are staying in someone else's household, or in a hostel or HMO accommodation. If they receive a summons in relation to non-payment, the first step is to write explaining their circumstances and attempt to negotiate payment in instalments.

8.213 Councils can obtain liability orders in the magistrates' court against asylum-seekers, despite their inability to pay.[296] Should enforcement procedures reach the stage of committal, a request can be made to the magistrates' court that the tax should be remitted on the ground that failure to pay is not blameworthy and the asylum-seeker/former asylum-seeker cannot afford to pay.[297]

Quick eligibility guides

8.214 The tables below, one for non-EEA nationals and one for EEA nationals, are a shorthand guide to the provisions. References in italics are to the legislation – except where otherwise noted references are to the Allocation of Housing and Homelessness (Eligibility) (England) Regulations.

296 *R v Hackney LBC ex p Adebiri* (1997) 31 July QBD.

297 Council Tax (Administration and Enforcement) Regulations 1992 SI No 613 reg 48(2), as amended.

Migrants housing eligibility guide

Part 1: non-EEA nationals (persons subject to immigration control)

Immigration status and documentation	*Other conditions*	*Habitual residence test applies?*	*Eligible for homelessness assistance*	*Eligible for a housing allocation*	*Other housing options*
Refugee – *Home Office status document and letter* (see appendix).	Must be recognised as such by UKBA.	No	Yes reg 5(1)(a)	Yes reg 3(a)	Could claim housing benefit and seek private rented housing.
Asylum-seeker, claimed asylum since 3 April 2000 – *ARC card.*	No final Home Office decision or appeal.	No	No	No	Support under IAA 1999 s95, or section 4 if asylum claim refused. NAA 1948 s21 support if care needs.
Asylum-seeker, claimed asylum before 3 April 2000 – *SAL 1/ ARC card/ IS 96/ Home Office letter.*	Must have claimed 'on arrival' or within three months of a country of upheaval direction and not yet have asylum decision or have claimed asylum before 4 February 1996 and was entitled to housing benefit on that date.	No	Yes reg 5(1)(e)	No	Support under IAA 1999 s95, or section 4 if claim refused. Section 21 support if care needs.
Discretionary leave (DL), humanitarian protection (HP) outside the rules, exceptional leave, or leave outside the rules – *Home Office status document and letter* (see appendix C).	Must not be subject to a 'no recourse to public funds' condition.	No	Yes reg 5(1)(b)	Yes reg 3(b)	If no recourse to public funds, can apply for Social Services assistance. Otherwise could claim housing benefit and seek private rented housing.

HP under immigration rules – *Home Office status document and letter* (see appendix C).		No	Yes reg 5(1)(d)	Yes reg 3(d)	Could claim housing benefit and seek private rented housing.
Indefinite leave to remain – *Home Office status document and letter* (see appendix C).	If sponsored, sponsor must have died or the sponsorship taken place at least five years ago.	Yes	Yes	Yes	If sponsor alive/ within five years, can apply for social services assistance.
A person who left Montserrat after 1 November 1995 because of the volcanic eruption – *passport with date stamp/ entry visa/ Home Office letter.*	Must have applied in England before 20 April 2006, or in Wales on or after 9 October 2006.	No	Yes reg 5(1)(d)	Yes reg 3(d)	Could claim housing benefit and seek private rented housing.
Leave to remain expired but applied to extend it before it expired – *Original Home Office letter or visa stamp showing leave and copy of application for further leave with proof of posting such as immigration solicitor letter and recorded delivery slip or (rarely available) Home Office acknowledgement.*	Same terms as previous leave.	Depends on terms of original leave.	Yes – depending on terms of original leave. IA 1971 s3A, as amended by IAA 1999 s3A provides for the extension of leave.	Yes – depending on terms of original leave. IA 1971 s3A, as amended by IAA 1999 s3A provides for the extension of leave.	HB and other mainstream rights. If late application for extension made, may be able to apply for NAA 1948 s21 assistance if claimed asylum on arrival or if returning home would interfere with their ECHR rights (see chapter 9).

A 'lawfully present' national of a state which has ratified the European Convention on Social and Medical Assistance (ECSMA) or the European Social Charter (ESC). This includes nationals of Turkey, Croatia or Macedonia and EEA nationals who do not have the right to reside and so are 'persons subject to immigration control' – *Identity card, passport or ARC to show nationality, Home Office letter such as IS 96 to show lawful presence.*	Applies to applications made in England or Wales before 20 April 2006, or in Wales only after 9 October 2006.	No	Yes Homelessness (England) Regulations 2000 reg 3(1)(e); Homelessness Wales Regulations	Yes Allocation of Housing (England) Regulations 2002 reg 4(d)(i)	If an asylum-seeker with outstanding claim or dependant child, UKBA accommodation under IAA 1999 s95.
In receipt of income support/IBJSA.	Only applies in Wales.	Yes	Yes Homelessness Wales Regulations 2006	No	Could claim housing benefit and seek private rented housing.

Part 2: EEA nationals and their family members

Status	*Other conditions*	*Habitual residence test applies?*	*Eligible for Part 6 assistance*	*Eligible for an allocation*	*Other options*
Initial three months right of residence or longer residence but has been economically inactive so does not fall within any other category below.	No other rights of residence.	n/a	No	No	Not entitled to housing benefit. They are excluded from most social services assistance by NIAA 2002 s54 and Sch 3 unless support is needed to avoid a breach of their ECHR rights or EU Treaty rights, eg if work was imminent. SS could provide a ticket back to their EU country of origin.
Jobseeker – *EEA passport. Registered at job-centre.*	Never worked in UK or has worked but has not retained worker status, no other rights of residence.	n/a	No	No	As above. NB if they can show a link to the labour market they may qualify for social assistance to obtain work such as housing benefit see para 2.60.

Worker – actually working and family members – *Identity card, passport or birth certificate and evidence of employment such as wage slips; if A8 national past or current worker's registration certificate; if A2 worker then work permit.*	If A8 national, must have Worker's Registration Certificate unless they have completed 12 months registered work. If A2 national subject to authorisation must be in authorised work.	No	Yes reg 6(2)(a) and (c)	Yes reg 4(2)(a) and (c)	Claim housing benefit for private rented housing. Not excluded from social services assistance by Sch 3.
Worker – previously worked and family members – *As above.*	If temporarily incapacitated, or if are involuntarily unemployed and registered as a jobseeker plus they worked for 12 months *or* they have been unemployed for less than six months *or* they have a genuine chance of getting a job or if they are on vocational training, which must be related to last job if they stopped working voluntarily. If A8 or A2 national requirement in box above also applies.	No	Yes reg 6(2)(a), (b) and (c), EEA Regs 2006 reg 6(2)	Yes reg 4(2)(a) and (c), EEA Regs 2006 reg 6(2)	Claim housing benefit for private rented housing. Not excluded from social services assistance by Sch 3.

Self-employed person and family members – *Identity card, passport or birth certificate and HMRC letter showing registration as self-employed person with evidence of self-employment such as accounts, invoices, letters from clients etc.*	Currently self-employed or previously self-employed but unable to work due to illness/accident. No separate rules for A2 or A8 nationals.	No	Yes reg 6(2)(b)	Yes reg 4(2)(b)	Claim housing benefit for private rented housing. Not excluded from social services assistance by Sch 3.
Previously self-employed in UK and family members – *As above.*	If temporarily incapacitated due to illness or accident.	No	Yes reg 6(2)(b), EEA Regs 2006 reg 6(3)	Yes reg 4(2)(b), EEA Regs 2006 reg 6(3)	Claim housing benefit for private rented housing. Not excluded from social services assistance by Sch 3.
Retired/ permanently incapacitated with permanent right to reside and family members – *Evidence of employment.*	If worked lawfully in UK for 12 months before retirement after three years living in UK or if lived here two years before incapacity, or if they receive occupational pension due to accident or illness in UK. Family member must have been living with them immediately before they died.	No	Yes EEA Regs 2006 reg 5(3)	Yes	As above.

Student (and certain family members) – *Student visa, insurance certificate, evidence of enrolment.*	On specified course. Must have sickness insurance and have declared they have sufficient resources to avoid becoming a burden on the (UK) state. Family members limited to dependent child/ spouse/civil partner.	Yes	Yes, provided the homelessness assistance is not a burden on UK EEA Regs 2006 reg 4	Yes, in theory but may be difficult to show that providing over-subscribed social housing is not a burden on the UK.	May be able to claim housing benefit temporarily for short-term private rented accommodation.
'Self-sufficient person' and family members – *insurance certificate.*	Must have sickness insurance and have sufficient resources to avoid becoming a burden on the (UK) state.	Yes	As above	As above	As above.
Has lived lawfully in the UK for five years, ie would qualify for the permanent right to reside and family member – *A residence card or certificate but this is not essential – evidence that previously had lawful residence, eg evidence of employment is sufficient.*	Family member must have lived with the EEA national or have had the right to reside for five years.	Yes	Yes EEA Regs 2006 reg 15(a), (b) and (f)	Yes	As above.

Family members including non-EEA nationals – of EEA nationals					
Living with EEA worker/ self-employed person who died due to work accident or disease or who had lived in the UK for two years before they died EEA Regs 2006, reg 15(e).	Family member must have lived with deceased a year before their death and now be a worker, self-employed or self-sufficient person (or their family member).	Yes	Yes	Yes	All entitlements.
If worker or self-employed person died or left UK and child still in prescribed education child and person with custody.	As above	Yes	Yes EEA Regs 2006, reg 10(3)–(4)	Yes	No exclusions.
Divorced/civil partnership terminated from qualifying person.	Marriage partnership must have lasted three years, of which one was spent in the UK, or former spouse/partner of qualified person must have rights of custody/ access to child in the UK or needs to stay in the UK due to difficult circumstances eg domestic violence. But must be non-EEA national who would qualify as worker, self-employed or self-sufficient person.	Yes	Yes	Yes	No exclusions.

Carer of child in school in UK whose EU partner/spouse was a worker or self-employed and has left UK or relationship has ended, or who was him/herself a worker		Yes	Yes potentially (see para 8.31)	Yes potentially (see para 8.31)	Could claim housing benefit and seek private rented housing; CA s17 1989 if needed to avoid a breach of EU Treaty rights.
Extended family members					
All must have EEA family permit, registration certificate or residence card from Home Office.			EEA Regs 2006 reg 8 applies		
Dependent relative who accompanied EEA national or their spouse/civil partner to UK.	Was dependent in country of origin or is dependent on them or a member of their household.	Yes	Yes	Yes	No exclusions.
Relative of EEA national/their spouse or civil partner who needs personal care from them 'on serious health grounds'.		Yes	Yes	Yes	No exclusions.

Relative of EEA national who would meet requirements of immigration rules for ILR as a dependent relative (eg dependent elderly relative).		Yes	No recourse to public funds issue.	No recourse to public funds issue.	NAA 1948 s21.
Partner of EEA national who can show they are in a durable relationship.		Yes	Yes	Yes	No exclusions.

CHAPTER 9

Community care services

continued

Introduction

9.1 The community care regime gives rise to two basic issues in the immigration context:

- in the case of asylum-seekers: is the Home Office or a local authority responsible for the provision of basic accommodation and support?
- in the case of other migrants such as EEA nationals and persons subject to immigration control (PSIC), to what extent are they ineligible for community care services?

9.2 Between 24 July 1996, when the Asylum and Immigration Act (AIA) 1996 excluded asylum-seekers who failed to claim asylum on arrival and other PSIC from income support and related state benefits, and the coming into force of the Immigration and Asylum Act (IAA) 1999 on 6 December 1999 (local authority interim support) and 3 April 2000 (Home Office support), community care services provided by local authorities constituted the only source of accommodation and subsistence for destitute asylum-seekers and other PSIC. A central purpose of the IAA 1999 was to establish a system for providing support to all asylum-seekers (but not to other PSIC) and, correspondingly, to withdraw both access to state benefits and community care services from asylum-seekers. Accordingly, the IAA 1999 set up the National Asylum Support Service (NASS) to provide centrally-administered asylum support (NASS was later subsumed within the Home Office and will henceforth be referred to as such). The IAA 1999 created a series of exclusions, which made PSIC ineligible for almost all state welfare benefits and for many local authority community care services. The exclusions from community care services were far from comprehensive. However, the Nationality, Immigration and Asylum Act (NIAA) 2002 s54 and Sch 3 introduced significantly broader community care exclusions and the Asylum and Immigration (Treatment of Claimants, etc) Act 2004 continued that process. On the other hand, the extension of the EEA to include many eastern European countries potentially increases eligibility for community care services provided such services are necessary to enable them to exercise their free movement rights (see para 2.53).

9.3 This chapter explains how the community care scheme now fits in with the asylum support scheme, with a summary of who is excluded from community care services and who is included. There follows a detailed examination of:

- the meaning of 'community care services';
- the machinery of assessment;
- exclusions affecting PSIC and EEA nationals; and
- the nature of services available.

In each case, services under the National Health Service and Community Care Act (NHSCCA) 1990 and services under the Children Act (CA) 1989 are considered separately.

9.4 This chapter concludes with an examination of problems due to changes of immigration or other status, and an outline of the remedies available.

Overview

Community care services

9.5 Community care services comprise a range of means of providing for the needs of people through the social services departments of local authorities and, in some cases, through health authorities or NHS trusts. Needs that can be met include needs for accommodation, subsistence, and care and support services. In practice, local authorities use their powers and duties under the community care statutes (particularly the National Assistance Act (NAA) 1948 s21) and the CA 1989 to provide accommodation and subsistence for destitute individuals who meet the criteria in the statutes and who are not excluded from eligibility. However, in general, while some community care statutes such as the NAA 1948 can give rise to individual rights (subject to an assessment of need), other statutes, such as the CA 1989, usually give rise to general duties and powers to promote the welfare of people in their area and define ways in which local authorities may meet those responsibilities. Whether or not an individual can apply to the courts when a local authority fails to make provision will usually depend on whether the authority has complied with its responsibilities in a public law sense, or (in exceptional cases) has acted compatibly with the European Convention on Human Rights (ECHR).

9.6 IAA 1999 Part 6 and NIAA 2002 s54 and Sch 3 have excluded asylum-seekers and others from community care services to a considerable extent, but important areas remain where eligibility for assistance is available. In particular, it should be noted that the exclusions referred to below never exclude any migrant from aftercare services for certain formerly detained patients under the

Mental Health Act (MHA) 1983 s117, which remain fully available irrespective of immigration status.

Who is excluded?

9.7 Healthy, able-bodied asylum-seeking adults with children receive accommodation and essential living needs from the Home Office under IAA 1999 s95 and the Asylum Support Regulations (AS Regs) 2000.[1] This applies even if the children are disabled or otherwise have special needs. Eligibility for asylum support continues even after a refusal of the asylum claim because IAA 1999 s94(5) defines a person whose household contains a dependent child under 18 as remaining an asylum-seeker for asylum support purposes for as long as they remain in the UK, notwithstanding the failure of their asylum claim, providing the Home Secretary has not certified under the Immigration and Asylum (Treatment of Claimants, etc) Act 2004 s9 that such families have not taken reasonable steps to leave the UK voluntarily (in which case the adults but not the children will be excluded from support under CA 1989, NAA 1948 and other community care services). Up until that point, if entitlement to asylum support ends for some other reason, the family is, in principle, eligible for support under CA 1989.[2]

9.8 Healthy, able-bodied, destitute adult asylum-seekers without dependent children also receive support from the Home Office under IAA 1999 s95 and the AS Regs 2000. This provision continues until a final decision is made upon their application for asylum (including by way of appeal). After that, accommodation will be available in limited cases under the IAA 1999 s4 scheme,[3] but there is no community care safety net unless they claimed asylum at port so are deemed lawfully in the UK or need support to avoid an ECHR breach, usually because they have an outstanding fresh claim.[4] If entitlement to asylum support ends for some other reason, there is also no community care safety net.

9.9 Asylum-seekers who require services on reaching the age of 18 after having been in local authority care, and who are healthy and able-bodied, receive Home Office support but with some local authority input.[5]

1 SI No 704.

2 See paras 4.33, 6.19 and 9.70.

3 See chapter 6.

4 See para 9.68.

5 See paras 9.139–9.159.

9.10 Adults who are citizens of other EEA countries, or who have been granted refugee status by other EEA countries, or who are failed asylum-seekers who have failed to co-operate with removal directions or who are present in the UK in breach of the immigration laws, are excluded from almost all community care services by NIAA 2002 s54 and Sch 3, except to the extent that EU law or the ECHR requires provision to be made.[6]

Who is included?

9.11 Unaccompanied asylum-seeking children are exclusively the responsibility of local authorities under CA 1989 Part 3[7] and are not covered by the Home Office support scheme.

9.12 In the case of families with dependent children, if services under the AS Regs 2000 are suspended or discontinued for any reason then the children may become eligible for assistance under CA 1989 Part 3, and under CA 1989 s17, that can and usually should include assistance for the whole family.[8] But normally an able-bodied adult asylum-seeker with a dependent child must receive asylum support rather than CA 1989 help.[9]

9.13 Adult asylum-seekers and other migrants who have a need for care as well as accommodation and subsistence (for example where old age, physical or mental illness, or disability have given rise to a need for care) are eligible for support under the community care regime, including accommodation and basic living requirements under NAA 1948 s21, as well as domiciliary help and other services under the usual community care provisions.[10] They should apply to the social services department of the local authority, and not to the Home Office.[11] If such adults have children then the adult may receive social services assistance but any child will be a Home Office and not a social services responsibility.[12]

9.14 Any migrant, including an asylum-seeker who has been detained for treatment under the MHA 1983 ss3, 37, 45A, 47 or 48 is entitled

6 See para 9.68.
7 See para 9.31.
8 See para 9.126.
9 IAA 1999 s122.
10 See para 9.92.
11 *R (Westminster) v NASS* (2002) 5 CCLR 511.
12 *R (O) v Haringey LBC* [2004] EWCA Civ 535, (2004) 7 CCLR 310.

to services including accommodation, subsistence and support under MHA 1983 s117[13] whether or not their current needs arise through destitution alone.[14]

9.15 Migrants who have (as children) been in local authority care are entitled to support on leaving care and there is no exclusion of persons from abroad from the children leaving care machinery in CA 1989.[15] In practice, however, if the children are asylum-seekers with an outstanding fresh claim, they will also be eligible for IAA 1999 s95 asylum support when they reach 18, and the Home Office will take over financial responsibility for the cost for accommodation and essential needs (on a standard cost basis).[16] Eligibility for support ceases by virtue of NIAA 2002 s54 and Sch 3 after the asylum claim has been refused,[17] but there may be an entitlement to IAA 1999 s4 support.[18] If the former children have care needs then they will continue to be entirely a local authority responsibility, under NAA 1948 s21.

Assessments and remedies

9.16 Access to community care services is via an 'assessment of need' followed by a 'care plan'.[19]

9.17 If a local authority fails or refuses to complete an assessment of need or a care plan in respect of a child or adult then, unless the person concerned is plainly ineligible for assistance, the most appropriate remedy is likely to be an application for judicial review to ensure that the local authority carries out its duty. If the assessment of need or care plan is unsatisfactory, the appropriate remedy will be either pursuing a formal complaint through the local authority complaints procedures to obtain a different decision or judicial review to correct errors of law, including failures to comply with the assessment procedures set out in the relevant statutory guidance.[20] In practice, the judicial review avenue is appropriate when the case is urgent, or there is an important point of law in issue.

13 See para 9.123.
14 See para 9.6.
15 See para 9.139.
16 See the Children (Leaving Care) Act 2000 Regulations and Guidance paras 2.7–2.11.
17 See para 9.172.
18 See chapter 6.
19 See para 9.31.
20 See para 9.39.

What are community care services?

9.18 Community care services are defined[21] as those services that a local authority may provide or arrange to be provided under:

- NAA 1948 Part 3;
- Health Services and Public Health Act (HSPHA) 1968 s45 (a range of services for the elderly including home help, meals and social work support);
- National Health Service Act (NHSA) 2006 s254 and Sch 20 (a range of services for the social care and aftercare of the ill including home helps and laundry but not accommodation); and
- MHA 1983 s117 (aftercare services for mentally ill persons discharged from detention in hospital can include accommodation, board where required, social work assistance and, in effect, anything that is needed).

9.19 Services provided under NAA 1948 Part 3 include residential accommodation under NAA 1948 s21 (accommodation and, where needed, board and other welfare services provided in connection with the accommodation). Additionally, a wide range of other services for disabled people can be provided under NAA 1948 s29 and also the Chronically Sick and Disabled Persons Act (CSDPA) 1970 s2.[22] These services include social work assistance, recreational facilities in the home (such as radios, televisions, telephones, etc) or, elsewhere, the provision of disability-related training, the provision of suitable employment, domiciliary care (for example help with dressing, washing, toileting, housework, shopping, cooking, etc), home adaptations and meals.

9.20 Services under CA 1989 Part 3 (a very wide range of services, which can include accommodation, cash, and assistance in kind) are not 'community care services' as defined by statute.[23] Nonetheless, many services for children under Part 3 are analogous to adult services under the NHSCCA 1990 and many of the procedures are very similar, so they are generally considered to be part of 'community care' in a broader sense.

9.21 Support or other community care-type provision might be available under the Local Government Act (LGA) 2000 s2, which

21 NHSCCA 1990 s46(3).

22 Services under CSDPA 1970 s2 qualify as 'community care services' because they are provided under NAA 1948 s29 (which is within NAA 1948 Part 3): *R v Kirklees MBC ex p Daykin* (1998) 1 CCLR 512.

23 NHSCCA 1990 s46(3).

places a target duty on local authorities, but cannot be used as a substitute if statute specifically prohibits entitlement.[24]

Which local authority to approach?

9.22 Many community care services are administered by the social services department of a unitary local authority. In the case of non-unitary authorities, the social services department will be part of the county council. Some services (under MHA 1983 s117 and the NHSA 2006) also involve NHS trusts in responsibility for service provision.

9.23 Sometimes, social services authorities are driven, usually by shortage of resources, to dispute with social services authorities in other areas which authority is responsible for a particular individual in need of services. So far as concerns most community care services, the authority responsible is usually the authority in whose area the individual is 'ordinarily resident'. A person will be ordinarily resident in an area if they can show a regular habitual mode of life in a particular place, the continuity of which has persisted despite any temporary absences.[25] There is no statutory definition of the term 'ordinarily resident' but there is central government guidance at LAC(93)7 (currently being reviewed).[26]

9.24 Importantly for asylum-seekers, ordinary residence will not be acquired where residence has not been voluntarily adopted, or where there has been no settled purpose in living in a particular residence.[27] Many asylum-seekers do not have 'ordinary residence' in any local authority area. But where they do, it is important to note that once provided with accommodation under NAA 1948 s21,[28] the person remains ordinarily resident in the area of the authority where they were living before that accommodation was provided.[29] In the case of *R (Mani) v Lambeth LBC*,[30] the court held that the relevant date

24 *R (J) v Enfield LBC* (2002) 5 CCLR 434.

25 *Shah v Barnet LBC* [1983] 2 AC 309.

26 The guidance, details of the DoH consultation on changing the guidance and issuing draft directions and copies of the secretary of states' determinations of ordinary residence disputes, can be found at www.dh.gov.uk/en/SocialCare/Deliveringadultsocialcare/Ordinaryresidence/index.htm.

27 *Al-Ameri v Kensington and Chelsea RLBC* [2004] UKHL 4.

28 See para 9.92.

29 NAA 1948 s24(5).

30 [2002] EWHC 735 (Admin), (2002) 5 CCLR 486.

for considering whether an asylum-seeker was ordinarily resident in a particular local authority area was the date he made his application (not the date judicial review proceedings were issued) and that an asylum-seeker living in temporary accommodation in Eurotower for six months had become ordinarily resident in that area.

9.25 In the case of provision under CA 1989 s17, however,[31] it is established that the duty is owed by an authority to children who are physically present 'within their area', whether or not the children are ordinarily resident in the area.[32]

9.26 For example, where authority A provides accommodation to an asylum-seeker in the area of authority B: if the asylum-seeker is an adult who was ordinarily resident in the area of authority A, they remain the responsibility of authority A if they lose the accommodation; if they are an adult asylum-seeker who had not established ordinary residence in area A, they will become the responsibility of authority B upon losing this accommodation; if they are an unaccompanied minor, they will become the responsibility of authority B if they lose their accommodation.[33]

Decision on which authority is responsible for a child in need

In *R (Stewart) v Wandsworth LBC, Hammersmith and Fulham LBC and Lambeth LBC*[34] there was a dispute between three authorities as to which of them should carry out a child in need assessment. Hammersmith and Fulham LBC had accommodated a woman and her two children in the area of Lambeth LBC pending a decision on her homeless application. The children attended school in the area of Wandsworth LBC. The woman was found to be intentionally homeless and the family then sought a child in need assessment with a view to obtaining accommodation under

31 See para 9.127.

32 *R (Stewart) v Wandsworth LBC, Lambeth LBC and Hammersmith and Fulham LBC* (2001) 4 CCLR 466, *R (Liverpool CC) v Hillingdon LBC* [2009] EWCA Civ 43.

33 The rules about ordinary residence are different in cases of provision under MHA 1984 s117. The relevant health authority is the health authority of the discharging hospital but the relevant social services authority is the authority for the area in which the person resides or where they are sent on discharge: see section 117(3).

34 [2001] EWHC 709 (Admin).

CA 1989 s17. Each of the three authorities denied that it had a duty to carry out an assessment. The court held that Hammersmith and Fulham LBC did not have a duty to carry out the assessment, as the children were not 'within their area'. The fact that they had investigated a homeless application did not place them under a duty to carry out a child in need assessment. It was both necessary and sufficient for the children to be 'physically present' in an area to create a duty to assess. Both Wandsworth LBC and Lambeth LBC had a duty to carry out assessments and were ordered to do so.

9.27 In relation to the provision of accommodation under NAA 1948 s21,[35] a local authority's duty to provide accommodation extends to those who are ordinarily resident in its area, but also to those who are not ordinarily resident in any area but are living in its area when the need arises, and to those (whether or not ordinarily resident anywhere) who are in urgent need.[36] In addition, the authority has power to provide for a person who is ordinarily resident in the area of another authority if that authority agrees.[37]

9.28 Disputes between authorities about ordinary residence in relation to NAA 1948 s21 are generally settled by referral to the secretary of state,[38] but they can be settled by the courts.[39] At the time of writing, the Department of Health had issued draft guidance to clarify the legal position for local authorities and primary care trusts so as to avoid and settle disputes. This proposed that before referring a matter to the Secretary of State, the local authorities must ensure they have taken all reasonable steps to resolve the dispute, including specified steps. If the dispute is not resolved after three or six months (the period of time is one of the matters subject to consultation), there would be a duty to refer it to the Secretary of State.[40] Under no circumstances should authorities fail to assess

35 See para 9.92.

36 NAA 1948 s24(3); Approvals and Directions LAC(93)10.

37 NAA 1948 s24(4).

38 NAA 1948 s32(3).

39 *R v Kent CC ex p Salisbury and Pierre* (2000) 3 CCLR 38.

40 'A consultation on the revision of guidance on the ordinary residence provisions in the National Assistance Act (NAA) 1948; and on the draft Ordinary Residence Disputes (NAA 1948) Directions 2009, the Ordinary Residence Disputes (Community Care (Delayed Discharges etc) Act 2003) Directions 2009 and the Ordinary Residence Disputes (Mental Capacity Act 2005) Directions 2009', April 2009, www.dh.gov.uk/en/Consultations/Liveconsultations/DH_098421.

or meet needs merely because there is a dispute about financial responsibility: the 'authority of the moment' should take the necessary steps, subject to the determination of financial responsibility later on.[41] Furthermore, ordinary residence is not generally relevant in deciding which local authority should conduct an assessment. The need for assessment is triggered by an application by a person to an authority or by that authority becoming aware that an individual may have a need for community care services which the authority has a power to provide. The authority cannot refuse to assess because a person is not ordinarily resident in its area.[42] The draft guidance confirms that an applicant who is of no settled residence (such as a refused asylum-seeker), or in urgent need is not ordinarily resident so will be the responsibility of the authority to which they present, by virtue of NAA 1948 s24(3).

Assessing applicants for community care services

9.29 In order to make decisions about whether or not to provide community care services, local authorities follow a set procedure for conducting an assessment and preparing a care plan. A person seeking such services triggers this procedure by requesting the authority to carry out an assessment of need and complete a care plan. The assessment of need identifies what needs the local authority considers the applicant has (including 'unmet needs', that the authority has no present intention of meeting). The care plan then sets out what needs the local authority has decided to meet and its plan for meeting them.

Accommodation pending the assessment

9.30 In urgent cases, eg where the applicant is street homeless, the local authority must consider exercising its power to make emergency provision for a person's needs pending the outcome of the assessment process.[43] A local authority may temporarily provide a service without carrying out a prior assessment of needs 'if, in the opinion of the authority, the condition of that person is such that he requires

41 See LAC(93)7.

42 *R v Berkshire CC ex p P* (1998) 1 CCLR 141, QBD.

43 NHSCCA 1990 s47(5); *R (AA) v Lambeth LBC* (2002) 5 CCLR 36.

those services as a matter of urgency'.[44] Where services are provided in an emergency, the duty to assess still remains and an assessment should be done as soon as reasonably practicable. Although it is a power rather than a duty to provide temporary urgent services, in obvious cases of urgent need the courts will order an authority to make provision pending an assessment.

Assessment for services under the NHSCCA 1990

9.31 When a local authority is aware that a person may be in need of community care services that it has a power to provide, it has a duty to carry out an assessment and a duty to make a decision on the basis of the assessment as to whether there are needs for the provision of services.[45] The failure of a local authority to complete an assessment or a care plan can be the subject of a formal complaint but, at least in urgent cases, is generally challenged by judicial review proceedings. In such cases, in practice, the matter is invariably resolved speedily, at or around the stage of applying for permission in such proceedings.

9.32 The threshold test for assessment (whether there 'may be' a need for services) is very low and the consequent duty to assess is absolute (in other words, does not depend on whether resources are available to carry out assessments, or on whether the local authority would be likely to provide relevant services).[46] So it would be difficult for a local authority to justify delay in completing an assessment for any reasons other than professional reasons inherent in the assessment process itself.[47]

9.33 If, during an assessment of need, it appears to the local authority that the person concerned is disabled, the local authority is required to make a decision as to the services the person requires under the Disabled Persons (Services, Consultation and Representation) Act 1986 s4, without their requesting the authority to do so.[48] This simply means that the local authority has to assess the person's needs for services under CSDPA 1970 s2. In addition, the local authority must inform them that it will be carrying out this assessment and of their rights under that Act, one of which is the right to have account taken

44 NHSCCA 1999 s47(5).
45 NHSCCA 1990 s47.
46 *R v Bristol CC ex p Penfold* (1998) 1 CCLR 315.
47 *R v Kirklees MBC ex p Daykin* (1998) 1 CCLR 512.
48 NHSCCA 1990 s47(2).

of the ability of any carer to continue to provide care on a regular basis.[49]

9.34 Carers who provide substantial amounts of care are entitled to participate in assessments and to request an assessment of their own ability to provide care without assistance under the Disabled Persons (Services, Consultation and Representation) Act 1986 and also under the Carers (Recognition and Services) Act 1995. There is guidance at LAC(96)7. Carers should be consulted by social services when a community care assessment is carried out and have the right to have their views taken into account by social services when considering how best to make provision for those for whom they care.[50] Under the Carers and Disabled Children Act 2000, carers are entitled to assessments of their ability to care and local authorities are given the power to provide services to carers to help them provide care.

9.35 If at any time during an assessment it appears to the local authority that the person concerned might need health services or housing services, the local authority must notify the relevant health authority or local housing authority and invite them to assist, as far as is reasonable in the circumstances, in completing the assessment. In making any decision as to the provision of services, the local authority must take into account any services that are likely to be made available by that health authority or the local housing authority.[51] Conversely, of course, the local authority would have to take into account the fact that services might not be likely to be forthcoming from the NHS trust or local housing authority, which could increase the needs that the social services authority would have to consider meeting. For example, if a disabled person has a need for housing that is not likely to be met by the housing department, and if as a result the person has unmet community care needs, including a need for suitable accommodation, then the local authority has at least to consider exercising its community care powers to meet such needs and may be under a duty to do so.[52]

49 Disabled Persons (Services, Consultation and Representation) Act 1986 s8.

50 Community Care Directions 2004 direction 2.

51 NHSCCA 1990 s47(4).

52 *R v Tower Hamlets LBC ex p Bradford* (1998) 1 CCLR 294; *R v Wigan MBC ex p Tammadge* (1998) 1 CCLR 581; *R v Lambeth LBC ex p K* (2000) 3 CCLR 141; *R v Bristol CC ex p Penfold* (1998) 1 CCLR 315; *R v Kensington and Chelsea LBC ex p Kujtim* (1999) 2 CCLR 340; *R (Batantu) v Islington LBC* (2001) 4 CCLR 445; *R (Wahid) v Tower Hamlets LBC* (2001) 5 CCLR 239.

9.36 Assessments under MHA 1983 s117 are multidisciplinary assessments involving both the social services authority and also the NHS trust.[53]

9.37 Assessments sometimes only address domiciliary needs, ie based on a person living in their home in the community, as opposed to residential accommodation needs but this is unlawful:[54]

> An assessment is something that is directed at the particular person who presents with an apparent need. One cannot be said to have been carried out unless the authority concerned has fully explored that need in relation to services it has the power to supply. In some cases the exercise will be very simple; in others more complex.

Assessment for services under the CA 1989

9.38 It is implicit in CA 1989 s17 and explicit in Sch 2 para 1 (the duty to identify the extent to which there are children in need within the area) that local authorities are required to assess the needs of children who might be 'children in need' for the purposes of CA 1989.[55]

Assessment procedures: adults

9.39 In exercising their social services functions, local authorities are regulated by directions and guidance issued by central government. In England, the Secretary of State has issued directions that require consultation, the provision of information and a reasonable attempt to reach agreement.[56] The Local Authority Social Services Act (LASSA) 1970 s7 provides that local authorities shall, in the exercise of their social services functions, including the exercise of any discretion conferred by any relevant legislation, act under the general guidance of the Secretary of State. 'Social services functions'[57] include the assessment procedures and the provision of all community care services, and services under CA 1989 Part 3. Guidance

53 HC(90)23/LASSL(90)11 (setting out 'the care programme approach' (CPA)), Effective Care and Co-ordination in Mental Health Services; modernising the care programme approach issued under the National Service Framework for Mental Health (HSC(1999)223; LAC(1999)34).

54 *R v Bristol CC ex p Penfold* (1997) 1 CCLR 315.

55 *R (W, A, G) v Lambeth and Barnet LBC* [2003] UKHL 57, [2004] 2 AC 208.

56 See the Community Care Assessment Directions 2004 and the accompanying Circular LAC (2004) 24.

57 Defined in LASSA 1970 Sch 1.

issued under LASSA 1970 s7 is known generally as 'statutory guidance' or 'mandatory guidance'. Circulars issued to local authorities almost always clearly state whether they have been issued under LASSA 1970 s7.

9.40 Guidance issued under LASSA 1970 s7 must be followed in substance. The duty under section 7 to 'act under' this type of guidance requires local authorities to follow the path charted by the guidance, with liberty to deviate from it where the local authority judges on admissible grounds that there is good reason to do so, but without the freedom to take a substantially different course.[58]

9.41 Much guidance that the practitioner comes across is not issued under LASSA 1970 s7 by the Secretary of State, but is 'departmental guidance' or 'practice guidance', issued by the relevant civil service department.[59] The local authority must *have regard* to this guidance[60] but can act differently if it has good reason. However, it cannot act contrary to the guidance simply because it does not agree with it. That would, in effect, be to disregard it.[61]

9.42 Until relatively recently, the main general guidance issued by the Secretary of State under LASSA 1970 s7, so far as concerns community care services has been the Circular 'Community Care in the Next Decade and Beyond'.[62] This is commonly referred to as the 'Policy Guidance'. The Policy Guidance has now been substantially supplemented by guidance called *Fair Access to Care Services* (FACS). Since the decision in *R v Islington LBC ex p Rixon*,[63] local authorities and other practitioners have operated on the basis that the Policy Guidance and FACS apply to assessments under NHSCCA 1990 s47 by virtue of LASSA 1970 s7. It has been decided that since NHSCCA 1990 s47(4) expressly provides that – subject to any directions made by the Secretary of State – authorities are free to carry out assessments in such manner and in such form as they consider appropriate, such guidance is not substantially binding by

58 *R v Islington LBC ex p Rixon* (1998) 1 CCLR 119.

59 See *Care management and assessment: a practitioner's guide* (HMSO, 1991); *Care management and assessment: a manager's guide* (HMSO, 1991); *Empowerment, assessment, care management and the skilled worker* (HMSO, 1993).

60 *R v Islington LBC ex p Rixon* (1998) 1 CCLR 119.

61 *R v North Derbyshire HA ex p Fisher* (1998) 1 CCLR 150.

62 HMSO, November 1990.

63 (1998) 1 CCLR 119.

virtue of LASSA 1970 s7.[64] This decision would appear, however, to fail to take into account the effect of LASSA 1970 Sch 1, as amended after the enactment of NHSCCA 1990, which is at variance with other decisions and is probably wrong.

9.43 In summary, the Policy Guidance on assessment procedures includes the following:

- the individual service user and, usually with their agreement, any carers, should be involved throughout the assessment and care management process and should feel that the process is aimed at meeting their wishes;[65]
- the local authority is required to publish readily accessible information about care services, criteria and policies to enable users and carers to exercise choice and participate properly;[66]
- the assessment and care management process should take into account particular risk factors for service users, carers and the community generally: abilities and attitudes, health (especially remediable conditions or chronic conditions requiring continuing healthcare) and accommodation and social subordinates;[67]
- once needs have been assessed, the services to be provided or arranged and the objectives of any intervention should be agreed in the form of a care plan which, so far as possible, should preserve or restore normal living;[68]
- the aim should be to secure the most cost-effective package of services that meets the user's care needs, taking account of the user's and carer's own preferences. Where agreement between all the parties is not possible, the points of difference should be recorded;[69]
- decisions on service provision should include clear agreement about what is going to be done, by whom and by when;[70]
- it is necessary to assess the needs of carers and the ability of carers to continue to cope;[71]
- care needs should be reviewed at regular intervals and should be reviewed if it is clear that community care needs have changed.[72]

64 *R (B and H) v Hackney LBC* [2003] EWHC 1654 (Admin).
65 Para 3.16.
66 Para 3.18.
67 Para 3.19.
68 Para 3.24.
69 Para 3.25.
70 Para 3.26.
71 Paras 3.27–3.29.
72 Para 3.51.

FACS contains guidance about assessment procedures that is to similar effect. Further and more detailed guidance is contained in the *Manager's guide care*[73] and the *Practitioner's Guide.*[74]

9.44 FACS prescribes the eligibility criteria that local authorities should adopt to determine who is eligible for community care services.[75]

Assessment procedures: children

9.45 The procedure for conducting children assessments is also based on guidance. The relevant guidance is again issued under LASSA 1970 s7[76] and so is substantially binding on local authorities. There are two main sources of guidance: the Children Act 1989 Regulations and Guidance (CA 1989 RG) (six volumes) and the Framework for the Assessment of Children in Need (FACN) (sometimes referred to as the 'lilac book').

9.46 Volume 2 of the CA 1989 RG contains the following relevant provisions summarised here:

- The definition of 'need' in section 17(10) of the Act is deliberately wide to reinforce the emphasis on preventative support and services to families. The child's needs will include physical, emotional and educational needs according to their age, sex, race, religion, culture and language and the capacity of the current carer to meet those needs. CA 1989 requires each authority to decide its own level and scale of services appropriate to the children in need within its area; however, a local authority cannot lawfully substitute any other definition of 'need', for example by confining services to children at risk of significant harm.[77]
- In assessing individual need, authorities must assess the existing strengths and skills of the families concerned and help them overcome identified difficulties and enhance strengths. Sometimes the needs will be found to be intrinsic to the child; at other times, however, it may be that parenting skills and resources are depleted.[78]

73 *Care Management and assessment: a manager's guide* (HMSO, 1991).
74 *Care management and assessment: a practitioners' guide* (HMSO, 1991).
75 FACS guidance can be found at: www.dh.gov.uk
76 See para 9.39.
77 Para 2.4.
78 Para 2.5.

- Good practice requires that the assessment of need should be undertaken in an open way and should involve those caring for the child, the child and other significant persons. Families with a child in need, whether the need results from family difficulties or the child's circumstances, have the right to receive sympathetic support and sensitive intervention.[79]
- In making an assessment, the local authority should take account of the particular needs of the child, that is, in relation to health, development, disability, education, religious persuasion, racial origin, cultural and linguistic background, etc.[80]
- Assessment must identify and find a way to provide as helpful a guide as is possible to the child's needs.[81] Once the need has been identified, a plan for the best service provision will be required.[82]

9.47 Volume 3 contains further provisions relevant to assessments:

- Assessments must cover the child's needs, the parents' abilities, the wishes and views of the child, and all factors relevant to the welfare of the individual child.[83]
- There is no prescribed format for a child care plan, but there should be such a plan recorded in writing, containing the child's and their family's social history and a number of key elements including the child's identified needs, how those needs might be met, the timescale, the proposed services, a contingency plan, details of the roles all relevant persons are to play, the extent to which the wishes and views of the child, their parents and anyone else with a sufficient interest in the child have been obtained and acted upon and explanations of why wishes or views have been discounted, dates for reviews and so forth.[84]

9.48 The FACN contains very detailed provisions for the holistic assessment of children in need, together with recommended assessment pro-formas.

Timescales and services pending assessment

9.49 The FACN guidance also makes it clear that a decision should be made whether, and if so how, to assess, and in other ways what

79 Para 2.7.
80 Para 2.8.
81 Para 2.9.
82 Para 2.10.
83 Paras 2.21–2.22; see also paras 2.56–2.57.
84 Para 2.62.

response may be required, within one working day; an initial assessment (as defined) should be completed within a maximum of seven working days, while a comprehensive assessment (as defined[85]) should be completed within a maximum of 35 working days. Appropriate services should be provided whilst awaiting the completion of the specialist assessment.[86] If services are not provided an application for judicial review and an injunction can be made. The High Court will normally order an authority to provide services on an interim basis pending full assessment in a case of obvious need.

9.50 Assistance under CA 1989 s17 may be provided unconditionally or subject to conditions as to the repayment of the assistance or of its value (in whole or in part).[87] Before giving any assistance, or imposing any conditions, the local authority has to have regard to the means of the child and their parents.[88] Charges cannot be made to persons in receipt of income support or child tax credit.

9.51 For the particular problems that arise in relation to assessing a child's age, see 9.134–9.137 below.

Where a need is identified, does a local authority have to meet it?

9.52 Local authorities have a duty to provide some community care services and a discretion as to whether to provide others. A duty can exist in relation to services under CSDPA 1970 s2 and NAA 1948 s21. Once a local authority has decided that a person needs services under these statutes, it has a duty to take steps to provide the services needed, without taking their resources situation into account, but the authority still has a discretion as how best and most cost-effectively to meet the assessed need. Where, however, provision is discretionary, or under a general duty, the authority must consider whether or not to meet the need. In deciding whether or not a need exists, the local authority must apply the language of the relevant statute, but in doing so must also have regard to its 'eligibility criteria'. Eligibility criteria is a system of placing individuals in a hierarchy of categories (or 'bands') according to levels of risk of harm if services are not provided. Eligibility criteria used to vary widely

85 See *R (MM) v Lewisham LBC* [2009] EWHC 416 (Admin).

86 FACN para 3.11.

87 CA 1989 s17(7).

88 CA 1989 s17(8).

from one local authority to another but now, as a result of FACS,[89] are all virtually identical and closely reflect the criteria in FACS.

Exclusion of PSIC and others from community care services

9.53 The IAA 1999 and the NIAA 2002 exclude certain migrants from certain community care services. Not all migrants are excluded, and the exclusion operates only in relation to certain services.

9.54 If a person is clearly excluded by IAA 1999 or NIAA 2002, there is no duty on the local authority to complete a formal assessment because the duty to complete an assessment and care plan only arises in relation to a person for whom a local authority might have the power to provide or arrange for the provision of community care services.[90] However, where – as is probably usually the case – it is not clear whether a person is excluded, at least some form of assessment, for example at least of the person's immigration status, would appear to be required. Where exclusion depends on whether or not support is needed to avoid a breach of ECHR rights, under the NIAA 2002 for example, it would appear that some form of assessment is required, so the local authority can decide whether or not it has the power to provide services. It will need to take into account immigration status, care needs, EU law rights and ECHR rights. In such cases, where it transpires that the applicant is ineligible, assessments can be expected to be relatively brief but would have to be fair, rational and properly reasoned to be lawful.

Community care services excluded by IAA 1999

9.55 The exclusions in the IAA 1999 are at sections 116–117 and apply only in relation to three kinds of services:

- NAA 1948 s21 (residential accommodation);
- HSPHA 1968 s45 (a range of services[91] for older people); and
- National Health Service Act (NHSA) 2006 Sch 20 (a range of services[92] for the social care and aftercare of the ill).

89 See para 9.39.

90 NHSCCA 1990 s47.

91 See para 9.109.

92 See para 9.113.

So there is no exclusion in relation to services under the following:

- NAA 1948 s29, including services under CSDPA 1970 s2 (a wide range of non-residential services for disabled people);[93]
- MHA 1983 s117 (a very wide range of services[94] including accommodation for the aftercare of mentally-ill persons discharged from hospital detention).

9.56 In the case of each of the three types of community care services where the exclusion operates, the exclusion from eligibility applies only to:

- PSIC as defined by IAA 1999 s115; who are also
- persons whose need for the service in question has arisen solely because they are destitute, or because of the physical effects or anticipated physical effects of their destitution.

9.57 A person is excluded if they are not an EEA national and if they:[95]

- require leave to enter or remain in the UK but do not have it; or
- have leave to enter or remain in the UK, which is subject to a condition that they do not have recourse to public funds; or
- have leave to enter or remain in the UK given as a result of a maintenance undertaking (a written undertaking given by another person in pursuance of the immigration rules to be responsible for that person's maintenance and accommodation); or
- have leave to enter or remain in the UK pending the conclusion of an appeal.

9.58 As mentioned above, a person is only excluded if, in addition to being a person to whom IAA 1999 s115 applies, their need for assistance has arisen solely because they are destitute, or because of the physical effects, or anticipated physical effects, of their being destitute.

9.59 The statutory criteria for residential accommodation under NAA 1948 s21 include needing 'care and attention ... not otherwise available' by reason of 'age, illness, disability or any other circumstances'. Before the IAA 1999, the courts held that destitution and the other difficulties that faced many asylum-seekers at that time could be 'any other circumstances', capable of giving rise to illness

93 See para 9.117.

94 See para 9.123.

95 For further explanation of these terms, see chapter 1.

and care needs and therefore a need for 'care and attention'.[96] It was established that destitution could result in conditions and needs that gave rise to a need for residential accommodation under NAA 1948 s21, and the same consideration would appear to apply to other community care services.

9.60 IAA 1999 ss116–117 ensure that people falling within section 115 may not be provided with community care services under NAA 1948 s21, HSPHA 1968 s45 or NHSA 1977 Sch 8 para 2 if their need arises solely because of destitution or because of the physical effects, or anticipated physical effects of destitution, but destitution can still be a cause, even the major cause, of the need for community care services, provided there is a need for 'looking after'.[97] The person is only excluded if destitution is the sole cause of the need. As a result, the courts have held that the following were eligible or potentially eligible for residential accommodation on account of being 'destitute plus':

- a man who required medical treatment for cancer[98] and a woman disabled by cancer;[99]
- a woman with chronic and relapsing depression with psychotic features during episodes of relapse;[100]
- men and women with HIV;[101]
- a woman vulnerable for 'other special reasons' as the result of historic but long-standing and severe domestic violence;[102] a similar argument could be made in the case of a woman who has been trafficked to the UK;
- a man with severe ankylosing spondylitis (leaving him with no movement in his neck and only slight movement in his spine);[103]
- a man disabled by thoracic spinal injury and a man disabled by the effects of polio, neither of whom were able to stand without

96 *R v Westminster CC ex p M, P, A and X* (1998) 1 CCLR 85.

97 See para 9.62.

98 *R v Wandsworth LBC ex p O* [2000] 1 WLR 2539, (2000) 3 CCLR 237.

99 Ibid.

100 Ibid.

101 *R (J) v Enfield LBC* [2002] EWHC 432; (2003) 5 CCLR 434; *R (Mani and others) v Lambeth LBC and others* [2002] EWHC 735; (2002) 5 CCLR 486, *R (H) v Kingston upon Thames* [2002] EWHC 3158 (Admin), (2003) 6 CCLR 240; *R (B and H) v Hackney LBC* [2003] EWHC 1654.

102 *R (Khan) v Oxfordshire CC* (2003) 5 CCLR 611 (reversed on the facts but not as to the principle in the Court of Appeal at [2004] EWCA Civ 309).

103 *R (Mani and others) v Lambeth LBC and others* [2002] EWHC 735, (2002) 5 CCLR 486.

crutches and callipers or perform everyday tasks without a wheelchair and special adaptations;[104]

- a man whose right leg was half the length of his left leg as the result of congenital disability.[105]

9.61 Other examples might include persons suffering from mental illness, old and frail persons, persons recovering from drug or alcohol dependency and persons suffering from significant illness or accident.

The effect of *R (M) v Slough*

9.62 The above cases now need to considered in the light of the leading case of *R (M) v Slough BC*[106] where the House of Lords reviewed the authorities on the meaning of section 21. Delivering the leading judgment, Baroness Hale emphasised that whilst a person might require 'care and attention' without requiring nursing or personal care, it was not sufficient merely to require accommodation and other support because of destitution. There had to be a need for at least some 'looking after':[107]

> I remain of the view which I expressed in [*R (Wahid) Tower Hamlets LBC* [2002] EWCA Civ 287 at para 32], that the natural and ordinary meaning of the words 'care and attention' in this context is 'looking after'. Looking after means doing something for the person being cared for which he cannot or should not be expected to do for himself: it might be household tasks which an old person can no longer perform or can only perform with great difficulty; it might be protection from risks which a mentally disabled person cannot perceive; it might be personal care, such as feeding, washing or toileting. This is not an exhaustive list. The provision of medical care is expressly excluded. Viewed in this light, I think it likely that all three of Mrs Y-Ahmed, Mrs O and Mr Bhikha needed some care and attention (as did Mr Wahid but in his case it was available to him in his own home, over-crowded though it was). This definition draws a reasonable line between the 'able bodied' and the 'infirm'.

9.63 It is important to note that the court considered their view was consistent with 'all the authorities, including *R (Mani) v Lambeth*

104 *R (Murua and Gichura) v Croydon LBC* (2002) 5 CCLR 51.

105 *R (Mani and others) v Lambeth LBC and others* [2002] EWHC 735, (2002) 5 CCLR 486 and in the Court of Appeal at [2003] EWCA Civ 836, (2003) 6 CCLR 376.

106 [2008] UKHL 52, [2008] 1 WLR 1808.

107 Baroness Hale at para 32.

LBC.[108] That case was argued on the assumption that the claimant did have a need for care and attention, but not a need that required the provision of residential accommodation. Mr Mani had one leg which was half the length of the other. He had difficulty walking and when in pain he could not undertake basic tasks such as bed-making, vacuum cleaning and shopping. He did need some looking after, going beyond the mere provision of a home and the wherewithal to survive.

9.64 The judgment makes it clear that section 21 accommodation may be provided for the purpose of preventing illness as well as caring for those who are ill. Baroness Hale also considered whether the approach the court was setting out contradicted the former approach in *ex p M* which suggested it should not be necessary for a person to wait for their health to deteriorate if this can reasonably be foreseen. Her response to this was:

> It would be possible to meet the need for care of an HIV positive person who is beginning to get sick before he becomes a great deal worse. But there must still be a need for some care and attention for section 21(1)(a) to apply at all.

Other decisions on the meaning of NAA 1948 s21

- In the first judgment after *M v Slough*, the High Court decided that a blind man, receiving help from two friends in connection with shopping, laundry, cooking and getting around, required a sufficient degree of 'looking after' to be in need of care and attention and so entitled to section 21 accommodation.[109]
- It was established in *R (G & D) v Leeds CC*[110] that expectant and nursing mothers who were refused asylum-seekers fell to be accommodated by the Secretary of State under IAA 1999 s4 and not under NAA 1948 s21(1)(aa) because those provisions are discretionary. In the light of the decision in the *Slough* case, it would seem that only expectant and nursing mothers who required 'looking after' would ever fall within NAA 1948 s21(1)(aa), so that other expectant and nursing mothers, who were asylum-seekers, would fall to be accommodated by the Secretary of State under IAA 1999 s95.

108 [2003] EWCA Civ 836, [2004] LGR 35.
109 *R (Zarzour) v Hillingdon LBC* [2009] EWHC 1398 (Admin).
110 [2008] EWHC 3275 (Admin).

- In the context of psychiatric care in *R (Pajaziti and Pajaziti) v Lewisham LBC and Secretary of State for the Home Department (Interested Party)*,[111] the Court of Appeal reviewed the authorities, concluding that the legal principles in this area were clear. They found that in, the relevant question was 'whether the appellants' need for section 21 care and attention by way of the provision of residential accommodation was made materially more acute by reason of their psychiatric disorder'. Mrs Pajaziti had a medical report stating she was suffering from a major depressive episode and recommending settlement in London. This was just before the decision in *R (M) v Slough* and was not referred to by the House of Lords so it needs to be considered in the context of Baroness Hale's approach to 'looking after'.

9.65 As to when a need for care and attention ('looking after') has arisen 'solely' because of destitution, the decision of the Court of Appeal in *R v Wandsworth LBC ex p O*[112] remains the leading case:

> In what circumstances, then, is it to be said that destitution is the sole cause of need? The local authorities contend that the approach should be this. First ask if the applicant has (a) somewhere to live ('adequate accommodation') and (b) means of support (the means to 'meet his other essential living needs') [see s95(3) of the Act of 1999]. Assuming the answer is 'no' to each of those questions, ask next whether, but for those answers, he would need section 21 assistance. If not, he does not qualify. In other words, it is only if an applicant would still need assistance even without being destitute that he is entitled to it.
>
> The applicants contend for an altogether different approach. They submit that if an applicant's need for care and attention is to any material extent made more acute by some circumstance other than mere lack of accommodation and funds, then, despite being subject to immigration control, he qualifies for assistance. Other relevant circumstances include, of course, age, illness and disability, all of which are expressly mentioned in section 21(1) itself. If, for example, an immigrant, as well as being destitute, is old, ill or disabled, he is likely to be yet more vulnerable and less well able to survive than if he were merely destitute.
>
> Given that both contended-for constructions are tenable, I have not the least hesitation in preferring the latter. The word 'solely' in the

111 [2007] EWCA Civ 1351.

112 [2000] 1 WLR 2539, (2000) 3 CCLR 237.

new section is a strong one and its purpose there seems to me evident. Assistance under the Act of 1948 is, it need hardly be emphasised, the last refuge of the destitute. If there are to be immigrant beggars on our streets, then let them at least not be old, ill or disabled (as per Simon Brown LJ).

Baroness Hale specifically stated in *M v Slough* that she still considered it likely that O was in need of care and attention, as were the claimants in subsequent cases in which O was followed.[113]

9.66 It should be noted that people who have needs that do not arise solely from destitution, and who therefore potentially qualify for these community care services, include not only asylum-seekers, but all other migrants, including EEA nationals, applicants for humanitarian protection or discretionary leave to remain, people lawfully here with leave and people unlawfully here (as was the case in fact in *ex p O*) and whether or not they are pursuing some form of immigration appeal. The principal aim of NIAA 2002 Sch 3 was further to restrict eligibility for community care services among such persons.

Community care services excluded by NIAA 2002 Sch 3

A refused asylum-seeker is *not* excluded from community care services by Sch 3 if he or she claimed asylum at the port and so is lawfully in the UK, *or* if he or she has an outstanding asylum or ECHR claim.[114]

9.67 The exclusions under NIAA 2002 s54 and Sch 3 relate principally to the following community care and other services described below at paras 9.92–9.115:[115]

- NAA 1948 ss21 and 29 (note that now NAA 1948 s29 is excluded, for the first time, so too is CSDPA 1970 s2 because services under s2 are performed in the exercise of functions under NAA 1948 s29);[116]
- HSPHA 1968 s45;

113 *R (Westminster) v NASS* (2002) 5 CCLR 511; *R (Mani) v Lambeth LBC* (2003) 5 CCLR 376.

114 See para 9.68 and *R (AW) v Croydon LBC; (D, A, Y) v Hackney LBC* [2005] EWHC 2950.

115 See NIAA 2002 Sch 3 para 1.

116 Services under CSDPA 1970 s2 qualify as 'community care services' because they are provided under NAA 1948 s29 (which is within NAA 1948 Part 3).

- NHSA 2006 s254 and Sch 20;
- CA 1989 ss17, 23C, 23CA, 24A, 24B;
- LGA 2000 s2.

There continues to be no exclusion as far as concerns MHA 1983 s117 (a very wide range of services, including accommodation and board, for the aftercare of certain mentally ill persons discharged from detention in hospital).

9.68 NIAA 2002 Sch 3 excludes defined categories of persons altogether[117] unless the person is also:

- a British citizen;
- a child;
- included by virtue of regulations; or
- unless it is necessary to provide a service in order to avoid a breach of the person's ECHR rights, or their rights under EEA treaties.[118]

9.69 So, for example, provision can be made for the children of ineligible adults (such as accommodation and support under CA 1989 s20 but cannot also be made for their parents, unless required by the ECHR or EEA treaties. This may lead social services to advise applicants that they can only accommodate a child without their parents, which may cause anxiety. In practice the authority must consider whether it has power to accommodate the family together to avoid an ECHR breach.

9.70 On the face of it, the ECHR can require the state to accommodate children with parents[119] and to support the destitute.[120] Having taken these potential obligations into account, however, the Court of Appeal held that the ECHR does not require any support to be provided to a destitute adult in the UK, even where necessary to enable the adult to enjoy family life with their child, if the adult can reasonably be expected to travel to their country of origin.[121] If the adult has an outstanding ECHR claim for leave to remain in the UK, case law suggests that the authority may not make its own decision on the merits of the Home Office claim, unless the fresh claim is

117 See NIAA 2002 Sch 3 para 2.

118 NIAA 2002 Sch 3 para 3.

119 *R (J) v Enfield LBC* [2002] EWHC 432, (2003) 5 CCLR 434.

120 *R (Q) v Secretary of State for the Home Department* [2003] EWCA Civ 364, [2003] 3 WLR 365.

121 *R (K) v Lambeth LBC* [2003] EWCA Civ 1150.

'manifestly unfounded'.[122] If there is no outstanding asylum or ECHR claim to the Home Office, the social services authority must still reach a decision as to whether it would be incompatible with the ECHR rights of one or more family members to be without support because they are unable to leave the UK (for example due to pregnancy) or their ECHR rights would be breached by returning to their country of origin.[123] There is further guidance on how local authorities should approach such cases in the decisions below.

Decisions on whether support is needed to avoid an ECHR breach

Children

- In the case of a Jamaican overstayer with two children who were British nationals,[124] the council carried out a 'human rights assessment' and decided that the family's needs could be met elsewhere. She had been married to a British national but was now divorced. Ms B-S had applied to the council for assistance under CA 1989 s17 arguing that she had an outstanding application to remain in the UK based on ECHR article 8, although no evidence of this was ever provided. After investigating, the council decided that she could return to Jamaica and find work to support her family there. There was no evidence that she could not support herself and her family if she returned. The council offered to meet the family's travel expenses to return to Jamaica or to accommodate the children alone under CA 1989 s20, in circumstances where their mother would be able to freely visit them and maintain contact with them. The court held that the council's decision was lawful. They had carried out an adequate assessment and had considered the article 8 rights of the family. There was no absolute duty for the council to provide accommodation for the claimant with her children under section 17.[125]

122 See *R (AW) v Croydon LBC; D, A, Y v Hackney LBC* [2005] EWHC 2950; *R (M) v Slough BC* [2006] EWCA Civ 655 at para 39 and footnote 128 below.

123 See *AC v Bimingham CC* [2008] EWHC 3038 (Admin), [2009] 1 All ER 1039.

124 A child born in the UK to a father with indefinite leave to remain can apply to be registered as a British citizen even if the parents are unmarried: see British Nationality Act 1981 ss1(1)(b) and s50(9A) and the British Nationality (Proof of Paternity) Regulations 2006 SI No 1496.

125 *R (Blackburn-Smith) v Lambeth LBC* [2007] EWHC 767 (Admin).

- There was a successful challenge to a refusal of CA 1989 s17 assistance to a homeless family in the context of NIAA 2002 Sch 3 in the case of C, a Jamaican national with four children who had come to the UK as a visitor. Her asylum claim was rejected but she was awaiting the outcome of her application for leave to remain based on her children having lived in the UK for seven years.[126] Allowing C's judicial review application, the court reviewed the case-law and found that the authority had failed properly to consider whether the refusal of accommodation would result in a breach of the family's ECHR article 8 rights. In particular the authority had not considered the policy underlying the seven-year rule, aimed at protecting family and private life under article 8.[127]
- PB was a depressed, homeless Jamaican woman who had overstayed her permission to stay in the UK and who the council had refused to assist. She had contact with her oldest child who lived with his father in the UK. Her other four children, all born in the UK, were the subject of care proceedings and not living with her. The High Court found that the council had applied an incorrect approach to their duty to accommodate her under NAA 1948 s21, in deciding she could return to Jamaica. They had failed to consider whether her rights to respect for family life under ECHR article 8 would be breached if she were forced to leave the UK whilst care proceedings were pending.[128]

Adults

- A council withdrew support from a 19-year-old refused asylum-seeker with mental health problems who had made a further application for leave to remain in the UK on the basis that it would be a breach of ECHR article 8 to return him to Uganda. The council had supported the claimant while he was a child and he argued that it continued to have a duty to provide services under CA 1989 ss23 and 24 (children leaving care

126 Under Home Office Policy DP 5/96 which has since been withdrawn: see para 1.172.

127 *R (C) v Birmingham CC* [2008] EWHC 3038 (Admin), [2009] 1 All ER 1039, June 2009 *Legal Action* 28.

128 *R (PB) v Haringey LBC and (1) Secretary of State for Health (2) Secretary of State for Communities and Local Government (Interested Parties)* [2006] EWHC 2255 (Admin).

services for adults) as well as under NAA 1948 s21. The Home Office had not yet recorded or made a decision on this application. The council argued that they were prohibited from providing services to the claimant by NIAA 2002 Sch 3 para 7 because he was an in-country asylum-seeker unlawfully in the UK. Their approach was that it was for them to decide whether there would be a violation of ECHR article 8 if the claimant were returned to Uganda, as it would be unlawful for them to provide services unless they were so satisfied. After reviewing the merits of the art 8 claim, they had concluded that there would be no breach if he were returned. The court held that the council's approach was incorrect. Where there is an outstanding application to the Home Office on the basis of ECHR article 8, the only question for the local authority was whether that application was manifestly unfounded. In all other cases the responsibility and expertise for making such decision lay with the Home Office. Pending that decision the authority would have to consider whether it was necessary to provide a service to prevent a breach of ECHR article 3.[129]

9.71 The wording of NIAA 2002 Sch 3 provides that a local authority has power to provide the excluded community care services if it is necessary in order to avoid a breach of their rights under the EU treaties. There is limited case law on the effect of this provision.[130] It would be necessary to provide community care services to avoid a breach of a person's right not be discriminated against under EU treaties if they are an EEA national and have a right to reside, for example as a worker, self-employed person or their family member.[131] Where a Spanish jobseeker with children had lost her accommodation in the UK, the court held that it was not necessary for the local authority to provide assistance under CA 1989 s17, and this would not be a breach of the applicant's treaty rights.[132] This was held to be

129 *R (Gordon Binomugisha) v Southwark LBC* [2006] EWHC 2254 (Admin); The same approach to fresh claims was taken in *R (N) v Lambeth* [2006] EWHC 3427 (Admin).

130 But see para 7.31–7.32.

131 See paras 2.65–2.101. EC Regulation 1612/68 and *Lebon* [1987] ECR 2811 and *R v IAT ex p Antonissen* [1991] 2 CMLR 373.

132 *R (Conde) v Lambeth LBC* (2005) 37 HLR 452, [2005] 2 FLR 198, but see also para 2.60.

the case even though it was accepted that the applicant had a right to reside as a work-seeker, but Collins J stated:

> The fact that a person is an EU national does not automatically apply para 5 of Schedule 3 . . . For a work seeker, as opposed to a worker, in a housing and Children Act cases it is likely that there will be no material right which has to be taken into account and which overrides the exclusion in para 5. But for a worker, and specifically for a worker who for whatever reason loses his job and needs to fall back on some sort of benefit, the situation is different. Indeed Article 7(2) of 1612/68 explicitly refers to that possible situation.

9.72 The categories of persons excluded by NIAA 2002 Sch 3 are as follows:

- persons granted refugee status by another EEA state and their dependants;[133]
- nationals of other EEA states and their dependants;[134]
- former asylum-seekers who have failed to co-operate with removal directions and their dependants;[135]
- persons in the UK in breach of the immigration laws within the meaning of NIAA 2002 s11 who are not asylum-seekers;[136]
- failed asylum-seeker families certified by the Secretary of State as not having taken reasonable steps to leave the UK.[137]

Unlawfully in the UK

9.73 A person is in the UK in breach of the immigration laws within the meaning of NIAA 2002 s11 if they:

- are present in the UK;
- do not have the right of abode;
- do not have a currently valid leave to enter or remain;
- are not entitled to remain in the UK without leave as an EEA citizen or their dependant; and
- are not exempted from the need to have leave (certain crew members, diplomats, forces personnel). It should be noted, however, that NIAA 2002 s11 applies IA 1971 s11, with the result that a person who has 'temporary admission' in the UK and who has not otherwise entered the UK (for example unlawfully or

133 NIAA 2002 Sch 3 para 4.
134 NIAA 2002 Sch 3 para 5.
135 NIAA 2002 Sch 3 para 6.
136 NIAA 2002 Sch 3 para 7.
137 NIAA 2002 Sch 3 para 7A; see para 4.123–4.127.

with leave) is not in the UK in breach of the immigration laws, and so a person who claims asylum on arrival, for example, and who is granted temporary admission, is not unlawfully in the UK for so long as that temporary admission lasts.[138]

Power to finance return travel to EEA countries

9.74 By virtue of NIAA 2002 Sch 3 paras 8, 9 and 10, the Secretary of State has made the Withholding and Withdrawal of Support (Travel Assistance and Temporary Accommodation) Regulations 2002 (WWS(TATA)R 2002). 'Dependant' is defined by WWS(TATA)R 2002 reg 2(2). A person married to an EEA national as the result of a marriage of convenience is still their dependant for these purposes.[139]

9.75 Furthermore, by virtue of NIAA 2002 Sch 3 para 2 and WWS-(TATA)R 2002 reg 4, the Secretary of State has issued guidance, to which local authorities must have regard, called the Nationality, Immigration and Asylum Act 2002 s54 and Sch 3 and the Withholding and Withdrawal of Support (Travel Assistance and Temporary Accommodation) Regulations 2002: Guidance to Local Authorities and Housing Authorities (the NIAA 2002 Guidance).[140]

9.76 WWS(TATA)R 2002 reg 3(1) empowers local authorities to make travel arrangements enabling EEA refugees and EEA nationals[141] to leave the UK to travel to the relevant EEA state. Providing the person in question has a dependent child with them, WWS(TATA)R 2002 reg 3(2) empowers local authorities to accommodate him/her, with their child, pending the implementation of such travel arrangements (at least until such time as they fail to co-operate with the travel arrangements: see reg 5).

Power to accommodate pending removal

9.77 However, WWS(TATA)R 2002 do not empower local authorities to make travel arrangements enabling former asylum-seekers who have not failed to co-operate with removal directions or persons unlawfully present in the UK[142] to travel to their countries of origin. Regulation 3(3) does, however, empower local authorities to accommodate persons unlawfully present in the UK who have not failed

138 *R (AW) v Croydon LBC* [2005] EWHC 2950 (Admin).
139 *R (Kimani) v Lambeth LBC* [2003] EWCA Civ 1150.
140 www.asylumsupport.info/witholdingandwithdrawing.htm
141 The categories of persons excluded by NIAA 2002 Sch 3 paras 4 and 5.
142 The categories of persons excluded by NIAA 2002 Sch 3 paras 6 and 7.

to co-operate with removal directions, providing such persons have a dependant child. In *R (M) v Islington LBC*,[143] the local authority decided that, in the light of the NIAA 2002 Guidance, it could only lawfully provide such accommodation for a very short period of ten days or so, and could then provide assistance with travel to the family's country of origin, but not other assistance under CA 1989 s17 on the basis that this was in the children's best interests. The court quashed this decision holding that local authorities have power under WWS(TATA)R 2002 to provide accommodation up until the unlawfully present adult fails to comply with removal directions. In considering how to exercise this power, regard had to be given to the ECHR, with reference to which it would be difficult not to see an offer of travel with an alternative of no accommodation (made not for social reasons but as an attempt to enforce immigration control other than by issuing removal directions) as an unjustifiable interference with article 8 rights.

The local authority/Home Office divide[144]

9.78 Where persons are not asylum-seekers, or failed asylum-seekers, no question of Home Office support arises and the individuals in question either will or will not qualify for local authority help, depending on the extent to which they are excluded by IAA 1999 and NIAA 2002. In the case of individual asylum-seekers, or families of asylum-seekers, however, the Home Office and local authorities have potentially overlapping responsibilities in relation to accommodation and basic support (although only local authorities have the power to provide more specialised forms of care).

Able-bodied adult asylum-seekers

9.79 Adult asylum-seekers who are healthy and able-bodied and who do not have children are the responsibility of the Home Office.[145]

9.80 When such persons cease to be asylum-seekers they may qualify for accommodation under IAA 1999 s4[146] but will not qualify for support under NAA 1948 s21, because they will not need 'looking after' because of care needs,[147] or for accommodation under WWS(TATA)R 2002 (because they do not have a child).

143 [2003] EWCA Civ 235.

144 See also table at para 4.139.

145 *R (Westminster) v NASS* (2002) 5 CCLR 511.

146 See chapter 6.

147 See para 9.92.

9.81 Adult asylum-seekers who are healthy and able-bodied and who have children are, together with their children, the responsibility of the Home Office,[148] irrespective of whether the children are healthy and able-bodied.[149] Only the local authority has the power to provide specialised care going beyond accommodation and support to disabled children, but the Home Office still has the duty to provide accommodation and basic support that meets the needs of disabled children, however complex, for example adapted accommodation and special diets.[150]

9.82 In a case where the Home Office is not under a duty to support such families under IAA 1999 s122, for example because they have failed to comply with conditions attached to support,[151] the families become a local authority responsibility under CA 1989 ss17 and 20.

Section 9 families[152]

9.83 An asylum-seeker with a child does not normally cease to be an asylum-seeker for the purposes of asylum support, even after the final adverse determination of their asylum claim or appeal.[153] There is an exception if the Secretary of State certifies that they have failed to take reasonable steps to return to their countries of origin, under NIAA 2002 Sch 3 para 7A. At that point, the family as a whole will be excluded from the Home Office support and the adults, but not the children, will be excluded from local authority support, except to the extent that the lack of support will give rise to a breach of ECHR or EEA treaty rights, but it will be difficult for a refused asylum-seeker to demonstrate that the family needs support to avoid a breach of their ECHR rights if there is no ECHR or Refugee Convention reason why they cannot return to their country of origin.[154]

Refused asylum-seekers with care needs

9.84 Adult asylum-seekers who do not have children but who need 'looking after' because of care needs not caused solely by destitution, are a local authority responsibility under NAA 1948 s21.[155]

148 Because of IAA 1999 s122.

149 *R (A) v (1) NASS and (2) Waltham Forest LBC* [2003] EWCA Civ 1473, (2003) 6 CCLR 538.

150 Although NASS can seek local authority assistance under IAA 1999 s100.

151 See AS Regs 2000 reg 20.

152 See also para 4.123.

153 See IAA 1999 s94(5).

154 *R (Kimani) v Lambeth LBC* [2003] EWCA Civ 1150, [2004] 1 WLR 272; and see paras 9.70–9.72 above.

155 *R (M) v Slough BC* [2008] UKHL 52, [2008] 1 WLR 1808.

9.85 When such persons cease to be asylum-seekers[156] they will continue to qualify for local authority support under NAA 1948 s21, rather than Home Office accommodation under IAA 1999 s4, if they claimed asylum at port unless and until they fail to co-operate with removal directions.[157] If such refused asylum-seekers are also unlawfully present in the UK within the meaning of NIAA 2002 s11, because they entered the UK unlawfully and claimed asylum 'in-country', they will be excluded from assistance under NAA 1948 s21 by NIAA 2002 Sch 3 para 7 unless they require continued assistance on ECHR grounds. This applies if they have made a further application for leave to remain on ECHR grounds that are not manifestly abusive (because they are unfit to travel or cannot obtain travel documents or cannot gain entry into another country).[158]

Refused asylum-seekers who are pregnant or nursing mothers

9.86 Local authorities have a *duty* to provide accommodation under s21 NAA 1948 to those in need of care and attention due to disability, mental illness, age etc, whereas in relation to pregnant and nursing mothers there is a *power*. Two pregnant mothers who were refused asylum-seekers applied for assistance under NAA 1948 s21(1)(aa) on the basis that they were in need of care and attention that was not otherwise available to them. The council refused on the basis that they qualified for support under IAA 1999 s4 either on the basis of an outstanding fresh claim or on the basis of being unable to travel home due to being pregnant/a nursing mother. Mitting J dismissed the claimants' application for judicial review.[159] He considered that the claimants were only in need of care and attention due to their destitution, not due to being an expectant or nursing mother. He considered they were excluded from assistance by section 21(1A), which excludes those who are solely in need of care and attention due to destitution. Secondly the judge considered that the Home Secretary's only duty was to take into account any other support which was available to the applicant and having done so could decide

156 See para 4.33.

157 See NIAA 2002 Sch 3 para 6 and see *R (AW) v Croydon LBC* [2005] EWHC 2950 (Admin) and in the Court of Appeal at [2007] EWCA Civ 266.

158 *R (AW) v Croydon LBC* [2005] EWHC 2950 (Admin) and see para 9.70.

159 *R (AG) v Leeds City Council; R (MD) v (1) Leeds City Council; (2) Secretary of State for the Home Department (interested party)* [2007] EWHC 3275 (Admin) March 2008 *Legal Action* 22.

to provide s4 support, rather than expect the local authority to do so.

9.87 Adult asylum-seekers who have children who are disabled or need looking after or special care are a Home Office responsibility together with their children.[160]

9.88 When such families cease to be asylum-seekers they are likely to remain a Home Office responsibility under IAA 1999 s95 until the children reach 18.

9.89 Unaccompanied children, whether or not they are asylum-seekers, are exclusively the responsibility of local authorities, under CA 1989 s20, since asylum support is only available to asylum-seekers aged 18 and over.[161]

9.90 Adult asylum-seekers who have (as children) been in local authority care are entitled to support on leaving care and there is no exclusion of persons from abroad from the children leaving care machinery in CA 1989.[162] In practice, however, since such children will also be eligible for asylum support when they reach 18, the Home Office will take over financial responsibility at least[163], but the local authority's duty to maintain a pathway plan and personal adviser and the local authority's overarching welfare duty remains. If the former children require 'looking after' then they will continue to be entirely a local authority responsibility under NAA 1948 s21.

9.91 When such persons (who are now adults) cease also to be asylum-seekers their eligibility for assistance under the children leaving care machinery of CA 1989 also ceases, by virtue of NIAA 2002 s54 and Sch 3, except where the person has an outstanding claim for LTR under the ECHR or for some other reason cannot be expected to leave the UK and except (in any event) in respect of the provision of a personal adviser and reviews of the pathway plan.[164] Otherwise, as refused asylum-seeker adults, they may be entitled to support under IAA 1999 s4 if they meet the criteria.[165]

160 *R (O) v Haringey* [2004] EWCA Civ 535, [2004] 2 FLR 476.

161 IAA 1999 s94(1).

162 See para 9.139.

163 See Children (Leaving Care) Act 2000 Regulations and Guidance chapter 2 paras 7–11.

164 *R (Binomugisha) v Southwark LBC* [2006] EWHC 2254 (Admin).

165 See chapter 6.

The nature and extent of community care services

Services under the NHSCCA 1990 subject to exclusions

Section 21 residential accommodation under NAA 1948

9.92 Asylum-seekers and other PSIC who have needs to be 'looked after', which derive at least in part from causes other than destitution or the physical effects of destitution (for example because they are elderly, disabled, physically or mentally ill, or pregnant, or because they are a nursing mother),[166] will be entitled to have their needs for accommodation and subsistence met by the local authority social services department under NAA 1948 s21.

9.93 Local authorities have duties and powers to provide residential accommodation under NAA 1948 s21, which are 'triggered' by approvals and directions made under section 21 by the Secretary of State for Health.[167] Migrants are excluded from these services in the circumstances described above.[168]

9.94 Most commonly, the duty arises under the combination of NAA 1948 s21(1)(a) and the direction at para 2(1)(b) of the approvals and directions, in respect of 'persons aged 18 or over who by reason of age, illness, disability or any other circumstances are in need of care and attention not otherwise available to them' and who are ordinarily resident in the local authority area or in urgent need. The duty is to provide 'residential accommodation' to those, not as may be expected in need of accommodation, but only to those in need of care and attention not otherwise available to them. In particular circumstances, an authority may be under a duty to provide accommodation to a person who, at the point of assessment, has accommodation available. In *R (Wahid) v Tower Hamlets LBC*,[169] Hale LJ stated that the 'natural and ordinary meaning' of the expression 'in need of care and attention' in this context was 'looking after'. She developed this concept in the case of *R (M) v Slough BC*[170] (in which she specifically referred to the *Wahid* case) by indicating that:

> Looking after means doing something for the person being cared for which he cannot or should not be expected to do for himself.

166 See NAA 1948 s21(1)(aa); but see para 9.86.
167 See LAC (93) 10 Appendix 1.
168 See para 9.53.
169 (2001) 5 CCLR 239.
170 [2008] UKHL 52, [2008] 1 WLR 1808.

9.95 In the *Wahid* case, Hale LJ provided the following introduction to NAA 1948 s21:

> Some basic points may deserve emphasis given the recent expansion of litigation in this field. Under section 21(1)(a) of the National Assistance Act 1948, local social services authorities have a duty to make arrangements for providing residential accommodation for people over 18 (who are ordinarily resident in their area or in urgent need) where three inter-related conditions are fulfilled:
>
> 1) the person is in need of care and attention;
> 2) that need arises by reason of age, illness, disability or any other circumstances; and
> 3) that care and attention is not available to him otherwise than by the provision of residential accommodation under this particular power.
>
> Three further points are also relevant:
>
> 1) it is for the local social services authority to assess whether or not these conditions are fulfilled and, if so, how the need is to be met, subject to the scrutiny of the court on the ordinary principles of judicial review;
> 2) section 21 does not permit the local social services authority to make provision which may or must be made by them or any other authority under an enactment other than Part 3 of the 1948 Act (see section 21(8)); but
> 3) having identified a need to be met by the provision of residential accommodation under section 21, the authority have a positive duty to meet it which can be enforced in judicial review proceedings.
>
> ... 'residential accommodation' can mean ordinary housing without the provision of any ancillary services.

9.96 Care and attention can be 'otherwise available' to a person if they have family members who can provide them with support and/or care or if there are charitable or other avenues of voluntary support. But emergency support provided, for example by, community members on a short-term basis in order to help a desperate person ought not to preclude eligibility.

9.97 Where residential accommodation is provided, there is a duty to meet needs for food and other welfare services, where required.[171] No assistance can be given, however, in the form of cash.[172]

171 NAA 1948 s21(5) and Approvals and Directions para 4.

172 *R v Secretary of State for Health ex p M and K* (1998) 1 CCLR 495.

9.98 For the duty under NAA 1948 s21 to arise in relation to a person subject to immigration control,[173] the need for care and attention must not arise solely because of destitution or the physical effects of destitution.[174] There would, therefore, have to be another element present, of the kind mentioned in section 21, ie age, illness, disability, pregnancy, nursing or some other circumstance giving rise to a need for care and attention.[175] Cases in which the court has found 'destitution plus' to be present include the following:

- a woman disabled by cancer;[176]
- men and women with HIV (although the cases now need to be read in the light of *R (M) v Slough LBC*);[177]
- a woman vulnerable as the result of historic but long-standing and severe domestic violence;[178]
- a man with severe ankylosing spondylitis (leaving him with no movement in his neck and only slight movement in his spine);[179]
- a man whose right leg was half the length of his left leg as the result of congenital disability.[180]

9.99 Other examples could include persons suffering from mental illness, old and frail persons, expectant and nursing mothers (specifically referred to in NAA 1948 s21(1)(aa) but see para 9.86), persons recovering from drug or alcohol dependency and persons suffering from significant illness or accident, providing in every case the person concerned did require at least some 'looking after' and not just accommodation, food and healthcare.

9.100 The approvals and directions set out a number of types of cases where there is a duty or power to provide residential accommodation. Local authorities will have published eligibility criteria, under NHSCCA 1990 s46 and FACS, by reference to which social workers

173 See para 9.53.

174 NAA 1948 s21(1)(A), introduced by IAA 1999 s116.

175 See para 9.60.

176 *R (Westminster) v NASS* (2002) 5 CCLR 511.

177 *R (J) v Enfield LBC* [2002] EWHC 432, (2003) 5 CCLR 434; *R (Mani and others) v Lambeth and others* [2002] EWHC 735, (2002) 5 CCLR 486; *R (H) v Kingston upon Thames* [2002] EWHC 3158 (Admin), (2003) 6 CCLR 240; *R (B and H) v Hackney LBC* [2003] EWHC 1654.

178 *R (Khan) v Oxfordshire CC* (2003) 5 CCLR 611 (reversed on the facts but not as to the principle in the Court of Appeal at [2004] EWCA Civ 309).

179 *R (Mani and others) v Lambeth and others* [2002] EWHC 735; (2002) 5 CCLR 486.

180 *R (Mani and others) v Lambeth and others* [2002] EWHC 735; (2002) 5 CCLR 486 and in the Court of Appeal at [2003] EWCA Civ 836, (2003) 6 CCLR 376.

generally decide whether a 'need' for residential accommodation exists, but those criteria have little if any application to the cases of asylum-seekers seeking assistance under NAA 1948 s21. Attempts to argue that the eligibility criteria should be applied to destitute asylum-seekers and PSIC have failed.[181] Once a local authority has assessed a need for residential accommodation as existing, then it must meet the need.[182]

9.101 'Residential accommodation' can be accommodation in an institution, a hostel or an ordinary house or flat.[183] It should be suitable, which in this context requires the local authority to have regard to the welfare of all persons for whom accommodation is provided, and to provide different descriptions of accommodation suited to different descriptions of persons.[184] It must meet whatever needs have been assessed as existing.[185] The authority should strive to meet the assisted person's preferences within its available resources.[186] It has to plan how best to meet the needs assessed and how best to meet preferences in accordance with the provisions of the Policy Guidance and FACS.[187]

9.102 Where the assisted person has a dependent child, the local authority has the power to accommodate them together with the child, if need be, by using its powers under CA 1989 s17. The local authority would be under a duty to exercise its powers under CA 1989 s17 in this way if not to do so would result in a breach of ECHR article 8.[188] It has been the long-standing practice of local authorities to accommodate assisted persons together with adult family members or carers (for example an elderly spouse).[189] However, where the

181 *R (N) v Lambeth LBC* [2006] EWHC 3427 (Admin) and *R (N) v Lambeth LBC* [2007] EWCA Civ 862.

182 *R v Kensington and Chelsea LBC ex p Kujtim* (1999) 2 CCLR 340; *R (Wahid) v Tower Hamlets LBC* (2001) 5 CCLR 239.

183 *R v Newham LBC ex p Medical Foundation for the Care of Victims of Torture* (1998) 1 CCLR 227; *R v Bristol City Council ex p Penfold* (1998) 1 CCLR 315; *R (Wahid) v Tower Hamlets LBC* (2001) 5 CCLR 239.

184 NAA 1948 s21(2).

185 *R v Avon CC ex p M* (1999) 2 CCLR 185.

186 Policy Guidance para 3.25.

187 See para 9.31.

188 *R (J) v Enfield LBC* (2003) 5 CCLR 434.

189 *R (Khana) v Southwark LBC* (2001) 4 CCLR 267; *R (Batantu) v Islington LBC* (2001) 4 CCLR 445; *R (Wahid) v Tower Hamlets LBC* (2002) 5 CCLR 239 and *R (O) v Haringey* [2004] EWCA Civ 535, [2004] 2 FLR 476 are some cases which refer to this practice.

assisted person is an asylum-seeker, the Home Office is financially responsible for the children, and potentially other dependants.[190]

Choice of accommodation

9.103 Even if the person with care needs is an asylum-seeker, they may have some input into where they are housed. The NAA 1948 (Choice of Accommodation) Directions 1992 provide that the assisted person has the right to choose their 'preferred accommodation' provided certain conditions are met. This could apply where, for example, the local authority has located accommodation some distance away, but the asylum-seeker has found cheaper accommodation located near relatives and friends. The conditions summarised here are that:[191]

- the preferred accommodation appears to the local authority to be suitable in relation to the person's needs as assessed by them;
- the cost of making arrangements at the preferred accommodation would not require the authority to pay more than it would usually expect to pay having regard to the assessed needs;
- the preferred accommodation is available;
- the persons in charge of the preferred accommodation provide it subject to the authority's usual terms and conditions.

If the accommodation would require the authority to pay more than it would usually expect to pay, third parties are permitted to 'top up' the difference.[192]

9.104 It is important to note that, while an authority absolutely must meet assessed needs, the way in which the authority meets those needs is largely a matter for the authority to decide, although it must strive to meet service provision preferences within available resources.[193] This is in stark contrast to the support system under the IAA 1999, where it is repeatedly stressed that no regard is to be had to an applicant's preferences.

9.105 Residential accommodation can be provided by the local authority entering into arrangements with the private sector, under NAA 1948 s29. Alternatively, it can be provided by the local authority using accommodation held for that purpose under NAA 1948 s21 itself.

190 *R (O) v Haringey* [2004] EWCA Civ 535, [2004] 2 FLR 476; and see Asylum Support Policy Bulletin 85.

191 Asylum Support Policy Bulletin 85, para 3.

192 Asylum Support Policy Bulletin 85, para 4.

193 Policy Guidance para 3.25.

The local authority can grant licences of its own housing stock for this purpose.[194]

9.106 It is only in an exceptional case that a local authority is entitled to treat its duty under section 21 as discharged, so that it does not have to offer further accommodation, for example on account of disruptive behaviour. In *R v Kensington and Chelsea LBC ex p Kujtim*,[195] the Court of Appeal emphasised that it was essential that local authorities should not reach the conclusion that their duty to provide residential accommodation was discharged unless satisfied that the applicant had unreasonably refused to accept accommodation provided, or that they had persistently and unequivocally refused to comply with the local authority's requirements (for example as to behaviour) so as in effect to reject the accommodation, coupled with a careful consideration of their current needs and circumstances (including any change of heart on the part of the applicant).

9.107 A local authority may charge for accommodation provided under s21. There is a detailed scheme of means testing and regulation.[196] These charging provisions are not usually relevant to asylum-seekers with limited resources, but may be relevant to other migrants such as EEA nationals.

9.108 NIAA 2002 Sch 3 and s54 exclude EEA refugees, EEA nationals, former asylum-seekers who have failed to co-operate with removal directions and certain persons unlawfully present in the UK from services under NAA 1948 s45, except where provision is required to avoid a breach of the ECHR or EU treaties.[197] Other persons from abroad are not excluded. As to which asylum-seekers are eligible for local authority support under NAA 1948 s21 and which are the responsibility of the Home Office see paras 4.139 and 9.78.

Services for older people under HSPHA 1968 s45

9.109 Asylum-seekers and other migrants who have needs that derive at least in part from causes other than destitution or the physical effects

194 The proscription on local authorities granting tenancies and licences to PSIC imposed by IAA 1999 s118 is lifted for the purposes of NAA 1948 s21 by the Persons Subject to Immigration Control (Housing Authority Accommodation and Homelessness) Order 2000 SI No 706 reg 4(1)(a).

195 [1999] 4 All ER 161.

196 See NAA 1948 s22, National Assistance (Assessment of Resources) Regulations 1992 SI No 2977 and Charging for Residential Accommodation Guide (LAC(95)7, as frequently amended).

197 See paras 9.67–9.77.

of destitution (for example because they are elderly, handicapped, disabled, physically or mentally ill) will be eligible for services under HSPHA 1968 s45.

9.110 The services provided under HSPHA 1968 s45 are miscellaneous services, which local authorities are empowered to provide for the elderly, in accordance with approvals and directions made under that section, that are found in circular LAC 19/71. The services include meals on wheels and recreation, in the home or elsewhere, social work assistance, practical assistance and adaptations in the home and warden services. Almost by definition, it might be thought, a person likely to qualify for this kind of service would not be in need solely by reason of destitution, but also by reason of old age.

9.111 The exclusion of certain PSIC by IAA 1999 will have little impact in relation to services under HSPHA 1968 s45, since there will be few people (if any) with a need for these services for whom destitution is the only cause of that need.

9.112 NIAA 2002 absolutely excludes EEA refugees, EEA nationals, former asylum-seekers who have failed to co-operate with removal directions and certain persons unlawfully present in the UK from services under HSPHA 1968 s45, except where provision is required to avoid a breach of the ECHR or EU treaties.[198]

Services for those with a long-term illness under the NHSA 2006

9.113 The services provided under NHSA 2006 s254 and Sch 20 relate to services that local authorities may, and in some cases must, provide for the prevention of illness, the care of people suffering from illness and the aftercare of people who have been suffering from illness, as well as non-accommodation services for pregnant and nursing mothers. Provision is made in accordance with approvals and directions.[199] The kinds of services involved are day centres and similar facilities, social services support, social and recreational facilities. Provision is discretionary.

9.114 Again, almost by definition, it might be thought, a person likely to qualify for these kinds of services would not be in need solely by reason of destitution, but also by reason of past or present illness and, so, the limited exclusion of PSIC by IAA 1999 described at paras 9.53–9.61 is likely to have little impact.

198 See paras 9.67–9.77.

199 LAC(93)10 Appendix 3.

9.115 It will be recollected, however, that NIAA 2002 absolutely excludes EEA refugees, EEA nationals, former asylum-seekers who have failed to co-operate with removal directions and certain persons unlawfully present in the UK from services under NHSA 1977 s21 and Sch 8 para 2, except where provision is required to avoid a breach of the ECHR or EU treaties.[200]

Services under the NHSCCA 1990 not subject to exclusions under IAA 1999

9.116 There is no exclusion in IAA 1999 of asylum-seekers or other PSIC from services under NAA 1948 s29, CSDPA 1970 s2, LGA 2000 s2 and MHA 1983 s117. Of these sets of provisions, only MHA 1983 s117 and LGA 2000 s2 offer the possibility of the provision of assistance with accommodation and subsistence. There are, however, exclusions under NIAA 2002 in respect of NAA 1948 s29, CSDPA 1970 s2 and LGA 2000 s2.

NAA 1948 s29, CSDPA 1970 s2 and LGA 2000 s2

9.117 These enactments apply only to substantially disabled persons:[201]

> persons aged 18 or over who are blind, deaf or dumb, or who suffer from mental disorder of any description and other persons aged 18 or over who are substantially and permanently handicapped by illness, injury, or congenital deformity or such other disabilities as may be prescribed by the Minister.

9.118 Services under NAA 1948 s29 are provided in accordance with approvals and directions made under that section[202] and, again, each local authority will have its own published eligibility criteria which, currently, can be expected to mirror the eligibility criteria in FACS.[203] The services provided include social work assistance, different types of day centres, holiday homes, travel, and warden schemes.

9.119 The services available under CSDPA 1970 s2 are set out in the section itself and include practical assistance in the home, various kinds of leisure provision, home adaptations, telephones and meals. The assessment process was considered by the House of Lords in

200 See paras 9.67–9.77.
201 NAA 1948 s29(1).
202 LAC(93)10 Appendix 2.
203 See para 9.39.

R v Gloucestershire CC ex p Barry.[204] The conclusion was that, in assessing needs and whether it was necessary to meet them, local authorities are entitled and obliged to have regard to:

- the current standards of living;
- the nature and extent of the disability;
- the extent and manner to which quality of life would be improved; and
- the cost of providing the service in the context of the resources available to the local authority.

The relative cost is to be weighed against the relative benefit and the relative need for that benefit, in the light of the local authorities' published community care criteria.

9.120 Additionally, in the case of persons from abroad, the local authority will inevitably have to pay particular attention to the effect on such persons of destitution.

9.121 LGA 2000 s2 empowers local authorities to do anything that they consider likely, among other things, to promote the social well-being of their area.[205] It is expressly provided that local authorities can make provision for individuals, including financial assistance and accommodation.[206] However, this power does not allow local authorities to do something to the extent prohibited or restricted by another enactment.[207] Furthermore, the power must be exercised having regard to the local authority's own strategy[208] and guidance issued by the Secretary of State.[209] However, the power under LGA 2000 s2 can be used to provide assistance or support required by the ECHR, for which there is no other statutory basis.[210]

9.122 It will be recollected that NIAA 2002 absolutely excludes EEA refugees, EEA nationals, former asylum-seekers who have failed to co-operate with removal directions, certain persons unlawfully present in the UK and section 9 'certified families' from services under NAA 1948 s29, CSDPA 1970 s2 and LGA 2000 s2, except where provision is required to avoid a breach of the ECHR or EU treaties.[211] LGA 2000 s2 is also excluded in respect of 'section 55'

204 LGA 2000 s2(2) and (4).
205 [1997] AC 584, (1997) 1 CCLR 40.
206 LGA 2000 s2(1).
207 LGA 2000 s2(2) and (4).
208 LGA 2000 s3.
208 LGA 2000 ss2(3) and 4.
209 LGA 2000 s3(5).
210 *R (J) v Enfield LBC* (2002) 5 CCLR 434.
211 See paras 9.67–9.77.

asylum-seekers who do not claim asylum as soon as reasonably practicable upon arrival.[212]

MHA 1983 s117 – mental patients

9.123 Asylum-seekers and PSIC who are so mentally ill as to have been 'sectioned' or compulsorily detained under MHA 1983 ss3, 37, 45A, 47 or 48 remain eligible for support irrespective of their immigration status, because there are no immigration exclusions from services under MHA 1983 s117. Detention under MHA 1983 s2, which is detention for four weeks for an assessment, or psychiatric treatment as a voluntary patient, is not included. Services under section 117 are 'aftercare' services provided for persons who cease to be detained under the treatment provisions of the MHA 1983.[213] They include 'social work, support in helping the ex-patient with problems of employment, accommodation or family relationships, the provision of domiciliary services and the use of day centre and residential facilities'.[214] The Guidance on the Mental Health (Patients in the Community) Act 1995 provides further authority to show that s117 services can include daytime activities, treatment, personal and practical support, 24-hour emergency cover and assistance in welfare rights and financial advice, as well as accommodation. They also include the provision of residential accommodation and charges cannot be made.[215] Responsibility for the provision of services rests jointly upon the health and social services authorities.

9.124 Before a mentally ill person is discharged from a psychiatric unit where they have been detained, there has to be a multidisciplinary assessment of their needs around the time of discharge, completed by relevant medical and social services officers.[216] The duty applies even if the detention occurred some time earlier. It is normally met

212 NIAA 2002 s55. And see para 4.105.

213 MHA 1983 s117 does not apply to those detained for assessment under section 2 or to those who become in-patients voluntarily.

214 *Clunis v Camden and Islington HA* (1998) 1 CCLR 215 at 225G-H.

215 *R (Stennett) v Manchester CC* [2002] UKHL 34, (2002) 5 CCLR 500.

216 See the Care Programme Approach at HC(90)23/LASSL(90)23 and in Effective Care and Co-ordination in Mental Health Services, issued under the relatively new National Service Framework for Mental Health at HSC(1999)223; see also LAC(1999)34 Guidance on the Discharge of Mentally Disordered People and their Continuing Care in the Community; Building Bridges: a Guide to Arrangements for the Inter-Agency Working for Care and Protection of Severely Mentally Ill People at LASSL(94)4), HSG(94)27; *R v Ealing LBC ex p Fox* [1993] 3 All ER 170; *R v Mental Health Review Tribunal ex p Hall* (1999) 2 CCLR 361.

jointly by the PCT and local authority social services, working jointly through the community mental health team.

9.125 So far as concerns all of these services, migrants are eligible for assistance on the same basis as British citizens. The only additional factor likely to arise is that the destitution of people from abroad may result in needs existing that would not otherwise have existed and may increase the needs that fall to be met under the community care scheme if physical or mental damage is to be avoided.

Services for children

9.126 The IAA 1999 marked a new departure by taking the subsistence and accommodation needs of children living with their families who are asylum-seekers outside the scope of the CA 1989,[217] except in highly residual cases.[218] NIAA 2002 Sch 3 goes further and excludes adults, but not children, from support under CA 1989 s17 if they are EEA refugees, EEA nationals, former asylum-seekers who have failed to co-operate with removal directions, certain categories of persons unlawfully present and 'certified families'. Apart from these exclusions, services for children are almost exclusively provided under the CA 1989. An exception is made where a child is disabled,[219] and so eligible for all of the services within CSDPA 1970 s2. Provision for unaccompanied children who claim asylum is made entirely under the CA 1989.

Children in need

9.127 Local authorities have powers and duties under CA 1989 Part 3 in relation to a 'child in need'. A child is defined as a person under 18 years of age.[220] The term 'child in need' is defined in CA 1989 s17(10) as being a child who is:

- unlikely to achieve or maintain, or to have the opportunity of achieving or maintaining, a reasonable standard of health[221] or development,[222] without the provision for them of services by the local authority under CA 1989 Part 3; or

217 IAA 1999 s122.
218 See para 9.81.
219 As defined in NAA 1948 s29.
220 CA 1989 s105(1).
221 'Health' is defined as including physical or mental health.
222 'Development' is defined as including physical, intellectual, emotional, social or behavioural development.

- likely to suffer significant impairment of health or development, or further impairment, without the provision for them of services by the local authority under CA 1989 Part 3; or
- disabled: that is a child who is blind, deaf or dumb or who suffers from mental disorder of any kind or who is substantially and permanently handicapped by illness, injury or congenital deformity.

Children of families of migrants with insecure immigration status lacking accommodation and the means of support, and/or whose parents have insecure immigration status are likely to fall within the scope of this definition.

Services for children in need living with their families

9.128 The services provided can include assistance in kind and also cash.[223] All of the services can be provided for the child or, where appropriate, for the child and their family.[224] Assistance in kind can include accommodation.[225] Where a child is homeless, the local authority is under a duty to provide assistance to the child,[226] but there is no absolute duty under section 17 to house homeless children together with their families. Rather, local authorities must take such steps as are reasonably practicable to enable a child to live with their family where it is necessary to promote and safeguard the child's welfare.[227] It is not unlawful for a local authority to have a general policy of not accommodating children with families, where its experience is that homeless families invariably make do.[228] However, each case must be considered individually and local authorities are subject to judicial review in accordance with ordinary public law principles.[229] ECHR article 8 can require local authorities to accommodate families together.[230] Local authorities can grant tenancies or licences to accommodate families under section 17.[231] Local authorities must

223 CA 1989 s17(6).

224 CA 1989 s17(3).

225 CA 1989 s17(6).

226 CA 1989 s20.

227 CA 1989 s17(1) and (3).

228 *R (W, A, G) v Lambeth LBC* [2003] UKHL 57.

229 *R (W, A, G) v Lambeth LBC* [2003] UKHL 57.

230 *R (J) v Enfield LBC* (2002) 5 CCLR 434.

231 The proscription on local authorities granting tenancies and licences to PSIC imposed by IAA 1999 s118 is lifted for the purposes of children in need by Persons Subject to Immigration Control (Housing Authority Accommodation and Homelessness) Order 2000 SI No 706 reg 4(1)(b).

make such provision as they consider appropriate in respect of advice, social activities, travel for the purpose of using services, and holidays.[232] This could include assistance with school clothing, books and other study materials, toys etc.

9.129 Prior to the IAA 1999, local authorities provided destitute asylum-seeker families with accommodation, food and other basic necessities under CA 1989 s17 on a very large scale. The great advantage of the CA 1989 regime is its flexibility. Once the authority has decided to provide assistance, there is no limit to the type of assistance that can be provided or the way in which it can be provided.

9.130 However, it is a flexibility that cuts both ways. Assistance under CA 1989 s17 confers no absolute right to services to meet an assessed need, far less to particular accommodation and services. Also, a local authority can discharge its duties in a variety of ways, as it considers appropriate in the circumstances. So, it may satisfy a need for accommodation by securing accommodation itself, or by providing assistance to parents to find accommodation in the private rented sector, such as a deposit. The assistance must, however, be effective in a case where the local authority has decided to provide assistance for a particular purpose.[233] As indicated above, however, local authorities have a considerable margin of judgment when deciding whether and if so what assistance to provide and for what purposes.

Unaccompanied asylum-seeker children (UASC)

9.131 This covers children under 18 years of age who arrive in the UK, claim asylum and are without close adult family members either accompanying them or already present in the UK and whom they can join. Such children are the responsibility of the social services department of the local authority in whose area they are for the time being, and should on arrival be referred immediately to the social services department for an assessment and for the immediate provision of assistance. Assistance provided ranges from accommodation and food to foster carers, leisure, language help and trauma counselling. Such children should be treated no differently from UK children who have been taken into care except, of course, that they may need extra help. There is a duty to take steps to trace the child's relatives (see para 4.14).

232 CA 1989 s17 and Sch 2 Part I para 8.

233 *R v Barking and Dagenham LBC ex p Ebuki* (2000) 5 December, QBD.

9.132 Assistance is provided to such children under CA 1989 s20. In *R (G) v Southwark LBC*[234] the House of Lords considered a number of earlier cases on this point and held that where a child satisfied the criteria in section 20 the authority had to accommodate the child under section 20 and could not provide them with 'accommodation assistance' under section 17 except when they refused accommodation under section 20. The authority must provide accommodation to any child in need who appears to require it as a result of there being no one who has parental responsibility for them, being lost or abandoned, or the child's carers being prevented for the time being from providing suitable accommodation or care. In addition to providing accommodation, the authority must maintain the child.[235] Provision must, so far as practicable, have regard to the wishes of the child[236] but otherwise local authorities are given a wide discretion as to how they discharge their duty.[237] Where the authority is also providing accommodation for a sibling, the children should be accommodated together.[238] Fostering arrangements with a family of the same refugee community are common.

9.133 Assessment takes place under CA 1989 s17 and Sch 2 Part 1 para 1,[239] and is subject to the guidance referred to at para 9.45. Provision must be reviewed regularly.[240]

Age assessments

9.134 In these case, a preliminary issue often arises as to whether applicants are in fact children, or adults. This issue is fraught. Approximately 3,000 unaccompanied children come to the UK each year and claim asylum.[241]

9.135 It is in the interests of young asylum-seekers to be treated as a child and looked after under CA 1989, because the CA 1989 regime is, in many respects relatively liberal, while children also have advantages in terms of asylum procedures. There are serious risks to a child of being supported through the adult system, and potentially

234 [2009] UKHL 26, [2009] 1 WLR 1299.
235 CA 1989 s23(1).
236 CA 1989 s22(4) and (5).
237 CA 1989 s23(2).
238 CA 1989 s23(7).
239 *R (W, A, G) v Lambeth and Barnet LBC* [2003] UKHL 57.
240 CA 1989 s26 and Review of Children's Cases Regulations 1991 SI No 895.
241 *Going it Alone: children in the asylum process*, The Children's Society, 2007.

subject to detention.[242] On the other hand, it is often seen as in the economic and practical interests of local authorities not to accept young asylum-seekers for long-term care under CA 1989 and it is often seen as in the practical interests of the Home Secretary to treat young asylum-seekers as adults whenever possible. The assessment of age is notoriously subjective, age documentation is often regarded with suspicion, it is easily possible to interview genuine children in such a way as to make them appear to have contradicted themselves or to have told untruths. So the whole process is notoriously fallible for a number of reasons. It is possible, and indeed common, to obtain paediatric reports on age: such reports generally have a margin of error of up to two years either way and for some time were usually (but not always and certainly not by all local authorities) treated as being reliable indicators of probable age, including in a number of decided cases. Those cases may now only be of largely historic interest because in *R (A) v Croydon LBC (Secretary of State for the Home Department (Interested party)* (which was subject to an appeal at the time of writing)[243] after having read extensive expert evidence and heard detailed argument, Collins J indicated that in general such reports had very little persuasive weight:

> I do not however think that local authorities or the Secretary of State can in general disregard reports from Dr Birch or any other paediatrician... It may be that a particular matter identified by the doctor has not been taken into account. In A's case, for example, it is said that Dr Birch identified his limited intellectual abilities and this had not been taken into account by the social workers.
>
> Whether that should have made a difference will have to be considered, but I have no doubt that in general Croydon's and the Secretary of State's approach is correct. However, it is for them to decide how much weight to attach to such a report and it is in a given case open to the decision maker to attach no weight. For the reasons I have given, I would expect that only in rare cases would such a report persuade the decision maker to reach a different view.

9.136 NASS Policy Bulletin 33 provides some guidance and the court gave detailed guidance in relation to age assessments in *R (B) v Merton LBC*, subsequently followed in a number of other cases:[244]

242 The treatment of Asylum-seekers, Joint Committee of Human Rights, 10th report of Session 2006–07, HL Paper 81-1; HC 60-1, para 203.

243 [2009] EWHC 939 (Admin).

244 [2003] EWHC 1689 (Admin), (2003) 6 CCLR 457.

- the social services department of a local authority cannot simply adopt a decision made by the Home Office. It must itself decide whether an applicant is a child in need: ie whether the applicant is a child and, if so, whether they are in need within the meaning of CA 1989 Part 3. A local authority may take into account information obtained by the Home Office, but it must make its own decision, and for that purpose must have available to it adequate information;
- except in clear cases, the decision-maker should not decide age solely on the basis of the appearance of the applicant;
- in general, the decision-maker must seek to elicit the general background of the applicant, including family circumstances and history, educational background, and activities during the previous few years. Ethnic and cultural information may also be important. If there is reason to doubt the applicant's statement as to age, the decision-maker will have to make an assessment of credibility, and they will have to ask questions designed to test credibility;
- if an applicant has previously stated that they were over 18, the decision-maker will take that previous statement into account and, in the absence of an acceptable explanation, it may, when considered with the other material available, be decisive;
- the appearance and demeanour of the applicant may justify a provisional view that they are indeed a child or an adult;
- where an interpreter is required, it is obviously greatly preferable for them to be present during the interview. Using a telephone interpreting service carries with it the risk of misunderstanding, and great care is required to ensure that no mistakes are made;
- the decision-maker must explain to an applicant the purpose of the interview. If the decision-maker forms the view, which must at that stage be a provisional view, that the applicant is lying about their age, the applicant must be given the opportunity to address the matters that have led to that view, so that they can explain themselves if possible;
- a local authority is obliged to give adequate reasons for its decision that an applicant claiming to be a child is not a child, and who is therefore refused support under CA 1989 Part 3. The consequences of such a decision may be drastic for the applicant, and they are entitled to know the basis for it, and to consider, if possible, with legal assistance if it is available to them whether the decision is a lawful one.

9.137 In *R (A) v Croydon LBC*[245] the Court of Appeal decided that an age assessment was not the determination of a civil right for the purposes of ECHR article 6 and, even if it were, judicial review was an appropriate method of judicial supervision. A had argued that because of the rights which an assessment gave rise to, he should be entitled to a fair and objective hearing, which was not provided by the current social services process. A judgment from the House of Lords in A's appeal was awaited at the time of publication.

Care-leavers

9.138 In the meantime, the Home Office is reviewing procedures for age assessment.

9.139 The Children (Leaving Care) Act 2000 amended CA 1989 so as to provide a detailed regime for managing the transition to adulthood of children who have been in public care.

9.140 By CA 1989 Sch 2 para 19A, it is the duty of a local authority looking after a child to 'advise, assist and befriend him with a view to promoting his welfare when they have ceased to look after him'.

9.141 By CA 1989 Sch 2 para 19B, a local authority must assess the needs of 'eligible children' that it is 'looking after' and prepare a 'pathway plan', addressing what advice, assistance and support it would be appropriate to provide the child with under the other CA 1989 functions,[246] while it is still looking after them and after it ceases to look after them. The local authority must keep this pathway plan under review.

9.142 By CA 1989 Sch 2 para 19C, a local authority must provide a 'personal adviser' to each eligible child it is looking after.

9.143 By virtue of CA 1989 Sch 2 para 19A and the Children Leaving Care (England) Regulations 2001[247] reg 3, a child is an 'eligible child' for present purposes if they are aged 16 or 17 and have been 'looked after' by a local authority for periods totalling at least 13 weeks, beginning on a day after the child reached the age of 14 and ending on a day after the child reached the age of 16 years.

9.144 Up until 7 November 2002, a child was 'looked after' by a local authority if it was provided with accommodation by the local authority in the exercise of any social services functions. Accordingly, up

245 [2008] EWCA Civ 1445, [2009] 1 FLR 1325.

246 See para 9.150 onwards.

247 SI No 2874.

until 7 November 2002, a child was a looked-after child whether they were accommodated by a local authority under CA 1989 s17 or s20.[248]

9.145 By virtue of amendments made to CA 1989 s22(1) by the Adoption and Children Act 2002 s116(2), effective on and from 7 November 2002, children are not 'looked-after' children if they are accommodated under, among other things, CA 1989 s17. However, in the light of the House of Lords' decision outlined at para 9.132, this distinction is less significant as most, if not all, unaccompanied asylum-seeker children will have been looked after under CA 1989 s20.

9.146 A 'relevant child' is a child who is not being looked after by any local authority but who was an eligible child before they last ceased to be looked after and is aged 16 or 17.[249]

9.147 The local authority is required to take reasonable steps to keep in touch with a relevant child and to appoint a personal adviser for them, to assess their needs and to prepare a pathway plan for them (and keep it under review), if it has not already done so.[250]

9.148 By CA 1989 s23B(8), the local authority must safeguard and promote the relevant child's welfare and, unless satisfied that their welfare does not require it, support them by maintaining them, or by providing them with suitable accommodation or by providing such other support as may be prescribed (ie under the Children Leaving Care (England) Regulations 2001).

9.149 There is then the 'former relevant child'. There are two types:

(1) a person who has been a relevant child and would be if they were still under 18 years;
(2) a person who was being looked after when they reached 18 and immediately before ceasing to be looked after was an eligible child.[251]

9.150 So far as concerns former relevant children, local authorities must take reasonable steps to keep in touch with them, they must continue the appointment of a personal adviser and they must keep the pathway plan under review.[252] Furthermore, they must give the former relevant child (broadly speaking, until they attain the age of 21 years):

248 CA 1989 s22(1).
249 CA 1989 s23A, subject to exclusions under Children Leaving Care (England) Regulations 2001 SI No 2874 reg 4.
250 CA 1989 s23B.
251 CA 1989 s23C(1).
252 CA 1989 s23C(2) and (3).

- the assistance referred to in s24(B)(1), to the extent that their welfare requires it;
- the assistance referred to in s24(B)(2), to the extent that their welfare and education or training needs require it;
- other assistance, to the extent that their welfare requires it.[253]

9.151 Assistance under CA 1989 s24(B)(1) comprises a contribution towards the cost of living near a place of actual or sought-after employment.

9.152 Assistance under CA 1989 s24(B)(2) comprises a contribution towards the cost of living near a place of education or training, or towards the cost of such education or training.

9.153 The 'other assistance' referred to in CA 1989 s23C(4)(c) is only defined to the extent that CA 1989 s23C(5) provides that it may be assistance in kind or, in exceptional circumstances, cash. This language precisely reflects the language found in CA 1989 s17(6), which has been regarded as broad enough to include any service within reason, including the provision of accommodation.[254]

9.154 Finally, there is the 'person qualifying for advice and assistance'. This person is under 21 years, is not currently being looked after but was looked after, at some point when they were 16 or 17.[255]

9.155 The local authority is under a duty to contact such persons to the extent it considers appropriate, with a view to discharging its functions under CA 1989 ss24A and 24B.

9.156 There are duties and powers to befriend and advise at CA 1989 s24A(1)–(3) and at section 24A(4) there is a power to provide assistance, which may be in kind or, in exceptional circumstances, may be cash or – providing CA 1989 s24B does not apply – accommodation.

9.157 CA 1989 s24B contains a power to provide assistance by contributing to the expense of living near employment, education or training and the associated expenses of education or training (up to the age of 24 years).

9.158 The Department of Health has issued guidance under the Local Social Services Act 1970 s7 called the Children (Leaving Care) Act 2000 Regulations and Guidance, which makes it clear that the provisions of the Children (Leaving Care) Act 2000 apply to unaccompanied asylum-seeking children and that when such

253 CA 1989 s23B(4)–(7).

254 *R (W) v Lambeth LBC* [2002] EWCA Civ 613, (2002) 5 CCLR 203.

255 CA 1989 s24(1).

children reach 18 the Home Office will contribute to the cost of their ongoing care (at their current location) up to a pre-set limit and *will not disperse them*.[256] It would appear that the local authority remains liable for maintaining a personal adviser and pathway plan and continues to have overarching responsibility for the former child's residual welfare needs.

9.159 NIAA 2002 Sch 3 excludes all former looked-after children who have become young adults from these leaving care provisions if they are EEA refugees, EEA nationals, former asylum-seekers who have failed to co-operate with removal directions and certain categories of persons unlawfully present, except to the extent necessary to avoid a breach of the ECHR or EU.[257]

Effects of changes of status

9.160 This section describes the consequences for the provision of services under the community care statutes and the CA 1989 of changes in the status of asylum-seekers. The following changes of status are considered:

- the grant of refugee status or humanitarian protection/discretionary leave to remain;
- the refusal of an asylum application or an appeal;
- the asylum-seeker and others reaching 18 years of age.

The grant of refugee status or humanitarian protection or discretionary leave to remain

9.161 A successful asylum application will conclude with a decision by the Home Secretary or at the conclusion of an appeal to grant the applicant refugee status or humanitarian protection (HP) or discretionary leave (DL) in the UK.[258]

9.162 People who have refugee status or HP/DL will be eligible to apply for assistance under HA 1996 Parts 6 and 7. Home Office support ends 28 days after the grant of asylum or other leave.[259] The

256 See chapter 2, paras 7–11.

257 See para 9.67 but the entitlement to a Pathway Plan is not excluded. See *R (PB) v Haringey LBC and (1) Secretary of State for Health (2) Secretary of State for Communities and Local Government (Interested Parties)* [2006] EWHC 2255 (Admin).

258 See para 1.143.

259 AS Regs 2000 reg 2(2A).

asylum-seeker, upon notification of a grant of refugee status or leave to remain, should at once apply to register on the housing register of the local authority and, upon becoming homeless or threatened with homelessness, apply for assistance under Part 7 as a homeless person.[260] Such people will also be entitled to work and to state benefits. If not working, they should immediately apply for employment support allowance (ESA (formerly income support) or jobseeker's allowance, tax credits and housing benefit and council tax benefit[261]), as appropriate.[262]

9.163 Where the asylum-seeker whose claim is determined is supported with accommodation and subsistence by the local authority under community care legislation (usually NAA 1948 s21 or CA 1989 s17), then – unless the asylum-seeker requires residential care, leaving aside entirely the question of destitution – the social services department is likely to take steps to terminate that support and transfer responsibility to the housing department, its own benefit department and to the relevant social security body.[263] However, there is no requirement to end support within 28 days as is the case with asylum support. The local authority should not terminate support until satisfied that, as the case may be, the applicant's needs are otherwise being met[264] or the child is no longer a child in need.[265] The change of circumstances occasioned by a grant of refugee status or HP/DL should give rise to a formal review of the community care or CA 1989 assessment and revision of the care plan before any changes are made to service provision. Peremptory termination of community care services in such cases could be challenged by judicial review.

9.164 There is commonly a practical problem when a decision is made by the Home Secretary, or on appeal, granting refugee status or HP/DR, because the applicant has not yet received documents proving their new immigration status. The Home Office or the social services department may, in such circumstances, terminate assistance, but on approaching the local housing authority or the Jobcentre Plus, the applicant is told that they will not be assisted until they can produce

260 See para 8.17.
261 See para 8.7.
262 See chapter 3.
263 See chapter 3.
264 NAA 1948 s21.
265 CA 1989 s17.

the standard documentation.[266] The most obvious remedies for the applicant are by way of judicial review, of the failure of the Home Office to issue the necessary status documentation and/or of the local authority social services department for breach of its duties under NAA 1948 s21 or under CA 1989 s17 or ss24, 24A and 24B.

9.165 Unaccompanied asylum-seeker children who are the subject of positive decisions on their applications will not have their support under the CA 1989 terminated in consequence. Those who are 16 years old or over may qualify for income-based JSA or ESA.[267] They will be eligible for housing assistance.[268]

Refusal of an asylum application or an appeal

9.166 An unsuccessful asylum application concludes with a refusal decision by the Home Secretary or a refusal on appeal. Two questions arise:

(1) What will be the effect of such a decision on services already being provided to the applicant?
(2) In what circumstances will such a decision lead to an applicant being entitled to community care services because of the withdrawal of other means of support?

9.167 NIAA 2002 Sch 3 paras 1 and 6 exclude former asylum-seekers from eligibility for services under:

- NAA 1948 ss21 and 29;
- CSDPA 1970 s2;
- HSPHA 1968 s45;
- NHSA 1977 s21 and Sch 8;
- CA 1989 ss17, 23C, 23CA, 24A and 24B;
- LGA 2000 s2;

but only if they have also failed to co-operate with removal directions. If they are also unlawfully present in the UK, as well as being a former asylum-seeker, they will be excluded by NIAA 2002 Sch 3 para 7, irrespective of whether they have failed to co-operate with removal directions.[269] Again, the exclusion is subject to any need to make provision to avoid a breach of ECHR or EU treaty rights, for

266 See para 3.157 for difficulties in processing benefit claims.
267 See paras 3.84–3.85.
268 See para 8.48.
269 *R (AW) v Croydon LBC* [2005] EWHC 2950 (Admin).

example where the person has made a further application for LTR on an ECHR ground, which is not manifestly abusive.[270]

9.168 Former asylum-seekers may be eligible for support under IAA 1999 s4[271] and will remain entitled to aftercare services including accommodation under MHA 1983 s117.[272]

9.169 In the case of unaccompanied asylum-seeker children, negative decisions on their applications will have no effect. The support described above[273] continues after a negative asylum decision, so long as the child remains under 18 and in the UK.

9.170 As far as concerns adults whose households include dependent children, asylum support will continue following an adverse asylum decision unless the youngest child reaches 18, or the dependent child leaves the household or the UK, or unless leave to remain is granted or the family becomes 'certified' as not having taken reasonable steps to leave the UK,[274] in which case the adults but not the children are excluded from support under CA 1989 and the other provisions set out above, except to the extent that provision is required to be made by the ECHR or Eu Law.

The asylum-seeker and others reaching 18 years of age

9.171 Unaccompanied asylum-seekers aged under 18 are excluded from support under the asylum support scheme[275] and are the responsibility of the social services department, which is under a duty to look after them under CA 1989 s20.[276] Where a child has been looked after under s20, the local authority remains under a duty under CA 1989 ss23A–23E and ss24A–24B to provide assistance where appropriate up to the age of 21 and in some cases beyond.[277]

9.172 If an asylum-seeker child (unaccompanied or not), on reaching their 18th birthday, has had their asylum application refused and has exhausted the appeal rights, then they will not be entitled to assistance from the Home Office because they will no longer be an asylum-seeker. They may be entitled to assistance with

270 NIAA 2002 Sch 3 para 3.
271 See chapter 6.
272 See para 9.123.
273 See para 9.131.
274 IAA 1999 s94(5).
275 IAA 1999 s94(1).
276 See para 9.131.
277 See para 9.139.

accommodation under NAA 1948 s21, if they need 'looking after', otherwise then solely because of destitution or the physical effects of destitution.[278] They will be excluded from continuing care under CA 1989 ss23A–23E and ss24A–24B by NIAA 2002 Sch 3 paras 6 and 7, only if they have also failed to co-operate with removal directions or are unlawfully present in the UK. Again, the exclusion is subject to any need to make provision to avoid a breach of ECHR or EU treaty rights, for example if he or she is unable to travel home or has outstanding human rights representations.[279] As a last resort, the scheme at IAA 1999 s4 may be available.[280]

9.173 If an asylum-seeker child (unaccompanied or not), on reaching their 18th birthday, has a pending asylum application or appeal, then they will be eligible for support from the Home Office. In the case of unaccompanied children, the social services department is advised to arrange for a Home Office application to be made two weeks before the child reaches their 18th birthday, and should provide evidence of destitution, including evidence of support provided under the CA 1989.[281] The Home Office and local authorities should then share the responsibility of continuing care for such young adults.[282]

Community care challenges

9.174 In practice, many challenges to a failure by a local authority to carry out an assessment or provide a community care service are likely to be by way of judicial review, on the basis that the local authority has misconstrued its statutory powers or acted irrationally or unfairly. Practitioners in this field will need little reminding of the paramount need to act in a proportionate and non-litigious manner: see, for example, *R (Anufrijeva) v Southwark LBC*[283] and *R (Cowl) v Plymouth CC*.[284]

9.175 If there is a generalised breakdown of local authority provision, then it is possible to ask the Home Secretary to exercise their default

278 See para 9.62.
279 NIAA 2002 Sch 3 para 3.
280 See chapter 6.
281 NASS Policy Bulletin 29.
282 See para 9.158.
283 [2003] EWCA Civ 1406.
284 (2002) 5 CCLR 42.

powers under LASSA 1970 s7D. It is rare for the existence of default powers to constitute an alternative remedy to judicial review and it is believed that the Secretary of State has never exercised such powers in an ordinary community care case.

Complaints: adults

9.176 Otherwise, many decisions can be challenged by way of the complaints procedures, which local authorities are required to set up under LASSA 1970 s7B. The current procedures for NHS and social services complaints are contained in the Local Authority Social Services and NHS Complaints (England) Regulations 2009, made under the Health and Social Care (Community Health and Standards) Act 2003.[285] Complaints ultimately result, if successful, in recommendations being made by the Review Panel. Although not binding, local authorities must have good reason for not complying with such recommendations[286] and are required by regulation 14 to notify the complainant in writing what action they propose to take in the light of the Review Panel's decision. The complaints procedure is well-suited to non-urgent cases where there is a dispute about the detail of service provision, ie whether accommodation is suitable, whether food is suitable, whether enough food or enough suitable clothing has been provided etc. The complainant can attend the Social Services Complaints Review Panel and present their predicament orally to the panel.

Complaints: children

9.177 There is a separate though similar procedure for complaints about how a local authority has discharged its duties under the Children Act.[287]

In either case, the complaints procedure is suitable where the issue relates to questions of fact and degree. It is not likely to constitute an alternative remedy to judicial review where a discrete issue of law arises;[288] however, a dispute can be suited to the

285 SI No 309. See further paras 10.67–10.71.

286 *R v Avon CC ex p M* (1999) 2 CCLR 185.

287 Children Act 1989 Representations Procedure (England) Regulations 2006 SI No 1738.

288 *R v Devon CC ex p Baker* [1995] 1 All ER 72; *R v Sutton LBC ex p Tucker* (1998) 1 CCLR 251.

complaints procedure, despite the existence of legal issues. Those advising claimants must always bear well in mind the very strong desirability of avoiding judicial review litigation wherever possible: *R (Cowl) v Plymouth CC*.[289]

9.178 The Local Government Ombudsman has power to intervene in community care cases, although in this context they will often not be able to act quickly enough. There can, however, sometimes be considerable advantages in involving the Local Government Ombudsman as they have power:

- to recommend that compensation is paid;
- to carry out investigations and ascertain facts that it might be difficult to ascertain in the course of judicial review;
- to review local authority procedures in the round;
- in effect to force local authorities to change procedures and to report back to demonstrate that change has occurred.[290] The Ombudsman can also be brought in if the local authority fails to implement the complaints procedure correctly or promptly.

9.179 In exceptional cases, where there has been a failure by a local authority to discharge community care functions it may be possible to make a claim for damages under ECHR article 3 or 8. Generally, there must be a clear interference with family life or serious damage bordering on inhuman and degrading treatment, which the authority knew or should have known about: *R v Enfield LBC ex p Bernard*[291] and *R (Anufrijeva) v Southwark LBC*.[292]

9.180 Where the Home Office's maladministration in failing to issue accurate immigration status documents meant that a migrant waited a year subject to an incorrect 'no recourse to public funds' condition and a refugee waited nine months after his asylum appeal for a status letter, Keith J found the Home Office owed each of them a duty of care and awarded damages in negligence to compensate them for their lost income support.[293]

289 (2002) 5 CCLR 42.

290 See, eg, Investigation into Complaint No 97/A/2959 against Hackney LBC.

291 [2002] EWHC 2282 (Admin), (2002) 5 CCLR 577.

292 [2003] EWCA Civ 1406, [2004] QB 1124.

293 *R ((1) A and (2) Kanidagli) v Secretary of State for the Home Department* [2004] EWHC 1585 (Admin).

CHAPTER 10

Healthcare

continued

Introduction

10.1 In recent years the government has introduced various statutory and policy measures designed to restrict migrants' access to free National Health Service (NHS) treatment. The resulting difficulties have led to a need for advisers, lawyers, and healthcare professionals to understand the relevant legislative provisions in this area and the ways in which they are implemented. This chapter gives an overview of the law as it affects access and entitlement to NHS treatment. It should be read with other chapters, particularly those dealing with immigration, European and community care law.

10.2 One of the founding principles of the NHS was that treatment would be provided free at the point of access. Subsequent legislation modified this, by providing that charges could be made for treatment provided to those not 'ordinarily resident' in the UK.

10.3 In 1989 regulations were made governing the charging of overseas visitors (defined as those 'not ordinarily resident in the UK'), but only for secondary (ie hospital) treatment.[1] One of many exemptions from charging (often known as the '12-month rule') covered patients who had been in the UK for more than 12 months, regardless of their immigration status. In practice, this generally meant that only short-term visitors (eg tourists and those here on medical visas) were charged for treatment.

10.4 In 2004 the Regulations were amended and the 12-month rule was modified, so that only those who had resided lawfully in the UK for over 12 months were exempt from charges. Guidance was issued to hospitals and this, coupled with prioritisation of the issue by both the Department of Health and the Home Office, meant that hospitals began enforcing the Regulations more rigorously. Access to primary care (eg GP treatment) was also affected in practice, even though the legislation in relation to primary care had not changed.

10.5 Access to primary care has remained untouched by legislation, but a Health Service circular[2] advised GPs that they had the discretion to register overseas visitors or to treat them as private patients. The circular is now obsolete, and at the time of writing it has not been replaced.

10.6 In this chapter we will cover:

1 National Health Service (Charges to Overseas Visitors) Regulations 1989 SI No 306. See appendix A.

2 Health Service Circular 1999/018.

- the structure of the NHS;
- access to primary care;
- entitlement to secondary care;
- post-hospital care;
- remedies.

Key features

- Refugees, people with leave to remain such as discretionary leave or humanitarian protection, asylum-seekers with outstanding claims and appeals and their dependants are entitled to free NHS treatment.
- Nobody is excluded from GP treatment because of their immigration status.
- Some migrants can be charged for hospital treatment, but everyone must be given 'immediately necessary' and 'urgent' hospital treatment regardless of their immigration status and ability to pay.

Structure of the NHS

Legislative framework

10.7 The basic framework for the NHS in England is provided by the National Health Service Act (NHSA) 2006, which consolidated amendments to the (now repealed) NHS Act 1977. Wales and Scotland have their own NHS Acts to reflect the devolution of decision-making in this area to the Scottish and Welsh assemblies. The Scottish legislation as it affects migrants' access to healthcare[3] is essentially identical to the English legislation, but Scottish guidance on the implementation of the legislation differs in some respects.[4] Welsh legislation on this issue[5] was identical to the English legislation until 15 July 2009, when the Welsh Regulations were

3 NHS (Scotland) Act 1978 s98 and NHS (Charges to Overseas Visitors) (Scotland) Regulations 1989 SI No 364.

4 The guidance can be accessed through the Scottish Office website: www.scotland.gov.uk/library/documents-w/guide-02.htm

5 NHS (Wales) Act 2006 s124 and NHS (Charges to Overseas Visitors) (Amendment) (Wales) Regulations 2004 SI No 1433.

amended so as to exempt refused asylum-seekers from charges for hospital treatment.[6]

10.8 The Secretary of State for Health has a duty to provide services to improve the physical and mental health of the people of England, and for the prevention, diagnosis and treatment of illness.[7] For Wales it is the Welsh ministers, rather than the Secretary of State, who are under that duty, and it applies, of course, to the people of Wales.[8] The services should be provided free of charge unless otherwise legislated.[9]

10.9 Although charges can be made for many kinds of services such as dentistry, prescriptions etc, NHSA 2006 s175[10] is the only provision that specifies that particular patients can be charged for treatment that would otherwise be free. Under that section the Secretary of State and the Welsh ministers have the power to make regulations providing for the making and recovery of charges for treatment provided to patients who are not ordinarily resident in the UK. The only regulations that have been made under NHSA 2006 s175 concern amendments to the NHS (Charges to Overseas Visitors) Regulations 1989,[11] which are discussed in more detail below.

Who provides NHS services?

10.10 The task of providing NHS services in England is delegated to primary care trusts (PCTs) and strategic or special health authorities by way of directions.[12] Special health authorities cover the whole of England and are generally concerned with a particular type of illness or treatment (eg the National Blood Authority). Strategic health authorities cover a regional area, and are responsible for, among other things, overseeing the implementation of national NHS policies within the region, developing local health plans and monitoring the performance of local health services. PCTs are responsible for commissioning specific services, such as GP treatment, within defined geographical areas which are often similar to areas of local government (for example Croydon has its own PCT, as does the

6 NHS (Charges to Overseas Visitors) (Amendment) (Wales) Regulations 2009 reg 2(a).

7 NHSA 2006 ss1 and 3.

8 NHS (Wales) Act 2006 s1.

9 Section 1(3) of both the English and Welsh Acts.

10 The equivalent provision in the Welsh Act is section 124.

11 SI No 306.

12 Made under NHSA 2006 s7.

London Borough of Waltham Forest). In Scotland NHS boards are responsible for commissioning services, and in Wales local health boards have that responsibility.

10.11 It can be difficult to know which body is responsible for providing treatment to a particular patient, and guidance has been issued to help identify the responsible commissioner.[13] In England it is generally the PCT in whose area a patient is registered with a GP that will be responsible for funding that patient's treatment, and in Wales it is likely to be the local health board in whose area a patient is registered with a GP.

10.12 The duties of PCTs are set out in secondary legislation in some detail, and include the provision of primary medical services (such as GP treatment) to 'practice patients' in their area (ie people registered with GPs in their area), and to people who are not practice patients of another PCT and who are either usually resident in the PCT's area or simply present in its area.[14] This should ensure that everyone is the responsibility of a PCT, and that patients cannot be the responsibility of two PCTs at the same time. Lists of practice patients have to be maintained by the PCT under the GMS Contracts Regulations.[15]

10.13 Hospital treatment is largely provided by NHS trusts, or NHS foundation trusts, and is commissioned by the PCT. Most treatment is provided under commissioning agreements whereby a hospital is paid to provide, for example, accident and emergency services, but in some areas specialised treatment will be provided by a particular hospital with expertise in that area. Patients will usually be referred for hospital treatment by their GP, unless they present at hospitals as an emergency.

Entitlement to primary care

What is primary care, and who is entitled to receive it?

10.14 Primary care is treatment provided to patients in the community. The most obvious example is GP treatment, but it also includes

13 *Who pays? Establishing the Responsible Commissioner*, Department of Health, September 2007.

14 NHS (Functions of Strategic Health Authorities and Primary Care Trusts and Administration Arrangements) (England) Regulations 2002 reg 3.

15 NHS (General Medical Services Contracts) Regulations 2004 SI No 291 Sch 6 para 14.

community-based nursing, dental treatment, eye tests from an optometrist or ophthalmic optician, and other community-based treatment that is not provided in a hospital. GP services play a crucial role beyond primary care, however. GPs function as a gateway to many NHS services, by referring patients for secondary treatment, and because patients who are registered with them become the responsibility of the local PCT.

10.15 Who is entitled to primary care? The short answer to the question is 'everyone'. This is because NHSA 2006 s175 is the only primary legislation permitting regulations to be made that allow people to be treated differently because of their immigration status or place of residence, and no such regulations have been made that affect entitlement to primary care.

10.16 So nobody is excluded from primary care because of their immigration status, as there is no law providing that anyone is entitled or not entitled to GP treatment. Under the GMS Contracts Regulations, GPs can manage their own practice lists, so they have the discretion to register whomsoever they choose (whether or not they live in the GP's catchment area) and to decide that their lists are open or closed.[16] On accepting an application from a patient the GP must inform the local PCT,[17] which must then update its list accordingly and inform the applicant that it has done so.[18] The PCT does not have the power to veto an application that has been accepted by a GP.

GP powers and duties

10.17 Although there is no law preventing any GP from registering anyone as a patient, irrespective of the patient's status, the GMS Contracts Regulations do restrict the reasons for which a GP can refuse to register a patient. A GP can only refuse an application if they have reasonable grounds for doing so that do not relate to the applicant's race, gender, social class, age, religion, sexual orientation, appearance, disability or medical condition. If a GP refused an application for a discriminatory reason, the patient could bring legal proceedings under the anti-discrimination legislation.[19] The only reasonable grounds specified by the Regulations are that the applicant does not

16 NHS (GMS Contracts) Regs 2004 SI No 91 reg 15(1).
17 NHS (GMS Contracts) Regs 2004 SI No 91 reg 15(5).
18 NHS (GMS Contracts) Regs 2004 SI No 91 reg 15(6).
19 See para 8.155.

live in the GP's practice area. If a GP whose list is open refuses an application they must, within 14 days of the decision, notify the applicant in writing of the refusal and the reason for it. The GP must also keep a written record of refusals of applications and of the reasons for them, and must make this record available to the PCT on request.[20]

10.18 This does not necessarily mean that a GP is obliged to register all applicants as permanent patients of the practice. If, for example, an applicant is temporarily resident away from his normal place of residence, or moving from place to place and not for the time being resident in any place the GP may, if his list of patients is open, accept that person as a temporary resident, so long as he is satisfied that the person intends to stay in the GP's area for more than 24 hours but less than three months. If the GP wishes to remove the patient from his list before the end of the three months, the patient must be notified either orally or in writing.[21]

10.19 GPs are also obliged to provide 'immediately necessary' treatment for up to 14 days to anyone who requests it and who is not registered with another GP in their area, even if the patient has already been refused registration as a permanent or temporary patient.[22] Of course, a GP can propose to register an applicant as a privately paying patient, and applicants are free to agree to this, but it is unlikely to be in their best interests to do so if they can get free treatment.

PCT powers and duties

10.20 If a patient cannot find a GP who is willing to register them, they can approach the local PCT, which has the power to assign such patients to practices whose lists are open,[23] and, in limited circumstances, to practices whose lists are closed.[24] In doing so the PCT must have regard to, amongst other things, the wishes and circumstances of the patient to be assigned and the distance between the patient's place of residence and the practice.[25] Conversely, PCTs have the power to

20 NHS (GMS Contracts) Regs 2004 SI No 91 reg 17.
21 NHS (GMS Contracts) Regs 2004 SI No 91 reg 16.
22 NHS (GMS Contracts) Regs 2004 SI No 91 reg 15.
23 NHS (GMS Contracts) Regs 2004 SI No 91 reg 32.
24 NHS (GMS Contracts) Regs 2004 SI No 91 reg 33.
25 NHS (GMS Contracts) Regs 2004 SI No 91 reg 34.

remove patients from a practice list if they are satisfied that the patient has moved and no longer resides in the area.[26]

10.21 As noted above, the PCT is responsible for people 'usually resident' in its area. The term has no statutory definition, and could either be interpreted to cover everyone who lives in the PCT area for the time being, or in the same way as 'ordinary residence'. However, ordinary residence has been examined by the courts on a number of occasions, and now means far more than simply 'where someone lives for the time being'. The common law definitions of the term pre-date the Regulations concerning PCTs, so it is arguable that if 'usual residence' had the same meaning as 'ordinary residence', the Regulations would have used the latter term rather than the former.

Free prescriptions and other charges

10.22 If a household is in receipt of IAA 1999 s95 asylum support, certain health benefits are passported.[27] The supported person should be provided with an HC2 certificate by UKBA, which allows free prescriptions, fares to and from hospital, dental treatment, sight tests, wigs and fabric supports. Vouchers for the cost of glasses or contact lenses and travel costs to and from hospital may also be available. Where prescriptions have already been paid for, a refund can be claimed within three months on form FP57, available in chemists. The HC2 lasts for six months (or 12 months for patients with HIV/AIDS). An application for a replacement then needs to be made to UKBA.

10.23 Where a migrant is not in receipt of asylum support, they can apply on form HC1 for an exemption from charges, which is simply based on a low income. They will need a postal address and it may take a few weeks for the application to be processed. There is a fast-tracking system for asylum-seekers applying for an HC2. Envelopes with the relevant address or other details may be obtained from the Health Benefits Division help desk or by writing to Prologistics at the Department of Health. The HC1 form is available at chemists, hospitals and surgeries, benefits offices or can be ordered online from the Prescription Pricing Authority,[28] which also arranges for exemptions for mothers who are pregnant or have a child under one year old.

26 NHS (GMS Contracts) Regs 2004 SI No 91 reg 23.
27 AS Regs 2000 Sch.
28 www.ppa.org.uk.

Common problems and practical solutions

Proof of identity and address

10.24 GPs often require applicants to provide specific identity documents and proof of address before they agree to register them as a patient. Many migrants will be unable to fulfil this requirement, for example because their documents are with the Home Office, or because they are staying with friends or are homeless. It is arguable that refusing to register a patient because of their immigration status breaches the GMS Contracts Regulations because it would be for reasons relating to the applicant's race (most refused applicants are likely to be from BME groups) and/or social class. Similarly, refusing to register someone because they cannot provide proof of their address could be discriminatory as it would be for reasons relating to the applicant's status, as a homeless person.[29]

10.25 In theory refusals to register patients can be challenged through the GP's complaints procedure. A complaint can also be made to the PCT. In practice, advocates can often negotiate with practice staff, many of whom are unaware of the content of the relevant regulations set out above. Because applications are usually received by receptionists and processed by practice managers, the GPs are often unaware that staff may be breaching the terms of the GMS Contracts Regulations and, if pressed, will often choose to exercise their discretion to register patients rather than risk further breaches, complaints or legal difficulties.

10.26 Tips for negotiating with receptionists include:

- avoiding mentioning nationality or immigration status;
- asking the name of the person on the phone/desk, as this will be useful when writing a GP registration letter for the service user, and will help to put on some pressure during negotiations;
- focusing on the medical needs of the client: the client needs medical help, what can be done to help them? (ie involve the receptionist in finding a solution);
- acknowledging the difficulty the receptionists face, eg 'I can see that this is a difficult situation for you, but the client is unable to get a proof of address and really needs to register with a GP – is there any way we can work something out?';

29 Following the reasoning of the House of Lords in *R (RJM) v Secretary of State for Work and Pensions* [2008] UKHL 63.

- stressing the positives – if they do have a visa but no proof of address, tell them that they have a visa;
- explaining why it is very difficult for the service user to get a proof of address:
  - for those with stable accommodation: bills integrated into tenancy agreement, only keys for electricity/gas, bills in the name of the other tenants, etc;
  - the service user is homeless: either sleeping rough or staying with friends (some people might be moving from friend to friend or whoever else offers them a place to sleep);
- asking for written reasons for the decision, pointing out that a failure to provide this breaches the GMS Contracts under which the GP operates, and puts the practice at risk of penal measures or legal proceedings;
- trying to speak to the practice manager, the person who has decided the registration procedure, or the GP.

10.27 When trying to persuade a GP to register a patient it may help to refer to the BMA's Ethics Department's guidance on this issue,[30] and to the General Medical Council's guidance on good medical practice.[31] Although not statutory guidance, both documents carry a lot of weight as GPs will be members of the BMA and will be registered with the GMC, and both documents make it clear that the care of the patient, whether they are an overseas visitor or not, should be the paramount consideration.

Counter fraud services

10.28 All PCTs are required to have a counter fraud officer whose task is to investigate and tackle fraudulent practices within its area, such as fake prescriptions or over-charging for services. Over the last couple of years registration of overseas visitors has become part of the counter fraud service's remit, even though accessing NHS treatment as an overseas visitor, or providing treatment to an overseas visitor, cannot be considered to be fraud.

10.29 Counter fraud officers are now responsible, within many PCTs in London, for the PCT policies on registration of overseas visitors, many of which may be unlawful as they fail to make a clear distinction between the rules on entitlement to primary and secondary

30 www.bma.org.uk/images/asylumhealthcare2008_tcm41-175519.pdf

31 www.gmc-uk.org/guidance/good_medical_practice/index.asp

care, and simply refer to entitlement to NHS treatment in general. Such policies may well be unlawfully misleading, and may also breach the PCT's race and other equality duties.

10.30 It has been reported that GPs, after accepting an application and sending the patient's details to the PCT, have subsequently been contacted by counter fraud services and told that the patient is not entitled to NHS treatment and should be taken off the list. As detailed earlier in this chapter the PCT has no statutory power to do this, and would be acting unlawfully if this was done.

Future changes?

10.31 The government has been proposing to change the rules on entitlement to primary care for several years, but none of the proposed changes has been implemented at the time of writing. In 2004, the Department of Health issued a consultation document proposing to exclude many foreign nationals from primary care. Since then the government has repeatedly stated that the matter is being reviewed, and since 2007 the review has reportedly been conducted in conjunction with the Home Office. It is not clear when the results of the review will be published, or whether the proposals will be implemented at all, but it is clear that the majority of respondents to the consultation were opposed to the proposals, and that none of the key stakeholders (including the British Medical Association, the Royal College of General Practitioners and the Royal College of Midwives) was in favour of the proposals.[32] It is also worth noting that, at the time of writing, the Department of Health was conducting an equality impact assessment of the current policy and practice relating to access to healthcare for migrants, while the Home Affairs Committee emphasised its opposition to the proposals:

> *3. The evidence we received during consideration of the Draft (Partial) Immigration and Citizenship Bill cautioned against any future restrictions on access to primary health services for those subject to immigration control. Medical professionals gave persuasive evidence that the risks—to public as well as individual health—outweighed the benefits of any such restriction.*[33]

32 www.medsin.org/ghap/wherestheconsultation.

33 Home Affairs Committee recommendation, para 27, June 2009, www.publications.parliament.uk/pa/cm200809/cmselect/cmhaff/425/42502.htm

Entitlement to secondary care

What is secondary care, and who is entitled to receive it?

10.32 Secondary care is treatment that is provided by or through hospitals, which are usually run by NHS trusts, or NHS foundation trusts. There are no absolute exclusions from entitlement to secondary treatment for people from abroad because some kinds of treatment must be provided regardless of immigration status, but there are detailed provisions that exclude some people from some kinds of free hospital treatment.

10.33 The relevant Regulations made pursuant to NHSA 2006 s175 are the NHS (Charges to Overseas Visitors) Regulations 1989[34] (The Charging Regulations 1989), which provide that people who are not ordinarily resident in the UK must be charged for certain kinds of treatment, unless they benefit from one of the exemptions from charging.[35] The Regulations apply to 'overseas visitors', who are defined as those not 'ordinarily resident' in the UK.[36] NHS trusts tend to employ overseas visitors managers, whose task is to identify overseas visitors, charge them for treatment and recover payments.

10.34 It is interesting to note that both primary and secondary legislation focus exclusively on charging for treatment, and make no mention of any power to withhold or refuse to provide treatment. However, case law has established that NHS trusts can refuse to provide treatment in some circumstances[37] and the Department of Health issued guidance to NHS trusts explaining how to apply the Charging Regulations 1989, and detailing the circumstances in which treatment can be refused.[38]

Ordinary residence

10.35 There is no statutory definition of 'ordinary residence', but there have been a number of cases in which its meaning has been considered. Lord Scarman defined it as 'a man's abode in a particular

34 SI No 306.

35 Charging Regulations 1989 reg 2.

36 Charging Regulations 1989 reg 1(2).

37 *R v Hammersmith Hospitals NHS Trust ex p Reffell* (2001) 4 CCLR 159.

38 Implementing the Overseas Visitors Hospital Charging Regulations, Department of Health, April 2004: www.dh.gov.uk/en/Publicationsandstatistics/Publications/PublicationsPolicyAndGuidance/DH_4080313

place or country which he has adopted voluntarily and for settled purposes as part of the regular order of his life for the time being, whether of short or of long duration', with the important proviso that he must be here lawfully.[39]

10.36 The Court of Appeal recently considered this in the context of entitlement to free secondary treatment for refused asylum-seekers, and decided that in this context a migrant must have leave to remain in the UK in order to be ordinarily resident (or lawfully resident) in the UK.[40]

10.37 Ordinary residence is not, however, defined by nationality, nor is it defined by national insurance contributions or payment of taxes. For example, a British citizen who has worked in the UK for most of his life but then moves abroad permanently will not be ordinarily resident in the UK once he has moved and will not, therefore, be automatically entitled to free NHS treatment should he return for a brief visit. Indeed, it can be easier to understand what ordinary residence means by looking at those do not meet the definition. Tourists are the most obvious example, whilst people who come to the UK to visit relatives, or have multiple entry working visas, would also not be ordinarily resident here.

10.38 How long does a person have to be in the UK before becoming ordinarily resident? There are no clear rules on this point, and in theory a person could be ordinarily resident in the UK on the first day of their arrival if he or she intended to stay here for a long period of time. In practice, however, he or she would have to demonstrate their intention to stay (by registering children in school, bringing all of his or her possessions, and having the other trappings of settling somewhere) before being able to persuade anyone of their ordinary residence in the UK. In this respect, establishing ordinary residence is similar to establishing habitual residence in the social security context.[41]

Exemptions from charging

Exempt categories of treatment

10.39 Regulation 3 of the Charging Regulations 1989 specifies a number of types of treatment for which charges cannot be made. These

39 *Shah v Barnet LBC* [1983] 1 All ER 226.

40 *R (YA) v Secretary of State for Health* [2009] EWCA Civ 225.

41 See *Nessa v Chief Adjudication Officer* [1999] 1 WLR 1937 and para 3.63.

include treatment provided in an accident and emergency or casualty department, any treatment that is not provided at or by a hospital (meaning that charges cannot be made for primary care), family planning services, treatment for a long list of infectious diseases set out in Sch 1 to the Regulations, and treatment provided to those detained under the Mental Health Act 1983. Treatment provided by STD or GUM clinics is also exempt from charging, with the important exception of HIV treatment. People with HIV only get the initial test and counselling for free. Charges can be made for any treatment required thereafter.

10.40 Another important exemption from charging is for a 'continuing course of treatment'.[42] NHS trusts cannot charge a patient for the rest of a course of treatment that has already started on the understanding that it would be provided for free, or if they were covered by an exemption on a date during the course of treatment. This is particularly helpful for asylum-seekers who, for example, may have started HIV treatment while their claim for asylum was under consideration. They must receive the rest of that course of treatment for free even if their asylum claim is refused in the meantime, and their appeal rights have been exhausted. 'Course of treatment' is not defined. It could apply to one particular procedure, or it could be considered to be all treatment for a particular illness.

Exempt categories of patient

10.41 Some kinds of people are exempt from charging, most notably:[43]

- asylum-seekers;
- refugees;
- people with exceptional, humanitarian or discretionary leave to remain;
- people who are lawfully employed or self-employed in the UK;
- people engaged in certain types of voluntary work providing services similar to health and social services, for example caring organisations. Note that asylum-seekers and refused asylum-seekers need permission from the Home Office to work lawfully, and voluntary work is included in this requirement;[44]

42 Charging Regulations 1989 reg 4(2) and (3).

43 Charging Regulations 1989 reg 4(1).

44 See paras 1.50 and 1.105.

- students on a full-time course that lasts longer than six months or is substantially funded by the UK government;
- missionaries;
- sailors;
- diplomats;
- various government employees including soldiers;
- UK pensioners based abroad for part of the year;
- patients who are lawfully taking up permanent residence in the UK, for example those with leave to enter the UK to join relatives here. Some migrants have conditions on their visa prohibiting 'recourse to public funds'. Note that NHS treatment is not listed in the immigration rules as 'public funds', so that would not be a lawful basis on which to refuse treatment;
- patients who have resided lawfully in the UK for a year or more, for example someone who came to the UK on a time-limited visa (eg; as a visitor), decided to stay here permanently and applied to extend the visa or applied for indefinite leave to remain before the visa ran out. As long as no decision has been made on the application, or an appeal is ongoing and was submitted in time, then they will still have leave to enter the UK[45] so they may be considered to be lawfully resident in the UK. Note that the Department of Health's guidance specifies the contrary[46] but this aspect of the guidance is not supported by the legislation. It is also worth noting that lawful residence is not the same as lawful presence,[47] so this does not help (for example, refused asylum-seekers who claimed asylum at port of entry and were granted temporary admission, such as the appellant in *Szoma v Secretary of State for Work and Pensions*;[48]
- victims of trafficking identified as such by UKBA;[49]
- immigration detainees and prisoners;
- family members (ie; spouse, civil partner and children) of a patient who is exempt under any of these categories.[50]

Exempt nationalities

10.42 Some nationalities are exempt from charges. This includes residents of Switzerland or an EEA country, and their family members, who

45 By virtue of Immigration Act 1971 s3C.

46 Para 6.18.

47 See *R (YA) v Secretary of State for Health* [2009] EWCA Civ 225.

48 [2005] UKHL 64.

49 Charging Regulations 1989 reg 4(1)(r).

50 Charging Regulations 1989 reg 4(4).

are 'insured' under their country's equivalent of the UK's national insurance contributions system. Under reg 5, if they are not insured they are entitled to receive all 'necessary' treatment, including 'treatment the need for which arose during the visit',[51] which includes treatment that is required to prevent a pre-existing condition from increasing in severity, and routine monitoring for chronic and existing illnesses. It does not include 'elective' treatment that they have travelled to the UK to receive.

10.43 Stateless people are also entitled to treatment the need for which arose during the visit,[52] as are nationals of states that have contracted to the European Convention on Social and Medical Assistance and who cannot afford to pay for the treatment.[53] Similarly, nationals of states which have signed the European Social Charter and who cannot afford to pay for treatment are exempt from charges for that treatment.[54]

10.44 There are also exemptions from charging for nationals of countries with reciprocal agreements with the UK, which are listed in Sch 1 to the Charging Regulations 1989 as Anguilla, Australia, Barbados, British Virgin Islands, Falkland Islands, Gibraltar, Guernsey and its bailiwick, Iceland, Isle of Man, Israel, Jersey, Montserrat, New Zealand, Russian Federation, St Helena, Sweden, Turks and Caicos Islands and the former Yugoslavia.

Treatment that must be provided irrespective of immigration status

Immediately necessary treatment

10.45 Even if a patient is chargeable and cannot afford to pay for the treatment, some kinds of treatment cannot be withheld. The most obvious example is 'immediately necessary' treatment. There is no statutory definition, but the Department of Health's guidance explains that:

> Trusts need to treat patients in need of immediately necessary care regardless of their ability to pay. This may be because their condition is life-threatening, or because if treatment is not given immediately it

51 Defined at Charging Regulations 1989 reg 1.

52 Defined at Charging Regulations 1989 reg 5(a).

53 See para 2.40, and appendix B.

54 See para 2.40, and appendix B.

> will become life-threatening, or because permanent serious damage will be caused by any delay. It is a matter of clinical judgment which should not be second-guessed by administrative staff .... Where immediately necessary treatment takes place and the Trust knows that payment is unlikely, treatment should be limited to that which is clinically necessary to enable the patient to return to their own country. This should not normally include routine treatment unless it is necessary to prevent a life-threatening situation. Any charge for such treatment will stand, but if it proves to be irrecoverable, then it should be written off.

10.46 There were widespread reports of very restrictive interpretations of the guidance, and of treatment for illnesses such as cancer being refused, so the guidance was challenged by the claimant in *YA*,[55] and was declared unlawful by the Court of Appeal. In relation to the guidance on 'immediately necessary treatment', the Court held that insufficient guidance was given as to the investigations that NHS trusts would need to make into when a patient could return home. At the time of writing, the Department of Health has not redrafted the guidance, but it responded to the judgment by writing to the chief executives of every NHS trust[56] to emphasise that immediately necessary treatment:

> *must never be withheld for any reason*. It should be limited to that which is necessary to enable the patient to return to their own country, *but* trusts should consider the *likelihood of the person returning home* when deciding what limits to place on the treatment.

The Department of Health intends to redraft the guidance in late 2009 once it has consulted with key stakeholders and taking into account NHS feedback on applying the initial advice.

10.47 All maternity treatment is considered by the Department of Health to be immediately necessary.[57]

Urgent treatment

10.48 Urgent treatment is defined by the Department of Health as treatment that is 'not immediately necessary, but cannot wait until the patient returns home'. The guidance advises NHS trusts that patients in need of such treatment:

55 See above.

56 www.dh.gov.uk/en/Publicationsandstatistics/Lettersandcirculars/Dearcolleagueletters/DH_097384

57 Page 42 of the guidance, see above.

> should be booked in for treatment, but the trust should use the intervening period to establish the patient's chargeable status. Wherever possible, if the patient is chargeable, trusts are strongly advised to seek deposits equivalent to the estimated full cost of treatment in advance of providing any treatment.

10.49 Again, there was widespread evidence that NHS trusts were interpreting the guidance very strictly and considering themselves obliged to demand payment in advance. Patients who could not pay were then denied the treatment that they needed, and their conditions worsened. This part of the guidance was therefore also challenged in *YA*, and was declared unlawful. Ward LJ stated:

> The problem here is that the Guidance is silent on what should happen when it is not possible to provide that deposit. No help is given in the case of those who cannot return home before the treatment does become necessary. What is to happen to the patient who cannot wait? In those respects the guidance is not clear and unambiguous and in so far as it purports to be dealing with a category of patients like those before us, the failed asylum seekers who cannot be returned, it is seriously misleading.

10.50 The Department of Health, in its letter to NHS trusts, has subtly redefined 'urgent treatment' as:

> That which clinicians do not consider immediately necessary, but which nevertheless cannot wait until the person can be reasonably expected to return home. This may be for conditions such as cancer. *It will be necessary for an assessment to be made as to when the patient is likely to return home in order for the clinician to establish if the need is therefore urgent.* If a Trust decides that the need for treatment is urgent and it is to go ahead, it should use any intervening period ahead of treatment to secure payment, but if this is not possible, *treatment should not be cancelled or delayed.* In doing this, Trusts should take care not to discourage those in need of urgent treatment from receiving it. Whilst Trusts have a duty to recover charges, this will not be possible in all cases, and they should not go beyond what is reasonable in pursuing them. Trusts have the option to write off debts where it proves impossible to recover them or where it would be futile to begin to pursue them, for instance when the person is known to be without any funds.

Non-urgent treatment

10.51 Non-urgent treatment was defined by the Department of Health as:

> Routine elective treatment which could in fact wait until the patient returns home. The patient's chargeable status should be established

> as soon as possible after first referral to the hospital. Where the patient is chargeable, the trust should not initiate treatment processes, eg by putting the patient on a waiting list, until a deposit equivalent to the estimated full cost of treatment has been obtained.

So the guidance effectively directed trusts to withhold treatment until the patient paid for it in advance. For destitute patients and those on low incomes this equated to a denial of treatment, although there were reports of patients taking out loans to try and pay the fees.

10.52 This aspect of the guidance was also challenged in *YA*, and the Court of Appeal again declared it unlawful because:

> The assumption has to be that the patient can return home before that routine elective treatment becomes necessary. Again, it is not clear what should be done for those who have no prospect of returning within a medically acceptable time. There is no suggestion that it may be necessary to treat in those circumstances or even that it may be necessary to investigate the likelihood and length of any undue delay. Once again the Guidance is not clear enough.

10.53 The Department of Health's response to this was to emphasise to NHS trusts that:

> *Once again, an assessment of how long the patient will likely remain in the UK will be necessary for the clinician to come to this conclusion.* If the patient is unlikely to return for some time, but the need for treatment remains non-urgent, then it should not be initiated until the full estimated amount has been received. If the patient's need for treatment becomes urgent, either because their condition unexpectedly increases in severity, or because their circumstances change and they are no longer able or likely to return home within a medically acceptable time, then they should be provided with the treatment even if payment cannot be secured in the meantime.

Future changes to secondary care?

10.54 At the time of writing, an appeal against the Court of Appeal's decision in *YA* is being contemplated, so the situation may yet change. However, some ambiguities remain in the guidance. The Department of Health concluded the part of its letter to NHS trusts concerning implementation of the Court of Appeal's judgment in *YA* by emphasising that an assessment would have to be made of each patient's ability to return home. This is likely to give rise to disputes in individual cases because NHS trusts may not be familiar with the immigration system, or with relevant common law principles, particularly those established in asylum support cases, which provide some definition of when people cannot reasonably be expected to return home (for example if a fresh claim is pending, or there is a legitimate practical impediment to return). It is also unclear what a 'medically acceptable time' might be, and this may be the subject of disputes between clinicians, overseas visitors managers and patients.

10.55 This matter may also be revisited by the Department of Health when it concludes the equality impact assessment that is being carried out in this area. Organisations representing patients and migrants have made representations about the need to amend the current regulations so as to exempt refused asylum-seekers and HIV treatment from charges, whilst the Joint Committee on Human Rights, in its recent report on the treatment of asylum-seekers, noted the government's failure to produce any evidence to support its assertions that the current restrictions are necessary to combat so-called 'health tourism'. It concluded:[58]

> No evidence has been provided to us to justify the charging policy whether on the grounds of costs saving or of encouraging asylum-seekers to leave the UK. We recommend that free primary and secondary healthcare be provided to all those who have made a claim for asylum or under ECHR whilst they are in the UK, in order to comply with the laws of common humanity and the UK's international human rights obligations, and to protect the health of the nation.

Post-hospital care

10.56 Some types of treatment span both primary and secondary care, and it can be difficult to identify the NHS body responsible for providing the treatment, and the relevant rules on eligibility. For example, a patient who has received hospital treatment as an in-patient may be well enough to leave hospital, but may still require nursing care in the community. A common problem for destitute migrants is the lack of appropriate accommodation to which they can be discharged, and the local authority may have a duty to provide it.[59] Some patients, however, remain too ill for independent or supported accommodation, and require a place in a residential nursing home. Disputes can arise

58 JCHR inquiry into the treatment of asylum-seekers HL 81-I/HC 60-I 10th Report 30 March 2007, para 170: www.publications.parliament.uk/pa/jt/jtrights.htm

59 See chapter 9.

at all stages of this process, and often a collaborative, problem-solving approach will prove successful, but on occasions more robust advocacy may be required.

Delaying discharge from hospital

10.57 The Community Care (Delayed Discharges etc) Act (CC(DD)A) 2003 provides that if hospital staff consider that a patient does not have accommodation to which he can be discharged safely, they can formally notify the relevant local authority's social services of this, thus delaying the patient's discharge from hospital whilst an assessment of the patient's community care needs is carried out and a care plan is put in place. Typically this would arise where an elderly person fell at home, and there were doubts over their ability to continue to live there safely without additional support.

10.58 The notice is commonly known as a section 2 notice, and the task is usually the responsibility of the hospital's discharge co-ordinator. Practice varies from hospital to hospital, and some have homeless patients co-ordinators who can be instrumental in liaising between clinicians and local authorities to achieve consensus and a practical solution. Hospitals can be reluctant formally to notify the local authority because the hospitals are then obliged to keep the patient on the ward when it is no longer clinically necessary to do so. The local authority will, however, be obliged to reimburse the hospital if discharge is delayed because community care services are not in place by the date of discharge.

10.59 It is important to note, however, that the CC(DD)A 2003 only applies to patients who are 'ordinarily resident' in the UK (see above). This requirement does not affect the local authority's duty to assess or provide services, but it does mean that the hospital cannot compel them to assess the patient or reimburse the hospital for any delays. If advocating for a patient in this situation, it is therefore essential to establish contact and communicate effectively with hospital staff in order to negotiate extra time for the patient while steps are taken to ensure that appropriate post-discharge services are put in place.

Residential nursing care

10.60 Some patients will be too ill to be discharged to independent or supported accommodation, and may require a placement in a residential nursing home. This is often known as 'continuing care', and there is a wealth of case law and guidance on who funds such placements. It is a subject that cannot be adequately covered here,[60] and it concerns the point at which a patient's care ceases to be the responsibility of the NHS (ie PCT), and becomes the responsibility of the local authority.

10.61 Disputes usually arise in the context of older people who are liable to pay charges towards local authority-funded placements, but not for NHS-funded placements. People from abroad may also have an interest in who assumes responsibility because local authority care is subject to exclusions on the basis of immigration status,[61] whilst continuing care is considered to be primary care, and is therefore not subject to an immigration test.

10.62 Broadly speaking, the PCT will be responsible for funding placements for patients whose need is primarily medical (assessed by reference to the complexity, intensity and frequency of medical or nursing care the patient requires), whilst the local authority will be responsible for funding placements for patients whose healthcare needs are 'incidental or ancillary' to the provision of accommodation under National Assistance Act 1948 s21.[62] There is a complex assessment process set out in the National Framework for NHS Continuing Healthcare and NHS-funded Nursing Care.[63] It is for the PCT to assess whether the need is primarily medical or not, and the local authority must abide by its assessment.[64]

Nursing care at home

10.63 Even if a patient is well enough to be discharged to independent or supported accommodation, they may still require nursing care at home. This would generally be provided by the district nursing service, which is funded by the PCT and is primary care. The rules on entitlement to primary care, set out above, will therefore apply.

60 For further resources and information see www.dh.gov.uk/en/SocialCare/Deliveringadultsocialcare/Continuingcare/DH_079404 and in particular the National Framework for NHS Continuing Healthcare and NHS-funded Nursing Care

61 Under NIAA 2002 s54 and Sch 3: see chapter 9.

62 *R (Coughlan) v North and East Devon Health Authority* [1999] EWCA Civ 1871, and *R (Grogan) v Bexley NHS Care Trust* [2006] EWHC 44 (Admin).

63 www.dh.gov.uk/en/Publicationsandstatistics/Publications/Publications-PolicyAndGuidance/DH_076288

64 *St Helens BC v Manchester PCT* [2008] EWCA Civ 931.

Mental health services

10.64 Mental health services are also considered to be primary care, and are exempt from charges for treatment. The responsibility for providing them is shared by the PCT and local authority, and is provided by jointly funded teams (eg community mental health team) under the auspices of mental health trusts. Whether it is the PCT or local authority's ultimate responsibility to provide treatment depends on the type of treatment needed. For example if independent or semi-independent accommodation must be provided under MHA 1983 s117 then the local authority will be responsible for providing it; but if more intensive treatment in highly supported accommodation in the community is required, then the PCT will be responsible for funding it. Note that if a migrant has been detained under the Mental Health Act 1983 (other than under section 2), they are entitled to free aftercare.[65]

Remedies

10.65 Some decisions to withhold treatment will have to be challenged urgently because of the risk of the illness worsening or irrevocably deteriorating, so they will have to be challenged by way of an application for judicial review. The most obvious examples of this are refusals of cancer treatment by hospitals, or refusals of home nursing care to a patient who cannot feed himself. Other decisions, however, may be challenged by way of a complaint.

10.66 Although no cases have been successfully brought on this point yet, it may be arguable that a refusal of treatment can give rise to a breach of the patient's ECHR rights.[66] However, given the Court of Appeal's decision in *YA*, it is likely that any such challenge to a refusal of hospital treatment could be brought on the basis that the NHS trust has failed lawfully to apply the revised guidance, assuming the guidance is redrafted properly.

NHS and adult social care complaints procedure

10.67 From 1 April 2009, both NHS bodies and local authority adult social care providers in England have been required to implement

65 See further para 9.123.

66 Most likely art 3, but possibly also articles 2 and 8 and 14.

complaints procedures to ensure that a single procedure is applied across all adult health and social care.[67] All PCTs, NHS trusts, health authorities, care trusts and GPs ('responsible bodies') must comply with this requirement, and must have a designated person responsible for dealing with complaints.[68]

10.68 Anyone affected by the responsible body can make a complaint, and complaints can be made on behalf of an affected person who has died, or an affected child, or an affected person who is incapable of complaining themselves, but in the latter two cases the complaint need not be investigated if the responsible body is satisfied that it is not being made in the best interests of the child or patient.[69] Complainants are, of course, free to conduct their complaints through representatives such as solicitors or advisers, and they can complain either directly to the responsible body or to the local PCT. If the complaint is made to the PCT and concerns another responsible body, the PCT can decide, with the complainant's consent, either to investigate the claim itself or refer it to the responsible body.[70] If information that is relevant to a complaint is held by another responsible body, there is a duty to co-operate by disclosing such information.[71]

10.69 Complaints need not be in writing,[72] but they must be made within 12 months of either the date on which the subject matter occurred, or the date on which the matter came to the attention of the complainant. The time limit can, however, be extended if there was good reason for the delay and it has not affected the responsible body's ability to investigate the matter.[73] On receipt of a complaint the responsible body must acknowledge it, either orally or in writing, within three working days, and must offer to discuss the matter with the complainant at a convenient time, in order to explain the manner in which the complaint will be handled, and the timescale within which a response will be sent.[74]

67 Local Authority Social Services and National Health Service Complaints (England) Regulations 2009 SI No 309 (Complaints Regulations 2009).

68 Complaints Regulations 2009 reg 4.

69 Complaints Regulations 2009 reg 5.

70 Complaints Regulations 2009 reg 7.

71 Complaints Regulations 2009 reg 9.

72 Complaints Regulations 2009 reg 13(1).

73 Complaints Regulations 2009 reg 12.

74 Complaints Regulations 2009 reg 13.

10.70 A response to the complaint must be provided as soon as reasonably practicable, but if it is not provided within six months (a deadline that can be extended by agreement with the complainant) the responsible body must provide a written explanation of the reason for the delay, and confirm when a response will be provided.[75] The responsible body must keep records of all complaints and responses thereto,[76] collate them in an annual report, send copies of the report to the local PCT and/or strategic health authority, and make them available to anyone on request.[77] If the complaint is not adequately resolved at this stage the matter can then be referred to the Parliamentary and Health Service Ombudsman for investigation. It often takes several months for the Ombudsman to investigate complaints, so this would not be an adequate remedy if the problem is time-sensitive.

10.71 In Wales the complaints procedure is different. Complaints must be made within six months rather than 12 months, although the deadline can be similarly extended. Complaints must be acknowledged within two working days of receipt, and a reply should be provided within four weeks. If this is not possible a written explanation for the delay should be provided, along with an explanation of how long it will take to resolve the complaint. If the complaint is not resolved at this stage complainants can request, within 28 days, an independent review. The Welsh Assembly then appoints an independent reviewer and a lay adviser to review the complaint along with, if appropriate, a clinical adviser. The complainant has a further 28 days to provide written evidence and submissions, and the reviewer will then either consider the complaint or set up an independent panel to consider the matter. The process can be lengthy, but the independent review should be completed within six months. If the complaint has still not been resolved the complaint can be referred to the Public Services Ombudsman for Wales.

Confidentiality

10.72 An increasing problem for migrants accessing both primary and secondary care is the tendency of hospital staff (in particular overseas visitors managers) and PCT staff (in particular counter fraud officers) to threaten to report patients to the Home Office if they try to access

75 Complaints Regulations 2009 reg 14.
76 Complaints Regulations 2009 reg 17.
77 Complaints Regulations 2009 reg 18.

treatment. There have been numerous reports of patients becoming so scared by this that they disengage from treatment, so it is important to know the limits on health bodies' ability to disclose information about patients.

10.73 Doctors have a duty of confidentiality towards their patients, which is a fundamental principle of the code to which they subscribe on qualification, and of registration with the General Medical Council. The duty of confidentiality extends to GPs' employees and to NHS employees, as NHS bodies can only disclose information relating to a patient without the patient's consent in extremely limited circumstances where the public interest outweighs the duty of confidentiality. A detailed code of practice on this issue has been issued by the NHS[78] in which no mention is made of disclosure to the Home Office for the purposes of enforcement of immigration law, even though the patient may be in the UK in breach of such law. This is not surprising, as examples are given of circumstances in which the duty of confidentiality can be breached in the interests of preventing crime, and the examples given are of the prevention of serious crimes such as murder, rape etc. Less serious crimes such as theft are considered unlikely to warrant a breach of the duty of confidentiality, as the public interest in preventing such crimes is likely to be outweighed by the public interest in maintaining confidence in the provision of healthcare on a confidential basis.

10.74 In short, it is unlikely that NHS bodies could justify a breach of confidentiality in these circumstances, but if they chose to do this, they would first have to obtain the approval of the body's appointed Caldicott Guardian, who is assigned to protect patient information. This can be an onerous and protracted process, so in practice an insistence on the procedure being followed, with the threat of legal action or a complaint if this is not done, may well ensure that no such disclosure is made.

10.75 In addition to the NHS-specific duty of confidentiality, the Data Protection Act 1998 protects personal information, and authorises both civil and criminal proceedings if the Act is breached. Again, there are a number of exceptions under which information can be disclosed, and they are similar to the ones mentioned in the NHS code of practice on this point, with the most relevant exception being that disclosure is necessary in the interests of preventing crime. On balance, it is unlikely that such disclosure will be considered to be

78 www.dh.gov.uk/en/Publicationsandstatistics/Publications/PublicationsPolicyAndGuidance/DH_4069253

justified given the competing public interest of maintaining the confidentiality of medical treatment.

Debt

10.76 Because so much secondary treatment must be provided irrespective of the patient's immigration status or ability to pay, many patients are left in debt, or are deterred from accessing treatment by the prospect of debt. It is therefore essential that good debt advice is provided so as to reassure patients, as many are under the misconception that they can be imprisoned or deported if they do not pay. Moreover, NHS trusts often pursue these debts very aggressively, and refer the matter to debt collection agencies, even where patients are destitute and there is no prospect of them ever being able to pay for the treatment. Collection tactics can amount to harassment, and both trusts and agencies often ignore the Department of Health guidance that advises them to write off debts that it would be futile to pursue.[79]

10.77 Patients should therefore be referred to a competent debt adviser as early as possible so that they can be given appropriate advice, and assisted either to negotiate with the trust and agree a repayment plan (which can be for as little as £2 per week) or defend any debt recovery action if the decision to charge them was wrong.

79 See above.

APPENDICES

APPENDIX A

Extracts from UK legislation[1]

1 As amended up to date to 11 September 2009. © Crown copyright. Reproduced with the kind permission of the Controller of HMSO and The Queen's Printer for Scotland.

IMMIGRATION AND ASYLUM ACT 1999

(extracts, as amended)

4 Accommodation

(1) The Secretary of State may provide, or arrange for the provision of, facilities for the accommodation of persons–
- (a) temporarily admitted to the United Kingdom under paragraph 21 of Schedule 2 to the 1971 Act;
- (b) released from detention under that paragraph; or
- (c) released on bail from detention under any provision of the Immigration Acts.

The Secretary of State may provide, or arrange for the provision of, facilities for the accommodation of persons–
- (a) temporarily admitted to the United Kingdom under paragraph 21 of Schedule 2 to the 1971 Act;
- (b) released from detention under that paragraph; or
- (c) released on bail from detention under any provision of the Immigration Acts.

(2) The Secretary of State may provide, or arrange for the provision of, facilities for the accommodation of a person if–
- (a) he was (but is no longer) an asylum-seeker, and
- (b) his claim for asylum was rejected.

(3) The Secretary of State may provide, or arrange for the provision of, facilities for the accommodation of a dependant of a person for whom facilities may be provided under subsection (2).

(4) The following expressions have the same meaning in this section as in Part VI of this Act (as defined in section 94)–
- (a) asylum-seeker,
- (b) claim for asylum, and
- (c) dependant.

(5) The Secretary of State may make regulations specifying criteria to be used in determining–
- (a) whether or not to provide accommodation, or arrange for the provision of accommodation, for a person under this section;
- (b) whether or not to continue to provide accommodation, or arrange for the provision of accommodation, for a person under this section.

(6) The regulations may, in particular–
- (a) provide for the continuation of the provision of accommodation for a person to be conditional upon his performance of or participation in community activities in accordance with arrangements made by the Secretary of State;
- (b) provide for the continuation of the provision of accommodation to be subject to other conditions;
- (c) provide for the provision of accommodation (or the continuation of the provision of accommodation) to be a matter for the Secretary of State's discretion to a specified extent or in a specified class of case.

(7) For the purposes of subsection (6)(a)–

(a) 'community activities' means activities that appear to the Secretary of State to be beneficial to the public or a section of the public, and
(b) the Secretary of State may, in particular–
   (i) appoint one person to supervise or manage the performance of or participationin activities by another person;
   (ii) enter into a contract (with a local authority or any other person) for the provision of services by way of making arrangements for community activities in accordance with this section;
   (iii) pay, or arrange for the payment of, allowances to a person performing or participating in community activities in accordance with arrangements under this section.

(8) Regulations by virtue of subsection (6)(a) may, in particular, provide for a condition requiring the performance of or participation in community activities to apply to a person only if the Secretary of State has made arrangements for community activities in an area that includes the place where accommodation is provided for the person.

(9) A local authority or other person may undertake to manage or participate in arrangements for community activities in accordance with this section.

(10) The Secretary of State may make regulations permitting a person who is provided with accommodation under this section to be supplied also with services or facilities of a specified kind.

(11) Regulations under subsection (10)–
(a) may, in particular, permit a person to be supplied with a voucher which may be exchanged for goods or services,
(b) may not permit a person to be supplied with money,
(c) may restrict the extent or value of services or facilities to be provided, and
(d) may confer a discretion.

...

PART VI: SUPPORT FOR ASYLUM-SEEKERS

Interpretation

94 Interpretation of Part VI

(1) In this Part–

'asylum-seeker' means a person who is not under 18 and has made a claim for asylum which has been recorded by the Secretary of State but which has not been determined;

'claim for asylum' means a claim that it would be contrary to the United Kingdom's obligations under the Refugee Convention, or under Article 3 of the Human Rights Convention, for the claimant to be removed from, or required to leave, the United Kingdom;

'the Department' means the Department of Health and Social Services for Northern Ireland;

'dependant', in relation to an asylum-seeker or a supported person, means a person in the United Kingdom who–

(a) is his spouse;
(b) is a child of his, or of his spouse, who is under 18 and dependent on him; or
(c) falls within such additional category, if any, as may be prescribed;

'the Executive' means the Northern Ireland Housing Executive;
'housing accommodation' includes flats, lodging houses and hostels;
'local authority' means–

(a) in England and Wales, a county council, a county borough council, a district council, a London borough council, the Common Council of the City of London or the Council of the Isles of Scilly;
(b) in Scotland, a council constituted under section 2 of the Local Government etc. (Scotland) Act 1994;

'Northern Ireland authority' has the meaning given by section 110(9);
'supported person' means–

(a) an asylum-seeker, or
(b) a dependant of an asylum-seeker,

who has applied for support and for whom support is provided under section 95.

(2) References in this Part to support provided under section 95 include references to support which is provided under arrangements made by the Secretary of State under that section.
(3) For the purposes of this Part, a claim for asylum is determined at the end of such period beginning–
(a) on the day on which the Secretary of State notifies the claimant of his decision on the claim, or
(b) if the claimant has appealed against the Secretary of State decision, on the day on which the appeal is disposed of,
as may be prescribed.
(4) An appeal is disposed of when it is no longer pending for the purposes of the Immigration Acts or the Special Immigration Appeals Commission Act 1997.
(5) If an asylum-seeker's household includes a child who is under 18 and a dependant of his, he is to be treated (for the purposes of this Part) as continuing to be an asylum-seeker while–
(a) the child is under 18; and
(b) he and the child remain in the United Kingdom.
(6) Subsection (5) does not apply if, on or after the determination of his claim for asylum, the asylum-seeker is granted leave to enter or remain in the United Kingdom (whether or not as a result of that claim).
(7) For the purposes of this Part, the Secretary of State may inquire into, and decide, the age of any person.
(8) A notice under subsection (3) must be given in writing.
(9) If such a notice is sent by the Secretary of State by first class post, addressed–
(a) to the asylum-seeker's representative, or
(b) to the asylum-seeker's last known address,
it is to be taken to have been received by the asylum-seeker on the second day after the day on which it was posted.

Provision of support

95 Persons for whom support may be provided

(1) The Secretary of State may provide, or arrange for the provision of, support for–

(a) asylum-seekers, or

(b) dependants of asylum-seekers,

who appear to the Secretary of State to be destitute or to be likely to become destitute within such period as may be prescribed.

(2) In prescribed circumstances, a person who would otherwise fall within subsection (1) is excluded.

(3) For the purposes of this section, a person is destitute if–

(a) he does not have adequate accommodation or any means of obtaining it (whether or not his other essential living needs are met); or

(b) he has adequate accommodation or the means of obtaining it, but cannot meet his other essential living needs.

(4) If a person has dependants, subsection (3) is to be read as if the references to him were references to him and his dependants taken together.

(5) In determining, for the purposes of this section, whether a person's accommodation is adequate, the Secretary of State–

(a) must have regard to such matters as may be prescribed for the purposes of this paragraph; but

(b) may not have regard to such matters as may be prescribed for the purposes of this paragraph or to any of the matters mentioned in subsection (6).

(6) Those matters are–

(a) the fact that the person concerned has no enforceable right to occupy the accommodation;

(b) the fact that he shares the accommodation, or any part of the accommodation, with one or more other persons;

(c) the fact that the accommodation is temporary;

(d) the location of the accommodation.

(7) In determining, for the purposes of this section, whether a person's other essential living needs are met, the Secretary of State–

(a) must have regard to such matters as may be prescribed for the purposes of this paragraph; but

(b) may not have regard to such matters as may be prescribed for the purposes of this paragraph.

(8) The Secretary of State may by regulations provide that items or expenses of such a description as may be prescribed are, or are not, to be treated as being an essential living need of a person for the purposes of this Part.

(9) Support may be provided subject to conditions.

(9A) A condition imposed under subsection (9) may, in particular, relate to–

(a) any matter relating to the use of the support provided, or

(b) compliance with a restriction imposed under paragraph 21 of Schedule 2 to the 1971 Act (temporary admission or release from detention) or paragraph 2 or 5 of Schedule 3 to that Act (restriction pending deportation).

(10) The conditions must be set out in writing.

(11) A copy of the conditions must be given to the supported person.

(12) Schedule 8 gives the Secretary of State power to make regulations supplementing this section.

(13) Schedule 9 makes temporary provision for support in the period before the coming into force of this section.

96 Ways in which support may be provided

(1) Support may be provided under section 95–

(a) by providing accommodation appearing to the Secretary of State to be adequate for the needs of the supported person and his dependants (if any);

(b) by providing what appear to the Secretary of State to be essential living needs of the supported person and his dependants (if any);

(c) to enable the supported person (if he is the asylum-seeker) to meet what appear to the Secretary of State to be expenses (other than legal expenses or other expenses of a prescribed description) incurred in connection with his claim for asylum;

(d) to enable the asylum-seeker and his dependants to attend bail proceedings in connection with his detention under any provision of the Immigration Acts; or

(e) to enable the asylum-seeker and his dependants to attend bail proceedings in connection with the detention of a dependant of his under any such provision.

(2) If the Secretary of State considers that the circumstances of a particular case are exceptional, he may provide support under section 95 in such other ways as he considers necessary to enable the supported person and his dependants (if any) to be supported.

(3)–(6) [Repealed.]

97 Supplemental

(1) When exercising his power under section 95 to provide accommodation, the Secretary of State must have regard to–

(a) the fact that the accommodation is to be temporary pending determination of the asylum-seeker's claim;

(b) the desirability, in general, of providing accommodation in areas in which there is a ready supply of accommodation; and

(c) such other matters (if any) as may be prescribed.

(2) But he may not have regard to–

(a) any preference that the supported person or his dependants (if any) may have as to the locality in which the accommodation is to be provided; or

(b) such other matters (if any) as may be prescribed.

(3) The Secretary of State may by order repeal all or any of the following–

(a) subsection (1)(a);

(b) subsection (1)(b);

(c) subsection (2)(a).

(4) When exercising his power under section 95 to provide essential living needs, the Secretary of State–

(a) must have regard to such matters as may be prescribed for the purposes of this paragraph; but
(b) may not have regard to such other matters as may be prescribed for the purposes of this paragraph.

(5) In addition, when exercising his power under section 95 to provide essential living needs, the Secretary of State may limit the overall amount of the expenditure which he incurs in connection with a particular supported person–
(a) to such portion of the income support applicable amount provided under section 124 of the Social Security Contributions and Benefits Act 1992, or
(b) to such portion of any components of that amount, as he considers appropriate having regard to the temporary nature of the support that he is providing.

(6) For the purposes of subsection (5), any support of a kind falling within section 96(1)(c) is to be treated as if it were the provision of essential living needs.

(7) In determining how to provide, or arrange for the provision of, support under section 95, the Secretary of State may disregard any preference which the supported person or his dependants (if any) may have as to the way in which the support is to be given.

98 Temporary support

(1) The Secretary of State may provide, or arrange for the provision of, support for–
(a) asylum-seekers, or
(b) dependants of asylum-seekers,
who it appears to the Secretary of State may be destitute.

(2) Support may be provided under this section only until the Secretary of State is able to determine whether support may be provided under section 95.

(3) Subsections (2) to (11) of section 95 apply for the purposes of this section as they apply for the purposes of that section.

Support and assistance by local authorities etc

99 Provision of support by local authorities

(1) A local authority or Northern Ireland authority may provide support for persons in accordance with arrangements made by the Secretary of State under section 4, 95 or 98.

(2) Support may be provided by an authority in accordance with arrangements made with the authority or with another person.

(3) Support may be provided by an authority in accordance with arrangements made under section 95 only in one or more of the ways mentioned in section 96(1) and (2).

(4) An authority may incur reasonable expenditure in connection with the preparation of proposals for entering into arrangements under section 4, 95 or 98.

(5) The powers conferred on an authority by this section include power to–
(a) provide services outside their area;

(b) provide services jointly with one or more other bodies;
(c) form a company for the purpose of providing services;
(d) tender for contracts (whether alone or with any other person).

100 Local authority and other assistance for Secretary of State

(1) This section applies if the Secretary of State asks–
(a) a local authority,
(b) a registered social landlord,
(c) a registered housing association in Scotland or Northern Ireland, or
(d) the Executive,
to assist him to exercise his power under section 95 to provide accommodation.

(2) The person to whom the request is made must co-operate in giving the Secretary of State such assistance in the exercise of that power as is reasonable in the circumstances.

(3) Subsection (2) does not require a registered social landlord to act beyond its powers.

(4) A local authority must supply to the Secretary of State such information about their housing accommodation (whether or not occupied) as he may from time to time request.

(5) The information must be provided in such form and manner as the Secretary of State may direct.

(6) 'Registered social landlord' has the same meaning as in Part I of the Housing Act 1996.

(7) 'Registered housing association' has the same meaning–
(a) in relation to Scotland, as in the Housing Associations Act 1985; and
(b) in relation to Northern Ireland, as in Part II of the Housing (Northern Ireland) Order 1992.

101 [Not reproduced here.]

Appeals

102 [Repealed.]

103 Appeals

(1) If, on an application for support under section 95, the Secretary of State decides that the applicant does not qualify for support under that section, the applicant may appeal to the First-tier Tribunal.

(2) If the Secretary of State decides to stop providing support for a person under section 95 before that support would otherwise have come to an end, that person may appeal to the First-tier Tribunal.

(2A) If the Secretary of State decides not to provide accommodation for a person under section 4, or not to continue to provide accommodation for a person under section 4, the person may appeal to the First-tier Tribunal.

(3) On an appeal under this section, the First-tier Tribunal may–
(a) require the Secretary of State to reconsider the matter;
(b) substitute its decision for the decision appealed against; or
(c) dismiss the appeal.

(4) [Repealed.]

(5) The decision of the First-tier Tribunal is final.

(6) If an appeal is dismissed, no further application by the appellant for support under section 4 or 95 is to be entertained unless the Secretary of State is satisfied that there has been a material change in the circumstances.

(7) The Secretary of State may by regulations provide for decisions as to where support provided under section 4 or 95 is to be provided to be appealable to the First-tier Tribunal under this Part.

(8) Regulations under subsection (7) may provide for any provision of this section to have effect, in relation to an appeal brought by virtue of the regulations, subject to such modifications as may be prescribed.

(9) The Secretary of State may pay any reasonable travelling expenses incurred by an appellant in connection with attendance at any place for the purposes of an appeal under this section.

104 [Repealed.]

Offences

105 False representations

(1) A person is guilty of an offence if, with a view to obtaining support for himself or any other person under any provision made by or under this Part, he–

(a) makes a statement or representation which he knows is false in a material particular,

(b) produces or gives to a person exercising functions under this Part, or knowingly causes or allows to be produced or given to such a person, any document or information which he knows is false in a material particular;

(c) fails, without reasonable excuse, to notify a change of circumstances when required to do so in accordance with any provision made by or under this Part; or

(d) without reasonable excuse, knowingly causes another person to fail to notify a change of circumstances which that other person was required to notify in accordance with any provision made by or under this Part.

(2) A person guilty of an offence under this section is liable on summary conviction to imprisonment for a term not exceeding three months or to a fine not exceeding level 5 on the standard scale, or to both.

106 Dishonest representations.

(1) A person is guilty of an offence if, with a view to obtaining any benefit or other payment or advantage under this Part for himself or any other person, he dishonestly–

(a) makes a statement or representation which is false in a material particular;

(b) produces or gives to a person exercising functions under this Part, or causes or allows to be produced or given to such a person, any document or information which is false in a material particular;

(c) fails to notify a change of circumstances when required to do so in accordance with any provision made by or under this Part; or

(d) causes another person to fail to notify a change of circumstances which that other person was required to notify in accordance with any provision made by or under this Part.

(2) A person guilty of an offence under this section is liable–

(a) on summary conviction, to imprisonment for a term not exceeding six months or to a fine not exceeding the statutory maximum, or to both; or

(b) on conviction on indictment, to imprisonment for a term not exceeding seven years or to a fine, or to both.

(3) In the application of this section to Scotland, in subsection (1) for 'dishonestly' substitute 'knowingly'.

107 Delay or obstruction

(1) A person is guilty of an offence if, without reasonable excuse, he–

(a) intentionally delays or obstructs a person exercising functions conferred by or under this Part; or

(b) refuses or neglects to answer a question, give any information or produce a document when required to do so in accordance with any provision made by or under this Part.

(2) A person guilty of an offence under subsection (1) is liable on summary conviction to a fine not exceeding level 3 on the standard scale.

108 Failure of sponsor to maintain

(1) A person is guilty of an offence if, during any period in respect of which he has given a written undertaking in pursuance of the immigration rules to be responsible for the maintenance and accommodation of another person–

(a) he persistently refuses or neglects, without reasonable excuse, to maintain that person in accordance with the undertaking; and

(b) in consequence of his refusal or neglect, support under any provision made by or under this Part is provided for or in respect of that person.

(2) A person guilty of an offence under this section is liable on summary conviction to imprisonment for a term not exceeding 3 months or to a fine not exceeding level 4 on the standard scale, or to both.

(3) For the purposes of this section, a person is not to be taken to have refused or neglected to maintain another person by reason only of anything done or omitted in furtherance of a trade dispute.

109 Supplemental

(1) If an offence under section 105, 106, 107 or 108 committed by a body corporate is proved–

(a) to have been committed with the consent or connivance of an officer, or

(b) to be attributable to neglect on his part,

the officer as well as the body corporate is guilty of the offence and liable to be proceeded against and punished accordingly.

(2) 'Officer', in relation to a body corporate, means a director, manager, secretary or other similar officer of the body, or a person purporting to act in such a capacity.

(3) If the affairs of a body corporate are managed by its members, subsection (1) applies in relation to the acts and defaults of a member in connection with his functions of management as if he were a director of the body corporate.

(4) If an offence under section 105, 106, 107 or 108 committed by a partnership in Scotland is proved–

(a) to have been committed with the consent or connivance of a partner, or

(b) to be attributable to neglect on his part,

the partner as well as the partnership is guilty of the offence and liable to be proceeded against and punished accordingly.

(5) 'Partner'includes a person purporting to act as a partner.

109A Arrest

An immigration officer may arrest without warrant a person whom the immigration officer reasonably suspects has committed an offence under section 105 or 106.

109B Entry, search and seizure

(1) An offence under section 105 or 106 shall be treated as–

(a) a relevant offence for the purposes of sections 28B and 28D of the Immigration Act 1971, and

(b) an offence under Part 3 of that Act (criminal proceedings) for the purposes of sections 28(4), 28E, 28G and 28H (search after arrest, etc) of that Act.

(2) The following provisions of the Immigration Act 1971 shall have effect in connection with an offence under section 105 or 106 of this Act as they have effect in connection with an offence under that Act–

(a) section 28I (seized material: access and copying),

(b) section 28J (search warrants: safeguards),

(c) section 28K (execution of warrants), and

(d) section 28L(1) (interpretation).

Expenditure

110 Payments to local authorities

[Not reproduced here.]

111 Grants to voluntary organisations

[Not reproduced here.]

112 Recovery of expenditure on support: misrepresentation etc

(1) This section applies if, on an application made by the Secretary of State, the court determines that–

(a) a person ('A') has misrepresented or failed to disclose a material fact (whether fraudulently or otherwise); and
(b) as a consequence of the misrepresentation or failure, support has been provided under section 95 or 98 (whether or not to A).

(2) If the support was provided by the Secretary of State, the court may order A to pay to the Secretary of State an amount representing the monetary value of the support which would not have been provided but for A's misrepresentation or failure.

(3) If the support was provided by another person ('B') in accordance with arrangements made with the Secretary of State under section 95 or 98, the court may order A to pay to the Secretary of State an amount representing the payment to B which would not have been made but for A's misrepresentation or failure.

(4) 'Court' means a county court or, in Scotland, the sheriff.

113 Recovery of expenditure on support from sponsor

[Not reproduced here.]

114 Overpayments

(1) Subsection (2) applies if, as a result of an error on the part of the Secretary of State, support has been provided to a person under section 95 or 98.

(2) The Secretary of State may recover from a person who is, or has been, a supported person an amount representing the monetary value of support provided to him as a result of the error.

(3) An amount recoverable under subsection (2) may be recovered as if it were a debt due to the Secretary of State.

(4) The Secretary of State may by regulations make provision for other methods of recovery, including deductions from support provided under section 95.

Exclusions

115 Exclusion from benefits

(1) No person is entitled to income-based jobseeker's allowance under the Jobseekers Act 1995 or to state pension credit under the State Pension Credit Act 2002 or to income-related allowance under Part 1 of the Welfare Reform Act 2007 (employment and support allowance) or to–

(a) attendance allowance,
(b) severe disablement allowance,
(c) carer's allowance,
(d) disability living allowance,
(e) income support,
(f)–(g) [Repealed.]
(h) a social fund payment,
(i) child benefit,
(j) housing benefit, or
(k) council tax benefit,

under the Social Security Contributions and Benefits Act 1992 while he is a person to whom this section applies.

(2) No person in Northern Ireland is entitled to–
(a) income-based jobseeker's allowance under the Jobseekers (Northern Ireland) Order 1995, or
(b) any of the benefits mentioned in paragraphs (a) to (j) of subsection (1),

under the Social Security Contributions and Benefits (Northern Ireland) Act 1992 while he is a person to whom this section applies.

(3) This section applies to a person subject to immigration control unless he falls within such category or description, or satisfies such conditions, as may be prescribed.

(4) Regulations under subsection (3) may provide for a person to be treated for prescribed purposes only as not being a person to whom this section applies.

(5) In relation to child benefit, 'prescribed' means prescribed by regulations made by the Treasury.

(6) In relation to the matters mentioned in subsection (2) (except so far as it relates to child benefit), 'prescribed' means prescribed by regulations made by the Department.

(7) Section 175(3) to (5) of the Social Security Contributions and Benefits Act 1992 (supplemental powers in relation to regulations) applies to regulations made by the Secretary of State of the Treasury under subsection (3) as it applies to regulations made under that Act.

(8) Sections 133(2), 171(2) and 172(4) of the Social Security Contributions and Benefits (Northern Ireland) Act 1992 apply to regulations made by the Department under subsection (3) as they apply to regulations made by the Department under that Act.

(9) 'A person subject to immigration control' means a person who is not a national of an EEA State and who–
(a) requires leave to enter or remain in the United Kingdom but does not have it;
(b) has leave to enter or remain in the United Kingdom which is subject to a condition that he does not have recourse to public funds;
(c) has leave to enter or remain in the United Kingdom given as a result of a maintenance undertaking; or
(d) has leave to enter or remain in the United Kingdom only as a result of paragraph 17 of Schedule 4.

(10) 'Maintenance undertaking', in relation to any person, means a written undertaking given by another person in pursuance of the immigration rules to be responsible for that person's maintenance and accommodation.

116 Amendment of section 21 of the National Assistance Act 1948

In section 21 of the National Assistance Act 1948 (duty of local authorities to provide accommodation), after subsection (1), insert–

'(1A) A person to whom section 115 of the Immigration and Asylum Act 1999 (exclusion from benefits) applies may not be provided with residential accommodation under subsection (1)(a) if his need for care and attention has arisen solely–
(a) because he is destitute; or
(b) because of the physical effects, or anticipated physical effects, of his being destitute.

(1B) Subsections (3) and (5) to (8) of section 95 of the Immigration and Asylum Act 1999, and paragraph 2 of Schedule 8 to that Act, apply for the purposes of subsection (1A) as they apply for the purposes of that section, but for the references in subsections (5) and (7) of that section and in that paragraph to the Secretary of State substitute references to a local authority.'

117 Other restrictions on assistance: England and Wales

(1) In section 45 of the Health Services and Public Health Act 1968 (promotion by local authorities of the welfare of old people), after subsection (4), insert–

'(4A) No arrangements under this section may be given effect to in relation to a person to whom section 115 of the Immigration and Asylum Act 1999 (exclusion from benefits) applies solely–

(a) because he is destitute; or

(b) because of the physical effects, or anticipated physical effects, of his being destitute.

(4B) Subsections (3) and (5) to (8) of section 95 of the Immigration and Asylum Act 1999, and paragraph 2 of Schedule 8 to that Act, apply for the purposes of subsection (4A) as they apply for the purposes of that section, but for the references in subsections (5) and (7) of that section and in that paragraph to the Secretary of State substitute references to a local authority.'

(2)–(4) [Repealed.]

(5) In the 1996 Act, omit section 186 (asylum-seekers and their dependants).

(6) In section 187(1) of the 1996 Act (provision of information by Secretary of State), in paragraph (a), for 'or has become an asylum-seeker, or a dependant of an asylum-seeker' substitute 'a person to whom section 115 of the Immigration and Asylum Act 1999 (exclusion from benefits) applies'.

118 Housing authority accommodation

(1) Each housing authority must secure that, so far as practicable, a tenancy of, or licence to occupy, housing accommodation provided under the accommodation provisions is not granted to a person subject to immigration control unless–

(a) he is of a class specified in an order made by the Secretary of State; or

(b) the tenancy of, or license to occupy, such accommodation is granted in accordance with arrangements made under section 4, 95 or 98.

(2) 'Housing authority' means –

(a) in relation to England and Wales, a local housing authority within the meaning of the Housing Act 1985;

(b) in relation to Scotland, a local authority within the meaning of the Housing (Scotland) Act 1987; and

(c) in relation to Northern Ireland, the Executive.

(3) 'Accommodation provisions' means –

(a) in relation to England and Wales, Part II of the Housing Act 1985;

(b) in relation to Scotland, Part I of the Housing (Scotland) Act 1987;

(c) in relation to Northern Ireland, Part II of the Housing (Northern Ireland) Order 1981.

(4) 'Licence to occupy', in relation to Scotland, means a permission or right to occupy.

(5) 'Tenancy', in relation to England and Wales, has the same meaning as in the Housing Act 1985.
(6) 'Person subject to immigration control' means a person who under the 1971 Act requires leave to enter or remain in the United Kingdom (whether or not such leave has been given).
(7) This section does not apply in relation to any allocation of housing to which Part VI of the Housing Act 1996 (allocation of housing accommodation) applies.

119 Homelessness: Scotland and Northern Ireland
[Not reproduced here.]

120 Other restrictions on assistance: Scotland
[Not reproduced here.]

121 Other restrictions on assistance: Northern Ireland
[Not reproduced here.]

122 Support for children
(1) In this section 'eligible person' means a person who appears to the Secretary of State to be a person for whom support may be provided under section 95.
(2) Subsections (3) and (4) apply if an application for support under section 95 has been made by an eligible person whose household includes a dependant under the age of 18 ('the child').
(3) If it appears to the Secretary of State that adequate accommodation is not being provided for the child, he must exercise his powers under section 95 by offering, and if his offer is accepted by providing or arranging for the provision of, adequate accommodation for the child as part of the eligible person's household.
(4) If it appears to the Secretary of State that essential living needs of the child are not being met, he must exercise his powers under section 95 by offering, and if his offer is accepted by providing or arranging for the provision of, essential living needs for the child as part of the eligible person's household.
(5) No local authority may provide assistance under any of the child welfare provisions in respect of a dependant under the age of 18, or any member of his family, at any time when–
(a) the Secretary of State is complying with this section in relation to him; or
(b) there are reasonable grounds for believing that–
(i) the person concerned is a person for whom support may be provided under section 95; and
(ii) the Secretary of State would be required to comply with this section if that person had made an application under section 95.
(6) 'Assistance' means the provision of accommodation or of any essential living needs.
(7) 'The child welfare provisions' means –

(a) section 17 of the Children Act 1989 (local authority support for children and their families);
(b) section 22 of the Children (Scotland) Act 1995 (equivalent provision for Scotland); and
(c) Article 18 of the Children (Northern Ireland) Order 1995 (equivalent provision for Northern Ireland).

(8) Subsection (9) applies if accommodation provided in the discharge of the duty imposed by subsection (3) has been withdrawn.
(9) Only the relevant authority may provide assistance under any of the child welfare provisions in respect of the child concerned.
(10) 'Relevant authority' means –
(a) in relation to Northern Ireland, the authority within whose area the withdrawn accommodation was provided;
(b) in any other case, the local authority within whose area the withdrawn accommodation was provided.

(11) In such circumstances as may be prescribed, subsection (5) does not apply.

123 [Repealed.]

Miscellaneous

124 Secretary of State to be corporation sole for purposes of Part VI

(1) For the purpose of exercising his functions under this Part, the Secretary of State is a corporation sole.
(2) Any instrument in connection with the acquisition, management or disposal of property, real or personal, heritable or moveable, by the Secretary of State under this Part may be executed on his behalf by a person authorised by him for that purpose.
(3) Any instrument purporting to have been so executed on behalf of the Secretary of State is to be treated, until the contrary is proved, to have been so executed on his behalf.

125 Entry of premises

(1) This section applies in relation to premises in which accommodation has been provided under section 95 or 98 for a supported person.
(2) If, on an application made by a person authorised in writing by the Secretary of State, a justice of the peace is satisfied that there is reason to believe that–
(a) the supported person or any dependants of his for whom the accommodation is provided is not resident in it,
(b) the accommodation is being used for any purpose other than the accommodation of the asylum-seeker or any dependant of his, or
(c) any person other than the supported person and his dependants (if any) is residing in the accommodation,

he may grant a warrant to enter the premises to the person making the application.

(3) A warrant granted under subsection (2) may be executed–
(a) at any reasonable time;
(b) using reasonable force.

(4) In the application of subsection (2) to Scotland, read the reference to a justice of the peace as a reference to the sheriff or a justice of the peace.

126 Information from property owners

(1) The power conferred by this section is to be exercised with a view to obtaining information about premises in which accommodation is or has been provided for supported persons.

(2) The Secretary of State may require any person appearing to him–
(a) to have any interest in, or
(b) to be involved in any way in the management or control of,
such premises, or any building which includes such premises, to provide him with such information with respect to the premises and the persons occupying them as he may specify.

(3) A person who is required to provide information under this section must do so in accordance with such requirements as may be prescribed.

(4) Information provided to the Secretary of State under this section may be used by him only in the exercise of his functions under this Part.

127 Requirement to supply information about redirection of post

(1) The Secretary of State may require any person conveying postal packets to supply redirection information to the Secretary of State–
(a) for use in the prevention, detection, investigation or prosecution of criminal offences under this Part;
(b) for use in checking the accuracy of information relating to support provided under this Part; or
(c) for any other purpose relating to the provision of support to asylum-seekers.

(2) The information must be supplied in such manner and form, and in accordance with such requirements, as may be prescribed.

(3) The Secretary of State must make payments of such amount as he considers reasonable in respect of the supply of information under this section.

(4) 'Postal packet' has the same meaning as in the Postal Services Act 2000.

(5) 'Redirection information' means information relating to arrangements made with any person conveying postal packets for the delivery of postal packets to addresses other than those indicated by senders on the packets.

NATIONALITY, IMMIGRATION AND ASYLUM ACT 2002

(extracts, as amended)

54 **Withholding and withdrawal of support**

Schedule 3 (which makes provision for support to be withheld or withdrawn in certain circumstances) shall have effect.

SCHEDULE 3: WITHHOLDING AND WITHDRAWAL OF SUPPORT

Section 54

1 **Ineligibility for support**

(1) A person to whom this paragraph applies shall not be eligible for support or assistance under–

(a) section 21 or 29 of the National Assistance Act 1948 (local authority: accommodation and welfare),

(b) section 45 of the Health Services and Public Health Act 1968 (local authority: welfare of elderly),

(c) section 12 or 13A of the Social Work (Scotland) Act 1968 (social welfare services),

(d) Article 7 or 15 of the Health and Personal Social Services (Northern Ireland) Order 1972 (SI 1972/1265 (NI 14)) (prevention of illness, social welfare, etc),

(e) section 254 of, and Schedule 20 to, the National Health Service Act 2006, or section 192 of, and Schedule 15 to, the National Health Service (Wales) Act 2006 (social services),

(f) section 29(1)(b) of the Housing (Scotland) Act 1987 (interim duty to accommodate in case of apparent priority need where review of a local authority decision has been requested),

(g) section 17, 23C, 24A or 24B of the Children Act 1989 (welfare and other powers which can be exercised in relation to adults),

(h) Article 18, 35 or 36 of the Children (Northern Ireland) Order 1995 (SI 1995/755 (NI 2)) (welfare and other powers which can be exercised in relation to adults),

(i) sections 22, 29 and 30 of the Children (Scotland) Act 1995 (provisions analogous to those mentioned in paragraph (g)),

(j) section 188(3) or 204(4) of the Housing Act 1996 (accommodation pending review or appeal),

(k) section 2 of the Local Government Act 2000 (promotion of well-being),

(l) a provision of the Immigration and Asylum Act 1999, or

(m) a provision of this Act.

(2) A power or duty under a provision referred to in sub-paragraph (1) may not be exercised or performed in respect of a person to whom this paragraph applies (whether or not the person has previously been in receipt of support or assistance under the provision).

(3) An approval or directions given under or in relation to a provision referred to in sub-paragraph (1) shall be taken to be subject to sub-paragraph (2).

2 Exceptions

(1) Paragraph 1 does not prevent the provision of support or assistance–
 (a) to a British citizen, or
 (b) to a child, or
 (c) under or by virtue of regulations made under paragraph 8, 9 or 10 below, or
 (d) in a case in respect of which, and to the extent to which, regulations made by the Secretary of State disapply paragraph 1, or
 (e) in circumstances in respect of which, and to the extent to which, regulations made by the Secretary of State disapply paragraph 1.

(2) Regulations under sub-paragraph (1)(d) may confer a discretion on the Secretary of State.

(3) Regulations under sub-paragraph (1)(e) may, in particular, disapply paragraph 1 to the provision of support or assistance by a local authority to a person where the authority–
 (a) has taken steps in accordance with guidance issued by the Secretary of State to determine whether paragraph 1 would (but for the regulations) apply to the person, and
 (b) has concluded on the basis of those steps that there is no reason to believe that paragraph 1 would apply.

(4) Regulations under sub-paragraph (1)(d) or (e) may confer a discretion on an authority.

(5) A local authority which is considering whether to give support or assistance to a person under a provision listed in paragraph 1(1) shall act in accordance with any relevant guidance issued by the Secretary of State under sub-paragraph (3)(a).

(6) A reference in this Schedule to a person to whom paragraph 1 applies includes a reference to a person in respect of whom that paragraph is disapplied to a limited extent by regulations under sub-paragraph (1)(d) or (e), except in a case for which the regulations provide otherwise.

3 Paragraph 1 does not prevent the exercise of a power or the performance of a duty if, and to the extent that, its exercise or performance is necessary for the purpose of avoiding a breach of–
 (a) a person's Convention rights, or
 (b) a person's rights under the Community Treaties.

4 First class of ineligible person: refugee status abroad

(1) Paragraph 1 applies to a person if he–
 (a) has refugee status abroad, or
 (b) is the dependant of a person who is in the United Kingdom and who has refugee status abroad.

(2) For the purposes of this paragraph a person has refugee status abroad if–
 (a) he does not have the nationality of an EEA State, and
 (b) the government of an EEA State other than the United Kingdom has determined that he is entitled to protection as a refugee under the Refugee Convention.

5 **Second class of ineligible person: citizen of other EEA State**
Paragraph 1 applies to a person if he–
(a) has the nationality of an EEA State other than the United Kingdom, or
(b) is the dependant of a person who has the nationality of an EEA State other than the United Kingdom.

6 **Third class of ineligible person: failed asylum-seeker**
(1) Paragraph 1 applies to a person if–
(a) he was (but is no longer) an asylum-seeker, and
(b) he fails to cooperate with removal directions issued in respect of him.
(2) Paragraph 1 also applies to a dependant of a person to whom that paragraph applies by virtue of sub-paragraph (1).

7 **Fourth class of ineligible person: person unlawfully in United Kingdom**
Paragraph 1 applies to a person if–
(a) he is in the United Kingdom in breach of the immigration laws within the meaning of section 11, and
(b) he is not an asylum-seeker.

7A(1) Paragraph 1 applies to a person if–
(a) he–
(i) is treated as an asylum-seeker for the purposes of Part VI of the Immigration and Asylum Act 1999 (c. 33) (support) by virtue only of section 94(3A) (failed asylum-seeker with dependent child), or
(ii) is treated as an asylum-seeker for the purposes of Part 2 of this Act by virtue only of section 18(2),
(b) the Secretary of State has certified that in his opinion the person has failed without reasonable excuse to take reasonable steps–
(i) to leave the United Kingdom voluntarily, or
(ii) to place himself in a position in which he is able to leave the United Kingdom voluntarily,
(c) the person has received a copy of the Secretary of State's certificate, and
(d) the period of 14 days, beginning with the date on which the person receives the copy of the certificate, has elapsed.
(2) Paragraph 1 also applies to a dependant of a person to whom that paragraph applies by virtue of sub-paragraph (1).
(3) For the purpose of sub-paragraph (1)(d) if the Secretary of State sends a copy of a certificate by first class post to a person's last known address, the person shall be treated as receiving the copy on the second day after the day on which it was posted.
(4) The Secretary of State may by regulations vary the period specified in sub-paragraph (1)(d).

8 **Travel assistance**
The Secretary of State may make regulations providing for arrangements to be made enabling a person to whom paragraph 1 applies by virtue of paragraph 4 or 5 to leave the United Kingdom.

9 Temporary accommodation

(1) The Secretary of State may make regulations providing for arrangements to be made for the accommodation of a person to whom paragraph 1 applies pending the implementation of arrangements made by virtue of paragraph 8.

(2) Arrangements for a person by virtue of this paragraph–

(a) may be made only if the person has with him a dependent child, and

(b) may include arrangements for a dependent child.

10(1) The Secretary of State may make regulations providing for arrangements to be made for the accommodation of a person if–

(a) paragraph 1 applies to him by virtue of paragraph 7, and

(b) he has not failed to cooperate with removal directions issued in respect of him.

(2) Arrangements for a person by virtue of this paragraph–

(a) may be made only if the person has with him a dependent child, and

(b) may include arrangements for a dependent child.

11 Assistance and accommodation: general

Regulations under paragraph 8, 9 or 10 may–

(a) provide for the making of arrangements under a provision referred to in paragraph 1(1) or otherwise;

(b) confer a function (which may include the exercise of a discretion) on the Secretary of State, a local authority or another person;

(c) provide that arrangements must be made in a specified manner or in accordance with specified principles;

(d) provide that arrangements may not be made in a specified manner;

(e) require a local authority or another person to have regard to guidance issued by the Secretary of State in making arrangements;

(f) require a local authority or another person to comply with a direction of the Secretary of State in making arrangements.

12(1) Regulations may, in particular, provide that if a person refuses an offer of arrangements under paragraph 8 or fails to implement or cooperate with arrangements made for him under that paragraph–

(a) new arrangements may be made for him under paragraph 8, but

(b) new arrangements may not be made for him under paragraph 9.

(2) Regulations by virtue of this paragraph may include exceptions in the case of a person who–

(a) has a reason of a kind specified in the regulations for failing to implement or co-operate with arrangements made under paragraph 8, and

(b) satisfies any requirements of the regulations for proof of the reason.

13 Offences

(1) A person who leaves the United Kingdom in accordance with arrangements made under paragraph 8 commits an offence if he–

(a) returns to the United Kingdom, and

(b) requests that arrangements be made for him by virtue of paragraph 8, 9 or 10.

(2) A person commits an offence if he–
  (a) requests that arrangements be made for him by virtue of paragraph 8, 9 or 10, and
  (b) fails to mention a previous request by him for the making of arrangements under any of those paragraphs.

(3) A person who is guilty of an offence under this paragraph shall be liable on summary conviction to imprisonment for a term not exceeding six months.

14 Information

(1) If it appears to a local authority that paragraph 1 applies or may apply to a person in the authority's area by virtue of paragraph 6, 7 or 7A, the authority must inform the Secretary of State.

(2) A local authority shall act in accordance with any relevant guidance issued by the Secretary of State for the purpose of determining whether paragraph 1 applies or may apply to a person in the authority's area by virtue of paragraph 6, 7 or 7A.

15 Power to amend Schedule

The Secretary of State may by order amend this Schedule so as–
  (a) to provide for paragraph 1 to apply or not to apply to a class of person;
  (b) to add or remove a provision to or from the list in paragraph 1(1);
  (c) to add, amend or remove a limitation of or exception to paragraph 1.

16 Orders and regulations

(1) An order or regulations under this Schedule must be made by statutory instrument.

(2) An order or regulations under this Schedule may–
  (a) make provision which applies generally or only in specified cases or circumstances or only for specified purposes;
  (b) make different provision for different cases, circumstances or purposes;
  (c) make transitional provision;
  (d) make consequential provision (which may include provision amending a provision made by or under this or another Act).

(3) An order under this Schedule, regulations under paragraph 2(1)(d) or (e) or other regulations which include consequential provision amending an enactment shall not be made unless a draft has been laid before and approved by resolution of each House of Parliament.

(4) Regulations under this Schedule to which sub-paragraph (3) does not apply shall be subject to annulment in pursuance of a resolution of either House of Parliament.

17 Interpretation

(1) In this Schedule–

'asylum-seeker' means a person–
  (a) who is at least 18 years old,
  (b) who has made a claim for asylum (within the meaning of section 18(3)), and

(c) whose claim has been recorded by the Secretary of State but not determined,

'Convention rights' has the same meaning as in the Human Rights Act 1998,

'child' means a person under the age of eighteen,

'dependant' and 'dependent' shall have such meanings as may be prescribed by regulations made by the Secretary of State,

'EEA State' means a State which is a contracting party to the Agreement on the European Economic Area signed at Oporto on 2nd May 1992 (as it has effect from time to time),

'local authority'–

(a) in relation to England and Wales, has the same meaning as in section 129(3),

(b) in relation to Scotland, has the same meaning as in section 129(4), and

(c) in relation to Northern Ireland, means a health service body within the meaning of section 133(4)(d) and the Northern Ireland Housing Executive (for which purpose a reference to the authority's area shall be taken as a reference to Northern Ireland),

'the Refugee Convention' means the Convention relating to the status of Refugees done at Geneva on 28th July 1951 and its Protocol, and

'removal directions' means directions under Schedule 2 to the Immigration Act 1971 (c 77) (control of entry, etc), under Schedule 3 to that Act (deportation) or under section 10 of the Immigration and Asylum Act 1999 (removal of person unlawfully in United Kingdom).

(2) For the purpose of the definition of 'asylum-seeker' in sub-paragraph (1) a claim is determined if–

(a) the Secretary of State has notified the claimant of his decision,

(b) no appeal against the decision can be brought (disregarding the possibility of an appeal out of time with permission), and

(c) any appeal which has already been brought has been disposed of.

(3) For the purpose of sub-paragraph (2)(c) an appeal is disposed of when it is no longer pending for the purpose of–

(a) Part 5 of this Act, or

(b) the Special Immigration Appeals Commission Act 1997.

(4) The giving of directions in respect of a person under a provision of the Immigration Acts is not the provision of assistance to him for the purposes of this Schedule.

ASYLUM SUPPORT REGULATIONS 2000 SI NO 704

(as amended)

General

1 Citation and commencement

These Regulations may be cited as the Asylum Support Regulations 2000 and shall come into force on 3rd April 2000.

2 Interpretation

(1) In these Regulations–
'the Act' means the Immigration and Asylum Act 1999;
'asylum support' means support provided under section 95 of the Act;
'civil partnership couple' means two people of the same sex who are civil partners of each other and who are members of the same household;
'dependant' has the meaning given by paragraphs (4) and (5);
'the interim Regulations' means the Asylum Support (Interim Provisions) Regulations 1999;
'married couple' means a man and woman who are married to each other and are members of the same household; and
'same-sex couple' means two people of the same sex who, though not civil partners of each other, are living together as if they were;
'unmarried couple' means a man and woman who, though not married to each other, are living together as if married.

(2) The period of 14 days is prescribed for the purposes of section 94(3) of the Act (day on which a claim for asylum is determined).

(3) Paragraph (2) does not apply in relation to a case to which the interim Regulations apply (for which case, provision corresponding to paragraph (2) is made by regulation 2(6) of those Regulations).

(4) In these Regulations 'dependant', in relation to an asylum-seeker, a supported person or an applicant for asylum support, means, subject to paragraph (5), a person in the United Kingdom ('the relevant person') who–

(a) is his spouse or civil partner;
(b) is a child of his or of his spouse or civil partner, is dependant on him and is, or was at the relevant time, under 18;
(c) is a member of his or his spouse's or civil partner's close family and is, or was at the relevant time, under 18;
(d) had been living as part of his household–
  (i) for at least six of the twelve months before the relevant time, or
  (ii) since birth, and is, or was at the relevant time, under 18;
(e) is in need of care and attention from him or a member of his household by reason of a disability and would fall within sub-paragraph (c) or (d) but for the fact that he is not, and was not at the relevant time, under 18;
(f) had been living with him as a member of an unmarried couple for at least two of the three years before the relevant time;
(fa) had been living with him as a member of a same-sex couple for at least two of the three years before the relevant time;

(g) is living as part of his household and was, immediately before 6th December 1999 (the date when the interim Regulations came into force), receiving assistance from a local authority under section 17 of the Children Act 1989;

(h) is living as part of his household and was, immediately before the coming into force of these Regulations, receiving assistance from a local authority under–

(i) section 22 of the Children (Scotland) Act 1995; or

(ii) Article 18 of the Children (Northern Ireland) Order 1995; or

(i) has made a claim for leave to enter or remain in the United Kingdom, or for variation of any such leave, which is being considered on the basis that he is dependant on the asylum-seeker;

and in relation to a supported person, or an applicant for asylum support, who is himself a dependant of an asylum-seeker, also includes the asylum-seeker if in the United Kingdom.

(5) Where a supported person or applicant for asylum support is himself a dependant of an asylum-seeker, a person who would otherwise be a dependant of the supported person, or of the applicant, for the purposes of these Regulations is not such a dependant unless he is also a dependant of the asylum-seeker or is the asylum-seeker.

(6) In paragraph (4), 'the relevant time', in relation to the relevant person, means–

(a) the time when an application for asylum support for him was made in accordance with regulation 3(3); or

(b) if he has joined a person who is already a supported person in the United Kingdom and sub-paragraph (a) does not apply, the time when he joined that person in the United Kingdom.

(7) Where a person, by falling within a particular category in relation to an asylum-seeker or supported person, is by virtue of this regulation a dependant of the asylum-seeker or supported person for the purposes of these Regulations, that category is also a prescribed category for the purposes of paragraph (c) of the definition of 'dependant' in section 94(1) of the Act and, accordingly, the person is a dependant of the asylum-seeker or supported person for the purposes of Part VI of the Act.

(8) Paragraph (7) does not apply to a person who is already a dependant of the asylum-seeker or supported person for the purposes of Part VI of the Act because he falls within either of the categories mentioned in paragraphs (a) and (b) of the definition of 'dependant' in section 94(1) of the Act.

(9) Paragraph (7) does not apply for the purposes of any reference to a 'dependant' in Schedule 9 to the Act.

Initial application for support

3 Initial application for support: individual and group applications

(1) Either of the following–

(a) an asylum-seeker, or

(b) a dependant of an asylum-seeker,

may apply to the Secretary of State for asylum support.

(2) An application under this regulation may be–
  (a) for asylum support for the applicant alone; or
  (b) for asylum support for the applicant and one or more dependants of his.

(3) The application must be made by completing in full and in English the form for the time being issued by the Secretary of State for the purpose.

(4) The application may not be entertained by the Secretary of State–
  (a) where it is made otherwise than in accordance with paragraph (3); or
  (b) where the Secretary of State is not satisfied that the information provided is complete or accurate or that the applicant is co-operating with enquiries made under paragraph (5).

(5) The Secretary of State may make further enquiries of the applicant about any matter connected with the application.

(5A) Where the Secretary of State makes further enquiries under paragraph (5) the applicant shall reply to those enquiries within five working days of his receipt of them.

(5B) The Secretary of State shall be entitled to conclude that the applicant is not co-operating with his enquiries under paragraph (5) if he fails, without reasonable excuse, to reply within the period prescribed by paragraph (5A).

(5C) In cases where the Secretary of State may not entertain an application for asylum support he shall also discontinue providing support under section 98 of the Act.

(6) Paragraphs (3) and (4) do not apply where a person is already a supported person and asylum support is sought for a dependant of his for whom such support is not already provided (for which case, provision is made by regulation 15).

(7) For the purposes of this regulation, working day means any day other than a Saturday, a Sunday, Christmas Day, Good Friday or a day which is a bank holiday under section 1 of the Banking and Financial Dealings Act 1971 in the locality in which the applicant is living.

4 Persons excluded from support

(1) The following circumstances are prescribed for the purposes of subsection (2) of section 95 of the Act as circumstances where a person who would otherwise fall within subsection (1) of that section is excluded from that subsection (and, accordingly, may not be provided with asylum support).

(2) A person is so excluded if he is applying for asylum support for himself alone and he falls within paragraph (4) by virtue of any sub-paragraph of that paragraph.

(3) A person is so excluded if–
  (a) he is applying for asylum support for himself and other persons, or he is included in an application for asylum support made by a person other than himself;
  (b) he falls within paragraph (4) (by virtue of any sub-paragraph of that paragraph); and
  (c) each of the other persons to whom the application relates also falls within paragraph (4) (by virtue of any sub-paragraph of that paragraph).

(4) A person falls within this paragraph if at the time when the application is determined–
(a) he is a person to whom interim support applies; or
(b) he is a person to whom social security benefits apply; or
(c) he has not made a claim for leave to enter or remain in the United Kingdom, or for variation of any such leave, which is being considered on the basis that he is an asylum-seeker or dependent on an asylum-seeker.

(5) For the purposes of paragraph (4), interim support applies to a person if–
(a) at the time when the application is determined, he is a person to whom, under the interim Regulations, support under regulation 3 of those Regulations must be provided by a local authority;
(b) sub-paragraph (a) does not apply, but would do so if the person had been determined by the local authority concerned to be an eligible person; or
(c) sub-paragraph (a) does not apply, but would do so but for the fact that the person's support under those Regulations was (otherwise than by virtue of regulation 7(1)(d) of those Regulations) refused under regulation 7, or suspended or discontinued under regulation 8, of those Regulations;

and in this paragraph 'local authority', 'local authority concerned' and 'eligible person' have the same meanings as in the interim Regulations.

(6) For the purposes of paragraph (4), a person is a person to whom social security benefits apply if he is–
(a) a person who by virtue of regulation 2 of the Social Security (Immigration and Asylum) Consequential Amendments Regulations 2000 is not excluded by section 115(1) of the Act from entitlement to–
(i) income-based jobseeker's allowance under the Jobseekers Act 1995;
(ii) income support, housing benefit or council tax benefit under the Social Security Contributions and Benefits Act 1992;or
(iii) income-related employment and support allowance payable under Part 1 of the Welfare Reform Act 2007;
(b) a person who, by virtue of regulation 2 of the Social Security (Immigration and Asylum) Consequential Amendments Regulations (Northern Ireland) 2000 is not excluded by section 115(2) of the Act from entitlement to–
(i) income-based jobseeker's allowance under the Jobseekers (Northern Ireland) Order 1995; or
(ii) income support or housing benefit under the Social Security Contributions and Benefits (Northern Ireland) Act 1992;

(7) A person is not to be regarded as falling within paragraph (2) or (3) if, when asylum support is sought for him, he is a dependant of a person who is already a supported person.

(8) The circumstances prescribed by paragraphs (2) and (3) are also prescribed for the purposes of section 95(2), as applied by section 98(3), of the Act as circumstances where a person who would otherwise fall within subsection (1) of section 98 is excluded from that subsection (and, accordingly, may not be provided with temporary support under section 98).

(9) For the purposes of paragraph (8), paragraphs (2) and (3) shall apply as if any reference to an application for asylum support were a reference to an application for support under section 98 of the Act.

Determining whether persons are destitute

5 Determination where application relates to more than one person, etc

(1) Subject to paragraph (2), where an application in accordance with regulation 3(3) is for asylum support for the applicant and one or more dependants of his, in applying section 95(1) of the Act the Secretary of State must decide whether the applicant and all those dependants, taken together, are destitute or likely to become destitute within the period prescribed by regulation 7.

(2) Where a person is a supported person, and the question falls to be determined whether asylum support should in future be provided for him and one or more other persons who are his dependants and are–

(a) persons for whom asylum support is also being provided when that question falls to be determined; or

(b) persons for whom the Secretary of State is then considering whether asylum support should be provided, in applying section 95(1) of the Act the Secretary of State must decide whether the supported person and all those dependants, taken together, are destitute or likely to become destitute within the period prescribed by regulation 7.

6 Income and assets to be taken into account

(1) This regulation applies where it falls to the Secretary of State to determine for the purposes of section 95(1) of the Act whether–

(a) a person applying for asylum support, or such an applicant and any dependants of his, or

(b) a supported person, or such a person and any dependants of his, is or are destitute or likely to become so within the period prescribed by regulation 7.

(2) In this regulation 'the principal' means the applicant for asylum support (where paragraph (1)(a) applies) or the supported person (where paragraph (1)(b) applies).

(3) The Secretary of State must ignore–

(a) any asylum support, and

(b) any support under section 98 of the Act,

which the principal or any dependant of his is provided with or, where the question is whether destitution is likely within a particular period, might be provided with in that period.

(4) But he must take into account–

(a) any other income which the principal, or any dependant of his, has or might reasonably be expected to have in that period;

(b) any other support which is available to the principal or any dependant of his, or might reasonably be expected to be so available in that period; and

(c) any assets mentioned in paragraph (5) (whether held in the United Kingdom or elsewhere) which are available to the principal or any dependant of his otherwise than by way of asylum support or support under section 98, or might reasonably be expected to be so available in that period.

(5) Those assets are–
(a) cash;
(b) savings;
(c) investments;
(d) land;
(e) cars or other vehicles; and
(f) goods held for the purpose of a trade or other business.

(6) The Secretary of State must ignore any assets not mentioned in paragraph (5).

7 Period within which applicant must be likely to become destitute

The period prescribed for the purposes of section 95(1) of the Act is–
(a) where the question whether a person or persons is or are destitute or likely to become so falls to be determined in relation to an application for asylum support and sub-paragraph
(b) does not apply, 14 days beginning with the day on which that question falls to be determined;
(c) where that question falls to be determined in relation to a supported person, or in relation to persons including a supported person, 56 days beginning with the day on which that question falls to be determined.

8 Adequacy of existing accommodation

(1) Subject to paragraph (2), the matters mentioned in paragraph (3) are prescribed for the purposes of subsection (5)(a) of section 95 of the Act as matters to which the Secretary of State must have regard in determining for the purposes of that section whether the accommodation of–
(a) a person applying for asylum support, or
(b) a supported person for whom accommodation is not for the time being provided by way of asylum support,
is adequate.

(2) The matters mentioned in paragraph (3)(a) and (d) to (g) are not so prescribed for the purposes of a case where the person indicates to the Secretary of State that he wishes to remain in the accommodation.

(3) The matters referred to in paragraph (1) are–
(a) whether it would be reasonable for the person to continue to occupy the accommodation;
(b) whether the accommodation is affordable for him;
(c) whether the accommodation is provided under section 98 of the Act, or otherwise on an emergency basis, only while the claim for asylum support is being determined;
(d) whether the person can secure entry to the accommodation;
(e) where the accommodation consists of a moveable structure, vehicle or vessel designed or adapted for human habitation, whether there is a place where the person is entitled or permitted both to place it and reside in it;

(f) whether the accommodation is available for occupation by the person's dependants together with him;
(g) whether it is probable that the person's continued occupation of the accommodation will lead to domestic violence against him or any of his dependants.

(4) In determining whether it would be reasonable for a person to continue to occupy accommodation, regard may be had to the general circumstances prevailing in relation to housing in the district of the local housing authority where the accommodation is.

(5) In determining whether a person's accommodation is affordable for him, the Secretary of State must have regard to–
(a) any income, or any assets mentioned in regulation 6(5) (whether held in the United Kingdom or elsewhere), which is or are available to him or any dependant of his otherwise than by way of asylum support or support under section 98 of the Act, or might reasonably be expected to be so available;
(b) the costs in respect of the accommodation; and
(c) the person's other reasonable living expenses.

(6) In this regulation–
(a) 'domestic violence' means violence from a person who is or has been a close family member, or threats of violence from such a person which are likely to be carried out; and
(b) 'district of the local housing authority' has the meaning given by section 217(3) of the Housing Act 1996.

(7) The reference in paragraph (1) to subsection (5)(a) of section 95 of the Act does not include a reference to that provision as applied by section 98(3) of the Act.

9 Essential living needs

(1) The matter mentioned in paragraph (2) is prescribed for the purposes of subsection (7)(b) of section 95 of the Act as a matter to which the Secretary of State may not have regard in determining for the purposes of that section whether a person's essential living needs (other than accommodation) are met.

(2) That matter is his personal preference as to clothing (but this shall not be taken to prevent the Secretary of State from taking into account his individual circumstances as regards clothing).

(3) None of the items and expenses mentioned in paragraph (4) is to be treated as being an essential living need of a person for the purposes of Part VI of the Act.

(4) Those items and expenses are–
(a) the cost of faxes;
(b) computers and the cost of computer facilities;
(c) the cost of photocopying;
(d) travel expenses, except the expense mentioned in paragraph (5);
(e) toys and other recreational items;
(f) entertainment expenses.

(5) The expense excepted from paragraph (4)(d) is the expense of an initial journey from a place in the United Kingdom to accommodation provided

by way of asylum support or (where accommodation is not so provided) to an address in the United Kingdom which has been notified to the Secretary of State as the address where the person intends to live.

(6) Paragraph (3) shall not be taken to affect the question whether any item or expense not mentioned in paragraph (4) or (5) is, or is not, an essential living need.

(7) The reference in paragraph (1) to subsection (7)(b) of section 95 of the Act includes a reference to that provision as applied by section 98(3) of the Act and, accordingly, the reference in paragraph (1) to 'that section' includes a reference to section 98.

Provision of support

10 Kind and levels of support for essential living needs

(1) This regulation applies where the Secretary of State has decided that asylum support should be provided in respect of the essential living needs of a person.

(2) As a general rule, asylum support in respect of the essential living needs of that person may be expected to be provided weekly in the form of cash, equal to the amount shown in the second column of the following Table opposite the entry in the first column which for the time being describes that person.

Table

Qualifying couple	£69.57
Lone parent aged 18 or over	£42.16
Single person aged 25 or over, excluding lone parent (where the decision to grant support is made prior to the 5th October 2009 and the person has or will have reached age 25 prior to that date)	£42.16
Any other single person aged 18 or over, excluding lone parent	£35.13
Person aged at least 16 but under 18 (except a member of a qualifying couple)	£38.18
Person aged under 16	£50.81

(3) In paragraph (1) and the provisions of paragraph (2) preceding the Table, 'person' includes 'couple'.

(3A) For the purposes of the table at regulation 10(2), a decision to grant support is made on the date recorded on the letter granting asylum support to the applicant.

(4) In this regulation–

(a) 'qualifying couple' means a married couple, an unmarried couple, a civil partnership couple or a same-sex couple, at least one of whom is aged 18 or over and neither of whom is aged under 16;
(b) 'lone parent' means a parent who is not a member of a married couple, an unmarried couple, a civil partnership couple or a same-sex couple;
(c) 'single person' means a person who is not a parent or a member of a qualifying couple;and
(d) 'parent' means a parent of a relevant child, that is to say a child who is aged under18 and for whom asylum support is provided.

(5) Where the Secretary of State has decided that accommodation should be provided for a person (or couple) by way of asylum support, and the accommodation is provided in a form which alsomeets other essential living needs (such as bed and breakfast, or half or full board), the amounts shown in the Table in paragraph (2) shall be treated as reduced accordingly.

(6) [Revoked.]

10A Additional support for pregnant women and children under 3

(1) In addition to the cash support which the Secretary of State may be expected to provide weekly as described in regulation 10(2), in the case of any pregnant woman or child aged under 3 for whom the Secretary of State has decided asylum support should be provided, there shall, as a general rule, be added to the cash support for any week the amount shown in the second column of the following table opposite the entry in the first column which for the time being describes that person.

TABLE

Pregnant woman	£3.00
Child aged under 1	£5.00
Child aged at least 1 and under 3	£3.00

(2) In this regulation, 'pregnant woman' means a woman who has provided evidence to satisfy the Secretary of State that she is pregnant.

11 [Revoked.]

12 Income and assets to be taken into account in providing support

(1) This regulation applies where it falls to the Secretary of State to decide the level or kind of asylum support to be provided for–
(a) a person applying for asylum support, or such an applicant and any dependants of his; or
(b) a supported person, or such a person and any dependants of his.

(2) In this regulation 'the principal' means the applicant for asylum support (where paragraph (1)(a) applies) or the supported person (where paragraph (1)(b) applies).

(3) The Secretary of State must take into account–
(a) any income which the principal or any dependant of his has or might reasonably be expected to have,
(b) support which is or might reasonably be expected to be available to the principal or any dependant of his, and

(c) any assets mentioned in regulation 6(5) (whether held in the United Kingdom or elsewhere) which are or might reasonably be expected to be available to the principal or any dependant of his, otherwise than by way of asylum support.

13 Accommodation

(1) The matters mentioned in paragraph (2) are prescribed for the purposes of subsection (2)(b) of section 97 of the Act as matters to which regard may not be had when exercising the power under section 95 of the Act to provide accommodation for a person.

(2) Those matters are–

(a) his personal preference as to the nature of the accommodation to be provided; and

(b) his personal preference as to the nature and standard of fixtures and fittings;

but this shall not be taken to prevent the person's individual circumstances, as they relate to his accommodation needs, being taken into account.

14 Services

(1) The services mentioned in paragraph (2) may be provided or made available by way of asylum support to persons who are otherwise receiving such support, but may be so provided only for the purpose of maintaining good order among such persons.

(2) Those services are–

(a) education, including English language lessons,

(b) sporting or other developmental activities.

Change of circumstances

15 Change of circumstances

(1) If a relevant change of circumstances occurs, the supported person concerned or a dependant of his must, without delay, notify the Secretary of State of that change of circumstances.

(2) A relevant change of circumstances occurs where a supported person or a dependant of his–

(a) is joined in the United Kingdom by a dependant or, as the case may be, another dependant, of the supported person;

(b) receives or gains access to any money, or other asset mentioned in regulation 6(5), that has not previously been declared to the Secretary of State;

(c) becomes employed;

(d) becomes unemployed;

(e) changes his name;

(f) gets married;

(fa) forms a civil partnership;

(g) starts living with a person as if married to that person;

(ga) starts living with a person as if a civil partner of that person;

(h) gets divorced;

(ha) becomes a former civil partner on the dissolution of his civil partnership;

- (i) separates from a spouse, or from a person with whom he has been living as if married to that person;
- (ia) separates from his civil partner or from the person with whom he has been living as if a civil partner of that person;
- (j) becomes pregnant;
- (k) has a child;
- (l) leaves school;
- (m) starts to share his accommodation with another person;
- (n) moves to a different address, or otherwise leaves his accommodation;
- (o) goes into hospital;
- (p) goes to prison or is otherwise held in custody;
- (q) leaves the United Kingdom; or
- (r) dies.

(3) If, on being notified of a change of circumstances, the Secretary of State considers that the change may be one–
- (a) as a result of which asylum support should be provided for a person for whom it was not provided before, or
- (b) as a result of which asylum support should no longer be provided for a person, or
- (c) which may otherwise affect the asylum support which should be provided for a person,

he may make further enquiries of the supported person or dependant who gave the notification.

(4) The Secretary of State may, in particular, require that person to provide him with such information as he considers necessary to determine whether, and if so, what, asylum support should be provided for any person.

16 Contributions

(1) This regulation applies where, in deciding the level of asylum support to be provided for a person who is or will be a supported person, the Secretary of State is required to take into account income, support or assets as mentioned in regulation 12(3).

(2) The Secretary of State may–
- (a) set the asylum support for that person at a level which does not reflect the income, support or assets; and
- (b) require from that person payments by way of contributions towards the cost of the provision for him of asylum support.

(3) A supported person must make to the Secretary of State such payments by way of contributions as the Secretary of State may require under paragraph (2).

(4) Prompt payment of such contributions may be made a condition (under section 95(9) of the Act) subject to which asylum support for that person is provided.

Recovery of sums by Secretary of State

17 Recovery where assets become realisable

(1) This regulation applies where it appears to the Secretary of State at any time (the relevant time)–

(a) that a supported person had, at the time when he applied for asylum support, assets of any kind in the United Kingdom or elsewhere which were not capable of being realised; but

(b) that those assets have subsequently become, and remain, capable of being realised.

(2) The Secretary of State may recover from that person a sum not exceeding the recoverable sum.

(3) Subject to paragraph (5), the recoverable sum is a sum equal to whichever is the less of–

(a) the monetary value of all the asylum support provided to the person up to the relevant time; and

(b) the monetary value of the assets concerned.

(4) As well as being recoverable as mentioned in paragraph 11(2)(a) of Schedule 8 to the Act, an amount recoverable under this regulation may be recovered by deduction from asylum support.

(5) The recoverable sum shall be treated as reduced by any amount which the Secretary of State has by virtue of this regulation already recovered from the person concerned (whether by deduction or otherwise) with regard to the assets concerned.

17A Recovery of asylum support

(1) The Secretary of State may require a supported person to refund asylum support if it transpires that at any time during which asylum support was being provided for him he was not destitute.

(2) If a supported person has dependants, the Secretary of State may require him to refund asylum support if it transpires that at any time during which asylum support was being provided for the supported person and his dependants they were not destitute.

(3) The refund required shall not exceed the monetary value of all the asylum support provided to the supported person or to the supported person and his dependants for the relevant period.

(4) In this regulation the relevant period is the time during which asylum support was provided for the supported person or the supported person and his dependants and during which he or they were not destitute.

(5) If not paid within a reasonable period, the refund required may be recovered from the supported person as if it were a debt due to the Secretary of State.

18 Overpayments: method of recovery

As well as being recoverable as mentioned in subsection (3) of section 114 of the Act, an amount recoverable under subsection (2) of that section may be recovered by deduction from asylum support.

Breach of conditions and suspension and discontinuation of support

19 Breach of conditions: decision whether to provide support

(1) When deciding–

(a) whether to provide, or to continue to provide, asylum support for any person or persons, or

(b) the level or kind of support to be provided for any person or persons, the Secretary of State may take into account the extent to which a relevant condition has been complied with.

(2) A relevant condition is one which makes the provision of asylum support subject to actual residence by the supported person or a dependant of his for whom support is being provided in a specific place or location.

20 Suspension or discontinuation of support

(1) Asylum support for a supported person and any dependant of his or for one or more dependants of a supported person may be suspended or discontinued if–

(a) support is being provided for the supported person or a dependant of his in collective accommodation and the Secretary of State has reasonable grounds to believe that the supported person or his dependant has committed a serious breach of the rules of that accommodation;

(b) the Secretary of State has reasonable grounds to believe that the supported person or a dependant of his for whom support is being provided has committed an act of seriously violent behaviour whether or not that act occurs in accommodation provided by way of asylum support or at the authorised address or elsewhere;

(c) the supported person or a dependant of his has committed an offence under Part VI of the Act;

(d) the Secretary of State has reasonable grounds to believe that the supported person or any dependant of his for whom support is being provided has abandoned the authorised address without first informing the Secretary of State or, if requested, without permission;

(e) the supported person has not complied within a reasonable period, which shall be no less than five working days beginning with the day on which the request was received by him, with requests for information made by the Secretary of State and which relate to the supported person's or his dependant's eligibility for or receipt of asylum support including requests made under regulation 15;

(f) the supported person fails, without reasonable excuse, to attend an interview requested by the Secretary of State relating to the supported person's or his dependant's eligibility for or receipt of asylum support;

(g) the supported person or, if he is an asylum seeker, his dependant, has not complied within a reasonable period, which shall be no less than ten working days beginning with the day on which the request was received by him, with a request for information made by the Secretary of State relating to his claim for asylum;

(h) the Secretary of State has reasonable grounds to believe that the supported person or a dependant of his for whom support is being provided has concealed financial resources and that the supported person or a dependant of his or both have therefore unduly benefited from the receipt of asylum support;

(i) the supported person or a dependant of his for whom support is being provided has not complied with a reporting requirement;

(j) the Secretary of State has reasonable grounds to believe that the supported person or a dependant of his for whom support is being provided has made a claim for asylum ('the first claim') and before the first claim has been determined makes or seeks to make a further claim for asylum not being part of the first claim in the same or a different name; or

(k) the supported person or a dependant of his for whom support is being provided has failed without reasonable excuse to comply with a relevant condition.

(2) If a supported person is asked to attend an interview of the type referred to in paragraph (1)(f) he shall be given no less than five working days notice of it.

(3) Any decision to discontinue support in the circumstances referred to in paragraph (1) above shall be taken individually, objectively and impartially and reasons shall be given. Decisions will be based on the particular situation of the person concerned and particular regard shall be had to whether he is a vulnerable person as described by Article 17 of Council Directive 2003/9/EC of 27th January 2003 laying down minimum standards for the reception of asylum seekers.

(4) No person's asylum support shall be discontinued before a decision is made under paragraph (1).

(5) Where asylum support for a supported person or his dependant is suspended or discontinued under paragraph (1)(d) or (i) and the supported person or his dependant are traced or voluntarily report to the police, the Secretary of State or an immigration officer, a duly motivated decision based on the reasons for the disappearance shall be taken as to the reinstatement of some or all of the supported person's or his dependant's or both of their asylum support.

(6) For the purposes of this regulation–

(a) the authorised address is–

(i) the accommodation provided for the supported person and his dependants (if any) by way of asylum support; or

(ii) if no accommodation is so provided, the address notified by the supported person to the Secretary of State in his application for asylum support or, where a change of address has been notified to the Secretary of State under regulation 15 or under the Immigration Rules or both, the address for the time being so notified;

(b) 'collective accommodation' means accommodation which a supported person or any ependant of his for whom support is being provided shares with any other supported person and includes accommodation in which only facilities are shared;

(c) 'relevant condition' has the same meaning as in regulation 19(2);

(d) 'reporting requirement' is a condition or restriction which requires a person to report to the police, an immigration officer or the Secretary of State and is imposed under–

(i) paragraph 21 of Schedule 2 to the Immigration Act 1971 (temporary admission or release from detention);

(ii) paragraph 22 of that Schedule; or

(iii) paragraph 2 or 5 of Schedule 3 to that Act (pending deportation).

(e) 'working day' has the same meaning as in regulation 3(7) save that the reference to the applicant shall be a reference to the supported person or his dependant.

20A Temporary Support

Regulations 19 and 20 shall apply to a person or his dependant who is provided with temporary support under section 98 of the Act in the same way as they apply to a person and his dependant who is in receipt of asylum support and any reference to asylum support in regulations 19 and 20 shall include a reference to temporary support under section 98.

21 Effect of previous suspension or discontinuation

(1) Subject to regulation 20(5) where–

(a) an application for asylum support is made,

(b) the applicant or any other person to whom the application relates has previously had his asylum support suspended or discontinued under regulation 20, and

(c) there has been no material change of circumstances since the suspension or discontinuation, the application need not be entertained unless the Secretary of State considers that there are exceptional circumstances which justify its being entertained.

(2) A material change of circumstances is one which, if the applicant were a supported person, would have to be notified to the Secretary of State under regulation 15.

(3) This regulation is without prejudice to the power of the Secretary of State to refuse the application even if he has entertained it.

Notice to quit

22 Notice to quit

(1) If–

(a) as a result of asylum support, a person has a tenancy or licence to occupy accommodation,

(b) one or more of the conditions mentioned in paragraph (2) is satisfied, and

(c) he is given notice to quit in accordance with paragraph (3) or (4),

his tenancy or licence is to be treated as ending with the period specified in that notice, regardless of when it could otherwise be brought to an end.

(2) The conditions are that–

(a) the asylum support is suspended or discontinued as a result of any provision of regulation 20;

(b) the relevant claim for asylum has been determined;

(c) the supported person has ceased to be destitute; or

(d) he is to be moved to other accommodation.

(3) A notice to quit is in accordance with this paragraph if it is in writing and–

(a) in a case where sub-paragraph (a), (c) or (d) of paragraph (2) applies, specifies as the notice period a period of not less than seven days; or

(b) in a case where the Secretary of State has notified his decision on the relevant claim for asylum to the claimant, specifies as the notice period a period at least as long as whichever is the greater of–

(i) seven days; or
(ii) the period beginning with the date of service of the notice to quit and ending with the date of determination of the relevant claim for asylum (found in accordance with section 94(3) of the Act).

(4) A notice to quit is in accordance with this paragraph if–
(a) it is in writing;
(b) it specifies as the notice period a period of less than seven days; and
(c) the circumstances of the case are such that that notice period is justified.

Meaning of 'destitute' for certain other purposes

23 Meaning of 'destitute' for certain other purposes

(1) In this regulation 'the relevant enactments' means–
(a) section 21(1A) of the National Assistance Act 1948;
(b) section 45(4A) of the Health Services and Public Health Act 1968;
(c) paragraph 2(2A) of Schedule 8 to the National Health Service Act 1977;
(d) sections 12(2A), 13A(4) and 13B(3) of the Social Work (Scotland) Act 1968;
(e) article 14 of the Mental Health (Care and Treatment) (Scotland) Act 2003 (Consequential Provisions) Order 2005; and
(f) Articles 7(3) and 15(6) of the Health and Personal Social Services (Northern Ireland) Order 1972.

(2) The following provisions of this regulation apply where it falls to an authority, or the Department, to determine for the purposes of any of the relevant enactments whether a person is destitute.

(3) Paragraphs (3) to (6) of regulation 6 apply as they apply in the case mentioned in paragraph (1) of that regulation, but as if references to the principal were references to the person whose destitution or otherwise is being determined and references to the Secretary of State were references to the authority or (as the case may be) Department.

(4) The matters mentioned in paragraph (3) of regulation 8 (read with paragraphs (4) to (6) of that regulation) are prescribed for the purposes of subsection (5)(a) of section 95 of the Act, as applied for the purposes of any of the relevant enactments, as matters to which regard must be had in determining for the purposes of any of the relevant enactments whether a person's accommodation is adequate.

(5) The matter mentioned in paragraph (2) of regulation 9 is prescribed for the purposes of subsection (7)(b) of section 95 of the Act, as applied for the purposes of any of the relevant enactments, as a matter to which regard may not be had in determining for the purposes of any of the relevant enactments whether a person's essential living needs (other than accommodation) are met.

(6) Paragraphs (3) to (6) of regulation 9 shall apply as if the reference in paragraph (3) to Part VI of the Act included a reference to the relevant enactments.

(7) The references in regulations 8(5) and 9(2) to the Secretary of State shall be construed, for the purposes of this regulation, as references to the authority or (as the case may be) Department.

SCHEDULE: APPLICATION FORM AND NOTES

Regulation 3(3)

[Revoked.]

NATIONAL HEALTH SERVICE (CHARGES TO OVERSEAS VISITORS) REGULATIONS 1989 SI NO 306

(as amended)

1 Citation, commencement and interpretation

(1) These Regulations may be cited as the National Health Service (Charges to Overseas Visitors) Regulations 1989 and shall come into force on 1st April 1989.

(2) In these Regulations, unless the context otherwise requires–

'the Act' means the National Health Service Act 1977;

'authorised child' means a child who has either been granted leave to enter the United Kingdom with his parent for the purpose of the parent obtaining a course of treatment in respect of which no charges are payable under regulation 6A or is the child of an authorised companion;

'authorised companion' means a person who has been granted leave to enter the United Kingdom to accompany a person who is obtaining a course of treatment in respect of which no charges are payable under regulation 6A;

'Authority' means, as the case may require, a Regional Health Authority, a District Health Authority, or a special health authority;

'child' means a person who is–

(a) under the age of sixteen; or

(b) under the age of nineteen and treated for the purposes of the Child Benefit Act 1975, or the Child Benefit (Northern Ireland) Order 1975, as receiving full-time education at an educational establishment recognised under that Act or that Order;

'Continental Shelf', except in reference to a designated area of the Continental Shelf, means the sea-bed and subsoil of the submarine area (other than in the Baltic or Mediterranean Seas, including the Adriatic and Aegean, or the Black Sea) adjacent to the coasts, lying north of the latitude of 25 degrees north and between the longtitude of 30 degrees west and 35 degrees east, of the territory (including islands) of–

(i) any country situated on the Continent of Europe, or

(ii) the Republic of Ireland,

where the submarine area is outside the seaward limits of the territorial limits of those countries and the Republic of Ireland and is an area with respect to which the exercise by any of them of sovereign rights in accordance with international law is recognised by Her Majesty's Government in the United Kingdom;

'designated area of the Continental Shelf' means any area which is for the time being designated by an Order in Council under the Continental Shelf Act 1964 as an area within which the rights of the United Kingdom with respect to the seated and subsoil and their natural resources may be exercised;

'member of the family', in relation to a national of a member State or a stateless person or refugee entitled to receive treatment by virtue of Regulations made by the Council of the European Communities under Article 51 of the Treaty establishing the European Economic Community, means a member of the family as defined for the purpose of such Regulations **3**;

'member State' means a State which is a Contracting Party to the Agreement on the European Economic Area European Economic Area Act 1993 but until that Agreement omes into force in relation to Liechtenstein does not include the State of Liechtenstein;

'NHS foundation trust' has the same meaning as in section 1(1) of the Health and Social Care (Community Health and Standards) Act 2003;

'NHS trust' means a National Health Service trust established under Part I of the National Health Service and Community Care Act 1990;

'overseas visitor' means a person not ordinarily resident in the United Kingdom;

'reciprocal agreement' means arrangements mutually agreed between the Government of the United Kingdom and the Government of a country or territory outside the United Kingdom for providing health care;

'refugee' means a person who is a refugee within the meaning of Article 1 of the Convention relating to the Status of Refugees 1951 and Article 1 of the Protocol relating to the Status of Refugees 1967 and any other person taking refuge in the territory of a member State with leave of the Government of that State;

'services forming part of the health service' means accommodations, services and other facilities provided under section 3(1) of the Act (the Secretary of State's duty to provide accommodation and services) and includes accommodation, services and other facilities provided by an NHS trust, but does not include any accommodation, service or facility made available or provided under section 65 of the Act (accommodation and services for private patients of health authorities), section 7(2) of the Health and Medicines Act 1988 (powers to make more income available for the health service) or paragraph 14 of Schedule 2 to the National Health Service and Community Care Act 1990 (accommodation and services for private patients of NHS trusts) or made available or provided by an NHS foundation trust to a patient other than for the purposes of the health service;

'ship or vessel' includes hovercraft;

'stateless person' has the meaning assigned to it in article 1 of the Convention relating to the Status of Stateless Persons 1954;

'treatment' includes medical, dental and nursing services required for the care of women who are pregnant or in childbirth or for the prevention or diagnosis of illness;

'treatment the need for which arose during the visit' means diagnosis of symptoms or signs occurring for the first time after the visitor's arrival in the United Kingdom and any other treatment which, in the opinion of a medical or dental practitioner employed by, or under contract with, an Authority or NHS trust or NHS foundation trust, is required promptly for a conditions which arose after the visitor's arrival in the United Kingdom, or became, or but for treatment would be likely to become, acutely exacerbated after such arrival;

'the United Kingdom Government' as referred to in regulation 4(1)(a)(iii) includes the National Assembly for Wales.

(3) In calculating, for the purpose of any provision of these Regulations, a period of residence in the United Kingdom, any interruption by reason of temporary absence of not more than three months shall be disregarded.

(4) Unless the context otherwise requires, in these Regulations any reference to a numbered regulation or Schedule is a reference to the regulation or Schedule bearing that number in these Regulations.

2 Making and recovery of charges

(1) Where an Authority or NHS trust or NHS foundation trust provides an overseas visitor with services forming part of the health service, that Authority or NHS trust or NHS foundation trust, having determined, by means of such enquiries as it is satisfied are reasonable in all the circumstances, including the state of health of that overseas visitor, that the case is not one in which these Regulations provide for no charge to be made, shall make and recover from the person liable under regulation 7 charges for the provision of those services.

(2) An Authority or NHS trust or NHS foundation trust which makes and recovers a charge in accordance with paragraph (1) of this regulation shall give or send to the person making the payment a receipt for the amount paid.

3 Services exempted from charges

No charge shall be made in respect of any services forming part of the health service provided for an overseas visitor–

(a) at a hospital accident and emergency department or, casualty department, unless and until he has been accepted as an in-patient at the hospital, for treatment of the condition in respect of which such services are provided; or

(b) otherwise than at, or by staff employed to work at, or under the direction of, a hospital; or

(bb) consisting of the provision of family planning services; or

(c) for treatment in respect of a disease listed in Schedule 1; or

(d) at a special clinic for the treatment of sexually transmitted diseases or in respect of a sexually transmitted disease by virtue of a reference from such a clinic, but in the case of services which relate to infection with any Human Immuno deficiency Virus, only to the extent that they consist of a diagnostic test for evidence of infection with any such Virus and counselling associated with that test or its result;

(e) who is detained in a hospital, or received into guardianship, under the Mental Health Act 1983 or any other enactment authorising orders for admission to, and detention in, hospital by reason of mental disorder; or

(f) with a view to the improvement of his mental condition where submission to the treatment is, under section 3(1) of the Powers of the Criminal Courts Act 1973, included by the Court in a probation order under section 2 of that Act.

4 Overseas visitors exempt from charges

(1) No charge shall be made in respect of any services forming part of the health service provided for an overseas visitor–

(a) who is shown to the satisfaction of the Authority or NHS trust or NHS foundation trust, or Primary Care Trust to be present in the United Kingdom or in a designated area of the Continental Shelf or, in or over any area of the Continental Shelf, or on a stationary structure within the territorial waters of the United Kingdom, for the purpose of–

(zi) engaging in employment with an employer which has its principal place of business in the United Kingdom or which is registered in the United Kingdom as a branch of an overseas company;

(i) being a self employed person whose principal place of business is in the United Kingdom;

(ii) working as a volunteer with a voluntary organisation that is providing a service similar to a relevant service as defined in sections 64 and 65 of the Health Services and Public Health Act 1968, or service to which Article 71 of the Health and Personal Social Services (Northern Ireland) Order 1972 applies;

(iii) pursuing a full time course of study which is substantially funded by the United Kingdom Government or is of at least six months duration;

(iv) taking up permanent residence in the United Kingdom; or

(b) who has resided lawfully in the United Kingdom for a period of not less than one year immediately preceding the time when the services are provided unless this period of residence followed the grant of leave to enter the United Kingdom for the purpose of undergoing private medical treatment or a determination under regulation 6A;

(c) who has been accepted as a refugee in the United Kingdom, or who has made a formal application for leave to stay as a refugee in the United Kingdom; or

(d) who is employed on a ship or vessel registered in the United Kingdom; or

(e) who is in receipt of any pension or other benefit under a Personal Injuries Scheme, service pensions instrument or a 1914–1918 War Injuries Scheme as defined in regulation 2(1) of the Social Security (Overlapping Benefits) Regulations 1979; or

(f) who is a diplomatic agent for the purposes of the Articles of the Vienna Convention on Diplomatic Regulations set out in Schedule 1 to the Diplomatic Privileges Act 1964; or

(g) who is a member of Her Majesty's United Kingdom Forces; or

(h) who is some other Crown servant employed in the right of Her Majesty's Government of the United Kingdom having been recruited in the United Kingdom; or

(i) who is an employee, recruited in the United Kingdom, of the British Council or the Commonwealth War Graves Commission; or

(j) who is working in employment that is financed in part by the Government of the United Kingdom in accordance with arrangements made with the Government of some other country or territory or a public body in such other country or territory; or

(k) who has at any time had not less than ten years continuous lawful residence in the United Kingdom and is engaged in employment as an employed or self-employed person outside the United Kingdom that has lasted for a period of no more than five years.

(l) who is employed in another member State and who is contributing as an employed or self-employed earner under the Social Security Act 1975 or the Social Security (Northern Ireland) Act 1975; or

(m) who, in the case of a national of a member State, a refugee or a stateless person, has entitlement to the provision of the services in question by virtue of Regulations made by the Council of the European Communities under Article 51 of the Treaty establishing the European Economic Community or, in the case of a national of another country, is entitled to be provided with such services by virtue of an agreement entered into between that Community and any other country; or

(n) whose detention in prison or in an institution provided by the Secretary of State under section 43(1) of the Prison Act 1952 is for the time being authorised by law; or who is detained under the provisions of the Immigration Act 1971; or

(o) in whose case the services are provided in circumstances covered by a reciprocal agreement with a country or territory specified in Schedule 2; or

(p) who-
   (i) is not a national of a Member State, and
   (ii) is a national of a State which is a signatory to the European Social Charter, and
   (iii) is not entitled to be provided with such services under a reciprocal agreement specified in Schedule 2, and
   (iv) is without sufficient resources to pay the charge, or

(q) who is working outside the United Kingdom as a missionary for an organisation that is established in the United Kingdom, regardless of whether he–
   (i) derives a salary or wage from the organisation, or
   (ii) receives any type of funding or assistance from the organisation for the purposes of working overseas for the organisation; or

(r) who the competent authorities of the United Kingdom for the purposes of the Council of Europe Convention on Action Against Trafficking in Human Beings (in this regulation 'the Convention'),
   (i) consider that there are reasonable grounds to believe is a victim within the meaning of Article 4 of the Convention, and the recovery and reflection period in relation to him under Article 13 of the Convention has not yet expired, or
   (ii) have identified as a victim within the meaning of Article 4 of the Convention.

(2) Where a person meets the residence qualification in paragraph (1)(b) on a date during a course of treatment for which charges could have been made prior to that date no charge shall be made in respect of services received subsequently;

(3) Where it is established that a person does not meet the residence qualification in paragraph (1)(b) and that person has already received services as part of a course of treatment on the basis that no charges would be made, no charges may be made for the remainder of that course of treatment.

(4) No charge is to be made in respect of any services forming part of the health service provided for–
   (a) in the case where sub-paragraph (g), (h), (i), (j), (q) or (r) of paragraph (1) applies to an overseas visitor, the spouse, civil partner or child of the overseas visitor; or

(b) in the case where any other sub-paragraph applies to an overseas visitor, the spouse, civil partner or child of the overseas visitor, if the spouse, civil partner or child lives on a permanent basis with the overseas visitor in the United Kingdom.

4A Exemption from charges during long term visits by United Kingdom pensioners

(1) No charge shall be made or recovered in respect of any overseas visitor who–

(a) is in receipt of a retirement pension under the Social Security Contributions and Benefits Act 1992 or the Social Security (Contributions and Benefits) (Northern Ireland) Act 1992;

(b) resides in the United Kingdom for at least six months and in another member State for less than six months each year; and

(c) is not registered as a resident of another member State; for services forming part of the health service which he receives during the period he resides in the United Kingdom.

(2) No charge shall be made in respect of any services forming part of the health service provided for the spouse, civil partner or child of an overseas visitor to whom this regulation applies where he lives on a permanent basis with the overseas visitor during the period they reside in the United Kingdom.

5 Exemption from charges for treatment the need for which arose during the visit

No charge for services forming part of the health service, provided only for the purpose of giving treatment the need for which arose during the visit, shall be made in respect of any overseas visitor who is–

(a) a national of a member State, or a refugee or a stateless person, or a member of the family of any of them, resident in each case in the territory of a member State; or

(b) a person, or the spouse, civil partner or child of a person, who has at any time had not less than ten years continuous lawful residence in the United Kingdom or not less than ten years continuous lawful service as a Crown servant employed in the right of Her Majesty's Government of the United Kingdom and is in receipt of a pension or benefit under the Social Security Act 1975 or the Social Security (Northern Ireland) Act 1975; or

(c) a person resident in a country, other than Israel, or territory specified in Schedule 2; or

(d) a person who is without sufficient resources to pay the charge and who is a national of a country which is a contracting party to the European Convention on Social and Medical Assistance 1954; or

(e) a person, or the spouse, civil partner or child of a person, who has at any time had not less than ten years continuous lawful residence in the United Kingdom and who is resident in a member State or in a country, other than Israel, or territory specified in Schedule 2, or

(f) an authorised child or an authorised companion.

6 Exemption from charges for treatment provided to a member of the forces of the North Atlantic Treaty Organisation

No charge shall be made or recovered for the provision of services forming part of the health services required for the treatment of a person to whom Article IX(5) of the North Atlantic Treaty Organisation Status of Forces Agreement applies, where such treatment cannot readily be provided by the medical services of the armed forces of his own country or of the United Kingdom.

6A Exemption from charges for exceptional humanitarian reasons

(1) Where an overseas visitor who has been granted leave to enter the United Kingdom for a course of treatment applies, or someone on his behalf applies, for exemption from charges for services forming part of the health service, the Secretary of State may determine where he considers that exceptional humanitarian reasons justify it, that no charge shall be made or recovered in respect of that person and that course of treatment.

(2) Such a determination may only be made by the Secretary of State if he is satisfied in the case of that person that–

(a) the treatment specified is not available in that person's home country;

(b) the necessary arrangements have been made for temporary accommodation for that person, the authorised companion (if any) and any authorised child for the duration of the course of treatment; and

(c) the necessary arrangements have been made for the return of that person, the authorised companion (if any) and any authorised child to their home country when the course of treatment is completed.

6B Regulation 6A as inserted for England shall additionally have effect in Wales subject to the modification that for the references to the 'Secretary of State' there shall be substituted references to the 'National Assembly for Wales.

7 Liability for payment of charges

The person liable to pay charges payable by virtue of these Regulations shall be the overseas visitor in respect of whom the services are provided except that–

(a) if the overseas visitor is employed to work on and for the purposes of a ship or vessel and is present in the United Kingdom in the course of such employment, the person liable to pay such charges shall be the owner of the ship or vessel on which the overseas visitor is employed; and

(b) if the overseas visitor is employed to work on and for the purposes of an aircraft and is present in the United Kingdom in the course of such employment, the person liable to pay such charges shall be his employer.

8 Repayments

(1) Where a sum has been paid as a charge for services forming part of the health service by or on behalf of a person who, at the time services were provided for such person, was not an overseas visitor in respect of whom,

or did not receive services for which, such a charge was payable, a claim for repayment of the sum may be made by presenting to the Authority or NHS trust or NHS foundation trust by which the charge was made and recovered–

(a) the receipt for payment of such sum;
(b) a declaration in support of the claim signed by or on behalf of the claimant; and
(c) such evidence in support of the declaration as the Authority or NHS trust or NHS foundation trust may require.

(2) The Authority or NHS trust or NHS foundation trust, if satisfied by the evidence so produced that the sum to which the receipt relates was not payable by virtue of these Regulations, shall repay to the claimant the amount of any such sum.

9 Revocation of Regulations

The Regulations specified in column 1 of Schedule 3 are hereby revoked.

SCHEDULE 1: DISEASES FOR THE TREATMENT OF WHICH NO CHARGE IS TO BE MADE

Regulation 3(c)

Part I: Notifiable Diseases Public Health (Control Of Disease) Act 1984 s10

Cholera
Food poisoning
Plague
Relapsing fever
Smallpox
Typhus

Part II: Diseases To Which Public Health Enactments Applied Public Health (Infectious Diseases) Regulations 1968

Acute encephalitis
Acute poliomyelitis
Amoebic dysentry
Anthrax
Bacillary dysentery
Diphtheria
Leprosy
Leptospirosis
Malaria
Measles
Meningitis
Meningococcal Septicaemia (without meningitis)
Mumps
Ophthalmia neonatorum

Paratyphoid fever
Rabies
Rubella
Scarlet fever
Tetanus
Tuberculosis
Typhoid fever
Viral haemorrhagic fever
Viral hepatitis
Whooping cough
Yellow fever

Part III: Food Poisoning And Food-Borne Infections Public Health (Infectious Diseases) Regulations 1968
Salmonella infections
Staphylococcal infections likely to cause food poisoning

PART IV: Other Diseases
Severe Acute Respiratory Syndrome.
Pandemic influenza (influenza caused by a new virus subtype that has an increased and sustained transmission during a global outbreak of influenza).

SCHEDULE 2: COUNTRIES OR TERRITORIES IN RESPECT OF WHICH THE UNITED KINGDOM GOVERNMENT HAS ENTERED INTO A RECIPROCAL AGREEMENT

Regulations 4 and 5
Anguilla
Australia
Barbados
British Virgin Islands
Falkland Islands
Gibraltar
Guernsey and its bailiwick
Iceland
Isle of Man
Israel
Jersey
Montserrat
New Zealand
Russian Federation
St Helena
Sweden
Turks and Caicos Islands
Union of Soviet Socialist Republics except the States of Estonia, Latvia, Lithuania and the Russian Federation
Yugoslavia

SCHEDULE 3: REVOCATIONS

Regulation 9

(1)	(2)
Regulations Revoked	***References***
The National Health Service (Charges to Overseas Visitors) (No. 2) Regulations 1982	SI 1982/863
The National Health Service (Charges to Overseas Visitors) (Amendment) Regulations 1982	SI 1982/1577
The National Health Service (Charges to Overseas Visitors) Amendment Regulations 1983	SI 1983/302
The National Health Service (Charges to Overseas Visitors) Amendment Regulations 1984	SI 1984/300
The National Health Service (Charges to Overseas Visitors) Amendment Regulations 1985	SI 1985/371
The National Health Service (Charges to Overseas Visitors) Amendment Regulations 1986	SI 1986/459
The National Health Services (Charges to Overseas Visitors) Amendment (No 2) Regulations 1986	SI 1986/950
The National Health Service (Charges to Overseas Visitors) Amendments Regulations 1987	SI 1987/371
The National Health Service (Charges to Overseas Visitors) Amendment Regulations 1988	SI 1988/8
The National Health Service (Charges to Overseas Visitors) Amendment (No 2) Regulations 1988	SI 1988/472

THE TRIBUNAL PROCEDURE (FIRST-TIER TRIBUNAL) (SOCIAL ENTITLEMENT CHAMBER) RULES 2008 SI NO 2685

PART 1: INTRODUCTION

1 Citation, commencement, application and interpretation

(1) These Rules may be cited as the Tribunal Procedure (First-tier Tribunal) (Social Entitlement Chamber) Rules 2008 and come into force on 3rd November 2008.

(2) These Rules apply to proceedings before the Tribunal which have been assigned to the Social Entitlement Chamber by the First-tier Tribunal and Upper Tribunal (Chambers) Order 2008.

(3) In these Rules–

'the 2007 Act' means the Tribunals, Courts and Enforcement Act 2007;

'appeal' includes an application under section 19(9) of the Tax Credits Act 2002;

'appellant' means a person who makes an appeal to the Tribunal, or a person substituted as an appellant under rule 9(1) (substitution of parties);

'asylum support case' means proceedings concerning the provision of support for an asylum seeker, a failed asylum seeker or a person designated under section 130 of the Criminal Justice and Immigration Act 2008 (designation), or the dependants of any such person;

'criminal injuries compensation case' means proceedings concerning the payment of compensation under a scheme made under the Criminal Injuries Compensation Act 1995;

'decision maker' means the maker of a decision against which an appeal has been brought;

'dispose of proceedings' includes, unless indicated otherwise, disposing of a part of the proceedings;

'document' means anything in which information is recorded in any form, and an obligation under these Rules to provide or allow access to a document or a copy of a document for any purpose means, unless the Tribunal directs otherwise, an obligation to provide or allow access to such document or copy in a legible form or in a form which can be readily made into a legible form;

'hearing' means an oral hearing and includes a hearing conducted in whole or in part by video link, telephone or other means of instantaneous two-way electronic communication;

'legal representative' means an authorised advocate or authorised litigator as defined by section 119(1) of the Courts and Legal Services Act 1990, an advocate or solicitor in Scotland or a barrister or solicitor in Northern Ireland;

'party' means–

(a) a person who is an appellant or respondent in proceedings before the Tribunal;

(b) a person who makes a reference to the Tribunal under section 28D of the Child Support Act 1991;

(c) a person who starts proceedings before the Tribunal under paragraph 3 of Schedule 2 to the Tax Credits Act 2002; or
(d) if the proceedings have been concluded, a person who was a party under paragraph (a), (b) or (c) when the Tribunal finally disposed of all issues in the proceedings;

'practice direction' means a direction given under section 23 of the 2007 Act;

'respondent' means–
(a) in an appeal against a decision, the decision maker and any person other than the appellant who had a right of appeal against the decision;
(b) in a reference under section 28D of the Child Support Act 1991–
  (i) the absent parent or non-resident parent;
  (ii) the person with care; and
  (iii) in Scotland, the child if the child made the application for a departure direction or a variation;
(c) in proceedings under paragraph 3 of Schedule 2 to the Tax Credits Act 2002, a person on whom it is proposed that a penalty be imposed; or
(d) a person substituted or added as a respondent under rule 9 (substitution and addition of parties);

'Social Entitlement Chamber' means the Social Entitlement Chamber of the First-tier Tribunal established by the First-tier Tribunal and Upper Tribunal (Chambers) Order 2008;

'social security and child support case' means any case allocated to the Social Entitlement Chamber except an asylum support case or a criminal injuries compensation case;

'Tribunal' means the First-tier Tribunal.

2 Overriding objective and parties' obligation to co-operate with the Tribunal

(1) The overriding objective of these Rules is to enable the Tribunal to deal with cases fairly and justly.
(2) Dealing with a case fairly and justly includes–
  (a) dealing with the case in ways which are proportionate to the importance of the case, the complexity of the issues, the anticipated costs and the resources of the parties;
  (b) avoiding unnecessary formality and seeking flexibility in the proceedings;
  (c) ensuring, so far as practicable, that the parties are able to participate fully in the proceedings;
  (d) using any special expertise of the Tribunal effectively; and
  (e) avoiding delay, so far as compatible with proper consideration of the issues.
(3) The Tribunal must seek to give effect to the overriding objective when it–
  (a) exercises any power under these Rules; or
  (b) interprets any rule or practice direction.
(4) Parties must–
  (a) help the Tribunal to further the overriding objective; and
  (b) co-operate with the Tribunal generally.

3 Alternative dispute resolution and arbitration

(1) The Tribunal should seek, where appropriate–
- (a) to bring to the attention of the parties the availability of any appropriate alternative procedure for the resolution of the dispute; and
- (b) if the parties wish and provided that it is compatible with the overriding objective, to facilitate the use of the procedure.

(2) Part 1 of the Arbitration Act 1996 does not apply to proceedings before the Tribunal.

PART 2: GENERAL POWERS AND PROVISIONS

4 Delegation to staff

(1) Staff appointed under section 40(1) of the 2007 Act (tribunal staff and services) may, with the approval of the Senior President of Tribunals, carry out functions of a judicial nature permitted or required to be done by the Tribunal.

(2) The approval referred to at paragraph (1) may apply generally to the carrying out of specified functions by members of staff of a specified description in specified circumstances.

(3) Within 14 days after the date on which the Tribunal sends notice of a decision made by a member of staff under paragraph (1) to a party, that party may apply in writing to the Tribunal for that decision to be considered afresh by a judge.

5 Case management powers

(1) Subject to the provisions of the 2007 Act and any other enactment, the Tribunal may regulate its own procedure.

(2) The Tribunal may give a direction in relation to the conduct or disposal of proceedings at any time, including a direction amending, suspending or setting aside an earlier direction.

(3) In particular, and without restricting the general powers in paragraphs (1) and (2), the Tribunal may–
- (a) extend or shorten the time for complying with any rule, practice direction or direction;
- (b) consolidate or hear together two or more sets of proceedings or parts of proceedings raising common issues, or treat a case as a lead case (whether in accordance with rule 18 (lead cases) or otherwise);
- (c) permit or require a party to amend a document;
- (d) permit or require a party or another person to provide documents, information, evidence or submissions to the Tribunal or a party;
- (e) deal with an issue in the proceedings as a preliminary issue;
- (f) hold a hearing to consider any matter, including a case management issue;
- (g) decide the form of any hearing;
- (h) adjourn or postpone a hearing;
- (i) require a party to produce a bundle for a hearing;
- (j) stay (or, in Scotland, sist) proceedings;

(k) transfer proceedings to another court or tribunal if that other court or tribunal has jurisdiction in relation to the proceedings and–
  (i) because of a change of circumstances since the proceedings were started, the Tribunal no longer has jurisdiction in relation to the proceedings; or
  (ii) the Tribunal considers that the other court or tribunal is a more appropriate forum for the determination of the case; or
(l) suspend the effect of its own decision pending the determination by the Tribunal or the Upper Tribunal of an application for permission to appeal against, and any appeal or review of, that decision.

6 Procedure for applying for and giving directions

(1) The Tribunal may give a direction on the application of one or more of the parties or on its own initiative.
(2) An application for a direction may be made–
  (a) by sending or delivering a written application to the Tribunal; or
  (b) orally during the course of a hearing.
(3) An application for a direction must include the reason for making that application.
(4) Unless the Tribunal considers that there is good reason not to do so, the Tribunal must send written notice of any direction to every party and to any other person affected by the direction.
(5) If a party or any other person sent notice of the direction under paragraph (4) wishes to challenge a direction which the Tribunal has given, they may do so by applying for another direction which amends, suspends or sets aside the first direction.

7 Failure to comply with rules etc.

(1) An irregularity resulting from a failure to comply with any requirement in these Rules, a practice direction or a direction, does not of itself render void the proceedings or any step taken in the proceedings.
(2) If a party has failed to comply with a requirement in these Rules, a practice direction or a direction, the Tribunal may take such action as it considers just, which may include–
  (a) waiving the requirement;
  (b) requiring the failure to be remedied;
  (c) exercising its power under rule 8 (striking out a party's case); or
  (d) exercising its power under paragraph (3).
(3) The Tribunal may refer to the Upper Tribunal, and ask the Upper Tribunal to exercise its power under section 25 of the 2007 Act in relation to, any failure by a person to comply with a requirement imposed by the Tribunal–
  (a) to attend at any place for the purpose of giving evidence;
  (b) otherwise to make themselves available to give evidence;
  (c) to swear an oath in connection with the giving of evidence;
  (d) to give evidence as a witness;
  (e) to produce a document; or
  (f) to facilitate the inspection of a document or any other thing (including any premises).

8 Striking out a party's case

(1) The proceedings, or the appropriate part of them, will automatically be struck out if the appellant has failed to comply with a direction that stated that failure by a party to comply with the direction would lead to the striking out of the proceedings or that part of them.

(2) The Tribunal must strike out the whole or a part of the proceedings if the Tribunal–

(a) does not have jurisdiction in relation to the proceedings or that part of them; and

(b) does not exercise its power under rule 5(3)(k)(i) (transfer to another court or tribunal) in relation to the proceedings or that part of them.

(3) The Tribunal may strike out the whole or a part of the proceedings if–

(a) the appellant has failed to comply with a direction which stated that failure by the appellant to comply with the direction could lead to the striking out of the proceedings or part of them;

(b) the appellant has failed to co-operate with the Tribunal to such an extent that the Tribunal cannot deal with the proceedings fairly and justly; or

(c) the Tribunal considers there is no reasonable prospect of the appellant's case, or part of it, succeeding.

(4) The Tribunal may not strike out the whole or a part of the proceedings under paragraph (2) or (3)(b) or (c) without first giving the appellant an opportunity to make representations in relation to the proposed striking out.

(5) If the proceedings, or part of them, have been struck out under paragraph (1) or (3)(a), the appellant may apply for the proceedings, or part of them, to be reinstated.

(6) An application under paragraph (5) must be made in writing and received by the Tribunal within 1 month after the date on which the Tribunal sent notification of the striking out to the appellant.

(7) This rule applies to a respondent as it applies to an appellant except that–

(a) a reference to the striking out of the proceedings is to be read as a reference to the barring of the respondent from taking further part in the proceedings; and

(b) a reference to an application for the reinstatement of proceedings which have been struck out is to be read as a reference to an application for the lifting of the bar on the respondent from taking further part in the proceedings.

(8) If a respondent has been barred from taking further part in proceedings under this rule and that bar has not been lifted, the Tribunal need not consider any response or other submission made by that respondent.

9 Substitution and addition of parties

(1) The Tribunal may give a direction substituting a party if–

(a) the wrong person has been named as a party; or

(b) the substitution has become necessary because of a change in circumstances since the start of proceedings.

(2) The Tribunal may give a direction adding a person to the proceedings as a respondent.

(3) If the Tribunal gives a direction under paragraph (1) or (2) it may give such consequential directions as it considers appropriate.

10 No power to award costs

The Tribunal may not make any order in respect of costs (or, in Scotland, expenses).

11 Representatives

(1) A party may appoint a representative (whether a legal representative or not) to represent that party in the proceedings.

(2) Subject to paragraph (3), if a party appoints a representative, that party (or the representative if the representative is a legal representative) must send or deliver to the Tribunal written notice of the representative's name and address.

(3) In a case to which rule 23 (cases in which the notice of appeal is to be sent to the decision-maker) applies, if the appellant (or the appellant's representative if the representative is a legal representative) provides written notification of the appellant's representative's name and address to the decision maker before the decision maker provides its response to the Tribunal, the appellant need not take any further steps in order to comply with paragraph (2).

(4) If the Tribunal receives notice that a party has appointed a representative under paragraph (2), it must send a copy of that notice to each other party.

(5) Anything permitted or required to be done by a party under these Rules, a practice direction or a direction may be done by the representative of that party, except signing a witness statement.

(6) A person who receives due notice of the appointment of a representative–

(a) must provide to the representative any document which is required to be provided to the represented party, and need not provide that document to the represented party; and

(b) may assume that the representative is and remains authorised as such until they receive written notification that this is not so from the representative or the represented party.

(7) At a hearing a party may be accompanied by another person whose name and address has not been notified under paragraph (2) or (3) but who, with the permission of the Tribunal, may act as a representative or otherwise assist in presenting the party's case at the hearing.

(8) Paragraphs (2) to (6) do not apply to a person who accompanies a party under paragraph (7).

12 Calculating time

(1) Except in asylum support cases, an act required by these Rules, a practice direction or a direction to be done on or by a particular day must be done by 5pm on that day.

(2) If the time specified by these Rules, a practice direction or a direction for doing any act ends on a day other than a working day, the act is done in time if it is done on the next working day.

(3) In this rule 'working day' means any day except a Saturday or Sunday, Christmas Day, Good Friday or a bank holiday under section 1 of the Banking and Financial Dealings Act 1971.

13 Sending and delivery of documents

(1) Any document to be provided to the Tribunal under these Rules, a practice direction or a direction must be–

(a) sent by pre-paid post or delivered by hand to the address specified for the proceedings;

(b) sent by fax to the number specified for the proceedings; or

(c) sent or delivered by such other method as the Tribunal may permit or direct.

(2) Subject to paragraph (3), if a party provides a fax number, email address or other details for the electronic transmission of documents to them, that party must accept delivery of documents by that method.

(3) If a party informs the Tribunal and all other parties that a particular form of communication (other than pre-paid post or delivery by hand) should not be used to provide documents to that party, that form of communication must not be so used.

(4) If the Tribunal or a party sends a document to a party or the Tribunal by email or any other electronic means of communication, the recipient may request that the sender provide a hard copy of the document to the recipient. The recipient must make such a request as soon as reasonably practicable after receiving the document electronically.

(5) The Tribunal and each party may assume that the address provided by a party or its representative is and remains the address to which documents should be sent or delivered until receiving written notification to the contrary.

14 Use of documents and information

(1) The Tribunal may make an order prohibiting the disclosure or publication of–

(a) specified documents or information relating to the proceedings; or

(b) any matter likely to lead members of the public to identify any person whom the Tribunal considers should not be identified.

(2) The Tribunal may give a direction prohibiting the disclosure of a document or information to a person if–

(a) the Tribunal is satisfied that such disclosure would be likely to cause that person or some other person serious harm; and

(b) the Tribunal is satisfied, having regard to the interests of justice, that it is proportionate to give such a direction.

(3) If a party ('the first party') considers that the Tribunal should give a direction under paragraph (2) prohibiting the disclosure of a document or information to another party ('the second party'), the first party must–

(a) exclude the relevant document or information from any documents that will be provided to the second party; and

(b) provide to the Tribunal the excluded document or information, and the reason for its exclusion, so that the Tribunal may decide whether the document or information should be disclosed to the second party or should be the subject of a direction under paragraph (2).

(4) The Tribunal must conduct proceedings as appropriate in order to give effect to a direction given under paragraph (2).

(5) If the Tribunal gives a direction under paragraph (2) which prevents disclosure to a party who has appointed a representative, the Tribunal may give a direction that the documents or information be disclosed to that representative if the Tribunal is satisfied that–
  (a) disclosure to the representative would be in the interests of the party; and
  (b) the representative will act in accordance with paragraph (6).

(6) Documents or information disclosed to a representative in accordance with a direction under paragraph (5) must not be disclosed either directly or indirectly to any other person without the Tribunal's consent.

15 Evidence and submissions

(1) Without restriction on the general powers in rule 5(1) and (2) (case management powers) the Tribunal may give directions as to–
  (a) issues on which it requires evidence or submissions;
  (b) the nature of the evidence or submissions it requires;
  (c) whether the parties are permitted or required to provide expert evidence;
  (d) any limit on the number of witnesses whose evidence a party may put forward, whether in relation to a particular issue or generally;
  (e) the manner in which any evidence or submissions are to be provided, which may include a direction for them to be given–
    (i) orally at a hearing; or
    (ii) by written submissions or witness statement; and
  (f) the time at which any evidence or submissions are to be provided.

(2) The Tribunal may–
  (a) admit evidence whether or not–
    (i) the evidence would be admissible in a civil trial in the United Kingdom; or
    (ii) the evidence was available to a previous decision maker; or
  (b) exclude evidence that would otherwise be admissible where–
    (i) the evidence was not provided within the time allowed by a direction or a practice direction;
    (ii) the evidence was otherwise provided in a manner that did not comply with a direction or a practice direction; or
    (iii) it would otherwise be unfair to admit the evidence.

(3) The Tribunal may consent to a witness giving, or require any witness to give, evidence on oath, and may administer an oath for that purpose.

16 Summoning or citation of witnesses and orders to answer questions or produce documents

(1) On the application of a party or on its own initiative, the Tribunal may–
  (a) by summons (or, in Scotland, citation) require any person to attend as a witness at a hearing at the time and place specified in the summons or citation; or
  (b) order any person to answer any questions or produce any documents in that person's possession or control which relate to any issue in the proceedings.

(2) A summons or citation under paragraph (1)(a) must–
  (a) give the person required to attend 14 days' notice of the hearing or such shorter period as the Tribunal may direct; and
  (b) where the person is not a party, make provision for the person's necessary expenses of attendance to be paid, and state who is to pay them.

(3) No person may be compelled to give any evidence or produce any document that the person could not be compelled to give or produce on a trial of an action in a court of law in the part of the United Kingdom where the proceedings are due to be determined.

(4) A summons, citation or order under this rule must–
  (a) state that the person on whom the requirement is imposed may apply to the Tribunal to vary or set aside the summons, citation or order, if they have not had an opportunity to object to it; and
  (b) state the consequences of failure to comply with the summons, citation or order.

17 Withdrawal

(1) Subject to paragraph (2), a party may give notice of the withdrawal of its case, or any part of it–
  (a) at any time before a hearing to consider the disposal of the proceedings (or, if the Tribunal disposes of the proceedings without a hearing, before that disposal), by sending or delivering to the Tribunal a written notice of withdrawal; or
  (b) orally at a hearing.

(2) In the circumstances described in paragraph (3), a notice of withdrawal will not take effect unless the Tribunal consents to the withdrawal.

(3) The circumstances referred to in paragraph (2) are where a party gives notice of withdrawal–
  (a) under paragraph (1)(a) in a criminal injuries compensation case; or
  (b) under paragraph (1)(b).

(4) A party who has withdrawn their case may apply to the Tribunal for the case to be reinstated.

(5) An application under paragraph (4) must be made in writing and be received by the Tribunal within 1 month after–
  (a) the date on which the Tribunal received the notice under paragraph (1)(a); or
  (b) the date of the hearing at which the case was withdrawn orally under paragraph (1)(b).

(6) The Tribunal must notify each party in writing of an withdrawal under this rule.

18 Lead cases

(1) This rule applies if–
  (a) two or more cases have been started before the Tribunal;
  (b) in each such case the Tribunal has not made a decision disposing of the proceedings; and
  (c) the cases give rise to common or related issues of fact or law.

(2) The Tribunal may give a direction–
  (a) specifying one or more cases falling under paragraph (1) as a lead case or lead cases; and
  (b) staying (or, in Scotland, sisting) the other cases falling under paragraph (1) ('the related cases').
(3) When the Tribunal makes a decision in respect of the common or related issues–
  (a) the Tribunal must send a copy of that decision to each party in each of the related cases; and
  (b) subject to paragraph (4), that decision shall be binding on each of those parties.
(4) Within 1 month after the date on which the Tribunal sent a copy of the decision to a party under paragraph (3)(a), that party may apply in writing for a direction that the decision does not apply to, and is not binding on the parties to, a particular related case.
(5) The Tribunal must give directions in respect of cases which are stayed or sisted under paragraph (2)(b), providing for the disposal of or further directions in those cases.
(6) If the lead case or cases lapse or are withdrawn before the Tribunal makes a decision in respect of the common or related issues, the Tribunal must give directions as to–
  (a) whether another case or other cases are to be specified as a lead case or lead cases; and
  (b) whether any direction affecting the related cases should be set aside or amended.

19 Confidentiality in child support or child trust fund cases

(1) Paragraph (3) applies to proceedings under the Child Support Act 1991 in the circumstances described in paragraph (2), other than an appeal against a reduced benefit decision (as defined in section 46(10)(b) of the Child Support Act 1991, as that section had effect prior to the commencement of section 15(b) of the Child Maintenance and Other Payments Act 2008).
(2) The circumstances referred to in paragraph (1) are that the absent parent, non-resident parent or person with care would like their address or the address of the child to be kept confidential and has given notice to that effect–
  (a) to the Secretary of State or the Child Maintenance and Enforcement Commission in the notice of appeal or when notifying any subsequent change of address;
  (b) to the Secretary of State or the Child Maintenance and Enforcement Commission, whichever has made the enquiry, within 14 days after an enquiry is made; or
  (c) to the Tribunal when notifying any change of address.
(3) Where this paragraph applies, the Secretary of State, the Child Maintenance and Enforcement Commission and the Tribunal must take appropriate steps to secure the confidentiality of the address, and of any information which could reasonably be expected to enable a person to identify the address, to the extent that the address or that information is not already known to each other party.
(4) Paragraph (6) applies to proceedings under the Child Trust Funds Act 2004 in the circumstances described in paragraph (5).

(5) The circumstances referred to in paragraph (4) are that a relevant person would like their address or the address of the eligible child to be kept confidential and has given notice to that effect, or a local authority with parental responsibility in relation to the eligible child would like the address of the eligible child to be kept confidential and has given notice to that effect–

(a) to HMRC in the notice of appeal or when notifying any subsequent change of address;

(b) to HMRC within 14 days after an enquiry by HMRC; or

(c) to the Tribunal when notifying any change of address.

(6) Where this paragraph applies, HMRC and the Tribunal must take appropriate steps to secure the confidentiality of the address, and of any information which could reasonably be expected to enable a person to identify the address, to the extent that the address or that information is not already known to each other party.

(7) In this rule–

'eligible child' has the meaning set out in section 2 of the Child Trust Funds Act 2004;

'HMRC' means Her Majesty's Revenue and Customs;

'non-resident parent' and 'parent with care' have the meanings set out in section 54 of the Child Support Act 1991;

'parental responsibility' has the meaning set out in section 3(9) of the Child Trust Funds Act 2004; and

'relevant person' has the meaning set out in section 22(3) of the Child Trust Funds Act 2004.

20 Expenses in criminal injuries compensation cases

(1) This rule applies only to criminal injuries compensation cases.

(2) The Tribunal may meet reasonable expenses–

(a) incurred by the appellant, or any person who attends a hearing to give evidence, in attending the hearing; or

(b) incurred by the appellant in connection with any arrangements made by the Tribunal for the inspection of the appellant's injury.

21 Expenses in social security and child support cases

(1) This rule applies only to social security and child support cases.

(2) The Secretary of State may pay such travelling and other allowances (including compensation for loss of remunerative time) as the Secretary of State may determine to any person required to attend a hearing in proceedings under section 20 of the Child Support Act 1991, section 12 of the Social Security Act 1998 or paragraph 6 of Schedule 7 to the Child Support, Pensions and Social Security Act 2000.

PART 3: PROCEEDINGS BEFORE THE TRIBUNAL

Chapter 1: Before the hearing

22 Cases in which the notice of appeal is to be sent to the Tribunal

(1) This rule applies to asylum support cases and criminal injuries compensation cases.

(2) An appellant must start proceedings by sending or delivering a notice of appeal to the Tribunal so that it is received–
  (a) in asylum support cases, within 3 days after the date on which the appellant received written notice of the decision being challenged;
  (b) in criminal injuries compensation cases, within 90 days after the date of the decision being challenged.

(3) The notice of appeal must be in English or Welsh, must be signed by the appellant and must state–
  (a) the name and address of the appellant;
  (b) the name and address of the appellant's representative (if any);
  (c) an address where documents for the appellant may be sent or delivered;
  (d) the name and address of any respondent;
  (e) details (including the full reference) of the decision being appealed; and
  (f) the grounds on which the appellant relies.

(4) The appellant must provide with the notice of appeal–
  (a) a copy of any written record of the decision being challenged;
  (b) any statement of reasons for that decision that the appellant has or can reasonably obtain;
  (c) any documents in support of the appellant's case which have not been supplied to the respondent; and
  (d) any further information or documents required by an applicable practice direction.

(5) In asylum support cases the notice of appeal must also–
  (a) state whether the appellant will require an interpreter at any hearing, and if so for which language or dialect; and
  (b) state whether the appellant intends to attend or be represented at any hearing.

(6) If the appellant provides the notice of appeal to the Tribunal later than the time required by paragraph (2) or by an extension of time allowed under rule 5(3)(a) (power to extend time)–
  (a) the notice of appeal must include a request for an extension of time and the reason why the notice of appeal was not provided in time; and
  (b) unless the Tribunal extends time for the notice of appeal under rule 5(3)(a) (power to extend time) the Tribunal must not admit the notice of appeal.

(7) The Tribunal must send a copy of the notice of appeal and any accompanying documents to each other party–
  (a) in asylum support cases, on the day that the Tribunal receives the notice of appeal, or

  (if that is not reasonably practicable) as soon as reasonably practicable on the following day;
  (b) in criminal injuries compensation cases, as soon as reasonably practicable after the Tribunal receives the notice of appeal.

23 Cases in which the notice of appeal is to be sent to the decision maker

(1) This rule applies to social security and child support cases (except references under the Child Support Act 1991 and proceedings under paragraph 3 of Schedule 2 to the Tax Credits Act 2002).

(2) An appellant must start proceedings by sending or delivering a notice of appeal to the decision maker so that it is received within the time specified in Schedule 1 to these Rules (time limits for providing notices of appeal to the decision maker).

(3) If the appellant provides the notice of appeal to the decision maker later than the time required by paragraph (2) the notice of appeal must include the reason why the notice of appeal was not provided in time.

(4) Subject to paragraph (5), where an appeal is not made within the time specified in Schedule 1, it will be treated as having been made in time if the decision maker does not object.

(5) No appeal may be made more than 12 months after the time specified in Schedule 1.

(6) The notice of appeal must be in English or Welsh, must be signed by the appellant and must state–

(a) the name and address of the appellant;

(b) the name and address of the appellant's representative (if any);

(c) an address where documents for the appellant may be sent or delivered;

(d) details of the decision being appealed; and

(e) the grounds on which the appellant relies.

(7) The decision maker must refer the case to the Tribunal immediately if–

(a) the appeal has been made after the time specified in Schedule 1 and the decision maker objects to it being treated as having been made in time; or

(b) the decision maker considers that the appeal has been made more than 12 months after the time specified in Schedule 1.

(8) Notwithstanding rule 5(3)(a) (case management powers) and rule 7(2) (failure to comply with rules etc.), the Tribunal must not extend the time limit in paragraph (5).

24 Responses and replies

(1) When a decision maker receives the notice of appeal or a copy of it, the decision maker must send or deliver a response to the Tribunal–

(a) in asylum support cases, so that it is received within 3 days after the date on which the Tribunal received the notice of appeal; and

(b) in other cases, as soon as reasonably practicable after the decision maker received the notice of appeal.

(2) The response must state–

(a) the name and address of the decision maker;

(b) the name and address of the decision maker's representative (if any);

(c) an address where documents for the decision maker may be sent or delivered;

(d) the names and addresses of any other respondents and their representatives (if any);

(e) whether the decision maker opposes the appellant's case and, if so, any grounds for such opposition which are not set out in any documents which are before the Tribunal; and

(f) any further information or documents required by a practice direction or direction.

(3) The response may include a submission as to whether it would be appropriate for the case to be disposed of without a hearing.

(4) The decision maker must provide with the response–

(a) a copy of any written record of the decision under challenge, and any statement of reasons for that decision, if they were not sent with the notice of appeal;

(b) copies of all documents relevant to the case in the decision maker's possession, unless a practice direction or direction states otherwise; and

(c) in cases to which rule 23 (cases in which the notice of appeal is to be sent to the decision maker) applies, a copy of the notice of appeal, any documents provided by the appellant with the notice of appeal and (if they have not otherwise been provided to the Tribunal) the name and address of the appellant's representative (if any).

(5) The decision maker must provide a copy of the response and any accompanying documents to each other party at the same time as it provides the response to the Tribunal.

(6) The appellant and any other respondent may make a written submission and supply further documents in reply to the decision maker's response.

(7) Any submission or further documents under paragraph (6) must be provided to the Tribunal within 1 month after the date on which the decision maker sent the response to

25 Medical and physical examination in appeals under section 12 of the Social Security Act 1998

(1) This rule applies only to appeals under section 12 of the Social Security Act 1998.

(2) At a hearing an appropriate member of the Tribunal may carry out a physical examination of a person if the case relates to–

(a) the extent of that person's disablement and its assessment in accordance with section 68(6) of and Schedule 6 to, or section 103 of, the Social Security Contributions and Benefits Act 1992; or

(b) diseases or injuries prescribed for the purpose of section 108 of that Act.

(3) If an issue which falls within Schedule 2 to these Rules (issues in relation to which the Tribunal may refer a person for medical examination) is raised in an appeal, the Tribunal may exercise its power under section 20 of the Social Security Act 1998 to refer a person to a health care professional approved by the Secretary of State for–

(a) the examination of that person; and

(b) the production of a report on the condition of that person.

(4) Neither paragraph (2) nor paragraph (3) entitles the Tribunal to require a person to undergo a physical test for the purpose of determining whether that person is unable to walk or virtually unable to do so.

26 Social security and child support cases started by reference or information in writing

(1) This rule applies to proceedings under section 28D of the Child Support Act 1991 and paragraph 3 of Schedule 2 to the Tax Credits Act 2002.

(2) A person starting proceedings under section 28D of the Child Support Act 1991 must send or deliver a written reference to the Tribunal.

(3) A person starting proceedings under paragraph 3 of Schedule 2 to the Tax Credits Act 2002 must send or deliver an information in writing to the Tribunal.

(4) The reference or the information in writing must include–

(a) an address where documents for the person starting proceedings may be sent or delivered;

(b) the names and addresses of the respondents and their representatives (if any); and

(c) a submission on the issues that arise for determination by the Tribunal.

(5) Unless a practice direction or direction states otherwise, the person starting proceedings must also provide a copy of each document in their possession which is relevant to the proceedings.

(6) Subject to any obligation under rule 19(3) (confidentiality in child support cases), the person starting proceedings must provide a copy of the written reference or the information in writing and any accompanying documents to each respondent at the same time as they provide the written reference or the information in writing to the Tribunal.

(7) Each respondent may send or deliver to the Tribunal a written submission and any further relevant documents within one month of the date on which the person starting proceedings sent a copy of the written reference or the information in writing to that respondent.

Chapter 2: Hearings

27 Decision with or without a hearing

(1) Subject to the following paragraphs, the Tribunal must hold a hearing before making a decision which disposes of proceedings unless–

(a) each party has consented to, or has not objected to, the matter being decided without a hearing; and

(b) the Tribunal considers that it is able to decide the matter without a hearing.

(2) This rule does not apply to decisions under Part 4.

(3) The Tribunal may in any event dispose of proceedings without a hearing under rule 8 (striking out a party's case).

(4) In a criminal injuries compensation case–

(a) the Tribunal may make a decision which disposes of proceedings without a hearing; and

(b) subject to paragraph (5), if the Tribunal makes a decision which disposes of proceedings without a hearing, any party may make a written application to the Tribunal for the decision to be reconsidered at a hearing.

(5) An application under paragraph (4)(b) may not be made in relation to a decision–

(a) not to extend a time limit;

(b) not to set aside a previous decision;

(c) not to allow an appeal against a decision not to extend a time limit; or

(d) not to allow an appeal against a decision not to reopen a case.

(6) An application under paragraph (4)(b) must be received within 1 month after the date on which the Tribunal sent notice of the decision to the party making the application.

28 Entitlement to attend a hearing

Subject to rule 30(5) (exclusion of a person from a hearing), each party to proceedings is entitled to attend a hearing.

29 Notice of hearings

(1) The Tribunal must give each party entitled to attend a hearing reasonable notice of the time and place of the hearing (including any adjourned or postponed hearing) and any changes to the time and place of the hearing.

(2) The period of notice under paragraph (1) must be at least 14 days except that–

(a) in an asylum support case the Tribunal must give at least 1 day's and not more than 5 days' notice; and

(b) the Tribunal may give shorter notice–

(i) with the parties' consent; or

(ii) in urgent or exceptional circumstances.

30 Public and private hearings

(1) Subject to the following paragraphs, all hearings must be held in public.

(2) A hearing in a criminal injuries compensation case must be held in private unless–

(a) the appellant has consented to the hearing being held in public; and

(b) the Tribunal considers that it is in the interests of justice for the hearing to be held in public.

(3) The Tribunal may give a direction that a hearing, or part of it, is to be held in private.

(4) Where a hearing, or part of it, is to be held in private, the Tribunal may determine who is permitted to attend the hearing or part of it.

(5) The Tribunal may give a direction excluding from any hearing, or part of it–

(a) any person whose conduct the Tribunal considers is disrupting or is likely to disrupt the hearing;

(b) any person whose presence the Tribunal considers is likely to prevent another person from giving evidence or making submissions freely;

(c) any person who the Tribunal considers should be excluded in order to give effect to a direction under rule 14(2) (withholding information likely to cause harm); or

(d) any person where the purpose of the hearing would be defeated by the attendance of that person.

(6) The Tribunal may give a direction excluding a witness from a hearing until that witness gives evidence.

31 Hearings in a party's absence

If a party fails to attend a hearing the Tribunal may proceed with the hearing if the Tribunal–

(a) is satisfied that the party has been notified of the hearing or that reasonable steps have been taken to notify the party of the hearing; and
(b) considers that it is in the interests of justice to proceed with the hearing.

Chapter 3: Decisions

32 Consent orders

(1) The Tribunal may, at the request of the parties but only if it considers it appropriate, make a consent order disposing of the proceedings and making such other appropriate provision as the parties have agreed.
(2) Notwithstanding any other provision of these Rules, the Tribunal need not hold a hearing before making an order under paragraph (1), or provide reasons for the order.

33 Notice of decisions

(1) The Tribunal may give a decision orally at a hearing.
(2) Subject to rule 14(2) (withholding information likely to cause harm), the Tribunal must provideto each party as soon as reasonably practicable after making a decision which finally disposes of all issues in the proceedings (except a decision under Part 4)–
(a) a decision notice stating the Tribunal's decision;
(b) where appropriate, notification of the right to apply for a written statement of reasons under rule 34(3); and
(c) notification of any right of appeal against the decision and the time within which, and the manner in which, such right of appeal may be exercised.
(3) In asylum support cases the notice and notifications required by paragraph (2) must be provided at the hearing or sent on the day that the decision is made.

34 Reasons for decisions

(1) In asylum support cases the Tribunal must send a written statement of reasons for a decision which disposes of proceedings (except a decision under Part 4) to each party–
(a) if the case is decided at a hearing, within 3 days after the hearing; or
(b) if the case is decided without a hearing, on the day that the decision is made.
(2) In all other cases the Tribunal may give reasons for a decision which disposes of proceedings (except a decision under Part 4)–
(a) orally at a hearing; or
(b) in a written statement of reasons to each party.
(3) Unless the Tribunal has already provided a written statement of reasons under paragraph (2)(b), a party may make a written application to the Tribunal for such statement following a decision which finally disposes of all issues in the proceedings.
(4) An application under paragraph (3) must be received within 1 month of the date on which the Tribunal sent or otherwise provided to the party a

decision notice relating to the decision which finally disposes of all issues in the proceedings.

(5) If a party makes an application in accordance with paragraphs (3) and (4) the Tribunal must, subject to rule 14(2) (withholding information likely to cause harm), send a written statement of reasons to each party within 1 month of the date on which it received the application or as soon as reasonably practicable after the end of that period.

PART 4: Correcting, setting aside, reviewing and appealing Tribunal decisions

35 Interpretation

In this Part–

'appeal' means the exercise of a right of appeal–

(a) under paragraph 2(2) or 4(1) of Schedule 2 to the Tax Credits Act 2002;

(b) under section 21(10) of the Child Trust Funds Act 2004; or

(c) on a point of law under section 11 of the 2007 Act; and

'review' means the review of a decision by the Tribunal under section 9 of the 2007 Act.

36 Clerical mistakes and accidental slips or omissions

The Tribunal may at any time correct any clerical mistake or other accidental slip or omission in a decision, direction or any document produced by it, by–

(a) sending notification of the amended decision or direction, or a copy of the amended document, to all parties; and

(b) making any necessary amendment to any information published in relation to the decision, direction or document.

37 Setting aside a decision which disposes of proceedings

(1) The Tribunal may set aside a decision which disposes of proceedings, or part of such a decision, and re-make the decision, or the relevant part of it, if–

(a) the Tribunal considers that it is in the interests of justice to do so; and

(b) one or more of the conditions in paragraph (2) are satisfied.

(2) The conditions are–

(a) a document relating to the proceedings was not sent to, or was not received at an appropriate time by, a party or a party's representative;

(b) a document relating to the proceedings was not sent to the Tribunal at an appropriate time;

(c) a party, or a party's representative, was not present at a hearing related to the proceedings; or

(d) there has been some other procedural irregularity in the proceedings.

(3) A party applying for a decision, or part of a decision, to be set aside under paragraph (1) must make a written application to the Tribunal so that it is received no later than 1 month after the date on which the Tribunal sent notice of the decision to the party.

38 Application for permission to appeal

(1) This rule does not apply to asylum support cases or criminal injuries compensation cases.

(2) A person seeking permission to appeal must make a written application to the Tribunal for permission to appeal.

(3) An application under paragraph (2) must be sent or delivered to the Tribunal so that it is received no later than 1 month after the latest of the dates that the Tribunal sends to the person making the application–

(a) written reasons for the decision;

(b) notification of amended reasons for, or correction of, the decision following a review;

or

(c) notification that an application for the decision to be set aside has been unsuccessful.

(4) The date in paragraph (3)(c) applies only if the application for the decision to be set aside was made within the time stipulated in rule 37 (setting aside a decision which disposes of proceedings) or any extension of that time granted by the Tribunal.

(5) If the person seeking permission to appeal sends or delivers the application to the Tribunal later than the time required by paragraph (3) or by any extension of time under rule 5(3)(a) (power to extend time)–

(a) the application must include a request for an extension of time and the reason why the application was not provided in time; and

(b) unless the Tribunal extends time for the application under rule 5(3)(a) (power to extend time) the Tribunal must not admit the application.

(6) An application under paragraph (2) must–

(a) identify the decision of the Tribunal to which it relates;

(b) identify the alleged error or errors of law in the decision; and

(c) state the result the party making the application is seeking.

(7) If a person makes an application under paragraph (2) when the Tribunal has not given a written statement of reasons for its decision–

(a) if no application for a written statement of reasons has been made to the Tribunal, the application for permission must be treated as such an application;

(b) unless the Tribunal decides to give permission and directs that this sub-paragraph does not apply, the application is not to be treated as an application for permission to appeal; and

(c) if an application for a written statement of reasons has been, or is, refused because of a delay in making the application, the Tribunal must only admit the application for permission if the Tribunal considers that it is in the interests of justice to do so.

39 Tribunal's consideration of application for permission to appeal

(1) On receiving an application for permission to appeal the Tribunal must first consider, taking into account the overriding objective in rule 2, whether to review the decision in accordance with rule 40 (review of a decision).

(2) If the Tribunal decides not to review the decision, or reviews the decision and decides to take no action in relation to the decision, or part of it, the Tribunal must consider whether to give permission to appeal in relation to the decision or that part of it.

(3) The Tribunal must send a record of its decision to the parties as soon as practicable.

(4) If the Tribunal refuses permission to appeal it must send with the record of its decision–

(a) a statement of its reasons for such refusal; and

(b) notification of the right to make an application to the Upper Tribunal for permission to appeal and the time within which, and the method by which, such application must be made.

(5) The Tribunal may give permission to appeal on limited grounds, but must comply with paragraph

(4) in relation to any grounds on which it has refused permission.

40 Review of a decision

(1) This rule does not apply to asylum support cases or criminal injuries compensation cases.

(2) The Tribunal may only undertake a review of a decision–

(a) pursuant to rule 39(1) (review on an application for permission to appeal); and

(b) if it is satisfied that there was an error of law in the decision.

(3) The Tribunal must notify the parties in writing of the outcome of any review, and of any right of appeal in relation to the outcome.

(4) If the Tribunal takes any action in relation to a decision following a review without first giving every party an opportunity to make representations, the notice under paragraph (3) must state that any party that did not have an opportunity to make representations may apply for such action to be set aside and for the decision to be reviewed again.

41 Power to treat an application as a different type of application

The Tribunal may treat an application for a decision to be corrected, set aside or reviewed, or for permission to appeal against a decision, as an application for any other one of those things.

SCHEDULE 1: TIME LIMITS FOR PROVIDING NOTICES OF APPEAL TO THE DECISION MAKER

Rule 23

Type of proceedings	*Time for providing notice of appeal*
cases other than those listed below	the latest of– (a) one month after the date on which notice of the decision being challenged was sent to the appellant; (b) if a written statement of reasons for the decision is requested, 14 days after the later of (i) the date on which the period at (a) expires; and (ii) the date on which the written statement of reasons was provided; or (c) where the appellant made an application for revision of the decision under– (i) regulation 17(1)(a) of the Child Support (Maintenance Assessment Procedure) Regulations 1992; (ii) regulation 3(1) or (3) or 3A(1) of the Social Security and Child Support (Decision & Appeals) Regulations 1999; or (iii) regulation 4 of the Housing Benefit and Council Tax Benefit (Decisions and Appeals) Regulations 2001 and that application was unsuccessful, one month of the date on which notice that the decision would not be revised was sent to the appellant.
appeal against a certificate of NHS charges under section 157(1) of the Health and Social Care (Community Health and Standards) Act 2003	(a) 3 months after the latest of– (i) the date on the certificate; (ii) the date on which the compensation payment was made; (iii) if the certificate has been reviewed, the date the certificate was confirmed or a fresh certificate was issued; or (iv) the date of any agreement to treat an earlier compensation payment as having been made in final discharge of a claim made by or in respect of an injured person and arising out of the injury or death; or

Type of proceedings	*Time for providing notice of appeal*
	(b) if the person to whom the certificate has been issued makes an application under section 157(4) of the Health and Social Care (Community Health and Standards) Act 2003, one month after– (i) the date of the decision on that application; or (ii) if the person appeals against that decision under section 157(6) of that Act, the date on which the appeal is decided or withdrawn
appeal against a waiver decision under section 157(6) of the Health and Social Care (Community Health and Standards) Act 2003	one month after the date of the decision
appeal against a certificate of NHS charges under section 7 of the Road Traffic (NHS Charges) Act 1999	3 months after the latest of– (a) the date on which the liability under section 1(2) of the Road Traffic (NHS Charges) Act 1999 was discharged; (b) if the certificate has been reviewed, the date the certificate was confirmed or a fresh certificate was issued; or (c) the date of any agreement to treat an earlier compensation payment as having been made in final discharge of a claim made by or in respect of a traffic casualty and arising out of the injury or death

Type of proceedings	*Time for providing notice of appeal*
appeal against a certificate of recoverable benefits under section 11 of the Social Security (Recovery of Benefits) Act 1997	one month after the latest of– (a) the date on which any payment to the Secretary of State required under section 6 of the Social Security (Recovery of Benefits) Act 1997 was made; (b) if the certificate has been reviewed, the date the certificate was confirmed or a fresh certificate was issued; or (c) the date of any agreement to treat an earlier compensation payment as having been made in final discharge of a claim made by or in respect of an injured person and arising out of the accident, injury or disease
appeal under the Vaccine Damage Payments Act 1979	no time limit
appeal under the Tax Credits Act 2002	as set out in the Tax Credits Act 2002
appeal under the Child Trust Funds Act 2004	as set out in the Child Trust Funds Act 2004
appeal against a decision in respect of a claim for child benefit or guardian's allowance under section 12 of the Social Security Act 1998	as set out in regulation 28 of the Child Benefit and Guardian's Allowance (Decisions and Appeals) Regulations 2003

SCHEDULE 2: ISSUES IN RELATION TO WHICH THE TRIBUNAL MAY REFER A PERSON FOR MEDICAL EXAMINATION UNDER SECTION 20(2) OF THE SOCIAL SECURITY ACT 1998

Rule 25(3)

An issue falls within this Schedule if the issue–

(a) is whether the claimant satisfies the conditions for entitlement to–
  (i) an attendance allowance specified in section 64 and 65(1) of the Social Security Contributions and Benefits Act 1992;
  (ii) severe disablement allowance under section 68 of that Act;
  (iii) the care component of a disability living allowance specified in section 72(1) and (2) of that Act;
  (iv) the mobility component of a disability living allowance specified in section 73(1), (8) and (9) of that Act; or
  (v) a disabled person's tax credit specified in section 129(1)(b) of that Act.

(b) relates to the period throughout which the claimant is likely to satisfy the conditions for entitlement to an attendance allowance or a disability living allowance;

(c) is the rate at which an attendance allowance is payable;

(d) is the rate at which the care component or the mobility component of a disability living allowance is payable;

(e) is whether a person is incapable of work for the purposes of the Social Security Contributions and Benefits Act 1992;

(f) relates to the extent of a person's disablement and its assessment in accordance with Schedule 6 to the Social Security Contributions and Benefits Act 1992;

(g) is whether the claimant suffers a loss of physical or mental faculty as a result of the relevant accident for the purposes of section 103 of the Social Security Contributions and Benefits Act 1992;

(h) relates to any payment arising under, or by virtue of a scheme having effect under, section 111 of, and Schedule 8 to, the Social Security Contributions and Benefits Act 1992 (workmen's compensation);

(i) is whether a person has limited capability for work or work-related activity for the purposes of the Welfare Reform Act 2007.

APPENDIX B

EU law

COUNCIL DIRECTIVE 2003/9/EC

of 27 January 2003

laying down minimum standards for the reception of asylum seekers[1]

THE COUNCIL OF THE EUROPEAN UNION,
Having regard to the Treaty establishing the European Community, and in particular point (1)(b) of the first subparagraph of Article 63 thereof,

Having regard to the proposal from the Commission,[2]

Having regard to the opinion of the European Parliament,[3]

Having regard to the opinion of the Economic and Social Committee,[4]

Having regard to the opinion of the Committee of the Regions,[5] Whereas:

(1) A common policy on asylum, including a Common European Asylum System, is a constituent part of the European Union's objective of progressively establishing an area of freedom, security and justice open to those who, forced by circumstances, legitimately seek protection in the Community.

(2) At its special meeting in Tampere on 15 and 16 October 1999, the European Council agreed to work towards establishing a Common European Asylum System, based on the full and inclusive application of the Geneva Convention relating to the Status of Refugees of 28 July 1951, as supplemented by the New York Protocol of 31 January 1967, thus maintaining the principle of non-refoulement.

(3) The Tampere Conclusions provide that a Common European Asylum System should include, in the short term, common minimum conditions of reception of asylum seekers.

(4) The establishment of minimum standards for the reception of asylum seekers is a further step towards a European asylum policy.

(5) This Directive respects the fundamental rights and observes the principles recognised in particular by the Charter of Fundamental Rights of the European Union. In particular, this Directive seeks to ensure full respect for human dignity and to promote the application of Articles 1 and 18 of the said Charter.

(6) With respect to the treatment of persons falling within the scope of this Directive, Member States are bound by obligations under instruments of international law to which they are party and which prohibit discrimination.

1 Reproduced from Official Journal of the European Union, 6 February 2003 L 31/19.

2 OJ C 213 E, 31 July 2001, p286.

3 Opinion delivered on 25 April 2002 (not yet published in the Official Journal).

4 OJ C 48, 21 February 2002, p63.

5 OJ C 107, 3 May 2002, p85.

(7) Minimum standards for the reception of asylum seekers that will normally suffice to ensure them a dignified standard of living and comparable living conditions in all Member States should be laid down.

(8) The harmonisation of conditions for the reception of asylum seekers should help to limit the secondary movements of asylum seekers influenced by the variety of conditions for their reception.

(9) Reception of groups with special needs should be specifically designed to meet those needs.

(10) Reception of applicants who are in detention should be specifically designed to meet their needs in that situation.

(11) In order to ensure compliance with the minimum procedural guarantees consisting in the opportunity to contact organisations or groups of persons that provide legal assistance, information should be provided on such organisations and groups of persons.

(12) The possibility of abuse of the reception system should be restricted by laying down cases for the reduction or withdrawal of reception conditions for asylum seekers.

(13) The efficiency of national reception systems and cooperation among Member States in the field of reception of asylum seekers should be secured.

(14) Appropriate coordination should be encouraged between the competent authorities as regards the reception of asylum seekers, and harmonious relationships between local communities and accommodation centres should therefore be promoted.

(15) It is in the very nature of minimum standards that Member States have the power to introduce or maintain more favourable provisions for third-country nationals and stateless persons who ask for international protection from a Member State.

(16) In this spirit, Member States are also invited to apply the provisions of this Directive in connection with procedures for deciding on applications for forms of protection other than that emanating from the Geneva Convention for third country nationals and stateless persons.

(17) The implementation of this Directive should be evaluated at regular intervals.

(18) Since the objectives of the proposed action, namely to establish minimum standards on the reception of asylum seekers in Member States, cannot be sufficiently achieved by the Member States and can therefore, by reason of the scale and effects of the proposed action, be better achieved by the Community, the Community may adopt measures in accordance with the principles of subsidiarity as set out in Article 5 of the Treaty. In accordance with the principle of proportionality, as set out in that Article, this Directive does not go beyond what is necessary in order to achieve those objectives.

(19) In accordance with Article 3 of the Protocol on the position of the United Kingdom and Ireland, annexed to the Treaty on European Union and to the Treaty establishing the European Community, the United Kingdom gave notice, by letter of 18 August 2001, of its wish to take part in the adoption and application of this Directive.

(20) In accordance with Article 1 of the said Protocol, Ireland is not participating in the adoption of this Directive. Consequently, and without prejudice to Article 4 of the aforementioned Protocol, the provisions of this Directive do not apply to Ireland.

(21) In accordance with Articles 1 and 2 of the Protocol on the position of Denmark, annexed to the Treaty on European Union and to the Treaty establishing the European Community, Denmark is not participating in the adoption of this Directive and is therefore neither bound by it nor subject to its application,

HAS ADOPTED THIS DIRECTIVE:

CHAPTER I: PURPOSE, DEFINITIONS AND SCOPE

Article 1: Purpose

The purpose of this Directive is to lay down minimum standards for the reception of asylum seekers in Member States.

Article 2: Definitions

For the purposes of this Directive:

(a) 'Geneva Convention' shall mean the Convention of 28 July 1951 relating to the status of refugees, as amended by the New York Protocol of 31 January 1967;

(b) 'application for asylum' shall mean the application made by a third-country national or a stateless person which can be understood as a request for international protection from a Member State, under the Geneva Convention. Any application for international protection is presumed to be an application for asylum unless a third-country national or a stateless person explicitly requests another kind of protection that can be applied for separately;

(c) 'applicant' or 'asylum seeker' shall mean a third country national or a stateless person who has made an application for asylum in respect of which a final decision has not yet been taken;

(d) 'family members' shall mean, in so far as the family already existed in the country of origin, the following members of the applicant's family who are present in the same Member State in relation to the application for asylum:

(i) the spouse of the asylum seeker or his or her unmarried partner in a stable relationship, where the legislation or practice of the Member State concerned treats unmarried couples in a way comparable to married couples under its law relating to aliens;

(ii) the minor children of the couple referred to in point (i) or of the applicant, on condition that they are unmarried and dependent and regardless of whether they were born in or out of wedlock or adopted as defined under the national law;

(e) 'refugee' shall mean a person who fulfils the requirements of Article 1(A) of the Geneva Convention;

(f) 'refugee status' shall mean the status granted by a Member State to a person who is a refugee and is admitted as such to the territory of that Member State;
(g) 'procedures' and 'appeals', shall mean the procedures and appeals established by Member States in their national law;
(h) 'unaccompanied minors' shall mean persons below the age of eighteen who arrive in the territory of the Member States unaccompanied by an adult responsible for them whether by law or by custom, and for as long as they are not effectively taken into the care of such a person; it shall include minors who are left unaccompanied after they have entered the territory of Member States;
(i) 'reception conditions' shall mean the full set of measures that Member States grant to asylum seekers in accordance with this Directive;
(j) 'material reception conditions' shall mean the reception conditions that include housing, food and clothing, provided in kind, or as financial allowances or in vouchers, and a daily expenses allowance;
(k) 'detention' shall mean confinement of an asylum seeker by a Member State within a particular place, where the applicant is deprived of his or her freedom of movement;
(l) 'accommodation centre' shall mean any place used for collective housing of asylum seekers.

Article 3: Scope

1. This Directive shall apply to all third country nationals and stateless persons who make an application for asylum at the border or in the territory of a Member State as long as they are allowed to remain on the territory as asylum seekers, as well as to family members, if they are covered by such application for asylum according to the national law.
2. This Directive shall not apply in cases of requests for diplomatic or territorial asylum submitted to representations of Member States.
3. This Directive shall not apply when the provisions of Council Directive 2001/55/EC of 20 July 2001 on minimum standards for giving temporary protection in the event of a mass influx of displaced persons and on measures promoting a balance of efforts between Member States in receiving such persons and bearing the consequences thereof[5] are applied.
4. Member States may decide to apply this Directive in connection with procedures for deciding on applications for kinds of protection other than that emanating from the Geneva Convention for third-country nationals or stateless persons who are found not to be refugees.

Article 4: More favourable provisions

Member States may introduce or retain more favourable provisions in the field of reception conditions for asylum seekers and other close relatives of the applicant who are present in the same Member State when they are dependent on him or for humanitarian reasons insofar as these provisions are compatible with this Directive.

6 OJ L 212, 7 August 2001, p12.

CHAPTER II: GENERAL PROVISIONS ON RECEPTION CONDITIONS

Article 5: Information

1. Member States shall inform asylum seekers, within a reasonable time not exceeding fifteen days after they have lodged their application for asylum with the competent authority, of at least any established benefits and of the obligations with which they must comply relating to reception conditions.

   Member States shall ensure that applicants are provided with information on organisations or groups of persons that provide specific legal assistance and organisations that might be able to help or inform them concerning the available reception conditions, including health care.
2. Member States shall ensure that the information referred to in paragraph 1 is in writing and, as far as possible, in a language that the applicants may reasonably be supposed to understand. Where appropriate, this information may also be supplied orally.

Article 6: Documentation

1. Member States shall ensure that, within three days after an application is lodged with the competent authority, the applicant is provided with a document issued in his or her own name certifying his or her status as an asylum seeker or testifying that he or she is allowed to stay in the territory of the Member State while his or her application is pending or being examined.

   If the holder is not free to move within all or a part of the territory of the Member State, the document shall also certify this fact.
2. Member States may exclude application of this Article when the asylum seeker is in detention and during the examination of an application for asylum made at the border or within the context of a procedure to decide on the right of the applicant legally to enter the territory of a Member State. In specific cases, during the examination of an application for asylum, Member States may provide applicants with other evidence equivalent to the document referred to in paragraph 1.
3. The document referred to in paragraph 1 need not certify the identity of the asylum seeker.
4. Member States shall adopt the necessary measures to provide asylum seekers with the document referred to in paragraph 1, which must be valid for as long as they are authorised to remain in the territory of the Member State concerned or at the border thereof.
5. Member States may provide asylum seekers with a travel document when serious humanitarian reasons arise that require their presence in another State.

Article 7: Residence and freedom of movement

1. Asylum seekers may move freely within the territory of the host Member State or within an area assigned to them by that Member State. The assigned area shall not affect the unalienable sphere of private life and shall allow sufficient scope for guaranteeing access to all benefits under this Directive.

2. Member States may decide on the residence of the asylum-seeker for reasons of public interest, public order or, when necessary, for the swift processing and effective monitoring of his or her application.
3. When it proves necessary, for example for legal reasons or reasons of public order, Member States may confine an applicant to a particular place in accordance with their national law.
4. Member States may make provision of the material reception conditions subject to actual residence by the applicants in a specific place, to be determined by the Member States. Such a decision, which may be of a general nature, shall be taken individually and established by national legislation.
5. Member States shall provide for the possibility of granting applicants temporary permission to leave the place of residence mentioned in paragraphs 2 and 4 and/or the assigned area mentioned in paragraph 1. Decisions shall be taken individually, objectively and impartially and reasons shall be given if they are negative.

   The applicant shall not require permission to keep appointments with authorities and courts if his or her appearance is necessary.
6. Member States shall require applicants to inform the competent authorities of their current address and notify any change of address to such authorities as soon as possible.

Article 8: Families

Member States shall take appropriate measures to maintain as far as possible family unity as present within their territory, if applicants are provided with housing by the Member State concerned. Such measures shall be implemented with the asylum seeker's agreement.

Article 9: Medical screening

Member States may require medical screening for applicants on public health grounds.

Article 10: Schooling and education of minors

1. Member States shall grant to minor children of asylum seekers and to asylum seekers who are minors access to the education system under similar conditions as nationals of the host Member State for so long as an expulsion measure against them or their parents is not actually enforced. Such education may be provided in accommodation centres.

   The Member State concerned may stipulate that such access must be confined to the State education system. Minors shall be younger than the age of legal majority in the Member State in which the application for asylum was lodged or is being examined.

   Member States shall not withdraw secondary education for the sole reason that the minor has reached the age of majority.
2. Access to the education system shall not be postponed for more than three months from the date the application for asylum was lodged by the minor or the minor's parents. This period may be extended to one year where specific education is provided in order to facilitate access to the education system.

3. Where access to the education system as set out in para- graph 1 is not possible due to the specific situation of the minor, the Member State may offer other education arrangements.

Article 11: Employment

1. Member States shall determine a period of time, starting from the date on which an application for asylum was lodged, during which an applicant shall not have access to the labour market.
2. If a decision at first instance has not been taken within one year of the presentation of an application for asylum and this delay cannot be attributed to the applicant, Member States shall decide the conditions for granting access to the labour market for the applicant.
3. Access to the labour market shall not be withdrawn during appeals procedures, where an appeal against a negative decision in a regular procedure has suspensive effect, until such time as a negative decision on the appeal is notified.
4. For reasons of labour market policies, Member States may give priority to EU citizens and nationals of States parties to theAgreement on the European Economic Area and also to legally resident third-country nationals.

Article 12: Vocational training

Member States may allow asylum seekers access to vocational training irrespective of whether they have access to the labour market.

Access to vocational training relating to an employment contract shall depend on the extent to which the applicant has access to the labour market in accordance with Article 11.

Article 13: General rules on material reception conditions and healthcare

1. Member States shall ensure that material reception conditions are available to applicants when they make their application for asylum.
2. Member States shall make provisions on material reception conditions to ensure a standard of living adequate for the health of applicants and capable of ensuring their subsistence.

   Member States shall ensure that that standard of living is met in the specific situation of persons who have special needs, in accordance with Article 17, as well as in relation to the situation of persons who are in detention.
3. Member States may make the provision of all or some of the material reception conditions and health care subject to the condition that applicants do not have sufficient means to have a standard of living adequate for their health and to enable their subsistence.
4. Member States may require applicants to cover or contribute to the cost of the material reception conditions and of the health care provided for in this Directive, pursuant to the provision of paragraph 3, if the applicants have sufficient resources, for example if they have been working for a reasonable period of time.

If it transpires that an applicant had sufficient means to cover material reception conditions and health care at the time when basic needs were being covered, Member States may ask the asylum seeker for a refund.

5. Material reception conditions may be provided in kind, or in the form of financial allowances or vouchers or in a combination of these provisions.

   Where Member States provide material reception conditions in the form of financial allowances or vouchers, the amount thereof shall be determined in accordance with the principles set out in this Article.

Article 14: Modalities for material reception conditions

1. Where housing is provided in kind, it should take one or a combination of the following forms:
   (a) premises used for the purpose of housing applicants during the examination of an application for asylum lodged at the border;
   (b) accommodation centres which guarantee an adequate standard of living;
   (c) private houses, flats, hotels or other premises adapted for housing applicants.
2. Member States shall ensure that applicants provided with the housing referred to in paragraph 1(a), (b) and (c) are assured:
   (a) protection of their family life;
   (b) the possibility of communicating with relatives, legal advisers and representatives of the United Nations High Commissioner for Refugees (UNHCR) and non-governmental organisations (NGOs) recognised by Member States.

   Member States shall pay particular attention to the prevention of assault within the premises and accommodation centres referred to in paragraph 1(a) and (b).
3. Member States shall ensure, if appropriate, that minor children of applicants or applicants who are minors are lodged with their parents or with the adult family member responsible for them whether by law or by custom.
4. Member States shall ensure that transfers of applicants from one housing facility to another take place only when necessary. Member States shall provide for the possibility for applicants to inform their legal advisers of the transfer and of their new address.
5. Persons working in accommodation centres shall be adequately trained and shall be bound by the confidentiality principle as defined in the national law in relation to any information they obtain in the course of their work.
6. Member States may involve applicants in managing the material resources and non-material aspects of life in the centre through an advisory board or council representing residents.
7. Legal advisors or counsellors of asylum seekers and representatives of the United Nations High Commissioner for Refugees or non-governmental organisations designated by the latter and recognised by the Member State concerned shall be granted access to accommodation centres and other housing facilities in order to assist the said asylum seekers. Limits on such access may be imposed only on grounds relating to the security of the centres and facilities and of the asylum seekers.

8. Member States may exceptionally set modalities for mate- rial reception conditions different from those provided for in this Article, for a reasonable period which shall be as short as possible, when:
   - an initial assessment of the specific needs of the applicant is required,
   - material reception conditions, as provided for in this Article, are not available in a certain geographical area,
   - housing capacities normally available are temporarily exhausted,
   - the asylum seeker is in detention or confined to border posts.

   These different conditions shall cover in any case basic needs.

Article 15: Health care

1. Member States shall ensure that applicants receive the necessary health care which shall include, at least, emergency care and essential treatment of illness.
2. Member States shall provide necessary medical or other assistance to applicants who have special needs.

CHAPTER III: REDUCTION OR WITHDRAWAL OF RECEPTION CONDITIONS

Article 16: Reduction or withdrawal of reception conditions

1. Member States may reduce or withdraw reception conditions in the following cases:
   (a) where an asylum seeker:
      - abandons the place of residence determined by the competent authority without informing it or, if requested, without permission, or
      - does not comply with reporting duties or with requests to provide information or to appear for personal interviews concerning the asylum procedure during a reasonable period laid down in national law, or
      - has already lodged an application in the same Member State.

   When the applicant is traced or voluntarily reports to the competent authority, a duly motivated decision, based on the reasons for the disappearance, shall be taken on the reinstallation of the grant of some or all of the reception conditions;

   (b) where an applicant has concealed financial resources and has therefore unduly benefited from material reception conditions.

   If it transpires that an applicant had sufficient means to cover material reception conditions and health care at the time when these basic needs were being covered, Member States may ask the asylum seeker for a refund.
2. Member States may refuse conditions in cases where an asylum seeker has failed to demonstrate that the asylum claim was made as soon as reasonably practicable after arrival in that Member State.
3. Member States may determine sanctions applicable to serious breaching of the rules of the accommodation centres as well as to seriously violent behaviour.

4. Decisions for reduction, withdrawal or refusal of reception conditions or sanctions referred to in paragraphs 1, 2 and 3 shall be taken individually, objectively and impartially and reasons shall be given. Decisions shall be based on the particular situation of the person concerned, especially with regard to persons covered by Article 17, taking into account the principle of proportionality. Member States shall under all circumstances ensure access to emergency health care.
5. Member States shall ensure that material reception conditions are not withdrawn or reduced before a negative decision is taken.

CHAPTER IV: PROVISIONS FOR PERSONS WITH SPECIAL NEEDS

Article 17: General principle

1. Member States shall take into account the specific situation of vulnerable persons such as minors, unaccompanied minors, disabled people, elderly people, pregnant women, single parents with minor children and persons who have been subjected to torture, rape or other serious forms of psychological, physical or sexual violence, in the national legislation implementing the provisions of Chapter II relating to material reception conditions and health care.
2. Paragraph 1 shall apply only to persons found to have special needs after an individual evaluation of their situation.

Article 18: Minors

1. The best interests of the child shall be a primary consideration for Member States when implementing the provisions of this Directive that involve minors.
2. Member States shall ensure access to rehabilitation services for minors who have been victims of any form of abuse, neglect, exploitation, torture or cruel, inhuman and degrading treatment, or who have suffered from armed conflicts, and ensure that appropriate mental health care is developed and qualified counselling is provided when needed.

Article 19: Unaccompanied minors

1. Member States shall as soon as possible take measures to ensure the necessary representation of unaccompanied minors by legal guardianship or, where necessary, representation by an organisation which is responsible for the care and well-being of minors, or by any other appropriate representation. Regular assessments shall be made by the appropriate authorities.
2. Unaccompanied minors who make an application for asylum shall, from the moment they are admitted to the territory to the moment they are obliged to leave the host Member State in which the application for asylum was made or is being examined, be placed:
   (a) with adult relatives;
   (b) with a foster-family;
   (c) in accommodation centres with special provisions for minors;
   (d) in other accommodation suitable for minors.

Member States may place unaccompanied minors aged 16 or over in accommodation centres for adult asylum seekers.

As far as possible, siblings shall be kept together, taking into account the best interests of the minor concerned and, in particular, his or her age and degree of maturity. Changes of residence of unaccompanied minors shall be limited to a minimum.

3. Member States, protecting the unaccompanied minor's best interests, shall endeavour to trace the members of his or her family as soon as possible. In cases where there may be a threat to the life or integrity of the minor or his or her close relatives, particularly if they have remained in the country of origin, care must be taken to ensure that the collection, processing and circulation of information concerning those persons is undertaken on a confidential basis, so as to avoid jeopardising their safety.
4. Those working with unaccompanied minors shall have had or receive appropriate training concerning their needs, and shall be bound by the confidentiality principle as defined in the national law, in relation to any information they obtain in the course of their work.

Article 20: Victims of torture and violence

Member States shall ensure that, if necessary, persons who have been subjected to torture, rape or other serious acts of violence receive the necessary treatment of damages caused by the afore-mentioned acts.

CHAPTER V: APPEALS

Article 21: Appeals

1. Member States shall ensure that negative decisions relating to the granting of benefits under this Directive or decisions taken under Article 7 which individually affect asylum seekers may be the subject of an appeal within the procedures laid down in the national law. At least in the last instance the possibility of an appeal or a review before a judicial body shall be granted.
2. Procedures for access to legal assistance in such cases shall be laid down in national law.

CHAPTER VI: ACTIONS TO IMPROVE THE EFFICIENCY OF THE RECEPTION SYSTEM

Article 22: Cooperation

Member States shall regularly inform the Commission on the data concerning the number of persons, broken down by sex and age, covered by reception conditions and provide full information on the type, name and format of the documents provided for by Article 6.

Article 23: Guidance, monitoring and control system

Member States shall, with due respect to their constitutional structure, ensure that appropriate guidance, monitoring and control of the level of reception conditions are established.

Article 24: Staff and resources

1. Member States shall take appropriate measures to ensure that authorities and other organisations implementing this Directive have received the necessary basic training with respect to the needs of both male and female applicants.
2. Member States shall allocate the necessary resources in connection with the national provisions enacted to implement this Directive.

CHAPTER VII: FINAL PROVISIONS

Article 25: Reports

By 6 August 2006, the Commission shall report to the European Parliament and the Council on the application of this Directive and shall propose any amendments that are necessary.

Member States shall send the Commission all the information that is appropriate for drawing up the report, including the statistical data provided for by Article 22 by 6 February 2006.

After presenting the report, the Commission shall report to the European Parliament and the Council on the application of this Directive at least every five years.

Article 26: Transposition

1. Member States shall bring into force the laws, regulations and administrative provisions necessary to comply with this Directive by 6 February 2005. They shall forthwith inform the Commission thereof.

   When the Member States adopt these measures, they shall contain a reference to this Directive or shall be accompanied by such a reference on the occasion of their official publication. Member States shall determine how such a reference is to be made.
2. Member States shall communicate to the Commission the text of the provisions of national law which they adopt in the field relating to the enforcement of this Directive.

Article 27: Entry into force

This Directive shall enter into force on the day of its publication in the Official Journal of the European Union.

Article 28: Addressees

This Directive is addressed to the Member States in accordance with the Treaty establishing the European Union.

Done at Brussels, 27 January 2003.

For the Council

The President
G PAPANDREOU

DIRECTIVE 2004/38/EC

OF THE EUROPEAN PARLIAMENT AND OF THE COUNCIL of 29 April 2004

on the right of citizens of the Union and their family members to move and reside freely within the territory of the Member States amending Regulation (EEC) No 1612/68 and repealing Directives 64/221/EEC, 68/360/EEC, 72/194/EEC, 73/148/EEC, 75/34/EEC, 75/35/EEC, 90/364/EEC, 90/365/ EEC and 93/96/EEC
(Text with EEA relevance)

THE EUROPEAN PARLIAMENT AND THE COUNCIL OF THE EUROPEAN UNION,

Having regard to the Treaty establishing the European Community, and in particular Articles 12, 18, 40, 44 and 52 thereof,

Having regard to the proposal from the Commission,

Having regard to the Opinion of the European Economic and Social Committee,

Having regard to the Opinion of the Committee of the Regions,

Acting in accordance with the procedure laid down in Article 251 of the Treaty,

Whereas:

(1) Citizenship of the Union confers on every citizen of the Union a primary and individual right to move and reside freely within the territory of the Member States, subject to the limitations and conditions laid down in the Treaty and to the measures adopted to give it effect.

(2) The free movement of persons constitutes one of the fundamental freedoms of the internal market, which comprises an area without internal frontiers, in which freedom is ensured in accordance with the provisions of the Treaty.

(3) Union citizenship should be the fundamental status of nationals of the Member States when they exercise their right of free movement and residence. It is therefore necessary to codify and review the existing Community instruments dealing separately with workers, self-employed persons, as well as students and other inactive persons in order to simplify and strengthen the right of free movement and residence of all Union citizens.

(4) With a view to remedying this sector-by-sector, piecemeal approach to the right of free movement and residence and facilitating the exercise of this right, there needs to be a single legislative act to amend Council Regulation (EEC) No 1612/68 of 15 October 1968 on freedom of movement for workers within the Community, and to repeal the following acts: Council Directive 68/360/EEC of 15 October 1968 on the abolition of restrictions on movement and residence within the Community for workers of Member States and their families, Council Directive 73/148/EEC of 21 May 1973 on the

abolition of restrictions on movement and residence within the Community for nationals of Member States with regard to establishment and the provision of services, Council Directive 90/364/EEC of 28 June 1990 on the right of residence, Council Directive 90/365/EEC of 28 June 1990 on the right of residence for employees and self-employed persons who have ceased their occupational activity and Council Directive 93/96/EEC of 29 October 1993 on the right of residence for students.

(5) The right of all Union citizens to move and reside freely within the territory of the Member States should, if it is to be exercised under objective conditions of freedom and dignity, be also granted to their family members, irrespective of nationality. For the purposes of this Directive, the definition of 'family member" should also include the registered partner if the legislation of the host Member State treats registered partnership as equivalent to marriage.

(6) In order to maintain the unity of the family in a broader sense and without prejudice to the prohibition of discrimination on grounds of nationality, the situation of those persons who are not included in the definition of family members under this Directive, and who therefore do not enjoy an automatic right of entry and residence in the host Member State, should be examined by the host Member State on the basis of its own national legislation, in order to decide whether entry and residence could be granted to such persons, taking into consideration their relationship with the Union citizen or any other circumstances, such as their financial or physical dependence on the Union citizen.

(7) The formalities connected with the free movement of Union citizens within the territory of Member States should be clearly defined, without prejudice to the provisions applicable to national border controls.

(8) With a view to facilitating the free movement of family members who are not nationals of a Member State, those who have already obtained a residence card should be exempted from the requirement to obtain an entry visa within the meaning of Council Regulation (EC) No 539/2001 of 15 March 2001 listing the third countries whose nationals must be in possession of visas when crossing the external borders and those whose nationals are exempt from that requirement or, where appropriate, of the applicable national legislation.

(9) Union citizens should have the right of residence in the host Member State for a period not exceeding three months without being subject to any conditions or any formalities other than the requirement to hold a valid identity card or passport, without prejudice to a more favourable treatment applicable to job-seekers as recognised by the case-law of the Court of Justice.

(10) Persons exercising their right of residence should not, however, become an unreasonable burden on the social assistance system of the host Member State during an initial period of residence. Therefore, the right of residence for Union citizens and their family members for periods in excess of three months should be subject to conditions.

(11) The fundamental and personal right of residence in another Member State is conferred directly on Union citizens by the Treaty and is not dependent upon their having fulfilled administrative procedures.

(12) For periods of residence of longer than three months, Member States should have the possibility to require Union citizens to register with the competent authorities in the place of residence, attested by a registration certificate issued to that effect.

(13) The residence card requirement should be restricted to family members of Union citizens who are not nationals of a Member State for periods of residence of longer than three months.

(14) The supporting documents required by the competent authorities for the issuing of a registration certificate or of a residence card should be comprehensively specified in order to avoid divergent administrative practices or interpretations constituting an undue obstacle to the exercise of the right of residence by Union citizens and their family members.

(15) Family members should be legally safeguarded in the event of the death of the Union citizen, divorce, annulment of marriage or termination of a registered partnership. With due regard for family life and human dignity, and in certain conditions to guard against abuse, measures should therefore be taken to ensure that in such circumstances family members already residing within the territory of the host Member State retain their right of residence exclusively on a personal basis.

(16) As long as the beneficiaries of the right of residence do not become an unreasonable burden on the social assistance system of the host Member State they should not be expelled. Therefore, an expulsion measure should not be the automatic consequence of recourse to the social assistance system. The host Member State should examine whether it is a case of temporary difficulties and take into account the duration of residence, the personal circumstances and the amount of aid granted in order to consider whether the beneficiary has become an unreasonable burden on its social assistance system and to proceed to his expulsion. In no case should an expulsion measure be adopted against workers, self-employed persons or job-seekers as defined by the Court of Justice save on grounds of public policy or public security.

(17) Enjoyment of permanent residence by Union citizens who have chosen to settle long term in the host Member State would strengthen the feeling of Union citizenship and is a key element in promoting social cohesion, which is one of the fundamental objectives of the Union. A right of permanent residence should therefore be laid down for all Union citizens and their family members who have resided in the host Member State in compliance with the conditions laid down in this Directive during a continuous period of five years without becoming subject to an expulsion measure.

(18) In order to be a genuine vehicle for integration into the society of the host Member State in which the Union citizen resides, the right of permanent residence, once obtained, should not be subject to any conditions.

(19) Certain advantages specific to Union citizens who are workers or self-employed persons and to their family members, which may allow these persons to acquire a right of permanent residence before they have resided five years in the host Member State, should be maintained, as these constitute acquired rights, conferred by Commission Regulation (EEC) No 1251/70 of 29 June 1970 on the right of workers to remain in the territory of a Member State after having been employed in that State and Council

Directive 75/34/EEC of 17 December 1974 concerning the right of nationals of a Member State to remain in the territory of another Member State after having pursued therein an activity in a self-employed capacity.

(20) In accordance with the prohibition of discrimination on grounds of nationality, all Union citizens and their family members residing in a Member State on the basis of this Directive should enjoy, in that Member State, equal treatment with nationals in areas covered by the Treaty, subject to such specific provisions as are expressly provided for in the Treaty and secondary law.

(21) However, it should be left to the host Member State to decide whether it will grant social assistance during the first three months of residence, or for a longer period in the case of job-seekers, to Union citizens other than those who are workers or self-employed persons or who retain that status or their family members, or maintenance assistance for studies, including vocational training, prior to acquisition of the right of permanent residence, to these same persons.

(22) The Treaty allows restrictions to be placed on the right of free movement and residence on grounds of public policy, public security or public health. In order to ensure a tighter definition of the circumstances and procedural safeguards subject to which Union citizens and their family members may be denied leave to enter or may be expelled, this Directive should replace Council Directive 64/221/EEC of 25 February 1964 on the coordination of special measures concerning the movement and residence of foreign nationals, which are justified on grounds of public policy, public security or public health.

(23) Expulsion of Union citizens and their family members on grounds of public policy or public security is a measure that can seriously harm persons who, having availed themselves of the rights and freedoms conferred on them by the Treaty, have become genuinely integrated into the host Member State. The scope for such measures should therefore be limited in accordance with the principle of proportionality to take account of the degree of integration of the persons concerned, the length of their residence in the host Member State, their age, state of health, family and economic situation and the links with their country of origin.

(24) Accordingly, the greater the degree of integration of Union citizens and their family members in the host Member State, the greater the degree of protection against expulsion should be. Only in exceptional circumstances, where there are imperative grounds of public security, should an expulsion measure be taken against Union citizens who have resided for many years in the territory of the host Member State, in particular when they were born and have resided there throughout their life. In addition, such exceptional circumstances should also apply to an expulsion measure taken against minors, in order to protect their links with their family, in accordance with the United Nations Convention on the Rights of the Child, of 20 November 1989.

(25) Procedural safeguards should also be specified in detail in order to ensure a high level of protection of the rights of Union citizens and their family members in the event of their being denied leave to enter or reside in another Member State, as well as to uphold the principle that any action taken by the authorities must be properly justified.

(26) In all events, judicial redress procedures should be available to Union citizens and their family members who have been refused leave to enter or reside in another Member State.

(27) In line with the case-law of the Court of Justice prohibiting Member States from issuing orders excluding for life persons covered by this Directive from their territory, the right of Union citizens and their family members who have been excluded from the territory of a Member State to submit a fresh application after a reasonable period, and in any event after a three year period from enforcement of the final exclusion order, should be confirmed.

(28) To guard against abuse of rights or fraud, notably marriages of convenience or any other form of relationships contracted for the sole purpose of enjoying the right of free movement and residence, Member States should have the possibility to adopt the necessary measures.

(29) This Directive should not affect more favourable national provisions.

(30) With a view to examining how further to facilitate the exercise of the right of free movement and residence, a report should be prepared by the Commission in order to evaluate the opportunity to present any necessary proposals to this effect, notably on the extension of the period of residence with no conditions.

(31) This Directive respects the fundamental rights and freedoms and observes the principles recognised in particular by the Charter of Fundamental Rights of the European Union. In accordance with the prohibition of discrimination contained in the Charter, Member States should implement this Directive without discrimination between the beneficiaries of this Directive on grounds such as sex, race, colour, ethnic or social origin, genetic characteristics, language, religion or beliefs, political or other opinion, membership of an ethnic minority, property, birth, disability, age or sexual orientation,

HAVE ADOPTED THIS DIRECTIVE:

CHAPTER I: GENERAL PROVISIONS

Article 1: Subject

This Directive lays down:

(a) the conditions governing the exercise of the right of free movement and residence within the territory of the Member States by Union citizens and their family members;

(b) the right of permanent residence in the territory of the Member States for Union citizens and their family members;

(c) the limits placed on the rights set out in (a) and (b) on grounds of public policy, public security or public health.

Article 2: Definitions

For the purposes of this Directive:

1) 'Union citizen' means any person having the nationality of a Member State;

2) 'Family member' means:
   (a) the spouse;
   (b) the partner with whom the Union citizen has contracted a registered partnership, on the basis of the legislation of a Member State, if the legislation of the host Member State treats registered partnerships as equivalent to marriage and in accordance with the conditions laid down in the relevant legislation of the host Member State;
   (c) the direct descendants who are under the age of 21 or are dependants and those of the spouse or partner as defined in point (b);
   (d) the dependent direct relatives in the ascending line and those of the spouse or partner as defined in point (b);
3) 'Host Member State' means the Member State to which a Union citizen moves in order to exercise his/her right of free movement and residence.

Article 3: Beneficiaries

1. This Directive shall apply to all Union citizens who move to or reside in a Member State other than that of which they are a national, and to their family members as defined in point 2 of Article 2 who accompany or join them.
2. Without prejudice to any right to free movement and residence the persons concerned may have in their own right, the host Member State shall, in accordance with its national legislation, facilitate entry and residence for the following persons:
   (a) any other family members, irrespective of their nationality, not falling under the definition in point 2 of Article 2 who, in the country from which they have come, are dependants or members of the household of the Union citizen having the primary right of residence, or where serious health grounds strictly require the personal care of the family member by the Union citizen;
   (b) the partner with whom the Union citizen has a durable relationship, duly attested.

   The host Member State shall undertake an extensive examination of the personal circumstances and shall justify any denial of entry or residence to these people.

CHAPTER II: RIGHT OF EXIT AND ENTRY

Article 4: Right of exit

1. Without prejudice to the provisions on travel documents applicable to national border controls, all Union citizens with a valid identity card or passport and their family members who are not nationals of a Member State and who hold a valid passport shall have the right to leave the territory of a Member State to travel to another Member State.
2. No exit visa or equivalent formality may be imposed on the persons to whom paragraph 1 applies.
3. Member States shall, acting in accordance with their laws, issue to their own nationals, and renew, an identity card or passport stating their nationality.

4. The passport shall be valid at least for all Member States and for countries through which the holder must pass when travelling between Member States. Where the law of a Member State does not provide for identity cards to be issued, the period of validity of any passport on being issued or renewed shall be not less than five years.

Article 5: Right of entry

1. Without prejudice to the provisions on travel documents applicable to national border controls, Member States shall grant Union citizens leave to enter their territory with a valid identity card or passport and shall grant family members who are not nationals of a Member State leave to enter their territory with a valid passport.

   No entry visa or equivalent formality may be imposed on Union citizens.
2. Family members who are not nationals of a Member State shall only be required to have an entry visa in accordance with Regulation (EC) No 539/2001 or, where appropriate, with national law. For the purposes of this Directive, possession of the valid residence card referred to in Article 10 shall exempt such family members from the visa requirement.

   Member States shall grant such persons every facility to obtain the necessary visas. Such visas shall be issued free of charge as soon as possible and on the basis of an accelerated procedure.
3. The host Member State shall not place an entry or exit stamp in the passport of family members who are not nationals of a Member State provided that they present the residence card provided for in Article 10.
4. Where a Union citizen, or a family member who is not a national of a Member State, does not have the necessary travel documents or, if required, the necessary visas, the Member State concerned shall, before turning them back, give such persons every reasonable opportunity to obtain the necessary documents or have them brought to them within a reasonable period of time or to corroborate or prove by other means that they are covered by the right of free movement and residence.
5. The Member State may require the person concerned to report his/her presence within its territory within a reasonable and non-discriminatory period of time. Failure to comply with this requirement may make the person concerned liable to proportionate and non-discriminatory sanctions.

CHAPTER III: RIGHT OF RESIDENCE

Article 6: Right of residence for up to three months

1. Union citizens shall have the right of residence on the territory of another Member State for a period of up to three months without any conditions or any formalities other than the requirement to hold a valid identity card or passport.
2. The provisions of paragraph 1 shall also apply to family members in possession of a valid passport who are not nationals of a Member State, accompanying or joining the Union citizen.

Article 7: Right of residence for more than three months

1. All Union citizens shall have the right of residence on the territory of another Member State for a period of longer than three months if they:
   (a) are workers or self-employed persons in the host Member State; or
   (b) have sufficient resources for themselves and their family members not to become a burden on the social assistance system of the host Member State during their period of residence and have comprehensive sickness insurance cover in the host Member State; or
   (c) – are enrolled at a private or public establishment, accredited or financed by the host Member State on the basis of its legislation or administrative practice, for the principal purpose of following a course of study, including vocational training; and
   – have comprehensive sickness insurance cover in the host Member State and assure the relevant national authority, by means of a declaration or by such equivalent means as they may choose, that they have sufficient resources for themselves and their family members not to become a burden on the social assistance system of the host Member State during their period of residence; or
   (d) are family members accompanying or joining a Union citizen who satisfies the conditions referred to in points (a), (b) or (c).
2. The right of residence provided for in paragraph 1 shall extend to family members who are not nationals of a Member State, accompanying or joining the Union citizen in the host Member State, provided that such Union citizen satisfies the conditions referred to in paragraph 1(a), (b) or (c).
3. For the purposes of paragraph 1(a), a Union citizen who is no longer a worker or self-employed person shall retain the status of worker or self-employed person in the following circumstances:
   (a) he/she is temporarily unable to work as the result of an illness or accident;
   (b) he/she is in duly recorded involuntary unemployment after having been employed for more than one year and has registered as a job-seeker with the relevant employment office;
   (c) he/she is in duly recorded involuntary unemployment after completing a fixed-term employment contract of less than a year or after having become involuntarily unemployed during the first twelve months and has registered as a job-seeker with the relevant employment office. In this case, the status of worker shall be retained for no less than six months;
   (d) he/she embarks on vocational training. Unless he/she is involuntarily unemployed, the retention of the status of worker shall require the training to be related to the previous employment.
4. By way of derogation from paragraphs 1(d) and 2 above, only the spouse, the registered partner provided for in Article 2(2)(b) and dependent children shall have the right of residence as family members of a Union citizen meeting the conditions under 1(c) above. Article 3(2) shall apply to his/her dependent direct relatives in the ascending lines and those of his/her spouse or registered partner.

Article 8: Administrative formalities for Union citizens

1. Without prejudice to Article 5(5), for periods of residence longer than three months, the host Member State may require Union citizens to register with the relevant authorities.
2. The deadline for registration may not be less than three months from the date of arrival. A registration certificate shall be issued immediately, stating the name and address of the person registering and the date of the registration. Failure to comply with the registration requirement may render the person concerned liable to proportionate and non-discriminatory sanctions.
3. For the registration certificate to be issued, Member States may only require that
   - Union citizens to whom point (a) of Article 7(1) applies present a valid identity card or passport, a confirmation of engagement from the employer or a certificate of employment, or proof that they are self-employed persons;
   - Union citizens to whom point (b) of Article 7(1) applies present a valid identity card or passport and provide proof that they satisfy the conditions laid down therein;
   - Union citizens to whom point (c) of Article 7(1) applies present a valid identity card or passport, provide proof of enrolment at an accredited establishment and of comprehensive sickness insurance cover and the declaration or equivalent means referred to in point (c) of Article 7(1). Member States may not require this declaration to refer to any specific amount of resources.
4. Member States may not lay down a fixed amount which they regard as 'sufficient resources', but they must take into account the personal situation of the person concerned. In all cases this amount shall not be higher than the threshold below which nationals of the host Member State become eligible for social assistance, or, where this criterion is not applicable, higher than the minimum social security pension paid by the host Member State.
5. For the registration certificate to be issued to family members of Union citizens, who are themselves Union citizens, Member States may require the following documents to be presented:
   (a) a valid identity card or passport;
   (b) a document attesting to the existence of a family relationship or of a registered partnership;
   (c) where appropriate, the registration certificate of the Union citizen whom they are accompanying or joining;
   (d) in cases falling under points (c) and (d) of Article 2(2), documentary evidence that the conditions laid down therein are met;
   (e) in cases falling under Article 3(2)(a), a document issued by the relevant authority in the country of origin or country from which they are arriving certifying that they are dependants or members of the household of the Union citizen, or proof of the existence of serious health grounds which strictly require the personal care of the family member by the Union citizen;
   (f) in cases falling under Article 3(2)(b), proof of the existence of a durable relationship with the Union citizen.

Article 9: Administrative formalities for family members who are not nationals of a Member State

1. Member States shall issue a residence card to family members of a Union citizen who are not nationals of a Member State, where the planned period of residence is for more than three months.
2. The deadline for submitting the residence card application may not be less than three months from the date of arrival.
3. Failure to comply with the requirement to apply for a residence card may make the person concerned liable to proportionate and non-discriminatory sanctions.

Article 10: Issue of residence cards

1. The right of residence of family members of a Union citizen who are not nationals of a Member State shall be evidenced by the issuing of a document called 'Residence card of a family member of a Union citizen' no later than six months from the date on which they submit the application. A certificate of application for the residence card shall be issued immediately.
2. For the residence card to be issued, Member States shall require presentation of the following documents:
   (a) a valid passport;
   (b) a document attesting to the existence of a family relationship or of a registered partnership;
   (c) the registration certificate or, in the absence of a registration system, any other proof of residence in the host Member State of the Union citizen whom they are accompanying or joining;
   (d) in cases falling under points (c) and (d) of Article 2(2), documentary evidence that the conditions laid down therein are met;
   (e) in cases falling under Article 3(2)(a), a document issued by the relevant authority in the country of origin or country from which they are arriving certifying that they are dependants or members of the household of the Union citizen, or proof of the existence of serious health grounds which strictly require the personal care of the family member by the Union citizen;
   (f) in cases falling under Article 3(2)(b), proof of the existence of a durable relationship with the Union citizen.

Article 11: Validity of the residence card

1. The residence card provided for by Article 10(1) shall be valid for five years from the date of issue or for the envisaged period of residence of the Union citizen, if this period is less than five years.
2. The validity of the residence card shall not be affected by temporary absences not exceeding six months a year, or by absences of a longer duration for compulsory military service or by one absence of a maximum of twelve consecutive months for important reasons such as pregnancy and childbirth, serious illness, study or vocational training, or a posting in another Member State or a third country.

Article 12: Retention of the right of residence by family members in the event of death or departure of the Union citizen

1. Without prejudice to the second subparagraph, the Union citizen's death or departure from the host Member State shall not affect the right of residence of his/her family members who are nationals of a Member State.

   Before acquiring the right of permanent residence, the persons concerned must meet the conditions laid down in points (a), (b), (c) or (d) of Article 7(1).
2. Without prejudice to the second subparagraph, the Union citizen's death shall not entail loss of the right of residence of his/her family members who are not nationals of a Member State and who have been residing in the host Member State as family members for at least one year before the Union citizen's death.

   Before acquiring the right of permanent residence, the right of residence of the persons concerned shall remain subject to the requirement that they are able to show that they are workers or self-employed persons or that they have sufficient resources for themselves and their family members not to become a burden on the social assistance system of the host Member State during their period of residence and have comprehensive sickness insurance cover in the host Member State, or that they are members of the family, already constituted in the host Member State, of a person satisfying these requirements. 'Sufficient resources' shall be as defined in Article 8(4).

   Such family members shall retain their right of residence exclusively on a personal basis.
3. The Union citizen's departure from the host Member State or his/her death shall not entail loss of the right of residence of his/her children or of the parent who has actual custody of the children, irrespective of nationality, if the children reside in the host Member State and are enrolled at an educational establishment, for the purpose of studying there, until the completion of their studies.

Article 13: Retention of the right of residence by family members in the event of divorce, annulment of marriage or termination of registered partnership

1. Without prejudice to the second subparagraph, divorce, annulment of the Union citizen's marriage or termination of his/her registered partnership, as referred to in point 2(b) of Article 2 shall not affect the right of residence of his/her family members who are nationals of a Member State.

   Before acquiring the right of permanent residence, the persons concerned must meet the conditions laid down in points (a), (b), (c) or (d) of Article 7(1).
2. Without prejudice to the second subparagraph, divorce, annulment of marriage or termination of the registered partnership referred to in point 2(b) of Article 2 shall not entail loss of the right of residence of a Union citizen's family members who are not nationals of a Member State where:
   (a) prior to initiation of the divorce or annulment proceedings or termination of the registered partnership referred to in point 2(b) of Article 2, the marriage or registered partnership has lasted at least three years, including one year in the host Member State; or

(b) by agreement between the spouses or the partners referred to in point 2(b) of Article 2 or by court order, the spouse or partner who is not a national of a Member State has custody of the Union citizen's children; or
(c) this is warranted by particularly difficult circumstances, such as having been a victim of domestic violence while the marriage or registered partnership was subsisting; or
(d) by agreement between the spouses or partners referred to in point 2(b) of Article 2 or by court order, the spouse or partner who is not a national of a Member State has the right of access to a minor child, provided that the court has ruled that such access must be in the host Member State, and for as long as is required.

Before acquiring the right of permanent residence, the right of residence of the persons concerned shall remain subject to the requirement that they are able to show that they are workers or self-employed persons or that they have sufficient resources for themselves and their family members not to become a burden on the social assistance system of the host Member State during their period of residence and have comprehensive sickness insurance cover in the host Member State, or that they are members of the family, already constituted in the host Member State, of a person satisfying these requirements. 'Sufficient resources' shall be as defined in Article 8(4).

Such family members shall retain their right of residence exclusively on personal basis.

Article 14: Retention of the right of residence

1. Union citizens and their family members shall have the right of residence provided for in Article 6, as long as they do not become an unreasonable burden on the social assistance system of the host Member State.
2. Union citizens and their family members shall have the right of residence provided for in Articles 7, 12 and 13 as long as they meet the conditions set out therein.
   In specific cases where there is a reasonable doubt as to whether a Union citizen or his/her family members satisfies the conditions set out in Articles 7, 12 and 13, Member States may verify if these conditions are fulfilled. This verification shall not be carried out systematically.
3. An expulsion measure shall not be the automatic consequence of a Union citizen's or his or her family member's recourse to the social assistance system of the host Member State.
4. By way of derogation from paragraphs 1 and 2 and without prejudice to the provisions of Chapter VI, an expulsion measure may in no case be adopted against Union citizens or their family members if:
   (a) the Union citizens are workers or self-employed persons, or
   (b) the Union citizens entered the territory of the host Member State in order to seek employment. In this case, the Union citizens and their family members may not be expelled for as long as the Union citizens can provide evidence that they are continuing to seek employment and that they have a genuine chance of being engaged.

Article 15: Procedural safeguards

1. The procedures provided for by Articles 30 and 31 shall apply by analogy to all decisions restricting free movement of Union citizens and their family members on grounds other than public policy, public security or public health.
2. Expiry of the identity card or passport on the basis of which the person concerned entered the host Member State and was issued with a registration certificate or residence card shall not constitute a ground for expulsion from the host Member State.
3. The host Member State may not impose a ban on entry in the context of an expulsion decision to which paragraph 1 applies.

CHAPTER IV: RIGHT OF PERMANENT RESIDENCE

Section I: Eligibility

Article 16: General rule for Union citizens and their family members

1. Union citizens who have resided legally for a continuous period of five years in the host Member State shall have the right of permanent residence there. This right shall not be subject to the conditions provided for in Chapter III.
2. Paragraph 1 shall apply also to family members who are not nationals of a Member State and have legally resided with the Union citizen in the host Member State for a continuous period of five years.
3. Continuity of residence shall not be affected by temporary absences not exceeding a total of six months a year, or by absences of a longer duration for compulsory military service, or by one absence of a maximum of twelve consecutive months for important reasons such as pregnancy and childbirth, serious illness, study or vocational training, or a posting in another Member State or a third country.
4. Once acquired, the right of permanent residence shall be lost only through absence from the host Member State for a period exceeding two consecutive years.

Article 17: Exemptions for persons no longer working in the host Member State and their family members

1. By way of derogation from Article 16, the right of permanent residence in the host Member State shall be enjoyed before completion of a continuous period of five years of residence by:
   (a) workers or self-employed persons who, at the time they stop working, have reached the age laid down by the law of that Member State for entitlement to an old age pension or workers who cease paid employment to take early retirement, provided that they have been working in that Member State for at least the preceding twelve months and have resided there continuously for more than three years.

   If the law of the host Member State does not grant the right to an old age pension to certain categories of self-employed persons, the age condition shall be deemed to have been met once the person concerned has reached the age of 60;

(b) workers or self-employed persons who have resided continuously in the host Member State for more than two years and stop working there as a result of permanent incapacity to work. If such incapacity is the result of an accident at work or an occupational disease entitling the person concerned to a benefit payable in full or in part by an institution in the host Member State, no condition shall be imposed as to length of residence;

(c) workers or self-employed persons who, after three years of continuous employment and residence in the host Member State, work in an employed or self-employed capacity in another Member State, while retaining their place of residence in the host Member State, to which they return, as a rule, each day or at least once a week.

For the purposes of entitlement to the rights referred to in points (a) and (b), periods of employment spent in the Member State in which the person concerned is working shall be regarded as having been spent in the host Member State.

Periods of involuntary unemployment duly recorded by the relevant employment office, periods not worked for reasons not of the person's own making and absences from work or cessation of work due to illness or accident shall be regarded as periods of employment.

2. The conditions as to length of residence and employment laid down in point (a) of paragraph 1 and the condition as to length of residence laid down in point (b) of paragraph 1 shall not apply if the worker's or the self-employed person's spouse or partner as referred to in point 2(b) of Article 2 is a national of the host Member State or has lost the nationality of that Member State by marriage to that worker or self-employed person.
3. Irrespective of nationality, the family members of a worker or a self-employed person who are residing with him in the territory of the host Member State shall have the right of permanent residence in that Member State, if the worker or self-employed person has acquired himself the right of permanent residence in that Member State on the basis of paragraph 1.
4. If, however, the worker or self-employed person dies while still working but before acquiring permanent residence status in the host Member State on the basis of paragraph 1, his family members who are residing with him in the host Member State shall acquire the right of permanent residence there, on condition that:

(a) the worker or self-employed person had, at the time of death, resided continuously on the territory of that Member State for two years; or

(b) the death resulted from an accident at work or an occupational disease; or

(c) the surviving spouse lost the nationality of that Member State following marriage to the worker or self-employed person.

Article 18: Acquisition of the right of permanent residence by certain family members who are not nationals of a Member State

Without prejudice to Article 17, the family members of a Union citizen to whom Articles 12(2) and 13(2) apply, who satisfy the conditions laid down therein, shall acquire the right of permanent residence after residing legally for a period of five consecutive years in the host Member State.

SECTION II: ADMINISTRATIVE FORMALITIES

Article 19: Document certifying permanent residence for Union citizens

1. Upon application Member States shall issue Union citizens entitled to permanent residence, after having verified duration of residence, with a document certifying permanent residence.
2. The document certifying permanent residence shall be issued as soon as possible.

Article 20: Permanent residence card for family members who are not nationals of a Member State

1. Member States shall issue family members who are not nationals of a Member State entitled to permanent residence with a permanent residence card within six months of the submission of the application. The permanent residence card shall be renewable automatically every ten years.
2. The application for a permanent residence card shall be submitted before the residence card expires. Failure to comply with the requirement to apply for a permanent residence card may render the person concerned liable to proportionate and non-discriminatory sanctions.
3. Interruption in residence not exceeding two consecutive years shall not affect the validity of the permanent residence card.

Article 21: Continuity of residence

For the purposes of this Directive, continuity of residence may be attested by any means of proof in use in the host Member State. Continuity of residence is broken by any expulsion decision duly enforced against the person concerned.

CHAPTER V: PROVISIONS COMMON TO THE RIGHT OF RESIDENCE AND THE RIGHT OF PERMANENT RESIDENCE

Article 22: Territorial scope

The right of residence and the right of permanent residence shall cover the whole territory of the host Member State. Member States may impose territorial restrictions on the right of residence and the right of permanent residence only where the same restrictions apply to their own nationals.

Article 23: Related rights

Irrespective of nationality, the family members of a Union citizen who have the right of residence or the right of permanent residence in a Member State shall be entitled to take up employment or self-employment there.

Article 24: Equal treatment

1. Subject to such specific provisions as are expressly provided for in the Treaty and secondary law, all Union citizens residing on the basis of this Directive in the territory of the host Member State shall enjoy equal treatment with the nationals of that Member State within the scope of the Treaty. The benefit of this right shall be extended to family members who

are not nationals of a Member State and who have the right of residence or permanent residence.

2. By way of derogation from paragraph 1, the host Member State shall not be obliged to confer entitlement to social assistance during the first three months of residence or, where appropriate, the longer period provided for in Article 14(4)(b), nor shall it be obliged, prior to acquisition of the right of permanent residence, to grant maintenance aid for studies, including vocational training, consisting in student grants or student loans to persons other than workers, self-employed persons, persons who retain such status and members of their families.

Article 25: General provisions concerning residence documents

1. Possession of a registration certificate as referred to in Article 8, of a document certifying permanent residence, of a certificate attesting submission of an application for a family member residence card, of a residence card or of a permanent residence card, may under no circumstances be made a precondition for the exercise of a right or the completion of an administrative formality, as entitlement to rights may be attested by any other means of proof.
2. All documents mentioned in paragraph 1 shall be issued free of charge or for a charge not exceeding that imposed on nationals for the issuing of similar documents.

Article 26: Checks

Member States may carry out checks on compliance with any requirement deriving from their national legislation for non-nationals always to carry their registration certificate or residence card, provided that the same requirement applies to their own nationals as regards their identity card. In the event of failure to comply with this requirement, Member States may impose the same sanctions as those imposed on their own nationals for failure to carry their identity card.

CHAPTER VI: RESTRICTIONS ON THE RIGHT OF ENTRY AND THE RIGHT OF RESIDENCE ON GROUNDS OF PUBLIC POLICY, PUBLIC SECURITY OR PUBLIC HEALTH

Article 27: General principles

1. Subject to the provisions of this Chapter, Member States may restrict the freedom of movement and residence of Union citizens and their family members, irrespective of nationality, on grounds of public policy, public security or public health. These grounds shall not be invoked to serve economic ends.
2. Measures taken on grounds of public policy or public security shall comply with the principle of proportionality and shall be based exclusively on the personal conduct of the individual concerned. Previous criminal convictions shall not in themselves constitute grounds for taking such measures.

   The personal conduct of the individual concerned must represent a genuine, present and sufficiently serious threat affecting one of the fundamental interests of society. Justifications that are isolated from the particulars of the case or that rely on considerations of general prevention shall not be accepted.

3. In order to ascertain whether the person concerned represents a danger for public policy or public security, when issuing the registration certificate or, in the absence of a registration system, not later than three months from the date of arrival of the person concerned on its territory or from the date of reporting his/her presence within the territory, as provided for in Article 5(5), or when issuing the residence card, the host Member State may, should it consider this essential, request the Member State of origin and, if need be, other Member States to provide information concerning any previous police record the person concerned may have. Such enquiries shall not be made as a matter of routine. The Member State consulted shall give its reply within two months.
4. The Member State which issued the passport or identity card shall allow the holder of the document who has been expelled on grounds of public policy, public security, or public health from another Member State to re-enter its territory without any formality even if the document is no longer valid or the nationality of the holder is in dispute.

Article 28: Protection against expulsion

1. Before taking an expulsion decision on grounds of public policy or public security, the host Member State shall take account of considerations such as how long the individual concerned has resided on its territory, his/her age, state of health, family and economic situation, social and cultural integration into the host Member State and the extent of his/her links with the country of origin.
2. The host Member State may not take an expulsion decision against Union citizens or their family members, irrespective of nationality, who have the right of permanent residence on its territory, except on serious grounds of public policy or public security.
3. An expulsion decision may not be taken against Union citizens, except if the decision is based on imperative grounds of public security, as defined by Member States, if they:
   (a) have resided in the host Member State for the previous ten years; or
   (b) are a minor, except if the expulsion is necessary for the best interests of the child, as provided for in the United Nations Convention on the Rights of the Child of 20 November 1989.

Article 29: Public health

1. The only diseases justifying measures restricting freedom of movement shall be the diseases with epidemic potential as defined by the relevant instruments of the World Health Organisation and other infectious diseases or contagious parasitic diseases if they are the subject of protection provisions applying to nationals of the host Member State.
2. Diseases occurring after a three-month period from the date of arrival shall not constitute grounds for expulsion from the territory.
3. Where there are serious indications that it is necessary, Member States may, within three months of the date of arrival, require persons entitled to the right of residence to undergo, free of charge, a medical examination to certify that they are not suffering from any of the conditions referred to in

paragraph 1. Such medical examinations may not be required as a matter of routine.

Article 30: Notification of decisions

1. The persons concerned shall be notified in writing of any decision taken under Article 27(1), in such a way that they are able to comprehend its content and the implications for them.
2. The persons concerned shall be informed, precisely and in full, of the public policy, public security or public health grounds on which the decision taken in their case is based, unless this is contrary to the interests of State security.
3. The notification shall specify the court or administrative authority with which the person concerned may lodge an appeal, the time limit for the appeal and, where applicable, the time allowed for the person to leave the territory of the Member State. Save in duly substantiated cases of urgency, the time allowed to leave the territory shall be not less than one month from the date of notification.

Article 31: Procedural safeguards

1. The persons concerned shall have access to judicial and, where appropriate, administrative redress procedures in the host Member State to appeal against or seek review of any decision taken against them on the grounds of public policy, public security or public health.
2. Where the application for appeal against or judicial review of the expulsion decision is accompanied by an application for an interim order to suspend enforcement of that decision, actual removal from the territory may not take place until such time as the decision on the interim order has been taken, except:
   - where the expulsion decision is based on a previous judicial decision; or
   - where the persons concerned have had previous access to judicial review; or
   - where the expulsion decision is based on imperative grounds of public security under Article 28(3).
3. The redress procedures shall allow for an examination of the legality of the decision, as well as of the facts and circumstances on which the proposed measure is based. They shall ensure that the decision is not disproportionate, particularly in view of the requirements laid down in Article 28.
4. Member States may exclude the individual concerned from their territory pending the redress procedure, but they may not prevent the individual from submitting his/her defence in person, except when his/her appearance may cause serious troubles to public policy or public security or when the appeal or judicial review concerns a denial of entry to the territory.

Article 32: Duration of exclusion orders

1. Persons excluded on grounds of public policy or public security may submit an application for lifting of the exclusion order after a reasonable period, depending on the circumstances, and in any event after three years from enforcement of the final exclusion order which has been validly adopted in

accordance with Community law, by putting forward arguments to establish that there has been a material change in the circumstances which justified the decision ordering their exclusion.

The Member State concerned shall reach a decision on this application within six months of its submission.

2. The persons referred to in paragraph 1 shall have no right of entry to the territory of the Member State concerned while their application is being considered.

Article 33: Expulsion as a penalty or legal consequence

1. Expulsion orders may not be issued by the host Member State as a penalty or legal consequence of a custodial penalty, unless they conform to the requirements of Articles 27, 28 and 29.
2. If an expulsion order, as provided for in paragraph 1, is enforced more than two years after it was issued, the Member State shall check that the individual concerned is currently and genuinely a threat to public policy or public security and shall assess whether there has been any material change in the circumstances since the expulsion order was issued.

CHAPTER VII: FINAL PROVISIONS

Article 34: Publicity

Member States shall disseminate information concerning the rights and obligations of Union citizens and their family members on the subjects covered by this Directive, particularly by means of awareness-raising campaigns conducted through national and local media and other means of communication.

Article 35: Abuse of rights

Member States may adopt the necessary measures to refuse, terminate or withdraw any right conferred by this Directive in the case of abuse of rights or fraud, such as marriages of convenience. Any such measure shall be proportionate and subject to the procedural safeguards provided for in Articles 30 and 31.

Article 36: Sanctions

Member States shall lay down provisions on the sanctions applicable to breaches of national rules adopted for the implementation of this Directive and shall take the measures required for their application. The sanctions laid down shall be effective and proportionate. Member States shall notify the Commission of these provisions not later than ......*[7] and as promptly as possible in the case of any subsequent changes.

Article 37: More favourable national provisions

The provisions of this Directive shall not affect any laws, regulations or administrative provisions laid down by a Member State which would be more favourable to the persons covered by this Directive.

7 Two years from the date of entry into force of this Directive.

Article 38: Repeals

1. Articles 10 and 11 of Regulation (EEC) No 1612/68 shall be repealed with effect from ... *.[8]
2. Directives 64/221/EEC, 68/360/EEC, 72/194/EEC, 73/148/EEC, 75/34/EEC, 75/35/EEC, 90/364/EEC, 90/365/EEC and 93/96/EEC shall be repealed with effect from .... *.[9]
3. References made to the repealed provisions and Directives shall be construed as being made to this Directive.

Article 39: Report

No later than.....*[10] the Commission shall submit a report on the application of this Directive to the European Parliament and the Council, together with any necessary proposals, notably on the opportunity to extend the period of time during which Union citizens and their family members may reside in the territory of the host Member State without any conditions. The Member States shall provide the Commission with the information needed to produce the report.

Article 40: Transposition

1. Member States shall bring into force the laws, regulations and administrative provisions necessary to comply with this Directive by ......**.[11]

   When Member States adopt those measures, they shall contain a reference to this Directive or shall be accompanied by such a reference on the occasion of their official publication. The methods of making such reference shall be laid down by the Member States.
2. Member States shall communicate to the Commission the text of the provisions of national law which they adopt in the field covered by this Directive together with a table showing how the provisions of this Directive correspond to the national provisions adopted.

Article 41: Entry into force

This Directive shall enter into force on the day of its publication in the Official Journal of the European Union.

Article 42: Addressees

This Directive is addressed to the Member States.
Done at Strasbourg, 29 April 2004.

For the European Parliament	For the Council
The President	The President
P. COX	M. McDOWELL

8 Two years from the date of entry into force of this Directive.
9 Two years from the date of entry into force of this Directive.
10 Four years from the date of entry into force of this Directive.
11 Two years from the date of entry into force of this Directive.

IMMIGRATION (EUROPEAN ECONOMIC AREA) REGULATIONS 2006 (as amended)[12]

PART 1: INTERPRETATION ETC

1 **Citation and commencement**

These Regulations may be cited as the Immigration (European Economic Area) Regulations 2006 and shall come into force on 30 April 2006.

2 **General interpretation**

(1) In these Regulations–

'the 1971 Act' means the Immigration Act 1971;

'the 1999 Act' means the Immigration and Asylum Act 1999;

'the 2002 Act' means the Nationality, Immigration and Asylum Act 2002;

'civil partner'does not include a party to a civil partnership of convenience;

'decision maker' means the Secretary of State, an immigration officer or an entry clearance officer (as the case may be);

'deportation order' means an order made pursuant to regulation 24(3);

'document certifying permanent residence' means a document issued to an EEA national, in accordance with regulation 18, as proof of the holder's permanent right of residence under regulation 15 as at the date of issue;

'EEA decision' means a decision under these Regulations that concerns a person's–

(a) entitlement to be admitted to the United Kingdom;

(b) entitlement to be issued with or have renewed, or not to have revoked, a registration certificate, residence card, document certifying permanent residence or permanent residence card; or

(c) removal from the United Kingdom;

'EEA family permit' means a document issued to a person, in accordance with regulation12, in connection with his admission to the United Kingdom;

'EEA national' means a national of an EEA State;

'EEA State' means–

(a) a Member State, other than the United Kingdom;

(b) Norway, Iceland or Liechtenstein; or

(c) Switzerland;

'entry clearance' has the meaning given in section 33(1) of the 1971 Act;

'entry clearance officer' means a person responsible for the grant or refusal of entry clearance;

'exclusion order' means an order made under regulation 19(1B);

'immigration rules' has the meaning given in section 33(1) of the 1971 Act;

'military service' means service in the armed forces of an EEA State;

'permanent residence card' means a card issued to a person who is not an EEA national, in accordance with regulation 18, as proof of the holder's permanent right of residence under regulation 15 as at the date of issue;

'registration certificate' means a certificate issued to an EEA national, in accordance with regulation 16, as proof of the holder's right of residence in the United Kingdom as at the date of issue;

12 As amended, up to date to 11 September 2009.

'relevant EEA national' in relation to an extended family member has the meaning given in regulation 8(6);

'residence card' means a card issued to a person who is not an EEA national, in accordance with regulation 17, as proof of the holder's right of residence in the United Kingdom as at the date of issue;

'spouse' does not include a party to a marriage of convenience;

'United Kingdom national' means a person who falls to be treated as a national of the United Kingdom for the purposes of the Community Treaties.

(2) Paragraph (1) is subject to paragraph 1(a) of Schedule 4 (transitional provisions).

(3) Section 11 of the 1971 Act (construction of references to entry) shall apply for the purpose of determining whether a person has entered the United Kingdom for the purpose of these Regulations as it applies for the purpose of determining whether a person has entered the United Kingdom for the purpose of that Act.

3 Continuity of residence

(1) This regulation applies for the purpose of calculating periods of continuous residence in the United Kingdom under regulation 5(1) and regulation 15.

(2) Continuity of residence is not affected by–

(a) periods of absence from the United Kingdom which do not exceed six months in total in any year;

(b) periods of absence from the United Kingdom on military service; or

(c) any one absence from the United Kingdom not exceeding twelve months for an important reason such as pregnancy and childbirth, serious illness, study or vocational training or an overseas posting.

(3) But continuity of residence is broken if a person is removed from the United Kingdom under these Regulations.

4 'Worker', 'self-employed person', 'self-sufficient person' and 'student'

(1) In these Regulations–

(a) 'worker' means a worker within the meaning of Article 39 of the Treaty establishing the European Community;

(b) 'self-employed person' means a person who establishes himself in order to pursue activity as a self-employed person in accordance with Article 43 of the Treaty establishing the European Community;

(c) 'self-sufficient person' means a person who has–

(i) sufficient resources not to become a burden on the social assistance system of the United Kingdom during his period of residence; and

(ii) comprehensive sickness insurance cover in the United Kingdom;

(d) 'student' means a person who–

(i) is enrolled at a private or public establishment, included on the Register of Education and Training Providers maintained by the Department for Innovation, Universities and Skills[13] or financed

13 The Register of Education and Training Providers is maintained by, and is available on the website of, the Department for Education and Skills.

from public funds, for the principal purpose of following a course of study, including vocational training;

(ii) has comprehensive sickness insurance cover in the United Kingdom; and

(iii) assures the Secretary of State, by means of a declaration, or by such equivalent means as the person may choose, that he has sufficient resources not to become a burden on the social assistance system of the United Kingdom during his period of residence.

(2) For the purposes of paragraph (1)(c), where family members of the person concerned reside in the United Kingdom and their right to reside is dependent upon their being family members of that person–

(a) the requirement for that person to have sufficient resources not to become a burden on the social assistance system of the United Kingdom during his period of residence shall only be satisfied if his resources and those of the family members are sufficient to avoid him and the family members becoming such a burden;

(b) the requirement for that person to have comprehensive sickness insurance cover in the United Kingdom shall only be satisfied if he and his family members have such cover.

(3) For the purposes of paragraph (1)(d), where family members of the person concerned reside in the United Kingdom and their right to reside is dependent upon their being family members of that person, the requirement for that person to assure the Secretary of State that he has sufficient resources not to become a burden on the social assistance system of the United Kingdom during his period of residence shall only be satisfied if he assures the Secretary of State that his resources and those of the family members are sufficient to avoid him and the family members becoming such a burden.

(4) For the purposes of paragraphs (1)(c) and (d) and paragraphs (2) and (3), the resources of the person concerned and, where applicable, any family members, are to be regarded as sufficient if they exceed the maximum level of resources which a United Kingdom national and his family members may possess if he is to become eligible for social assistance under the United Kingdom benefit system.

5 'Worker or self-employed person who has ceased activity'

(1) In these Regulations, 'worker or self-employed person who has ceased activity' means an EEA national who satisfies the conditions in paragraph (2), (3), (4) or (5).

(2) A person satisfies the conditions in this paragraph if he–

(a) terminates his activity as a worker or self-employed person and–

(i) has reached the age at which he is entitled to a state pension on the date on which he terminates his activity; or

(ii) in the case of a worker, ceases working to take early retirement;

(b) pursued his activity as a worker or self-employed person in the United Kingdom for at least twelve months prior to the termination; and

(c) resided in the United Kingdom continuously for more than three years prior to the termination.

(3) A person satisfies the conditions in this paragraph if–
(a) he terminates his activity in the United Kingdom as a worker or self-employed person as a result of a permanent incapacity to work; and
(b) either–
(i) he resided in the United Kingdom continuously for more than two years prior to the termination; or
(ii) the incapacity is the result of an accident at work or an occupational disease that entitles him to a pension payable in full or in part by an institution in the United Kingdom.
(4) A person satisfies the conditions in this paragraph if–
(a) he is active as a worker or self-employed person in an EEA State but retains his place of residence in the United Kingdom, to which he returns as a rule at least once a week; and
(b) prior to becoming so active in that EEA State, he had been continuously resident and continuously active as a worker or self-employed person in the United Kingdom for at least three years.
(5) A person who satisfies the condition in paragraph (4)(a) but not the condition in paragraph (4)(b) shall, for the purposes of paragraphs (2) and (3), be treated as being active and resident in the United Kingdom during any period in which he is working or self-employed in the EEA State.
(6) The conditions in paragraphs (2) and (3) as to length of residence and activity as a worker or self-employed person shall not apply in relation to a person whose spouse or civil partner is a United Kingdom national.
(7) For the purposes of this regulation–
(a) periods of inactivity for reasons not of the person's own making;
(b) periods of inactivity due to illness or accident; and
(c) in the case of a worker, periods of involuntary unemployment duly recorded by the relevant employment office,

shall be treated as periods of activity as a worker or self-employed person, as the case may be.

6 'Qualified person'

(1) In these Regulations, 'qualified person' means a person who is an EEA national and in the United Kingdom as–
(a) a jobseeker;
(b) a worker;
(c) a self-employed person;
(d) a self-sufficient person; or
(e) a student.
(2) A person who is no longer working shall not cease to be treated as a worker for the purpose of paragraph (1)(b) if–
(a) he is temporarily unable to work as the result of an illness or accident;
(b) he is in duly recorded involuntary unemployment after having been employed in the United Kingdom, provided that he has registered as a jobseeker with the relevant employment office and–
(i) he was employed for one year or more before becoming unemployed;
(ii) he has been unemployed for no more than six months; or
(iii) he can provide evidence that he is seeking employment in the United Kingdom and has a genuine chance of being engaged;

(c) he is involuntarily unemployed and has embarked on vocational training; or

(d) he has voluntarily ceased working and embarked on vocational training that is related to his previous employment.

(3) A person who is no longer in self-employment shall not cease to be treated as a self-employed person for the purpose of paragraph (1)(c) if he is temporarily unable to pursue his activity as a self-employed person as the result of an illness or accident.

(4) For the purpose of paragraph (1)(a), 'jobseeker' means a person who enters the United Kingdom in order to seek employment and can provide evidence that he is seeking employment and has a genuine chance of being engaged.

7 Family member

(1) Subject to paragraph (2), for the purposes of these Regulations the following persons shall be treated as the family members of another person–

(a) his spouse or his civil partner;

(b) direct descendants of his, his spouse or his civil partner who are–

(i) under 21; or

(ii) dependants of his, his spouse or his civil partner;

(c) dependent direct relatives in his ascending line or that of his spouse or his civil partner;

(d) a person who is to be treated as the family member of that other person under paragraph (3).

(2) A person shall not be treated under paragraph (1)(b) or (c) as the family member of a student residing in the United Kingdom after the period of three months beginning on the date on which the student is admitted to the United Kingdom unless–

(a) in the case of paragraph (b), the person is the dependent child of the student or of his spouse or civil partner; or

(b) the student also falls within one of the other categories of qualified persons mentioned in regulation 6(1).

(3) Subject to paragraph (4), a person who is an extended family member and has been issued with an EEA family permit, a registration certificate or a residence card shall be treated as the family member of the relevant EEA national for as long as he continues to satisfy the conditions in regulation 8(2), (3), (4) or (5) in relation to that EEA national and the permit, certificate or card has not ceased to be valid or been revoked.

(4) Where the relevant EEA national is a student, the extended family member shall only be treated as the family member of that national under paragraph (3) if either the EEA family permit was issued under regulation 12(2), the registration certificate was issued under regulation 16(5) or the residence card was issued under regulation 17(4).

8 'Extended family member'

(1) In these Regulations 'extended family member' means a person who is not a family member of an EEA national under regulation 7(1)(a), (b) or (c) and who satisfies the conditions in paragraph (2), (3), (4) or (5).

(2) A person satisfies the condition in this paragraph if the person is a relative of an EEA national, his spouse or his civil partner and–
   (a) the person is residing in an EEA State in which the EEA national also resides and is dependent upon the EEA national or is a member of his household;
   (b) the person satisfied the condition in paragraph (a) and is accompanying the EEA national to the United Kingdom or wishes to join him there; or
   (c) the person satisfied the condition in paragraph (a), has joined the EEA national in the United Kingdom and continues to be dependent upon him or to be a member of his household.

(3) A person satisfies the condition in this paragraph if the person is a relative of an EEA national or his spouse or his civil partner and, on serious health grounds, strictly requires the personal care of the EEA national his spouse or his civil partner.

(4) A person satisfies the condition in this paragraph if the person is a relative of an EEA national and would meet the requirements in the immigration rules (other than those relating to entry clearance) for indefinite leave to enter or remain in the United Kingdom as a dependent relative of the EEA national were the EEA national a person present and settled in the United Kingdom.

(5) A person satisfies the condition in this paragraph if the person is the partner of an EEA national (other than a civil partner) and can prove to the decision maker that he is in a durable relationship with the EEA national.

(6) In these Regulations 'relevant EEA national' means, in relation to an extended family member, the EEA national who is or whose spouse or civil partner is the relative of the extended family member for the purpose of paragraph (2), (3) or (4) or the EEA national who is the partner of the extended family member for the purpose of paragraph (5).

9 Family members of United Kingdom nationals

(1) If the conditions in paragraph (2) are satisfied, these Regulations apply to a person who is the family member of a United Kingdom national as if the United Kingdom national were an EEA national.

(2) The conditions are that–
   (a) the United Kingdom national is residing in an EEA State as a worker or self-employed person or was so residing before returning to the United Kingdom; and
   (b) if the family member of the United Kingdom national is his spouse or civil partner, the parties are living together in the EEA State or had entered into the marriage or civil partnership and were living together in that State before the United Kingdom national returned to the United Kingdom.

(3) Where these Regulations apply to the family member of a United Kingdom national the United Kingdom national shall be treated as holding a valid passport issued by an EEA State for the purpose of the application of regulation 13 to that family member.

10 'Family member who has retained the right of residence'

(1) In these Regulations, 'family member who has retained the right of residence' means, subject to paragraph (8), a person who satisfies the conditions in paragraph (2), (3), (4) or (5).

(2) A person satisfies the conditions in this paragraph if–

(a) he was a family member of a qualified person when the qualified person died;

(b) he resided in the United Kingdom in accordance with these Regulations for at least the year immediately before the death of the qualified person; and

(c) he satisfies the condition in paragraph (6).

(3) A person satisfies the conditions in this paragraph if–

(a) he is the direct descendant of–

(i) a qualified person who has died;

(ii) a person who ceased to be a qualified person on ceasing to reside in the United Kingdom; or

(iii) the person who was the spouse or civil partner of the qualified person mentioned in sub-paragraph (i) when he died or is the spouse or civil partner of the person mentioned in sub-paragraph (ii); and

(b) he was attending an educational course in the United Kingdom immediately before the qualified person died or ceased to be a qualified person and continues to attend such a course.

(4) A person satisfies the conditions in this paragraph if the person is the parent with actual custody of a child who satisfies the condition in paragraph (3).

(5) A person satisfies the conditions in this paragraph if–

(a) he ceased to be a family member of a qualified person on the termination of the marriage or civil partnership of the qualified person;

(b) he was residing in the United Kingdom in accordance with these Regulations at the date of the termination;

(c) he satisfies the condition in paragraph (6); and

(d) either–

(i) prior to the initiation of the proceedings for the termination of the marriage or the civil partnership the marriage or civil partnership had lasted for at least three years and the parties to the marriage or civil partnership had resided in the United Kingdom for at least one year during its duration;

(ii) the former spouse or civil partner of the qualified person has custody of a child of the qualified person;

(iii) the former spouse or civil partner of the qualified person has the right of access to a child of the qualified person under the age of 18 and a court has ordered that such access must take place in the United Kingdom; or

(iv) the continued right of residence in the United Kingdom of the person is warranted by particularly difficult circumstances, such as he or another family member having been a victim of domestic violence while the marriage or civil partnership was subsisting.

(6) The condition in this paragraph is that the person–
(a) is not an EEA national but would, if he were an EEA national, be a worker, a self-employed person or a self-sufficient person under regulation 6; or
(b) is the family member of a person who falls within paragraph (a).
(7) In this regulation, 'educational course' means a course within the scope of Article 12 of Council Regulation (EEC) No. 1612/68 on freedom of movement for workers12.
(8) A person with a permanent right of residence under regulation 15 shall not become a family member who has retained the right of residence on the death or departure from the United Kingdom of the qualified person or the termination of the marriage or civil partnership, as the case may be, and a family member who has retained the right of residence shall cease to have that status on acquiring a permanent right of residence under regulation 15.

PART 2: EEA RIGHTS

11 Right of admission to the United Kingdom

(1) An EEA national must be admitted to the United Kingdom if he produces on arrival a valid national identity card or passport issued by an EEA State.
(2) A person who is not an EEA national must be admitted to the United Kingdom if he is a family member of an EEA national, a family member who has retained the right of residence or a person with a permanent right of residence under regulation 15 and produces on arrival–
(a) a valid passport; and
(b) an EEA family permit, a residence card or a permanent residence card.
(3) An immigration officer may not place a stamp in the passport of a person admitted to the United Kingdom under this regulation who is not an EEA national if the person produces a residence card or permanent residence card.
(4) Before an immigration officer refuses admission to the United Kingdom to a person under this regulation because the person does not produce on arrival a document mentioned in paragraph (1) or (2), the immigration officer must give the person every reasonable opportunity to obtain the document or have it brought to him within a reasonable period of time or to prove by other means that he is–
(a) an EEA national;
(b) a family member of an EEA national with a right to accompany that national or join him in the United Kingdom; or
(c) a family member who has retained the right of residence or a person with a permanent right of residence under regulation 15.
(5) But this regulation is subject to regulations 19(1) and (2).

12 Issue of EEA family permit

(1) An entry clearance officer must issue an EEA family permit to a person who applies for one if the person is a family member of an EEA national and–

(a) the EEA national–
   (i) is residing in the UK in accordance with these Regulations; or
   (ii) will be travelling to the United Kingdom within six months of the date of the application and will be an EEA national residing in the United Kingdom in accordance with these Regulations on arrival in the United Kingdom; and

(b) the family member will be accompanying the EEA national to the United Kingdom or joining him there and–
   (i) is lawfully resident in an EEA State; or
   (ii) would meet the requirements in the immigration rules (other than those relating to entry clearance) for leave to enter the United Kingdom as the family member of the EEA national or, in the case of direct descendants or dependent direct relatives in the ascending line of his spouse or his civil partner, as the family member of his spouse or his civil partner, were the EEA national or the spouse or civil partner a person present and settled in the United Kingdom.

(2) An entry clearance officer may issue an EEA family permit to an extended family member of an EEA national who applies for one if–
   (a) the relevant EEA national satisfies the condition in paragraph (1)(a);
   (b) the extended family member wishes to accompany the relevant EEA national to the United Kingdom or to join him there; and
   (c) in all the circumstances, it appears to the entry clearance officer appropriate to issue the EEA family permit.

(3) Where an entry clearance officer receives an application under paragraph (2) he shall undertake an extensive examination of the personal circumstances of the applicant and if he refuses the application shall give reasons justifying the refusal unless this is contrary to the interests of national security.

(4) An EEA family permit issued under this regulation shall be issued free of charge and as soon as possible.

(5) But an EEA family permit shall not be issued under this regulation if the applicant or the EEA national concerned [is subject to a deportation or exclusion order or]13 falls to be excluded from the United Kingdom on grounds of public policy, public security or public health in accordance with regulation 21.

13 Initial right of residence

(1) An EEA national is entitled to reside in the United Kingdom for a period not exceeding three months beginning on the date on which he is admitted to the United Kingdom provided that he holds a valid national identity card or passport issued by an EEA State.

(2) A family member of an EEA national residing in the United Kingdom under paragraph (1) who is not himself an EEA national is entitled to reside in the United Kingdom provided that he holds a valid passport.

(3) But–
   (a) this regulation is subject to regulation 19(3)(b); and
   (b) an EEA national or his family member who becomes an unreasonable burden on the social assistance system of the United Kingdom shall cease to have the right to reside under this regulation.

14 Extended right of residence

(1) A qualified person is entitled to reside in the United Kingdom for so long as he remains a qualified person.

(2) A family member of a qualified person residing in the United Kingdom under paragraph (1) or of an EEA national with a permanent right of residence under regulation 15 is entitled to reside in the United Kingdom for so long as he remains the family member of the qualified person or EEA national.

(3) A family member who has retained the right of residence is entitled to reside in the United Kingdom for so long as he remains a family member who has retained the right of residence.

(4) A right to reside under this regulation is in addition to any right a person may have to reside in the United Kingdom under regulation 13 or 15.

(5) But this regulation is subject to regulation 19(3)(b).

15 Permanent right of residence

(1) The following persons shall acquire the right to reside in the United Kingdom permanently–

(a) an EEA national who has resided in the United Kingdom in accordance with these Regulations for a continuous period of five years;

(b) a family member of an EEA national who is not himself an EEA national but who has resided in the United Kingdom with the EEA national in accordance with these Regulations for a continuous period of five years;

(c) a worker or self-employed person who has ceased activity;

(d) the family member of a worker or self-employed person who has ceased activity;

(e) a person who was the family member of a worker or self-employed person where–

(i) the worker or self-employed person has died;

(ii) the family member resided with him immediately before his death; and

(iii) the worker or self-employed person had resided continuously in the United Kingdom for at least the two years immediately before his death or the death was the result of an accident at work or an occupational disease;

(f) a person who–

(i) has resided in the United Kingdom in accordance with these Regulations for a continuous period of five years; and

(ii) was, at the end of that period, a family member who has retained the right of residence.

(2) Once acquired, the right of permanent residence under this regulation shall be lost only through absence from the United Kingdom for a period exceeding two consecutive years.

(3) But this regulation is subject to regulation 19(3)(b).

PART 3: RESIDENCE DOCUMENTATION

16 Issue of registration certificate

(1) The Secretary of State must issue a registration certificate to a qualified person immediately on application and production of–

(a) a valid identity card or passport issued by an EEA State;
(b) proof that he is a qualified person.

(2) In the case of a worker, confirmation of the worker's engagement from his employer or a certificate of employment is sufficient proof for the purposes of paragraph (1)(b).

(3) The Secretary of State must issue a registration certificate to an EEA national who is the family member of a qualified person or of an EEA national with a permanent right of residence under regulation 15 immediately on application and production of–
(a) a valid identity card or passport issued by an EEA State; and
(b) proof that the applicant is such a family member.

(4) The Secretary of State must issue a registration certificate to an EEA national who is a family member who has retained the right of residence on application and production of–
(a) a valid identity card or passport; and
(b) proof that the applicant is a family member who has retained the right of residence.

(5) The Secretary of State may issue a registration certificate to an extended family member not falling within regulation 7(3) who is an EEA national on application if–
(a) the relevant EEA national in relation to the extended family member is a qualified person or an EEA national with a permanent right of residence under regulation 15; and
(b) in all the circumstances it appears to the Secretary of State appropriate to issue the registration certificate.

(6) Where the Secretary of State receives an application under paragraph (5) he shall undertake an extensive examination of the personal circumstances of the applicant and if he refuses the application shall give reasons justifying the refusal unless this is contrary to the interests of national security.

(7) A registration certificate issued under this regulation shall state the name and address of the person registering and the date of registration and shall be issued free of charge.

(8) But this regulation is subject to regulation 20(1).

17 Issue of residence card

(1) The Secretary of State must issue a residence card to a person who is not an EEA national and is the family member of a qualified person or of an EEA national with a permanent right of residence under regulation 15 on application and production of–
(a) a valid passport; and
(b) proof that the applicant is such a family member.

(2) The Secretary of State must issue a residence card to a person who is not an EEA national but who is a family member who has retained the right of residence on application and production of–
(a) a valid passport; and
(b) proof that the applicant is a family member who has retained the right of residence.

(3) On receipt of an application under paragraph (1) or (2) and the documents that are required to accompany the application the Secretary of State shall immediately issue the applicant with a certificate of application for

the residence card and the residence card shall be issued no later than six months after the date on which the application and documents are received.

(4) The Secretary of State may issue a residence card to an extended family member not falling within regulation 7(3) who is not an EEA national on application if–

(a) the relevant EEA national in relation to the extended family member is a qualified person or an EEA national with a permanent right of residence under regulation 15; and

(b) in all the circumstances it appears to the Secretary of State appropriate to issue the residence card.

(5) Where the Secretary of State receives an application under paragraph (4) he shall undertake an extensive examination of the personal circumstances of the applicant and if he refuses the application shall give reasons justifying the refusal unless this is contrary to the interests of national security.

(6) A residence card issued under this regulation may take the form of a stamp in the applicant's passport and shall be valid for–

(a) five years from the date of issue; or

(b) in the case of a residence card issued to the family member or extended family member of a qualified person, the envisaged period of residence in the United Kingdom of the qualified person,

whichever is the shorter.

(6A) A residence card issued under this regulation shall be entitled 'Residence card of a family member of an EEA national' or 'Residence card of a family member who has retained the right of residence', as the case may be.

(7) A residence card issued under this regulation shall be issued free of charge.

(8) But this regulation is subject to regulations 20(1) and (1A).

18 Issue of a document certifying permanent residence and a permanent residence card

(1) The Secretary of State must issue an EEA national with a permanent right of residence under regulation 15 with a document certifying permanent residence as soon as possible after an application for such a document and proof that the EEA national has such a right is submitted to the Secretary of State.

(2) The Secretary of State must issue a person who is not an EEA national who has a permanent right of residence under regulation 15 with a permanent residence card no later than six months after the date on which an application for a permanent residence card and proof that the person has such a right is submitted to the Secretary of State.

(3) Subject to paragraph (5), a permanent residence card shall be valid for ten years from the date of issue and must be renewed on application.

(4) A document certifying permanent residence and a permanent residence card shall be issued free of charge.

(5) A document certifying permanent residence and a permanent residence card shall cease to be valid if the holder ceases to have a right of permanent residence under regulation 15.

(6) But this regulation is subject to regulation 20.

PART 4: REFUSAL OF ADMISSION AND REMOVAL ETC

19 Exclusion and removal from the United Kingdom

(1) A person is not entitled to be admitted to the United Kingdom by virtue of regulation 11 if his exclusion is justified on grounds of public policy, public security or public health in accordance with regulation 21.

(1A) A person is not entitled to be admitted to the United Kingdom by virtue of regulation 11 if that person is subject to a deportation or exclusion order.

(1B) If the Secretary of State considers that the exclusion of an EEA national or the family member of an EEA national is justified on the grounds of public policy, public security or public health in accordance with regulation 21 the Secretary of State may make an order for the purpose of these Regulations prohibiting that person from entering the United Kingdom.

(2) A person is not entitled to be admitted to the United Kingdom as the family member of an EEA national under regulation 11(2) unless, at the time of his arrival–

(a) he is accompanying the EEA national or joining him in the United Kingdom; and

(b) the EEA national has a right to reside in the United Kingdom under these Regulations.

(3) Subject to paragraphs (4) and (5), an EEA national who has entered the United Kingdom or the family member of such a national who has entered the United Kingdom may be removed if–

(a) that person does not have or ceases to have a right to reside under these Regulations; or

(b) the Secretary of State has decided that the person's removal is justified on grounds of public policy, public security or public health in accordance with regulation 21.

(4) A person must not be removed under paragraph (3) as the automatic consequence of having recourse to the social assistance system of the United Kingdom.

(5) A person must not be removed under paragraph (3) if he has a right to remain in the United Kingdom by virtue of leave granted under the 1971 Act unless his removal is justified on the grounds of public policy, public security or public health in accordance with regulation 21.

20 Refusal to issue or renew and revocation of residence documentation

(1) The Secretary of State may refuse to issue, revoke or refuse to renew a registration certificate, a residence card, a document certifying permanent residence or a permanent residence card if the refusal or revocation is justified on grounds of public policy, public security or public health.

(1A) The removal of a person from the United Kingdom under these Regulations invalidates a registration certificate, residence card, document certifying permanent residence or permanent residence card held by that person or an application made by that person for such a certificate, card or document.

(2) The Secretary of State may revoke a registration certificate or a residence card or refuse to renew a residence card if the holder of the certificate or card has ceased to have a right to reside under these Regulations.

(3) The Secretary of State may revoke a document certifying permanent residence or a permanent residence card or refuse to renew a permanent residence card if the holder of the certificate or card has ceased to have a right of permanent residence under regulation 15.

(4) An immigration officer may, at the time of a person's arrival in the United Kingdom–

(a) revoke that person's residence card if he is not at that time the family member of a qualified person or of an EEA national who has a right of permanent residence under regulation 15, a family member who has retained the right of residence or a person with a right of permanent residence under regulation 15;

(b) revoke that person's permanent residence card if he is not at that time a person with a right of permanent residence under regulation 15.

(5) An entry clearance officer or immigration officer may at any time revoke a person's EEA family permit if–

(a) the revocation is justified on grounds of public policy, public security or public health; or

(b) the person is not at that time the family member of an EEA national with the right to reside in the United Kingdom under these Regulations or is not accompanying that national or joining him in the United Kingdom.

(6) Any action taken under this regulation on grounds of public policy, public security or public health shall be in accordance with regulation 21.

21 Decisions taken on public policy, public security and public health grounds

(1) In this regulation a 'relevant decision' means an EEA decision taken on the grounds of public policy, public security or public health.

(2) A relevant decision may not be taken to serve economic ends.

(3) A relevant decision may not be taken in respect of a person with a permanent right of residence under regulation 15 except on serious grounds of public policy or public security.

(4) A relevant decision may not be taken except on imperative grounds of public security in respect of an EEA national who–

(a) has resided in the United Kingdom for a continuous period of at least ten years prior to the relevant decision; or

(b) is under the age of 18, unless the relevant decision is necessary in his best interests, as provided for in the Convention on the Rights of the Child adopted by the General Assembly of the United Nations on 20th November 1989.[14]

(5) Where a relevant decision is taken on grounds of public policy or public security it shall, in addition to complying with the preceding paragraphs of this regulation, be taken in accordance with the following principles–

(a) the decision must comply with the principle of proportionality;

(b) the decision must be based exclusively on the personal conduct of the person concerned;

14 Cmd 1976.

(c) the personal conduct of the person concerned must represent a genuine, present and sufficiently serious threat affecting one of the fundamental interests of society;

(d) matters isolated from the particulars of the case or which relate to considerations of general prevention do not justify the decision;

(e) a person's previous criminal convictions do not in themselves justify the decision.

(6) Before taking a relevant decision on the grounds of public policy or public security in relation to a person who is resident in the United Kingdom the decision maker must take account of considerations such as the age, state of health, family and economic situation of the person, the person's length of residence in the United Kingdom, the person's social and cultural integration into the United Kingdom and the extent of the person's links with his country of origin.

(7) In the case of a relevant decision taken on grounds of public health–

(a) a disease that does not have epidemic potential as defined by the relevant instruments of the World Health Organisation[15] or is not a disease to which section 38 of the Public Health (Control of Disease) Act 1984[16] applies (detention in hospital of a person with a notifiable disease) shall not constitute grounds for the decision; and

(b) if the person concerned is in the United Kingdom, diseases occurring after the three month period beginning on the date on which he arrived in the United Kingdom shall not constitute grounds for the decision.

PART 5: PROCEDURE IN RELATION TO EEA DECISIONS

22 Person claiming right of admission

(1) This regulation applies to a person who claims a right of admission to the United Kingdom under regulation 11 as–

(a) a person, not being an EEA national, who is a family member of an EEA national, a family member who has retained the right of residence or a person with a permanent right of residence under regulation 15; or

(b) an EEA national, where there is reason to believe that he may fall to be excluded under regulation 19(1) or (1A).

(2) A person to whom this regulation applies is to be treated as if he were a person seeking leave to enter the United Kingdom under the 1971 Act for the purposes of paragraphs 2, 3, 4, 7, 16 to 18 and 21 to 24 of Schedule 2 to the 1971 Act (administrative provisions as to control on entry etc), except that–

(a) the reference in paragraph 2(1) to the purpose for which the immigration officer may examine any persons who have arrived in the United Kingdom is to be read as a reference to the purpose of determining

15 The relevant instrument of the World Health Organisation for these purposes is currently the International Health Regulations (2005).

16 Section 38 applies to a 'notifiable disease', as defined in section 10 of the Act and has been applied to an additional list of diseases by the Public Health (Infectious Diseases) Regulations SI 1988/1546.

whether he is a person who is to be granted admission under these Regulations;

(b) the references in paragraphs 4(2A), 7 and 16(1) to a person who is, or may be, given leave to enter are to be read as references to a person who is, or may be, granted admission under these Regulations; and

(c) a medical examination is not be carried out under paragraph 2 or paragraph 7 as a matter of routine and may only be carried out within three months of a person's arrival in the United Kingdom.

(3) For so long as a person to whom this regulation applies is detained, or temporarily admitted or released while liable to detention, under the powers conferred by Schedule 2 to the 1971 Act, he is deemed not to have been admitted to the United Kingdom.

23 Person refused admission

(1) This regulation applies to a person who is in the United Kingdom and has been refused admission to the United Kingdom–

(a) because he does not meet the requirement of regulation 11 (including where he does not meet those requirements because his EEA family permit, residence card or permanent residence card has been revoked by an immigration officer in accordance with regulation 20); or

(b) in accordance with regulation 19(1), (1A) or (2).

(2) A person to whom this regulation applies, is to be treated as if he were a person refused leave to enter under the 1971 Act for the purpose of paragraphs 8, 10, 10A, 11, 16 to 19 and 21 to 24 of Schedule 2 to the 1971 Act, except that the reference in paragraph 19 to a certificate of entitlement, entry clearance or work permit is to be read as a reference to an EEA family permit, residence card or a permanent residence card.

24 Person subject to removal

(1) If there are reasonable grounds for suspecting that a person is someone who may be removed from the United Kingdom under regulation 19(3), that person may be detained under the authority of an immigration officer pending a decision whether or not to remove the person under that regulation, and paragraphs 17 and 18 of Schedule 2 to the 1971 Act shall apply in relation to the detention of such a person as those paragraphs apply in relation to a person who may be detained under paragraph 16 of that Schedule.

(2) Where a decision is taken to remove a person under regulation 19(3)(a), the person is to be treated as if he were a person to whom section 10(1)(a) of the 1999 Act applied, and section 10 of that Act (removal of certain persons unlawfully in the United Kingdom) is to apply accordingly.

(3) Where a decision is taken to remove a person under regulation 19(3)(b), the person is to be treated as if he were a person to whom section 3(5)(a) of the 1971 Act (liability to deportation) applied, and section 5 of that Act (procedure for deportation) and Schedule 3 to that Act(supplementary provision as to deportation) are to apply accordingly.

(4) A person who enters the United Kingdom in breach of a deportation or exclusion order shall be removable as an illegal entrant under Schedule 2 to the 1971 Act and the provisions of that Schedule shall apply accordingly.

(5) Where such a deportation order is made against a person but he is not removed under the order during the two year period beginning on the date on which the order is made, the Secretary of State shall only take action to remove the person under the order after the end of that period if, having assessed whether there has been any material change in circumstances since the deportation order was made, he considers that the removal continues to be justified on the grounds of public policy, public security or public health.

(6) A person to whom this regulation applies shall be allowed one month to leave the United Kingdom, beginning on the date on which he is notified of the decision to remove him, before being removed pursuant to that decision except–

(a) in duly substantiated cases of urgency;

(b) where the person is detained pursuant to the sentence or order of any court;

(c) where a person is a person to whom regulation 24(4) applies.

24A Revocation of deportation and exclusion orders

(1) A deportation or exclusion order shall remain in force unless it is revoked by the Secretary of State under this regulation.

(2) A person who is subject to a deportation or exclusion order may apply to the Secretary of State to have it revoked if the person considers that there has been a material change in the circumstances that justified the making of the order.

(3) An application under paragraph (2) shall set out the material change in circumstances relied upon by the applicant and may only be made whilst the applicant is outside the United Kingdom.

(4) On receipt of an application under paragraph (2), the Secretary of State shall revoke the order if the Secretary of State considers that the order can no longer be justified on grounds of public policy, public security or public health in accordance with regulation 21.

(5) The Secretary of State shall take a decision on an application under paragraph (2) no later than six months after the date on which the application is received.

PART 6: APPEALS UNDER THESE REGULATIONS

25 Interpretation of Part 6

(1) In this Part–

'Asylum and Immigration Tribunal' has the same meaning as in the 2002 Act;

'Commission' has the same meaning as in the Special Immigration Appeals Commission Act 1997;

'the Human Rights Convention' has the same meaning as 'the Convention' in the Human Rights Act 1998; and

'the Refugee Convention' means the Convention relating to the Status of Refugees done at Geneva on 28th July 1951 and the Protocol relating to the Status of Refugees done at New York on 31st January 1967.

(2) For the purposes of this Part, and subject to paragraphs (3) and (4), an appeal is to be treated as pending during the period when notice of appeal is given and ending when the appeal is finally determined, withdrawn or abandoned.

(3) An appeal is not to be treated as finally determined while a further appeal may be brought; and, if such a further appeal is brought, the original appeal is not to be treated as finally determined until the further appeal is determined, withdrawn or abandoned.

(4) A pending appeal is not to be treated as abandoned solely because the appellant leaves the United Kingdom.

26 Appeal rights

(1) Subject to the following paragraphs of this regulation, a person may appeal under these Regulations against an EEA decision.

(2) If a person claims to be an EEA national, he may not appeal under these Regulations unless he produces a valid national identity card or passport issued by an EEA State.

(3) If a person claims to be the family member or relative of an EEA national he may not appeal under these Regulations unless he produces–

(a) an EEA family permit; or

(b) other proof that he is related as claimed to an EEA national.

(4) A person may not bring an appeal under these Regulations on a ground certified under paragraph (5) or rely on such a ground in an appeal brought under these Regulations.

(5) The Secretary of State or an immigration officer may certify a ground for the purposes of paragraph (4) if it has been considered in a previous appeal brought under these Regulations or under section 82(1) of the 2002 Act.

(6) Except where an appeal lies to the Commission, an appeal under these Regulations lies to the Asylum and Immigration Tribunal.

(7) The provisions of or made under the 2002 Act referred to in Schedule 1 shall have effect for the purposes of an appeal under these Regulations to the Asylum and Immigration Tribunal in accordance with that Schedule.

27 Out of country appeals

(1) Subject to paragraphs (2) and (3), a person may not appeal under regulation 26 whilst he is in the United Kingdom against an EEA decision–

(a) to refuse to admit him to the United Kingdom;

(aa) to make an exclusion order against him;

(b) to refuse to revoke a deportation or exclusion order made against him;

(c) to refuse to issue him with an EEA family permit; or

(d) to remove him from the United Kingdom after he has entered the United Kingdom in breach of a deportation or exclusion order.

(2) Paragraphs (1)(a) and (aa) do not apply where the person is in the United Kingdom and–

(a) the person held a valid EEA family permit, registration certificate, residence card, document certifying permanent residence or permanent residence card on his arrival in the United Kingdom or can otherwise prove that he is resident in the United Kingdom;

(b) the person is deemed not to have been admitted to the United Kingdom under regulation 22(3) but at the date on which notice of the decision to refuse to admit him is given he has been in the United Kingdom for at least 3 months or;

(c) a ground of the appeal is that, in taking the decision, the decision maker acted in breach of his rights under the Human Rights Convention or the Refugee Convention, unless the Secretary of State certifies that that ground of appeal is clearly unfounded.

(3) Paragraph (1)(d) does not apply where a ground of the appeal is that, in taking the decision, the decision maker acted in breach of the appellant's rights under the Human Rights Convention or the Refugee Convention, unless the Secretary of State certifies that that ground of appeal is clearly unfounded.

28 Appeals to the Commission

(1) An appeal against an EEA decision lies to the Commission where paragraph (2) or (4) applies.

(2) This paragraph applies if the Secretary of State certifies that the EEA decision was taken–

(a) by the Secretary of State wholly or partly on a ground listed in paragraph (3); or

(b) in accordance with a direction of the Secretary of State which identifies the person to whom the decision relates and which is given wholly or partly on a ground listed in paragraph (3).

(3) The grounds mentioned in paragraph (2) are that the person's exclusion or removal from the United Kingdom is–

(a) in the interests of national security; or

(b) in the interests of the relationship between the United Kingdom and another country.

(4) This paragraph applies if the Secretary of State certifies that the EEA decision was taken wholly or partly in reliance on information which in his opinion should not be made public–

(a) in the interests of national security;

(b) in the interests of the relationship between the United Kingdom and another country; or

(c) otherwise in the public interest.

(5) In paragraphs (2) and (4) a reference to the Secretary of State is to the Secretary of State acting in person.

(6) Where a certificate is issued under paragraph (2) or (4) in respect of a pending appeal to the Asylum and Immigration Tribunal the appeal shall lapse.

(7) An appeal against an EEA decision lies to the Commission where an appeal lapses by virtue of paragraph (6).

(8) The Special Immigration Appeals Commission Act 1997 shall apply to an appeal to the Commission under these Regulations as it applies to an appeal under section 2 of that Act to which subsection (2) of that section applies (appeals against an immigration decision) but paragraph (i) of that subsection shall not apply in relation to such an appeal.

29 Effect of appeals to the Asylum and Immigration Tribunal

(1) This Regulation applies to appeals under these Regulations made to the Asylum and Immigration Tribunal.

(2) If a person in the United Kingdom appeals against an EEA decision to refuse to admit him to the United Kingdom, any directions for his removal from the United Kingdom previously given by virtue of the refusal cease to have effect, except in so far as they have already been carried out, and no directions may be so given while the appeal is pending.

(3) If a person in the United Kingdom appeals against an EEA decision to remove him from the United Kingdom, any directions given under section 10 of the 1999 Act or Schedule 3 to the 1971 Act for his removal from the United Kingdom are to have no effect, except in so far as they have already been carried out, while the appeal is pending.

(4) But the provisions of Part I of Schedule 2, or as the case may be, Schedule 3 to the 1971 Act with respect to detention and persons liable to detention apply to a person appealing against a refusal to admit him or a decision to remove him as if there were in force directions for his removal from the United Kingdom, except that he may not be detained on board a ship or aircraft so as to compel him to leave the United Kingdom while the appeal is pending.

(5) In calculating the period of two months limited by paragraph 8(2) of Schedule 2 to the 1971 Act for–

(a) the giving of directions under that paragraph for the removal of a person from the United Kingdom; and

(b) the giving of a notice of intention to give such directions,

any period during which there is pending an appeal by him under is to be disregarded.

(6) If a person in the United Kingdom appeals against an EEA decision to remove him from the United Kingdom, a deportation order is not to be made against him under section 5 of the 1971 Act while the appeal is pending.

(7) Paragraph 29 of Schedule 2 to the 1971 Act (grant of bail pending appeal) applies to a person who has an appeal pending under these Regulations as it applies to a person who has an appeal pending under section 82(1) of the 2002 Act.

PART 7: GENERAL

30 Effect on other legislation

Schedule 2 (effect on other legislation) shall have effect.

31 Revocations, transitional provisions and consequential amendments

(1) The Regulations listed in column 1 of the table in Part 1 of Schedule 3 are revoked to the extent set out in column 3 of that table, subject to Part 2 of that Schedule and to Schedule 4.

(2) Schedule 4 (transitional provisions) and Schedule 5 (consequential amendments) shall have effect.

SCHEDULE 1: APPEALS TO THE ASYLUM AND IMMIGRATION TRIBUNAL

Regulation 26(7)

The following provisions of, or made under, the 2002 Act have effect in relation to an appeal under these Regulations to the Asylum and Immigration Tribunal as if it were an appeal against an immigration decision under section 82(1) of that Act:

section 84(1) except paragraphs (a) and (f);
sections 85 to 87;
sections 103A to 103E;
section 105 and any regulations made under that section; and
section 106 and any rules made under that section.

SCHEDULE 2: EFFECT ON OTHER LEGISLATION

Regulation 30

1 Leave under the 1971 Act

(1) In accordance with section 7 of the Immigration Act 1988, a person who is admitted to or acquires a right to reside in the United Kingdom under these Regulations shall not require leave to remain in the United Kingdom under the 1971 Act during any period in which he has a right to reside under these Regulations but such a person shall require leave to remain under the 1971 Act during any period in which he does not have such a right.

(2) Subject to sub-paragraph (3), where a person has leave to enter or remain under the 1971 Act which is subject to conditions and that person also has a right to reside under these Regulations, those conditions shall not have effect for as long as the person has that right to reside.

(3) Where the person mentioned in sub-paragraph (2) is an accession State national subject to worker authorisation working in the United Kingdom during the accession period and the document endorsed to show that the person has leave is an accession worker authorisation document, any conditions to which that leave is subject restricting his employment shall continue to apply.

(4) In sub-paragraph (3)–

(a) 'accession period' has the meaning given in regulation 1(2)(c) of the Accession (Immigration and Worker Authorisation) Regulations 2006;

(b) 'accession State national subject to worker authorisation' has the meaning given in regulation 2 of those Regulations; and

(c) 'accession worker authorisation document' has the meaning given in regulation 9(2) of those Regulations.

2 Persons not subject to restriction on the period for which they may remain

(1) For the purposes of the 1971 Act and the British Nationality Act 1981, a person who has a permanent right of residence under regulation 15 shall be regarded as a person who is in the United Kingdom without being subject under the immigration laws to any restriction on the period for which he may remain.

(2) But a qualified person, the family member of a qualified person and a family member who has retained the right of residence shall not, by virtue of that status, be so regarded for those purposes.

3 Carriers' liability under the 1999 Act

For the purposes of satisfying a requirement to produce a visa under section 40(1)(b) of the 1999 Act (charges in respect of passenger without proper documents), 'a visa of the required kind' includes an EEA family permit, a residence card or a permanent residence card required for admission under regulation 11(2).

4 Appeals under the 2002 Act and previous Immigration Acts

(1) The following EEA decisions shall not be treated as immigration decisions for the purpose of section 82(2) of the 2002 Act (right of appeal against an immigration decision)–

(a) a decision that a person is to be removed under regulation 19(3)(a) by way of a direction under section 10(1)(a) of the 1999 Act (as provided for by regulation 24(2));

(b) a decision to remove a person under regulation 19(3)(b) by making a deportation order under section 5(1) of the 1971 Act (as provided for by regulation 24(3));

(c) a decision to remove a person mentioned in regulation 24(4) by way of directions under paragraphs 8 to 10 of Schedule 2 to the 1971 Act.

(2) A person who has been issued with a registration certificate, residence card, a document certifying permanent residence or a permanent residence card under these Regulations or a registration certificate under the Accession (Immigration and Worker Registration) Regulations 2004, or an accession worker card under the Accession (Immigration and Worker Authorisation) Regulations 2006, or a person whose passport has been stamped with a family member residence stamp, shall have no right of appeal under section 2 of the Special Immigration Appeals Commission Act 1997 or section 82(1) of the 2002 Act. Any existing appeal under those sections of those Acts or under the Asylum and Immigration Appeals Act 1993, the Asylum and Immigration Act 1996 or the 1999 Act shall be treated as abandoned.

(3) Subject to paragraph (4), a person may appeal to the Asylum and Immigration Tribunal under section 83(2) of the 2002 Act against the rejection of his asylum claim where–

(a) that claim has been rejected, but

(b) he has a right to reside in the United Kingdom under these Regulations.

(4) Paragraph (3) shall not apply if the person is an EEA national and the Secretary of State certifies that the asylum claim is clearly unfounded.

(5) The Secretary of State shall certify the claim under paragraph (4) unless satisfied that it is not clearly unfounded.

(6) In addition to the national of a State which is a contracting party to the Agreement referred to in section 84(2) of the 2002 Act, a Swiss national shall also be treated as an EEA national for the purposes of section 84(1)(d) of that Act.

(7) An appeal under these Regulations against an EEA decision (including an appeal made on or after 1st April 2003 which is treated as an appeal under these Regulations under Schedule 4 but not an appeal made before that date) shall be treated as an appeal under section 82(1) of the 2002 Act against an immigration decision for the purposes of section 96(1)(a) of the 2002 Act.

(8) Section 120 of the 2002 Act shall apply to a person if an EEA decision has been taken or may be taken in respect of him and, accordingly, the Secretary of State or an immigration officer may by notice require a statement from that person under subsection (2) of that section and that notice shall have effect for the purpose of section 96(2) of the 2002 Act.

(9) In sub-paragraph (1), 'family member residence stamp' means a stamp in the passport of a family member of an EEA national confirming that he is the family member of an accession State worker requiring registration or an accession State national subject to worker authorisation working in the United Kingdom with a right of residence under these Regulations as the family member of that worker; and in this sub-paragraph 'accession State worker requiring registration' has the same meaning as in regulation 2 of the Accession (Immigration and Worker Registration) Regulations 2004 and 'accession State national subject to worker authorisation' has the meaning given in regulation 2 of the Accession (Immigration and Worker Authorisation) Regulations 2006.

SCHEDULE 3: REVOCATIONS AND SAVINGS

Regulation 31(2)

PART 1: TABLE OF REVOCATIONS

1	2	3
Regulations revoked	**References**	**Extent of revocation**
The Immigration (European Economic Area) Regulations 2000	SI 2000/2326	The whole Regulations
The Immigration (European Economic Area) (Amendment) Regulations 2001	SI 2001/865	The whole Regulations
The Immigration (Swiss Free Movement of Persons) (No 3) Regulations 2002	SI 2002/1241	The whole Regulations
The Immigration (European Economic Area) (Amendment) Regulations 2003	SI 2003/549	The whole Regulations
The Immigration (European Economic Area) (Amendment No 2) Regulations 2003	SI 2003/3188	The whole Regulations

1	2	3
Regulations revoked	**References**	**Extent of revocation**
The Accession (Immigration and Worker Registration) Regulations 2004	SI 2004/1219	Regulations 3 and 6
The Immigration (European Economic Area) and Accession (Amendment) Regulations 2004	SI 2004/1236	Regulation 2
The Immigration (European Economic Area) (Amendment) Regulations 2005	SI 2005/47	The whole Regulations
The Immigration (European Economic Area)(Amendment) (No 2) Regulations 2005	SI 2005/671	The whole Regulations

PART 2: SAVINGS

1 The–

(a) Immigration (Swiss Free Movement of Persons) (No 3) Regulations 2002 are not revoked insofar as they apply the 2000 Regulations to posted workers; and

(b) the 2000 Regulations and the Regulations amending the 2000 Regulations are not revoked insofar as they are so applied to posted workers;

and, accordingly, the 2000 Regulations, as amended, shall continue to apply to posted workers in accordance with the Immigration (Swiss Free Movement of Persons) (No 3) Regulations 2002.

2. In paragraph 1, 'the 2000 Regulations' means the Immigration (European Economic Area) Regulations 2000 and 'posted worker' has the meaning given in regulation 2(4)(b) of the Immigration (Swiss Free Movement of Persons) (No 3) Regulations 2002.

SCHEDULE 4: TRANSITIONAL PROVISIONS

Regulation 31(2)

1 **Interpretation**

In this Schedule–

(a) the '2000 Regulations' means the Immigration (European Economic Area) Regulations 2000 and expressions used in relation to documents issued or applied for under those Regulations shall have the meaning given in regulation 2 of those Regulations;

(b) the 'Accession Regulations' means the Accession (Immigration and Worker Registration) Regulations 2004.

2 Existing documents

(1) An EEA family permit issued under the 2000 Regulations shall, after 29th April 2006, be treated as if it were an EEA family permit issued under these Regulations.

(2) Subject to paragraph (4), a residence permit issued under the 2000 Regulations shall, after 29th April 2006, be treated as if it were a registration certificate issued under these Regulations.

(3) Subject to paragraph (5), a residence document issued under the 2000 Regulations shall, after 29thApril 2006, be treated as if it were a residence card issued under these Regulations.

(4) Where a residence permit issued under the 2000 Regulations has been endorsed under the immigration rules to show permission to remain in the United Kingdom indefinitely it shall, after 29thApril 2006, be treated as if it were a document certifying permanent residence issued under these Regulations and the holder of the permit shall be treated as a person with a permanent right of residence under regulation 15.

(5) Where a residence document issued under the 2000 Regulations has been endorsed under the immigration rules to show permission to remain in the United Kingdom indefinitely it shall, after 29th April 2006, be treated as if it were a permanent residence card issued under these Regulations and the holder of the permit shall be treated as a person with a permanent right of residence under regulation 15.

(6) Paragraphs (4) and (5) shall also apply to a residence permit or residence document which is endorsed under the immigration rules on or after 30thApril 2006 to show permission to remain in the United Kingdom indefinitely pursuant to an application for such an endorsement made before that date.

3 Outstanding applications

(1) An application for an EEA family permit, a residence permit or a residence document made but not determined under the 2000 Regulations before 30 April 2006 shall be treated as an application under these Regulations for an EEA family permit, a registration certificate or a residence card, respectively.

(2) But the following provisions of these Regulations shall not apply to the determination of an application mentioned in sub-paragraph (1)–

(a) the requirement to issue a registration certificate immediately under regulation 16(1); and

(b) the requirement to issue a certificate of application for a residence card under regulation 17(3).

4 Decisions to remove under the 2000 Regulations

(1) A decision to remove a person under regulation 21(3)(a) of the 2000 Regulations shall, after 29th April 2006, be treated as a decision to remove that person under regulation 19(3)(a) of these Regulations.

(2) A decision to remove a person under regulation 21(3)(b) of the 2000 Regulations, including a decision which is treated as a decision to remove a person under that regulation by virtue of regulation 6(3)(a) of the

Accession Regulations, shall, after 29th April 2006, be treated as a decision to remove that person under regulation 19(3)(b) of these Regulations.

(3) A deportation order made under section 5 of the 1971 Act by virtue of regulation 26(3) of the 2000 Regulations shall, after 29thApril 2006, be treated as a deportation made under section 5 of the 1971 Act by virtue of regulation 24(3) of these Regulations.

5 Appeals

(1) Where an appeal against an EEA decision under the 2000 Regulations is pending immediately before 30th April 2006 that appeal shall be treated as a pending appeal against the corresponding EEA Decision under these Regulations.

(2) Where an appeal against an EEA decision under the 2000 Regulations has been determined, withdrawn or abandoned it shall, on and after 30th April 2006, be treated as an appeal against the corresponding EEA decision under these Regulations which has been determined, withdrawn or abandoned, respectively.

(3) For the purpose of this paragraph–

(a) a decision to refuse to admit a person under these Regulations corresponds to a decision to refuse to admit that person under the 2000 Regulations;

(b) a decision to remove a person under regulation 19(3)(a) of these Regulations corresponds to a decision to remove that person under regulation 21(3)(a) of the 2000 Regulations;

(c) a decision to remove a person under regulation 19(3)(b) of these Regulations corresponds to a decision to remove that person under regulation 21(3)(b) of the 2000 Regulations, including a decision which is treated as a decision to remove a person under regulation 21(3)(b) of the 2000 Regulations by virtue of regulation 6(3)(a) of the Accession Regulations;

(d) a decision to refuse to revoke a deportation order made against a person under these Regulations corresponds to a decision to refuse to revoke a deportation order made against the 2000 Regulations, including a decision which is treated as a decision to refuse to revoke a deportation order under the 2000 Regulations by virtue of regulation 6(3)(b) of the Accession Regulations;

(e) a decision not to issue or renew or to revoke an EEA family permit, a registration certificate or a residence card under these Regulations corresponds to a decision not to issue or renew or to revoke an EEA family permit, a residence permit or a residence document under the 2000 Regulations, respectively.

6 Periods of residence under the 2000 Regulations

(1) Any period during which a person carried out an activity or was resident in the United Kingdom in accordance with the 2000 Regulations shall be treated as a period during which the person carried out that activity or was resident in the United Kingdom in accordance with these Regulations for the purpose of calculating periods of activity and residence under these Regulations.

SCHEDULE 5: CONSEQUENTIAL AMENDMENTS

Regulation 31(2)

Statutory Instruments The Channel Tunnel (International Arrangements) Order 1993

1(1) The Channel Tunnel (International Arrangements) Order 199359 is amended as follows.

(2) In Schedule 4, in paragraph 5–

(a) at the beginning of the paragraph, for 'the Immigration (European Economic Area) Regulations 2000' there is substituted 'the Immigration (European Economic Area) Regulations 2006';

(b) in sub-paragraph (a), for 'regulation 12(2)' there is substituted 'regulation 11(2)' and for 'residence document or document proving family membership' there is substituted 'residence card or permanent residence card';

(c) for sub-paragraph (b) there is substituted–

'(b) in regulations 11(4) and 19(2) after the word 'arrival' and in regulations 20(4) and (5) after the words 'United Kingdom' insert 'or the time of his production of the required documents in a control zone or a supplementary control zone'.

The Travel Restriction Order (Prescribed Removal Powers) Order 2002

2(1) The Travel Restriction Order (Prescribed Removal Powers) Order 2002 is amended as follows.

(2) In the Schedule, for 'Immigration (European Economic Area) Regulations 2000 (2000/2326)' in the first column of the table there is substituted 'Immigration (European Economic Area) Regulations 2006' and for 'Regulation 21(3)' in the corresponding row in the second column of the table there is substituted 'Regulation 19(3)'.

The Immigration (Notices) Regulations 2003

3(1) The Immigration (Notices) Regulations 2003 are amended as follows.

(2) In regulation 2, in the definition of 'EEA decision'–

(a) at the end of paragraph (b), 'or' is omitted;

(b) in paragraph (c), after 'residence document;', there is inserted 'or'; and

(c) after paragraph (c), there is inserted–

'(d) on or after 30th April 2006, entitlement to be issued with or have renewed, or not to have revoked, a registration certificate, residence card, document certifying permanent residence or permanent residence card;'

The Nationality, Immigration and Asylum Act 2002 (Juxtaposed Controls) Order 2003

4(1) The Nationality, Immigration and Asylum Act 2002 (Juxtaposed Controls) Order 2003 is amended as follows.

(2) In article 11(1), for sub-paragraph (e) there is substituted–

'(e) the Immigration (European Economic Area) Regulations 2006.'.

(3) In Schedule 2, in paragraph 5–

(a) at the beginning of the paragraph, for 'the Immigration (European Economic Area) Regulations 2000' there is substituted 'the Immigration (European Economic Area) Regulations 2006';

(b) in sub-paragraph (a), for 'in regulation 2, at the beginning insert' there is substituted 'in regulation 2(1), after the definition of 'civil partner' insert';

(c) in sub-paragraph (b), for 'regulation 12(2)' there is substituted 'regulation 11(2)' and for 'residence document or document proving family membership' there is substituted 'residence card or permanent residence card';

(d) for sub-paragraph (c) there is substituted–

'(c) in regulations 11(4) and 19(2) after the word 'arrival' and in regulations 20(4) and (5) after the words 'United Kingdom' insert 'or the time of his production of the required documents in a Control Zone'.

The Immigration and Asylum Act 1999 (Part V Exemption: Relevant Employers) Order 2003

5(1) The Immigration and Asylum Act 1999 (Part V Exemption: Relevant Employers) Order 2003 is amended as follows.

(2) In Article 2, in the definition of 'EEA national' and 'family member of an EEA national', for 'Immigration (European Economic Area) Regulations 2000' there is substituted 'Immigration (European Economic Area) Regulations 2006'.

The Immigration (Restrictions on Employment) Order 2004

6(1) The Immigration (Restrictions on Employment) Order 2004 is amended as follows.

(2) In Part 1 of the Schedule (descriptions of documents for the purpose of article 4(2)(a) of the Order)–

(a) for paragraph 4 there is substituted–

'**4.**

A registration certificate or document certifying permanent residence within the meaning of regulation 2 of the Immigration (European Economic Area) Regulations 2006, including a document which is treated as a registration certificate or document certifying permanent residence by virtue of Schedule 4 to those Regulations.';

(b) for paragraph 5 there is substituted–

'**5.**

A residence card or a permanent residence card within the meaning of regulation 2 of the Immigration (European Economic Area) Regulations 2006, including a document which is treated as a residence card or a permanent residence card by virtue of Schedule 4 to those Regulations'.

The Accession (Immigration and Worker Registration) Regulations 2004

7(1) The Accession (Immigration and Worker Registration) Regulations 200460 are amended as follows.

(2) In regulation 1(2) (interpretation)–
(a) after paragraph (b) there is inserted–
'(ba) 'the 2006 Regulations' means the Immigration (European Economic Area) Regulations 2006;';
(b) in paragraph (j), for 'regulation 3 of the 2000 Regulations' these is substituted 'regulation 4 of the 2006 Regulations'.
(3) In regulation 2 ('accession State worker requiring registration')–
(a) [Revoked.]
(b) paragraph (9)(a) is omitted;
(c) for paragraph (9)(c) there is substituted–
'(c) 'family member' has the same meaning as in regulation 7 of the 2006 Regulations.'.
(4) In regulation 4 (right of residence of work seekers and workers from relevant acceding States during the accession period)–
(a) in paragraph (1), before 'Council Directive' there is inserted 'Council Directive 2004/38/EC of the European Parliament and of the Council on the right of citizens of the Union and their family members to move and reside freely within the territory of the Member States,[17] insofar as it takes over provisions of';
(b) in paragraph (3), for '2000 Regulations' there is substituted '2006 Regulations';
(c) in paragraph (4), for 'An' there is substituted 'A national of a relevant accession State who is seeking employment and an' and for '2000 Regulations' there is substituted '2006 Regulations'.
(5) For regulation 5 (application of 2000 Regulations in relation to accession State worker requiring registration) there is substituted–

'5 Application of 2006 Regulations in relation to accession State worker requiring registration

(1) The 2006 Regulations shall apply in relation to a national of a relevant accession State subject to the modifications set out in this regulation.
(2) A national of a relevant accession State who is seeking employment in the United Kingdom shall not be treated as a jobseeker for the purpose of the definition of 'qualified person' in regulation 6(1) of the 2006 Regulations and an accession State worker requiring registration shall be treated as a worker for the purpose of that definition only during a period in which he is working in the United Kingdom for an authorised employer.
(3) Subject to paragraph (4), regulation 6(2) of the 2006 Regulations shall not apply to an accession State worker requiring registration who ceases to work.

17 OJ L158, 30 April 2004, p77 (the full title of the Directive is Council Directive 2004/38/EC of the European Parliament and the Council on the rights of citizens of the Union and their family members to move and reside freely within the territory of the member States amending Regulation (EEC) No 1612/68 and repealing Directives 64/221/EEC, 68/360/EEC, 72/194/EEC, 75/34/EEC, 90/364/EEC, 90/365/EEC and 93/96/EEC).

(4) Where an accession State worker requiring registration ceases working for an authorised employer in the circumstances mentioned in regulation 6(2) of the 2006 Regulations during the one month period beginning on the date on which the work begins, that regulation shall apply to that worker during the remainder of that one month period.

(5) An accession State worker requiring registration shall not be treated as a qualified person for the purpose of regulations 16 and 17 of the 2006 Regulations (issue of registration certificates and residence cards).'

The Asylum and Immigration Tribunal (Procedure) Rules 2005

8(1) The Asylum and Immigration Tribunal (Procedure) Rules 2005 are amended as follows.

(2) In regulation 18(1)(b), after '('the 2000 Regulations')' there is inserted 'or, on or after 30April 2006, paragraph 4(2) of Schedule 2 to the Immigration (European Economic Area) Regulations 2006 ('the 2006 Regulations')'.

(3) In regulation 18(2), after '2000 Regulations' there is inserted 'or paragraph 4(2) of Schedule 2 to the 2006 Regulations'.

EUROPEAN SOCIAL CHARTER

Treaty open for signature by the member States of the Council of Europe

Opening for signature
Place: Turin
Date : 18/10/1961

Entry into force
Conditions: 5 Ratifications.
Date : 26/2/1965

Status as of: 15/9/2009

Member States of the Council of Europe

States	Signature	Ratification	Entry into force	Notes	R.	D.	A.	T.	C.	O.
Albania				52						
Andorra				52						
Armenia				52						
Austria	22/7/1963	29/10/1969	28/11/1969	51		X				
Azerbaijan				52						
Belgium	18/10/1961	16/10/1990	15/11/1990	52		X				
Bosnia and Herzegovina				52						
Bulgaria				52						
Croatia	8/3/1999	26/2/2003	28/3/2003			X				
Cyprus	22/5/1967	7/3/1968	6/4/1968	52		X				
Czech Republic	27/5/1992	3/11/1999	3/12/1999	51		X				
Denmark	18/10/1961	3/3/1965	2/4/1965	51		X		X		
Estonia				52						
Finland	9/2/1990	29/4/1991	29/5/1991	52		X				
France	18/10/1961	9/3/1973	8/4/1973	52	X	X				
Georgia				52						
Germany	18/10/1961	27/1/1965	26/2/1965	51		X		X		
Greece	18/10/1961	6/6/1984	6/7/1984	51		X				
Hungary	13/12/1991	8/7/1999	7/8/1999	52		X				
Iceland	15/1/1976	15/1/1976	14/2/1976	51		X				
Ireland	18/10/1961	7/10/1964	26/2/1965	52		X				
Italy	18/10/1961	22/10/1965	21/11/1965	52		X				
Latvia	29/5/1997	31/1/2002	2/3/2002	51		X				
Liechtenstein	9/10/1991									
Lithuania				52						
Luxembourg	18/10/1961	10/10/1991	9/11/1991	51		X				

States	Signature	Ratification	Entry into force	Notes	R.	D.	A.	T.	C.	O.
Malta	26/5/1988	4/10/1988	3/11/1988	52		X				
Moldova				52		X		X		
Monaco				51						
Montenegro				51						
Netherlands	18/10/1961	22/4/1980	22/5/1980	52		X		X		
Norway	18/10/1961	26/10/1962	26/2/1965	52	X	X		X		
Poland	26/11/1991	25/6/1997	25/7/1997	51		X				
Portugal	1/6/1982	30/9/1991	30/10/1991	52	X	X				
Romania	4/10/1994			52						
Russia				51						
San Marino				51						
Serbia				51						
Slovakia	27/5/1992	22/6/1998	21/7/1998	52		X				
Slovenia	11/10/1997			52						
Spain	27/4/1978	6/5/1980	5/6/1980	51		X				
Sweden	18/10/1961	17/12/1962	26/2/1965	52		X				
Switzerland	6/5/1976									
the former Yugoslav Republic of Macedonia	5/5/1998	31/3/2005	30/4/2005	51		X				
Turkey	18/10/1961	24/11/1989	24/12/1989	52		X				
Ukraine	2/5/1996			52						
United Kingdom	18/10/1961	11/7/1962	26/2/1965	51		X		X		

Total number of signatures not followed by ratifications:	5
Total number of ratifications/accessions:	27

Notes:
(51) State signatory to the European Social Charter (revised) (ETS 163). (52) State Party to the European Social Charter (revised) (ETS 163). a: Accession - s: Signature without reservation as to ratification - su: Succession - r: Signature 'ad referendum'. R.: Reservations - D.: Declarations - A.: Authorities - T.: Territorial Application - C.: Communication - O.: Objection.

Source : Treaty Office on http://conventions.coe.int

EUROPEAN CONVENTION ON SOCIAL AND MEDICAL ASSISTANCE

Treaty open for signature by the member States and for accession by non-member States

Opening for signature
Place: Paris
Date : 11/12/1953

Entry into force
Conditions: 2 Ratifications.
Date : 1/7/1954

Status as of: 15/9/2009

Member States of the Council of Europe

States	Signature	Ratification	Entry into force	Notes	R.	D.	A.	T.	C.	O.
Albania										
Andorra										
Armenia										
Austria										
Azerbaijan										
Belgium	11/12/1953	24/7/1956	1/8/1956		X	X				
Bosnia and Herzegovina										
Bulgaria										
Croatia										
Cyprus										
Czech Republic										
Denmark	11/12/1953	30/6/1954	1/7/1954			X				
Estonia	1/12/1999	20/7/2004	1/8/2004			X				
Finland										
France	11/12/1953	30/10/1957	1/11/1957			X				
Georgia										
Germany	11/12/1953	24/8/1956	1/9/1956		X	X				
Greece	11/12/1953	23/6/1960	1/7/1960			X				
Hungary										
Iceland	11/12/1953	4/12/1964	1/1/1965			X				
Ireland	11/12/1953	31/3/1954	1/7/1954			X				
Italy	11/12/1953	1/7/1958	1/8/1958			X				
Latvia										
Liechtenstein										
Lithuania										

Luxembourg	11/12/1953	18/11/1958	1/12/1958		X	X				
Malta	7/5/1968	6/5/1969	1/6/1969			X				
Moldova										
Monaco										
Montenegro										
Netherlands	11/12/1953	20/7/1955	1/8/1955			X				
Norway	11/12/1953	9/9/1954	1/10/1954		X	X				
Poland										
Portugal	27/4/1977	4/7/1978	1/8/1978			X				
Romania										
Russia										
San Marino										
Serbia										
Slovakia										
Slovenia										
Spain	9/2/1981	21/11/1983	1/12/1983			X				
Sweden	11/12/1953	2/9/1955	1/10/1955			X				
Switzerland										
the former Yugoslav Republic of Macedonia										
Turkey	11/12/1953	2/12/1976	1/1/1977		X	X				
Ukraine										
United Kingdom	11/12/1953	7/9/1954	1/10/1954		X	X				

Non-member States of the Council of Europe

States	Signature	Ratification	Entry into force	Notes	R.	D.	A.	T.	C.	O.

Total number of signatures not followed by ratifications:	
Total number of ratifications/accessions:	18

Notes:
a: Accession - s: Signature without reservation as to ratification - su: Succession - r: Signature 'ad referendum'. R.: Reservations - D.: Declarations - A.: Authorities - T.: Territorial Application - C.: Communication - O.: Objection.

Source : Treaty Office on http://conventions.coe.int

CONTRACTING PARTIES TO THE AGREEMENT ON THE EUROPEAN ECONOMIC AREA[18]

THE EUROPEAN COMMUNITY,[19]
THE KINGDOM OF BELGIUM,
THE REPUBLIC OF BULGARIA
THE CZECH REPUBLIC,
THE KINGDOM OF DENMARK,
THE FEDERAL REPUBLIC OF GERMANY,
THE REPUBLIC OF ESTONIA,
IRELAND,
THE HELLENIC REPUBLIC,
THE KINGDOM OF SPAIN,
THE FRENCH REPUBLIC,
THE ITALIAN REPUBLIC,
THE REPUBLIC OF CYPRUS,
THE REPUBLIC OF LATVIA,
THE REPUBLIC OF LITHUANIA,
THE GRAND DUCHY OF LUXEMBOURG,
THE REPUBLIC OF HUNGARY,
MALTA,
THE KINGDOM OF THE NETHERLANDS,
THE REPUBLIC OF AUSTRIA,
THE REPUBLIC OF POLAND,
THE PORTUGUESE REPUBLIC,
ROMANIA
THE REPUBLIC OF SLOVENIA,
THE SLOVAK REPUBLIC,
THE REPUBLIC OF FINLAND,
THE KINGDOM OF SWEDEN,
THE UNITED KINGDOM OF GREAT BRITAIN AND NORTHERN IRELAND,
AND
[ ][20]
ICELAND,
THE PRINCIPALITY OF LIECHTENSTEIN,
THE KINGDOM OF NORWAY,

18 As amended by the Adjusting Protocol and subsequently by the 2004 EEA Enlargement Agreement (OJ No L 130, 29 April 2004, p3 and EEA Supplement No 23, 29 April 2004, p1), eif 1 May 2004, and subsequently by the 2007 EEA Enlargement Agreement (OJ No L [to be published]), provisionally applicable as of 1 August 2007, eif pending.

19 As amended by the 2004 EEA Enlargement Agreement (OJ No L 130, 29 April 2004, p3 and EEA Supplement No 23, 29 April 2004, p1), eif 1 May 2004, and subsequently by the 2007 EEA Enlargement Agreement (OJ No L [to be published]), provisionally applicable as of 1August 2007, eif pending.

20 Austria, Finland and Sweden acceded the European Union on 1 January 1995.

MEMBER STATES OF THE EUROPEAN UNION

Belgium	1958
France	1958
(West) Germany	1958
Italy	1958
Luxembourg	1958
Netherlands	1958
Denmark	1973
Ireland	1973
United Kingdom	1973
Greece	1981
Portugal	1986
Spain	1986
Austria	1995
Finland	1995
Sweden	1995
Cyprus	2004
Czech Republic	2004
Estonia	2004
Hungary	2004
Latvia	2004
Lithuania	2004
Malta	2004
Poland	2004
Slovakia	2004
Slovenia	2004
Romania	2007
Bulgaria	2007

APPENDIX C

UKBA immigration status documents: samples[1]

NON-UKBA FORMS

APPLICATION REGISTRATION CARD (ARC)

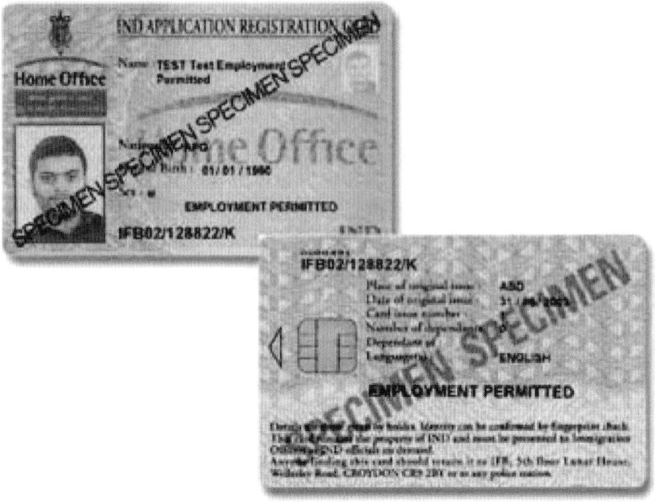

UK RESIDENCE PERMIT (SAMPLES)

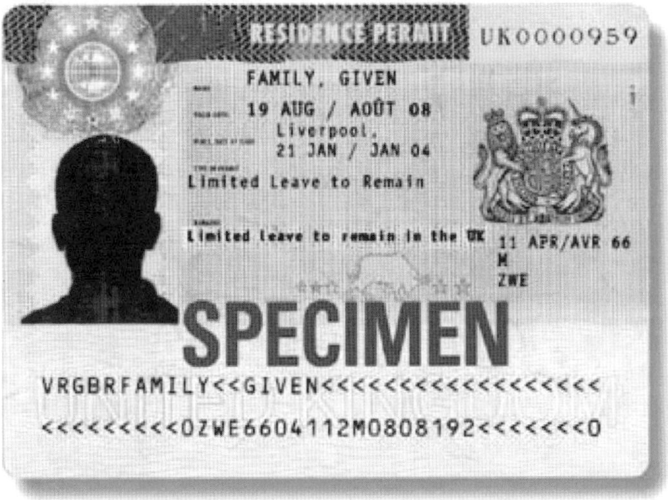

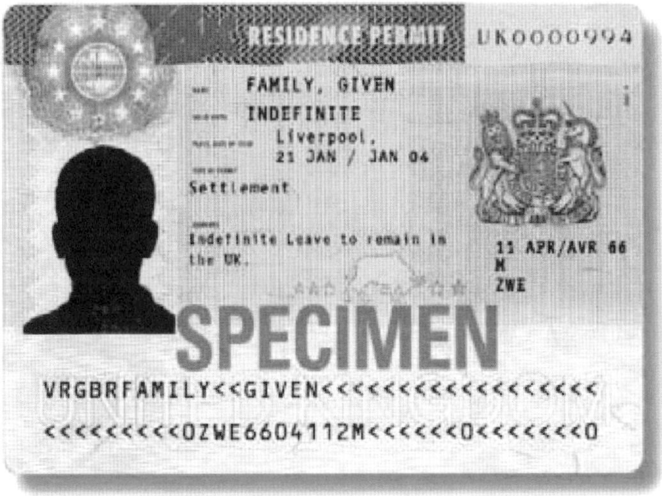

GRANT OF INDEFINITE LEAVE TO REMAIN

Home Office
UK Border Agency

UK Border Agency
Lunar House
40 Wellesley Road
Croydon
CR9 2BY
Tel
Fax
Email @ukba.gsi.gov.uk
Web www.ukba.homeoffice.gov.uk

Our Ref

Your Ref Your Ref

Date 03 August 2009

Dear Miss

GRANT OF INDEFINITE LEAVE TO REMAIN

Your case has been reviewed. Having fully considered the information you have provided, and because of the individual circumstances of your case, it has been decided to grant you indefinite leave to remain in the United Kingdom. This leave has been granted exceptionally, outside the Immigration Rules. This is due to yourstrength of connections in the United Kingdom, and compassionate circumstances

This means that you are free to stay in this country permanently.

THIS LETTER IN ITSELF CONFERS NO LEAVE TO REMAIN IN THE UNITED KINGDOM AND DOES NOT CONSTITUTE PROOF OF YOUR STATUS.

Please find enclosed the Immigration Status Document for you. This has been endorsed with indefinite leave to remain in the United Kingdom. It is this endorsement that constitutes proof of your immigration status in the United Kingdom

On reviewing your case it is noted that you have an outstanding Further Representation claim. Unless you contact us within the next 14 calendar days we will assume you wish to withdraw the outstanding claim.

ENTITLEMENTS

You are permitted to work and do not need the permission of any Government Department before doing so. If you do not already have a National Insurance Number, you must contact the Department for Work and Pensions in order to apply for one.

Information may be obtained by telephoning 0845 600 0643 between 8.00am and 6.00pm, Monday to Friday. You will be required to attend an interview in order to verify your identity and that you have permission to work. You will need to bring this letter and Immigration Status Document/Passport with you to the interview.

You are free to use the National Health Service and the social services, and other services provided by local authorities as you need them.

TRAVEL ABROAD

You may travel out of the Common Travel Area any number of times during the validity of the leave you have been granted. The Common Travel Area comprises the United Kingdom, the Channel Islands, the Isle of Man and the Republic of Ireland. On your return, you will be re-admitted to the United Kingdom without having to obtain fresh leave to enter unless you have been absent from the United Kingdom for a continuous period of more than two years. Nevertheless, an investigation into your circumstances may be carried out upon your return to the United Kingdom, in order to determine whether or not the leave you have been granted should be revoked

DEPENDANTS

If you are the principal sponsor and you are married and/ or have children under the age of 18 who are outside the UK the normal requirements of the Immigration Rules regarding support and accommodation would have to be satisfied to entitle them to join you in the United Kingdom. If your spouse and minor children wish to apply to join you, they will need to approach a British Embassy, High Commission or Consulate abroad to make an application for entry clearance to the United Kingdom. Dependants are required to make their application before travelling to the United Kingdom

CAUTION

You should understand, however, that you may not be allowed to remain in the United Kingdom if, during your stay, you take part in any criminal activities or activities such as support for or encouragement of terrorist organisations, or you otherwise endanger national security or public order You may also not be allowed to remain in the United Kingdom if it is decided for some other reason that your presence here is not conducive to the public good.

Yours sincerely,

J Gladstone
Legacy CRT - South 17

Acting on behalf of the Secretary of State

Home Office
UK Border Agency

IMMIGRATION STATUS DOCUMENT

Personal Details

Full Name

Nationality
ETHIOPIA

Date of Birth

Place of Birth
ETHIOPIA

Gender
FEMALE

Case ID

'This leave has been granted exceptionally, outside the Immigration Rules.'

The period for which leave to enter or remain in the United Kingdom has been granted or the duration of the right of residence in the United Kingdom is indicated in the endorsement

This Immigration Status Document has been endorsed in place of a valid national passport or travel document and confers upon the person named leave to enter or remain in the United Kingdom or a right of residence in the United Kingdom for the period indicated. It does not certify the accuracy of the personal particulars, which are those supplied by the person who made the application. It remains the property of Her Majesty's Government and may be withdrawn at any time. It should not be tampered with or passed to an unauthorised person. Any case of loss or destruction should be immediately reported to the nearest police station and to the UK Border Agency at the address below; only after exhaustive enquiries can a replacement be issued in such circumstances. The Immigration Status Document of a deceased person should be returned to the UK Border Agency for cancellation.

Enquiries about the purpose, use, or validity of this document should be made to the UK Border Agency at:

Lunar House, 40 Wellesley Road, Croydon, CR9 2BY (Telephone 0870 606 7766)

ASL 2150

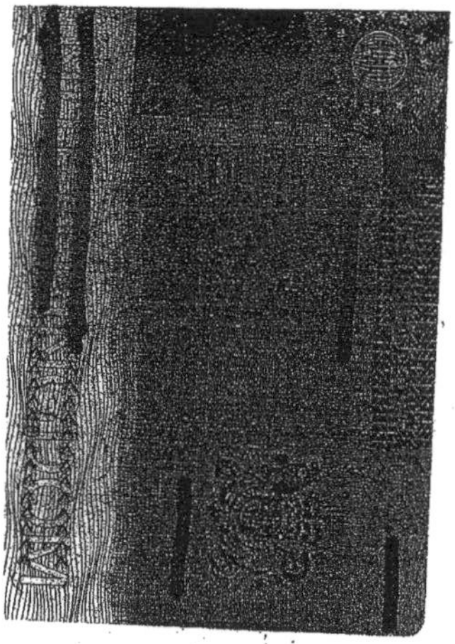

EEA NATIONAL REGISTRATION CERTIFICATE

EEA NATIONAL FAMILY MEMBER RESIDENCE CARD

A8 WORKER REGISTRATION SCHEME

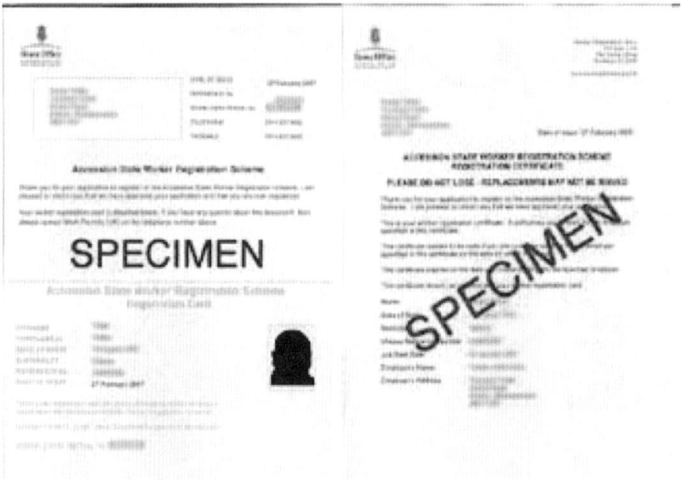

A2 NATIONAL (BLUE) (EXEMPT)

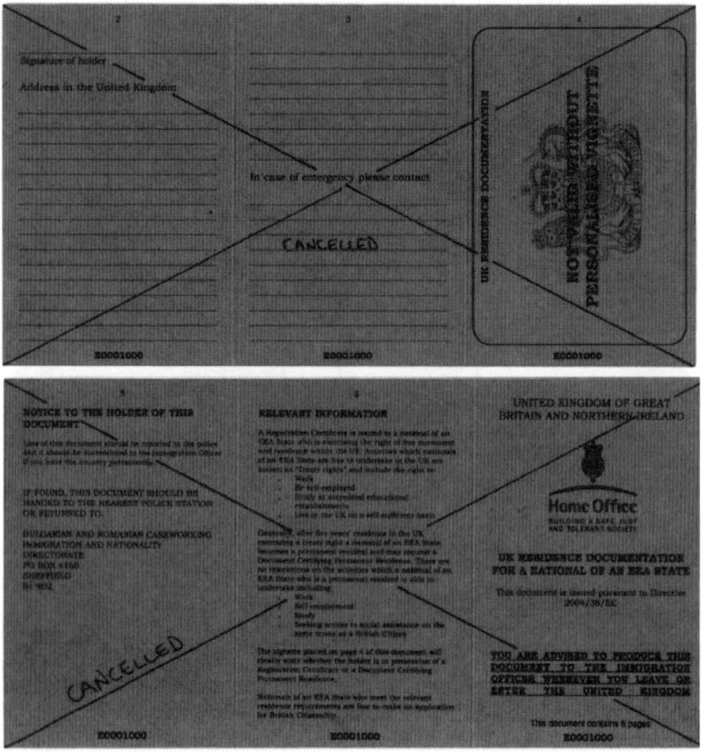

A2 NATIONAL (YELLOW) (STUDENT / SELF-EMPLOYED)

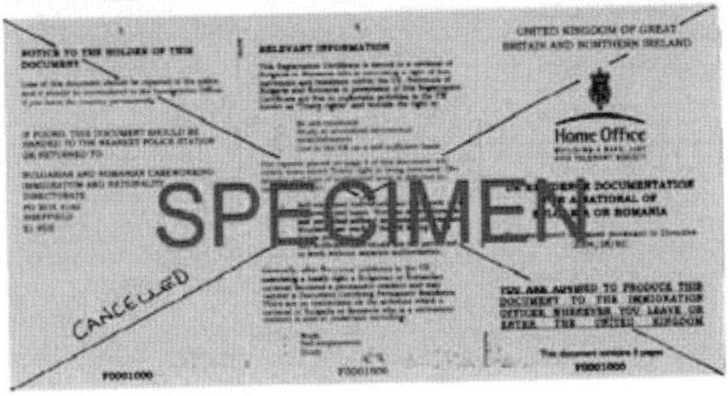

A2 NATIONAL (PURPLE) (ACCESSION WORKER CARD)

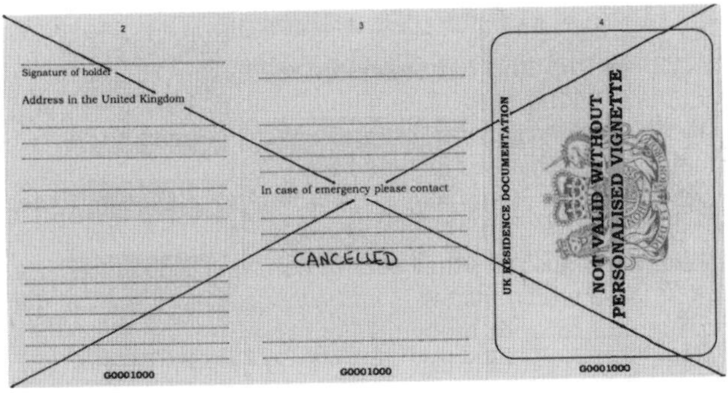

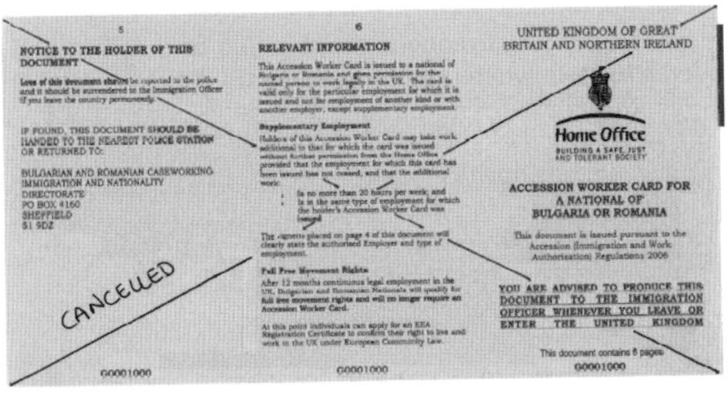

FIRST-TIER TRIBUNAL (ASYLUM SUPPORT): NOTICE OF APPEAL

2nd Floor
Anchorage House
2 Clove Crescent
London
E14 2BE

T: 020 7538 6171
F: 020 7538 6200

FIRST-TIER TRIBUNAL
ASYLUM SUPPORT

Notice of Appeal

See the Guidance Notes for further information on completing this form

SECTION 1: YOUR PERSONAL DETAILS

Full Name: ....

Date of Birth: .... Nationality: ....

Your UKBA Support reference number: ....

Do you have a disability? **YES** ☐ **NO** ☐ *Please tick the appropriate box*

If **YES**, do you have additional requirements: ....

SECTION 2: YOUR CONTACT DETAILS

Please give an address, daytime telephone number and/or fax (if you have one) in the United Kingdom where you can be contacted:

Address and Post Code ....
....

Telephone: .... Fax: ....

SECTION 3: UKBA DECISION LETTER

Please give the date of the UKBA decision letter against which you are appealing.

Date: ....

NOTE: You must attach a full copy of the UKBA decision letter to this form.
Failure to do so may result in your appeal being treated as invalid.

SECTION 4: TYPE OF HEARING AND LANGUAGE

Please tick the appropriate box for the type of hearing you require. If you need an interpreter, you must specify the language and dialect in which you wish to give evidence.

I want my appeal determined on the papers	**YES**	☐	NO	☐
I want an oral hearing of my appeal	**YES**	☐	NO	☐
I want to attend the oral hearing of my appeal	**YES**	☐	NO	☐
I require an interpreter to assist me at the hearing	**YES**	☐	NO	☐

If so, in what language and dialect?

....

SECTION 5: REPRESENTATIVE

Do you have a representative assisting you with this appeal?	**YES**	☐	NO	☐
Will your representative be attending the oral hearing of your appeal	**YES**	☐	NO	☐

If you have answered "yes" to either question you must provide your representative's contact details in the box below, together with any reference number the representative has given your case.

Name: ....

Address: ....

Post Code: ....

Ref No: ....

Telephone: ....

Fax: ....

SECTION 6: GROUNDS OF APPEAL

You must complete this section. Failure to do so may result in your appeal being treated as invalid.

1. What are the grounds of your appeal?
2. What matters in the UKBA decision letter do you disagree with? (Please use a separate A4 sheet if required)
3. If your appeal is late, please explain the reason and why you should be allowed to appeal out of time.

Signed: .... Date: ....
(Appellant/Representative)

GUIDANCE NOTES

1. Please ensure that you complete all sections as fully as possible.
2. You MUST enclose a copy of the UKBA decision letter, or your appeal may be treated as invalid.
3. If you have requested an oral hearing and need an interpreter please ensure that you tell us the language you require.
4. If you have requested an oral hearing, it is in your interests to attend. Please note that UKBA will provide and send you your travel documents up to two days before your hearing date.
5. You MUST include your grounds of appeal at SECTION 6 or your appeal may be treated as invalid.
6. If you have further information, which you would like the Judge to take into account when making a decision about your appeal, you should send this together with copies of any documents with this form.
7. If you have any problems in understanding or filling out this form please seek out a voluntary refugee organisation within your area, which may be able to assist you.
8. **RETURN THIS FORM TO:**

   Tribunals Service
   Asylum Support
   2nd Floor
   Anchorage House
   2 Clove Crescent
   London
   E14 2BE

9. You may also return this form by fax. Our fax number is **020 7538 6200.**
10. The Asylum Support's freephone number for appellants who wish to discuss any aspect of the appeal process is: **0800 681 6509.**
11. Further information about Asylum Support appeals is available on: **www.asylum-support-tribunal.gov.uk**

APPENDIX D

Education rights for migrants

A migrant parent living in the UK has the same duty as any other parent to ensure his or her dependent child receives full-time education if aged between five and 16 years old. Previously the Home Office published *Asylum Support Policy Bulletin 63: Education* which gave an overview of education facilities for households it supported, eg explaining pre-school children of asylum-seekers may be entitled to nursery provision from the age of three. The bulleting has been withdrawn from the UKBA website and there is now a short page stressing an asylum-seeker parent's duties to ensure their child attends school, or otherwise receives full-time education.

Education for children

Asylum-seekers' children of school age are entitled to primary and secondary education under the Education Act (EA) 1996 s14, which places a duty on each local education authority to secure adequate places in primary and secondary schools for children residing temporarily or permanently in its area. The duty covers education appropriate to the age, aptitude, abilities and any special educational needs the child may have up to the age of 16. There are two Codes of Practice on school admissions, which were revised and reissued on 10 February 2009.[1] The School Admissions Code, Annex B states 'All children of compulsory school age in the UK have a right of access to education'. It goes on to refer to the children of asylum-seekers and unaccompanied asylum-seeking children as included in this right. The School Admissions Appeal Code explains the procedures for appealing against a refusal of a school to admit a pupil, but it makes no reference to immigration or asylum-seeker status.

The School Admissions Code prohibits admission authorities from using admission arrangements which directly or indirectly disadvantage children from any particular social or racial group or those with disabilities or special educational needs. It requires local authorities to provide a Choice Advice Service to those parents who are most in need of support during the secondary school admissions process, particularly those from disadvantaged groups. The Code expects school governing bodies to ensure that other

1 See www.dcsf.gov.uk/sacode/index/shtml

policies and procedures, for example the school uniform policy, do not discourage certain groups of parents from applying to the school.

Fair Access Protocols exist to ensure that education is secured quickly for 'hard-to-place' children, but that no school in the area is required to admit more than its fair share of pupils with challenging behaviour. The revised School Admissions Code specifies the groups of children that may have difficulty securing a place outside the normal admission round, which must be covered by a Protocol including children of asylum-seekers and refugees, children with special educational needs but without a statement, children with disabilities and medical conditions.

Special needs

The Special Education Needs Code of Practice[2] sets out detailed procedures for the identification of special educational needs and the provisions that should be made to meet those needs. Responsible bodies, such as local education authorities, schools, government-funded nursery providers and associated agencies such as social services and health trusts have a statutory duty to have regard to the code.

Asylum-seeker parents have a duty to ensure their child receives full-time education whether by attendance at school or otherwise[3] and may face prosecution if they fail to do this. EA 1996 requires local education authorities and governors of maintained schools to admit a child to the school of their parents' choice, subject to resource considerations and the consequences for other pupils, ie potential prejudice to efficient education. Parents may appeal to the relevant admissions authority if refused a school place. The appeal right in relation to infant classes (reception, year 1 and year 2) is restricted by the Education (Infant Class Sizes) England) Regulations 1998, as amended,[4] which limit the maximum number of children in a class to 30 for each qualified teacher. The admission authority must make and fund the necessary arrangements when appellants request the services of a translator at the appeals hearing. But there is no legal requirement on admission appeals to translate documents provided by the local authority or the parent.

Shortage of school places

In some parts of the country, and particularly in London, there is a shortage of school places. This problem commonly affects the children of asylum-seekers who move into an authority area between admission rounds. Local education authorities have a duty[5] to make suitable educational provision available to a pupil who is out of school due to illness, exclusion or otherwise. A parent could consider making an application for judicial review where a local education authority fails to provide either an adequate school

2 DfES/581/2001.
3 EA 1996 s7.
4 SI No 1973.
5 EA 1996 s19.

place for an asylum-seeker child or alternative interim provision under EA 1996 s19.

Education benefits

Local education authorities must provide free school meals to children of asylum-seekers receiving section 95 asylum support under IAA 1999 Part 6.[6] There is no such provision for those supported under IAA 1999 s4. This exclusion should only affect a small number of households because a refused asylum-seeker continues to qualify for section 95 support if there is a dependent child in their household at the time his or her asylum claim/ appeal is finally decided. Grants for school uniforms and travel passes are discretionary, but the authority should consider the exercise of its discretion fairly and taking into account the asylum-seeker child's rights under article 8 and article 14 (freedom from discrimination). Where an authority refuses assistance, reasons should be given. A local authority would also need to consider its discretion to make provision under the Children Act 1989 s17 or Local Government Act 2000 s2. In making a decision, the authority should take into account its general duty to promote equality of opportunity and good race relations between different racial groups,[7] which might be adversely affected if asylum-seeker pupils were stigmatised by the inability to purchase school uniform worn by British pupils.

Education for adults[8]

The Home Office may provide 'services' to adult asylum-seekers in the form of education including English language classes and 'developmental activities' such as sport but only 'for the purpose of maintaining good order' among supported persons.[9]

Further education

Mainstream Discretionary Support funds are available for migrants with leave to remain, EEA nationals and asylum seekers aged 16 to 18 years old who are on a course funded by the Learning and Skills Council.[10] Asylum-seekers are not eligible for student support, access funds or hardship loans. A migrant or asylum-seeker on a low income may qualify for an Educational Maintenance Allowance of £30 per week for full-time (12 hours or more) post- 16 further education in a sixth form or college.[11]

An Adult Learning Grant may be available to those 19 years old or over who are studying on a Level 2 course (qualifications are equivalent to five

6 IAA 1999 Sch 14, para 117 amended EA 1996 s512(3).

7 Race Relations Act 1976 s71 as amended.

8 The UK Council for International Student Affairs provides more detailed information and advice on this subject: see www.ukcosa.org.uk

9 AS Regs 2000 reg 14.

10 www.direct.gov.uk/en/EducationAndLearning/AdultLearning/FinancialHelpForAdultLearners/DG_10033131

11 http://ema.directgov.uk

or more GCSEs at grades A* to C or NVQ level 2) or Level 3 course (qualifications are equivalent to two A levels or NVQ level 3). Both these grants are currently administered by Capita.

The Learning and Skills Council funds tuition fees on further education courses for asylum-seekers on s95 and s4 support, or supported by social services, as well as refugees and former asylum-seekers with exceptional leave to remain (ELR), humanitarian protection (HP) or discretionary leave (DL who are in receipt of income support or income-based JSA.[12]

The college or school will require evidence of immigration status and income. Asylum-seekers aged 16–18 and people with ELR, HP or DL who do not meet the three-year residence requirement are entitled to the Learner Support Fund.

Higher education

The rules about who pays the home student rate for higher education (university) and who pays the more expensive overseas student rate are complex. The relevant date for the purpose of calculating entitlement is the first day of the academic year in which the potential student wishes to study. The rules for the academic year beginning on or after 1 September 2010 are contained in Schedule 1 to The Education (Fees and Awards) (EFA) Regulations 2009.[13] These regulations are updated each year. The rules for entitlement to student loans are slightly different and are contained in The Education (Student Support) Regulations 2007.[14]

An asylum-seeker, refused asylum-seeker or person unlawfully in the UK is liable to pay university tuition fees at the same rate as an overseas student. A person who has been granted indefinite leave to remain as a refugee, their spouse, civil partner or child is assessed as a home student provided he or she has been ordinarily resident in the UK from the date when indefinite leave is granted. A person who claimed asylum but was granted ELR, DL or HP is in the same position, including an unaccompanied minor whose leave has been extended following an in-time appeal or application to extend their leave (see above). But unlike a refugee he or she is not entitled to a student loan until they have been ordinarily resident in the UK for three years.

An EEA or Swiss national or his or her dependant(s) must have a right to reside in the UK and have been ordinarily resident in the EEA or the UK for three years preceding the relevant date to be treated as a home student. The children of Turkish migrant workers also benefit from this approach.[15]

12 www.lsc.gov.uk/news docs/Funding Guidance-FE.pdf

13 SI No 1555.

14 SI No 777.

15 Decision 1/80 of the Association Council (established by the Association Agreement between the EC and Turkey) in relation to certain education matters, article 9.

APPENDIX E

Asylum Support Partnership

refugee action · North of England Refugee Service · Refugee Council · scottish refugee council · Welsh Refugee Council / Cyngor Ffoaduriaid Cymru

One Stop Service Locations

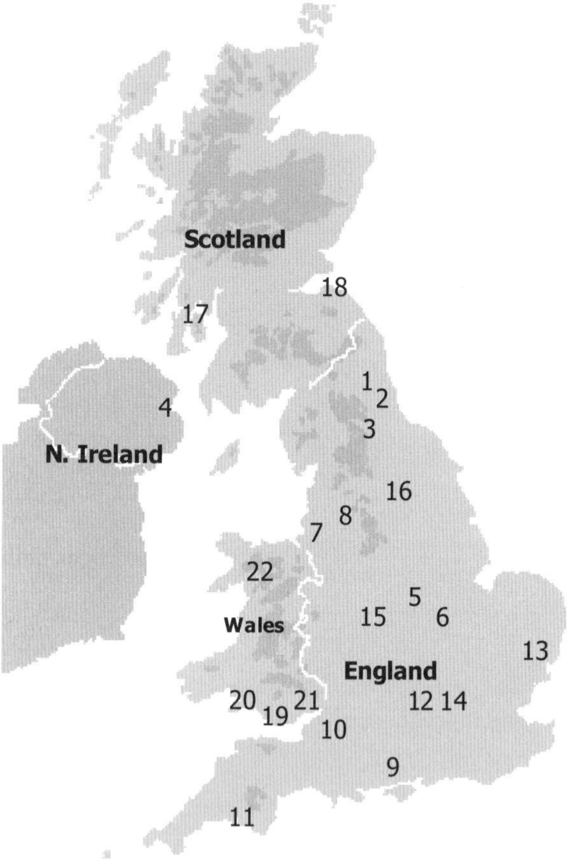

July 2009

ASP is a partnership project hosted by the British Refugee Council

British Refugee Council, (commonly called the Refugee Council) is a company limited by guarantee registered in England and Wales, [No 2727514] and a registered charity, [No 1014576]. Registered office: 240-250 Ferndale Road, London SW9 8BB, United Kingdom

One Stop Service Locations

	ORGANISATION	OPENING TIMES	ADDRESS	TELEPHONE
1	**NERS** (North of England Refugee Service)	Mon – Fri: 09:30 – 13:00 Appointments only: Mon-Fri *(not Wed)* 14:00 – 16:30	19 The Bigg Market Newcastle NE1 1UN	Tel - 0191 222 0406
2	**NERS** (North of England Refugee Service)	Mon – Fri: 09:30 – 13:00 14:00 – 16:30 *(not Wed)*	19 Villiers Street Sunderland Tyne & Wear SR1 1EJ	Tel - 0191 510 8685
3	**NERS** (North of England Refugee Service)	Mon – Fri: 09:30 – 13:00 Appointments only: Mon-Fri *(not Wed)* 14:00 – 16:30	3rd Floor, Sylvan House 12-16 Woodlands Road Middlesbrough TS1 3BE	Tel - 01642 217 447 Fax - 01642 232414
4	**MCRC** (Multi-Cultural Resource Centre)		9 Lower Crescent Belfast BT7 1NR	Tel - 02890 238 645
5	**REFUGEE ACTION** Nottingham	Mon - Fri (**Not Wed**) 10:00 - 12:30 14:00 - 16:00 Mon & Thur: Drop in (am) / Appt's (pm) Tue: Appt's Fri: Appt's (am) Advice Line - Nottingham Office (Mon, Tues, Thurs, Fri) 10:00 - 12:30 14:00 - 16:00 Derby outreach service (appt's. only) Tue & Thur 10:00 - 13:00 14:00 - 16:00	Castle Court, 59 Castle Boulevard, Nottingham, NG7 1FD	Tel: 0115 941 8552 Fax: 0115 950 9980
6	**REFUGEE ACTION** Leicester	Office hours 0900-1300 & 1400-1700 Monday - Thursday 0900-1300 & 1330-1630 Friday Open to clients Mon: Drop In 1000-1230 & 1400-1600 Tue: Appts/Advice Line 1000-1300 & 1400-1600	Chancery House 7 Millstone Lane Leicester LE1 5JN	Tel - 0116 261 6200 Fax - 0116 261 6226 Telephone Advice Line - 0116 261 6223

One Stop Service Locations

		Wed: Emergencies only Thu: Appointments 1000-1300 & 1400-1600 Fri: Advice Line 1000-1300 & 1400-1600		
7	**REFUGEE ACTION** North West	Monday: 9.45 - 12.30 and 2 - 3.30 for drop in sessions and appointments. Tuesday: 9.45 - 12.30 and 2-3.30 for drop in sessions and appointments. Wednesday - closed. Thursday: 9.45 - 12.30 and 2-3.30 for drop in sessions and appointments. Friday: 9.45 - 12.30 - drop in session and appointments.	64 Mount Pleasant Liverpool L3 5SD	Tel - 0151 702 6300 Fax – 0151 709 6684
8	**REFUGEE ACTION** North West	Mon-Fri (not Wed): 10:00 – 13:00 14:00 – 16:30 Closed Wed Drop in service on Monday and Thursday from 9.30 a.m. and 2.00 p.m. Appointments only on Tuesday, Wednesday and Friday. Our advice line is open Mon - Fri 10.00 a.m. - 4.30 p.m. and will return messages left on this number later that day or the next working day.	23-37 Edge Street, Manchester M4 1HW	Free client advice line: 0800 917 2719 Main Tel – 0161 831 5420 Casework Fax – 0161 831 5496 Office Fax – 0161 834 7715
9	**REFUGEE ACTION** South Central	PORTSMOUTH Mon - Fri 10:00-13:00	Third Floor Venture Tower Fratton Road	Tel: 023 9229 7407 Fax: 023 9285

One Stop Service Locations

14	**BRITISH REFUGEE COUNCIL** London Office (Head Office)	Mon-Fri (not Wed a.m.): 09.00 – 17.00 Wed: 09:00 – 14:00 emergencies & appointments only	240-250 Ferndale Rd Brixton London SW9 8BB	Tel - 020 7346 6700/ 020 7346 6777 (advice line) Fax – 0207 346 6774
15	**BRITISH REFUGEE COUNCIL** West Midlands Office	Mon, Tues, Thurs, Fri 0930–1300; 1400–1730 Wednesday emergencies only Outreach in Stoke-on-Trent (in various locations, please contact OSS) Drop-in Tues & Fri 0930–1300; 1400–1730 Fortnightly on Monday, appointments only	3 Lionel Street Birmingham B3 1AG	Tel - 0121 234 1950 (switchboard/ advice line) Fax – 0121 236 7864
16	**BRITISH REFUGEE COUNCIL** Yorkshire & Humberside Office	Mon, Tues, Thurs. & Fri. – 09:00 to 16:00 Wed. – Emergencies or appointments only	Ground Floor Hurley House 1 Dewsbury Road Leeds LS11 5DQ	Tel - 0113 244 9404 Advice Line - 0113 386 2210 Fax – 0113 246 5229
17	**SCOTTISH REFUGEE COUNCIL**	Mon, Tues, Thurs & Fri: 09:30 – 13:00 & 14:00 – 16:00 Wed: 13:00 – 16:00	5 Cadogan Square (170 Blythswood Court) Cadogan Street Glasgow G2 7PH	Tel - 0141 248 9799 Free phone number - 0800 0856 087 Fax number - 0141 243 2499
18	**SCOTTISH REFUGEE COUNCIL**	Monday AM Thursday ALL DAY	Citizens Advice Bureau 58 Dundas Street Edinburgh	Appointments via freephone number: 0800 085 6087
19	**WELSH REFUGEE COUNCIL**	Monday Drop – in between 10.30am – 12.30pm and 2pm – 3.30pm Tuesday Appointments only	Phoenix House 389 Newport Road Cardiff CF24 1TP	Tel - 02920 489 800 Fax - 02920 432 980

One Stop Service Locations

		Wednesday Women's Only Drop-in between 10.30am – 12.30pm Thursday Drop – in between 10.30am – 12.30pm and 2pm – 3.30pm Friday Appointments only *Ring 029 2048 9800 to make an appointment or for general queries between 9am – 1pm and 2pm – 5pm*		
20	**WELSH REFUGEE COUNCIL**	Mon, Tue, Thu: 10:00 – 12:30 14:00 – 15:30 Fri:10:30 – 12:30 Telephone advice: Mon – Fri 9:00 – 13:00 14:00 – 17:00	3rd Floor, Grove House Grove Place Swansea SA1 5DF	Tel - 01792 630 180 Fax - 01792 630 181
21	**WELSH REFUGEE COUNCIL**	Monday 10:00 – 12:30 14:00 – 15:30 Tuesday 11.00 – 12.30 2.00 – 3.30 Wednesday : Closed Thursday 10:00 – 12:30 14:00 – 15:30 Friday 10:00 – 12:30 PM Closed	High Street Chambers 51 High Street Newport NP20 1GB	Tel – 01633 266 420 Fax - 01633 266 421
22	**WELSH REFUGEE COUNCIL**	Mon, Tue, Thu: 10:00 – 12:30 14:00 – 15:30 Fri:10:00 – 12:30	Trinity House Trinity Street Wrexham LL11 1NL	Tel - 01978 367890 Fax - 01978 367 891

Asylum Support Partnership

refugee action

REFUGEE COUNCIL

scottish refugee council

Welsh Refugee Council
Cyngor Ffoaduriaid Cymru

Initial Accommodation Service Locations

Addresses and Opening Times of Initial Accommodation Services

	Organisation	Opening Times	Address	Telephone
1	Refugee Council (subcontracted to Bryson) – Belfast	9am – 5pm Monday to Friday Closed between 1-2pm daily	9 Lower Crescent Belfast BT7 NR1	Tel: 028 90439226 Fax: 028 90329539
2	Refugee Action – Liverpool	9.30 – 4pm Monday to Friday: drop in service for Initial Accommodation Residents	27 Greenbank Drive Sefton Park Liverpool L17 1AS	Tel: 0151 7347570 Fax: 0151 7343625
3	Refugee Council - Belmont, Barnsley	Monday to Friday 9 – 5pm. Closed Wednesday morning	Cross Street, Monk Bretton Barnsley, S71 2DY	Tel: 01226 320544 Fax: 01226 323670
4	Refugee Council – Birmingham	Monday, Tuesday Thursday and Friday 9.30 to 1.00 p.m. 2.00 p.m. to 5.30 p.m. Wednesday closed am except for emergencies open from 2.00pm -5.30pm	Address 3 Stone Road, Edgbaston, Birmingham. B15 2HH	Tel: 0121 446 5118 Fax: 0121 4467299
5	Refugee Council – Hillside, Leeds	Monday to Friday 9 – 5pm. Closed Wednesday morning	602 Leeds & Bradford Rd Bramley, Leeds, LS13 1HQ	Tel: 0113 2396440 Fax: 0113 2393165
6	Refugee Council – Angel Lodge, Wakefield	Monday to Friday 9 – 5pm. Closed Wednesday morning	Angel Lodge, Love Lane Wakefield, WF2 9AF	Tel: 01924 234070 Fax: 01924 364674
7	Scottish Refugee Council – Glasgow	Monday – Friday 9.30 - 13.00 14.00 - 16.00	Scottish Induction Service Flat 29/3 33 Petershill Drive Glasgow G21 4 QQ	Tel: 0141 248 9799 Fax: 0141 558 9397
8	Welsh Refugee Council – Cardiff	Monday, Tuesday and Thursday 10:00 – 16:00 Wednesday and Friday 10:00 – 13:00	Lynx House 385 Newport Road Cardiff CF24 1RN	Tel – 029 2048 0150 Fax- 029 2047 1592

Information on Partnership agencies Initial Accommodation Services

Refugee Action

The Refugee Action Wraparound service provides assistance for newly arrived asylum seekers within Initial Accommodation in Liverpool. It assists with applications for more long-term support and housing, Orientation Briefings and Dispersal Briefings, as well as providing a daily drop-in service dealing with issues including clients whose age is disputed, accessing health services, maternity benefits, and problems with support and accommodation.

Through the One Stop Services Refugee Action also offer advice and support to newly arrived asylum seekers who may need to access Initial Accommodation and also work with asylum seekers who have made an asylum application and are supported by UKBA.

Refugee Council

Through Refugee Council's 'Wraparound Service' they offer advice and support to newly arrived people seeking asylum residing in Initial Accommodation Sites in Wakefield (accommodates up to 220), Barnsley and Leeds (both accommodating up to 75 clients each).

Clients generally stay in the centres for 3 to 4 weeks, before being dispersed into Yorkshire and Humberside or the North East. Whilst there the Wraparound services team deliver the following sessions:

- Orientation Briefing – The briefing explains the process and rules whilst the client is in the centre. This is also an opportunity to identify health needs, and make appropriate referrals.
- NASS 1 –This is a briefing to apply for accommodation from the Home Office for when the client is dispersed. Any health needs that affect the accommodation are highlighted here.
- Asylum Process – This briefing explains the entire asylum process to the client.
- Dispersal – This briefing is given just before a client leaves the centre, it gives information and advice about support, education, harassment and emergency services.

From April 07 to April 08 the Wraparound Services Team, delivered 24,000 advice sessions to asylum seekers residing within the three centres.

Scottish Refugee Council

Scottish Refugee Council provide information briefings and advice sessions for new asylum seekers routed to Glasgow by UKBA routing team, Liverpool and for families accommodated in IA after presenting at their OSS in Cadogan Square, Glasgow. Scottish Refugee Council induction team is located on site. They arrange legal representation and GP registration and also complete NASS 1 applications for IA residents who are generally dispersed within Glasgow around 3 weeks after arrival. Scottish Refugee Council have an on site weekly midwife service and basic English classes for new arrivals with no English.

Welsh Refugee Council

Welsh Refugee Council have a dedicated Initial Accommodation Team that provide full advice sessions and briefings for those asylum seekers who have just claimed asylum and have arrived (sent by UKBA) in Cardiff. The briefings and sessions are provided on site in the hostel where asylum seekers are housed by UKBA for the first few weeks of their asylum claim. The sessions are aimed to help asylum seekers understand the asylum process, access UKBA longer term housing, access solicitors, social care, essential living needs and family reunion or tracing.

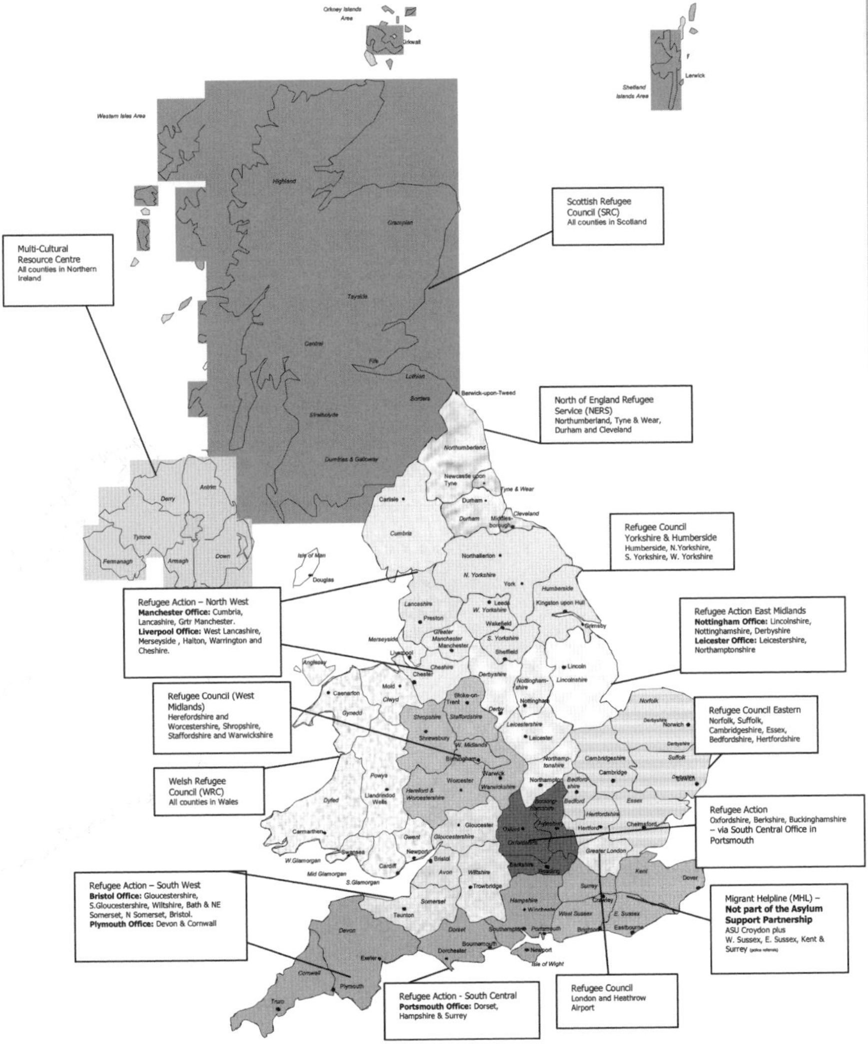
Multi-Cultural Resource Centre
All counties in Northern Ireland
Scottish Refugee Council (SRC)
All counties in Scotland
North of England Refugee Service (NERS)
Northumberland, Tyne & Wear, Durham and Cleveland
Refugee Council Yorkshire & Humberside
Humberside, N.Yorkshire, S. Yorkshire, W. Yorkshire
Refugee Action – North West
Manchester Office: Cumbria, Lancashire, Grtr Manchester.
Liverpool Office: West Lancashire, Merseyside , Halton, Warrington and Cheshire.
Refugee Action East Midlands
Nottingham Office: Lincolnshire, Nottinghamshire, Derbyshire
Leicester Office: Leicestershire, Northamptonshire
Refugee Council (West Midlands)
Herefordshire and Worcestershire, Shropshire, Staffordshire and Warwickshire
Refugee Council Eastern
Norfolk, Suffolk, Cambridgeshire, Essex, Bedfordshire, Hertfordshire
Welsh Refugee Council (WRC)
All counties in Wales
Refugee Action
Oxfordshire, Berkshire, Buckinghamshire – via South Central Office in Portsmouth
Refugee Action – South West
Bristol Office: Gloucestershire, S.Gloucestershire, Wiltshire, Bath & NE Somerset, N Somerset, Bristol.
Plymouth Office: Devon & Cornwall
Migrant Helpline (MHL) –
Not part of the Asylum Support Partnership
ASU Croydon plus
W. Sussex, E. Sussex, Kent & Surrey
Refugee Action - South Central
Portsmouth Office: Dorset, Hampshire & Surrey
Refugee Council
London and Heathrow Airport
Orkney Islands Area
Kirkwall
Shetland Islands Area
Lerwick
Western Isles Area
Highland
Grampian
Tayside
Central
Fife
Lothian
Borders
Strathclyde
Dumfries & Galloway
Berwick-upon-Tweed
Northumberland
Newcastle upon Tyne
Tyne & Wear
Durham
Cleveland
Carlisle
Cumbria
Derry
Antrim
Tyrone
Fermanagh
Armagh
Down
Isle of Man
Douglas
Northallerton
N. Yorkshire
York
Humberside
Kingston upon Hull
Grimsby
Lancashire
Preston
Leeds
W. Yorkshire
Wakefield
S. Yorkshire
Sheffield
Greater Manchester
Manchester
Merseyside
Liverpool
Cheshire
Chester
Lincoln
Lincolnshire
Anglesey
Caenarfon
Mold
Clwyd
Gynedd
Derbyshire
Nottinghamshire
Nottingham
Derby
Stoke-on-Trent
Shropshire
Staffordshire
Shrewsbury
Leicestershire
Leicester
Norfolk
Norwich
Suffolk
W. Midlands
Birmingham
Warwick
Warwickshire
Worcester
Powys
Llandrindod Wells
Hereford & Worcestershire
Dyfed
Northamptonshire
Northampton
Cambridgeshire
Cambridge
Bedford
Essex
Hertfordshire
Hertford
Chelmsford
Carmarthen
Gloucester
Gloucestershire
Oxford
Oxfordshire
Aylesbury
Gwent
Newport
Swansea
Cardiff
Bristol
Avon
Wiltshire
Trowbridge
Berkshire
Reading
Greater London
W.Glamorgan
Mid Glamorgan
S.Glamorgan
Kent
Dover
Somerset
Taunton
Hampshire
Winchester
Surrey
Crawley
West Sussex
E. Sussex
Brighton
Eastbourne
Devon
Exeter
Dorset
Dorchester
Bournemouth
Southampton
Portsmouth
Newport
Isle of Wight
Cornwall
Plymouth
Truro

APPENDIX F

UKBA Policy Bulletins[1]

Access to support
Policy Bulletin 4 – Determining whether persons who apply for asylum support are destitute
Policy Bulletin 11 – Mixed households
Policy Bulletin 37 – Maternity payments
Policy Bulletin 67 – Overpayments
Policy Bulletin 70 – Domestic violence
Policy Bulletin 73 – Provisions of emergency accommodation
Policy Bulletin 75 – Section 55 (late claims) 2002 Act guidance – revised version
Policy Bulletin 76 – Asylum support applications from nationals of a European Economic Area State or from persons who have refugee status abroad (New)
Policy Bulletin 78 – Additional payments to pregnant women and children
Policy Bulletin 79 – Section 57 (applications for support: false or incomplete information) 2002 Act guidance
Policy Bulletin 80 – Back payment on asylum support
Policy Bulletin 83 – Duty to offer support, family unity, vulnerable persons, withdrawing support
Policy Bulletin 84 – Entertaining a further application for support
Policy Bulletin 87 – The Civil Partnership Act 2004

Children
Policy Bulletin 29 – Transition at age 18
Policy Bulletin 33 – Age disputes

Dispersal
Policy Bulletin 31 – Dispersal guidelines
Policy Bulletin 61 – Pregnancy

General
Policy Bulletin 23 – Asylum support appeals process
Policy Bulletin 47 – Judicial review

1 All policy bulletins listed are available for download in PDF format at www.ukba.homeoffice.gov.uk/policyandlaw/guidance/asylumsuppbull/

Policy Bulletin 64 – Has been withdrawn. In the interim please use the 'Bail flowcharts' below for assistance in deciding support arrangements for bail cases.
Bail flowchart – The applicant was not already in IND accommodation before being taken into detention
Bail flowchart – The applicant was already in IND accommodation before being taken into detention
Bail flowchart – The applicant has already been released from immigration or police detention and now wishes to access IND accommodation as a bail address
Policy Bulletin 72 – Employment & voluntary activity
Policy Bulletin 81 – Racist incidents
Policy Bulletin 82 – Asylum seekers with care needs
Policy Bulletin 86 – Possessions

Medical
Policy Bulletin 43 – HC2 certificates
Policy Bulletin 59 – Help with the cost of funerals
Policy Bulletin 85 – Dispersing asylum seekers with health care needs

Travel
Policy Bulletin 17 – Failure to travel
Policy Bulletin 28 – Providing travelling expenses and reimbursing essential travel

APPENDIX G

Support entitlements

TABLE OF SUPPORT ENTITLEMENTS FOR ASYLUM-SEEKERS ACCORDING TO IMMIGRATION STATUS

ADULTS/FAMILIES

Category	Status	Entitlement	Provider	Type of support
Recently arrived asylum-seeker	Arrived in UK lawfully or unlawfully, not yet claimed asylum.	If able-bodied, no right to housing or support until makes asylum claim at Asylum Screening Unit. If pregnant or clear care needs can access emergency overnight accommodation.	none	none
Asylum-seeker	Recently arrived and claimed asylum on arrival.	Emergency accommodation for household under IAA 1999 s98 initially.	UKBA via voluntary sector agent	Full-board normally in hostel.
Asylum-seeker	Entered UK unlawfully, eg in lorry or on fake passport and then claimed asylum 'in-country', ie after arrival. No child/ special needs.	NIAA 2002 s55 means he or she must show that they claimed asylum as soon as reasonably practicable or must show support is needed to avoid a breach of his or her human rights, eg they are homeless. Will then qualify for section 98 support initially and then section 95 support.	UKBA	Ordinary support and accommodation (see below). UKBA usually refuses support if applicant stays with friends and claims cash-only support.

Category	Status	Entitlement	Provider	Type of support
Asylum-seeker	Has made first claim for asylum or under ECHR article 3 and is awaiting decision. Able-bodied/ no care needs.	Support under IAA 1999 s95 until final refusal of claim or appeal. Covers asylum-seeker and any dependants.	UKBA	Cash of about 70% of income support rate for adults and notionally 100% for a child Asylum-seeker may seek cash only support and stay with friends or be dispersed.
Asylum-seeker with care needs	Has made first claim for asylum or under ECHR article 3 and is awaiting decision. Has a need for 'looking after' due to a disability, long term health need, old age mental illness	Accommodation under National Assistance Act 1948 s21	Local Authority Social Services	Normally accommodation and full board or vouchers. Personal/home care if needed.
Rejected asylum-seeker with child	Asylum claim has been refused and there is no outstanding appeal. Asylum-seeker living with a child who was born before asylum claim or appeal finally refused.	Family normally continues to receive support under Immigration and Asylum Act 1999 s95.	UKBA	Accommodation and cash support continue.

Category	Status	Entitlement	Provider	Type of support
Rejected asylum-seeker no child at time of asylum claim	Asylum claim has been refused and there is no outstanding appeal. Able-bodied/no care needs. No child under 18 born before date of final asylum refusal/ appeal.	Support continues until 21 days after final decision/ appeal. After that no support unless qualifies for section 4 support (see next box)	None	
Rejected asylum-seeker no child at time of asylum claim	Asylum claim has been refused and there is no outstanding appeal. Able-bodied/ no care needs. No child born at date of final refusal. Unable to travel home because physically unable to travel (eg late stage of pregnancy), or UKBA says no safe route, or he or she has applied for a judicial review of the asylum appeal decision, or they have made a fresh asylum or human rights claim which has not yet been recorded by UKBA or they are taking reasonable steps to leave the UK.	Support under IAA 1999 s4	UKBA	Board and lodging or shared room in private rented accommodation plus £35 per week equivalent supermarket vouchers. No cash. Minimal provision for extra support for children's, clothes, travel etc.

Category	Status	Entitlement	Provider	Type of support
Rejected asylum-seeker	Asylum claim/appeal refused. Has care needs for 'looking after'. Applied for asylum on arrival in the UK.	Accommodation under National Assistance Act 1948 s21.	Local Authority Social Services	Accommodation and support continue unless there are removal directions.
Rejected asylum-seeker with care needs	Asylum claim/appeal refused. Has care needs. Applied for asylum in-country.	None unless can show accommodation needed to avoid a breach of human rights. If claim refused and no fresh claim, Social Services may argue applicant should go home to avoid human rights breach.	None	None
Rejected asylum-seeker has made fresh claim	Asylum claim/appeal refused. Has made fresh asylum claim. No child during original claim/appeal.	Section 4 support until/unless UKBA agree to 'record' the fresh claim, ie accept it is sufficiently different from original claim. Once it is recorded, applicant become asylum-seeker with right to ordinary section 95 support or Social Services support if care need.	UKBA/Social Services	

UNACCOMPANIED ASYLUM-SEEKING CHILDREN

Category	Status	Entitlement	Provider	Type of support
Unaccompanied asylum-seeking child under 18	Has claimed or is about to claim asylum.	Support under Children Act 1989 s20.	Local authority Social Services	Should be designed to meet child's needs, normally foster care if under 16, supported hostel if 16/17.
Previously unaccompanied asylum-seeking child 18 or over	Asylum/ human rights claim outstanding.	Support under IAA 1999 s95 until final refusal of claim or appeal. Children Leaving Care help under Children Act s23. If he or she was granted leave to remain until 18 and applied for a 'variation of leave' before 18, existing support entitlement should continue, which could be mainstream housing and benefits.	UKBA and/or Social Services/ or Department for Work and Pensions Local Authority Housing Services	Accommodation and cash

Category	Status	Entitlement	Provider	Type of support
Rejected previous unaccompanied asylum-seeking child 18 or over	Asylum/ human rights claim/ final appeal refused.	None unless can show support needed to avoid a breach of human rights eg if a fresh asylum claim has been made or applicant is unable to travel home or unless he or she claimed on arrival and has temporary admission (see adults above).		
Successful previous unaccompanied asylum-seeking child 18 or over	Asylum/ human rights claim accepted and leave to remain granted.	Housing as a homeless person, social security benefits, right to work. Children Leaving care help.	DWP/ local authority	Suitable housing, social security benefits, Social Services assistance

SUMMARY OF OTHER WELFARE ENTITLEMENTS BASED ON IMMIGRATION STATUS[1]

Services	Asylum-seeker section 95 support (see chapter 3)	Asylum-seeker supported by Social Services or other means (eg relatives)	Refused asylum-seeker awaiting removal directions	Former asylum-seeker granted indefinite leave to remain as a refugee	Former asylum-seeker granted discretionary or other leave to remain	Former asylum-seeker now A8 national
Free NHS hospital treatment	Yes	Yes	No, unless needs treatment for emergency or specified illnesses or other exemption. Entitled to urgent and immediately necessary treatment but may be charged later (see chapter10).	Yes	Yes	Yes but may need EU ID as proof of entitlement.

1 This table is intended as a basic outline. Please refer to relevant chapters for a fuller explanation

Services	**Asylum-seeker section 95 support (see chapter 3)**	**Asylum-seeker supported by Social Services or other means (eg relatives)**	**Refused asylum-seeker awaiting removal directions**	**Former asylum-seeker granted indefinite leave to remain as a refugee**	**Former asylum-seeker granted discretionary or other leave to remain**	**Former asylum-seeker now A8 national**
NHS GP treatment	Yes	Yes	Yes, subject to discretion of GP (see chapter 10).	Yes	Yes	Yes but may need EU ID as proof of entitlement.
Free prescriptions	Yes with HC2 certificate.	Need to apply on form HC1 on basis of low income.	Yes, may apply on form HC1 on basis of low income.	Apply on form HC1 if on benefits/low income.	Apply on form HC1 if on benefits/low income.	Apply on form HC1 if on benefits/ low income.
Early years provision	Yes	Yes	Yes	Yes	Yes	Yes
School provision 5-16	Yes	Yes	Yes	Yes	Yes	Yes
Free school meals	Yes	No	No	If on income support	If on income support	If on income support

Services	Asylum-seeker section 95 support (see chapter 3)	Asylum-seeker supported by Social Services or other means (eg relatives)	Refused asylum-seeker awaiting removal directions	Former asylum-seeker granted indefinite leave to remain as a refugee	Former asylum-seeker granted discretionary or other leave to remain	Former asylum-seeker now A8 national
16-18 years education benefits	Yes – see further appendix D on education rights.	Yes – see further appendix D on education rights.	Yes – see further appendix D on education rights.	Yes – see further appendix D on education rights.	Yes – see further appendix D on education rights.	Yes – see further appendix D on education rights.
Further education	Yes	Yes	Learning and Skills Council does not cover fees.	Yes	Yes	Yes if self-supporting or child of someone with right o reside who has lived in EEA state for 3 years.
Higher education (university)	No funding and overseas student fees.	no funding and overseas student fees.	No	Eligible for any loan/ grant funding on same basis as British Citizen without waiting for a qualifying period.	3-year qualifying period for any grant funding.	Yes if self-supporting or child of someone with right o reside who has lived in EEA state for 3 years.

Services	Asylum-seeker section 95 support (see chapter 3)	Asylum-seeker supported by Social Services or other means (eg relatives)	Refused asylum-seeker awaiting removal directions	Former asylum-seeker granted indefinite leave to remain as a refugee	Former asylum-seeker granted discretionary or other leave to remain	Former asylum-seeker now A8 national
Social Security benefits	Eligible for contributory benefits if has or had permission to work and has paid sufficient contributions but income must be below destitution threshold to retain section 95 entitlement.	eligible for relevant contributory benefits if has permission to work and has paid sufficient contributions	No	Yes	Yes	If s/he has right to reside eg is working and registered to work, or has been working and registered for a continuous period of 12 months or is dependant of the above or is self-employed. Otherwise is entitled to child benefit and disability living allowance/ carer's allowance.

Services	**Asylum-seeker section 95 support (see chapter 3)**	**Asylum-seeker supported by Social Services or other means (eg relatives)**	**Refused asylum-seeker awaiting removal directions**	**Former asylum-seeker granted indefinite leave to remain as a refugee**	**Former asylum-seeker granted discretionary or other leave to remain**	**Former asylum-seeker now A8 national**
Social housing	No, except as part of an eligible household.	No, except as part of an eligible household.	No, except as part of an eligible household.	Yes	Yes	If s/he has right to reside eg is working and registered to work, has been working and registered for a continuous period of 12 months or is self-employed.
Social services help (community care)	Yes for 'non-destitution needs'.	Yes for 'non-destitution needs'.	Yes for 'non-destitution needs', but excluded if Schedule 3 applies (see chapter 9).	Yes	Yes	Only if provision is necessary to avoid a breach of rights under EU treaty or ECHR.

Services	**Asylum-seeker section 95 support (see chapter 3)**	**Asylum-seeker supported by Social Services or other means (eg relatives)**	**Refused asylum-seeker awaiting removal directions**	**Former asylum-seeker granted indefinite leave to remain as a refugee**	**Former asylum-seeker granted discretionary or other leave to remain**	**Former asylum-seeker now A8 national**
Asylum support	Yes	Yes, eg for family members not supported by social services.	Yes if has dependent child under 18 who was in household during asylum application/ appeal, unless refusing to co-operate with departure. Otherwise section 4 support if meet criteria (chapter 6).	Ends 28 days after notice of decision.	Ends 28 days after notice of decision.	No

APPENDIX H

Resources

GENERAL

Finding legislation and case-law

- www.statutelaw.gov.uk/
- www.parliament.the-stationery-office.co.uk
- www.direct.gov.uk

Statutes, statutory instruments and information about government departments can be found at the above sites.

- www.bailii.org/

Free access to important UK and EU judgments.

Advice and information

Advisory Centre for Education (ACE)
www.ace-ed.org.uk
Tel: 020 7354 8321

Community Legal Service
www.communitylegaladvice.org.uk/
Tel: 0845 345 4 345
How to find a local solicitor eg doing immigration or community care law

Equality and Human Rights Commission
www.equalityhumanrights.com/
Advice line: England 0845 604 6610; Scotland 0845 604 5510; Wales 0845 604 8810
Advice and information on discrimination and human rights issues

Liberty
www.liberty-human-rights.org.uk
Advisers' helpline on human rights: tel 0808 808 4546

Public Law Project
www.publiclawproject.org.uk
Advice line for advisers: tel 0808 800 4546 or 020 7697 2194
Specialist legal advice about public law and human rights issues.

Law Centres' Federation
www.lawcentres.org.uk
Tel: 020 7387 8570

Complaints

UK Borders Agency
For complaints see UKBA website (below) as different customer service units deal with different types of complaint

Parliamentary and Health Service Ombudsman
www.ombudsman.org.uk
Tel 0845 015 4033
The Parliamentary Ombudsman considers complaints against UKBA (as part of the Home Office)

Local Government Ombudsman
www.lgo.gov.uk/
Advice line 0845 6021983
Considers complaints about local authority maladministration

Office of the Information Commissioner
www.informationcommissioner.gov.uk
Helpline 01625 545745 333
Considers complaints about the handling of information under the Data Protection Act 1998 and Freedom of Information Act 2000

ASYLUM AND IMMIGRATION LAW RESOURCES

Publications

- *Butterworths' Immigration Law Service,* Butterworths.
- *Immigration, Nationality and Refugee law Handbook,* JCWI 2006
- *MacDonald's Immigration Law and Practice,* MacDonald and Toal, Lexis-Nexis Butterworths,7th edition, 2009
- *Asylum Law & Practice,* Mark Symes and Peter Jorro, Butterworths, 2003 (2nd edition forthcoming Jan 2010 (Bloomsbury Professional))
- *Immigration Law Handbook,* Margaret Phelan and James Gillespie, OUP, 6th edition, 2009
- *Putting children first,* Jane Coker, Nadine Finch and Alison Stanley, Legal Action Group, 2002

Advice and information

Asylum Aid
www.asylumaid.org.uk
Tel: 020 7377 5123
Campaigns and provides immigration advice

Immigration Advisory Service (IAS)
County House
190 Great Dover Street
London SE1 4YB
www.iasuk.org
Tel: 020 7967 1200 **E-mail:** advice@ias.org

Government funded advice and representation

Greater Manchester Immigration Aid
Unit 400 Cheetham Hill Road
Manchester M8 7EL
www.gmiau.org
Tel: 0161 740 7722

Immigration advice and campaigning

Immigration Advisory Service
www.iasuk.org/home.aspx
National body providing immigration and asylum advice and representation to those eligible for legal aid

Joint Council for the Welfare of Immigrants (JCWI)
115 Old Street
London EC1V 9RT
www.jcwi.org.uk

Legal advice on immigration and nationality law

Refugee and Migrant Justice (formerly the Refugee Legal Centre)
153-157 Commercial Road,
London E8 2DA

www.refugee-migrant-justice.org.uk/
Tel: 020 7780 3200
Advice and representation on asylum and asylum appeals

UK Lesbian & Gay Immigration Group (formerly known as the Stonewall Immigration Group)
www.uklig.org.uk
Campaigns for immigration rights for same-sex couples and asylum-seekers.

General information and government bodies

Electronic Immigration Network
www.ein.org.uk
Tel 0845 458 4151 (0161 2737515)
Electronic Immigration network has extensive links to organisations andlegal sources.

UN High Commissioner for Refugees
www.unhcr.ch
UN High Commissioner for Refugees' website holds international refugee law, up to date country and guidance on the protection of refugees.

Home Office UK Border Agency
Lunar House
40 Wellesley Road
Croydon CR9 2BY
www.ukba.homeoffice.gov.uk

Home Office's UKBA website publishes immigration law, policy and guidance including the full text of the Immigration rules, country assessments, prescribed application forms and Asylum Support policy bulletins.

For immigration enquiries contact: 0870 606 7766
See website for regional offices and contact centres

Research Development Statistics : www.homeoffice.gov.uk/rds

Home Office statistics, research and publications on asylum and immigration Quarterly statistics showing asylum and UKBA applications

The Office of the Immigration Services Commissioner
5th Floor, Counting House 53 Tooley Street London SE1 2QN
www.oisc.gov.uk
General enquiries: 0845 000 0046; Tel: 020 7211 1500
Regulates provision of immigration advice

Immigration Law Practitioners Association
Lindsey House
40–42 Charterhouse Street
London EC1M 6JH
www.ilpa.org.uk
Tel: 020 7251 8363
Professional association of immigration lawyers and academics

EU RESOURCES

Publications

- *Free Movement of Persons in the Enlarged European Union*, Rogers and Scannell, Sweet & Maxwell, 2005
- *Immigration, Nationality and Refugee law Handbook*, JCWI 2006
- *Migration and Social Security Handbook*, Child Poverty Action Group, 4th edition
- *Asylum Support: a practitioners' guide to the EU Reception Directive*, Baldaccini, Justice, 2005

EU websites and links

Europa
www.europa.eu
Comprehensive European law site with legislation and case-law.

Directive 2004/38/EC on the Right of Citizens of the Union and their Family Members to Move and Reside Freely within the Territory of the Member States at: http://europa.eu.int/eur-lex/pri/en/oj/dat/2004/l_229/l_22920040629en00350048.pdf

Council of Europe
www.coe.int/
For treaties and institutions, for example you can find a copy of and the list of signatories and ratifications of the European Convention on Social and Medical Assistance and the Council of Europe Social Charter (see appendix B). For ECHR cases: www.echr.coe.int/

Curia
http://curia.europa.eu/en/
Case-law of the European Court of Justice

Eur-lex
http://eur-lex.europa.eu/en/index.htm
Direct free access to EU law including the Official Journal of the European Union (OJ) and treaties, legislation, case-law and legislative proposals

UK Office of the European Parliament
www.europarl.org.uk/office/WelcomeMain.htm
The European Parliament's office in the UK exists to provide information to the public, the media, government, regional agencies and the business community about the role and activities of the Parliament itself and the European Union more generally

Directive laying down minimum standards for the reception of asylum seekers
http://www.ecre.org/eu_developments/reception/recdirfinal.pdf

Domestic resources

Office of Public Sector Information
www.opsi.gov.uk
For Acts of Parliament and statutory instruments

Includes:
Immigration (European Economic Area) Regulations 2006 (unamended): www.opsi.gov.uk/si/si2006/20061003.htm

Accession (Immigration and Worker Registration) Regulations 2004: www.opsi.gov.uk/si/si2004/20041219.htm

The Accession (Immigration and Worker Authorisation) Regulations 2006: www.opsi.gov.uk/si/si2006/20063317.htm

The Accession (Immigration and Worker Authorisation) (Amendment) Regulations 2007: www.opsi.gov.uk/SI/si2007/20070475.htm

Employment

UKBA
www.ukba.homeoffice.gov.uk/workingintheuk/eea/wrs/
Home Office website explaining the workers' registration and authorisation schemes with forms and guidance in European languages.

Her Majesty's Revenue and Customs
www.hmrc.gov.uk/selfemployed/
Inland Revenue website – info regarding registering as self-employed for tax/NI purposes

Immigration and Nationality Directorate
www.ind.homeoffice.gov.uk/6353/11406/49552/wrsapril07.doc
For the worker's registration form for A8 nationals

Advice and Information

CPAG
Advisers' advice line: 020 7837 7979 (Mon-Thurs 2-4pm)
Advice on welfare benefits and EU law

Advice on Individual Rights in Europe
(AIRE Centre)
www.airecentre.org.uk
Advice line 0207 831 3850

Interrights
www.interrights.org.default.asp
Tel: 020 7278 3230
Advice and information about European and international human rights law.

BENEFITS RESOURCES

Publications

See generally, publications by CPAG: www.cpag.org.uk

- *Social Security Legislation 2009,* Sweet and Maxwell, 2009 (published annually)
- *Welfare Benefits and Tax Credits Handbook,* CPAG (published annually)
- *Migration and Social Security Handbook,* 4th edition, CPAG
- *Housing Benefit and Council Tax Benefit Legislation 2008-9,* CPAG (published annually)

Websites

www.osscsc.org.uk
Commissioners' decisions and guidance.

www.hywels.demon.co.uk
Commissioners' decisions up to 18/9/00 only

www.dwp.gov.uk
DWP website with guidance, manuals and Commissioners' decisions.

www.irssf.gov.uk
Independent review service publishes social fund directions.

Government offices and agencies

Department for Work and Pensions (benefits)
www.hmrc.gov.uk/nic/
For information on NI contributions or National Insurance Contributions
Benton Park View
Newcastle upon Tyne NE98 1ZZ
Telephone 0845 302 1479 (Monday to Friday 8am to 5pm)

The Tribunals Service
www.tribunals.gov.uk/Tribunals/Upper/upper.htm
For information and guidance about the new Upper Tribunal, replacing the former social security commissioners

Advice and Information

London Advice Services Alliance
Universal House
88-94 Wentworth Street
London E1 7SA
www.lasa.org.uk.
Tel: 020 7377 2738

Welfare benefits information and Training for advisers
www.rightsnet.org.uk
LASA's welfare rights website with discussion and current information about asylum support issues. Contains good links to other legal sites.

Child Poverty Action Group (CPAG)
94, White Lion Street
London N1 9PF
www.cpag.org.uk
Tel 0207 837 7979
Advice line (for advisers only) 0207 833 4627 (Monday to Friday 2pm – 4pm)
Welfare benefits information, training and publications (inc *Welfare Rights Bulletin*)

Citizens Advice
Myddleton House
115-123 Pentonville Road
London N1 9LZ
www.citizensadvice.org.uk
Tel: 020 7833 2181
For details of the local Citizens' Advice Bureau

ASYLUM SUPPORT RESOURCES

Publications

There are numerous publications about the effect of the asylum support scheme and other aspects of support on asylum-seekers. Many of these can be accessed via the websites and organisations below:

- Information Centre about Asylum and Refugees in the UK includes list of research publications: www.icar.org.uk
- The Refugee Council has website has numerous research publications and resources including translated leaflets and guides about asylum support. Information service details at: www.refugeecouncil.org.uk/practice/asylum/information/
- The Islington-based No recourse to Public Funds network provides information to support local authorities' work on migrants with no entitlement to mainstream support: www.islington.gov.uk/Health/ServicesForAdults/nrpf_network/default.asp
- *Legal Action* monthly magazine has an update on asylum support developments usually published each December and June: www.lag.org.uk/legalaction

List of reports on destitution

Deserving Dignity: The Independent Asylum Commission's Third Report on Conclusions and Recommendations, July 2008: www.independentasylumcommission.org.uk/

JCHR inquiry into the treatment of asylum-seekers
The Joint Committee on Human Rights has published its report on the treatment of asylum-seekers with chapters on asylum support, children, healthcare, detention and the media: (1HL 81-I/HC 60-I 0th Report 30 March 2007): www.publications.parliament.uk/pa/jt/jtrights.htm

Unreasonably Destitute? Asylum Support Appeals Project (ASAP), July 2008: www.asaproject.org/web/images/PDFs/news/unreasonably_destitute.pdf

Failing the Failed? How NASS Decision-making is letting down destitute rejected asylum-seekers, Asylum Support Appeals Project, February 2007, www.asaproject.org.uk).
Not moving on: Still destitute in Leeds, David Brown, Joseph Rowntree Charitable Trust, July 2008: www.jrct.org.uk

'More Token Gestures': A Refugee Council report into the use of vouchers for asylum seekers claiming Section 4 support, October 2008: www.refugeecouncil.org.uk

Websites

UK Borders Agency
www.ukba.homeoffice.gov.uk

The asylum support part of the UKBA website has forms for applying for section 95 and section 4 support and guidance. It has latest news about asylum support and Asylum Support Policy Bulletins. Navigate there from asylum support or law and policy.

Advice and information
(see also list of national one-stop services at appendix E)

Asylum Support Appeals Project (ASAP)
www.asaproject.org.uk
Helpline: 020 8684 5972.
Provides advice to agencies and refugee community organisations on asylum support/community care cases. Fact sheets and information on asylum support can be downloaded. They also operate a duty scheme at the AST.

Refugee Council
3 Bondway
London SW8 1SJ
www.refugeecouncil.org.uk
Tel: 020 7820 3000
E-mail: info@refugeecouncil.org.uk
Information, advice, training and publications

Tribunals Service: asylum support
www.asylum-support-tribunal.gov.uk
The First-tier tribunal (Asylum Support) website with useful information including appeal forms and appeal decisions.

Government offices and agencies
First-tier Tribunal (asylum support)
2nd Floor, Anchorage House
2 Clove Crescent
East India Dock
London E14 2BE
www.asylum-support-tribunal.gov.uk/
Tel: 020 7538 6171
Fax: 020 7538 6200
Freephone for appellants: 0800 681 6509

UK Borders Agency
Voyager House
30 Wellesley Road
Croydon CR0 2AD
www.ukba.homeoffice.gov.uk
Telephone enquiry bureau: 0845 602 1739

HOUSING RESOURCES

Publications

- *Encyclopedia of Housing Law and Practice*, Arden, Sweet and Maxwell
- *Housing law: an adviser's handbook*, Astin, 2008, Legal Action Group
- *Homelessness and Allocations*, Arden and Hunter, 2006, 7th edition, Legal Action Group (new edition 2010)
- *Repairs: tenants' rights*, Luba and Knafler, 1999, 3rd edition, Legal Action Group (new edition December 2009)
- *Legal Action*, monthly updates on housing law: www.lag.org.uk/magazine

Reports

Discussion paper: *No place like home? Addressing the issues of housing and migration*, O'Hara, Shelter, 2008

Websites

Department of Communities and Local Government
Codes of Guidance at:
www.communities.gov.uk/publications/housing/homelessnesscode
www.communities.gov.uk/publications/housing/allocationaccommodation code

Also publishes housing regulations and guidance, eg relating to the dispersal scheme.

Government offices and agencies

Independent Housing Ombudsman
Norman House
105–109 The Strand
London WC2R 0AA
www.ihos.org.uk
Tel: 020 7836 3630
E-mail: ombudsman@ihos.org.uk

Advice and information (see also general advice)

Shelter
88 Old Street
London EC1V 9HU
www.shelter.org.uk
Shelterline advice line 0808 800 4444; Tel: 020 7505 2000
National housing organisation offering housing advice, information, training, and publications.

COMMUNITY CARE RESOURCES

Publications

- *Community Care and the Law,* Clements and Thompson, 2007, 4th edn, Legal Action Group
- *Community Care Law Reports,* Legal Action Group, quarterly.

For more information on these publications see www.lag.org.uk

Children (UASCs)

The Health of Refugee Children: Guidelines for Paediatricians published by the Royal College of Paediatrics and Child Health, (Levenson and Sharma)

For assistance in assessing the age of unaccompanied minors: www.rcph.ac.uk

Guidance on Support for Asylum-seekers with care needs, April 2004: www.alg.gov.uk

Better Outcomes: the way forward – Improving the Care of Unaccompanied Asylum-seeking Children, Home Office Border and Immigration Agency, January 2008
This paper contains the government's response and proposals following its consultation paper 'Planning Better Outcomes and Support for Unaccompanied Asylum Seeking Children', March 2007.

Going it Alone: children in the asylum process (The Children's Society, 2007)
When is a child not a child? Asylum, age disputes and the process of age assessment, Heaven Crawley May 2007, ILPA

Seeking asylum alone, UK, Bhabha and Finch, November 2006: www.gardencourtchambers.co.uk/
This report on the treatment of separated and trafficked refugee children also forms part of an investigation into the situation in the U.S. and Australia.

Family Rights Group
www.frg.org.uk
Advice line: 0800 731 1696 (10 am -12 pm and 1.30 pm – 3.30 pm Monday – Friday)
Advice by email: advice@frg.org.uk
Advises families who are involved with social services about any care and protection issue. There are a number of advice sheets on various aspects of SS law and practice.

Victims of human trafficking

Human Trafficking- human rights: law and practice, Sandhya Drew, Legal Action Group, 2009

The Council of Europe Convention against Trafficking in Human Beings (CETS No. 197) came into force in the UK on 1 April 2009.

Home Office
www.crimereduction.homeoffice.gov.uk/humantrafficking

UK Human Trafficking Centre
www.ukhtc.org/
UK Human Trafficking Centre for information and advice

ECPAT
www.ecpat.org.uk/
Organisation campaigning against child trafficking

HEALTHCARE RESOURCES

Publications and reports

- *JCHR report on human rights' implications of Health Bill 2009*: www.publications.parliament.uk/pa/jt200809/jtselect/jtrights/78/78.pdf
- *The Myth of HIV Health Tourism*, National Aids Trust, October 2008. This report refutes the claim that there is a pattern of migrants coming to the UK in order to access life saving HIV treatment which is not available to them in their country of origin.
- *Access to health care for asylum seekers and refused asylum-seekers*, Guidance from the BMA's Medical Ethics Department, September 2008. The British Medical Association (BMA)'s interpretation of the current law in relation to access to primary care, as well as recommendations for good practice and useful reference materials.
- *Health Protection Agency Report on Migrant Health*: www.hpa.org.uk/publications/2006/migrant_health/migrant_health.pdf
- *First do no harm: Denying healthcare to people whose asylum claims have failed*, Oxfam and Refugee Council, June 2006: www.refugeecouncil.org.uk/downloads/rc_reports/Health_access_report_jun06.pdf

Guidance

The Secretary of State for Health interim guidance on the charging regulations saying that the situation will be monitored for six months and the guidance will then be amended: www.dh.gov.uk/en/Publicationsandstatistics/Lettersandcirculars/Dearcolleagueletters/DH_097384

Advice

Government Agencies

Asylum Seeker Coordination Team Department of Health Room 8E10 Quarry House
Quarry Hill
Leeds LS2 7UE
Tel: 0113 2546605
Fax: 0113 2545481
For questions about general asylum seeker health issues

Department of Health
For questions about access to primary care for overseas visitors which the PCT cannot answer:
E-mail: foreignnationals@dh.gsi.gov.uk

For any questions specifically relating to eligibility for free NHS hospital treatment for overseas visitors which cannot be resolved by the PCT, the Department provides a helpline number:
Tel: 0113 254 5819
If using this helpline, please note that it is not for questions about general asylum seeker health issues, or questions relating to personal medical services
E-mail: overseasvisitors@dh.gsi.gov.uk

Department of Health, Health Benefits Division processes applications for exemption from prescription charges for asylum-seekers (and others) on a low income that are not supported by UKBA:
Prologistics
Department of Health
PO Box 777
London SE1 6XN
Tel 0191 203 5555.

Websites

Department of Health
www.doh.gov.uk
For wide range of resources and publications.

Department of Health Overseas Visitors Policy Unit
www.gov.uk/overseasvisitors 01132
For queries about charges for GP or hospital treatment.

Health Services Ombudsman
www.ombudsman.org.uk
Tel 0845 015 4033
E-mail: OHSC.Enquiries@ombudsman.gsi.gov.uk
For complaints about the NHS.

Prescription Pricing Authority
www.ppa.org.uk
Tel: 0191 203 5100
For enquiries about exemption from prescription and other charges.

HARP
www.harpweb.org.uk
Information about health issues affecting asylum-seekers and refugees includes standard letters interpreted into various languages.

Medact
www.medact.org.uk
Tel: 02027 271 2020
Medact is a network of health workers who exchange information and resources to improve conditions for asylum-seekers and refugees.

Medical Foundation for the Care of Victims of Torture
www.torturecare.org.uk
Tel: 0207 813 7777
Medical Foundation for the Care of Victims of Torture provides counseling and other services for torture survivors.

Practical assistance

Project London
Tel: 0207 516 9103
Runs a drop-in clinic for help accessing healthcare in London

Medecins du Monde UK
E-mail: projectlondon@medecinsdumonde.org.uk

Medical Justice
www.medicaljustice.org.uk/
Independent medical advice and resources for immigration detainees.

National AIDS Trust
www.nat.org.uk
Information and resources on HIV/AIDS.

Crusaid
www.crusaid.org.uk/
Advice and support for people with HIV/AIDS. Operate a hardship fund

Terrence Higgins Trust
www.tht.org.uk
Information and resources for people with HIV/AIDS.

Index